War and Justice in the 21st Century

War and Justice in the 21st Century

A Case Study on the International Criminal Court and its Interaction with the War on Terror

LUIS MORENO OCAMPO

Founder Chief Prosecutor of the International Criminal Court

With the collaboration of Joanna Frivet and Francisco J. Quintana and the assistance of Dolores Neira

OXFORD
UNIVERSITY PRESS

Oxford University Press is a department of the University of Oxford. It furthers the University's objective of excellence in research, scholarship, and education by publishing worldwide. Oxford is a registered trade mark of Oxford University Press in the UK and certain other countries.

Published in the United States of America by Oxford University Press
198 Madison Avenue, New York, NY 10016, United States of America.

Library of Congress Cataloging-in-Publication Data
Names: Moreno Ocampo, Luis, author.
Title: War and justice in the 21st century : a case study on the International Criminal Court and its interaction with the war on terror / by Luis Moreno Ocampo.
Description: New York, NY : Oxford University Press, 2022. | Includes index.
Identifiers: LCCN 2022000230 (print) | LCCN 2022000231 (ebook) | ISBN 9780197628973 (hardback) | ISBN 9780197628997 (epub) | ISBN 9780197628980 (updf) | ISBN 9780197629000 (online)
Subjects: LCSH: Prosecution (International law) | International Criminal Court. | Terrorism (International law) | Moreno Ocampo, Luis Gabriel. | Public prosecutors—Biography.
Classification: LCC KZ7332 .M67 2022 (print) | LCC KZ7332 (ebook) | DDC 345/.01262—dc23/eng/20220202
LC record available at https://lccn.loc.gov/2022000230
LC ebook record available at https://lccn.loc.gov/2022000231

DOI: 10.1093/oso/9780197628973.001.0001

1 3 5 7 9 8 6 4 2

Printed by Sheridan Books, Inc., United States of America

Note to Readers
This publication is designed to provide accurate and authoritative information in regard to the subject matter covered. It is based upon sources believed to be accurate and reliable and is intended to be current as of the time it was written. It is sold with the understanding that the publisher is not engaged in rendering legal, accounting, or other professional services. If legal advice or other expert assistance is required, the services of a competent professional person should be sought. Also, to confirm that the information has not been affected or changed by recent developments, traditional legal research techniques should be used, including checking primary sources where appropriate.

(Based on the Declaration of Principles jointly adopted by a Committee of the American Bar Association and a Committee of Publishers and Associations.)

You may order this or any other Oxford University Press publication
by visiting the Oxford University Press website at www.oup.com.

To Hejewa Adam and Nadia Murad, two women fighting for justice
To Sergio Vieira de Mello, who gave his life for humanity
To Ben Ferencz, an exemplary life to be followed
To Invisible Children, the misunderstood innovators
To the people that created and worked at the International Criminal Court

Contents

SECOND PART: *JUS AD CURIAM* AND *JUS AD BELLUM* DECISIONS ADOPTED BY THE UN SECURITY COUNCIL, THE US, AND CÔTE D'IVOIRE

Preface

The Challenge for the modern Prosecutor is to become a lawyer for the people. It is your duty to build an effective relationship with the community and to ensure that the rights of the victims are protected. It is your duty to prosecute fairly and effectively according with the rule of law and to act in a principled way without fear, favor or prejudice. It is your duty to build a prosecution service that is an effective deterrence to crime and is known to demonstrate great compassion and sensitivity to the people it serves.

Nelson Mandela, 2000[1]

It is a failure by design. The legal architecture created in the eighteenth century and adjusted by the UN Charter in 1945 is not equipped to deal efficiently with transnational problems like genocide or international terrorism. Two legal models challenging the traditional concept of national sovereignty were developed to face those crimes at the beginning of the twenty-first century: the Rome Statute system, including the International Criminal Court (ICC); and the War on Terror policy.

The efforts to implement international criminal justice and to control global terrorism were not integrated. Thus, the current global order is not consistent, and the number of victims is unprecedented. Since 2009 civil wars and massive violence drove worldwide forced displacement to new records, surpassing the situation after World War II and still growing each year.[2] The war in Ukraine opening a second Cold War exacerbated the problem.

For nine years, I was one of the persons making efforts to control massive crimes. As the first chief prosecutor of the International Criminal Court, I had a role that no one performed before. In a world organized by nations, my duty was to protect the victims "of the most serious crimes of concern to the international community as a whole." Following Nelson Mandela's vision, I had to build a relationship with a dispersed global community and protect the rights of victims of massive atrocities from different parts of the world.[3]

I was not involved in the discussion either of the Rome Statute or the War on Terror. Still, I had to make strategic legal decisions and became a participant and a privileged witness of how they were implemented during their first years. This book describes my unique practice.

In 1998 at Rome, mindful that during the twentieth century, "millions of children, women, and men have been victims of unimaginable atrocities that deeply shock the conscience of humanity," 120 nations took an unmatched decision. They adopted the Rome Statute "to put an end to impunity for the perpetrators" of "the most serious crimes of concern to the international community as a whole" to "contribute to their prevention."

The Rome Statute created more than a court. It produced a peculiar confederation of nation-states connected with a permanent International Criminal Court. States assumed primary responsibility to prevent, investigate, and prosecute the crimes and requested the Office of the Prosecutor to trigger the ICC intervention if they fail to act. Professor James Crawford, the chair of the UN International Law Commission (ILC) working group that produced the Draft Statute in 1994, described the final version adopted in Rome as "a distinct and to a considerable extent an autonomous criminal justice system."[4]

My role was unprecedented because in the past prosecutors have had represented national or local communities and have had no authority to investigate crimes committed beyond national borders. At Nuremberg, Yugoslavia, and Rwanda *ad hoc* international tribunals, prosecutors represented the international community and could investigate specific situations selected by states.

The Rome Statute provided an additional and disruptive mandate to the ICC prosecutor: to trigger criminal proceedings in sovereign countries when the states parties failed to act. Article 15 conferred *proprio motu* authority to the prosecutor and established a specific procedure, a *preliminary examination*, to identify situations that should be investigated. This was the most innovative part of my practice. The book describes my strategic legal decisions to decide where the court should intervene.

The Clinton administration opposed the *proprio motu* independent authority of the ICC prosecutor. The United States Constitution guarantees a fair trial to any defendant in national courts and the US had promoted previous international criminal justice efforts. Still, it wanted to control the ICC interventions through the United Nations Security Council (UNSC).

After the September 11, 2001, terrorist attack, the conflict heightened when the United States adopted a different model to control violence: *War on Terror*. Terrorist suspects in foreign countries were no longer treated as criminals to be investigated. Instead, to protect the United States, they were regarded as enemies to be killed.

To shield its soldiers from criminal investigations, the US Congress prohibited cooperation with the ICC and even authorized an eventual invasion of the Netherlands to rescue US prisoners. Furthermore, in March 2003, the United States led an international military intervention in Iraq, multiplying its efforts to undermine the Rome Statute system.

I was appointed a month later by the then seventy-eight states parties of the statute. I took office on June 2003, and there were doubts about the International Criminal Court's viability. Many states parties were "apprehensive about being perceived as an adversary to the United States."[5] Even those working at the court had reservations.[6] The book describes how, in a few years, the most innovative international legal system overcame the obstacles, became operational, and yet, was accepted by states non-parties like the United States, Russia, and China.

During my term, the prosecution conducted seventeen preliminary examinations: two in Asia (Korea and Afghanistan), one in the Middle East (Palestine), one at the crossroads of Western Asia and Eastern Europe (Georgia), two in Africa (Nigeria and Guinea), one in Central America (Honduras), two in South America (Colombia and Venezuela), and one in Europe (UK personnel involved in Iraq).

The office also conducted seven other preliminary examinations in Africa, analyzing the commission of crimes under the ICC jurisdiction and the existence of national proceedings. The prosecution opened investigations in four states parties, Democratic Republic of Congo, Uganda, Central African Republic, and Kenya, in Darfur and Libya after the UN Security Council referred those situations and in Ivory Coast, after its government accepted ICC jurisdiction.

The Office of the Prosecutor scrupulously respected the Rome Statute's legal framework. In all the cases presented, the chambers confirmed the prosecution delimitation of the ICC jurisdiction. The fears of a frivolous prosecutor or an ever-expanding International Criminal Court were not confirmed.

But the ICC operations in the proper jurisdictions created new political challenges. We had to investigate ongoing conflicts, and security for our investigators and witnesses became a primary concern. In any case, we obtained the evidence required through the cooperation of states parties and non-parties of the statute.

Overall, we requested arrest warrants and summons to appear for thirty-one individuals identified as those most responsible for the massive crimes committed, including militia leaders such as Joseph Kony and heads of state Omar al Bashir, Muammar Gaddafi, and Laurent Gbagbo. The pre-trial chambers, in turn, reviewed the prosecutor's evidence and issued all of them.[7]

The Office of the Prosecutor participated in seven confirmations of charges before the pre-trial chamber to review the evidence before going to trial[8] and in three trials.[9]

At the end of my term, after nine years of operations, forty-three additional states ratified the statute and joined the system, reaching 121 states parties.[10] They spent hundreds of million euros in building the court's permanent seat at The Hague. In February 2011, the UN Security Council, by consensus, referred the Libya situation to the ICC. On September 24, 2012, the UN General Assembly recognized the ICC's central role for all states.[11] On October 17, 2012, the UN Security Council held a meeting to discuss "Peace and justice, with a special focus on the role of the International Criminal Court." In that meeting, states non-parties like China, the United States, Russia, and even Sudan, a country presided over by a person indicted by the ICC for genocide, ended up recognizing the International Criminal Court's importance.[12]

The ICC became part of the institutional landscape, and its existence is no longer at risk. However, what is up for debate is the Rome Statute's relevance to *contribute to the prevention* of future crimes.

Measuring Relevance

How to measure the preventive impact of an autonomous criminal justice system that works worldwide, combining national institutions and a permanent court working under the complementarity principle? Counting the number of cases before a court created to act by default does not provide a proper evaluation of the Rome Statute autonomous criminal justice system.[13]

Jenny Martinez, Stanford University Law School professor and dean, provides an insight into the relationship between courts and the efforts and time needed to control a global problem. She described a forgotten movement promoted by the Quakers and led by the United Kingdom during the nineteenth century to end the slave trade.[14] The transformation included treaties and international courts' creation, but it also required a coalition of different public and private sector actors. Religious groups like the Quakers promoted the idea. Governments made the system operational, and even the British West Indian planters that owned slaves participated in expanding the model. Its success required massive popular support and included financial incentives, private enforcement, and military efforts. It took more than sixty years, but the complex action ended the slave trade globally.[15]

Taking into consideration such a precedent, a proper Rome Statute's evaluation should consider the actions of all the members of the treaty and other relevant actors preventing, investigating, and punishing the crimes.[16] In June 2003, during my swearing in, I proposed such a method to evaluate the ICC relevance: "The effectiveness of the International Criminal Court should not be measured by the number of cases that reach it. On the contrary, complementarity implies that the absence of trials before this Court, as a consequence of the regular functioning of national institutions, would be a major success."[17]

This book further develops such a criterion. It is a case study covering the commission of crimes and the procedures adopted by different actors to launch or prevent international criminal justice initiatives and some of their consequences. It describes the Office of the Prosecutor's preliminary examination activities in seventeen different situations, the decisions to open investigations in seven of them, pertinent rulings, and relevant national and international actors' decisions.

The book maps the Rome Statute system facilitating a discussion on its relevance.[18]

Hejewa Adams Demands

From my office in The Hague, I perceived the lack of a common criterion to manage transnational violence. There was no single frame to harmonize citizen demands for justice, political decisions adopted by national leaders, humanitarian assistance, peace negotiations, military operations, and court interventions. Different actors could choose the legal system to apply.

Hejewa Adam, a Darfur's victim, unveiled the problem. Her lack of international protection was the normal consequence of a legal design based on sovereign states. I never met Hejewa Adam personally, but I could not ever forget her comments in the documentary film *Darfur Now*.[19] She was at home cooking when she heard explosions. The Sudanese Army had surrounded her village. Then, *Janjaweed* militias integrated into the state forces burned houses, destroyed water mills, killed the men and boys, and took away the girls. Her friends' throats were slit in front of her eyes.

Hejewa Adam tried to escape, but they beat her and killed her one-year-old son, Nassareldeen, strapped to her back. What can you do if security forces attack you at your home?

The national state, instead of protecting Hejewa Adam, was attacking her. There were no Sudanese authorities, neither police, no prosecutor, and no judge ready to care for her. Hejewa Adam had to protect herself *from* her own state. She joined a rebel group and learned how to use automatic weapons. Holding a Kalashnikov rifle in her arms, she requested a solution before the cameras: "Fighting alone will not solve the problem in Darfur. Those people who went to school and got an education are the ones who will solve the problem. Fighting with guns will not solve it. Even in a hundred years."

Her message was so clear that I want to start this book by amplifying her voice. Who could protect a person attacked by her own national state? In 2003 Hejewa Adam should not expect other nations to intervene in Darfur. As the International Court of Justice (ICJ) has observed, "The principle of non-intervention involves the right of every sovereign State to conduct its affairs without outside interference."[20] Hejewa Adams's lack of international protections was the legal design's normal outcome.

However, in March 2005, nine Rome Statute states party and members of the UN Security Council, led by France, forced the United States to accept Darfur's referral to the ICC. The ICC investigated Darfur's crimes and issued arrest warrants against militia leaders, ministers, and President Bashir himself, but the court's efforts were not enough to stop the violence. Even some experts alleged that our intervention in Sudan was counterproductive.[21]

There was no concerted effort to implement the arrest warrants. The council decided not to impose such a duty. Therefore, states' non-parties had the discretion to choose whatever they consider convenient on the matter. For instance, President Obama took advantage of the ICC's arrest warrants against President Bashir to increase his leverage in a negotiation to facilitate South Sudan's independence and boost Sudan's support in the War on Terror.

The Obama administration was integrated by people fully committed to Darfur's victims, but it decided that stopping the genocide was not its priority. The inaction by nations in arresting individuals *abroad* is not a failure; they have the right to decide their foreign policies by design.

The beginning of the change was domestic. After a decade, President Bashir was removed by a coup d'état, he is in jail, and one of the suspects is on trial at The Hague. Showing the institutional work, Fatou Bensouda, the second ICC chief prosecutor; and her successor, Karim Kahn, visited Sudan and discussed cooperation.

Criminals or Enemies?

For five thousand years, violence was the mechanism to solve conflicts between communities; tribes had no legal constraints to attack their enemies. Peace was just the time between wars.[22] The Rome Statute is the peak of a millennial evolution, expanding the legal protection from cities to national states to an international community.

Ancient Athens, fifth century B.C., protected rights at *home* and required a trial to execute a citizen.[23] But, as Thucydides's famous "Melian dialogue" described, Athenians had no mercy and slaughtered and enslaved foreigners when acting abroad.[24]

It took twenty-two centuries to transform the meaning of *home* and *abroad*, expanding citizens' legal protection from cities like Athens to entire nations. Since the seventeenth century, a new legal design was emerging: the nation-state. Since its creation in the nineteenth century, the Greek state prevents violence between Athens and Melos.

The national state's borders defined the mechanism for violence management: "Modernity has generally been characterized by a strict distinction between internal and external relationships to sovereignty in which threats are posed by criminals when they occur at home and enemies when they occur abroad."[25] The national legal system avoided conflicts between cities, provided a shared territory and national identity to diverse communities unifying tribes.

The nation-state became the "guarantor of domestic order."[26] Harvard University Professor Steven Pinker reviewed five thousand years of human history and concluded that the most consistent violence reducer has been "a state that uses a monopoly of force to protect its citizens from one another."[27]

But sovereign nations are also the "legitimizer of external war"; they preserved a right to attack other nations.[28] States forces killed more than one hundred million persons during the twentieth-century wars.

The UN Charter, adopted to avoid new world wars between nations, cannot efficiently prevent many other problems. There is a growing global consensus on fundamental values, but states' commitment to respecting some principles does not include adopting an independent enforcement mechanism that could interfere with their sovereignty.[29]

Since 1948, when the Universal Declaration of Human Rights[30] was approved, many international treaties establishing individuals' rights were adopted.[31] But their enforcement is the prerogative of national authorities, exposing them to be criticized as *idealism* or *utopia*.[32]

A cruel example: Sudan signed the Genocide Convention in 2003 while committing genocide in Darfur. And the United States reinterpreted that "A determination that genocide has occurred in Darfur would have no legal—as opposed to moral, political, or policy—consequences for the United States."[33]

By design, the nation-state model cannot control violence inside other sovereign country or between them. We have been left to observe their repetition. In 1945, after the Nazi regime systematically killed millions, national leaders pledged "never again."

The promise was repeated during the 1990s after the failures to stop the Srebrenica and Rwanda genocides, which saw millions more slaughtered in the face of failing diplomacy. The call was raised again in the context of the genocide in Darfur. But the Afghanistan and Iraq conflicts, the Arab Spring, and concern for Libyan citizens deflected attention away from Darfur. Then came the use of chemical weapons in the Syrian conflict, overshadowing the Libyan victims. Later, the appearance of ISIS and the forced displacement of millions of Syrian and Iraqi citizens shifted attention once again.

Killing enemies is still an accepted method of resolving conflicts. The media keep denouncing new genocides—against the Yazidi and the Rohingya—but there is no global grand strategy to integrate the efforts to control and stop transnational crimes.

In her 2018 Nobel Prize lecture, Nadia Murad, a Yazidi victim of genocide, stressed "the need to define a new roadmap to protect women, children, and minorities from persecution, in particular victims of sexual violence."[34] The first time Nadia Murad had to talk in public, she received the advice to keep it simple. "Tell your own story." But she explained: "That was a terrifying idea. I knew that if my story were to have any impact, I would have to be as honest as I could stand to be. As calmly as I could, I told them about how I had been raped and beaten repeatedly and how I eventually escaped. I told them about my brothers who had been killed. I want to be the last girl in the world with a story like mine."[35]

How many girls should be raped to produce a change?

The War on Terror

The crimes against humanity committed by Al Qaeda on September 11, 2001, presented a different limitation of the nation-state model. The crimes were carefully planned *abroad* and executed by Al Qaeda, a transnational network of individuals based in different countries, involved in previous conflicts in Afghanistan and the Balkans, and unified by a peculiar interpretation of Islam.

They were following Osama bin Laden's directives, convinced that Muslim communities worldwide were the United States' victims. They felt the duty to retaliate. Bin Laden invoked the protection of his community to justify the attacks: "Because you attacked us and continue to attack us. Your forces occupy our countries. It is commanded by our religion and intellect that the oppressed have a right to return the aggression. Do not await anything from us but Jihad, resistance, and revenge."[36]

The United States, the most powerful nation in the world, was not prepared to protect its own citizens at *home* from this criminal network. National Security Adviser Condoleezza Rice recognized, "Our entire concept of what constituted security had been shaken. The governmental institutions simply didn't exist to deal with a threat of this kind."[37]

The United States improvised its reaction, blurring the distinctions between enemies and criminals, peace and war, and national and international security.[38]

"For decades, the US government had officially viewed terrorism as a law enforcement problem." Still, it took President Bush just a few minutes on the very morning of 9/11 to decide "that the conflict with Islamist terrorists must be viewed as a war."[39] President Bush did not treat bin Laden as a criminal but instead as an enemy.

"The clash between freedom and tyranny," President Bush said, is "an issue which can only be tried by war and decided by victory . . . The war on terror would be the same."[40]

Legal designs define an individual's rights and the duties of the security forces. "The criminal is not the enemy; the enemy is not the criminal."[41] Two videos showing US officers killing civilians expose the crucial distinction between the behavior accepted at *home* and *abroad*. One shows a Minneapolis police officer choking and killing George Floyd on May 25, 2020. The United States Constitution protects any person's rights at *home*, and the police officer was prosecuted and convicted.[42]

In contrast, the video of a US Apache helicopter flying over Baghdad on July 12, 2007, shooting people, including a Reuters' photographer, his assistant, and a father with his two kids, exposed the different legal treatment *abroad*. The US rules of engagement applied in Iraq, and the United States did not charge its soldiers. The video shows that the soldiers mistakenly assumed that the victims were enemy combatants who could be killed according to the law of war.

The US Constitution, as most domestic legal systems, does not protect aliens living in foreign countries. As an occupying authority, the United States decided that its soldiers operating in Iraq were under its exclusive jurisdiction and should not be charged.[43] By design, Iraqi criminal law did not protect Iraqis affected by US soldiers on Iraqi soil.

Global Problems and National Solutions

Cybercrimes are another clear example of a sovereign state model's limitation to control violence in the twenty-first century. Technology "makes less relevant many of the traditional concepts around which our laws and political organization for security have evolved." "National border, jurisdictional boundaries, citizenship, and the distinction between national and international, between act of war and crime, and between state and private action all offer divides less sharp than they used to."[44]

Whether national or international, no single authority can deliver effective solutions to protect civilians from genocide or international terrorism. And the most powerful countries, particularly the United States, are against any design change that can reduce their sovereignty.

Transnational crimes are not the only problems that require a global solution. Greta Thunberg, a Swedish girl demanding action on climate change, became the keynote speaker at a UN meeting on September 23, 2019. She challenged the national leaders: "We are at the beginning of a mass extinction . . . Yet you all come to us young people for hope. How dare you! You have stolen my dreams and my childhood with your empty words."[45]

Hejewa Adam, Nadia Murad, and Greta Thunberg represent new generations demanding solutions for problems beyond national authorities' reach. It is not about a lack of leadership. It is a lack of collective action by design.

On December 22, 2020, Norway's Supreme Court showed the limits of the most advanced national legal systems. It ruled that Norway's constitutional right to a clean environment does not preclude new oil exploration licenses in the Arctic, "the effects of global warming are only relevant to the extent that they affect Norway." Commenting on the decision, Greta Thunberg recognized that "we need a whole new way of thinking."[46]

The COVID pandemic management is the latest example of a global problem without global authorities to confront it. Mayors, governors, presidents, and the World Health Organization debated what to do, and no one was in charge of the entire problem. Growing vaccine nationalism "isn't just immoral—it's medically self-defeating."[47]

There is not yet clarity on how to control the dangers "we have introduced into the world through our endeavors to benefit from certain technologies. . . . We live, think and act in terms of concepts that are historically obsolete but that nonetheless continue to govern our thinking and acting."[48]

Between the two world wars, there were discussions on new ideas to manage violence. Albert Einstein wrote to Sigmund Freud, "The quest of international security involves the unconditional surrender by every nation, in a certain measure, of its liberty of action—its sovereignty that is to say."[49]

International Relations *Realist* scholars rightly point out that international law did not stop the Nazi regime. Instead of improving the League of Nations' legal architecture, they disregarded the entire exercise. They concluded that international law is a utopian mistake, "harmful in directing attention away from the need to prepare to the inevitable aggression when it came."[50]

However, *realists* should not commit a parallel mistake and direct attention away from the urgency to develop solutions to face the challenges presented by new technologies and new threats. But the legal architecture is not a relevant part of the academic discussions on global affairs. Chapter 5 analyzes how the law is more than idealism. It also confers power.

From a different angle, Harvard Professor Kathryn Sikkink presented quantitative and qualitative data exposing "an interrelated, dramatic new trend in world politics toward holding individual state officials, including heads of state, criminally accountable for gross human rights violations."[51] She describes three kinds of judicial enforcement: domestic (like the trials in Argentina), international (like Nuremberg, the International Criminal

Tribunal for the former Yugoslavia (ICTY), the International Criminal Tribunal for Rwanda (ICTR), and ICC), and foreign (as the UK intervention in the Pinochet case at the request of Spanish Judge Baltasar Garzon). Professor Sikkink calls this trend "the Justice Cascade" and measures its impact and consistent growth. One question that remains to be answered is why were there criminal investigations in one country and not in another, why in Argentina and not in Brazil? Justice demand is universal, but its implementation is case specific.

Demands define the supply of the product in a market economy. Instead, the justice demands are not always finding a consistent supply. Justice delivery is not homogeneous because national authorities should primarily enforce it. Global values are still at the mercy of domestic authorities.

New technologies based on artificial intelligence are a critical new variable. Netflix transformed the production and distribution of narratives. Amazon changed shopping. Google renovated how to do research. Facebook and Instagram enable us to connect with friends.

In the twenty-first century, we celebrate innovations in technology and dismiss innovations in global institutions. Can artificial intelligence serve a public purpose? The national model justifies the use of artificial intelligence to kill the enemies more efficiently. But it could change. Currency, like the criminal justice system, was the exclusive domain of a nation. Bitcoin changed that. Global governance requires a new design, incorporating new technologies to serve the people.

Scholars are not proposing comprehensive options to the practitioners. Similar to a chef or a film producer, my ICC practice required combining elements. We had to make decisions considering the security conditions, cooperation, understanding the legal requirements, finding a creative way to obtain evidence, keeping our budget, and reaching local communities.

The specialized knowledge developed by diverse disciplines analyzes those variables in isolation. International relations, political science, international law, international criminal law, humanitarian law, and military strategy focus on specific paradigms ignoring fundamental problems to protect the field boundaries.[52] Knowledge is produced within "echo chambers" according to nationality and profession. "Echo chambers can lead people to believe in falsehoods, and it may be difficult or impossible to correct them."[53]

To assist new generations in developing new solutions, I will describe the Rome Statute system's functioning.[54] The Rome Statute was discussed for decades, and it has now been operational for almost twenty years. It combines a network of national authorities applying similar standards monitored by the Office of the Prosecutor, an independent and international actor.[55]

The Rome Statute's model challenges constitutional ideas about representation, transforming the concept of national sovereignty and the international paradigm. It introduces individuals' responsibility as a permanent part of international order.

The unique legal architecture of the Rome Statute need not be the last institutional innovation. It could be the model upon which new types of institutions can be built. The new solutions have to respect local and national decisions and at the same time confront global problems, such as international terrorism, cybercrimes, climate change, and global pandemics: problems a single country cannot face in isolation.

The book describes our specific ICC practice, but it aims to help create the solutions that Hejewa Adam, Nadia Murad, and Greta Thunberg are demanding.

Notes

1. President Nelson Mandela, Former President of South Africa, Speech when receiving the Medal of Honor from the International Association of Prosecutors (Aug. 31, 2000). *International Association of Prosecutors: A History*, IAP, https://www.iap-asso ciation.org/getattachment/About/Sub-Page-1/History_PartI.pdf.aspx (last visited Jan. 8, 2021).

2. *Global Trends, Forced Displacement in 2019*, UNHCR, https://www.unhcr.org/globa ltrends2019/ (last accessed July 3, 2021).

3. Carlo Ginzburg presented human morality difficulties to relate with distant problems. He quoted Aristoteles: "Men also pity those who resemble them in age, character, habits, position, or family; for all such relations make a man more likely to think that their misfortune may befall him as well. "And: 'We agreed,' Diderot writes, 'that perhaps distance in space or time weakened all feelings and all sorts of guilty conscience, even of crime." Carlo Ginzburg, *Killing a Chinese Mandarin: The Moral Implications of Distance*, 208 NEW LEFT REV. 107, 107 (1994).

4. James Crawford, *The Drafting of the Rome Statute*, in FROM NUREMBERG TO THE HAGUE, THE FUTURE OF INTERNATIONAL CRIMINAL JUSTICE 109, 154 (Phillippe Sands ed., 2003).

5. Didier Pfirter, *The Position of Switzerland with Respect to the ICC Statute and in Particular the Elements of Crimes*, 32 CORNELL INT'L L.J. 499, 505 (1999)

6. "Those working inside the new institution felt its fragility acutely. One of the first judges elected recalled that he and his colleagues 'were not at all sure about whether this new baby would be able to survive all the hostility shown by the big powers.'"

DAVID BOSCO, ROUGH JUSTICE, THE INTERNATIONAL CRIMINAL COURT IN A WORLD
OF POWER POLITICS 81 (Kindle ed. 2014).

7. Our policy was to focus our investigation on those who bear the greatest responsibility, aiming to disrupt the group committing the crimes and maximizing our contribution to the prevention of future crimes. We requested thirty-one arrest warrants
and summons to appear: Joseph Kony (July 8, 2005), Okot Odhiambo (July 8, 2005–
Unsealed on October 13, 2005), Raska Lukwiya (July 8, 2005), Dominic Ongwen
(July 8, 2005–Unsealed on October 13, 2005), Vincent Otti (July 8, 2005–Unsealed on
October 13, 2005), Thomas Lubanga Dyilo (February 10, 2006–Unsealed on March
17, 2006), Bosco Ntaganda (August 22, 2006–Unsealed on April 28, 2008; Second
warrant: July 13, 2012), Ali Muhammad Ali Abd-Al-Rahman (April 27, 2007),
Ahmad Muhammad Harun (April 27, 2007), Mathieu Ngudjolo Chui (July 6, 2007–
Unsealed on February 7, 2008), Germain Katanga (July 2, 2007–Unsealed on October
15, 2007), Jean Pierre Bemba Gombo (June 10, 2008), Omar Hassan Ahmad Al Bashir
(March 4, 2009–July12, 2010), Bahar Idriss Abu Garda (May 7, 2009–Unsealed on
May 17, 2009), Abdallah Banda Abakaer Nourain (Issued under seal on August 27,
2009, Unsealed on June 15, 2010. Arrest warrant: 11, September 2014), Sylvestre
Mudacumura (August 27, 2009–Unsealed on June 15, 2010), Saleh Mohamed
Jerbo Jamus (August 27, 2009–Unsealed on June 15, 2010), Callixte Mbarushimana
(September 25, 2010–Unsealed on October 11, 2010), Mohamed Hussein Ali
(March 8, 2011), Joshua Arap Sang (March 8, 2011), William Samoei Ruto (March
8, 2011), Francis Kirimi Mutaura (March 8, 2011), Henry Kiprono Kosgey (March
8, 2011), Uhuru Muigai Kenyatta (March 8, 2011), Saif Al-Islam Gaddafi (June 27,
2011), Muammar Mohammed Abu Minyar Gaddafi (June 27, 2011), Abdullah Al-
Senussi (June 27, 2011), Laurent Gbagbo (November 23, 2011), Charles Ble Goude
(December 21, 2011), Simone Gbagbo (February 29, 2012–Unsealed on November
22, 2012), Abdel Raheem Muhammad Hussein (March 1, 2012)).

8. Thomas Lubanga Dyilo, Germain Katanga and Mathieu Ngujolo Chui, Bemba,
Francis Kirimi Mutaura, Uhuru Muigai Kenyatta and Mohammed Hussein Ali,
William Samoei Ruto, Henry Kiprono Kosgey and Joshua Arap Sang, Callixte
Mbarushimana and Abu Garda.

9. Lubanga, Katanga and Ngujolo Chui, and Bemba.

10. The Philippines and Burundi withdraw from the statute in 2017 and 2018 aiming to
protect their leaders allegedly involved in crimes under the court's jurisdiction.

11. "We recognize the role of the International Criminal Court in a multilateral system
that aims to end impunity and establish the rule of law, and in this respect, we wel-
come the States that have become parties to the Rome Statute of the International
Criminal Court, and call upon all States that are not yet parties to the Statute to consider ratifying or acceding to it, and emphasize the importance of cooperation with
the Court." G.A. Res. 67/1, ¶ 23, U.N. Doc. A/RES/67/1 (Nov. 30, 2012).

12. U.N. SCOR, 67 Sess., 6849th mtg., U.N. Doc. S/PV.6849 (Resumption 1) (Oct. 17,
2012) and U.N. SCOR, 67 Sess., 6849th mtg., U.N. Doc. S/PV.6849 (Oct. 17, 2012).
See the concept paper at Permanent Rep. of Guatemala to the U.N., Letter dated Oct.

1, 2012 from the Permanente Rep. of Guatemala to the United Nations addressed to the Secretary-General, U.N. S/2012/731 (Oct. 1, 2012).

13. Eric Posner, *The Absurd International Criminal Court*, WALL ST. J. (June 10, 2012, 5:57 PM), https://www.wsj.com/articles/SB10001424052702303753904577452122153205162. *See also* ERIC POSNER, THE TWILIGHT OF HUMAN RIGHTS LAW (Inalienable Rights) 54 (Kindle ed. 2014).

14. JENNY S. MARTINEZ, THE SLAVE TRADE AND THE ORIGINS OF INTERNATIONAL HUMAN RIGHTS LAW 34–35 (Kindle reprint ed. 2011).

15. *Id.*

16. Michael Reisman explained that courts are "in all but a few sectors, marginal and episodic forums for effective decisions." W. MICHAEL REISMAN, THE QUEST FOR WORLD ORDER AND HUMAN DIGNITY IN THE TWENTY-FIRST CENTURY: CONSTITUTIVE PROCESS AND INDIVIDUAL COMMITMENT (2012).

17. Luis Moreno Ocampo, Chief Prosecutor of the International Criminal Court, Statement made at the Ceremony of the solemn undertaking of the Chief Prosecutor of the International Criminal Court (June 16, 2003).

18. In 2018, Ruti Teitel organized a small meeting at New York Law School with Rob Howse, Jack Snyder, and other colleagues to discuss a draft of this Preface. She suggested to add the mapping concept.

19. *Darfur Now* is a documentary directed by Ted Braun, filmed in 2006 and 2007 released on 2008©2007. All Rights Reserved. DARFUR NOW (Warner Independent Pictures, Crescendo, Mandalay Independent Pictures and Participant Productions, Nov. 2, 2007).

20. Military and Paramilitary Activities in and against Nicaragua (Nicaragua. v. US), Judgment, 1986 I.C.J. Rep. 14 (June 27).

21. Julie Flint & Alex De Waal, *To Put Justice before Peace Spells Disaster for Sudan*, THE GUARDIAN (Mar. 6, 2009), https://www.theguardian.com/commentisfree/2009/mar/06/sudan-war-crimes.

22. During most of humanity's history, peace was a "period when war was neither imminent nor actually being fought/" MICHAEL HOWARD, THE INVENTION OF PEACE: REFLECTION ON WAR AND INTERNATIONAL ORDER (New ed. 2001).

23. P. J. Rhodes, *Ancient Athens: Democracy and Empire* 1, 16 EU. REV. HISTORY: REV. EU. D'HISTOIRE 201 (2009).

24. In 416 B.C.E., the Athenians invaded Melos, a small island in the Aegean that sought to remain neutral and avoided joining the Athenian empire. The Athenians offered the Melians a choice: become a subject of Athens or resist and be annihilated. The Melians presented their arguments including that justice was on their side. The Athenians dismissed arguments of justice as irrelevant and replied: "We both alike know that in human reckoning the question of justice only enters where there is equal power to enforce it, and that the powerful exact what they can, and the weak grant what they must." The Athenians killed all of the Melian men they had captured and enslaved the children and women. Adriaan Lanni, *The Laws of War in Ancient Greece* (Harv. Pub. L. Working Paper No. 07-24, 1 2007).

25. Samuel Moyn summarized Kahn's views. Samuel Moyn, *Drones and Imagination: A Response to Paul Kahn*, 24 Eur. J. Int'l L. 227, 228 (2013).

26. Michael Howard, The Invention of Peace: Reflections of War and International Order (2000).

27. Steven Pinker, The Better Angels of Our Nature: Why Violence Has Declined 680 (Kindle ed. 2011).

28. Michael Howard, The Invention of Peace: Reflections of War and International Order (2000).

29. In 1993 the UN General Assembly created the High Commissioner of Human Rights and the UN Human Rights Council (A/RES/60/251) was created in March 2006. They produced reports and promoted accountability through peer control and exposing the reputation of the states denounced. But they still had to respect the national state sovereignty. Libya under the Gaddafi regime, for instance, "was elected to the Human Rights Council in 2010." Hillel Neuer, Executive Director of UN Watch. *UN Should Apologize for "Legitimizing" Gaddafi with Key Posts*, UN Watch (Oct. 20, 2011), http://blog.unwatch.org/index.php/2011/10/20/un-should-apologize-for-legitimiz ing-gaddafi-with-key-posts/. *See also* Jose Luis Morin, *Global and Regional Human Rights Commissions, in* International Crime and Justice (Mangai Natarajan ed., 2011).

30. The Universal Declaration of Human Rights (UDHR) was adopted by the United Nations General Assembly on December 10, 1948.

31. The list of the treaties registered with the UN Secretariat pursuant to Article 102 of the UN Charter includes Convention on the Political Rights of Women. New York, 31 March 1953; International Convention on the Elimination of All Forms of Racial Discrimination. New York, 7 March 1966; International Covenant on Economic, Social and Cultural Rights. New York, 16 December 1966; International Covenant on Civil and Political Rights. New York, 16 December 1966; Convention on the non-applicability of statutory limitations to war crimes and crimes against humanity. New York, 26 November 1968; International Convention on the Suppression and Punishment of the Crime of Apartheid. New York, 30 November 1973; Convention on the Elimination of All Forms of Discrimination against Women. New York, 18 December 1979; Convention against Torture and Other Cruel, Inhuman or Degrading Treatment or Punishment. New York, 10 December 1984; International Convention against Apartheid in Sports. New York, 10 December 1985; Convention on the Rights of the Child. New York, 20 November 1989; Second Optional Protocol to the International Covenant on Civil and Political Rights, aiming at the abolition of the death penalty. New York, 15 December 1989; International Convention on the Protection of the Rights of All Migrant Workers and Members of their Families. New York, 18 December 1990; Convention on the Rights of Persons with Disabilities. New York, 13 December 2006; International Convention for the Protection of All Persons from Enforced Disappearance. New York, 20 December 2006.

32. *See* Martti Koskenniemi, The Politics of International Law 79 (Kindle ed. 2001). "A utopia critique argues that a given decision is too far divorced from political power, thus potentially lacking effectiveness." Sophie T. Rosenberg, *The International*

Criminal Court in Côte d'Ivoire, Impartiality at Stake?, 15 J. INT'L CRIM. JUST. 471, 486 (2017).

33. Rebecca Hamilton, *Inside Colin Powell Decision to Declare Genocide in Darfur*, ATLANTIC (Aug. 2011), https://www.theatlantic.com/international/archive/2011/08/inside-colin-powells-decision-to-declare-genocide-in-darfur/243560/.

34. "After the failure of the Government of Iraq and the Government of Kurdistan to protect us, the international community also failed to save us from ISIS and to prevent the occurrence of the genocide against us, and stood idly by watching the annihilation of a complete community. Our homes, our families, our traditions, our people, our dreams were all destroyed." Nadia Murad, Nobel Peace Prize Laureate 2018, Nobel lecture (Dec. 10, 2018).

35. NADIA MURAD, THE LAST GIRL: MY STORY OF CAPTIVITY, AND MY FIGHT AGAINST THE ISLAMIC STATE 300 (Kindle ed. 2017).

36. *Full Text: Bin Laden's Letter to America*, GUARDIAN (Nov. 24, 2002), HTTPS://WWW.THEGUARDIAN.COM/WORLD/2002/NOV/24/THEOBSERVER. The letter first appeared on the internet in Arabic and has since been translated and circulated by Islamists in Britain.

37. CONDOLEEZZA RICE, NO HIGHER HONOR: A MEMOIR OF MY YEARS IN WASHINGTON 79–80 (Kindle ed. 2011).

38. Ulrich Beck, *The Silence of Words: On Terror and War*, 34 SEC. DIALOGUE 255 (2003).

39. JACK GOLDSMITH, THE TERROR PRESIDENCY: LAW AND JUDGMENT INSIDE THE BUSH ADMINISTRATION 103 (Kindle ed. 2007).

40. GEORGE W. BUSH, DECISION POINTS 140 (Kindle ed. 2010).

41. "Criminals and enemies may do the same violent acts, destroying property and persons. Nevertheless, the modern political imagination carefully maintained the distinction as a matter of both formal law and informal representation." Paul W. Kahn, *Criminal and Enemy in the Political Imagination*, 99 YALE REV. 148, 148 (2011).

42. The prosecutor charged three other arresting officers with aiding and abetting murder. *See George Floyd Murder Suspect Derek Chauvin Has Bail Set at 1.25m*, BBC NEWS (June 8, 2020), https://www.bbc.com/news/world-us-canada-52961599.

43. "CPA Order 17, Status of the Coalition Provisional Authority, MNF - Iraq, Certain Missions and Personnel in Iraq, established that all personnel of the multinational force (MNF) and the CPA, and all International Consultants, are immune from Iraqi legal process, and are subject to the exclusive jurisdiction of their 'Sending States.'" R. CHUCK MASON, CONG. RESEARCH SERV., R400011 US-IRAQ WITHDRAWAL/STATUS OF FORCES AGREEMENT: ISSUES FOR CONGRESSIONAL OVERSIGHT 2 (July 13, 2009).

44. BENJAMIN WITTES & GABRIELLA BLUM, THE FUTURE OF VIOLENCE: ROBOTS AND GERMS, HACKERS AND DRONES—CONFRONTING A NEW AGE OF THREAT (2015).

45. Roger Harrabin, *Greta Thunberg: What Climate Summit Achieved after Outburst*, BBC NEWS (Sept. 24, 2019), https://www.bbc.com/news/science-environment-49807745.

46. Henrik Pryser Libell & Derrick Bryson Taylor, *Norway's Supreme Court Makes Way for More Artic Drilling*, N.Y. TIMES (Dec. 22, 2020), https://www.nytimes.com/2020/12/22/world/europe/norway-supreme-court-oil-climate-change.html?algo=combo_lda_channelsize20_unique_edimp_fye_step50_diversified&block=1&camp

aign_id=142&emc=edit_fory_20201222&fellback=false&imp_id=207650329&inst
ance_id=25317&nl=for-you&nlid=68113768&rank=3&regi_id=68113768&req_
id=755386262&segment_id=47616&surface=for-you-email-wym&user_id=2ec76
2efaded436e9996163f4f78cc58&variant=1_combo_lda_channelsize20_unique_e
dimp_step50_diversified.

47. Tedros Adhanom Ghebreyesus, *Vaccine Nationalism Harms Everyone and Protects No One*, Foreign Policy (Feb. 2, 2021), https://foreignpolicy.com/2021/02/02/vaccine-nationalism-harms-everyone-and-protects-no-one/.

48. Ulrich Beck, *The Silence of Words: On Terror and War*, 34 Security Dialogue 255 (2003).

49. Walter Isaacson, Einstein: His Life and Universe (Kindle ed. 2008).

50. Martti Koskenniemi, *The Place of Law in Collective Security*, 17 Mich. J. Int'l L. 455, 455 (1996).

51. Kathryn Sikkink, The Justice Cascade: How Human Rights Prosecutions are Changing World Politics 3–7 (Kindle ed. 2011).

52. To link knowledge with action it could be useful to import from the area of sustainability the concept of "boundary work": "The central idea of boundary work is that tensions arise at the interface between communities with different views of what constitutes reliable or useful knowledge." William C. Clark et al., *A Boundary Work for Sustainable Development: Natural Resource Management at the Consultative Group on International Agricultural Research (CGIAR)*, 11 Proc. Nat. Acad. Sciences 4615, 4615 (Pamela A. Matson ed. 2016).

53. Cass R. Sunstein, #Republic: Divided Democracy in the Age of Social Media 11 (Kindle ed. 2017).

54. A study in opinion dynamics and game theory both in regular and complex networks shows the impact of the Rome Statute's legal design. Éder M. Schneider et al., *Crimes against Humanity: The Role of International Courts*, 9 PLoS One (2014).

55. Anne-Marie Slaughter, A New World Order 4 (Kindle ed. 2009).

Introduction

This book is a case study of my nine-year practice as the first Chief Prosecutor of the International Criminal Court (ICC). It presents the functioning of the autonomous criminal justice system created by the Rome Statute.

The book depicts the Rome Statute operations, its interaction with the War on Terror, and their relationship with national legal systems and the UN Security Council. It comments on regional organizations, including the mechanisms to protect human rights established during the 1950s in Europe, afterward in the Americas, and more recently in Africa.[1]

Since the end of my tenure, have I felt the duty to transform my particular experiences into valuable data. I decided to present our strategic legal decisions,[2] implementing an unprecedented international mandate that transformed the meaning of sovereignty.

I don't have a thesis to prove. The book describes how the ICC Office of the Prosecutor and other relevant actors made specific legal decisions to launch or prevent the ICC's intervention in different situations and presents some of their consequences.

The Office of the Prosecutor's resolutions described in this book are the result of a collective effort. The entire office implemented our mandate. We absorbed ideas from court colleagues, states, international organizations, NGOs, academics, and journalists; following our legal duty, we paid particular attention to the victims' interests.

I learned from each member of the office, and, as an orchestra director, my role was to ensure that we followed the "symphonic score" and decide the timing of our different interventions. I had to approve many decisions when I was the prosecutor; this book presents some of them and our interactions with other relevant actors.

To put it simply, our job was to implement the Rome Statute. The Office of the Prosecutor's first duty is to conduct a *"preliminary examination,"* a process regulated by Articles 12, 15, 42, and 53 to identify situations under the court's jurisdiction and trigger the ICC intervention.

War and Justice in the 21st Century. Luis Moreno Ocampo, Oxford University Press. © Oxford University Press 2022.
DOI: 10.1093/oso/9780197628973.003.0001

The ICC prosecution is required to analyze multiple legal systems with overlapping jurisdictions.[3] The office had to identify crimes committed in the territory or by nationals of states parties and respect relevant national proceedings. After the UN Security Council referrals, the prosecution also analyzed Darfur and Libya's crimes and national proceedings. And the prosecutor had to respect the council's authority to suspend our investigations.

Informed by my firsthand perspective, the book portrays the facts that the Office of the Prosecutor considered and the rationale behind opening preliminary examinations in seventeen different situations and triggering the ICC jurisdiction in seven of them. I also comment on the pertinent rulings of the ICC judges on jurisdiction and admissibility.

The Office of the Prosecutor applied the statute consistently, and still, the outcomes varied.

The range is the result of the activity of many other actors. More than a century ago, Leo Tolstoy explained in *War and Peace*: "The movement of nations is caused not by power, nor by intellectual activity, nor even by a combination of the two as historians have supposed, but by the activity of all the people who participate in the events."[4]

As a privileged observer, I describe the decisions adopted by the *people who participate in the events* preventing or promoting the international criminal justice intervention. Some of them, including national authorities and the UN Security Council members, have a legal mandate to participate. The suspects, NGOs, and commentators participated in trying to influence the proceedings according to their vision.

I explain the rationale of our decisions and the circumstances that defined the outcomes. As Harold Koh, former US State Department legal adviser, said, "outsiders cannot fully evaluate the lawfulness of any state's conduct until they know the precise factual circumstances under which it chooses to take action."[5]

The sum of the particular decisions provides a glimpse of the complex interaction between different legal frames. I want to describe particularities to portray the universals.

My life taught me that legal designs are almost invisible and still a matter of life or death. When I was fourteen years old, I witnessed the clash between two very different sides of my family at teatime at my grandmother's house.

Two of my uncles were colonels supporting the military coup perpetrated in 1966, and my father was trying to dissuade them. His passionate defense of democracy and freedom did not change the mind of my mother's brothers.

They were sure that a military regime would be more efficient. While I loved my uncles and knew they were honest and sincere, I considered them wrong. Such conversation convinced me to study law.

Following *Normative Systems*, a seminal book published in 1971 by Carlos Alchourron and Eugenio Bulygin, I consider that a legal system is "a set of sentences that has (some) normative consequence for some Universe of cases (UC) and some Universe of Solutions (US)."[6]

The Rome Statute prescribes that when genocide, crimes against humanity, or war crimes are committed under the ICC's jurisdiction, the suspects should be investigated and prosecuted at the national level or in a complementary way by the ICC.

The UN Charter establishes that the UN Security Council is the only global authority responsible for international peace and security. It could include international criminal investigations and military interventions as optional methods and requests political negotiations as a solution.

The War on Terror is focused on killing alleged *enemy combatants* as the solution to control international terrorism. This model influences the council's decisions, and it conflicts with the Rome Statute to avoid judicial control.

The legal systems interact. The War on Terror model transformed US interests and exposed its personnel to international criminal justice, increasing US opposition to the ICC.

Many states parties to the Rome Statute also participated in the War on Terror. The International Security Assistance Force (ISAF)[7] deployment in Afghanistan counted fifty troop-contributing nations at its height. Out of them, thirty-nine were parties to the Rome Statute, and many of them reviewed their rules of engagement, taking into consideration the statute.

States parties, including the United Kingdom, Poland, and Australia, participated in Iraq's intervention from the beginning. Thirty-nine countries deployed troops to assist the US-led War in Iraq in either the initial invasion or the "Multi-National Force—Iraq" set up in 2004. Among these, twenty-four countries were parties to the Rome Statute. Many European leaders abandoned their initial criticisms and started to follow the War on Terror model.[8]

There are multiple legal systems demanding obedience or providing power to different actors simultaneously at the international level.[9] Although sometimes it is challenging to predict the outcomes, there is no chaos, just complexity.[10]

French Professor Mireille Delmas-Marty explains: "The interaction already occurring between multiple and heterogeneous legal systems does not offer the same image of legal certainty as that which results from the principle of hierarchy in the standard representation of legal systems. And yet, these are indeed legal, and therefore normative, interactions."[11] This book can help to elucidate such complexity.

The Rome Statute Established a New Field of Practice

The Rome Statute created a new field of practice.[12] States parties took the sovereign decision to delegate to the Office of the Prosecutor, a nonstate actor, the unprecedented authority to trigger the ICC's intervention for crimes committed in their own territory or by their own personnel. The book presents the Office of the Prosecutor's unique role as the *"gatekeeper"* of the Rome Statute, making decisions to activate or not the court's intervention.[13] The statute provoked an evolution of the concept of sovereignty and transformed an international legal system ruled exclusively by national states.

In Nuremberg, ICTY, and ICTR, political leaders decided the intervention of those ad hoc tribunals. The ICC follows a different model. Since 2003, a judicial actor,[14] the Office of the Prosecutor, became a decision maker in what was for decades an exclusive political scenario. There is no comprehensive academic field analyzing such a practice, and many scholars reject the model. For example, David Bosco produced the first complete description of the Rome Statute from an international relations perspective and considered that the ICC is "an unprecedented and anomalously designed institution."[15]

A miscomprehension about the ICC Office of the Prosecutor's role in triggering the court's jurisdiction created the perception of undue political activity for some commentators and a legal nuisance interfering with political decisions for other experts.

To clarify the scope of this unprecedented and emerging field of practice, I propose to use the expression *jus ad Curiam* to facilitate a dialogue between different academic disciplines.

I build on the well-known distinction between *jus ad Bellum* and *jus in Bello*. *Jus ad Bellum* establishes the conditions under which states may resort to war or the use of armed force in general.[16] *Jus in Bello* governs the conduct of parties engaged in an armed conflict, regardless of whether the hostilities' initiation was just.[17]

Following the same logic, *jus ad Curiam* comprises the political and legal decisions determining an international criminal justice intervention in specific situations. *Jus in Curiae* could be defined as the substantial and procedural body of law regulating the actors engaged in litigation to prove the defendant's responsibility.

The labels *jus ad Curiam* and *jus in Curia* help distinguish the Office of the Prosecutor's *preliminary examination* activities from its litigation before the chambers, highlighting a different legal practice.

Since 2003, national states and the UN Security Council lost their exclusivity to adopt *jus ad Curiam* decisions. The ICC Office of the Prosecutor also has authority in the field.

David Bosco accurately distinguished the two roles of the ICC prosecutor: what he called the "*initiation*" [preliminary examination] and the *investigation* function. He concluded: "In performing these two functions, [initiation/preliminary examination and investigation] the prosecutor has demonstrated quite distinct approaches to the major powers."[18]

Bosco rightly evaluated that in the investigation function, the prosecution was "increasingly loud" but "in the initiation function, however, the prosecutor has been remarkably quiet." He accurately assessed that the prosecution did "not challenge the Council's restrictions of the court's freedom of action or campaigned for expanded jurisdiction." And he observed that "In selecting this strategy, court officials have limited their ability to deploy the Court's moral authority."[19]

Bosco did not realize that the "*initiation*" function is part of the *jus ad Curiam*, and the UN Security Council has ample discretion to decide to refer or not a situation to the court. The Office of the Prosecutor has no authority to request referrals or to interfere in the Council prerogatives.

The *jus ad Curiam* field includes political actors considering their own interests, victims demanding justice, NGOs promoting specific values, and the ICC Office of the Prosecutor. This judicial actor should act impartially and follow legal procedures. There is no central authority to limit the different actors' selection of the legal frames, but the ICC Office of the Prosecutor must apply the Rome Statute exclusively. The judges would review some aspects of the prosecution's *jus ad Curiam* decisions in specific cases presented to prove a defendant's criminal responsibility.

The labels could also help to discuss the statute's relevance. The *jus ad Curiam* is about applying international criminal justice in a situation. The *jus in Curiae* concerns the individual responsibility of a defendant. Both aspects should be discussed and measured.

The *jus ad Curiam* label clarifies the international criminal justice relationship with *jus ad Bellum* decisions. One of the consequences of using the US Army to intervene in Afghanistan is that such a decision created clashes between the United States and the ICC after Afghanistan became a state party. Another example: the United States and Russia's intervention in Syria excluded the possibility of a *jus ad Curiam* resolution by the UN Security Council referring the situation to the ICC. The council would not be able to provide impartial international criminal justice to the Syrian victims. The Rome Statute consolidated the *jus ad Curiam* emerging legal field and, at the same time, the War on Terror against nonstate actors transformed *jus ad Bellum* and blocked *jus ad Curiam* decisions.

Outline of the Book

The background is an introduction describing my appointment, the Rome Statute and the War on Terror models, and the Office of the Prosecutor's first organizational decisions, including developing the preliminary examination process.

The first part presents the *jus ad Curiam* standards implemented in the four different situations opened in states parties' jurisdiction (DRC, Uganda, CAR, and Kenya) and nine of the other ten preliminary examinations conducted during my tenure. The office rejected three (Palestine, Venezuela, and UK personnel in Iraq), evaluated the crimes committed in three (Honduras, Korea, and Nigeria), and the national proceedings conducted in three (Guinea, Georgia, and Colombia). Each chapter presents various aspects of the preliminary examination, and in Chapter 8, the policy on the interest of justice; and Chapter 9, the interaction between justice and the peace negotiations with a militia called Lord Resistance Army (LRA).

The second part describes the *jus ad Curiam* and the *jus ad Bellum* decision adopted by the UN Security Council in nonstate parties, including Iraq, Darfur, Libya, and Syria. It also includes President Obama's renewal of the War on Terror policy and Afghanistan's military intervention, ICC preliminary examination in Afghanistan, and the interaction between Cote d'Ivoire, African regional organizations like the African Union (AU) and Economic

Community of West African States (ECOWAS), the UN Security Council, and the ICC.

Method of the Book

The book crosses academic disciplines and geographic areas to cover our practice diversity.

These are my observations as a participant, providing some new data and combining it with information already available in books, media, and academic papers but divided by topics.

Participant observation is a method used by ethnology scholars to describe the norms and conventions of specific groups. Instead, my global practice required me to apply various sets of norms, including national and international legal systems, and interact worldwide with many groups promoting their own legal models, from the Acholi in Northern Uganda to diplomats at the UN Security Council.

I prefer to describe the book as a *data fusion* exercise. It combines my participant explanations with multiple data sources and describes the interaction of multiple legal systems during the *jus ad Curiam* phase.

I am connecting dots to present a comprehensive picture of the formal and informal proceedings to launch the ICC interventions. The *data fusion* approach helps to transcend academic boundaries and to perceive the complexity of the international legal order.

The book aims to produce more relevant information than that provided by any single discipline. With an outstanding carrier as a practitioner and professor, Jose Alvarez considered, "The teaching of public international law has not caught up with its practice."[20] He submitted that international legal studies should focus on how the law is implemented by different actors and institutions rather than an exclusive analysis of the legal text.[21] The book is following his proposal.

I hope that commentators could help to add relevant data, correct my mistakes, and complete my analysis.

Measuring Efficiency

The Rome Statute system articulated activities across time and space, creating a shared goal and forming a global "*shadow*" (see Chapter 9). The strict judicial role during the *jus in Curiae* could be analyzed but the enforcement of the court's decisions is not in the judges' hands. Alexander Hamilton, one of the Founding Fathers of the US Constitution, graphically explained that the Judiciary "has no influence either over the sword or the purse" and "must ultimately depend upon the aid of the executive arm even for the efficacy of its judgments."[22]

The peculiarity of an ICC operating without an international government is that the enforcement depends on the nations' decisions. Implementing the court's resolutions is a sovereign responsibility.

The compliance with court orders was much higher in the treaty jurisdiction than in the jurisdiction provided by UN Security Council referrals. Article 59 establishes states parties' obligation to arrest.[23] States nonparties did not take such a commitment.

In the situations referred by the UN Security Council, the rate of fugitives in the cases presented during the first nine years is at the moment of writing this book 62.5%: five fugitives in eight cases.[24] Instead, the rate is more than ten times lower for the treaty jurisdiction cases: 5.5%. There is only one fugitive in eighteen cases.[25]

Beth A. Simmons and Hyeran Jo made a quantitative analysis confirming different deterrence impacts within the treaty jurisdiction and the UN Security Council referrals. They found that the Rome Statute had a deterrence impact within the state parties' jurisdiction, particularly on members of the governments but even on militias like the LRA.

Nonetheless, they also discovered that the ICC intervention did not have a similar impact on states' nonparties of the Rome Statute like Sudan and Libya, situations referred by the UN Security Council.[26]

Experts are discussing some aspects of Jo and Simmons's analysis. Still, there is no comparison between the limited and nuanced deterrence impact of the Rome Statute and the War on Terror's negative deterrence impact.

The data is revealing: despite the United States spending more than $6.4 trillion on a military-dominated approach to countering terrorism since September 2001, the violent extremist movement has metastasized.[27]

The number of deaths from terrorism in 2017 was three times the number in 2001, and the number of Islamist extremist fighters in 2018 was 270% higher than in 2001.[28] The book quotes many experts, including General Stanley McChrystal, confirming that the War on Terror, rather than deterred, expanded the support for international terrorism.

General Mc Chrystal, who commanded operations in Iraq and Afghanistan, mentioned the insurgents' community's duty of revenge, including their friends and family, members of the same tribe, or religion. He explained: "If you killed two out of ten insurgents, you don't end up with eight insurgents. You might end up multiplying the number of fighters aligned against you." "You're going to have something like twenty."[29] He labeled this paradoxical impact of the military operations against terrorism as the "insurgent math."[30]

An example of the duty of revenge when there is no justice mechanism is the case of Mohammad Sidique Khan, a British primary school teaching assistant, married and with one daughter. On December 7, 2005, he became a suicide bomber killing himself and six others. He said: "Your democratically elected governments continuously perpetuate atrocities against my people all over the world. And your support of them makes you directly responsible, just as I am directly responsible for protecting and avenging my Muslim brothers and sisters."[31]

After almost two decades, the War on Terror became *legitimate*, a "new normal" demanding to kill *enemies* abroad. Bombing in sovereign states, using proxy forces, and assassination became a dangerous common practice.

The world's community of experts and scholars is not proposing new and integrated legal solutions to manage international violence's challenges.

In 2015, Stephen Walt denounced a massive, collective failure of the entire US foreign-policy establishment, including Democrats and Republicans, to propose new strategies to deal with international terrorism in the Middle East.[32]

The problem did not disappear. In December 2018, President Trump announced his intention to withdraw all American troops from Syria and half from Afghanistan, uniting the US "left and right against" his plan but receiving no indication of what to do instead.[33]

Three years later, President Biden received no new plans. The US expert community knows that the military model to face international terrorism is not working, but it cannot discuss a different paradigm.

The twenty-first century did not produce a comprehensive legal framework and a grand strategy to deal with international terrorism. Analyzing how political, military, and judicial authorities implemented different legal systems during the first decade of the twenty-first century could do the following: (a) help to improve the functioning of the Rome Statute system

and (b) contribute to developing something new: a different and more efficient model to deal with international terrorism and other violence global
problems.

The book proposes connecting principles with reality.[34]

Notes

1. The first system allowing an individual to present cases before international human
   rights courts demanding the responsibility of the state was established in Europe
   during the 1950s by the European Convention on Human Rights. The second was
   established in Latin America by the American Declaration of the Rights and Duties
   of the persons (May 1948), and making it operational in 1960 when the Council of
   the OAS approved the Statute of the Inter-American Commission on Human Rights.
   In November 1969 the American Convention on Human Rights was adopted and
   entered into force on July 18, 1978, establishing the Inter-American Court of Human
   Rights. Both systems are now very well established and there are incipient efforts in
   Africa during the twenty-first century to create a similar model. Interestingly these
   three regions, Europe, Latin America, and Africa took the lead to adopt the Rome
   Statute. See KATHRYN SIKKINK, EVIDENCE FOR HOPE: MAKING HUMAN RIGHTS
   WORK IN THE 21ST CENTURY (Kindle ed. 2017). See also Jose Luis Morin, *Global and
   Regional Human Rights Commissions, in* INTERNATIONAL CRIME AND JUSTICE 386
   (Mangai Natarajan ed., Kindle ed. 2010).
2. *See* Yola Verbruggen, *Strategic Litigation: Opportunities and Pitfalls*, INTERNATIONAL
   BAR ASSOCIATION, https://www.ibanet.org/article/0dd39f54-34c7-4989-87b1-d94ab
   6d14def (last accessed July 3, 2021).
3. "One of the ways in which international law is affected by the complex and contradictory nature of international governance is through the emergence of several overlapping and competing normative orders." IGE F. DEKKER & WOTER G. WERNER,
   GOVERNANCE AND INTERNATIONAL LEGAL THEORY 23 (Nova et Vetera Iuris
   Gentium, Publications of the Institute of Public International Law of the University of
   Utrecht, 2004).
4. LEO TOLSTOY, WAR AND PEACE 24718 (Kindle ed. 2010).
5. He considered that government lawyers have a "duty to explain." Harold H. Koh, *The
   Legal Adviser's Duty to Explain*, 41 YALE J. INT'L L. 189, 203 (2016).
6. CARLOS ALCHOURRON & EUGENIO BULYGIN, NORMATIVE SYSTEMS 4–5 (1st ed. 1971).
7. The International Security Assistance Force was created and mandated by the UN
   Security Council Resolution 1386 to help the Afghan authorities to stabilize the
   country and ensure that it would not be a safe haven for terrorists anymore.
8. "In France, a constitutional state of emergency was in force for almost two years after
   a series of terrorist attacks in 2015; subsequently, many of the powers then issued
   for the police and military have been permanently enshrined in a new anti-terror
   law. Britain had one of its citizens killed in Iraq using a drone attack without even

attempting to provide any legal justification." Johannes Thimm, *From Exception to Normalcy*, STIFTUNG WISSENSCHAFT UND POLITIK 5 (Oct. 2018), https://www.swp-berlin.org/fileadmin/contents/products/research_papers/2018RP07_tmm.pdf.

9. The International Law Commission produced a report on "Fragmentation of international law: Difficulties arising from the diversification and expansion of international law" analyzing the problem. Rep.t of the Study Group of the Int'l L. Comm., 58th Sess., May 1, June 9, and July 3–Aug. 11, 2006, U.N. Doc. A/CN.4/L.682 (Apr. 13, 2006) (finalized by Martti Koskenniemi).

10. "[G]lobalization and international governance are not simple and linear developments, but rather complex and contradictory processes in which "homogenization goes hand in hand with differentiation, integration with fragmentation, centralization with decentralization, universalization with particularization." SUSAN MARKS, THE RIDDLE OF ALL CONSTITUTIONS: INTERNATIONAL LAW, DEMOCRACY AND THE CRITIQUE OF IDEOLOGY 78 (2000).

11. "At first glance, the answer to the challenge of the great legal complexity of the world seems to link together legal ensembles (national and international) that history has separated and will not accept hegemonic fusion." MIREILLE DELMAS-MARTY, ORDERING PLURALISM. A CONCEPTUAL FRAMEWORK FOR UNDERSTANDING THE TRANSNATIONAL LEGAL WORLD 14–15 (Naomi Norbergm trans., 2009).

12. Christine Bell, *Transitional Justice, Interdisciplinarity and the State of the "Field" or "Non-Field*,*" 3 INT'L J. TRANSITIONAL JUST. 5, 8–10 (2009).

13. Héctor Olásolo, *The Prosecutor of the ICC before the Initiation of Investigations: A Quasi-Judicial or a Political Body?*, 3 INT'L CRIM. L. REV. 87 (2003).

14. "In the Rome Statute, the Office of the Prosecutor should be considered a judicial authority, it is not part of any political body, is rooted in the civil law traditions and it could contravene other models were the Prosecutors are part of the Executive branch." PROSECUTORS AND DEMOCRACY: A CROSS-NATIONAL STUDY (ASCL STUDIES IN COMPARATIVE LAW) 311 (Maximo Langer & David Alan Sklansky eds., Kindle ed. 2017).

15. DAVID BOSCO, ROUGH JUSTICE, THE INTERNATIONAL CRIMINAL COURT IN A WORLD OF POWER POLITICS 17 (2014).

16. *What Are Jus ad Bellum and Jus in Bello?*, ICRC (Jan. 22, 2015), https://www.icrc.org/en/document/what-are-jus-ad-bellum-and-jus-bello-0.

17. *Id.*

18. DAVID BOSCO, ROUGH JUSTICE, THE INTERNATIONAL CRIMINAL COURT IN A WORLD OF POWER POLITICS 184 (2014).

19. "Prosecution officials insist that doing so would be impermissibly 'political.' That interpretation is understandable but not at all inevitable . . . Major states do not face a prosecutor actively (and, in some cases, embarrassingly) calling attention to situations where the court lacks jurisdiction. A quiet approach has also prevailed in other respects. Neither the prosecutor nor other court officials have challenged the way in which the Security Council has referred situations to the court . . ." *Id.* at 185.

20. JOSÉ E. ALVAREZ, THE IMPACT OF INTERNATIONAL ORGANIZATIONS ON INTERNATIONAL LAW 2 (Lam ed., 2017).

21. He highlighted a different method to analyze national legal systems "In the U.S., the teaching of national law usually means a focus on institutions." It involves the relations between "the executive, legislature, and judiciary." "It requires studying the interactions between the chief executive and the Congress" and also "various levels of courts" and "diverse governmental agencies that are delegated power by the executive and legislative branches of government to issue regulations on specific topics." José E. Alvarez, The Impact of International Organizations on International Law 2 (Lam ed., 2017).

22. Alexander Hamilton, Selected Works of Alexander Hamilton 2436 (Kindle ed. 2018).

23. It indicates that a state party *"shall immediately take steps to arrest the person in question in accordance with its laws and the provisions of Part 9."*

24. Three summon of appears and eight arrest warrants were issued in the situations referred by the UN Security Council. Libya leader's Muammar Gaddafi and Darfur rebel Saleh Mohammed Jerbo were killed. Abd-Al-Rahman (a.k.a. Ali Kushayb) surrendered to the ICC in June 2020. Five individuals remain as ICC fugitives, including former President al Bashir, former Sudan's Ministers Ahmed Harun and Abdel Raheem Muhammad Hussein, Darfur rebel Abdallah Banda, and informal Libya's leader Saif Al-Islam Gaddafi. The charges against Darfur rebel Abu Garda were not confirmed and the ICC accepted that Libya's national proceedings against Abdullah Al-Senussi made that case inadmissible.

25. Eighteen individuals were sought by the ICC in the states parties' jurisdiction during the first nine years. Of them, Joseph Kony is the only fugitive. Four were killed in action, (Raska Lukwiya, Vincent Otti, Okot Odhiambo, and Sylvestre Mudacumura), five were arrested and surrendered to the court by states parties like the DRC, Belgium, and France (Thomas Lubanga, Germain Katanga, Mattew Ngudjolo, Jean Pierre Bemba, Calixte Mbarushimana), six prominent Kenyans including the former deputy prime minister and current president appeared voluntarily before the court (Mohamed Hussein Ali, Joshua Arap Sang, William Samoei Ruto, Francis Kirimi Mutaura, Henry Kiprono Kosgey, Uhuru Muigai Kenyatta), and two militia leaders from DRC and Uganda surrendered to the United States and were transferred to the court (Bosco Ntaganda and Dominic Ongwen).

26. Hyeran Jo & Beth A. Simmons, *Can the International Criminal Court Deter Atrocity?*, 70 Int'l Org. 443 (2016).

27. *Economic Costs, Costs of War*, Watson Inst. Int'l & Pub. Aff., Brown U., https://watson.brown.edu/costsofwar/costs/economic (last updated Jan. 2020).

28. Eirc Rosand & Alistar Millar, *Nearly 20 Years Later: It's Time to Reset Our Approach to Countering Terrorism*, Just Security (Nov. 14, 2019), https://www.justsecurity.org/67270/nearly-20-years-later-its-time-to-reset-our-approach-to-countering-terrorism/.

29. Michael Hastings, The Operators 141 (Kindle ed. 2012). Stanley McChrystal's, *Gen. MacChrystal's Speech on Afghanistan*, Real Clear Politics (Oct. 1, 2009), https://www.realclearpolitics.com/articles/2009/10/01/gen_mcchrystals_address_on_afghanistan_98537.html..

30. Stanley McChrystal's, *Gen. McChrystal's Speech on Afghanistan*, REAL CLEAR POLITICS (Oct. 1, 2009), https://www.realclearpolitics.com/articles/2009/10/01/gen_mcchrystals_address_on_afghanistan_98537.html.

31. *London Bomber: Text in Full*, BBC NEWS (Sept. 1, 2005, 10:01 PM), http://news.bbc.co.uk/2/hi/uk/4206800.stm.

32. Stephen M. Walt, *Just Say No*, FOREIGN POLICY (Mar. 31, 2015, 11:39 AM) https://foreignpolicy.com/2015/03/31/just-say-no-us-war-on-terror-yemen-iraq/.

33. Mark Landler, *Trump Unites Left and Right Against Troop Plans, but Puts Off Debate on War Aims*, N.Y. TIMES (Dec. 27, 2018), https://www.nytimes.com/2018/12/27/us/politics/trump-syria-afghanistan-withdraw.html.

34. Ian Shapiro identified a dissociation between the study and practice of the law in medieval England that could apply to the study of international law in the twenty-first century. Legal French was the hybrid language used in the English courts and Latin was the language of jurisprudence in Oxford and Cambridge. "Whatever the reason, English jurisprudence developed in literal ignorance of the practice of English law." Shapiro affirms that "[a] comparable disjunction afflicts the human sciences today" scholars "see themselves as engaged in interpretation rather than explanation." IAN SHAPIRO, THE FLIGHT FROM REALITY 2 (Kindle ed. 2005).

BACKGROUND

1

The Appointment and the First Days

An Unexpected Proposition

The Call to Become the First Global Prosecutor

In November 2002, I was parking my car in downtown Buenos Aires when my phone rang. It was a collaborator of Prince Zeid, then Jordan's Permanent Representative to the United Nations[1] and president of the Assembly of States Parties of the Rome Statute.

My national experience prosecuting massive crimes had placed my name at the top of a list of potential candidates for the ICC Chief Prosecutor position. Prince Zeid wanted to meet me in New York to discuss whether I would be interested in the job.

The call took me by surprise. I was not involved in any of the Rome Statute's discussions, and I never proposed my name for any position in the court. At the time, I felt that my most significant professional achievement laid well behind me.

In 1985 I was the deputy prosecutor of the "Trial of the Juntas," a case against nine members of the different military juntas that ruled Argentina between 1976 and 1982 and the peak of profound national transformation.[2]

Between 1928 and 1983, military coups had ousted all the democratically elected governments in Argentina before the end of their constitutional terms.[3] All of Argentina's previous dictators enjoyed absolute immunity after they left power. But in 1983, 52% of the electorate supported the proposal of one of the candidates, Raul Alfonsin, to investigate the crimes.

It was the beginning of a transition from a military system of enemies to a democratic system that included a truth commission and a criminal investigation of the Army leaders and other perpetrators. The 1985 judicial hearings unveiled a secret "counterinsurgency" criminal campaign and transformed the dictatorship's public perception. The trial was an

War and Justice in the 21st Century. Luis Moreno Ocampo, Oxford University Press. © Oxford University Press 2022.
DOI: 10.1093/oso/9780197628973.003.0002

investigative and legal challenge and a critical piece of my country's transition to democracy.[4]

Argentina's experience had international repercussions. Harvard Professor Kathryn Sikkink visited the courtroom in Buenos Aires during the "Trial of the Juntas" and presented it as a critical part of the global "Justice Cascade."[5] She explained: "Argentina helped invent the two main accountability mechanisms that are the focus of much of the debate on transitional justice: truth commissions and high-level human rights prosecutions."[6]

Priscilla Hayner, who did seminal research on truth commissions, stated that Argentine's CONADEP was the first of five of the "most substantial—judged by the size, the impact they had on their respective political transitions, and the national and international attention they received . . ." It was followed by "Chile, El Salvador, South Africa, and Guatemala."[7]

My Junta trial experience taught me about counterinsurgency military plans and, at the same time, the complex process of a transition to democracy, something very different than my legal studies at Buenos Aires University Law School. My law professors emphasized principles, legal texts, and scholar analysis; implementation was not relevant.

My criminal law courses were based on German theories. One of my classmates said, "Professor, the legal analysis is fascinating, but what is its relevance? There is a police station in the corner of my house, and each night I hear from my bedroom how the suspects are tortured." The professor, who had researched at the Max Planck Institute in Germany, said, "I'm sorry, what happens in the corner of your house is irrelevant; this is a normative science."

I saw the gap between teaching and my country's practice, but I enjoyed the theoretical precision, and so I became a criminal law professor's assistant. Philosophy of law also attracted my attention. My professors, Carlos Alchourron and Eugenio Bulygin, challenged Hans Kelsen, an Austrian scholar with enormous influence in Europe. They created a new field analyzing "Normative Systems" following a Finnish author, Georg Henrik von Wright's influential work on "deontic logic."

After my graduation in 1980, one of my criminal law professors, Enrique Paixao, invited me to join the Solicitor General Office as a clerk. Argentine Constitution is based on the US Constitution, our judges quoted US precedents, and my work preparing solicitor general's briefs gave me some understanding of the US criminal justice system.

In 1984, Julio Strassera, *Junta trial*'s prosecutor, asked me to be his deputy. I felt honored, but I explained that I had no practical experience; all my previous work was analytical. He considered that my lack of involvement in Argentina's inquisitive criminal procedure was actually to my advantage.

The military code regulated the junta's case, and the prosecutor was responsible for the investigation. That was unusual; in those days, in Argentina's federal system, the judge of instruction was in charge of investigating.

We had to prove before a court of law the responsibility of three former dictators and six other top commanders in thousands of abductions, tortures, and killings committed by their subordinates.

"You understand how the US Prosecutors prepare their cases," Strassera told me, so "We had to invent something new for the Junta case. We cannot ask the police to investigate; many of them were involved in the crimes."

We assembled a small team to transform the information obtained by the truth commission (CONADEP) into evidence. This is when I learned the importance of understanding the facts and how to analyze military operations against civilians.

During the following seven years, I had been an Argentine prosecutor involved in critical cases related to our transition to democracy. I led the prosecution against other leaders of the Army and security forces involved in the counterinsurgency crimes; grand corruption cases against business-people and politicians; the review of a military malpractice case against the Malvinas/Falkland war commanders; and two military rebellion cases, including the last and final one in 1990.

Those cases developed my ability to be involved in highly controversial disputes without letting criticism or support influence my legal decisions.

In 1992, I resigned as the top Buenos Aires federal prosecutor and established my own law firm, but I continued to participate in public life as a private citizen. I had ten years of fascinating practice as a private lawyer, organizing methods to control corruption in big private companies and governments. My law firm included investigators, sociologists, and IT experts. I learned how private managers run big organizations.

I recognized that grand corruption is an international business with banks and hidden partners in different parts of the world. Until the 1990s, European companies could deduct bribes payments from their taxes. In 1995 I participated in the first meeting at the Organisation for Economic Co-operation and Development (OECD) to discuss the matter, and in 1998 I supported World Bank president James Wolfensohn to include anticorruption efforts in the international financial agenda.[8]

After that, I was advising the World Bank and the Inter-American Development Bank on strategies to control corruption.

I participated as a citizen in the development of national and international NGOs focused on civic participation and anticorruption. I visited more than forty countries, learning and discussing how to control corruption.

I realized that my legal education was not enough to understand crime's and justice's different dimensions. For two years, I joined a group of political science and communication scholars studying the role of criminal justice during Argentina's transition to democracy.[9]

As part of such an effort, I published a book in 1996 using the evidence collected during the Junta trial to explain the political and social background of the crimes.[10]

In 1999, in a paper in the *Journal of International Affairs*, I stated, "measuring the whole process by the number of convictions, would be a mistake. The information about the crimes and the trials themselves effectively demarcated the line between dictatorship and democracy."[11]

I learned from my mother the relationship between trials and public perceptions. While investigating the junta case in 1984, I failed to convince her that the junta members should be prosecuted. My mother admired General Videla; she went to church with him; and he reminded her of my grandfather, who was also a general. She thought that the generals were protecting her from the guerrillas and that I was wrong.

The witnesses changed my mother's mind. During the trial, even the most conservative Argentine newspapers published every day at least two pages with the chronicles of their testimonies. Reading their stories, my mother changed her mind. After just two weeks of the beginning of the trial, she told me: "I still love General Videla, but you are right; he has to be in jail."

Her reaction was an example of how the respectful judicial ritual of exposing the suffering of the victims influenced the perception of the "truth,"[12] blurring the scholars' distinctions between punitive and restorative justice.[13]

The trial has to fulfill all the legal requirements. Still, its relevance, including establishing the truth and promoting a different culture, is a different matter and will not be defined in the courtroom. The narratives about crimes and justice will determine its impact on society. "Sociologists have long argued that knowledge about the world, including crimes, is socially constructed."[14] Winning a case in court is just a contribution to a social process. In 2022, Amazon presented a feature film about our activities as prosecutors in the Junta trial, my youngest sons learned about my work from it.

Viet Thanh Nguyen presented a concept that could also be applied to trials of massive atrocities; he said, "all wars are fought twice, the first time on the battlefield, the second time in memory."[15]

Public memory is the focus of a particular academic field.[16] In 1997, I explored how to use massive communication to explain the legal systems. I hosted a TV show presenting cases and exploring how to disseminate fundamental knowledge about justice and conflict negotiation.[17]

In 2002 I was sure that I had already reached my most significant professional achievement as the deputy prosecutor of the junta trial. I had accepted offers to be a visiting professor at Stanford University and Harvard University to conceptualize my practice. I now realize that my varied previous professional activities were my training to be the ICC Chief Prosecutor.

The very nature of Prince Zeid's call exposed a new legal design. He was not calling me on behalf of Jordan, a state member of the UN committed to protecting human rights in its territory, but as president of the Assembly of States Parties of the Rome Statute. Prince Zeid was officially representing a states' network.

I was highly skeptical about my chances of being appointed as the ICC prosecutor, but I was unwilling to reject his invitation.

On a cold morning in December 2002, I visited the Jordanian embassy in New York.

Prince Zeid is a charming and skillful diplomat who was not yet forty, whose grandfather fought with Lawrence of Arabia, and whose mother was Swedish. During the nineties, he worked with the UN peacekeeping forces in the Balkans under Kofi Annan's direction and became a leader in the Rome Conference discussions.

He was trying to reach a rapid consensus to appoint the prosecutor before February 2003, when selecting the eighteen judges would start. We had an exciting conversation, exploring the challenges of the ICC prosecutor role and my national experience. But I remained highly skeptical about being appointed.

The Previous Proposal to Become the ICTY Prosecutor

Almost ten years before, I had learned how complex the process to appoint an international prosecutor was. The UN Security Council created the International Criminal Tribunal for the former Yugoslavia (ICTY) and reached an informal agreement to appoint me as the first chief prosecutor.

The Argentinian government was invited to propose my name, but the Menem administration refused. As a national prosecutor, I had led several investigations into public corruption, and my government considered me a political enemy.[18] Argentina's minister of foreign affairs informed me that someone else would be put forth as Argentina's candidate.

I did not resent Argentina's lack of support. In those days, I was not ready to accept an international position. In 1992 I had resigned as Buenos Aires's top federal criminal prosecutor after being involved in the conviction of the leaders of the last military rebellion in 1990, and I felt that Argentina's transition to democracy was complete.

I had established my law firm, and I had to focus on my family. I had a teenager son and daughter from my first marriage, and I had just remarried.

In August 1993, the UN Secretary-General proposed Cherif Bassiouni as the first chief prosecutor of the ICTY. He had been the leading force behind the UN Commission of Enquiry's working on the Balkans and became the obvious choice.[19] But his candidacy did not obtain the support needed.

In October 1993, the UN Security Council appointed Venezuela's general prosecutor Ramon Escobar Salom as the first chief prosecutor of the ICTY, who resigned just a few months later.[20] After complex negotiations, the UN Security Council appointed a prestigious judge from South Africa, Richard Goldstone, as the first ICTY prosecutor.[21]

My Appointment as the ICC Prosecutor

In 2002, my situation was different. After ten years of private practice, I took sabbatical leave from my law firm to conceptualize my experience at the national and international levels. I had accepted two offers as a visiting professor. In 2002 I spent time at Stanford University while preparing to pass a year at Harvard Law School.

After my conversation with Prince Zeid, I contacted the new president of Argentina, Eduardo Duhalde. I was informed that Argentina presented a supreme court's justice as a candidate to be appointed as an ICC's judge and would neither promote nor oppose my appointment. My country's position reduced my limited chances even further. States were competing to appoint their candidates, and it was difficult to imagine that Argentina would have both a judge and the chief prosecutor.

In any case, to understand the process and the expectations involved, I met Silvia Fernandez de Gurmendi in Buenos Aires for the first time.[22] She was an Argentinian diplomat who had played a critical role before, during, and after the Rome Conference. We had lunch, and her brilliance and sense of humor impressed me.

She knew everything about the process to adopt the statute and explained the crucial details of the negotiations. She emphasized the states' most significant concerns: the prosecutor's independence to trigger the court's jurisdiction.

In January 2003, I left Buenos Aires's summer and moved to Cambridge, Massachusetts. I remember walking through ten inches of snow in Harvard yard, thinking how lucky I was to be there reflecting on cutting-edge legal issues.

I was to co-teaching a course with Philip Heyman on corruption problems and running a small seminar discussing how to establish the rule of law globally. Meanwhile, Prince Zeid informed me that it had not been possible to reach an agreement on the candidate for prosecutor's position before the judges' selection and urged me to keep considering the possibility.

On March 11, 2003, Prince Zeid, as the president of the Assembly of States Parties; and Queen Beatrix of the Netherlands, representing the host country, presided the ICC's judges' swearing-in at The Hague. A skillful senior Canadian diplomat, Ambassador Philippe Kirsch, who presided over the Rome Conference, was elected president of the court. A prosecutor had to be selected in April.

The Argentine candidate for the judge position was not elected, and I was invited to discuss the possibility of being appointed. During Harvard's spring break week, I took up invitations from London, The Hague, and Oslo to be interviewed by members of the ministries of foreign affairs deciding on the nominations. All of them played important roles before and during the Rome Conference.

I went to the Ministry of Foreign Affairs in London and Elizabeth Wilmshurst, the UK Foreign Office Deputy Legal Adviser, interviewed me. She was very thoughtful and asked about my experience and my vision. I felt the conversation went well, but she resigned a few days later when the Iraq conflict started.

I traveled to The Hague and had a more informal conversation during lunch in a restaurant with the Dutch Ambassador in charge of the Rome

Statute and the Legal Advisor of the Netherlands' Minister of Foreign Affairs. More than interviewing me, they were explaining what they were planning.

At the Hague, I also visited the ICC's temporary premises. I met Sam Muller, who was working in the registry, and Morten Bergsmo,[23] the acting legal adviser of the Office of the Prosecutor. Morten coordinated further meetings for me in Germany, France, and Spain.

In Oslo, I met Ambassador Rolf Fife, then legal advisor of the Ministry of Foreign Affairs, who led the opposition to the US proposal to delay the vote at the end of the Rome Conference. He offered me a frugal Norwegian lunch at his office, and we had a long conversation. I had the impression that I was confusing him with my explanations about international criminality by showing a network analysis that I was using at my Harvard course.

My meeting in Berlin didn't go too well. In 2002, I denounced journalistic malpractice by one of the leading media groups in an Argentina's controversial case. The media group started to publish information against me.

Ambassador Hans Peter Kaul, who led the German delegation at the Rome Conference, showed me some Argentine newspapers' front pages attacking me. He was a diplomat and was concerned about such types of media attacks.

Ambassador Kaul also considered a problem that I was a Transparency International's board member, a global NGO against corruption. He believed Transparency International was a US group. It was difficult to convince him that its founder was Peter Eigen, a German citizen, and its headquarters were in Berlin, twenty blocks away from his own office.

The following day, at the building at Quai d' Orsay in Paris, I met the French legal advisor, Ronny Abraham, and we discussed some general ideas about the court. The statute established French and English as working languages, and I knew that for France, my ability to speak its language was essential.

During the meeting, I found that my recently acquired habit of speaking poor English had an unexpected consequence: it completely erased my previous decent French proficiency. I tried to convince the French legal adviser that I could understand his words even though I could not articulate a line in his language.

After a general conversation in Madrid with Ambassador Yañez Barrionuevo, then legal adviser of the Ministry of Foreign Affairs who was also involved at the Rome Conference, I flew back to Buenos Aires to spend a few days with my family. After my trip, I was even more skeptical about any appointment.

That Sunday, I was having breakfast at my house in Buenos Aires, still tired after my intense travel week. I told my wife, "I am glad I made an effort, but I don't think they will appoint me. States don't like independent prosecutors. Carla del Ponte has relevant experience after her work in Switzerland and ICTY/ICTR, and she would probably be interested in the job, but no one is considering her. Don't worry; our lives will not change."

She was reading an Argentina newspaper. Five minutes later, she showed me a short article on page 6: "Informal consensus reached: Luis Moreno Ocampo will be the Prosecutor of the new International Criminal Court."[24] Our lives did change.

I sold my law firm to my partners, we bought a house in The Hague, but my family stayed in Buenos Aires. I commuted each month for nine years to visit my wife and my children.

Defining my Priorities

While waiting for my official appointment, I went back to Harvard to complete my teaching while planning my next steps. My responsibility as the first ICC Chief Prosecutor was to build the institution. I had to identify the most critical issues and define my priorities. I sought advice from Fernando Oris de Roa on using the private sector's efficiency to build an international organization.

Fernando was a successful Argentinian businessman who worked in senior positions in multinational companies in New York, Paris, and Argentina who decided to take a sabbatical year to do a master's in public policy at the Kennedy School when he was fifty years old.

I thought he had the personal maturity and the combination of experience and theoretical knowledge that I needed, but he said:

"I would love to help, but I have no experience in legal institutions."

"The legal issues are not my biggest problem. I could hire lawyers with experience in international law, and I can consult the best world experts. My responsibility is to build the ICC Office of the Prosecutor from scratch and transform it into a permanent institution."

"You are a startup."

"Yes, but a unique start-up. At the national level, the Office of the Prosecutor is part of the state apparatus, but we are different. We are a stateless Prosecutor. We have to deal with conflicts in different parts of the world without a foreign affairs ministry, a justice ministry, or a police force. There is no benchmark for that. I need to plan how to combine the different pieces."

Fernando invited me to his house near Harvard Square to analyze the problems I was facing. We were sitting very formally in his living room. He offered me coffee and asked me:

"Start with the basics. What is your mandate?"

"In the words of the Statute: to ensure the end of impunity for "the most serious crimes to the international community as a whole" and "to contribute to the prevention of such crimes." The Statute is very clear on the first part, and there is less clarity on how the International Criminal Court could prevent such crimes. For me, this is a critical part: how do we contribute to prevention?"

"In this context, what is your specific mission?"

"I have to build an institution: the Office of the Prosecutor. The Office mandate is to identify situations under the Court's jurisdiction and trigger its intervention to investigate and prosecute before the court. The Office will be the main driver of the Court during the first period."

"OK. What are your main problems?"

"I have to put the system in motion very quickly, and I have no human resources, no clarity on the policies, and my main constituencies have conflicting expectations. States are worried about a very active prosecutor affecting their agendas while eighteen judges from all over the world are waiting for a case. They had previous prominent positions: they were Supreme Court judges, Ambassadors, and they decided to leave those positions to join the Court. Now they want to be involved in judicial proceedings as soon as possible. Additionally, I learned that some of them feel that the entire ICC project could be interrupted at any moment. Starting a trial could be the way to consolidate the institution."

"They are probably right. Operations should begin as soon as possible. Can you present a case in a short time?"

"I have no chance. Today the entire office comprises three people: a legal advisor, a manager, and an assistant. There is no security system to protect witnesses; there is no investigator and no lawyer with prosecutorial experience. I should appoint people on their merits, and the recruitment process will take at least six months. I don't want to make mistakes. The office should attract the best people from all over the world; it should be the "Olympus" of all national Prosecutors' offices. Professionalism is the only way to ensure respect for our mission."[25]

"How did the other international prosecutors address this?"

"In the beginning, the ICTY Prosecutor had many resource problems and bureaucratic obstacles to hire staff. Richard Goldstone had few options. The only way to start investigations was to rely on a few friends and accept gratis personnel from the US. The ICTY needed years to overcome such improvisation and its personnel's lack of diversity. We need to learn from such a lesson."

"Do you have similar resource problems?"

"Not at all. States parties appointed an advance team to prepare an entire building to host the Court and acquire the required equipment. There are six floors fully equipped at my disposal and a budget."

"Can you use your resources to explore transitional solutions? Can you appoint a small team to develop a case while you are recruiting the permanent staff?"

"The first decision is not how to collect evidence but rather where to investigate. I have to identify a situation under the Court's jurisdiction."

"Can you appoint a special team just to conduct such a process? What did you call it? Preliminary examination?"

"I am focusing on that, but we need some clear policies. Triggering the Court jurisdiction is the most controversial part of the ICC project. Everyone is worried about how the Office of the Prosecutor will do it. We should respect the 'principle of complementarity,' which is the cornerstone of the system created by the Rome Statute."

"Why is that so controversial?"

"Because it is challenging the pillar of our international legal order which has existed for three centuries: absolute sovereignty. The Office should have a clear policy before making any decision, a policy that should be sustained in the long run. I cannot move ahead and then backtrack. I would never do that."

"OK. Let me focus on what I know: management. That is the area where I can be more helpful," said Fernando. "Can you decide on your human and financial resources?"

"I have total independence: the Statute provided me with "full authority over the management and administration of the Office."[26] I have the responsibility to foresee the activities required and petition a specific budget. Additionally, because I am the first Prosecutor, I have the unique opportunity to design a structure for the Office to fulfill its mandate and to present it for approval to the Assembly of States Parties."

"Do you expect problems to approve your budget? Who will pay the costs?"

"The state parties will pay, and we are now in a honeymoon period. Every indication I received is that states are ready to resolve financial problems. In any case, I have to be very cost-efficient in the structure proposed to ensure stability in the long term. After the end of the honeymoon, the situation will be different. I have the chance to build the most efficient public office."

"Talking about efficiency: How big will your administrative section be?"

"Almost inexistent. The Registry is in charge of the administration of the entire Court. They are in charge of the back office. Additionally, they have to provide security, protection to our witnesses, and outreach."

Suddenly, Fernando lost his calm. He could not accept that situation.

"Does the Registry report to you?"

"No, it is a different organ. It provides services to us, but also the defense, the victims, and the judges. The Registrar reports to the Presidency of the Court."

"You should change that. You could be paralyzed. It is a basic concept: you cannot have the responsibility without authority. Change that should be your priority."

"I am sorry I cannot change it. That is the legal design."

He insisted on changing the administration system. "It will be a nightmare." He accepted to move on but still thought nothing could work. "Is there any other problem that you should take into consideration?"

"The most important: how to get cooperation from states parties, nonparties, the UN, and NGOs? As soon we leave the building, we are in international jurisdiction, and we need States' cooperation. We need visas, security, and support to interview witnesses and to collect evidence. I am not sure if state parties will provide the support needed. I am not quite sure how much they can resist the US' hostility and how the UN's cooperation would be impacted."

"Are states willing to cooperate with the Office of the Prosecutor?"

"There is a whole part of the Statute defining the state parties' legal duties to cooperate with the ICC's investigations and prosecutions. But there is nothing about preventing crimes or arresting individuals in a foreign territory. These are two areas without solutions."

"I don't like to discourage you, but you are facing a complicated situation. You don't control your operations' basic functions, and you have to rely on external actors' goodwill. How can you organize them? You cannot plan a network. As you explained, each node makes decisions independently, following their interests. I am not sure how I can help you."

"On the contrary, thank you for this exercise. It helped me organize my mind. As you just said, I have to plan my office but also to create a network. I should take advantage of the high value of our mission to attract the other actors' support. I see three choices:

(a) To start immediately with an investigation to launch the entire exercise. But there is a high risk of failure because the office is not ready, and such failure could be the end of the institution.
(b) To consult with states, NGOs, and the different stakeholders to align their interests and ensure their support. The risk is becoming paralyzed by the search for consensus.
(c) To prioritize internal matters and focus our efforts on the Office's policies and structure and staff selection. The risk is losing time to launch the institution and then support our activities.

"And what you will do?"

"I cannot prioritize. I have to face the three issues at the same time. Before taking office, I will focus on structure and policies. The acting legal advisor is working on that. He is collecting over one hundred expert opinions on how to deal with these issues. I will consolidate them and prepare a first draft describing our draft policy and structure. The day I am sworn in, I will take advantage of the strategic planning process to simultaneously consult our constituencies. I will invite states representatives, experts, NGOs, and national and international prosecutors and judges to receive their comments on our plans in a public hearing. I will appoint a small team of experts and rely on them to identify the first situations to be investigated and trigger the Court's intervention as soon as I can."

Creating Support for the Office

Meeting States Parties

Before my appointment became official, I wanted to meet states parties to offer them the possibility of asking questions. I wanted to express my commitment to respect the Rome Statute fully. It was a mistake. I did not realize that I should not reopen the process. The decision to appoint me was already adopted in the capitals.

In any case, following my request, the Argentine's UN permanent representative in New York agreed to organize informal meetings to allow states parties to meet me. I had four different sessions with ambassadors and legal advisors from all the regions, but they were just polite conversations without substantial analysis. Most of the diplomats had no interest in the intricacies of the statute.

However, in the meeting with countries from Europe, a legal advisor from a civil law country asked me, "Do you consider yourself a civil law or a common-law lawyer? I am asking because you come from a civil law country, but you spent time working in the US, a common law country."

I thought he was offering me an excellent opportunity to make my point about respect for the rules adopted in Rome. I took my statute book, raised it, and said, "I am a lawyer and this, the Rome Statute, is the law that I should apply. I do not care about civil law or common law."

I was very proud of my answer, but the legal advisor was disturbed. At the end of the meeting, he approached me and said, "You are wrong. You are appointed to represent the civil law countries."

Diplomats have a particular mission: to promote the agenda of their own country. Consequently, a state's network behaves peculiarly; reasons and facts on the specific matters are not the most critical factors. As it happens with any network, each node follows its own interest. That is why it was very complex to align them with our legal decisions.

Meeting the NGOs

NGOs provided crucial support for adopting the Rome Statute, and I was expecting their help to make the system operational. I knew Aryeh Neier from his time in the American Civil Liberty Union. I followed his role in creating Human Rights Watch and then as president of the Open Society Foundation. He agreed with me on the need to quickly articulate the relationship between the court and NGOs. He convened many of them in April 2003 at the New York headquarters of Open Society.

I had significant experience working with Argentinean and international NGOs.[27] Still, I failed to realize that international NGOs working for global justice did not have the tradition of maintaining a close relationship with international prosecutors.

The Argentinian NGOs I had worked with were primarily composed of parents who lost their sons and daughters under the military junta. They were always supportive and respectful of our efforts, as prosecutors, to obtain justice in the courts. They helped us contact the victims and provided copies of the "habeas corpus" petitions they had filed to locate their relatives. They wanted justice for their children.

At the international level, Transparency International had a strategy to be close to the authorities to support them while retaining its independence criticizing what was wrong.

The Open Society meeting gave me a better understanding of the various interests among the different NGOs involved in the international justice project. There was no single agenda. Each NGO approached me to promote its specific topic, and they didn't like any compromise.

Some groups concentrated on the idea of punishing perpetrators, others on advancing the gender agenda or the protection of children. Humanitarian groups supported the role of justice, but they were afraid of exposing their operations on the ground in conflict-affected areas. Other NGOs were interested in being involved with the investigations underpinning international criminal prosecution or interested in the concept of victims' participation in justice proceedings.

The umbrella organization, the Coalition for the International Criminal Court,[28] led by Bill Pace, harmonized NGOs' agendas during the Rome Conference and transformed them into a powerful promotor for adopting the statute.

The coalition was trying to ensure that the NGOs would continue working together during this new phase while respecting their different interests and expectations. Building this diversified coalition with a loose goal was likely the only strategy to maintain cooperation among NGOs with divergent interests. They support the ICC work but also want the prosecutor to follow their specific agenda.

Some of them were suspicious of my interest in being close to them; they were not used to having access to the prosecutors and felt that I threatened their independence. Additionally, these groups worked for almost ten years on creating the court, facing massive opposition, and focusing on the court's problems. They had reasonable doubts about whether I was prepared to meet the challenge and fulfill their expectations.

Nonetheless, I considered the NGOs a critical constituency. They represented civil society with a vested interest in our work, and I promised to maintain a regular dialogue with them. Therefore, I adopted a ritual of periodic meetings. Every six months, we received them at the office of the prosecutor to discuss our plans and interaction for my entire tenure. Later it became a practice adopted by the other ICC's organs.

The Cambridge Retreat

On April 21, 2003, the Assembly of States parties met in New York and unanimously appointed me. I organized a retreat to discuss the office's strategy and structure. I invited Morten Bergsmo, the office's acting legal advisor; and Silvia Fernandez to stay at the house I was renting in Cambridge, Massachusetts. While cooking, I had learned about the operational aspects of the ICTY and fully understood the expectations of the states parties.

Based on Morten Bergsmo's previous extensive consultation, we started to prepare a draft document to be discussed at the public hearing immediately after my swearing-in.

We adopted three main innovations compared to the ICTY/ICTR structure of the office of the prosecutor: (1) a specialized area of the office that would deal with the complementarity and the cooperation challenges,[29] (2) joint teams integrating the investigators and litigators from the beginning of the case to avoid the lack of coordination of the ICTY/ICTR investigations,[30] and (3) the creation of a victim unit with a particular focus on gender and children's issues.[31]

Silvia Fernandez had a critical role as the vice president of the Rome Conference and kept a good relationship with all the relevant actors. She knew how to achieve results in the diplomatic arena representing a country like Argentina, which was not a significantly influential one.

I had no experience in diplomatic relations, so I asked her to take a leave of absence from Argentina's minister of foreign affairs and join the office as chief of cabinet. This position did not require a formal process of selection and could be filled immediately.[32]

My Interaction with the US Administration

In those days, a Harvard colleague advised me to reject the offer I had received: "Luis, it would be a great honor to be the first ICC's chief prosecutor," he said, "but without the US support, the Court would not be able to investigate or to arrest." "It will not work and it will be a shame. You will spend nine years in The Hague receiving a salary for doing nothing."

He had a point. The Bush administration's hostility could reduce much-needed support from states parties and international organizations. I was thinking of a strategy to manage the relationship with the United States when I received a phone call from a friend who proudly informed me that he was going to take a high-level position in the Bush administration.

I explained my situation, and he told me that he could easily organize a couple of meetings within the US administration to clarify those matters. He was very confident that any problem could be resolved. Three days later, he called me back: "Luis, your place is radioactive! As soon as I mentioned the words "International Criminal Court," people turned away and let me talk alone."

I was intrigued by such a reaction and checked with some other contacts. The results were similar; no US government officials would agree to even meet me. In a private conversation, a former US State Department legal advisor explained that it was not personal. "We believe that you can do a good job," he said, "but this will be bad for US interests." They preferred a court without legitimacy, unable to constrain US options.

Understanding the US perspective so early into my tenure was very useful for me. I concluded that there was nothing I could do to change the US position concerning the court. I should disregard its concerns and focus on building the office, learning how to work with states that wanted to create the Rome Statute justice system.

Sergio Vieira de Mello: An Unusual Head of an International Organization

I received a phone call from Sergio Vieira de Mello. He identified himself as the UN High Commissioner for Human Rights. He was flattering me, expressing his admiration for my work in Argentina, which he said he followed closely and wanted to offer me his full support. After five minutes of conversation, he talked to me as if I was an old friend, making jokes and telling me stories about his work in Congo and East Timor. He spoke about the need to prevent massive crimes and invited me to meet him in Geneva to discuss how we could complement each other's work.

Sergio was a rising star in the UN. He was born in Rio de Janeiro but had studied philosophy at the Sorbonne University, where he had participated in the social revolt of May 1968 in Paris. Brazil had a dictatorship in those days, and Sergio did not return. Instead, he started a long career at the UN.

Sergio worked in conflict zones like Bangladesh, Sudan, Zimbabwe, Mozambique, Peru, Cambodia, the former Yugoslavia, Congo, and East Timor. He knew how to interact with politicians and diplomats in the UN corridors and with victims and perpetrators.

In mid-May, I went to Geneva to meet Sergio in person for the first time. His office was very formal; a driver and a protocol person met me at the airport and took me to Sergio's office through a series of security checkpoints. There, everything changed.

Sergio interrupted his phone conversation, smiled, and gave me a big hug. Then he passed the phone to me and said: "Talk to her. She is Carolina, the love of my life. She is also Argentinian."

After a short conversation with Carolina Larriera, I returned the phone to Sergio.

He spoke with her for a few minutes more while showing me a *New York Times* article saying that the Bush administration was asking Kofi Annan to allow Sergio to go to Iraq. He ended his phone call, talked for ten minutes about his feelings for Carolina, and then explained that he had no intention of going to Iraq and that we should plan on how to cooperate.

Sergio then introduced his team to me and insisted that we coordinate our activities while respecting our respective mandates. Our offices would be involved in the same conflicts, and he was proposing to mobilize states and do the political work that my office needed while I took care of the investigations and prosecutions. He smiled and said, "I am sorry, but I will be the good cop and you the bad one."

For me, it was the perfect division of labor. In order "to contribute to the prevention of future crimes," the office needed more than judicial cooperation; it needed diplomatic campaigns galvanizing support for justice to isolate and arrest criminals and to include in peace negotiations victims' rights to justice. I needed partners to help develop political and diplomatic networks to prevent crimes, and Sergio was perfect for doing that.

A few days later, Sergio called to inform me that he had to accept the UN position in Iraq. It was a critical part of a deal between the United States and the UN. He promised it would be a short-term assignment, insisting on keeping our planning for future interaction.

The last time I talked to Sergio was at the end of July 2003. He called from his office in Baghdad, joking about how badly things were going there. I told him that I needed him in Geneva, and he pledged that he would be back as the High Commissioner for Human Rights very soon.

A few weeks later, on August 19, 2003, a car packed with explosives destroyed part of Baghdad's hotel that was serving as headquarters for the United Nations. Sergio died among the debris with twenty-one other people. Carolina was there, and she miraculously escaped. I am still shocked by Sergio's sacrifice, and I missed him during my nine-year term. He would have been the perfect partner for my journey, but I never had the chance to work with him.

Notes

1. Prince Zeid bin Ra'ad after was Jordanian ambassador to the United States and later the United Nations High Commissioner for Human Rights.
2. The nine defendants were the members of the different "military juntas" integrated by the top commanders of the Armed Forces that ruled the country in the period between 1976 and 1982, including three former Argentinian dictators, General Jorge Rafael Videla, General Roberto Viola, and General Alfredo Galtieri. *See* Luis Moreno Ocampo, *Beyond Punishment: Justice in the Wake of Massive Crimes in Argentina*, 52 J. INT'L AFF. 669 (1999).
3. General Juan Domingo Peron completed his first term in 1946–1952 but was ousted in the middle of his second term in 1955. Maximo Langer, *Revolution in Latin American Criminal Procedure: Diffusion of Legal Ideas from the Periphery*, 55 AM. COMP. L. 617 (2007).
4. Argentina experience led the creation of the field of transitional justice. Laurel Fletcher & Harvey Weinstein *Writing Transitional Justice: An Empirical Evaluation of Transitional Justice Scholarship in Academic Journals*, 7 J. HUM. RTS. PRACT. 177 (2015).
5. KATHRYN SIKKINK, THE JUSTICE CASCADE: HOW HUMAN RIGHTS PROSECUTIONS ARE CHANGING WORLD POLITICS 3–7 (Kindle ed. 2011).
6. *Id.* at 87.
7. PRISCILLA HAYNER, UNSPEAKABLE TRUTH, FACING THE CHALLENGE OF TRUTH COMMISSIONS (2002).

8. FRANK VOGL, WAGING WAR ON CORRUPTION: INSIDE THE MOVEMENT FIGHTING THE ABUSE OF POWER 2899 (Kindle ed. 2012).

9. Between 1988 and 1990, I joined a research team at the Center for the Study of the State and Society (CEDES) a distinguished academic center in Argentina, learning about political science's methods of analysis and expanding my understanding of what happened. https://www.cedes.org/sobre-cedes/. The research team included C. H. Acuña, I. González Bombal, E. Jelin, O. Landi, L. A. Quevedo, C. Smulovitz, and A. Vacchieri, a group of political scientists, scholars on communication, and sociologists who analyzed the different aspects of the Trial of the Juntas in a project financed by the MacArthur Foundation.

10. LUIS MORENO OCAMPO, CUANDO EL PODER PERDIO EL JUICIO (1996).

11. Luis Moreno Ocampo, *Beyond Punishment: Justice in the Wake of Massive Crimes in Argentina*, 52 J. INT'L AFFAIRS, 669–89; Seeking International Justice The Role of Institutions (Spring 1999).

12. Mark Ossiel analyzed the expressive function of the trials reviewing experiences of Germany, Japan, France, Israel, and Argentina and concluded that courts' debates "can signally contribute to the special sort of solidarity-through civil dissensus-to which a modern pluralistic society may properly aspire." Mark J. Osiel, *Ever Again: Legal Remembrance of Administrative Massacre,* 144 U. PA. L. REV. 463–2537 (1995)

13. "The restorative justice model finds strong support too from activists and legal scholars who have long criticized harsh retributive punishment in their domestic legal systems as counterproductive. But the argument here is that the restorative and retributive justice models have not in practice been mutually exclusive. Rather, restorative justice, like truth commissions and reparations, has often been used very effectively together with retributive justice, such as domestic and foreign prosecutions. So, although some advocates like to stress the differences between them, it is perfectly legitimate both theoretically and practically to see these as complementary ideas that form part of the broader movement for accountability for past human rights violations." KATHRYN SIKKINK, THE JUSTICE CASCADE: HOW HUMAN RIGHTS PROSECUTIONS ARE CHANGING WORLD POLITICS 257 (The Norton Series in World Politics, Kindle ed., W. W. Norton & Company, 2011) See also ELMAR G. M. WEITEKAMP & HANS J. KERNER, RESTORATIVE JUSTICE, THEORETICAL FOUNDATIONS (Routledge 2012).

14. Joachim Savelsberg & Hollie Nyseth Brehm, *Representing Human Rights Violations in Darfur: Global Justice, National Distinctions,* 121 AM. J. SOCIOLOGY 564 (2015).

15. VIET THANH NGUYEN, NOTHING EVER DIES 4 (Kindle ed., Harvard University Press, 2016).

16. "The question of the 'reception' (by individuals) of memory produced by 'states,' 'actors' or other memory 'entrepreneurs'" became a critical part of an academic field developed since the 80s specifically adapted to the study of "memory," which is now considered a research object in itself." Sarah, Gensburger, "*Halbwachs' studies in collective memory: A founding text for contemporary 'memory studies'?,*" 16 J. CLASSICAL SOCIOLOGY 396 (2016)

17. According with a Gallup Argentina survey 10% of Argentina population (meaning 4 million people) learned how to solve problems with such show.

18. DAVID SCHEFFER, ALL THE MISSING SOULS: A PERSONAL HISTORY OF THE WAR CRIMES TRIBUNALS 34 (Kindle ed. Princeton University Press, 2013). Aryeh Neier mentioned that President Menem was "also trying to oust the Buenos Aires prosecutor, Luis Moreno Ocampo, who prosecuted the juntas and who secured the extradition of General Suarez-Mason." Aryeh Neier, *Menem's Pardons And Purges*, N.Y. TIMES (Oct. 2, 1989), https://www.nytimes.com/1989/10/02/opinion/menems-pardons-and-purges.html.

19. An informal vote at the UN Security Council to appoint Bassiouni revealed a division of seven to seven with one abstention. He was described as too victim-oriented and thus biased because he was a Muslim. Cherif Bassiouni, *Foreword* to PIERRE HAZAN, JUSTICE IN TIME OF WAR: THE TRUE STORY BEHIND THE INTERNATIONAL CRIMINAL TRIBUNAL FOR THE FORMER YUGOSLAVIA 84 (Kindle ed., Texas A&M University Press, 2004). INTRODUCTION TO INTERNATIONAL CRIMINAL LAW (Cherif Bassiouni ed., 2nd rev. ed., Koninklijke Brill NV, 2013).

20. He had a long career as an academic and a politician but was not interested in the international Prosecutor's role. I met him in 1992 when I was invited to advise the Venezuelan Prosecutors in their investigations on corruption. In March 1993 Escobar Salom had indicted Venezuela's President Carlos Andres Perez and when he received the offer to be the ICTY Prosecutor he informed the UN that before taking on that role he had to finish the Perez case. He went to The Hague on January 1994 for few days, met with Graham Blewitt, appointed him as acting Deputy Prosecutor and informed UN Secretary-General Boutros-Gali that he had accepted an invitation to become the Minister of Home Affairs in Venezuela. On February 3 1994, he resigned as the ICTY Prosecutor. INTERNATIONAL PROSECUTORS (Luc Reydams, Jan Wouters et al eds., Oxford University Press, 2012).

21. He had made an enormous contribution to his country's transition to democracy by leading the "Goldstone Commission," a key instrument to peacefully manage violent riots during the last years of apartheid.

22. Silvia Fernandez de Gurmendi, as an Argentine diplomat, was involved since 1994 in the creation of the Court. She was the legal advisor of the Argentine Permanent mission before the UN in New York, one of the first members of the "like minded group," she led the preparatory work of the Statute and was a very active Vice President of the Rome Conference leading the working group that wrote Parts V-VIII of the Statute. She was later the head of the Jurisdiction, Complementarity and Cooperation Division of the ICC Office of the Prosecutor (2003-2008), became an ICC Judge and the President of the Court and the President of the Assembly of States Parties.

23. In April 2003 Morten Bergsmo was the acting Legal Advisor of the Office of the Prosecutor, seconded by Klaus Rackwitz as the senior manager, one assistant and six interns. He was collecting documents from more than one hundred experts on the lessons learned at the Ad Hoc tribunals and on the ways to organize the new Office. Bergsmo had relevant experience of more than ten years practicing international criminal law. As a very young lawyer his government seconded him to assist the UN Commission that investigated crimes in the Balkans. After working for eight years in the legal advisory section of the ICTY he participated in all the preparatory work of

the Rome Statute, was active during and after the Conference, and was the entire advance team of the Office the Prosecutor of the International Criminal Court.

24. On March 21, agreement was reached in New York that Luis Moreno-Ocampo (Argentina) would be appointed as the first chief prosecutor. Hans-Peter Kaul, *Construction Site for More Justice: The International Criminal Court after Two Years*, 99 THE AM. J. OF INT'L L. 370, 370 (2005).

25. Rome Statute of the International Criminal Court, Article 44 establishes that the Prosecutor and the Registrar shall appoint such qualified staff as may be required to their respective offices, They shall ensure the highest standards of efficiency, competency and integrity.

26. Rome Statute of the International Criminal Court, Article 42.

27. I was a founding member of "Poder Ciudadano" in 1987 one of the first NGOs working on anti-corruption and later became deeply involved in Transparency International. Since 1995 I was member of the TI Advisory Board, Chairman of the Latin American and Caribbean branch and later member of the board of directors. I was also a member of "New Tactics for Human Rights" project.

28. Our Story, COALITION FOR THE ICC, http://www.coalitionfortheicc.org/about/our-story (last visited Apr. 7, 2020).

29. The ICTY and ICTR Prosecutor Offices were comprised of an investigation division and a prosecution division. We decided to add a section with a mandate to analyze jurisdictional issues including complementarity as well as carry out preliminary examinations. This decision had been described by a sector of the literature as privileging diplomatic considerations over legal ones. Jens Meierhenrich contends that these decisions constitute "*the expression of an operational strategy that deemed the international relations of prosecution to be of equal significance to the international law of prosecution.*" Jens Meierhenrich, *The Evolution of the Office of the Prosecutor at the International Criminal Court Insights from Institutional Theory, in* THE FIRST GLOBAL PROSECUTOR (Law, Meaning, And Violence) 97 (Martha Minow, C. C True-Frost et al eds, Kindle ed., University of Michigan Press, 2015). Following advice of an external consultant and Morten Bergsmo, the section was transformed into a Division: The Jurisdiction, Complementarity and Cooperation Division. Within the division the "Analysis Section" had the responsibility to conduct preliminary examinations. The "International cooperation section" provided the function that the Minister of Justice and the Minister of Foreign Affairs offer in the national settings: the facilitation of international cooperation from international organizations and states.

30. We adopted a matrix system, operational task forces with different lines of report. Joint Teams were comprised of investigators, prosecutors and an international cooperation advisor. My goal was to create a flexible model, able to deal with an increasing number of situations under investigation, as well as to force people from different divisions within the Office of the Prosecutor to consult with each other and avoid the disconnection between investigators and prosecutors that I observed in the Ad Hoc Tribunals' practice.

31. Article 43 (9) establishes that the Prosecutor shall appoint advisers with legal expertise on specific issues, including, but not limited to, sexual and gender violence and
violence against children.

32. She later competed to be the Head of the Jurisdiction, Complementarity and
Cooperation Division.

2

The Rome Statute Creating a
New Legal Field

Jus ad Curiam

To fulfill my mission to establish the Office of the Prosecutor and to launch
the International Criminal Court (ICC) activities, putting the entire Rome
Statute system in motion, I had to study the Rome Statute system and its roots.

The Versailles Treaty was the origin of international criminal justice, it established its basic ideas: an investigative commission, an international criminal tribunal, and a system of complementarity.

The Nuremberg trial had a peculiar champion: Soviet Union premier
Joseph Stalin. Stalin forced US president Franklin Roosevelt and UK prime
minister Winston Churchill to change their position to execute Nazi leaders
without trial. The three political leaders made *a jus ad Curiam* decision and
adopted the Nuremberg Charter, creating the first ad hoc international criminal tribunal. However, they did not create a global justice system; their limited goal was to ensure Nazi leaders' retribution through a criminal trial.

The Cold War suspended international criminal justice support.

In 1993 and 1994, the UN Security Council recovered the Nuremberg
legacy and established the International Criminal Tribunal for the former
Yugoslavia (ICTY) and the International Criminal Tribunal for Rwanda
(ICTR). The ad hoc international tribunals had independent prosecutors and
judges. Still, they were confined to prosecuting cases in a particular territory and at times defined by the UN Security Council. In any case, the creation and functioning of the ad hoc tribunals paved the way for a series of
discussions preparing for the Rome Conference in 1998.

The most divisive topic during the Rome Conference was a *jus ad Curiam*
matter: the prosecutor *proprio motu* authority (by its own motion or initiative) to trigger the ICC intervention into a sovereign country member.

The United States supported establishing a permanent ICC if and only if
the UN Security Council had control of the *jus ad Curiam* decisions. The

War and Justice in the 21st Century. Luis Moreno Ocampo, Oxford University Press. © Oxford University Press 2022.
DOI: 10.1093/oso/9780197628973.003.0003

opposition to an Office of the Prosecutor with *proprio motu* authority was the primary US delegation's objection. During the Rome Conference, 120 states decided to contradict the US proposal and provided independent power to the Office of the Prosecutor to trigger the court's jurisdiction.

The ICC is part of two coexisting and interrelated models of international criminal justice: a system integrated by 193 states UN members, led by UN Security Council; and a subsystem under the Rome Statute integrated by two-thirds of those states that ratified the Statute and the ICC.

A combination of three different norms created the autonomous criminal justice system recognized by Professor Crawford: the states parties' duty to prosecute, the complementarity principle, and the prosecutor's *proprio motu* authority.

Part One: The Way to Rome

Versailles

The Preliminary Peace Conference of Paris faced World War I's carnage and adopted the Versailles Treaty. It created the League of Nations, an international model of permanent coordination to overcome national state legal architecture's limitations. States adopted the duty to protect each other against aggression from other countries.

The Versailles Treaty also established the basic ideas for the international criminal justice system adopted decades later: an investigative commission;[1] an international criminal tribunal to prosecute the kaiser, considered the most responsible;[2] and the intervention of a Leipzig Court working under some sort of system of complementarity.[3]

Although neither the proposal to prosecute the kaiser nor the Leipzig Court worked efficiently, those decisions planted the seed of international criminal justice.[4]

But the national state's absolute sovereignty was protected by the expert community. In 1921, Raphael Lemkin, the Polish Jewish lawyer who developed the concept of genocide, discussed the lack of justice for Armenian victims with one of his professors. The professor used a metaphor to explain sovereignty: "Consider the case of a farmer who owns a flock of chickens," he said, "he kills them, and this is his business. If you interfere, you are trespassing."[5]

The Adoption of the UN Charter

The League of Nation's failure to deter Italy's aggressive war against Ethiopia in 1935 and then Hitler in 1938 convinced many international relations experts that international law is "counterproductive."[6]

Without analyzing how to improve the model, they concluded that it is a form of "idealism,"[7] a utopian mistake. *Realists* propose that "states must provide security for themselves because no one else will."[8]

The central concept for *realists* is that only the most powerful states can organize the world. "Law can matter for realists, but only because it helps to construct a self-enforcing equilibrium through ones that reflect the preferences of the powerful."[9] Following such a principle, World War II winners led the adoption of the UN Charter.[10]

The UN Charter was signed on June 26, 1945, in San Francisco by fifty nations to ensure peace. The UN Charter contributed to ending colonialism and multiplying the number of sovereign states, but the UN Security Council's rules do not respect equality. By legal design, the permanent members can control the Council Resolutions and even use their veto power to protect their allies.

The Charter establishes each UN state member "to refrain from violating human rights." Still, *it* did not adopt any independent international mechanism to protect individuals and did not even mention international criminal justice. The investigation and prosecution of crimes remained a national activity, a critical part of sovereignty.[11]

Nuremberg

During a meeting at Quebec in September 1944, US president Franklin Roosevelt and UK prime minister Winston Churchill agreed to execute Nazi leaders without trial. But then the decision had to be changed, taking into consideration Soviet Union premier Joseph Stalin's vision.[12]

Stalin became the main promotor of international justice. He wanted to use trials as a propaganda mechanism, as he had done before in the Soviet Union with the *Moscow Trials* against his internal enemies.[13] Finally, Roosevelt, Churchill, and Stalin took the *jus ad Curiam* decision to prosecute the Nazi's defeated leaders before an international military tribunal.

Legal discussions followed the political choices, and, in August 1945, the Nuremberg Charter was signed.[14] It allowed prosecutors and judges from four different countries to investigate and adjudicate the Nazi crimes.[15]

At Nuremberg, US Chief Prosecutor Justice Robert Jackson suggested using individual criminal responsibility to manage international conflicts between states. He explained at the opening of the trial: "This principle of personal liability is a necessary as well as logical one if international law is to render a real help to the maintenance of peace." He mentioned that in the past, "The only answer to recalcitrance was impotence or war. Only sanctions which reach individuals can peacefully and effectively be enforced."[16]

The Cold War

The Genocide Convention approved in 1948 mentioned the role of a permanent international penal tribunal, and the same year the UN General Assembly mandated the International Law Commission (ILC) to draft one.[17] However, the subsequent Cold War dynamic suspended those efforts, affected the UN Security Council's efficiency, and expanded the gap between international principles and their enforcement.

During the first Cold War, the fear of a nuclear conflict prevented an open war between the United States and the Soviet Union. However, the first Cold War was hot in Asia, Africa, and Latin America. As a result of the UN Charter legal design, there are no institutional solutions to solve problems between the Council's permanent members.

A divided UN Security Council did not protect millions of victims in Cambodia. To balance the Soviet Union's influence in the region, the United States and China opposed the Vietnam intervention in 1978, which stopped the massive atrocities and removed the Khmer Rouge. Still, the United States refused to recognize the new Cambodian government and supported the previous criminal regime until the end of the first Cold War in 1990.[18]

During the 1970s, South America's Armed Forces became US *proxy forces* in the fight against leftist guerrillas inspired by Cuba. Argentina was one of many bloody battlefields, and a divided UN Security Council did not protect thousands of Argentineans from their own army during the military junta "dirty war" against a communist "subversion."

Instead, the legal design of the Organization of American States (OAS)' Inter-American Commission on Human Rights helped stop the dictatorship crimes. The military junta ordered the closing of all the secret detention centers when the Inter-American Commission visited Argentina in 1979.[19]

The legal architecture can facilitate or control violence.

The Creation of the ICTY

The Berlin Wall fell in 1989, the first Cold War ended, and there have been different initiatives to establish international criminal courts.[20]

Between 1991 and 1993, the UN Security Council changed its own standards without a UN Charter reform. It expanded its role of controlling interstate aggressors to include citizens' protection from their own governments.

As the Iraqi forces cracked down on Kurdish separatists, the Council considered that internal attacks against civilians threatened international peace.[21] The Security Council used its powers under Article 41 of the Charter to adopt, in other cases, "smart"[22] sanctions such as arms embargoes, freezing of assets, or the issuance of travel bans against individuals.

Since 1989, the Yugoslavia war has been one of the biggest challenges for the UN Security Council.[23] During the summer of 1992, world media circulated pictures of concentration camps in the Balkans, evoking the Nazi regime and awakening the *Never again* promise. The Council reacted by establishing a Commission of Experts to gather evidence of war crimes in Yugoslavia.[24]

The Commission received no support; it had no office, no personnel, and no budget.[25] Cherif Bassiouni, the most active commissioner, considered that the UN Security Council's goal was "appeasing world public opinion."[26] Under Bassiouni's leadership, the Commission overcame many difficulties, produced a comprehensive report, and recommended creating an international tribunal.

A diplomatic negotiation was France's strategy to end the Balkans conflict. Without changing that plan, the French Minister of Foreign Affairs Roland Dumas convinced a reluctant President Mitterrand to propose an ad hoc international criminal tribunal.[27]

Richard Holbrooke, the lead US negotiator to end the armed conflict in the Balkans, explained that when the ICTY was created, "the tribunal was widely viewed as little more than a public relations device."[28]

"The cynicism of the Security Council was not complete: Madeleine Albright, America's UN ambassador, herself a former Czech refugee from both Nazism and Communism, fought hard for a strong tribunal."[29]

"It was against this background—nightmare images from Bosnia, coupled with a fundamental Western unwillingness to stop the Serb rampage—"[30] that in May 1993, the UN Security Council made a *jus ad Curiam* decision.

Acting under Chapter VII of the UN Charter, the Council adopted Resolution 827 establishing an "international tribunal for the sole purpose of prosecuting persons responsible for serious violations of international humanitarian law committed in the territory of the former Yugoslavia since 1991 and a date to be determined by the Security Council upon the restoration of peace." It also adopted the statute of the tribunal.[31]

A few years later, the ICTY prosecutor Louise Arbour's actions exposed the bias of the Council, creating a tribunal against no friendly leaders. She mentioned that the NATO campaign to protect Kosovo from March to June 1999 carried out by Western forces could be investigated for war crimes.

Legally, the ICTY prosecutor had the authority to investigate NATO forces. Their intervention happened within the territorial and temporal limits imposed by the Council. But the NATO spokesman Jamie Shea expressed the distance between political thinking and judicial duties: "I am certain that when Prosecutor Arbour returns to Kosovo and sees the facts, she will indict the Yugoslavian nationals and no other nationalities." He recommended the following to Ms. Arbour: "Don't bite the hand that feeds you."[32]

The Establishment of the ICTR

Since the beginning of the Rwandan genocide, in April 1994, the UN Security Council has regularly issued calls for political negotiations between the parties, as if there were a conflict between mutually stubborn parties rather than a deliberate campaign of extermination.[33]

After the killing of ten Belgian peacekeepers, the Security Council exposed no interest in protecting the victims of the genocide. President Clinton, affected by US soldiers' recent slaughter in Somalia, requested clarity on the UN peacekeeping mission's goal.[34] The Council issued a press statement calling all parties to end violence and subsequently reduced the number of peacekeepers deployed in Rwanda.

In April 1994, New Zealand and Czech ambassadors proposed that the UN Security Council issue a presidential statement using the term "genocide" to describe Rwanda's incidents. The Czech ambassador questioned the Council's intense focus on achieving a new ceasefire, which he likened to asking the Jews to reach a truce with Hitler.

The British ambassador was concerned that the Council would be a "laughingstock" if it called the crisis a genocide but did nothing to stop it. For some US officials, too, the Genocide Convention established a duty to act, and they were not ready to do so. In the end, a compromise was reached; there was no action, but a presidential statement was issued using words from the definition of the term "genocide" but not the word itself.[35]

In June 1994, the "Rwandan Patriotic Front," the Tutsi forces led by Paul Kagame, took control of the country and stopped the genocide. Then the UN Security Council established a Commission of Experts, which produced a preliminary report.[36]

The UN Security Council finally recognized the crimes committed and adopted a *jus ad Curiam* decision. Council Resolution 955 (1994) created the International Criminal Tribunal for Rwanda (ICTR) to prosecute "persons responsible for serious violations of international humanitarian law committed in the territory of Rwanda and Rwandan citizens responsible for such violations committed in the territory of neighboring States between 1 January 1994 and 31 December 1994." There was just one dissenting vote: that of Rwanda.[37]

Rwanda proposed to limit the temporal jurisdiction until July 1994 to avoid the investigation of alleged crimes committed by Tutsi troops. The Council did not accept the Rwanda proposal and included investigating the crimes allegedly committed by the Tutsi forces led by Paul Kagame at the end of 1994.[38]

Years later, the Council did not support ICTY/ICTR Prosecutor Carla Del Ponte when investigating those crimes. To stop her, the Council divided the ICTY and the ICTR Office of the Prosecutor.[39]

The events show the tension between the different legal mandates. A diplomat's mandate is to protect their state, instead a prosecutor must follow the law. The Council's decisions result from diplomatic and political agreements without the participation of judicial authorities.

Since 1999, the UN Security Council has adopted *jus ad Curiam* decisions creating "hybrid tribunals" combining national and international judges in East Timor[40] and Sierra Leone[41] to "prosecute serious violations international humanitarian law." And by Resolution 1757 (2007), the Council created the Special Tribunal for Lebanon to prosecute a specific incident.[42] In 2003 the UN General Assembly approved the creation of the "Extraordinary Chambers in the Courts of Cambodia."[43] Other *jus ad Curiam*'s decisions have established hybrid national/international courts by UN authorities in Kosovo[44] and Bosnia and Herzegovina.[45]

In August 2012, the African Union (AU) and Senegal created a special court, the Extraordinary African Chambers (EAC).[46]

The Way to the Rome Conference

The creation of a permanent International Criminal Tribunal was reintroduced in the international agenda in 1989 at Trinidad and Tobago's request, and the UN General Assembly instructed the International Law Commission (ILC) to start preparing a statute once again.[47]

In July 1994, in the middle of the Rwanda Genocide, the ILC finished its "draft Statute for an International Criminal Court," at the disposal of the UN Security Council and recommended convening an international conference of plenipotentiaries to discuss the project.[48]

The ILC Draft comprised two main concepts that remained in the final version adopted in 1998. It established that the "court is intended to be complementary to national criminal justice systems." And it is restricted only to "the most serious crimes of concern to the international community as a whole," including aggression crime.[49]

The ILC Draft respected the UN Charter architecture based on sovereign states and the UN Security Council's supreme authority.[50] There were only two mechanisms to initiate a case: either a state party or the UN Security Council had to present a complaint. In any case, the UN Security Council received the authority to stop any prosecution.[51]

The ILC Draft did not propose an autonomous criminal justice system but rather an accountability mechanism to serve as a new Council tool: "The purpose of the establishment of the court . . . is to provide a venue for the fair trial of persons accused of crimes of an international character."[52]

As a follow-up mechanism to study the project, the UN General Assembly established the ad hoc Committee on the Establishment of an International Criminal Court, which met twice in 1995 and produced a review consolidating "the principle of complementarity as an essential element."[53]

In December 1995, the UN General Assembly created the Preparatory Committee on the Establishment of an International Criminal Court to prepare a "widely acceptable consolidated text."[54] The "ICC seemed to be a natural extension of the ad hoc tribunals," and as a consequence, "skeptical major powers were reluctant to openly oppose the initiative."[55]

The Preparatory Committee met from 1996 to 1998, and all states participated in the debate, including the United States, and it was also open to NGOs.[56] The idea of the prosecutor's *proprio motu* power emerged during those discussions. Such a provision created the most significant conflict with the US delegates because justice requirements could prevail over any UN Security Council decision.

The people that participated in those events transformed the outcome. The appointment of Robin Cook as the UK Secretary of State for Foreign and Commonwealth Affairs, in 1997, under the new Labour government led by Prime Minister Blair, divided the five permanent members. The United Kingdom started to support the ICC concept to show a new foreign affairs policy based on ethics.[57]

In the last session held in April 1998, two delegates that later became ICC judges, Silvia Fernández representing Argentina and Hans Peter Kaul, the German representative, "proposed a system of judicial control, to be exercised by the Pre-trial Chamber."[58]

The Preparatory Committee Draft presented many options on different topics and included the prosecutor's *proprio motu* power subject to judicial review in Articles 12 and 13.[59] After this participatory drafting process, the UN General Assembly decided to hold the "United Nations Diplomatic Conference of Plenipotentiaries on the Establishment of an International Criminal Court."[60]

The global political context was favorable. Since the establishment of the European Union in 1993, the European states that had for centuries been using wars to resolve their conflicts developed a regional legal system redefining *home* and *abroad*, harmonizing their interests, and managing the disputes between them. They were trying to control the Balkans' conflict, the last war in Europe.

The 1997 UK Labour Party manifesto promised to support the ICC based "on an ethical foreign policy and the promotion of human rights."[61] At the end of the 1990s, all the South American countries were democracies and interested in avoiding their return to military dictatorships and political violence. Since 1995, Nelson Mandela had been leading African countries, aiming to protect the region from violence and colonialism.

The UN press release announcing the beginning of the Rome Conference highlighted "the authority of the Prosecutor to initiate cases is at the heart of the debate on the role of the court in the international legal system."[62]

Part Two: The Rome Conference

Delegations from 160 countries arrived in Rome during the summer of 1998 to participate in the Conference. They had five weeks to decide on more than one thousand contentious issues marked between brackets in the Draft. Representatives were aware that the window of opportunity could be closed if the Conference failed "to finalize and adopt a convention on the establishment of an international criminal court."[63]

The entire world was watching: 17 intergovernmental organizations, 14 specialized agencies and funds of the United Nations, and 124 NGOs were also participating in the side events. Four hundred seventy-four journalists were accredited to cover the Conference.[64]

On June 15, 1998, Kofi Annan, as the UN Secretary-General, opened the Conference expressing its relevance: "We have an opportunity to create an institution that can save lives and serve as a bulwark against evil. So, let us rise to this challenge. Let us give succeeding generations this gift of hope."[65]

The Serb attacks against Kosovo marked the moment. While Kofi Annan was talking, "more than 80 NATO warplanes from 15 European bases flew . . . to demand that Serbia stop using military force against civilians in Kosovo province."[66] A few months later, NATO intervened in the conflict.

What Are the Most Serious Crimes of "Concern to the International Community?"

During the Rome Conference, a consensus was reached that Nuremberg crimes plus genocide were "the most serious crimes of concern to the international community as a whole." They were already defined by previous conventions and customary international law when the Rome Statute was adopted.[67] The Rome Statute explicitly defined gender[68] and established a whole range of gender crimes.[69]

The crime of aggression was included in the ICC jurisdiction in 1998, albeit its definition was adopted in 2010, and a specific legal procedure was defined only in 2017. Current Article 8 *bis* describes this crime. At the end of the twentieth century, those were the only crimes considered unacceptable for any culture and any religion.[70]

Israel was a strong supporter of the establishment of the ICC. However, the inclusion of Article 8(2)(b)(viii) defining as a war crime "The transfer, directly or indirectly, by the Occupying Power of parts of its own civilian population into the territory it occupies (. . .)" blocked its acceptance of the Statute.[71]

The Rome Conference did not include several crimes suggested by the Preparatory Committee in the ICC jurisdiction.[72] Its focus on atrocity crimes set the Rome Statute apart from other mechanisms. Human rights violations remain exclusively under national states' jurisdiction and, in some instances, under regional organizations.[73]

The Discussion on the Role of the Prosecutor during the Rome Conference

A *jus ad Curiam* matter was the most divisive issue during the Rome Conference. David Scheffer, the head of the US delegation, explained that in "early June 1998, we had decided . . . to highlight our objection to the Proprio Motu prosecutor at the beginning of the Rome Conference."[74] The United States rejected the possibility of creating an international organization depriving the UN Security Council of control and putting US personnel at risk of independent investigations.[75]

US Ambassador Bill Richardson presented the core US position in his inaugural speech: maintaining the UN Security Council's central role in the international system. "A permanent Court cannot stand alone. It must be part of the international order and supported by the international community. The United Nations Security Council remains a vital part of that world order."[76]

Ambassador Richardson then challenged the *jus ad Curiam* role of the Prosecutor:

[I]t is essential that there be some screen to distinguish between crimes which do rise to the level of concern to the international community and those which do not. The only rational and workable proposal to date is to look to States, and in appropriate cases, the Security Council, to speak for what is 'of concern to the international community' as a whole.[77]

And finally, following the ad hoc tribunals model, the United States argued that the ICC Prosecutor should be able to independently select cases and suspects, a *jus in curiae* matter. But only among the situations referred by the UN Security Council or states, the classical actors in the *jus ad Curiam* field.[78]

In a cover page article on the Rome Conference's inauguration, the *New York Times* described the conflict between four Council's permanent members and forty-two like-minded states, including the United Kingdom, Canada, Germany, the Netherlands, Italy, Scandinavian countries, Australia, Greece, Argentina, and Costa Rica,[79] proposing an independent Court.[80] The Italian Foreign Minister put forth their position.[81] They were supported by African countries, led by Nelson Mandela, and reinforced by the NGOs Coalition. They won.

The Statute establishing the Prosecutor independent authority to trigger the Court jurisdiction subject to judicial review was adopted during the last day of the Conference by 120 states.

The Rome Statute model

The *jus ad Curiam* category helps identify decisions adopted by political and judicial actors as part of that same field.

Against some states and many NGOs' wishes, universal jurisdiction was rejected; the Court's intervention requires the previous state's consent.[82] National states, parties, and nonparties continue to be *jus ad Curiam* key players. Articles 12, 13 (a), and 14 consider that "*A State Party may refer to the Prosecutor a situation*" in any state party. Article 12 (3) defines that a State not a Party to this Statute may accept the Court's exercise of jurisdiction.

The Rome Statute recognized the UN Security Council authority in the *jus ad Curiam* phase, providing the possibility to use the ICC in a specific situation and also the power to suspend investigations.

Article 13(b) establishes the UN Security Council's authority to refer a situation to the ICC Prosecutor in any UN's 193 members (including more than sixty states nonparties of the Statute). Respecting the UN Security Council's mandate on international peace and security, Article 16 establishes the Council's authority to suspend any ICC investigation or prosecution for one year. The Council could paralyze the ICC investigations, but it would need nine Council member votes and no veto.

The UN Security Council had the discretion to approve the use of armed forces or to include international justice in any conflict affecting international peace and security.

The ICC is part of the UN Security Council model and the Rome Statute system

The entire book will help distinguish between two coexisting and interrelated models of international criminal justice: a system integrated by 193 states UN members, led by UN Security Council, and a subsystem under the Rome Statute integrated by two-thirds of those states combined with the ICC. International criminal justice in the UN system is a state or a Council's choice. In the Rome Statute system, justice is mandatory.

The UN Security Council has the option and the authority to refer situations to the ICC in the territories of states not a party to the Rome Statute. The five permanent members can veto such decisions. In this model, the ICC plays a role like the previous ad hoc international criminal tribunals at Nuremberg, Yugoslavia, and Rwanda: to conduct impartial investigations and fair trials. This was the formula proposed by the US delegation in Rome in 1998: the UN Security Council would decide where and when to investigate. The caveat is that the Office of the Prosecutor still must conduct a preliminary examination to filter the political decision following Article 53 and to trigger the Court's jurisdiction.

The states parties of the Rome Statute created an autonomous criminal justice system by making the sovereign decision to accept the ICC intervention in their territories when they failed to intervene. International criminal justice would be mandatory if states parties are not conducting genuine proceedings.

The *jus ad Curiam* Prosecutor *proprio motu* authority was limited to crimes committed in the territory or by nationals of states that have voluntarily joined the Rome Statute or deposited an ad hoc declaration. They adjusted their sovereignty and conferred authority to a permanent and independent ICC that "shall be complementary to national criminal jurisdictions."

States have primacy to conduct genuine proceedings, and the ICC is bound to act only by default. The Prosecutor is the *gatekeeper* connecting isolated national institutions with the permanent ICC. The positive decisions on jurisdiction by the Office of the Prosecutor would be reviewed in specific cases by the chambers.

The similarities with the Theodore Roosevelt proposal
On May 5, 1910, former US president Theodore Roosevelt, during his lecture accepting the Nobel Peace Prize, proposed an international model to control violence with some similarities to the Rome Statute system. He spoke "as a practical man" and proposed achieving global peace by establishing rules through agreements between sovereign states. He suggested authorizing "The Hague Courts and conferences" to decide the conflicts, creating "a species of world federation for international peace and justice."[83]

As an analogy, Theodore Roosevelt suggested studying "what has been done in the United States by the Supreme Court." He considered that "the methods adopted in the American Constitution to prevent hostilities between the states, and to secure the supremacy of the Federal Court in certain classes of cases, are well worth the study of those who seek at The Hague to obtain the same results on a world scale."[84]

He rightly foresaw: "The supreme difficulty in connection with developing the peace work of The Hague arises from the lack of any executive power, of any police power to enforce the decrees of the court."

To face the problem, Theodore Roosevelt suggested creating some "form of international police power competent and willing to prevent violence as between nations."[85]

As Roosevelt mentioned, rules and courts define the authority's boundaries between states like California or Alabama and the US federal government. The US Constitution established common standards, and the Supreme Court slowly affirmed its jurisdiction to solve conflicts between the states and the federal government.

Analogously, the Rome Statute redefined the limits between crimes under the national authorities' exclusive jurisdiction and those of "concern to the international community as a whole." The Rome Statute provided a global model to manage violence with some similarities to the one proposed by Roosevelt.

Ratification Process

The Statute was open to signature until the end of December 2000. One hundred thirty-nine countries finally signed it, including Russia, Israel, and the United States.[86] The Rome Statute required ratifications to enter into force. Senegal was the first to ratify it. In most countries, congresses and parliaments had to debate and approve the Statute. Some countries amended their constitutions.

For instance, France and Colombia included a new article in their Constitutions. Germany reformulated specific Constitution principles, and the Netherlands created a particular procedure to approve the Statute even where there were some conflicts between its Constitution and the Statute. Spain's *Consejo de Estado* interpreted the Statute to avoid a confrontation with its Constitution.[87]

In only four years, the ratification threshold was reached. Ten countries deposited their instrument of ratification simultaneously at a special ceremony at the UN on April 11, 2002. The Statute entered into force on July 1, 2002.

Notes

1. The Commission on the Responsibilities of the Authors of War and Enforcement of Penalties could be considered an embryo of the *UN Commissions of inquiry* model further developed at the end of the twentieth century. Int'l Law Comm'n, Rep. on the Question of International Criminal Jurisdiction by Ricardo J. Alfaro (Special Rapporteur), ¶ 1, U.N. Doc. A/CN.4/15 (Mar. 3, 1950). The Commission recommended "all persons belonging to enemy countries ... including heads of states, who have been guilty of offences against the law and customs of the war or the laws of humanity, are liable to criminal prosecutions." Commission on the Responsibility of the Authors of the War and on Enforcement of Penalties, *Report Presented to the Preliminary Peace Conference*, 14 AM. J. INT'L L. 95, 117 (1920).

2. There was an attempt to prosecute the German kaiser, Wilhelm II, before an international tribunal. He was considered the most responsible "for a supreme offence against international morality and the sanctity of treaties," Treaty of Versailles, art. 227 (June 28, 1919). The Kaiser escaped from Germany in 1919 and received asylum in the Netherlands, which refused to surrender him. The Netherlands stated, "[i]f a future international jurisdiction is created by the League of Nations as a competent judge of facts classified as crimes and punishable by statute it will rest with Holland to associate herself with the new system." It considered that it "has any other duty than that imposed by the laws of the state and national tradition. These have made Holland at all times a refuge for those vanquished in international conflicts." *Ex-Kaiser's Asylum*, MORNING BULLETIN, Jan. 29, 1920, 5.

3. The Versailles treaty accepted Germany's commitment to bringing many of its soldiers to trial before its own Court in Leipzig. It affirmed the right of the Allies

to prosecute war crimes, but Germany refused to hand over the 900 suspects. After negotiations, the Allies decided that if German justice proved faulty, they would reassert their jurisdiction. BENJAMIN FERENCZ, AN INTERNATIONAL CRIMINAL COURT, A STEP TOWARD WORLD PEACE: A DOCUMENTARY HISTORY AND ANALYSIS 33 (1980). Only six individuals were finally convicted, and almost none of them served time. THEODOR MERON, THE MAKING OF INTERNATIONAL CRIMINAL JUSTICE. A VIEW FROM THE BENCH: SELECTED SPEECHES 82 (1st ed. 2011).

4. Int'l Law Comm'n, Rep. on the Question of International Criminal Jurisdiction by Ricardo J. Alfaro (Special Rapporteur), ¶ 1, U.N. Doc A/CN.4/15 (Mar. 3, 1950). At its second meeting in London, in February 1920, the Council of the League appointed a committee of experts to plan the establishment of the PCIJ. The Commission unanimously recommended creating a High Court of International Justice "competent to try crimes constituting a breach of international public order or against the universal law of nations, referred to it by the Assembly or by the Council of the League of Nations." The creation of an International Criminal Court was also discussed at the International Law Association, at its conference of 1922 in Buenos Aires. The Inter-Parliamentary Union in 1925 discussed the prevention of wars and the International Association of Penal Law between 1926 and 1928 promoted the adoption of international codes and tribunals to enforce them.

5. SAMANTHA POWER, A PROBLEM FROM HELL 820 (Kindle ed. 2013).

6. "Realists of all types agree that the traditional view of international law held by many lawyers not only ignores or obfuscates power and interests but can be destabilizing and counterproductive." Stephen D. Krasner, Realist Views of International Law, 96 PROC. ANN. MEETING AM. SOC'Y INT'L L. 265, 268 (2002).

7. Stephen Walt, The Enduring Relevance of the Realist Tradition, in POLITICAL SCIENCE, STATE OF THE DISCIPLINE III 197, 199 (Ira Katznelson & Helen V. Milner eds., 2003). See Jack Goldsmith & Stephen D. Krasner, The Limits of Idealism, 132 DAEDALUS 47 (2003). JUDITH N. SHKLAR, LEGALISM: LAW, MORALS, AND POLITICAL TRIALS (1986).

8. Stephen Walt, The Enduring Relevance of the Realist Tradition, in POLITICAL SCIENCE, STATE OF THE DISCIPLINE III (Ira Katznelson & Helen V. Milner eds., 2003).

9. Stephen D. Krasner, Realist Views of International Law, 96 PROC. ANN. MEETING AM. SOC'Y INT'L L. 265, 268 (2002).

10. SAMUEL MOYN, THE LAST UTOPIA: HUMAN RIGHTS IN HISTORY (2012).

11. In 1948 Hans Morgenthau considered: "the ultimate decision as to whether and how to engage in a law enforcing action lies with the individual state." Hans J. Morgenthau, The Problem of Sovereignty Reconsidered, 48 COLUM. L. REV., 341, 344–45 (1948).

12. ARIEH J. KOCHAVI, PRELUDE TO NUREMBERG. ALLIED WAR CRIMES POLICY AND THE QUESTION OF PUNISHMENT 333–43 (1st ed. 1998).

13. The Soviets preferred rigged show trials, along the lines of the 1936–1938 Moscow purge trials. GARY JONATHAN BASS, STAY THE HAND OF VENGEANCE 195 (Kindle ed. 2000). For background on the Great Terror's transformation and integration into Soviet society see WENDY Z. GOLDMAN, TERROR AND DEMOCRACY IN THE AGE OF STALIN: THE SOCIAL DYNAMICS OF REPRESSION (2007); and SHELIA FITZPATRICK,

Everyday Stalinism: Ordinary Life in Extraordinary Times: Soviet Russia in the 1930s (1999).

14. Agreement by the Government of the United Kingdom of Great Britain and Northern Ireland, the Government of the United States of America, the Provisional Government of the French Republic and the Government of the Union of Soviet Socialist Republics for the Prosecution and Punishment of the Major War Criminals of the European Axis, art. 1, Aug. 8, 1945, 82 U.N.T.S. 279.

15. The International Military Tribunal integrated by judges and prosecutors from the United States, the United Kingdom, the Soviet Union, and France decided on the individual responsibility of 22 Nazi leaders. An additional 12 trials were conducted by the US Nuremberg Military Tribunal (NMT) by prosecutors and judges from the US *Nuremberg Trials*, US Holocaust Memorial Museum, https://encyclopedia. ushmm.org/content/en/article/the-nuremberg-trials (last visited Jan. 19, 2021).

16. Trial of the Major War Criminals before the International Military Tribunal. Volume II. Proceedings: 11/14/1945–11/30/1945. [Official text in the English language.] 98–102, Nuremberg: IMT (1947) as quoted in *Opening Statement before the International Military Tribunal*, Robert H. Jackson Center, https://www. roberthjackson.org/speech-and-writing/opening-statement-before-the-internatio nal-military-tribunal/ (last visited Jan. 19, 2021).

17. G.A. Res. 260 (III), B: Study by the International Law Commission of the Question of an International Criminal Jurisdiction (Dec. 9, 1948).

18. Vietnam's intervention in Cambodia at the end of 1978, supported by the Soviet Union, removed the Khmer Rouge's criminal regime. But China was not ready to accept their influence on its borders. In those days, the United States was forging its alliance with China, so Secretary of State Vance called for the Vietnamese to immediately "remove their forces from Cambodia" and began loudly condemning Vietnam. The United States knew very well that the Khmer Rouge had slaughtered more than two million Cambodians, but for political reasons there was no interest to do justice for those crimes. The US support to the Khmer Rouge regime ended with the end of the Cold War in 1990. Samantha Power, A Problem from Hell 3453 (Kindle ed. 2013).

19. Robert K. Goldman, *History and Action: The Inter-American Human Rights System and the Role of the Inter-American Commission on Human Rights*, 31 Hum. Rts. Quarterly 856, 873 (2009).

20. On March 2, 1989, the US House of Representatives passed a resolution calling for "the creation of an [i]nternational [c]riminal [c]ourt with jurisdiction over internationally recognized crimes of terrorism, illicit international narcotics trafficking, genocide, and torture, as those crimes are defined in various international conventions." The proposal excluded crimes against the peace. Chris Mahony, *The Justice Pivot: US International Criminal Law Influence from Outside the Rome Statute*, 46 Geo. J. Int'l L. 1071, 1078 (2015). "The Clinton administration explored several avenues to investigate and issue indictments against Saddam and his regime, including creation of an ad hoc international criminal tribunal by the Security Council similar to ICTY and ICTR, but these efforts met firm opposition from some Security Council members."

Lee Feinstein, & Tod Lindberg, Means to an End 34 (Kindle ed. 2011). In 1991, the European Community proposed the intervention of an international court to hold Saddam Hussein "personally responsible for genocide and "war crimes." Pierre Hazan, Justice in Time of War: The True Story behind the International Criminal Tribunal for the Former Yugoslavia 285 (James Thomas Snyder trans., Kindle ed. 2004). In August 1992, Germany's foreign minister suggested the creation of an international tribunal. David Scheffer, All the Missing Souls (Human Rights and Crimes against Humanity) 16 (Kindle ed. 2012).

21. UN Security Council Resolution 688 "[c]ondemns the repression of the Iraqi civilian population in many parts of Iraq, including most recently in Kurdish populated areas, the consequences of which threaten international peace and security in the region." The Security Council considered that the repression produced a "flow of refugees towards and across international frontiers and to cross-border incursions, which threaten international peace and security in the region." S.C. Res. 688/91, U.N. Doc. S/RES/688 (Apr. 5, 1991).

22. See Daniel W. Drezner, Sanctions Sometimes Smart: Targeted Sanctions in Theory and Practice, 13 Int'l Stud. Rev. 96 (2011). See also Devika Hovell, The Power of Process: The Value of Due Process in Security Council Sanctions Decision-Making (2016).

23. David Scheffer, All the Missing Souls (Human Rights and Crimes against Humanity) 15 (Kindle ed. 2012).

24. S.C. Res. 780, U.N. Doc. S/RES/780 (Oct. 6, 1992).

25. "Although France and Britain were not bold enough to vote against the resolution, they from the first saw the issue of war criminals as a potential impediment to making peace in ex-Yugoslavia, binding the hands of policymakers who might have to cut deals with criminal leaders." Gary Jonathan Bass, Stay the Hand of Vengeance 206–11 (Kindle ed. 2000).

26. Pierre Hazan, Justice in Time of War: The True Story behind the International Criminal Tribunal for the Former Yugoslavia 72 (James Thomas Snyder trans., Kindle ed. 2004).

27. Id. at 373.

28. Richard Holbrooke, To End a War 425 (Kindle ed. 2011).

29. During the debate Ambassador Albright highlighted the legacy of Nuremberg: "There is an echo in this chamber today. The Nuremberg principles have been reaffirmed." David Scheffer, All the Missing Souls (Human Rights and Crimes against Humanity) 22 (Kindle ed. 2012).

30. Gary Jonathan Bass, Stay the Hand of Vengeance 206–11 (Kindle ed. 2000).

31. S.C. Res. 827, U.N. Doc. S/RES/827 (May 25, 1993).

32. Pierre Hazan, Justice in Time of War: The True Story behind the International Criminal Tribunal for the Former Yugoslavia 2034 (James Thomas Snyder trans., Kindle ed. 2004).

33. David Bosco, Five to Rule Them All 195 (2009).

34. "In recent weeks in the Security Council, our Nation has begun asking harder questions about proposals for new peacekeeping missions: Is there a real threat to

international peace?" President Bill Clinton, Address to the UN General Assembly (Sept. 27, 1993).

35. DAVID BOSCO, FIVE TO RULE THEM ALL 190 (2009).

36. United Nations, *Chapter V – Subsidiary Organs of the Security Council*, REPERTOIRE OF THE SECURITY COUNCIL, SUPPLEMENT 1993–95, https://www.un.org/en/sc/rep ertoire/93-95/93-95_05.pdf#page=4.

37. The ICTR was established by the Security Council pursuant to Chapter VII of the UN Charter in accordance with U.N. Doc. S/RES/955 (1994).

38. The new Rwandan government proposed to create an international tribunal with jurisdiction from Oct. 1, 1990, until end of the war on July 17, 1994, thereby including previous attacks against the Tutsis and excluding the possibility of investigating the actions of the Rwandan Patriotic Front against Hutus after it took power. CARLA DEL PONTE, MADAME PROSECUTOR 184–85, 225 (Kindle ed. 2011).

39. *Id.* at 231–32.

40. The Special Panels of the Dili District Court (also called the East Timor Tribunal) was established by Sergio Vieira de Mello acting as United Nations Transitional Administration in East Timor (UNTAET) in 2000 to try cases of "serious criminal offences"—including murder, rape, and torture—which took place in East Timor in 1999. The authority invoked was the UN Security Council resolution 1272 (1999) of Oct. 25, 1999. Regulation No. 2000/15 on the Establishment of Panels with Exclusive Jurisdiction Over Serious Criminal Offences, UNTAET/REF/200/15 (June 6, 2000).

41. In August 2000 by, Resolution 1315 (2000), the UN Security Council provided a mandate to the UN Secretary-General to finalize an agreement with the President of Sierra Leone to establish an independent Special Court. The Special Court for Sierra Leone (SCSL) was established "to prosecute persons who bear the greatest responsibility for serious violations of international humanitarian law, and Sierra Leonean law committed in the territory of Sierra Leone since 30 November 1996"; arti. 1, *Agreement between the United Nations and the Government of Sierra Leone on the Establishment of the Special Court for Sierra Leone*, signed on Jan. 16, 2002. Press Release, Security Council, Security Council asks Secretary-General, Sierra Leone to negotiate agreement for creation of independent special court UN Press Release SC/6910 (Aug. 14, 200).

42. On January 23, 2007, the UN and the Lebanese government signed an agreement to create the Special Tribunal for Lebanon. It was created on May 30, 2007, by the UN Security Council Resolution 1757 (2007) "to prosecute persons responsible for the attack of Feb. 14, 2005 resulting in the death of former Lebanese Prime Minister Rafiq Hariri and the death or injury of other persons" and other connected cases. Article 1, Statute of the Special Tribunal for Lebanon, S/RES/1757. The purpose was defined by a "document" annexed to the Resolution and originally destined to form the text of an "Agreement between the United Nations and the Lebanese Republic on the establishment of a Special Tribunal for Lebanon." Mario Odoni, *The Establishment of the Special Tribunal for Lebanon and Domestic Jurisdiction*, 4 HAGUE JUSTICE J./J. JUDICIAIRE DE LA HAYE 171 (2009), published by Eleven International Publishing

(2010),   https://www.elevenjournals.com/tijdschrift/hjj/2009/3/HJJ_187-4202_2
009_004_003_002.pdf

43. In 2001, the Cambodian National Assembly passed a law to create the Extraordinary Chambers in the Courts of Cambodia for the Prosecution of Crimes Committed during the Period of Democratic Kampuchea (Extraordinary Chambers or ECCC). Its jurisdiction reached "senior leaders of Democratic Kampuchea and those who were most responsible for the crimes and serious violations of Cambodian penal law, international humanitarian law and custom, and international conventions recognized by Cambodia, that were committed during the period from 17 April 1975 to 6 January 1979." Article 1, Law on the Establishment of the Extraordinary Chambers. UN General Assembly Resolution 57/228(B) of May 13, 2003, approved a UN/Cambodia Agreement. The Agreement entered into force, in accordance with its art. 32, on Apr. 29, 2005, following the fulfillment of the legal requirements for ratification by both the Royal Government of Cambodia and the United Nations. The Extraordinary Chambers included foreigners proposed by the UN Secretary General to act as one of the two investigative judges, one of the two co-prosecutors and five of the twelve judges.

44. After the Kosovo War ended, Bernard Kourchner as head of the UN Interim Administration Mission in Kosovo (UNMIK) pursuant to the authority provided by UN Security Council resolution 1244 (1999) of June 10, 1999, and "For the purpose of ensuring the independence and impartiality of the judiciary and the proper administration of justice" adopted UNMIK Regulation 2000/64. It provided for panels consisting of at least two international and one judge from Kosovo that should take up cases where it is "necessary to ensure the independence and impartiality of the judiciary or the proper administration of justice."

45. In 2003, the ICTY and the Office of the High Representative (OHR), an ad hoc international institution responsible for overseeing implementation of the Dayton Peace Agreement ending the war in Bosnia and Herzegovina, agreed on a plan to establish a "war crimes chamber" within the Court of Bosnia and Herzegovina. International judges and prosecutors will serve in these institutions only for an initial period followed by a transition to a fully domestic complement of staff. http://www.internat ionalcrimesdatabase.org/courts/hybrid

46. Sarah Williams, *The Extraordinary African Chambers in the Senegalese Courts: An African Solution to an African Problem?*, 11 J. INT'L CRIMINAL JUSTICE 5, 1139 (2013).

47. By Resolution 36/106 of Dec. 10, 1981, the General Assembly, invited the International Law Commission to resume its work with a view to elaborating the draft Code of Offences against the Peace and Security of Mankind. In 1983, the Commission proceeded to a general debate and concluded that "the draft code should cover only the most serious international offences" and requested the General Assembly to indicate "whether the Commission's mandate extends to the preparation of the statute of a competent international criminal jurisdiction for individuals." G.A. 36/106, U.N. Docs. A/RES/36/106 (Dec. 10, 1981).

48. *Report on the work of its 46th Sess. Draft statute for an international Criminal Court with Commentaries* [1994] Y.B. Int'l L. Comm'n , vol. II, Part 2 26, A/CN.4/SER.A/1994/Add.l (Part 2).

49. *Id.*

50. "The court is envisaged as a facility available to States parties to its statute, and in certain cases to the Security Council." *Id.* at 45.

51. Article 23.3 provided "No prosecution may be commenced under this Statute arising from a situation which is being dealt with by the Security Council as a threat to or breach of the peace or an act of aggression under Chapter VII of the Charter, unless the Security Council other- wise decides." *Id.* at 43.

52. *Id.* at 27.

53. G.A. Res. 49/53, ¶ 2, U.N. Doc. A/RES/49/53 (Dec. 9, 1994). *Report of the Ad Hoc Committee on the Establishment of an International Criminal Court,* U.N. Doc. A/50/22, GAOR, 50th Sess., Sepp. No. 22 (1995).

54. G.A. Res. 50/46, ¶ 2 U.N. Doc. A/RES/50/46 (Dec. 11, 1995).

55. David Bosco, Rough Justice: The International Criminal Court in a World of Power Politics 43 (Kindle ed. 2014).

56. Claude E. Welch & Ashley F. Watkins, *Extending Enforcement: The Coalition for the International Criminal Court,* 33 Hum. Rts. Quarterly 927 (2011).

57. "Blair's Labour Party platform promised that 'we will make protection and promotion of human rights a central part of our foreign policy,' a move that was intended to distinguish itself from the realpolitik that marked Conservative governments from Margaret Thatcher to John Major." The principle and its contradictory applications are presented by Christopher Rudolph, Power and Principle: The Politics of International Criminal Courts 95 (Kindle ed. 2017).

58. Situation in the Republic of Cote D'Ivoire, ICC-02/11, Corrigendum to "Judge Fernandez de Gurmendi's separate and partially dissenting opinion to the Decision Pursuant to Article 15 of the Rome Statute on the Authorisation of an Investigation into the Situation in the Republic of Côte d'Ivoire" (Oct. 5, 2011), https://www.icc-cpi.int/CourtRecords/CR2011_16840.PDF.

59. UN Diplomatic Conference of Plenipotentiaries on the Establishment of an Int'l Crim. Court, Rep. of the Preparatory Comm. on the establishment of an Int'l Crim. Court, U.N Doc. A/CONF.183/2/Add.1-EN (Apr. 14, 1998).

60. G.A. Res. 51/207, ¶ 4 U.N. Doc. A/RES/51/207 (Dec. 17, 1996).

61. The manifesto clearly states, "We will work for the creation of an International Criminal Court to investigate genocide, war crimes, and crimes against humanity." Christopher Rudolph, Christopher, Power and Principle: The Politics of International Criminal Courts 89–112 (Kindle ed. 2017).

62. Press Release, UN Diplomatic conference to establish International Criminal Court to convene in Rome, June 15–July 17, UN Press Release, L/2867 (June 8, 1998).

63. *Rome Statute of the International Criminal Court, Overview,* UN Office of Legal Affairs, https://legal.un.org/icc/general/overview.htm (last visited Jan. 19, 2021).

64. Press Release, UN Diplomatic conference concludes in Rome with decision to establish permanent International Criminal Court, UN Press Release L/2889 (Jul. 20, 1998).

65. *World: Europe. Annan calls for strong world criminal court*, BBC NEWS (June 15, 1998, 10:50 AM), http://news.bbc.co.uk/2/hi/europe/112664.stm.

66. *NATO Air Exercise Sends Warning to Serbs*, N.Y. TIMES, June 16, 1998, at 2.

67. Article 6 defined Genocide following the Convention adopted by the UN General Assembly in 1948. Article 7 codified Crimes against humanity, transforming the jurisprudence developed by Nuremberg and ICTY and ICTR into an international treaty. Article 8 defined War crimes following the Geneva Convention and jurisprudence established by different experts, ICTY, ICTR and other tribunals. As Kirsch and Holmes explained: "It was understood that the statute was not to create new substantive law, but only to include crimes already prohibited under international law." See, e.g., 1 Report of the Preparatory Committee on the Establishment of an International Criminal Court, U.N. GAOR, 51st Sess., Supp. No. 22 at 16, U.N. Doc. A/51/22 (1996).

68. There were heated debates at Rome on the definition of the term "gender." In the end a definition was adopted: "gender" refers to the two sexes, male and female, within the context of society.

69. The Statute expanded the crime of persecution beyond the previously accepted grounds of race, ethnicity, nationality, religion, and politics to include persecution based on "gender." The Statute, following the ICTY and ICTR jurisprudence, listed rape as a crime against humanity, and added it as a war crime. It included "rape, sexual slavery, enforced prostitution, forced pregnancy . . . enforced sterilization or any other form of sexual violence also constituting" either "grave breaches" or violations of Common Article 3 of the Geneva Conventions as war crimes in international and internal war. The Statute also commands to take the protection of gender into consideration across the Prosecutor and Court procedures.

70. Fifty years before, Raphael Lemkin was worried about mixing the basic human rights and crimes like genocide. "If every abuse were to become a subject of international concern, Lemkin worried, states would recoil against international law and would not respond to the greatest crime of all." SAMANTHA POWER, A PROBLEM FROM HELL 1913 (Kindle ed. 2013).

71. "The Israeli representative noted that his country would have voted in favor of adopting the Statute had Article 8(2)(b)(viii) not been included." Hannes Jöbstl, *An Unlikely Day in Court?: Legal Challenges for the Prosecution of Israeli Settlements under the Rome Statute*, 51 ISRAEL L. REV. 339 (2013).

72. They were the following: the Crime of terrorism, Crimes against United Nations and associated personnel, and Crimes involving the illicit traffic in narcotic drugs and psychotropic substances G.A. 50/46, ¶ 2, U.N. Doc A/RES/50/46 (Dec. 11, 1995).

73. Isolated cases of political prisoners, police brutality, non-systematic assassinations, restrictions of free speech, unfair trials, media censorship, coup d'etat, corruption, terrorism, narcotics traffic, serious violations of economic or social human rights are not part of the ICC material jurisdiction. The Rome Statute is a unique diagnosis of what values are common to the entire humanity and what others did not reach such a level of acceptance. Using the language of French Professor Mireille Delmas-Marty the debate at Rome was a moment of "ordering pluralism." MIREILLE AUTERUR DELMAS, ORDERING PLURALISM. A CONCEPTUAL FRAMEWORK FOR UNDERSTATING THE TRANSITIONAL LEGAL WORLD (New ed., Naomi Norbergm trans., 2009).

74. David Scheffer, *False Alarm about the* Proprio Motu *Prosecutor, in* THE FIRST GLOBAL PROSECUTOR: PROMISE AND CONSTRAINTS (LAW, MEANING AND VIOLENCE) 29, 30 (Martha Minow et al. eds., Kindle ed. 2015).

75. "Statement of the United States Delegation Expressing Concerns Regarding the Proposal for a Proprio motu Prosecutor: The Concerns of the United States Regarding the Proposal for a Proprio motu Prosecutor," dated June 22, 1998 (the "US delegation statement"). *Is a U.N. International Criminal Court in the US National Interest? Hearing Before the Subcomm. on Int'l of the Comm. on Foreign Relations*, 105th Cong. 147–150 (1998).

76. Because of the Council's legal responsibilities for maintaining international peace and security, the United States believes that the Council must play an important role in the work of a permanent court, including as a court's trigger mechanism.

77. "To be sure, the United States regards all violations of human rights and international humanitarian law as reprehensible. But we must not turn an International Criminal Court—Prosecutor—into a human rights ombudsman open to, and responsible for responding to, any and all complaints from any source. If we do, the Court will be flooded with every imaginable complaint, hindering its investigation into the most serious crimes and undermining its scope and relevance. The only way the office of the Prosecutor could manage such an onrush would be by making decisions that inevitably will be regarded as political." Bill Richardson, Ambassador Extraordinary and Plenipotentiary US Permanent Representative to the United Nations, Statement at the UN Plenipotentiaries Conference on the Establishment of an International Criminal Court (transcript available in II Summary Records of the plenary meetings and of the meetings of the Committee of the Whole) UN Press Release #108 (98) (June 17, 1998).

78. "At the same time, however, we support giving maximum independence and discretion to the prosecutor in his or her proper sphere." Bill Richardson, Ambassador US Permanent Representative to the United Nations, Statement at the UN Plenipotentiaries Conference on the Establishment of an International Criminal Court *(transcript available in II* Summary Records of the plenary meetings and of the meetings of the Committee of the Whole) UN Press Release #108 (98) (June 17, 1998) in David Scheffer, *False Alarm about the* Proprio Motu *Prosecutor* in THE FIRST GLOBAL PROSECUTOR: PROMISE AND CONSTRAINTS (LAW, MEANING AND VIOLENCE) 29, 31 (Martha Minow et al. eds., 2015).

79. "The Clinton Administration, and most particularly the Pentagon, fear that unless the court is in some way answerable before the world's leading democracies, American soldiers around the globe could be hauled before international judges on politically motivated charges. Four of the permanent members of the United Nations Security Council—the United States, China, France, and Russia—want the Council to decide which cases should be prosecuted. Only Britain, the fifth member, does not. On the other side of the debate, at least 42 nations in what has been called the "like-minded group" are battling for an independent court, arguing that unless the court and its prosecutors are free from interference from the Security Council, its authority would be toothless." "No country is openly opposed to the notion of an international

court. Today, Pope John Paul II gave his blessing to the project." Alessandra Stanley, *Conference Opens on Creating Court to Try War Crimes*, N.Y. TIMES (June 15, 1998), http://www.nytimes.com/1998/06/15/world/conference-opens-on-creating-court-to-try-war-crimes.html.

80. "Initially, the [like-minded] group was heavily European, but it enjoyed the support of several Latin American states. Australia, New Zealand, and Canada were also enthusiastic. Two Canadian diplomats described the like-minded as dominated by "middle powers that were not directly involved in any conflicts, and had relatively little historical baggage to compromise the credibility of their search for humanitarian solutions." "Because they were not global powers, they thought of themselves as more able to construct international architecture that would be perceived as fair and legitimate by the rest of the world. The usually unstated corollary of this thesis was clear: powerful states with complex interests had limited ability to advance impartial international justice." DAVID BOSCO, ROUGH JUSTICE: THE INTERNATIONAL CRIMINAL COURT IN A WORLD OF POWER POLITICS 39 (Kindle ed. 2014).

81. "[A]n independent Prosecutor must not only be empowered to institute proceedings when individual States or the Security Council report a crime, but also to take the initiative to start investigations independently." H. E. Mr. Lamberto Dini, Minister of Foreign Affairs for Italy, Address at UN Plenipotentiaries Conference on the Establishment of an International Criminal Court (transcript available in II Summary Records of the plenary meetings and of the meetings of the Committee of the Whole) UN Press Release #108 (91) (June 17, 1998).

82. Philippe Kirsch, the Chairman of the Rome Conference, explained that "A German proposal providing universal jurisdiction for the court enjoyed strong support among some states and the vast majority of NGOs. A Korean proposal that provided for somewhat narrower, but still broad jurisdiction also enjoyed wide support. It suggested that the court could exercise jurisdiction if any of four states were party to the statute (the territorial state, the state of nationality of the accused or the victim, and the custodial state). Philippe Kirsch & John T. Holmes, *The Rome Conference on an International Criminal Court: The Negotiating Process*, 93 AM. J. INT'L L., 2, 8–9 (1999).

83. On Dec. 10, 1906, President Theodore Roosevelt was awarded the Peace Nobel Prize. He was unable to be present, and he delivered his speech of acceptance in 1910. Theodore Roosevelt, 26th President of the United States of American, Nobel Lecture: International Peace (May 5, 1910) (transcript available at https://www.nob elprize.org/prizes/peace/1906/roosevelt/lecture/).

84. *Id.*

85. *Id.*

86. The United States and Israel withdrew their signature months later and Russia in 2014 after the conflict in Ukraine.

87. *See* the analysis of the Colombian Constitutional Court, Cases C-614 and C-578 2002. Corte Constitucional [C.C.] [Constitutional Court], Sala Plena, julio 30 2002, Sentencia C-578/02, Gaceta de la Corte Constitucional [G.C.C.] (Colom.).

3

The New *Jus ad Bellum*

The War on Terror

President George W. Bush could have chosen to prosecute the September 11, 2001, attack's responsible. The decision to treat Al Qaeda terrorists as enemies that could be killed in any country rather than consider them as criminals that should be arrested distorted *jus ad Bellum*, increased US tensions with the Rome Statute, and transformed world order.

First, the chapter analyzes the options to face the conflict that the Bush administration did not contemplate, including making efforts to arrest and prosecute Osama bin Laden and the Taliban government members that supported him before US courts. The Noriega precedent demonstrated the possibility of using military forces to arrest individuals in a foreign country.

Second, the chapter discusses how the War on Terror strategy was improvised to face the 9/11 attacks. The US Congress transformed the *jus ad Bellum* standards. It authorized military forces' use against nonstate actors, without defining either a time limit or a specific battlefield. To protect the *home,* Congress authorized different US administrations to kill individuals *abroad,* even against the will of sovereign countries that were not at war with the United States, without occupying them and *exercising sovereign rights* abroad.[1] The exceptional character of humanitarian law authorizing to kill replaced the national legal system that protects life.

In a few weeks, a relatively small US military operation acting in partnership with local militias destroyed Al Qaeda camps and removed the Taliban administration.[2] Afterward, the United States faced a different problem: insurgency. The US plans ignored the Vietnam lessons on counterinsurgency and the previous Russian failure in Afghanistan.

Third, the chapter presents the tension between two normative models: *jus ad Bellum* and *jus ad Curiam.* The War on Terror increased the US opposition to an independent International Criminal Court (ICC). The US Congress adopted the American Service Members Protection Act (ASPA) prohibiting US cooperation with the court, including funding or sharing classified information.

War and Justice in the 21st Century. Luis Moreno Ocampo, Oxford University Press. © Oxford University Press 2022.
DOI: 10.1093/oso/9780197628973.003.0004

The ICC was also a primary concern for White House counsel Alberto Gonzalez, Secretary of Defense Donald Rumsfeld, and other administration members like John Bolton. The United States used its veto power to force the UN Security Council (UNSC) to adopt resolutions under Article 16 of the Rome Statute to protect its personnel from any ICC investigation.

Part One

September 11, 2001, Attacks

Al Qaeda attacks took the US government by surprise. On that very early Tuesday morning, George W. Bush had received a CIA's Presidential Daily Briefing, "which combined highly classified intelligence with in-depth analysis of geopolitics. . . . The September 11 briefing covered Russia, China, and the Palestinian uprising in the West Bank and Gaza Strip."[3] There was not even a mention of the possibility of a terrorist attack on the United States.

President Bush was visiting an elementary school in Sarasota, Florida, that morning when he received the information that "an airplane had crashed into the World Trade Center." He was talking to the students when he was told, "A second plane hit the second tower . . . America is under attack."[4]

He remained calm, finished the conversation with the students, and then went to a private room.

"I watched in horror as the footage of the second plane hitting the south tower replayed in slow motion . . . The country would be shaken, and I needed to get on TV right away. I wanted to assure the American people that the government was responding and that we would bring the perpetrators to justice."[5] The meaning of *justice* would change just fifteen minutes later. President Bush was on his way to the airport when he learned that "there had been a third plane crash, this one into the Pentagon." President Bush then made up his mind: "The first plane could have been an accident. The second was definitely an attack. The third was a declaration of war."[6]

Bin Laden: Moving from a Friendly Proxy Force to Be a Criminal

The mastermind behind the attack was Osama bin Laden, Al Qaeda's leader.[7] To fight the Soviet Union, the United States tolerated that Pakistan armed and funded a conservative movement: the "students of Islam," or Taliban,"[8] and promoted *mujahidin* forces.

Osama bin Laden contributed to the US-friendly *mujahidin* forces.[9] He was supported by Saudi Arabia funds exposing one of the war approach's main weaknesses: the United States created its future enemies.[10] The enemy of the US enemy became a US friend.[11]

Backed by the United States, the *mujahidin* rebellion grew, spreading to all parts of the country and forcing the Soviets to withdraw in 1989.[12] Osama bin Laden saw the defeat of the Soviets as a victory against "the foundation head of atheism and unbelief"[13] *and* focused his attention on the relationship between the United States and the Islamic world.

When Iraq invaded Kuwait, bin Laden offered to rally freedom fighters to protect the Saudi regime, but the kingdom instead asked the United States for military protection. *To bin Laden, corrupt princes were welcoming infidels to desecrate holy ground.*[14] He led a fundamentalist conspiracy attacking US personnel abroad.

The nationality of the victims and the attacks against embassies provided jurisdiction to US prosecutors. In June 1999, bin Laden was indicted in the United States on "charges of training the people involved in the 1993 attack that killed 18 US servicemen in Somalia and in connection with the August 7, 1998, bombings of the United States embassies in Dar es Salaam, Tanzania, and the Nairobi, Kenya attacks that killed over 200 people."[15] The US grand jury also determined that bin Laden was trying to develop chemical and nuclear weapons.[16] Osama bin Laden then became one of the FBI's ten most wanted individuals.

The Law Enforcement Options

How to bring bin Laden to justice? There was no need for international courts. The 9/11 crimes were planned in Afghanistan but executed in the United States. The US prosecutors and courts had jurisdiction and could have expanded bin Laden's indictments to cover the September 11 attack. US prosecutors could also have indicted other Al Qaeda members, even those in the Taliban government that were aiding and abetting the terrorist group.

The problem was how to enforce the grand jury's decision. National governments have the exclusive authority to arrest people in their territory, and the Taliban regime was unwilling to capture bin Laden.

There was already a US precedent for enforcing an arrest warrant through a military operation. In 1989, under the George H. W. Bush administration, US troops invaded Panama and arrested its leader, Manuel Noriega, who had been indicted in Miami for drug trafficking and racketeering.[17]

For years, like Osama bin Laden, Noriega was considered a US "friend" fighting against enemies. Noriega worked for the United States, helping to transfer weapons for the "Nicaraguan contras" in their guerrilla war against the Sandinistas.[18] US agencies were ignoring Noriega's crimes taking advantage of his contributions against the Sandinistas enemies.[19]

The Noriega arrest required the mobilization of 23,000 US soldiers,[20] more than fifty times the number needed to remove the Taliban government in 2001. The Panama military operation was not invoking self-defense as required by Article 51 of the UN Charter, and the UN General Assembly and the Organization of American States opposed it.[21] However, this would probably not have been the case regarding bin Laden. Although it is counterfactual, it is easy to predict that the UNSC could have authorized an operation to arrest bin Laden.

One day after the attack, on September 12, 2001, the UNSC unanimously adopted resolution 1368 (2001), calling "on all States to work together urgently to bring to justice the perpetrators, organizers, and sponsors of these terrorist attacks."[22] In the aftermath of 9/11, the Bush administration could have obtained a UNSC's authorization to use the armed forces to *bring the perpetrators to justice*, as stated by Resolution 1368.

Part Two

The *Jus ad Bellum* Decision against Al Qaeda and the Taliban

Bin Laden turned from a criminal into an enemy. President George W. Bush improvised a strategy: "There is no textbook on how to steady a nation rattled by a faceless enemy. I relied on instincts and background."[23]

The top members of the Bush administration met on September 12 to devise a plan: "removing the Taliban, denying sanctuary to al Qaeda, and helping a democratic government emerge."[24] By legal design, President George W. Bush was not responsible for Afghanistan and other nations' citizens. His duty was to protect US soil and US people. However, the final phase of the operation was to "stabilize the country and help the Afghan people build a free society,[25] including stopping gender discrimination in Afghanistan.[26]

Back to the Old World Order?

Dutch lawyer and philosopher Hugo Grotius's ideas from the seventeenth century supported President Bush's decision to launch the War on Terror in 2001. In his 1625 book *The Law of War and Peace*, Grotius coined a legal framework claiming that the reasons to wage war are identical to those that prompt lawsuits. "War is a substitute for courts, because courts are the original substitutes for war . . . The function of war is to right wrongs."[27] Grotius explained: "states are permitted to wage war against each other in order to enforce their legal rights."[28]

In *The Internationalists: How a Radical Plan to Outlaw War Remade the World*, Oona Hathaway and Scott Shapiro reviewed the struggle to make war illegal. They concluded that the signing of the Paris Peace Pact (also known as the Briand-Kellogg or Kellogg-Briand Pact) in 1928 marked the end of the Grotius's Old World Order. A New World Order started: war became just a defensive mechanism, and states could not use it when they felt aggrieved. *States should not right wrongs with force.*[29] Article 51 of the UN Charter confirmed the prohibition of aggressive war by the Paris Peace Pact.

President George W. Bush's proposal went back to the Old War Order. Grotius affirmed that war could be "useful for punishing criminals. If someone has engaged in egregious wrongdoing and is evading justice, war may be used to achieve retribution."[30]

President George W. Bush explained in his memoirs that criminal law would eventually not deter suicide attackers. However, the claim ignores other dimensions of the law. The law helps to coordinate different interests and provides a common framework to galvanize international cooperation.

Fundamentally, a legal system could reduce the need for revenge. Moral values as reconciliation are not the critical factor of peaceful coexistence. If someone kills my daughter, I should not attack him, but I should demand the best criminal investigation. No one can force me to reconcile with my hypothetical daughter killer, but I must respect the prohibition to use violence. The legal architecture could allow victims and criminals to live in peace together. Instead, the War on Terror prompted the *duty* of revenge mentioned in the introduction.

Congress's Authorization to use Military Forces

On September 18, 2001, Congress considered it necessary "to protect United States citizens both at home and abroad"[31] and passed a joint resolution by a vote of 98 to nil in the Senate and 420 to 1 in the House. Congress's resolution read:

> That the President is authorized to use all necessary and appropriate force against those nations, organizations, or persons he determines planned, authorized, committed, or aided the terrorist attacks that occurred on September 11, 2001, or harbored such organizations or persons, in order to prevent any future acts of international terrorism against the United States by such nations, organizations or persons.[32]

The US Congress did not establish a time limit; the 2001 authorization was used during the following decades by the Bush, Obama, Trump, and Biden administrations. Congress did not define a specific battlefield. The Bush and the Obama administrations considered that the United States had the right to conduct lethal operations even in a nation "which is not at war with US,"[33] when such a country was " 'unwilling and unable' to take 'appropriate action' to address" international terrorism.[34] Congress's authorization was limited to *those that planned, authorized, committed or aided the terrorist attacks on September 11, 2001*. With time, this limitation was expanded by the Bush and Obama administrations into *forces associated* with Al Qaeda and the Taliban.[35] The Trump administration considered that the 2001 authorization also covered Iran, alleging that it allowed Al Qaeda to transit its territory.[36]

There was one single vote against the 2001 Congress's authorization. It was cast by Barbara Lee, representing California's East Bay district and a US lieutenant colonel's daughter. She said, "However difficult this vote maybe, some of us must urge the use of restraint . . . think on the implications of our actions today, so this does not spiral out of control." She quoted a clergy member saying, "as we act, let us not become the evil that we deplore."[37]Ten days after her vote, Barbara Lee further explained her preference for bringing the terrorists to face US Justice: "It was a blank check to the president to attack anyone involved in the Sept. 11 events—anywhere, in any country . . . and without time limit." "We must respond, but the character of that response will determine for us and for our children the world that they will inherit." "We must develop our intelligence and bring those who did this to justice."[38] No one listened to her.

The Beginning of the War on Terror Operations

The UN Security Council Support

In 2001, the international community strongly supported the US government. On September 12, 2001, the council adopted Resolution 1368 (2001), expressing "its deepest sympathy and condolences to the victims and their families and the People and Government of the United States of America." Two weeks later, the UNSC supported US intervention in Afghanistan, "Reaffirming the inherent right of individual . . . self-defense as recognized" by the UN Charter.[39]

The war rationale did not include efforts to arrest bin Laden. A 2009 Report to Members of the Committee on Foreign Relations considered that "The US military operation executed in Afghanistan could had been focused on the specific mission to arrest Bin Laden."[40] There was a fierce two-week battle (December 3–17, 2001) in Tora Bora between Al Qaeda and Afghan militias allied with the United States, but US forces did not participate.

Bin Laden is thought to have left Tora Bora for Pakistan on horseback on December 16.[41] "The decision not to deploy American forces to go after bin Laden or block his escape was made by Secretary of Defense Donald Rumsfeld and his top commander, Gen. Tommy Franks. Rumsfeld said at the time that he was concerned that too many US troops in Afghanistan would create an anti-American backlash and fuel a widespread insurgency."[42]

In parallel, UN special envoy Lakhdar Brahimi, one of the top UN negotiators, traveled to Afghanistan to forge a consensus among various warring Afghan factions for a "homegrown" solution to the post-Taliban era.[43] On December 5, 2001, in Bonn, an agreement was reached between different Afghan leaders, establishing an interim administration led by Hamid Karzai, a Pashtun.[44]

Just two weeks later, the council adopted Resolution 1386 (2001), welcoming the new Afghan government, and creating the International Security Assistance Force (ISAF).[45] It was a collective military effort led by the United Kingdom to help the Afghan Interim Authority maintain security in Kabul and its surrounding areas.[46] The UN would not participate in a war. The new Afghan administration requested assistance to face an internal rebellion.[47]

As mentioned, 78% of all ISAF contributing nations were also state parties of the Rome Statute.[48] Their rules of engagement took into consideration the

Rome Statute's limits. The War on Terror and the Rome Statute worked together, influencing the behavior of the troops involved.

Furthermore, on February 10, 2003, Abdullah Abdullah, the new Afghanistan minister of foreign affairs, made a *jus ad Curiam* decision in the middle of the War on Terror: Afghanistan ratified the Rome Statute.[49] The minister wanted to have his country commit to human rights principles.

Jus in Bello during the War on Terror

After defeating the Taliban government and bombing Al Qaeda's training camps through conventional warfare, the US military faced a problem that the Soviet Union had already confronted in Afghanistan: increased insurgency. "Unlike traditional armies, insurgents did not expect to hold territory, as their priority was to play for time rather than hold space, allowing them to gain in support while the enemy was drained of patience and credibility."[50]

President Bush had to show leadership, but his improvised decision prevented the United States from learning from previous counterinsurgency experiences.[51] The United States ignored its own history. Instead, Vietnam leader Ho Chi Minh fought against the United States following George Washington's strategy: "wear down the enemy, avoid catastrophic defeat, keep the army in being and simply make it too expensive for your superior enemy to continue the war."[52]

The United States ignored the similarities between Soviet mistakes in Afghanistan and US miscalculations in the "Vietnam War." In both experiences, the support for the insurgency increased. A May 1989 US Army declassified report on "Lessons from the War in Afghanistan" exposed "Soviet failure to learn from the US experience [in Vietnam] caused them to make many of the same errors."[53]

The US Army evaluated that Soviet Afghanistan's invasion was "the strongest unifying factor for the insurgents" in Afghanistan. Similar to what would happen after US intervention in 2001, the Afghans "had invading infidels against whom to unite."[54] The US Army accurately identified the Soviet Union's mistakes in Afghanistan, but twenty years later, the War on Terror strategy fell into the same trap.

Chinese leader Mao Zedong explained that the insurgents must move among the people "like fish swimming in the water of the population."[55] Following Mao's principles, Al Qaeda consolidated a safe haven in Muslim communities, spreading to Pakistan, Iraq, Syria, and many other countries. To face the challenge, the United States needed information to discriminate between the fish and the water. Alberto Gonzales, then White House Counsel, discussed methods to obtain intelligence from prisoners.

There were six different *jus in Bello* decisions that became highly controversial: (1) The interception of private communications of aliens living in foreign countries that included communications within US territory. The US interceptions of foreign leader allies, including Brazil's president Dilma Rousseff and Germany's chancellor Angela Merkel, were considered legal by President Obama. (2) The adoption of "enhanced interrogation techniques" as a CIA method for investigation. (3) Cooperation with other national intelligence services to abduct people in foreign countries, a practice called "exceptional renditions." (4) The creation of "black sites," secret detention centers in Poland and Romania operated by the CIA, (5) Maintaining individuals in Guantanamo and other prisons for long periods without charges or access to due process. (6) Authorizing military officers to decide who should be executed without providing the targets with a right to present evidence and challenge their responsibility.

All these tactics were debated with selected US lawyers and then authorized. Jack Goldsmith, a crucial player in some of those debates,[56] explained that the Bush administration "has been strangled by law, and since September 11, 2001, this war has been lawyered to death."[57] The Bush administration took seriously into consideration the ICC's role.[58] It should be interesting to find the way to quantify the Clinton and, in particular, the Bush administrations levels of opposition to the ICC to evaluate the constraints it imposed or to measure its deterrence impact.

Part Three

The US Opposition to the ICC after September 11

The Bush Administration's Withdrawal of the Rome Statute's Signature
Since the end of World War II, the United States adopted a national defense strategy focused on protecting "home" through military deployment "abroad." Such a national defense strategy exposed US soldiers to be investigated "abroad," opening a confrontation with a permanent ICC's operation.

"The United States is the only country whose military has a global "defense" perimeter . . . Central Command is not in charge of defending" the US territory. "Rather, it is in charge of maintaining—and, if necessary, creating—conditions that Washington considers secure in the Middle East, North Africa, and Central Asia."[59]

The United States had been trying to obtain protection from the ICC since the 1996 negotiations at the UN.[60] President Clinton had signed the Rome Statute on the last possible day, openly recognizing that his goal was to protect US personnel from the court's intervention rather than ratify it.[61]

During the Bush administration, the National Security Council coordinated a new review.[62] But 9/11 produced a turning point. On October 2, 2001, Senator Jesse Helms introduced the ASPA at the US Senate. Alerting the US senators that the Rome Statute was going to be ratified and become operational, he stated:

> Our soldiers and decision-makers will be all the more exposed to the risk of illegitimate prosecution as they proceed . . . against those who on September 11 committed mass murder against innocent American civilians . . . . We have a responsibility as Senators to enact an insurance policy for our troops and our officials—such as Secretary of State Powell—to protect them from a U.N. Kangaroo Court where the United States has no veto.

Under the Vienna Convention on Treaties, a state that has signed but not ratified a treaty can send a letter of declaration not to ratify and ask to be removed from its obligations. In May 2002, John Bolton, then undersecretary of state for arms control and international security, sent such a letter to Kofi Annan, the UN secretary-general. The letter stated, "The United States does not intend to become a party to the treaty," and that, "[a]ccordingly, the United States has no legal obligations arising from its signature on December 31, 2000."

In a press briefing the same day, defense secretary Donald Rumsfeld argued that the ICC model was escaping the UNSC control.[63]

Marc Grossman, undersecretary for political affairs, expressed additional concerns:

> The United States has a unique role and responsibility to help preserve international peace and security. At any given time, US forces are located in close to 100 nations around the world conducting peacekeeping and

humanitarian operations and fighting inhumanity. We must ensure that our soldiers and government officials are not exposed to the prospect of politicized prosecutions and investigations.[64]

The European Union reacted with a statement expressing its disappointment with this action.[65]

In July 2002, the Rome Statute became operational when more than sixty states ratified it. A month later, the ASPA was enacted, prohibiting US cooperation with the court, including funding or sharing classified information.[66]

ASPA also restricted the US role in peacekeeping missions unless the UN specifically exempted US troops from prosecution by the ICC. It blocked US aid to allies unless they signed accords to shield US troops on their soil from being turned over to the ICC. It also authorized the president to take any necessary action to rescue US personnel handed over to the ICC, a direct threat to invade the Netherlands. ASPA is still defining the US vote at the UNSC and blocking any possibility to finance ICC operations through the UN.

The Impact of the ASPA Deliberation on the UN Security Council Decisions

On June 30, 2002, while the Bush administration was planning the Iraq intervention, precisely one day before the ICC jurisdiction came into effect, the United States decided to show its determination to protect its personnel from the court's jurisdiction. It vetoed a resolution to extend the UN mission in Bosnia and Herzegovina, affecting peacekeepers' deployment and police forces' training.[67]

That position led to clashes between American diplomats and some of their closest allies, including Britain and Canada, whose diplomats charged that the United States was engaged in an "abuse of power."[68]

US Ambassador Negroponte explained the veto: "With our global responsibilities, we are and will remain a special target and cannot have our decisions second-guessed by a court whose jurisdiction we do not recognize." He requested a resolution providing immunity from the ICC to non-state parties.[69]

In agreement with the United Kingdom, the French ambassador suggested a way forward respecting the statute's legal architecture. He proposed that the

United States sign a bilateral agreement with the host country or use Article 16 of the Rome Statute, suspending the ICC investigations as a solution. Both were legal mechanisms available under the Rome Statute.

On July 10, 2002, twenty states that were not members of the UNSC requested permission to discuss the proposed resolution applying Article 16.[70] The ensuing debate lasted more than five hours, with the majority of states opposing the immunity provision.[71]

Nevertheless, on July 12, 2002, the Security Council unanimously adopted Resolution 1422 (2002), invoking Article 16 of the Rome Statute and instructing the ICC not to commence proceedings against any personnel in a UN peacekeeping operation from a state nonparty to the statute for twelve months beginning on the July 1, 2002.

The United States was committed to defending itself not only from terrorism but also from the international legal community. At the stakeout, US ambassador John D. Negroponte explained: "The President of the United States is determined to protect our citizens—soldiers and civilians, peacekeepers and officials—from the ICC." He made the point clear: "We will not permit the imposition on our citizens of a novel legal system they have never accepted or approved, and which their government has explicitly rejected." And Amb. Negroponte promised this: "The American system of justice can be trusted to punish crimes, including war crimes or crimes against humanity, committed by an American—and we pledge to do so."[72] Answering a journalist's question, Ambassador Negroponte further explained that the United States planned "to seek renewal of this resolution on an annual basis."[73]

In August 2002, John Yoo, then deputy assistant attorney general, produced a memo showing a particular concern of the Bush administration: how to protect from the ICC US personnel implementing coercive techniques? Yoo considered that the torture's victims could not be regarded as civilians. He presented any interpretation against his opinion as a problem of a rogue prosecutor.[74]

In September 2002, the Bush administration officially adopted a US National Security Strategy and exposed the ICC as a fundamental constraint that should be faced:

> We will take the actions necessary to ensure that our efforts to meet our global security commitments and protect Americans are not impaired by the potential for investigations, inquiry, or prosecution by the International

Criminal Court (ICC), whose jurisdiction does not extend to Americans and which we do not accept.[75]

The transatlantic controversy aggravated following the promulgation of the ASPA. The Bush administration promoted the signing of Bilateral Immunity Agreements (BIA) worldwide. Nations have to accept that current or former US government officials, military and other personnel, and US nationals would not be transferred to the ICC jurisdiction.

The United Kingdom, Italy, and Spain initially considered negotiating a BIA with the United States while other countries, notably Germany and France, refused. As a compromise, the EU presidency elaborated some guidelines that set out the parameters for negotiation.[76]

Similar requests were presented to countries from other regions. Many states rejected the proposal, and President Bush announced on July 1, 2003, the suspension of military aid to thirty-five state parties to the court that had not entered into a BIA with the United States.[77]

Over the next three years, twelve Latin American countries (including Brazil, Bolivia, Ecuador, and Mexico) lost funding totaling over $10 million. In 2005, Mercosur, the South American regional trade organization, issued a joint presidential declaration opposing US BIA policy.

The Nethercutt Amendment of 2005 increased the penalties for BIA non-compliance and broadened the ASPA penalties to include prohibitions on economic aid provided under the Economic Support Funds (ESF) program.[78]

Human Rights Watch sent a letter to secretary of state Colin Powell denouncing US "bully tactics" pressing small, vulnerable, and often-fragile democratic governments to sign BIAs with Washington.[79]

Between 2002 and 2007, the Office of Security Negotiations and Agreements in the State Department negotiated and secured Article 98 agreements from over one hundred countries.[80] According to a report produced by the Coalition for the ICC in December 2006, forty-six of them were states parties of the Rome Statute.[81]

Rumsfeld's Concerns

For years, the Pentagon analyzed as a risk that "weak enemies like Al Qaeda used or misused the law to attack a critical US value: respect for the law." General Charles Dunlap considered it improper to challenge US personnel operations' legality. He assumed that US troops would always respect legal limits and labeled the use of legal complaints to achieve operational object-ives as "Lawfare."[82]

Henry Kissinger had already raised the possibility of pursuing US po-litical leaders for crimes committed abroad in July 2001.[83] In France, Chile, Argentina, and Spain, judges tried to ask Kissinger questions about "Operation Condor," South American coordinated intelligence service activ-ities that included assassinations conducted in Europe and the United States. A British judge refused to authorize to interrogate Kissinger on the issue when he visited London.[84]

After a meeting with Kissinger, Donald Rumsfeld asked Jack Goldsmith, newly appointed to the Department of Defense, to find a solution to "the judicialization of international politics."[85] Goldsmith perceived that:

> [T]he weak "enemy: using asymmetric legal weapons was not al Qaeda, but rather our very differently motivated European and South American allies and the human rights industry that supported their universal jurisdiction aspirations. Rumsfeld saw this form of lawfare as a potentially powerful check on American military power. He also saw it in more personal terms. He was leading the Department of Defense in a controversial war against al Qaeda and its affiliates and was about to take it into a more controversial war in Iraq. [A]s the widely detested critic of 'Old Europe' he could expect to be at the top of the target list.[86]

In 2003, Rumsfeld demanded action. Several years of NSC meetings among lawyers and deputies followed. But a concrete plan never emerged.[87] Rumsfeld acted alone, setting down a marker in the 2005 National Defense Strategy:

> Describing US "vulnerabilities" in the "changing security environment," the Strategy noted that "our strength as a nation-state will continue to be challenged by those who employ a strategy of the weak using international forums, judicial processes, and terrorism.[88]

The War on Terror model perceives only friends or enemies and therefore included between the enemy tag those proposing multilateralism; justice; and in particular, the ICC. Years later, Fatou Bensouda, the second ICC chief prosecutor, announced an investigation on US crimes in Afghanistan and was *designated*, a sanction applied to drug dealers and terrorists. The War on Terror and the Rome Statute are two opposite models.

Notes

1. Such a policy is impacting "two basic building blocks of international law ... the principles of reciprocity, that one nation should be entitled to exercise the same rights as those enjoyed by another nation." DAVID SCHEFFER, ALL THE MISSING SOULS: A PERSONAL HISTORY OF THE WAR CRIMES TRIBUNALS (HUMAN RIGHTS AND CRIMES AGAINST HUMANITY) 164 (Kindle ed. 2011)(ebook). US sovereignty was going to be expanded allowing the killing of people in foreign countries while the sovereignty of countries like Pakistan or Yemen could be affected. As Morgenthau explained: "... in a given territory only one state can have sovereignty, that is, supreme authority, and that no other state has the right to perform governmental acts within that territory without the consent of the state which has sovereignty over it. War as the extreme form of law enforcement under international law is the only exception to that rule; for it is of the very essence of war to penetrate the territory of the enemy while safeguarding the 'impenetrability' of one own's, and international law allows the occupying state to exercise sovereign rights in the territory occupied by its military force." Hans J. Morgenthau, *The Problem of Sovereignty Reconsidered*, 48 COLUM. L. REV. 341, 344–45 (1948).
2. "That war proved, in the short term, to be one of the easiest, cheapest, and most successful campaigns in American military history." MICHAEL MANDELBAUM, MISSION FAILURE 162 (Kindle ed. 2016).
3. GEORGE W. BUSH, DECISION POINTS 126 (Kindle ed. 2010).
4. *Id.* at 127.
5. *Id.* at 128.
6. *Id.* at 127–128.
7. The FBI investigation into the 9/11 attacks identified the nineteen hijackers on the plane and linked them to Al Qaeda. The United Kingdom and the United States also obtained electronic intercepts indicating that bin Laden's deputy Mohammed Atef was involved in the planning of the 9/11 attacks. CNN (Sept.17, 2001, 11:21 AM), http://edition.cnn.com/2001/US/09/16/inv.binladen.denial/.
8. *Id.* at 28.
9. In 1984, Congress passed a resolution, which called for "effective" US material aid for the rebels "in their fight for freedom from foreign domination" in Afghanistan. Steve Galster, *The September 11th Sourcebooks, Afghanistan: The Making of U.S. Policy, 1973–1990*, NAT. SECURITY ARCHIVE (Oct. 9, 2001), https://nsarchive2.gwu.edu/NSAEBB/NSAEBB57/essay.html.
10. RONAN FARROW, WAR ON PEACE: THE END OF DIPLOMACY AND THE DECLINE OF AMERICAN INFLUENCE 170–72 (Kindle ed. 2018).
11. In accordance with US intelligence community, bin Laden was financing the recruitment, transportation, and training of Arab nationals who volunteered to fight

alongside the Afghan mujahidin;*Osama Bin Laden: Islamic Extremist Financier*, NAT. SECURITY ARCHIVE, https://nsarchive2.gwu.edu/NSAEBB/NSAEBB55/ciaubl.pdf (last visited Jan. 18, 2021).

12. *Soviet Invasion of Afghanistan*, BRITANNICA, https://www.britannica.com/event/Sov iet-invasion-of-Afghanistan (last visited Jan. 18, 2021).

13. Meredith Taylor, *A Rhetorical Analysis of Messages to America by Osama bin Laden*, COMMUNICATION HONORS PROJECTS. Paper 1 (2013).

14. Mark Hosenball, *War on Terror: The Road to September 11*, NEWSWEEK (Sept. 30, 2001, 8:00 PM), https://www.newsweek.com/war-terror-road-september-11-151771.

15. *FBI Most Wanted Fugitive*, WEB ARCHIVE (June 1999), https://web.archive.org/web/ 20070515210241/http://www.fbi.gov/wanted/topten/fugitives/laden.htm.

16. Grand Jury Indictment, United States of America v. Usama Bin Laden, NY, S.D.N.Y.R. (1998), S(2) 98 Cr. 1023 (LBS).

17. Vice president Dick Cheney and secretary of state Colin Powell were also involved in the decision-making process in the Noriega case as secretary of defense and national security advisor, respectively COLIN L. POWELL & JOSEPH E. PERSICO, MY AMERICAN JOURNEY 7110 (Kindle ed. 2003). DICK CHENEY, IN MY TIME: A PERSONAL AND POLITICAL MEMOIR 167–68 (Kindle ed. 2011).

18. "We ourselves were using him as a conduit to get arms to the Nicaraguan contras in their guerrilla war against the Sandinistas." COLIN L. POWELL & JOSEPH E. PERSICO, MY AMERICAN JOURNEY 7005–10 (Kindle ed. 2003).

19. COLLIN POWELL & JOSEPH E. PERSICO, MY AMERICAN JOURNEY 7021 (Kindle ed. 2003).

20. "[O]n December 20, 10,000 US troops backed by gunships and fighter-bombers flew into Panama to rendezvous with the 13,000 soldiers already stationed at the American bases in the canal area." Douglas G. Brinley, *The Bush Administration and Panama* in FROM COLD WAR TO NEW WORLD ORDER: THE FOREIGN POLICY OF GEORGE H. W. BUSH 2850–1 (Meena Bose & Rosanna Perotti eds., Kindle ed., Greenwood Press, 2002).

21. Douglas G. Brinley, *The Bush Administration and Panama*, in FROM COLD WAR TO NEW WORLD ORDER: THE FOREIGN POLICY OF GEORGE H. W. BUSH 2871 (Meena Bose & Rosanna Perotti eds., Kindle ed. 2002).

22. S.C. Res. 1368, ¶ 3, U.N. Doc. S/RES/1368 (Sept. 12, 2001).

23. GEORGE W. BUSH, DECISION POINTS 140 (Kindle ed. 2010).

24. *Id.* at 194–19.

25. *Id.* at 194.

26. CONDOLEEZZA RICE, NO HIGHER HONOR: A MEMOIR OF MY YEARS IN WASHINGTON 79 (Kindle ed. 2011).

27. "These causes include not only self-defense and the punishment of crimes, but also matters of a completely commercial nature, such as the collection of 'debts arising from a contract' and 'defence of one's property. Because the function of war is to right wrongs, property seized in a just war belongs to the captor. Prize, booty, and conquest are merely the recovery of goods already due the attacker: Having been wronged, the victim has the right to go to war precisely because he cannot go to court." [OONA A

Hathaway & Scott Shapiro, The internationalists: How a Radical Plan to Outlaw War Remade the World 10 (1st. hardcover ed. 2017).

28. *Id.*

29. *Id.*

30. *Id.* at 9–10.

31. H.R.J. Res. 64, 107th Cong. (2001).

32. H.R.J. Res. 64, 107th Cong. (2001).

33. Jack Goldsmith, Power and Constraint: The Accountable Presidency after 9/11 13–15 (Kindle ed. 2012). *See Civilian Casualties & Collateral Damage,* Lawfare, https://www.lawfareblog.com/civilian-casualties-collateral-damage (last visited Mar. 10, 2020).

34. Rosa Brooks, How Everything Became War and the Military Became Everything: Tales from the Pentagon 285 (Kindle ed. 2016).

35. At the same time, the US Congress did not accept the additional mission defined in 2001 by the executive aiming to counter all terrorist threats generally. The original Bush administration project included a different language: "to deter and pre-empt any future acts of terrorism or aggression against the United States." Matthew C. Weed, Cong. Research Serv., R43983, 2001 Authorization for use of military Force: Issues Concerning Its Continued Application (2015).

36. *Report on the Legal and Policy Frameworks Guiding the United States' Use of the of Military Force and Related National Security Operations,* The White House, https://obamawhitehouse.archives.gov/sites/whitehouse.gov/files/documents/Legal_Policy_Report.pdf.

37. Conor Friedersdorf, *Against the War on Terror,* Atlantic (Sept. 14, 2014), https://www.theatlantic.com/politics/archive/2014/09/the-vindication-of-barbara-lee/380084/.

38. "In granting these overly broad powers, the Congress failed its responsibility to understand the dimensions of its declaration." Barbara Lee, *Why I Opposed the Resolution to Authorize Force,* SF Gate (Sept. 23, 2001, 4:00 PM), https://www.sfgate.com/opinion/article/Why-I-opposed-the-resolution-to-authorize-force-2875410.php.

39. S.C. Res. 1373, U.N. Doc S/RES/1373 (Sept. 28, 2001).

40. *Tora Bora Revisited: How We Failed to Get Bin Laden and Why It Matters Today. A Report to Members of the Comm. On Foreign Relations, United States Senate,* 111th Cong. (2009).

41. Max Boot, *U.S. Troop Withdrawal from Afghanistan: What Are Biden's Options?,* Council on Foreign Relations (Feb. 9, 2021), https://www.cfr.org/in-brief/us-troop-withdrawal-afghanistan-what-are-bidens-options.

42. *Tora Bora Revisited: How We Failed to Get Bin Laden and Why It Matters Today. A Report to Members of the Comm. On Foreign Relations, United States Senate,* 111th Cong. (2009).

43. Florian Krampe, *The Liberal Trap—Peacemaking and Peacebuilding in Afghanistan after 9/11* (2013), https://www.researchgate.net/publication/267335098

44. Steven Erlanger, *A NATION CHALLENGED: NEGOTIATIONS; Talks in Bonn End with Deal on Leadership for Afghans,* N.Y. Times (Dec. 5, 2001), https://www.nytimes.

com/2001/12/05/world/nation-challenged-negotiations-talks-bonn-end-with-deal-leadership-for-afghans.html.

45. The International Security Assistance Force was created and mandated by the UN Security Council Resolution 1386 with the aim of helping the Afghan authorities to stabilize the country and ensure that it would not be a safe haven for terrorists anymore.

46. S.C. Res. 1386, U.N. Doc S/Res/1386 (Dec. 20, 2001).

47. *Nato's Role in Afghanistan*, NATO (Apr. 9, 2009), https://www.nato.int/summit2009/topics_en/03-afghanistan.html.

48. *ISAF Troop Contributing Nations*, NATO (Oct. 21, 2009), https://www.nato.int/isaf/structure/nations/index.html.

49. Assembly of States Parties » States Parties to the Rome Statute » Asia-Pacific States » Afghanistan, ICC (Nov. 17, 2003), https://asp.icc-cpi.int/en_menus/asp/states%20parties/asian%20states/Pages/afghanistan.aspx.

50. Lawrence Freedman, The Future of War 193 (Kindle ed. 2017).

51. President John F. Kennedy tried *to shore up friendly governments in the developing world threatened by communist-inspired insurgency and subversion.* Vietnam war and Argentina's *dirty war* were some of the consequences of such a policy. In the early 1980s, a different counterinsurgency effort was conducted in Center America, under President Ronald Reagan. Noriega was a US friend in that effort." Alan J. Vick, Adam Grissom, William Rosenau, Beth Grill, & Karl P. Mueller, *The Challenge of Counterinsurgency: Lessons from the Cold War and After, in* Air Power in the New Counterinsurgency Era 27, 28 (2006)

52. "Christopher Woolf, *The Little-Known Story of Vietnamese Communist Leader Ho Chi Minh's Admiration for the US*, PRI (Sept. 18, 2017, 6:30 PM), https://www.pri.org/stories/2017-09-18/little-known-story-vietnamese-communist-leader-ho-chi-minh-s-admiration-us.

53. "Many lessons from the Soviet COIN [Counter Insurgency] experience will appear very familiar to students of the US involvement in Vietnam." Lessons from the War in Afghanistan, May 1989 (Army Department Declassification Release) (available at Nat. Security Archive: https://nsarchive2.gwu.edu/NSAEBB/NSAEBB57/us11.pdf).

54. *Id.*

55. Lawrence Freedman, The Future of War 203 (Kindle ed. 2017).

56. He was legal adviser to the general counsel of the Department of Justice (September 2002–October 2003) and US assistant attorney general (October 2003–July 2004).

57. Jack Goldsmith, The Terror Presidency: Law and Judgment Inside the Bush Administration 69 (Kindle ed. 2007).

58. "The nature of the new war places a high premium on other factors, such as the ability to quickly obtain information from captured terrorists and their sponsors in order to avoid further atrocities against American civilians," but he told the president that "It is difficult to predict the motives of prosecutors and independent counsels who may in the future decide to pursue unwarranted charges." Jack Goldsmith, The Terror

PRESIDENCY: LAW AND JUDGMENT INSIDE THE BUSH ADMINISTRATION 68 (Kindle ed. 2007).

59. NUNO P. MONTEIRO, THEORY OF UNIPOLAR POLITICS 1 (Kindle ed. 2014).

60. *See* Christopher Hall, *The First Two Sessions of the UN Preparatory Committee on the Establishment of an International Criminal Court*, 91 AM. J. INT. L. 177 (1997); Christopher Hall, *The Third and Fourth Sessions of the UN Preparatory Committee on the Establishment of an International Criminal Court*, 92 AM. J. INT. L. 124 (1998); Christopher Hall, *The Fifth Session of the UN Preparatory Committee on the Establishment of an International Criminal Court*, 92 AM. J. INT. L. 331 (1998); Christopher Hall, *The Sixth Session of the UN Preparatory Committee on the Establishment of an International Criminal Court*, 92 AM. J. INT. L. 54 (1998).

61. "We are concerned that when the court comes into existence, it will not only exercise authority over personnel of states that have ratified the treaty but also claim jurisdiction over personnel of states that have not. With a signature, however, we will be in a position to influence the evolution of the court. Without a signature, we will not . . . I will not, and do not recommend that my successor, submit the treaty to the Senate for advice and consent until our fundamental concerns are satisfied." William Clinton, 42nd President of the United States of America, Statement on the Rome Treaty on the International Criminal Court (Dec. 31, 2000).

62. Jean Galbraith, *The Bush Administration's Response to the International Criminal Court*, FACULTY SCHOLARSHIP AT PENN LAW, 1449 (2003), https://scholarship.law.upenn.edu/faculty_scholarship/1449.

63. Curtis A. Bradley, *US Announces Intent Not to Ratify International Criminal Court Treaty*, 7 (7) ASIL INSIGHTS (May 11, 2002), https://www.asil.org/insights/volume/7/issue/7/us-announces-intent-not-ratify-international-criminal-court-treaty.

64. Marc Grossman, Under Secretary of State for Political Affairs, Address delivered at Center for Strategic and International Studies (May 6, 2002).

65. Martijn Gorenleer, *The United States, the European Union, and the International Criminal Court: Similar Values, Different Interests?* 13 INT'L J. CONST. L. 930 (2015).

66. American Servicemembers Protection Act of 2002, Pub. L. 107–206 (amended by Pub. L. No. 110–181, enacted Jan. 28, 2008).

67. U.N. SCOR, 57th Sess., mtg. 4563 712 S/PV.4563, U.N. Doc. S/2002/712 (June 30, 2002).

68. DAVID BOSCO, ROUGH JUSTICE, THE INTERNATIONAL CRIMINAL COURT IN A WORLD OF POWER POLITICS 74 (Kindle ed., Oxford University Press, 2014).

69. "It strikes us as more than perplexing that others that are parties to the ICC can use the provision of the Treaty to exempt their forces for an extended period from the purview of the Court for war crimes and then suggest that our attempt to use other provisions of the Treaty similarly to provide protection for our forces either violates their Treaty obligations or does unacceptable damage to the spirit of the Treaty." S.C. meeting 4563, U.N. Doc. S/PV.4563 (June 30, 2002).

70. The states were Bosnia and Herzegovina, Brazil, Canada, Costa Rica, Croatia, Denmark, Fiji, Germany, India, the Islamic Republic of Iran, Jordan, Liechtenstein, Malaysia, Mongolia, New Zealand, Samoa, South Africa, Thailand, Ukraine, and Venezuela.

71. U.N. SCOR 57th Sess., 4568 mtg., U.N. Doc. S/PV.4568(July 10, 2002).

72. John. D. Negroponte, US Permanent Representative to the United Nations, Remarks at stakeout following UN Security Council vote on Resolution 1422, including text explanation of vote (July 12, 2002).

73. *Id.*

74. "We believe that the ICC cannot take action based on such interrogations. The United States' campaign against al Qaeda is an attack on a non-state terrorist organization, not a civilian population. If anything, the interrogations are taking place to elicit information that could prevent attacks on civilian populations. As we have explained elsewhere, members of al Qaeda cannot receive the protections accorded to POWs under GPW because al Qaeda is a non-state terrorist organization that has not signed the Conventions." Letter from John C. Yoo, Deputy Assistant Attorney General to Honorable Alberto R. Gonzales Counsel to the President (Aug. 1, 2002). https://www.justice.gov/sites/default/files/olc/legacy/2010/08/05/memo-gonzales-aug1.pdf

75. THE WHITE HOUSE, 2002 NATIONAL SECURITY STRATEGY OF THE UNITED STATES OF AMERICA (Sept. 17, 2002).

76. Martijn Gorenleer, *The United States, the European Union, and the International Criminal Court: Similar Values, Different Interests?*, 13 INT'L J. CONST. L. 930 (2015).

77. Elena Aoun, *Beyond EU/US Early Contentions Over the International Criminal Court: The Development of the EU's Loyalty to the ICC*, 61 STUDIA DIPLOMATICA 164 (2008).

78. LEE FEINSTEIN & TOD LINDBERG, MEANS TO AN END 51–52 (Kindle 2011).

79. The letter dated June 30, 2003, mentioned conflicts with Croatia, Bahamas, foreign ministers of the CARICOM, and others. *Letter to US Secretary of State Colin Powell on US Bully Tactics against the International Criminal Court*, HUMAN RIGHTS WATCH (June 30, 2003, 8:00 PM), https://www.hrw.org/news/2003/06/30/letter-us-secretary-state-colin-powell-us-bully-tactics-against-international.

80. LEE FEINSTEIN & TOD LINDBERG, MEANS TO AN END 51–52 (Kindle ed. 2011).

81. *Status of US Bilateral Immunity Agreements*, COALITION FOR THE INTERNATIONAL CRIMINAL COURT (Dec. 11, 2006), http://www.iccnow.org/documents/CICCFS_BIAstatus_current.pdf.

82. Major General Charles J. Dunlap, Jr., *Lawfare Today: A Perspective*, YALE J. INT'L AFF. 146, 146 (Winter 2008).

83. Henry A. Kissinger, *The Pitfalls of Universal Jurisdiction: Risking Judicial Tyranny*, FOREIGN AFF., July/Aug., at 86, 92 (2001).

84. JACK GOLDSMITH, THE TERROR PRESIDENCY: LAW AND JUDGMENT INSIDE THE BUSH ADMINISTRATION 57–58 (Kindle ed. 2007).

85. *Id.* at 59–60.

86. "Rumsfeld believed that opponents incapable of checking American military power would increasingly rely on lawfare weapons instead." *Id.* at 59–60.

87. "The Department of State argued that any effort by the United States to oppose the increasingly powerful institutions of international justice would seem like a defensive admission of the very war crimes charges it wanted to avoid. The effort would also smack of hypocrisy, the State Department emphasized, since the United States aggressively used human rights institutions—including universal jurisdiction lawsuits—to

check human rights abuses by other nations. The Department of Justice also opposed any anti–universal jurisdiction campaign on the ground that it would jeopardize its ability to bring its own universal jurisdiction prosecutions against foreign leaders and terrorists. The NSC remained worried about the threat of foreign judges. But in the face of the bureaucratic squabbling, and preoccupied with weightier concerns, it couldn't figure out what to do about it." *Id.* at 63.

88. *Id.* at 53.

4

Building the Office of the Prosecutor

This chapter explains how the Office of the Prosecutor was established, policies were planned, and operations were executed. It describes the swearing in and the public hearing convened to discuss the office's plans. It also presents the initial decisions to recruit the personnel.

A highly qualified and committed group of persons became members of the Office of the Prosecutor. They interacted with the rest of the court and our diverse constituencies to make the statute a reality. My colleagues had different professional backgrounds and experiences. Part of my work was learning from them and establishing policies and an operational manual to create a homogeneous practice. While I wrote this book, it is impossible to fully recognize all the people's efforts and ideas that built the Office of the Prosecutor. This book is exposing just a little part of their work.

My Swearing In

The solemn courtroom of the International Court of Justice in the Peace Palace was the stage for the ceremony of my swearing in as the chief prosecutor. Beautiful gardens surround the majestic building, a gift from Andrew Carnegie and the alternative because the ICC courtroom was not ready.

Around three hundred people attended the ceremony, including my four children and my wife; a few friends, my former Argentinian partners in the law firm; then Dutch Princess Maxima, who born in Argentina; former Nuremberg prosecutors, and dozens of ambassadors.

For the first time in my life, I wore the traditional long black robe used by lawyers in some European and African countries. I was seated in front of a vast desk, and the ICC eighteen judges were observing me.

Prince Zeid, president of the Assembly of States Parties, opened the ceremony:

War and Justice in the 21st Century. Luis Moreno Ocampo, Oxford University Press. © Oxford University Press 2022.
DOI: 10.1093/oso/9780197628973.003.0005

We are here in this magnificent location: the Peace Palace in The Hague, to witness the making by Luis Moreno-Ocampo of his solemn undertaking, an occasion unique in the affairs of humankind, for the legal power we are about to entrust to him meets no historical equal in breadth and significance.[1]

He added:

For his prosecutorial record in his own country has been judged by the Assembly to be uniformly distinguished. His treatment of cases was marked by rigor and an approach that was clearly meticulous, with considerable attention having been accorded by him to the victims themselves. All of this was accomplished in often the most trying of political circumstances.

I walked to the side of the room. I raised my right hand; and, after practicing for two days, I said in French: "*I*, Luis Moreno Ocampo, solemnly undertake that I will perform my duties and exercise my powers as prosecutor of the International Criminal Court, honorably, faithfully impartially, and conscientiously."

Then Philippe Kirsch, the president of the Court; Ben Ferencz, a former Nuremberg prosecutor; Getachew Kitaw, a lawyer representing the defense; Billon Ung Boun-Hor, a victim of the Khmer Rouge; and Bill Pace, the convenor of the Coalition for the ICC took the floor.[2] Bruno Cathala, a French judge who later became the first registrar of the court, choreographed the ceremony carefully.

I took advantage of my first speech as the prosecutor to outline my three central policies. First, I underscored that, as mentioned in its preamble, the Rome Statute's final objective is to prevent future crimes and protect the victims. "Our common mission is to ensure that the most serious crimes of concern to humanity are investigated and punished, thus contributing to the protection of millions of individuals."[3]

Second, I wanted to fully express my commitment to respect complementarity and consider states' actions as an indicator of the Rome Statute's success. I presented the idea of "positive complementarity"—encouraging and assisting states in fulfilling their missions to prosecute crimes that could fall under the Rome Statute jurisdiction. As mentioned, I linked the principle of complementarity with the evaluation of the entire Rome Statute system: "the absence of trials by the ICC, as a consequence of the effective functioning of national systems, would be a major success."

Third, to avoid misunderstandings and build consensus, I promised a continuous dialogue with all our stakeholders.[4] Following such a promise and as planned during my conversations with Fernando, I spent the following two days at a public hearing held in the Peace Palace's modern annex.

Engaging My Constituencies

I was seated at the front table with Morten Bergsmo in front of almost two hundred people, including many ambassadors and legal advisers, scholars, NGOs' members, activists, and the most prominent experts in the field. They came to present their views and comments on the Office of the Prosecutor's priorities and policies.[5]

Whitney Harris, a member of Robert Jackson's team during the first Nuremberg trial, gave us advice on using documents to prove a case in Court. Delegates at the Rome Conference, including Elizabeth Willmhurst (UK), David Scheffer (USA), Hakan Friman (Sweden), and Juan Antonio Yañez–Barrionuevo (Spain), presented their views about how to implement the Statute that they had helped draft. Bertrand Ramcharan, acting UN High Commissioner for Human Rights in the absence of Sergio, explained the synergies between the UN High Commissioner for Human Rights and the ICC Office of the Prosecutor. Antônio Cançado Trinidade, a Brazilian judge of the Inter-American Court of Human Rights and later of the International Court of Justice; James Hamilton, Ireland's Director of Public Prosecutions; and Antonio Cassese, former president of the ICTY, provided their insights. Members of the ICTY's Office of the Prosecutor shared their experience. Members of civil society organizations presented comments on issues ranging from victims' participation to crime prevention. Professors, including Otto Triffterer, Goran Sluitter, and Bruce Broomhall, also added their insights to the discussion.

The room was full of energy. It was the first time that all of these actors had met to discuss with an ICC officer the statute's implementation. It was one of the richest experiences of my work as the prosecutor, not just intellectually but in particular because it fostered the feeling that we were representing a community; that there was a group of individuals from all over the world who cared about international justice.

Everyone was very thankful for the transparency we exhibited by presenting our plans in public, and for the openness we demonstrated in listening to their opinions.

I received many frank comments, including criticism—for example, Bill Pace strongly questioned the "zero case" approach: "I don't think we should see the fact that there are trials as not a success. I note some of the leadership in the judges' chambers also frames it this way, and I just think that it should be reconsidered."[6]

Elizabeth Wilmshurst summarized the comments received during the hearing perfectly:

> First, I've been very impressed by the extent to which the two draft papers have been supported and endorsed by the speakers in all of their principal aspects. This does credit to the care with which your staff, particularly Morten, has been consulting before presenting the drafts. And it also shows that we do agree that the papers follow the Statute. They don't go beyond.
>
> I've been particularly struck by the endorsement of the fundamental proposal because it is quite fundamental that it should be prosecutorial policy to investigate those who bear the greatest responsibility for the offenses; for example, the leaders of the state or organization. And there's been wide agreement on your complementarity proposals.
>
> There's your much-quoted statement that the success of the ICC should not be measured by the number of cases that reach the Court but by the absence of the ICC trials as a consequence of the effective functioning of national systems.
>
> Bill Pace criticized that yesterday; indeed, he was quite grumpy about it . . . it really is very important, the strong aspirations that the national jurisdictions will operate effectively and that the ICC will have some influence towards that . . .
>
> My third remark. I think that everyone would like to see the first investigation begin as soon as possible, but I guess that most if not all of us here would share the remarks made by Bill Pace yesterday, that it's better to get things right than to get it wrong because it's done too quickly.

We produced a written comment identifying the suggestions received, the areas of consensus, and discrepancies, and we promised to include those ideas into our policies.[7]

Starting Operations

On June 19, 2003, I climbed the stairs of the ICC provisional building at Maanweg 174 on The Hague's outskirts for the first time as the ICC prosecutor. It was time to start operations.

I had an office on the corner of the twelfth floor with a view of a highway, tiny houses, and green fields. Morten Bergsmo was on the same floor, and Klaus Rackwitz on the seventh floor. We had a very efficient assistant and six brilliant young interns supporting our work. That was the entire office.

Silvia Fernandez arrived a few days later and occupied an office on the eleventh floor. She prepared the policies and selected the best possible team to manage the jurisdictional analysis and the required cooperation. Our decisions in the nascent field of *jus ad Curiam* had to be fully supported by the law.

I was impressed by Elizabeth Wilmshurst's clarity summarizing the public hearings convened at the Peace Palace Academy. Silvia convinced her to join us as a consultant for six months to work on the first policy paper considering the advice received.

Morten Bergsmo and some of the interns worked on the first draft of the regulations of the office. They were also analyzing the communications received, demanding our intervention in different situations.

Selecting the Office of the Prosecutor Members

Art. 42 of the statute said that "The Prosecutor shall be assisted by one or more Deputy Prosecutors." At the beginning of my tenure, I decided to appoint two deputies to put them in charge of the investigation and the prosecution division. One of my priorities was selecting my first deputy in charge of investigations and invited Carla del Ponte, the ICTY chief prosecutor, to join me at the selection panel.

After a public call for candidates, ultimately attracting 133 applicants from forty-seven countries, we preselected a list of twelve, interviewed them, and presented three nominees to the assembly. Delegates had to choose one of them to be the deputy prosecutor. Spanish Judge Baltasar Garzon was the only candidate I knew before, he had great experience investigating massive crimes, but he didn't have the language proficiency required.

We had only one female candidate preselected. She was impressive but with no experience in conducting investigations. As Serge Brammertz, she was from Belgium. I thought that it was not possible to present two persons from the same country. We discussed with Carla, and finally, I decided that he was more suited for the job.

On August 11, 2003, I nominated Hassan Bubacarr Jallow from The Gambia, Serge Brammertz from Belgium, and Vladimir Tochilovsky from Ukraine as candidates for the position of deputy prosecutor of the ICC.

A few days before the assembly's meeting, Hassan Jallow informed me that UN secretary-general Kofi Annan offered him to be the new chief prosecutor of the ICTR. As a consequence, he withdrew from the short list. Vladimir Tochilovsky obtained twenty-two votes and sixty-five votes elected Serge Brammertz as deputy prosecutor for a six-year term.

Serge had relevant experience as a prosecutor in Belgium coordinating prosecutors and interacting with the gendarmerie. He was young, intelligent, and fluent in French, German, and English. He was so competent that after leading the Lubanga investigation, in January 2007, Kofi Annan appointed him as the head of the UN International Independent Investigation Commission into the murder of former Lebanese prime minister Rafic Hariri. I gave him a leave of absence, but he never returned and eventually replaced Carla del Ponte as the ICTY chief prosecutor.

With Serge on board, we made efforts to recruit the best possible candidates. The ICC basically followed the UN system to appoint personnel. We had to advertise the positions offered, explaining the competences and the years of experience required. We had to provide a window of time for applicants to present their information; we would then review the candidates, make the first selection, and call them for an interview before a panel.

Each decision was made looking for the "highest standards of efficiency, competency, and integrity" as required by Art. 44 with due respect for gender and geographical balance. We recruited all the office personnel by open and transparent competition. There was no exception.[8] None of them knew me before Prince Zeid's call. I had no previous friends as staff—no one that had worked with me before.

Silvia Fernandez's reputation attracted young and brilliant professionals.[9] When Silvia resigned to go back to her diplomatic carrier, Beatrice Le Frapper du Hellen, who led the French delegation at Rome and had significant experience in battling international matters with big countries, replaced her. She is exceptionally brilliant and committed to justice and helped navigate difficult times, particularly during the arrest warrants' issuance against Bashir.

Phakiso Mokochoko replaced Beatrice in February 2011. During the Rome Conference, he represented Lesotho, and since 2002 was part of the ICC Advance Team created to set up the court in The Hague. For the nine previous years, he was the senior legal adviser in the ICC Registry. His vast experience significantly contributed to the office and helped us integrate our work within the court and with the rest of the Rome Statute network.

Serge recruited Michel De Smedt as his second in command, a highly talented officer of the Belgium gendarmerie with unique investigative, security, and strategic planning experience. After a few years, Michel became the head of the division that selected the investigators and analysts.

My experience in Argentina taught me the possibility of building the case from the victims' testimonies. I insisted on integrating into the investigation division young people with NGOs and UN fieldwork experience to interact with the victims. They were called the "softies," and it was not easy to integrate them with police or military investigators coming from ICTY following the traditional police method to obtain information from insiders. So we finally integrated both approaches.

We also filled the senior lawyer positions. We were together with Serge in the panel to appoint our first senior trial lawyer: Christine Chung. She is a top lawyer from the United States who had a very distinguished career reaching the prominent position of chief of appeal at the best US prosecutor office, the US's Southern District of Manhattan. Christine left New York to live at The Hague and then travel every two weeks to Uganda to interview LRA victims. She made a crucial contribution in establishing the highest standards of practice for the office.

At a similar moment in time, we selected Fabricio Guariglia as the senior appeal lawyer. He had been deeply involved in the legal discussions before, during, and after the Rome Conference and later served as legal adviser and appeals lawyer at the ICTY. He and Christine combined their different experiences and created a uniquely qualified team.[10]

After a few years, Sarah Criscitelli, who was in the US Department of Justice's international area, became a special adviser coordinating senior trial attorneys' work.

Our children and gender unit's perfect leader was Gloria Atiba Davis, a brave former prosecutor from Sierra Leone. She had gone into exile when people she investigated led a *coup d'etat* in her country. She had firsthand experience in being removed from her country and the knowledge and maturity to ensure proper interaction with victims.

Under Article 42.9, the prosecutor shall appoint advisers with legal expertise on specific issues, including, but not limited to, sexual and gender violence and violence against children. I took advantage of the new institution's attraction and the world's top experts, including Catharine MacKinnon, Juan Mendez, Tim McCormack, Jose Alvarez, and Christopher Stone, accepted to be our advisers.

In 2004, I requested applications for a second deputy prosecutor. We had many qualified candidates; we prepared a solid short list, and Fatou Bensouda was elected to the position by an overwhelming majority (fifty-eight votes of a total of seventy-eight).

Fatou had been a young attorney general in her native Gambia. After spending a short time working in the private sector, she moved on to work at the ICTR. She combined a very sharp mind and experience in national and international criminal law with a unique ability to interact with people ranging from presidents to victims. She never lost her calm; she could be steadfast without losing her composure.

The office's growth was exponential, challenging our ability to play as one consistent team: fivefold the first year, from five professionals to twenty-seven. In June 2005, we were sixty-six professionals, more than double the figures for the previous year.[11] We were still growing by 25% in the third year. At the end of my tenure, the office had around three hundred members.

We attracted the most talented young personnel from Sri Lanka to Saint Kitts and Navis.

We appointed a lawyer from Korea who resigned from his well-paid work in a corporation to join us. A young lawyer from Uganda became our spokesperson, and a human resource manager from Singapore became in charge of the area. My professional assistants came from Japan, Mexico, Colombia, and Mauritius. They had PhDs from the best universities and internships in international tribunals. One of them told me that she saw the ICC building from the freeway and considered it the Olympus mount, the top peak of global justice.

It was more challenging to propose high-quality and top-ranking national experts to interrupt their domestic carriers and join us. We were lucky that highly successful national prosecutors from Germany, Canada, the United States, and South Africa were willing to join us. A Peruvian expert on international cooperation with ten years of experience working for Switzerland

and a former businessman from Brazil managing the organizational aspects also joined our team.

The entire prosecution team came from ninety different countries, from national and international institutions, and had different kinds of expertise: successful investigators, lawyers, diplomats, activists, and analysts. In an office without any established best practices, they brought their own practice and strong opinions. It was a huge challenge to integrate them precisely because of every staff member's commitment to justice and belief in their own experiences' applicability.

The Uganda investigation provided an example of the complex interaction. As a federal US prosecutor, Christine Chung led the police during the investigations. The top investigators in the Uganda case were a talented UK military expert and a senior French policeman. In their national experience, the police collect evidence almost independently and provide a report at the end to the prosecutor. Both were feeling that Christine was intruding on their professional work. Christine, on the contrary, thought that they were excluding her from the case.

One day they came to my office looking for a solution to their different views on approaching the case. I used a metaphor to try to inspire them. "We have to be the best. We have to work together as a 'Ferrari' team."

The British investigator, frustrated by my comment, said, "I got it. We are mechanics, and Christine is Schumacher." Then he asked, "Can you tell Schumacher to tell us what the wheel that should be changed is? Normally, she just leaves the cockpit and changes the wheel herself."

We tried to devote time to discuss our experiences and train our teams. We received support from law firms and key actors from other countries like South African prosecutors, the US attorney general Loretta Lynch, and lawyers and judges from New York.

The adoption of the internal operations manual in 2010 transformed the interactions among all of us. It was a massive collective effort to assemble the office's best practices during its first seven years and transform them into a very detailed manual prescribing methods to ensure success at work.[12]

Interacting with the Other Organs

Although I had full authority over the Office of the Prosecutor, I needed to coordinate our activities alongside the court's other organs. I regularly met with Philippe Kirsch, the president of the court and former president of the Rome Conference, in his office on the ICC building's fifteenth floor. He was responsible for the court's general external relations while I had the authority over the specific Office of the Prosecutor mandate.

An extremely experienced diplomat and international lawyer, Philippe chose his words very carefully and strategically planned his meetings, meticulously setting the agenda and evaluating the outcomes. These personal characteristics were a crucial asset in Rome, where he had to combine the views of a variety of actors from one hundred sixty states. His skills also proved invaluable at the ICC, not just as a judge but also as a strategic leader.

Philippe had to manage three different fronts: he had the critical authority to call the appointed judges to come to The Hague and to lead their legal debates; to supervise the registry and its services; and to represent the entire court before the world, navigating the world of diplomacy and establishing relations with states and international organizations.

The lack of a state bureaucracy to implement its decisions forces the entire court to rely on national and international institutions' cooperation. Under Philippe's leadership, in less than two years, and despite the US' intense pressure, the court could sign a binding agreement of cooperation with the UN.[13]

In the beginning, one of Philippe's biggest concerns was to manage the expectations of the remaining seventeen appointed judges. There was no case yet to review, and the judges had to limit themselves to observing our preliminary examination decisions. Philippe was very respectful of my independent mandate and managed the problem by calling the judges to discuss the court's regulations.

During the first months, we had some misunderstandings. I surprised Philippe by proposing to discuss issues that I considered essential even if they were not on our agenda. But within a short time frame and despite our differences, we managed to understand each other very well. We learned to take advantage of our different characteristics to put the entire court into motion.[14]

A French judge on leave, Bruno Cathala, was appointed registrar of the court a few days after my swearing in and became the third member of the initial "troika." He had experience in administrative matters at the ICTY, where he had been the deputy registrar and had a clear vision for the Rome Statute. He was highly committed to victim participation and upholding the principles of fairness and the defendant's rights.

Bruno's job was incredibly complex; he had to manage a prison, a relatively small security unit, vehicles, courtrooms, translations, and records. He also had to supervise financial systems; human resources; victim participation; defense lawyers; outreach; and at the same time, provide efficient services to the judges and the Office of the Prosecutor. If everything worked correctly, no one would recognize the registry work, but any mistake would result in strong criticism.

It was very complicated, but we made progress in defining our respective responsibilities in many areas, including administration and outreach. In other areas, like security for witnesses, such consensus was not possible.[15] We ended up litigating these issues before the judges, but Bruno was always committed to resolving those questions with the victims' interests in mind.

The regulations of the court adopted by the judges provided for the establishment of a Coordination Council (CoCo), aiming to coordinate the independent activities of the presidency, the registry, and the prosecutor's office.

The CoCo met each week and became a critical space to overcome the difficulties that Fernando foresaw in our conversations at Harvard. It forced all of us to maintain an ongoing inter-organ dialogue and to discuss administrative and operational matters.[16] Nevertheless, the tensions between the court's different organs never disappeared, and our increasing operations exacerbated the challenges.

Besides, the leaders were regularly changing. In 2008, Silvana Arbia, a judge from Italy with significant experience as a senior trial attorney at the ICTR, was appointed as the new registrar. In 2009, Judge Sang-Huyn Song, a very distinguished law professor from Korea who was also teaching at Harvard in 2003, became the new president.

Thinking about how much energy we spent discussing different matters in that building on Maanweg 174 during those initial years now brings a smile to my face. We were hundreds of people, divided by our roles and professional backgrounds, with different ideas and styles, discussing and confronting each other relentlessly but with a deep sense of commitment to the enormous mission that we had to carry out.

Policies and Strategic Plans

We promised to analyze the comments received during the public hearing. We conducted internal discussions with the new members of the office, and in September 2003, we published the "Paper on some policy issues before the Office of the Prosecutor." The paper reiterated our careful application of the principle of complementarity.[17]

We also insisted on promoting genuine national proceedings, a policy that we call "Positive complementarity." In 2013 the assembly of the states parties approved a definition of *Positive Complementarity* and encouraged states parties to assist each other.[18]

In my Argentina experience after the Junta trial, we struggled with selecting the defendants in the cases against subordinates. We had evidence against many officers, and there were not legal criteria to choose a few defendants between them. From the generals to the sergeants, all those involved in the crimes could be prosecuted. Since Nuremberg, it is clear that due obedience does not provide a legal justification.

How do you select a few suspects in cases with a massive number of perpetrators? The matter always bothered me, and at the ICC, I knew we had to present a clear standard before starting any case.

In 1989 I had the chance to consult on the matter with Ben Ferencz, a former Nuremberg prosecutor, at a Benjamin Cardoso Law School meeting in New York. He explained that at Nuremberg, they had documents proving more than one million killings committed by thousands of people and that they choose twenty-two for the trial.

I was delighted to find a criterion, and I asked, for me, the crucial question: *Why twenty-two?* Ben said, *Well, the dock at Nuremberg had space for twenty-two chairs, so we choose twenty-two defendants.* There was no criterion, just pure discretion.

Silvia Fernandez suggested using the Sierra Leone court's formula, which already had international support.[19] The policy paper stated that as a general rule, "the Office of the Prosecutor should focus its investigative and prosecutorial efforts and resources on those who bear the greatest responsibility, such as the leaders of the State or organisation allegedly responsible for those crimes."[20]

Such a policy provided an explicit criterion, recognized the need to deal with the impunity gap, and made our intervention more relevant. Still, the policy made the investigations and, in particular, the arrest more complicated and more challenging for the political leaders.

The policy paper was just the beginning of our efforts to make our work transparent. Four years later, the office would make public its policy on

"Interest of Justice,"[21] and in 2010 on "Victims Participation" followed by a discussion on the draft of its "Policy on Preliminary Examination."[22]

Internally, the office discussed several other drafts, including policy papers on gender crimes, public information, selection of cases, positive complementarity, protection of witnesses and persons at risk, disclosure, and investigative methods.

In 2003, I met Christopher Stone. He had helped build prosecutors' offices in the United States, Chile, and South Africa and the British Serious Fraud office. In November 2003, I asked him to help produce a strategic plan defining the office's goals and the broader network of international criminal justice. I devoted a considerable part of the office's time to prepare such plans. The first draft was completed in February 2004, and it was discussed by the entire office divided into groups of ten.

During the meetings, I used metaphors to explain our main problems. For instance, to explain the need for a strategic plan, I said we were sailing in unchartered waters. We needed a map. I also noted that complementarity forced us to land when there is no airport, or the airport is under state criminals' control. I encouraged attendance to express their opinions freely. A young professional from Croatia with a severe face but smiling eyes raised her hand and said, "I am confused. Are we a boat or a plane?"

In 2006 the office produced its three-year report presenting its past activities and the Report on Prosecutorial Strategy.[23] Those documents were discussed during a second public hearing with sessions in The Hague and New York.[24] A new strategy was articulated for the period 2006 to 2009[25] and adjusted for 2009 to 2012.[26]

Fatou Bensouda, as the new prosecutor, continued the tradition and presented her plans for 2012 to 2015 and 2015 to 2018.[27]

In April 2009, after five years of practice, the office made public its regulations.[28] We officially adopted Serge's suggestion to create an executive committee comprised of the prosecutor and the heads of the three divisions to ensure interdisciplinary coordination, bridging the strengths of different parts of the office.

The executive committee provided strategic oversight to the entire office, adopted the office's policies, and supervised the project-driven joint teams' operations. We met every week to discuss and review all our plans and activities.

At the beginning of my tenure, I embarked on open discussions with my staff to understand their problems, learn from their experiences, and explain my views. I was trying to promote collective thinking. It was a process I enjoyed, but it also created problems. I found that younger officers used our conversations to challenge their immediate supervisors' instructions.

After a few years, I realized that the only way to integrate the varying approaches and professional differences between the office staff was intense supervision, including detailed operational instructions. It was not my style. It was hugely frustrating for all of us and occasionally created frictions. Still, it was necessary to create consistency and avoid some of the problems we suffered in collecting evidence in the Lubanga case.

We were investigating in Ituri, Democratic Republic of Congo, during an ongoing conflict at a moment in which the national authorities had no control over the territory. Our senior investigators were trying to obtain as much information as possible while balancing the security risks. They had friends in MONUC and informally collected thousands of documents from the UN and NGOs describing different militias' activities. Those documents helped us to organize our investigations.

After the arrest of Thomas Lubanga, we started the disclosure process. It was only then that the trial lawyers in charge of the case found these informally collected documents. They initially determined that around ninety-three of these informally obtained documents contained information that could be material to the defense's case and had to be disclosed. The documents indicated that the Ugandan army occupied the Ituri region during the alleged crimes committed by Lubanga, potentially enabling him to invoke this circumstance to his defense.

Our Jurisdiction, Complementarity and Cooperation Division (JCCD) tried to obtain formal authorization to possess such documents from the UN and some NGOs. But the providers were worried about the security of their personnel and requested confidentiality under Article 54(3)(e) as a condition for supplying the information officially. After months of negotiations, we had to accept such a strict confidential duty.

The Office of the Prosecutor informed the trial chamber that these documents contained information that could be regarded as material for the defense and they were in its possession but could not be disclosed. We explained that the ninety-three documents could be considered redundant as similar information establishing the exact circumstance was already disclosed. Additionally, the office was ready to accept that the Ugandan army was occupying the Ituri region. The trial chamber requested to review the documents itself. The prosecution refused to provide the documents because the chamber did not have a duty to maintain the confidentiality established by Article 54(3)(e).

We were candid about presenting the problem to the judges, exposing ourselves to external observers' criticism suggesting we behaved like a reckless prosecution. It was paradoxical because we were attached to our two conflicting obligations to disclose and at the same time respect our confidentiality commitment, risking never to start our first trial but fully respecting our legal mandate.

The trial chamber considered that the review was part of its authority and requested the UN permit to see the documents. The UN legal adviser called me saying, *Luis, the Judges are blackmailing me!* My answer was, *Yes, what will you do?* He proposed a mechanism allowing the chamber to review the documents. But the judges rejected it.

On June 13, 2008, the trial chamber decided to impose a stay on the proceedings and ordered Thomas Lubanga's release. Our first case was finished before the trial started! Finally, the appeal chamber established a mechanism to respect our confidentiality duties, we were able to submit the documents requested, and the pre-trial chamber lifted the stay.[29]

I realized that each Office of the Prosecutor member made the best possible decision, but the collective outcome was very poor. We ensure that there was no further document collected informally or under Article 54(3)(e).

Can a Network Plan Its Activities?

With the support of Jonathan F. Fanton, then-president of the MacArthur Foundation, Christopher Stone, after being appointed professor of the practice of criminal justice at the Kennedy School of Government, organized a Consultative Conference on International Criminal *Justice* in September 2009 at the United Nations Headquarters in New York.

He proposed to develop the connections among different areas of the international justice network, increasing the coordination between states and NGOs.[30]

During the consultations, many institutions[31] were present, exploring how to coordinate with one another in pursuing related goals. The promise of an emerging global justice system depends on the development of those networks.[32] A new world order is waiting for new participants.

Notes

1. H.R.H. Prince Zeid Ra'ad Zeid Al-Hussein of Jordan, President of the Assembly of States Parties to the Rome Statute of the International Criminal Court, Statement at Ceremony for the solemn undertaking of the Chief Prosecutor of the International Criminal Court (June 16, 2003).
2. Philippe Kirsch, president of the court, talked in the name of the judges showing that prevention was also in his mind: "We are part of humanity's response to the countless victims and their plight. The ICC is a humanitarian, judicial and practical imperative and as such it must succeed."
3. Luis Moreno Ocampo, Chief Prosecutor of the International Criminal Court, Statement at Ceremony for the solemn undertaking of the Chief Prosecutor of the International Criminal Court (June 16, 2003).
4. "There are so many divergent interests in the world today that there is not even consensus about the basic goal of punishing genocide." *Id.*
5. Commentators included the following: Dicker, Richard; Leanza, Umberto; Wierda, Marieke; Sluiter, Göran; Donat-Cattin, David; Ellis, Mark; Chhay, Hoc Pheng; Yañez–Barrionuevo, Juan Antonio; Pace, William R.; Cassese, Antonio; Hall, Christopher; Scheffer, David; Murphy, Peter; Zeverin-McLean, Diane; Rezek, Francisco; Ung Boun-Hor, Billon; Nainer, Vahida; Broomhall, Bruce; Prost, Kim; Guevara, Jose; McKay, Fiona; Nicholson, Peter; Aguirrezabal, Irune; Kebe, Mohamed; Ziauddin, Ahmed; Tochilovsky, Vladimir; Braune, Bernhard; Guariglia, Fabricio; Agirre, Xabier; Bertram Nothnagel, Jutta; Friman, Håkan; Grosse, Laurent; Figá-Talamanca, Nicçoló; Baraybar, Jose-Pablo; Hamilton, James; Scheffer, David; Ferstman, Carla; O'Donahue, Jonathan; Mundis, Darryl; Bernard, Antoine; Schifter-Sharratt, Sara; Duverger, Emmanuelle; Sulzer, Jeanne; Schrag, Minna; Verfuss, Thomas; Triffterer, Otto; Robla Ucieda, Sonia; Schense, Jennifer; Hall, Wanda; Bevers, Hans; Vámos-Goldman, András; O'Donnell, Bernard; du Toit, J. J.; Dahl, Arne W.; Rübesame, Anne; Wilmshurst, Elizabeth; Ramcharan, Bertrand G. See all the transcripts at http://www.icc-cpi.int/en_menus/icc/structure of the court/office%20of%20the%20prosecutor/network%20with%20partners/public%20hearings/Pages/first%20public%20hearing.aspx. (visited June 17, 2012).
6. He stated: *I wanted to respectfully disagree with framing the issue that the absence of trials would equal success.*
7. Office of the Prosecutor, *Summary of recommendations received during the first Public Hearing of the Office of the Prosecutor, convened from 17–18 June 2003 at the Hague, Comments and conclusions of the Office of the Prosecutor,* ICC (June 2003), http://www.icc-cpi.int/iccdocs/otp/ph1_conclusions.pdf.
8. By office policy, all positions were required to be renewed and filled by open and transparent competition based on the statute's requirements. The initial filling of the legal adviser and the chief of cabinet positions were the only ones provisionally filled without competition and there was no doubt about the appropriateness of the appointees. Still, a public competition process was established to renew the contracts. Morten Bergsmo decided to go to an academic position and Silvia Fernandez won the

competition for the head of the JCCD. In 2007 all of the office's posts will have been recruited through a process of public competition.

9. Darryl Robinson, who combined his experience working for NGOs and the Canadian government, was a young diplomat at the Rome Conference. Gavin Hood, a young diplomat from the United Kingdom, experienced in intelligence and investigative matters. Pascal Turlan, a French lawyer, who worked for an NGO in Sierra Leone, completed the first team. Paul Seils, a Scottish lawyer with previous experience as the chief of the Rule of Law and Democracy Unit at the UN Office of the High Commissioner for Human Rights in Geneva, was the first head of the situation analysis section in charge of the preliminary examination. A French expert, Emeric Rogier, with a strong background in analysis, replaced him and led the area for many years.

10. Christine's experience investigating organized crime and financial fraud in New York contributed enormously to developing best practices at the office. As a US prosecutor, she was used to commanding the investigation and, in addition, she was brilliant in analyzing the law and arguing before the judges. Fabricio had no practical experience as investigator or crossing a witness in court but compensated for Christine's lack of expertise on international law; Fabricio has a PhD (Summa Cum Laude) in criminal law from the University of Münster (Germany) and had lectured on international criminal law at the London School of Economics. He was entirely committed to the court, knew the Rome Statute in detail, and loved to explain and discuss its legal aspects. Months later, two senior trial lawyers from the ICTY, Ekkehard Whitpkof, a former state judge from Germany; and Andrew Cayley, an English barrister with previous experience in the British Army, completed the senior team.

11. Office of the Prosecutor, *Report on the activities performed during the first three years (June 2003–June 2006)*, ICC (Sept. 12, 2006), https://www.icc-cpi.int/nr/rdonlyres/d76a5d89-fb64-47a9-9821-725747378ab2/143680/otp_3yearreport20060914_english.pdf.

12. "Moreno Ocampo first requested a compilation of protocols and standard operating procedures (SOP) in 2005. Yet, as the SOP were not yet uniform and easily accessible to all staff, ExCom, in August 2006, established a SOP working group with an eye toward creating a database of documents for everyday use. On March 16, 2007, ExCom then established a Standing Committee on Regulations. Eventually, on October 31, 2007, ExCom has the LAS compile and review all internal OTP documents with the goal of producing an Operational Manual. According to the OTP's Three-Year Report, published in 2006, it had 'formulated over 130 draft policies, guidelines and standard operation procedures' related to more than eleven major aspects of its work. After wafting though these documents, LAS produced a first draft of a manual on January 31, 2008. After several rounds of additions and revisions, ExCom, in the fall of 2008, decided to appoint an interdivisional committee to take over the drafting process, with assistance from LAS. This interdivisional committee presented iterative drafts in November and December 2009. On February 12, 2010, after approval by ExCom, a draft of the Operational Manual was circulated to all OTP staff members. Finally in September of 2011, the OTP published—if only for internal use—the currently binding Operational Manual. At 185 pages in length, it is organized into fourteen

chapters and covers OTP activities ranging from public information and outreach to the screening and handling of information, and from evidence review and disclosure to the protection of and support for witnesses and others persons at risk." Jens Meierheinrich, *The Evolution of the Office of the Prosecutor at the International Criminal Court, in* The First Global Prosecutor: Promise and Constraints (Law, Meaning and Violence) 97, 121 (Martha Minow & C. Core True-Frost et al. eds., Kindle ed. 2015).

13. *Relationship Agreement Between the ICC and the United Nations,* ICC Now (Nov. 14, 2004), http://iccnow.org/documents/CICCFS-UNRelationshipAgmt_12Nov04.pdf.

14. Philippe Kirsch, President of the International Criminal Court, Address to the UN General Assembly, New York (Nov. 8, 2005).

15. For instance, the prosecution needed to protect a witness in Congo, a registry role, and we explored the issue with Bruno and an Australian expert who was managing the witness protection area. The expert wanted specific evidence of threats against the witness before establishing protective measures, as he was used to in Sydney. For us, it was enough to know that the witness would be at risk as soon as his community, the Hema, learned that he provided testimony against Thomas Lubanga, the leader of the Hema. It was difficult for the expert to grasp the way in which differences in the context, and its consequences on security, could justifiably lead to establish a different protocol that the one used in Australia.

16. Philippe Kirsch, President of the International Criminal Court, Speech at Information session for diplomatic representations (June 8, 2005).

17. "*As a* "general rule . . . the policy of the Office in the initial phase of its operations will be to take action only where there is a clear case of failure to take national action." Office of the Prosecutor, *Paper on some policy issues before the Office of the Prosecutor,* ICC (Sept. 1, 2003), https://www.icc-cpi.int/nr/rdonlyres/1fa7c4c6-de5f-42b7-8b25-60aa962ed8b6/143594/030905_policy_paper.pdf.

18. In 2010, at the Kampala review conference, a working group discussed "Taking stock of the principle of complementarity: bridging the impunity gap." Representatives of Denmark and South Africa, acting as focal points, noted that the global challenge was for states to assist each other to fight impunity where it began, that is, at the national level. Professor William Schabas, moderating the panel conveyed that "once the Statute entered into force, a new approach evolved. . . . The concept of positive complementarity then emerged, in the Prosecutorial strategy and in the documentation before the Conference." Review Conference of the Rome Statute, Stocktaking of international criminal justice, Complementarity ¶ 4, RC/11 Annex V (c).

For years, the Assembly of the States Parties tasked the secretariat to work on the topic. Assembly of States Parties of the ICC, Report of the Secretariat on complementarity, ICC-ASP/11/25 (Oct. 16, 2012).

The ASP approved a template letter to be directed by its secretariat to all states parties explaining the following: *positive complementarity refers to all activities/actions whereby national jurisdictions are strengthened and enabled to conduct genuine national investigations and trials of crimes included in the Rome Statute, without involving the Court in capacity building, financial support and technical assistance, but instead leaving these actions and activities for States, to assist each other on a voluntary basis.* Assembly of States Parties of the ICC, Note verbale on complementarity—information on any capacity-building needs in the area of the investigation and prosecution of serious international crimes, ICC-ASP/12/S/012 (Apr. 12, 2013).

19. We presented a caveat: "In some cases the focus of an investigation by the Office of the Prosecutor may go wider than high-ranking officers if, for example, investigation of certain types of crimes or those officers lower down the chain of command is necessary for the whole case." Office of the Prosecutor, *Paper on some policy issues before the Office of the Prosecutor,* ICC (Sept. 1, 2003), https://www.icc-cpi.int/nr/rdonlyres/1fa7c4c6-de5f-42b7-8b25-60aa962ed8b6/143594/030905_policy_paper.pdf.

20. *Id.*

21. *Id.*

22. Fatou Bensouda issued the final version of such policy during her tenure.

23. Office of the Prosecutor, *Report on the activities performed during the first three years (June 2003–June 2006),* ICC (Sept. 12, 2006), https://www.icc-cpi.int/nr/rdonlyres/d76a5d89-fb64-47a9-9821-725747378ab2/143680/otp_3yearreport20060914_english.pdf.

24. The office analysis of the comments received are in the Office of the Prosecutor, *Annex to the Three Year Report and the Report on the Prosecutorial Strategy,* ICC (Sept. 20, 2006), http://www.icc-cpi.int/NR/rdonlyres/B3608F87-C550-42CA-9824-A68AE76C2DCC/143696/OTP_ProsecutorialStrategyAnnex_En.pdf.

25. Office of the Prosecutor, *Report on Prosecutorial Strategy,* ICC (Sept. 14, 2006), http://www.icc-cpi.int/NR/rdonlyres/D673DD8C-D427-4547-BC69-2D363E07274B/143708/ProsecutorialStrategy20060914_English.pdf.

26. Office of the Prosecutor, *Prosecutorial Strategy 2009–2012, 1 February 2010 The Hague* (Feb. 1, 2010), http://www.icc-cpi.int/NR/rdonlyres/66A8DCDC-3650-4514-AA62-D229D1128F65/281506/OTPProsecutorialStrategy20092013.pdf.

27. Office of the Prosecutor, *Strategic plan June 2012–2015* (Oct. 11, 2013), http://www.icc-cpi.int/en_menus/icc/structure%20of%20the%20court/office%20of%20the%20prosecutor/reports%20and%20statements/statement/Documents/OTP%20Strategic%20Plan.pdf.

28. Regulations of the Office of the Prosecutor, Apr. 23, 2009, ICC-BD/05-01-09.

29. The chamber considered that it had been prevented from exercising its jurisdiction and as a consequence it was unable to determine whether or not the nondisclosure of this potentially exculpatory material constituted a breach of the accused's right to a fair trial. Following the prosecutions' appeal, the appeals chamber suspended Lubanga's release and later, on October 21, 2008, decided that the trial chamber had to be granted access to any material information in possession of the prosecution that was subject to a confidentiality agreement under Article 54(3)(e). But it added a critical point: Any chamber receiving such information must never order its disclosure without the prior agreement of the information provider.

The appeals chamber settled the tension between the respect for the confidentiality of the information provided under Article 54(3)(e) and the duty to disclose the information to the defense. With this legal certainty in place, the prosecution was able to place all the material in question before the trial chamber and the stay was lifted.

30. Christopher Stone considered, "The aim of the conference was to further strengthen international criminal justice by taking seriously the conception of these institutions and networks as a "system of justice." Yet the networks on which this "system" depends—networks among states, among NGOs, among international bodies—are unevenly developed and only tenuously connected to one another. If the system of international criminal justice is to continue to mature over the next decade, these networks, too, must be strengthened and aligned." Memorandum from Christopher Stone to Participants in the Preparatory Meeting for the September 2009 Consultative Conference on International Criminal Court. May 5, 2009.

31. 24 Hours for Darfur, Africa Centre for Open Governance, African Commission on Human and Peoples' Rights, Afrikan Community Empowerment, Program AIDS-Free World, American Bar Association, American Society of International Law, Amnesty International, Assembly of State Parties to the Rome Statute of the ICC, Austrian Mission to the United Nations, Beijing Normal University, British Mission to the United Nations, Carr Center for Human Rights, Harvard University Center for International Human Rights, Northwestern University Center for International Law, Central African Coalition for ICC, China University of Political Science and Law, Chinese Mission to United Nations, Civil Resource Development & Documentation Centre, Nigeria, Coalition for the International Criminal Court (CICC) Colombian Embassy, Columbia Human Rights Institute, Columbia Law School, Comisión Colombiana de Juristas, Corte Suprema de Justicia de Colombia, Council of the European Union, Crisis Action, Danish Institute for Human Rights, Delegation of the European Commission to the United Nations, DePaul University College of Law, ENOUGH Project, European Court of Human Rights, Faculdade de Direito de Vitoria, Brazil, FIDH, Fiji Mission to the United Nations, Ford Foundation, Fordham Law School, French Mission to the UN, Genocide Intervention Network, George Washington University Law School, Harvard Humanitarian Initiative, Harvard Kennedy School, Harvard Law School, Hauser Center for Nonprofit Organizations Harvard University, Holy See Mission Human Rights Center, University of California, Berkeley, Human Rights First, Human Rights Watch, Humanity United, ICTY, Institute for Security Studies, International Coalition for the Responsibility to Protect, International Bar Association, International Center for Transitional Justice (ICTJ), International Commission on Jurists, International Committee of the Red Cross, International Criminal Court Student Network, ICTR, International Refugee Rights Initiative, International Rescue Committee, Invisible Children, the Permanent Missions before the UN of Iran, Albania, Kenya, Guatemala, Poland, the Bolivarian Republic of Venezuela, Ukraine, Austria, Benin, Brazil, Burkina Faso, Canada, Colombia, Costa Rica, DR CONGO, Ecuador, Finland, Italy, Mexico, Nigeria, Peru, Poland, Slovakia, South Africa, Sweden of Switzerland, the Kingdom, Swaziland, the Kingdom, the Netherlands, the Republic, Croatia, the Republic, Zambia, the United Republic, Tanzania, to United Nations Permanent Representation of Belgium, United Nations Roosevelt House Public Policy Institute at Hunter College, Russian Mission to the United Nations, Save the Children, Skylight Pictures, Special Court for Sierra Leone, The African Union, The Czech Permanent Mission to the United

Nations, Timor-Leste Mission to the United Nations, Trinidad and Tobago Mission to the United Nations, the US Department of State, UCLA School of Law, the United Nations Office of the Special Adviser on prevention of Genocide, United Nations Association of the USA, United Nations High Commissioner for Refugees, University of Ottawa, University of Pittsburg School of Law, University of Winnipeg, the United States Mission to the United Nations, Washington College of Law, Wellspring Advisors, LLC, WITNESS Women's Initiatives for Gender Justice World Vision.

32. Memorandum from Christopher Stone to Participants in the Preparatory Meeting for the September 2009 Consultative Conference on International Criminal Court. May 5, 2009.

5

The Prosecutor's Authority in the *Jus ad Curiam* Phase

This chapter presents the distinction between the authority of the political actors and the ICC Prosecutor during the *jus ad Curiam* phase, describing the concept of "power-conferring" norms develop by H. L. A. Hart and Hans Kelsen. International law provided power to the ICC prosecutor to be a new judicial actor in the political arena.

The chapter also describes the "preliminary examination" standards developed by the Office of the Prosecutor. And finally, it summarizes the prosecution *jus ad Curiam* decisions and the chambers' rulings.

Political and Judicial Actors in the *Jus ad Curiam* Field

During the twentieth century, political leaders and state representatives had the exclusive authority to choose legal options during the *jus ad Curiam* phase. Martti Koskenniemi explained how political and legal decisions blend. "International law is what international lawyers make of it," and "every move they make is both law and politics simultaneously."[1] Koskenniemi described the dynamic: international law is "constructing the field of opportunities open for participants and determining their relative bargaining power in a formally egalitarian system of concepts and institutions."[2]

The Nuremberg Charter is an excellent example of a legal document implementing a political decision. The United States, United Kingdom, and the Soviet Union had the bargaining power to protect their personnel involved in alleged crimes and to prosecute the defeated enemies.

But such a dynamic changed after June 2003. Whereas political leaders could continue making decisions following their own interests during the *jus ad Curiam* phase, they lost their monopoly. The Office of the Prosecutor became a new judicial actor in the states parties' political scenario transforming "the field of opportunities open for participants" portrayed by Koskenniemi.[3]

War and Justice in the 21st Century. Luis Moreno Ocampo, Oxford University Press. © Oxford University Press 2022.
DOI: 10.1093/oso/9780197628973.003.0006

The Law Is Conferring Power

States provided an enormous authority to the ICC Office of the Prosecutor. Law could be more than idealism; it could confer power. Decades ago, H. L. A. Hart, a professor of jurisprudence at Oxford University, who had a significant influence on the common law tradition, presented a distinction that could help observe two legal system's dimensions. Hart distinguished between "duty-imposing" and "power-conferring" norms.[4] In the civil law tradition, Hans Kelsen reached a similar conclusion.[5]

"Duty-imposing" norms dictate what the ruled are legally obligated to do and what consequences attach to their disobedience. Except for the regional human rights systems, international conventions do not establish independent mechanisms to apply sanctions. Thus, *realists* would consider *duty-imposing* international legal norms as *idealism*.

However, the human rights movement showed that national and international law could strengthen social changes to protect people even without formal punishment. Martin Luther King presented the constitutional rights to speak, meet, and petition as the difference between the US civil rights movement in the 1960s and the struggle against South Africa apartheid.[6] He used his rights to obtain more rights influencing changes in society.

Albie Sachs, who was fighting against the South African apartheid and became later a member of the Supreme Court during Mandela time, explained the importance of *withdrawing specific questions from the political arena* and transforming them into legal matters.[7] An International Convention against *Apartheid* entered into force in July 1976, allowing South Africans to leverage their equality fight.[8]

The civil rights movement led by Dr. King crossed borders, and the UN Security Council supported Mandela's struggle.

Regardless of *duty-imposing* international legal norms' assessment, Hart also identified other types of legal standards that he called "power-conferring." They could not be characterized as idealism. Instead, they empower individuals and institutions to act as rulers.[9]

"Power-conferring" norms define the authority and procedures to create and alter "duty-imposing" norms. Rulers can obtain "the execution of their will by others"[10] as soon as their instructions are issued under their legal authority.[11]

The book already mentioned one example: the UN Charter provided authority to five permanent members to veto the UN Security Council

Resolutions. As an opposite example, the diplomatic conference that approved the Rome Statute provided relevance to each vote; it included neither veto power nor consensus.[12]

At Rome in 1998, 120 states' representatives took advantage of their bargaining power. They decided to establish an Office of the Prosecutor with authority to trigger the court jurisdiction independently. By the rules, neither the United States nor China could stop them.[13]

My appointment as the Chief Prosecutor by the Assembly of States Parties is another example of how law confers power. From June 16, 2003, until June 15, 2012, I received the exclusive authority to trigger the court's jurisdiction in states parties' territory. The ICC Office of the Prosecutor received the sole right to open and conduct a preliminary examination of any situation that, by its exclusive estimation, could fall under the court's jurisdiction. No previous prosecutor or international civil servant had such authority.

The unprecedented authority received by the ICC Office of the Prosecutor shows that law, including international law, confers power. The ICC Office of the Prosecutor received such power from international law that it became a concern in the *2002 National Defense Strategy of the United States*.

The prohibition of genocide, crimes against humanity, and war crimes, "duty-imposing" norms, could not be considered anymore as idealism. The Rome Statute includes *"power-conferring"* norms creating the ICC as an independent enforcement mechanism.

The Preliminary Examination

The ICC prosecutor power must respect a specific legal mandate, and it should be differentiated from the political actors' discretion described by Koskenniemi. Article 42 (7) and 21(3) of the statute provides that the prosecutor has a nonpolitical mandate; she should be independent[14] and impartial.[15]

The statute provides a precise mandate to the Office of the Prosecutor during the *jus ad Curiam* phase: "It shall be responsible for receiving referrals and any substantiated information on crimes within the jurisdiction of the Court, for examining them."[16]

By Articles 12, 15, and 53 (1), the Office of the Prosecutor must conduct a preliminary examination of (1) jurisdiction (temporal, material, and either territorial or personal jurisdiction); (2) admissibility (complementarity and gravity); and (3) the interests of justice.

The office should apply consistent methods and criteria in every situation, irrespective of the states or parties involved.[17]

The statute establishes the Office of the Prosecutor obligation to conduct a "preliminary examination," but it does not provide a detailed procedure on how to do it. The office developed a filtering process comprising four phases:

Phase 1 provides an initial assessment of all information on alleged crimes received ("communications") under Article 15 to filter out all information on crimes that are manifestly outside the court's jurisdiction like corruption, coup d'état, tax evasion, and individual homicides.

Phase 2 constitutes the formal commencement of the preliminary examination. It involves scrutinizing all information on alleged crimes, including "communications" that were not rejected in Phase 1.

The process starts by analyzing whether the preconditions to the exercise of jurisdiction under Article 12 are satisfied. We concluded in 2012 that Palestine was not considered a "state" by the relevant authorities, and the prosecution declined to intervene.

Then, and per Article 15 and 53(1) (a)–(c), the Office of the Prosecutor shall consider:

1. Jurisdiction relates to whether a crime within the court's jurisdiction has been or is being committed.
   a) Temporal jurisdiction: The office has no authority to intervene in any situation where crimes were committed before July 1, 2002. It has to assess the date of entry into force for any acceding state, the date specified in a Security Council referral, or a declaration lodged under Article 12(3).
   b) Subject matter-jurisdiction: the Office of the Prosecutor has to determine, based on third parties' information, the existence of a reasonable basis to believe that genocide, crimes against humanity, or war crimes have been committed in the temporal, and territorial or personal jurisdiction of the Court.

We dismissed the Venezuela situation in 2006, considering that the alleged crimes did not constitute crimes against humanity. However, such decisions are not final, and the preliminary examination could be reopened in light of new information.

    c) Territorial or personal jurisdiction. The prosecution has to evaluate that the alleged crimes were committed: on the territory or by a national of a state party; or a state not party that has lodged a declaration accepting the court's jurisdiction; or otherwise arises from a situation referred by the Security Council.

For instance, the office has no authority in the territory of Iraq, a non-state party. However, because the United Kingdom is a state party, we analyzed alleged crimes committed in Iraq by UK personnel.

Phase 3 analyzes the admissibility of a situation reviewing complementarity and gravity:

1. Admissibility

Once the office is satisfied that crimes under the jurisdiction of the court appear to have been committed, it examines

    a) Complementarity: analyzes the existence of relevant national proceedings concerning the potential cases being considered for the office's investigation. Where appropriate domestic investigations or prosecutions exist, the office will assess their genuineness.

What cases should be considered for investigation? The policy to focus on *those most responsible for the most serious crimes* provided a rational approach to the admissibility test.

There were no national proceedings in any of the seven situations opened during my tenure. This respect for national efforts is also apparent from the preliminary examinations conducted in Colombia, Guinea, and Georgia. There the office did not open an investigation but monitored the national efforts. The chambers ruled that the Kenya situation was admissible even if there were investigations against low-level perpetrators.

The Office of the Prosecutor is constantly analyzing situations involving massive crimes, and it would always be possible to find a small case that the national authorities did not investigate. If the number of cases would measure the court's relevance, the Office of the Prosecutor should focus the investigation on lower-level perpetrators. But that approach would make less clear the complementarity test. Focus on low-level perpetrators will invite the court's jurisdiction to expand and make unaffordable the financial costs of the institution.

2. "The gravity of the crime" includes an assessment of the scale, nature, manner of commission of the crimes, and their impact.

Regarding war crimes, the office took into consideration that Article 8 emphasizes that the court shall have jurisdiction "in particular when committed as part of a plan or policy or as part of a large-scale commission." For that reason, in 2006, we dismissed the allegations against UK personnel in Iraq.

Phase 4 examines the interests of justice.

1. The "interests of justice" is a countervailing consideration. The office must assess whether there are substantial reasons to believe that an investigation would not serve "the interests of justice."

We reduced our discretion by adopting a policy paper on the requirement of the "interest of justice," distinguishing it from the interest of peace under the UN Security Council's authority.[18] Following such criteria, we refused to interfere with states or the council authority during the negotiations for peace with Joseph Kony, Sudan, or Muammar Gaddafi.

The standard of proof is very low: "a reasonable basis" to believe that "a crime within the jurisdiction of the Court has been or is being committed."

The Office of the Prosecutor has two opposite duties at the end of the preliminary examination phase. According to the complementary principle, the prosecution has to refrain from opening investigations when national authorities have conducted genuine proceedings. But, if national authorities fail to do so, and the Office of the Prosecutor concludes that a situation fulfills all the Article 53 criteria, *the Prosecutor has a duty to open an investigation.*[19] It is the guarantee to *"end of impunity."*[20] The only remaining variables subject to the prosecutor's discretion are the timing and the mode of triggering an investigation.

In October 2010, the Office of the Prosecutor made public a "Draft policy paper on Preliminary Examinations" and asked for comments.[21] In December 2011, the office made public for the first time a "Report on

Preliminary Examination Activities."[22] Chief prosecutor Fatou Bensouda continued with the publication of a report in 2012 and, in November 2013, adopted a final version of the "Policy Paper on Preliminary Examinations," including the office's commitment to publish a yearly report.[23]

The Prosecutor Judicial Mandate

My first challenge as the ICC Prosecutor was to firmly represent the interest of the victims in the international scenario and, at the same time, ignore the different audiences' expectations, including states and NGOs, while receiving cooperation from them. In April 2003, in my acceptance speech, I promised that "[a]s Prosecutor of the International Criminal Court, I will be in charge of triggering the international jurisdiction. I will use this power with responsibility and firmness, ensuring strict compliance of the Statute."[24]

In 2015 Harvard Law School's dean Martha Minow and Professors Cora True-Frost and Alex Whiting made a sophisticated effort to integrate the statute's different dimensions. They concluded that "the prosecutor sought to engage all potential constituencies—governmental and nongovernmental—both to gain cooperation for the work of the OTP and to inculcate in future leaders the Court's central principles and values."[25]

Allison Danner rightly foresaw in 2003 that "The ICC Prosecutor sits at a critical juncture in the structure of the Court, where the pressures of law and politics converge."[26] As the ICC's Chief Prosecutor, I insisted that "Our mandate is to investigate the facts with impartiality and apply the law with integrity. To contribute to peace and security, the Office of the Prosecutor has to hold the legal limits firmly. It should not adjust to political considerations."[27]

The Office of the Prosecutor produced clear public guidelines to implement the *preliminary examination's* process.

As our work progressed in strict compliance with the announced policies, the Office of the Prosecutor's commitment to transparency and its adherence to its legal mandate produced a peculiar outcome; it became an explosive formula fueling public debates. Many commentators ignored the possibility that the Office of the Prosecutor made decisions based on the facts and the law. They were judging our intervention, comparing it with their own preferences.[28] The office's decisions were criticized from many sides.

Chapter 7 presents the uproar from NGOs and local communities created by my meeting with President Museveni to receive Uganda's referral

publicly. Justice supporters had concerns about a prosecutor meeting a political leader considered a suspect of the crimes to be investigated.[29] Many
commentators presented a different view and were disappointed by our le-
galistic position. Although regard for the limits of the law should be a normal
practice for a prosecutor, many political actors, international relations, and
legal experts resisted such a basic idea for the prosecutor of the International
Criminal Court.

For instance, David Bosco challenged our respect for the council's authority to refer or not situations in non-state parties. Bosco rightly assessed
that the prosecution had not "campaigned for expanded jurisdiction," challenging political actors' prerogatives.[30]

Professor William Burke-White suggested the opposite; a prosecutor
should follow states decisions and argued that the problem was that our approach had not been political.[31] Mark Kersten, a prolific commentator of international justice, said, *Indeed, the Office of the Prosecutor exhibits a certain
phobia to being seen as political.*[32]

Sarah Nouwen, deputy director of the Lauterpacht Centre for International
Law at Cambridge University, presented a different view assuming that the
prosecutor is part of the struggle described by Koskeniemi. Following Carl
Schmitt's binary characterization, she considered that the ICC "is inherently
political by making a distinction between the friends and enemies of the international community which it purports to represent."[33]

She did not define "political," and she did not register that the ICC
Prosecutor should not be assimilated to other international actors. She did
not analyze the rationale of our decision-making and did not even contemplate the possibility of an Office of the Prosecutor respecting its impartial
legal mandate to collect evidence and apply the law.[34]

Darryl Robinson labeled the confusion created by attributing a political role to the prosecutor as an "inescapable dyad." He considers that any
ICC Prosecutor legal decision can always "convincingly be portrayed as
'political.'"[35]

I always insisted that the ICC Prosecutor has not a political role because the word is ambiguous and could be derogative to describe any
prosecutor's activity. "Political" could mean, "acting in the interests of status
or power... rather than as a matter of principle."[36] Calling political to a prosecutor suggests biased and partisan decisions.

Those alleging political decisions are assuming our rationale without analyzing the facts and dismissing our respect for the prosecutor's legal duties.

I had no personal or state agenda, and my only goal was to build the best possible institution. I explained our standards, reduced our discretion, and followed no instruction, neither from states nor NGOs. David Bosco recognized that "there is ample evidence of the prosecutor being willing to rebuff pressures from powerful states."[37]

Unlike an agent, the ICC Prosecutor does not represent or follow the instructions of any principal. Even the Assembly of States Parties that appoints the prosecutor has no authority to give instructions to her.

As Karen Alter forcefully argued, international adjudicators act as trustees. "Under the trusteeship model, trustees are actors who are given authority to make meaningful decisions according to their own best judgment and professionalism on behalf of a beneficiary."[38]

She considers that the principal/trustee relation "provides a theoretical basis to question the expectations' claim that ICs are tailoring their decisions to reflect the wishes of powerful states and avoid adverse re-contracting."[39]

The principal/trustee relation adequately describes the type of original mandate provided by the Rome Statute and the rationale of our decision-making process. Discrepancies between the principals' position, the states' parties; and the trustee, the ICC Prosecutor, are not only possible but inevitable.

Summary of Our Practice during the *Jus ad Curiam* Phase

The bulk of the communications received when I took office involved allegations that the United States committed a crime of aggression in Iraq. A US professor visiting the office told me, "There is so much pressure that you should be paralyzed." But it was not so difficult. We just followed the rules adopted by the Rome Statute and implemented the "preliminary examination" process for the first time.

In those days, the statute did not allow the crime of aggression's investigation. Besides, the allegations of war crimes committed in Iraq by US troops were also outside the ICC's jurisdiction since neither Iraq nor the United States is a state party to the statute.

To manage the expectations, we publicly explained the lack of jurisdiction in the Iraq conflict when announcing our first investigation. That opened a different question: Where should the first investigation be opened?

The first decision was to be proactive, to not wait for a state referral. We didn't have so many options. We had to investigate crimes under the ICC jurisdiction committed after July 1, 2002. All previous conflicts were outside our reach.

There were demands to open investigations against individuals from the United States, Iraq, Israel, Sri Lanka, Zimbabwe, or Sudan. Still, those states were not parties to the Rome Statute, and, consequently, they were outside our jurisdiction.

An initial evaluation showed that in terms of the numbers of victims of alleged crimes under ICC jurisdiction, the Democratic Republic of Congo (DRC) and Colombia appeared to be the gravest situations within state parties' territories.

In each of them, at least five thousand people had been killed in the same period. Uganda was next, with approximately two thousand five hundred killings and a similar number of abductions.

However, there was an essential difference in the situations' admissibility: There were national proceedings in Colombia that required further analysis, whereas there were no investigations of the DRC crimes. The Office of the Prosecutor considered that the gravest situation admissible was the Democratic Republic of Congo (DRC), followed by Uganda.

After the Office of the Prosecutor reached such a conclusion, during the 2003 Assembly of States Parties, we used our proprio motu power to invite all states parties to refer to the ICC the DRC situation. A few weeks later, we asked Uganda to refer its own situation.

We received the referrals requested and opened a DRC investigation in June 2004 and Uganda in July 2004, triggering the court's operations in a non-controversial style. Such interaction with the territorial states facilitated cooperation during the investigation and created the Darfur referral opportunity.

Some scholars challenged our policy to invite states to refer their own situations. They considered that "self-referrals" constituted an improper mechanism that tainted the Office of the Prosecutor judicial mandate. Chapters 6 and 7 clarify the circumstances surrounding DRC and Uganda referrals. In any case, invitations to refer the situation were part of the prosecutor's authority.

Led by nine state parties, in March 2005, the Security Council referred the Darfur situation to the ICC. The United States mentioned that the ICC was operating in DRC and Uganda as one reason to explain its decision to accept the referral. After three months of a preliminary examination, the Office of the Prosecutor opened an investigation in Darfur.

After his indictment in 2009, a *jus in Curiae* decision, Al Bashir launched a media campaign neglecting his crimes and alleging that the court operated with an "African bias."[40] The *jus ad Curiam* category could help to clarify such an allegation. Equal geographical or ethnic representation of suspects is not a Rome Statute criterion to select situations and cases, but it became the standard of many good faith commentators.

In the meantime, the Central African Republic referred its own situation to our office, encouraged by an NGO, the International Federation of Human Rights (FIDH). We conducted a preliminary examination for more than two years to assess the national proceedings before opening the investigation.

In 2010, we used our *proprio motu* authority for the first time to request the approval of the Pre-Trial Chamber to open an investigation in Kenya. Previously we had invited Kenya's president to refer the situation to the ICC. He declined the invitation, but he and Kenyan's prime minister appeared with me in the presidential palace garden when I announced the Office of the Prosecutor's decision to open an investigation into Kenya post-electoral violence.

Later, Kenyan leaders objected to the suspects' selection during the *jus in Curiae* phase and joined the African bias campaign. By accepting to lead the War on Terror's regional efforts in Somalia, Kenya's leaders obtained support from the United States and United Kingdom.

In 2011, the UN Security Council took a unanimous *jus ad Curiam* decision. It referred the situation in Libya to the ICC just nine days after the beginning of the rebellion against Gaddafi.[41] The office conducted a preliminary examination, and a few days later, it opened an investigation.

Furthermore, a state non-party to the statute like Cote d'Ivoire took a *jus ad Curiam* decision and accepted the court's intervention. We requested and obtained authorization from the Pre-Trial Chamber to start an investigation.

We took other *jus ad Curiam* resolutions when the office decided not to open an investigation in Venezuela, against UK personnel involved in Iraq and in Palestine. We analyzed the Honduras, Nigeria, Korea, Georgia, Guinea, Colombia, and Afghanistan situations.

After the end of my tenure, Comoros, Mali, Gabon, Palestine, and Venezuela also referred their own situations. In September 2018, for the first time, a group of states parties (Argentine, Canada, Colombia, Chile, Paraguay, and Peru) referred to the ICC the situation of another state party: Venezuela.

In every situation opened by the ICC, hundreds or thousands of persons were killed or raped, and, in many, millions were displaced. The cases before the court are indeed the most serious crimes of concern to the international community as a whole.

The Role of the ICC Chambers

As in Nuremberg, ICTY, and ICTR, the ICC Chambers are the *jus in Curiae*'s final decision makers. Judges rule on *jus ad Curiam* in cases against specific individuals. Article 19 (1) establishes that "The Court shall satisfy itself that it has jurisdiction in any case brought before it." All *jus ad Curiam* decisions made by the Office of the Prosecutor to trigger the court's jurisdiction during my tenure were in full respect of the Rome Statute and confirmed by the chambers in the specific cases.[42]

Following our specific duty to focus on gender crimes and crimes against children, the prosecution's first case exposed boys and girls abused as child soldiers. It demonstrated how they were trained to kill, to rape, and to be raped. Australian Professor Tim Mc Cormack, the office's special adviser on International Humanitarian Law, helped submit a novel interpretation: commanders could commit war crimes raping their own soldiers. Each case before the court has highlighted a further aspect of gender crimes.[43]

The judges have established the court's jurisprudence scrupulously respecting the rights of the accused. They are independent, and as a new bench integrated by magistrates with different nationalities, gender, and professional background, they did not always agree between them.

In any case, the ICC judges ignored political pressures and focused on their different legal views. The trial chamber showed independence and stayed the proceedings of the first ICC case against Thomas Lubanga, dismissing our explanations. Separate pre-trial chambers refused to confirm the charges against four individuals.[44] During my term, we obtained the conviction of Thomas Lubanga.[45] The challenges set by an active and serious International Criminal Court replaced the fears of a frivolous prosecutor.

Notes

1. MARTTI KOSKENNIEMI, FROM APOLOGY TO UTOPIA, THE STRUCTURE OF INTERNATIONAL LEGAL ARGUMENT 617 (2005).
2. *Id.* at 614.
3. In 2009, I described my role: "I am putting a legal limit to the politicians. That's my job. I police the border-line and say, if you cross this, you're no longer on the political side, you are on the criminal side. I am the border control." Patrick Smith, *Interview: Luis Moreno Ocampo, ICC Prosecutor*, AFRICA REPORT (Sept. 21, 2009, 9:23 AM), https://www.theafricareport.com/9342/interview-luis-moreno-ocampo-icc-prosecutor/.
4. Hart's ideas were influenced by the previous Hans Kelsen work, with great importance on the civil law tradition. H. L. A. HART, THE CONCEPT OF LAW 81, 40–41 (Kindle ed. 2012). *See also* H. L. A. HART, THE LAW AS A UNION OF PRIMARY AND SECONDARY RULES (3rd ed. 1961).
5. Hans Kelsen, one of the main philosophers of law in the civil law tradition, agreed with Hart that *competence norms* are "power conferring norms." EUGENIO BULYGIN, ESSAYS IN LEGAL PHILOSOPHY 272 (1st ed. 2015).
6. "... in Mississippi, we can organize to register Negro voters, we can speak to the press, we can, in short, organize the people in non-violent action." Dr. Martin Luther King Jr. Speech on South Africa in London—December 1964 http://www.rfksafilm.org/html/speeches/africaking.php.
7. "At an earlier stage of my life, I was hostile to a Bill of Rights because it took out of the political arena issues that were really political in character. I believed it was far better to allow such matters to be resolved through struggle and democratic processes than to convert them into juridical questions to be settled by elite and usually conservative lawyers. Today I see withdrawing certain questions from the political arena as being the principal virtue of a Bill of Rights." ALBIE SACHS & VANESSA SEPTEMBER, THE FREE DIARY OF ALBIE SACHS (2004).
8. International Convention on the Suppression and Punishment of the Crime of Apartheid, *open for signature* Nov. 30, 1973, U.N.T.S. 243 (entered into force July 18, 1976).
9. This distinction is crossing the discussion between Professor Ruti Teitel and Professor Marti Koskenniemi. Prof. Teitel harmonized the "duty imposing" international legal norms. (RUTI G. TEITEL, HUMANITY'S LAW (2011). Marti Koskenniemi challenged her proposal asking "who is it that rules the process?" Martti Koskenniemi, *Humanity's Law by Ruti G. Teitel*, 26 ETHICS & INT'L AFF. 395, 396–397 (2012)(book review).
10. "Power, from the standpoint of experience, is merely the relation that exists between the expression of someone's will and the execution of that will by others." LEO TOLSTOY, WAR AND PEACE (Kindle ed. 2017).
11. Michael Reiman explained how rulers can establish what he called "operational codes," authorizing even prohibited behaviors. He highlighted that any normative system includes *mythical norms*, defining the citizens' expected behavior, what is prohibited, and what is permitted. They are the "duty imposing" norms in Hart's

language. Reisman also identified *operational codes*, which define what actors in what circumstances are authorized to perform such prohibited behavior. The operational codes are adopted by the rulers. The Military Junta plans, the authorizations to torture prisoners, the payment of bribes as a business policy are different examples of operational codes adopted by rulers. Michael Reisman explained the idea in FOLDED LIES: BRIBERY, CRUSADES AND REFORMS(1979). He also mentioned it in W. M. REISMAN, INTERNATIONAL AFFAIRS THE QUEST FOR WORLD ORDER AND HUMAN DIGNITY IN THE TWENTY FIRST CENTURY: CONSTITUTIVE PROCESS AND INDIVIDUAL COMMITMENT 98–99 (2012)

12. *Rome Statute of the International Criminal Court, Some Questions and Answers*, UN OFFICE OF INTERNATIONAL AFFAIRS, http://legal.un.org/icc/statute/iccq&a.htm (last visited Jan. 19, 2021). Quoting Lloyd Gruber, Stephen Krasner observed that "powerful states" can use their "go-it-alone power" to present weaker states with a *fait accompli* that leaves them worse off than they were in the *status quo*. But what Krasner and Gruber didn't anticipate is that a specific legal design could provide power to a group of weaker states to use the "go it alone" strategy and present stronger states with a fait accompli of their own, as happened with the Rome Statute. Stephen D. Krasner, *Realist Views of International Law*, 96 PROCEEDINGS OF THE ASIL ANNUAL MEETING, 266, 266 (2002). Similarly, the Convention on the Prohibition of the Use, Stockpiling, Production and Transfer of Anti-Personnel Mines and on their Destruction (1997) was signed by 122 states against the will of the United States, China and Russia.

13. Press Release, UN Diplomatic conference concludes in Rome with decision to establish permanent International Criminal Court, UN Press Release L/2889 (July 20, 1998).

14. "Several countries in Europe, Latin America, and elsewhere consider prosecutors as impartial officials who have to look equally for inculpatory and exculpatory elements of proof; have to document all their procedural activity and do not consider the elements of proof that they gather as elements of the prosecutor, but rather of the state's impartial investigation; do not consider that they lose if the defendant is acquitted; and may even appeal a conviction in favor of the defendant." In contrast the '. . . adversarial systems tend to consider the prosecutor as a party that is opposed to the defense"; MAXIMO LANGER & DAVID ALAN SKLANSKY, PROSECUTORS AND DEMOCRACY: A CROSS-NATIONAL STUDY (ASCL Studies in Comparative Law) (Kindle ed. 2017).

15. Article 67 (2).

16. Art. 42 of the Rome Statue of the International Criminal Court.

17. Office of the Prosecutor, *Policy Paper on Preliminary Examinations*, ICC (Nov. 2013), https://www.icc-cpi.int/iccdocs/otp/OTP-Policy_Paper_Preliminary_Examinations_2013-ENG.pdf.

18. *See* Office of the Prosecutor of the ICC, *Policy Paper on the Interests of Justice*, ICC (Sept. 1, 2007), https://www.icc-cpi.int/NR/rdonlyres/772C95C9-F54D-4321-BF09-73422BB23528/143640/ICCOTPInterestsOfJustice.pdf.

19. Emeric Rogier, *The Ethos of "Positive Complementarity,"* EJIL: TALK! BLOG (Dec. 11, 2018), https://www.ejiltalk.org/the-ethos-of-positive-complementarity/.

20. "The Statute has set clear criteria governing the process, and once these criteria are met, the duty of the Prosecutor is to proceed." Fabricio Guariglia & Emeric Rogier, *The*

Selection of Situations and Cases by the OTP of the ICC, in THE LAW AND PRACTICE OF THE INTERNATIONAL CRIMINAL COURT (Carsten Stahn ed., Kindle ed. 2015).

21. Office of the Prosecutor, *Draft Policy Paper on Preliminary Examinations*, ICC (Oct. 10, 2010), https://www.icc-cpi.int/NR/rdonlyres/9FF1EAA1-41C4-4A30-A202-174B18DA923C/282515/OTP_Draftpolicypaperonpreliminaryexaminations04101.pdf.

22. Office of the Prosecutor, *Report on Preliminary Examination activities*, ICC (Dec. 13, 2011), https://www.icc-cpi.int/NR/rdonlyres/63682F4E-49C8-445D-8C13-F310A4F3AEC2/284116/OTPReportonPreliminaryExaminations13December2011.pdf.

23. Office of the Prosecutor, *Policy Paper on Preliminary Examinations*, ICC (Nov. 25, 2013), https://www.icc-cpi.int/iccdocs/otp/otp-policy_paper_preliminary_examinations_2013-eng.pdf.

24. Luis Moreno Ocampo, Chief Prosecutor to the International Criminal Court, Statement before the Assembly of the States Parties (Apr. 23, 2003).

25. Martha Minow et al., *Conclusion, in* THE FIRST GLOBAL PROSECUTOR: PROMISE AND CONSTRAINTS (LAW, MEANING AND VIOLENCE) 360, 363 (Martha Minow & C. Core True-Frost. et al eds., Kindle ed. 2015).

26. "The ICC will inevitably be subject to charges that it is a purely political institution, remote from both the rule of law and the places where the crimes it adjudicates occur." Allison Marston Danner, *Enhancing the Legitimacy and Accountability of Prosecutorial Discretion at the International Criminal Court*, 97 AJIL, 3 510 (2003).

27. Speech at the Assembly of States Parties, December 2011.

28. KATHRYN SIKKINK, EVIDENCE FOR HOPE 17 (Kindle ed. 2017).

29. "The Prosecutor regularly insists that his actions and decisions are based on judicial and not political factors. But if this is really the case, then we need a better explanation for the current choice of situations. In reality, what we have at the ICC is a political determination but with less transparency, not more. This is not to suggest that the Prosecutor receives instructions from some clandestine committee of political advisors and foreign intelligence agencies, only that he is compelled to select situations where objective, judicial criteria alone do not suffice." William A. Schabas, *Victor's Justice: Selecting "Situations" at the International Criminal Court*, 43 JOHN MARSHALL L. REV. 535, 549 (2010).

30. DAVID BOSCO, ROUGH JUSTICE, THE INTERNATIONAL CRIMINAL COURT IN A WORLD OF POWER POLITICS 22 (Kindle ed. 2014).

31. He argued: "This desire to remain apolitical has led the prosecutor and the Court as a whole to frame its efforts as purely legal, driven by the provisions of the Rome Statute. The result is that the Court has often been caught politically off-guard, seen as disconnected from realities on the ground, and unable to garner the necessary support *from national governments to make the arrests necessary to fully realize the Court's deterrent and crime prevention capabilities.*" William Burke-White, *Maximizing the ICC's Crime Prevention Impact through Positive Complementarity and Hard-Nosed Diplomacy*, ICC FORUM (Jan. 31, 2014; 10:30 PM), http://iccforum.com/prevention.)

32. Mark Kersten, *The Politics of a Prosecutor: Getting the Context Right*, JUSTICE IN CONFLICT (Apr. 15, 2020), https://justiceinconflict.org/2020/04/15/the-politics-of-a-prosecutor-getting-the-context-right/.

33. Sarah M. H. Nouwen & Wouter G. Werner, *Doing Justice to the Political: The International Criminal Court in Uganda and Sudan*, 21 EJIL 941 (2010).

34. She refused to ". . . cry foul play, hypocrisy or conspiracy." As legal anthropologists or international lawyers who have reconciled themselves with Koskenniemi's analysis of the indeterminacy of (international) law will immediately react, 'of course': actors—whether politicians, ICC officials, community leaders or NGOs—invoke and use complementarity for their political agenda." SARAH M. H NOUWEN, COMPLEMENTARITY IN THE LINE OF FIRE (CAMBRIDGE STUDIES IN LAW AND SOCIETY) 33 (Kindle ed. 2013). *See also* Sarah M. H. Nouwen & Wouter G. Werner, *Doing Justice to the Political: The International Criminal Court in Uganda and Sudan*, 21 EJIL 4, 941–65 (2010).

35. "You are either (a) 'political' because you are acting on the presumed wishes of states or (b) 'political' because you are not acting on the presumed wishes of states. Similarly, you are either (a) 'political' because you are too concerned about external consequences, or (b) 'political' because you are insufficiently concerned about external consequences." Darryl Robinson, *Inescapable Dyads: Why the ICC Cannot Win*, 28 LEIDEN J. INT'L L. 323 (2015).

36. https://en.oxforddictionaries.com/definition/political

37. DAVID BOSCO, ROUGH JUSTICE: THE INTERNATIONAL CRIMINAL COURT IN A WORLD OF POWER POLITICS 186 (Kindle ed. 2013).

38. Karen J. Alter, *Agents or Trustees? International Courts in their Political Context*, 14 EU. J. INT'L RELATIONS 33 (2008).

39. Karen J. Alter, *Agents or Trustees? International Courts in their Political Context*, 14 EU. J. INT'L RELATIONS 33 (2008). See also Nineteenth Annual Herbert Rubin and Justice Rose Luttan Rubin International Law Symposium: The Function of Judges and Arbitrators in International Law presented in cooperation with PluriCourts. The Legitimate Roles of the Judiciary in the Global Order at the Faculty of Law of the University of Oslo: Geir Ulfstein, *International Courts and Judges: Independence, Interaction, And Legitimacy*, 46 N.Y.U. J. INT'L L. & POL. 849 (2014). *See also* Erik Voeten, *The Impartiality of International Judges: Evidence from the European Court of Human Rights*, 102 AM. POL. SCIENCE REV. 417–433 (2008); and in particular Sebastien Jodoin, *Understanding the Behavior of International Courts: An Examination of Decision-Making at the Ad Hoc International Criminal Tribunals*, 6 J. INT'L L & INT'L REL. 1 (2010). *See also* the comment at the ICC forum by a UCLA student Alma Pekmezovic, *Comment to the Oversight Question*, ICC FORUM (May 6, 2011), http://iccforum.com/forum/oversight.

40. See a discussion on the topic at *Africa Question: Is the International Criminal Court (ICC) Targeting Africa Inappropriately?*, ICC FORUM, https://iccforum.com/africa (last accessed July 5, 2021).

41. See U.N. Security Council, 6491st Mtg, U.N Doc. S/Res/1970 (Feb. 26, 2011).

42. After our intervention, Libya conducted national proceedings and the ICC considered inadmissible the case against Al-Senussi. Prosecutor v. Saif Al-Islam Gaddafi and Abdullah Al-Senussi, ICC-01/11-01/11 OA 6, Judgment on the appeal of Mr. Abdullah Al-Senussi against the decision of Pre-Trial Chamber I of October 11, 2013, entitled "Decision on the admissibility of the case against Abdullah

Al-Senussi'" (July 24, 2014), https://www.icc-cpi.int/CourtRecords/CR2014_06 755.PDF.

43. Including the case against Joseph Kony and other Lord Resistance Army's (LRA) leaders, and the command responsibility asserted for an organized campaign of rape alleged in the case against Jean Pierre Bemba.

44. Mohammed Hussein Ali and Henry Kiprono Kosgey in the Kenya situation, Abu Garda in Darfur and Callixte Mbarushimana in the DRC.

45. After the end of my tenure, Mathieu Ngudjolo Chui was acquitted, Germain Katanga convicted, and Jean Pierre Bemba acquitted.

FIRST PART

Preliminary Examinations in the States Parties'
Jurisdiction

6

Selecting DRC as the First Situation
to Be Investigated

This chapter presents the implementation for the first time of a preliminary examination. It explains the criterion adopted to select the first
situation to be opened and the policy to invite states to refer situations
to the ICC. Our first decision to open an investigation, which in 1998
was expected to be highly conflictive, turned out to be a smooth process
in agreement with the territorial state and supported by all the relevant
actors.

First, this chapter describes the proactive policy to identify a situation to be investigated, the criteria to select DRC as the gravest situation under ICC jurisdiction, and the information obtained about crimes
against humanity and war crimes committed. The next issue was the criterion to assess whether the situation was admissible. The office followed
an expert report proposing that the lack of national proceedings made
the situation admissible without the need to debate if the state was "unwilling" or "unable."

Second, it explains the office's conclusion that the DRC situation fulfilled all the elements required by the statute and the internal discussions
to select the most convenient mechanism to trigger the court's jurisdiction. It presents a two-step policy: a prosecution's independent legal decision followed by activities to obtain cooperation and support to conduct
the investigations.

The legal standards adopted by the Office of the Prosecutor in 2003
were reviewed and approved during the following years by twenty ICC
judges in different cases, laying solid foundations for the court's future
operations.

War and Justice in the 21st Century. Luis Moreno Ocampo, Oxford University Press. © Oxford University Press 2022.
DOI: 10.1093/oso/9780197628973.003.0007

Implementing for the First Time Our Legal Mandate

Defining the Preliminary Examination Process While Making Decisions

Even before my arrival, citizens, NGOs, and other associations sent information to the Office of the Prosecutor demanding our intervention in various situations. I remember a Mongolian teacher who encouraged her students to send us letters, regularly, denouncing crimes committed worldwide.

We promoted such connections with individuals adopting a protocol to answer each of them. I spent most of the first week of my tenure reviewing 499 "communications"[1] received from sixty-six different countries requesting the office to open investigations into several situations.[2] The question was, what should the criterion be to select the first situation to investigate?

During the public hearing at the Peace Palace, Xavi Agirre, an analyst working at the ICTY, suggested using gravity as the criterion to identify the first investigation. He proposed to prepare a matrix comparing the different possible situations. We analyzed our legal mandate and concluded that such an idea was supported by the statute's wording and provided an evolving standard.

The statute aims to end the impunity of the "most serious crimes," and Article 17 excludes the admissibility of the case if it "is not of sufficient gravity to justify further action by the Court." We extrapolated the criterion, and the comparison between states parties' situations would define gravity. The office found DRC as the gravest situation within the states parties' jurisdiction.[3]

The next issue was the criterion to assess whether the situation was admissible. Before my swearing in, a distinguished group of experts integrated by the former president of ICTY Antonio Cassese, former representatives at the Rome Conference, scholars, and members of NGOs,[4] were invited by the court to propose a reflection on "complementarity in practice."[5]

Scholars were discussing and are still debating the interpretation of "unwilling" and "unable." However, the group highlighted that "the most straightforward scenario is where no State has initiated any investigation (the inaction scenario). Thus, there is no need to examine the factors of unwillingness or inability; the case is simply admissible under the clear terms of Article 17.[6] We applied such a criterion in the DRC situation. The DRC's provisional government had only been established in June 2003 and was not conducting national proceedings. The new authorities had no absolute control over the country's east, particularly Ituri and the Kivus, limiting their capacity to implement accountability mechanisms.

By July 2003, our small team reached the provisional conclusion that the DRC' situation was the gravest of all admissible situations before us. We were ready to announce our plans.

Other Actors Requesting Investigations into DRC

Other actors were heading in the same direction. On July 7, 2003, deputy high commissioner for human rights, Bertrand Ramcharan, said during a UNSC session on the DRC that his "fervent hope that the Prosecutor of the International Criminal Court will consider the situation [in the DRC] seriously."[7]

This was echoed in a July 2003 report by Human Rights Watch (HRW) entitled "Ituri: Covered in Blood," with eye-witness accounts of the crimes committed, including the use of child soldiers in Ituri.[8] The report specifically recommended that the prosecutor exercise his *proprio motu* powers to investigate crimes committed in the Ituri region of the DRC.[9]

Our Public Announcement about Ituri

On July 16, 2003, just one month after my appointment, we held a press conference to fulfill my commitment to inform the public about the communications received.[10] Seated in front of dozens of journalists in The Hague's center, I explained that we had received over fifty communications containing allegations of acts committed before July 1, 2002, which therefore fell outside the court's temporal jurisdiction.

Several communications alleged criminal acts that, by their very nature, lay outside the subject-matter jurisdiction of the court, such as drug trafficking, money laundering, tax evasion, and judicial corruption.

I reported that the office had received sixteen communications with no detailed information relating to acts allegedly committed by US troops on Iraq's territory. It was our opportunity to clarify that neither Iraq nor the United States was a state party to the statute, and as a consequence, the ICC had no jurisdiction in these matters.

There were two brief communications with no detailed information about the Israeli-Palestinian conflict, which in those days fell outside the ICC jurisdiction. The office also received communications alleging civilians' killing by army soldiers in Cote d'Ivoire, which again fell outside the court's territorial jurisdiction because Cote d'Ivoire at that time was not a state party.[11]

After disregarding those communications, I announced that "The Office of the Prosecutor has selected the situation in Ituri, Democratic Republic of Congo, as the most urgent situation to be followed."[12] "The report on the latest of four Security Council missions to the Democratic Republic of Congo, issued on 16 June 2003, described the occurrence of gross violations of human rights in the eastern part of the country."

I considered that "These crimes could constitute genocide, crimes against humanity or war crimes, and could thus, fall within the jurisdiction of the International Criminal Court."[13] I stated that "[I]f necessary, the Office of the Prosecutor will seek authorization from a Pre-Trial Chamber to start an investigation."[14]

I felt that we launched our boat into the water, and we were sailing. Some states publicly recognized the gravity of the DRC situation and the need to do justice immediately after the press conference.

Two days after the press release, representatives of Germany and Bulgaria spoke encouragingly about our DRC announcement during a UN Security Council meeting.[15] The DRC representative did not specifically mention the ICC. He mentioned the need to end impunity "once and for all"[16] and establishing a national Truth and Reconciliation Commission and a National Observatory for Human Rights. A 2002 political settlement called the *Accord Global et Inclusive* proposed both initiatives.[17]

A further indicator of the perception of the gravity of the situation was that the UNSC passed Resolution 1493 on July 28, 2003. The resolution adopted under Chapter VII of the UN Charter focused specifically on Ituri and two other provinces and provided a mandate for peacekeeping troops.

How to Trigger the Jurisdiction in the DRC Situation?

The UN Security Council Option

The Office of the Prosecutor assessed that the statutory requirements to initiate an investigation under Article 53(1) were, in principle, satisfied. The question was no longer whether we would open an investigation into the Ituri situation but simply how to trigger it.

David Scheffer, the former US ambassador-at-large for war crimes, sent a memorandum to our office, recommending an investigation into the DRC situation through a UN Security Council referral. He explained that the council could provide enforcement mechanisms under Chapter VII of the UN Charter that neither a state referral nor a *proprio motu* action would be able to offer any.

I liked the idea. In those initial days, I believed that the council's authority would facilitate the states' support for our investigations and suspects' arrest. Later, I learned that the UN Security Council's main goal was to promote political agreements and to coordinate states' interests at each moment. It could authorize or not international justice interventions, but the enforcement of its own decisions would require a new political agreement.

In any case, at the beginning of my tenure, I thought that the proper way to do our job was to make efforts to align the international peace and security system led by the UN Security Council and the Rome Statute justice model. But after a lot of discussions, we concluded that our role did not include the possibility of requesting UN Security Council action. Besides, the council's dynamics did not seem favorable to refer a situation to the court. We concluded that during my nine years term, we would see no referral.

The States Parties' Referral Option

Looking for options, we started to think about a collective referral from states parties to launch the court investigation. We assumed that acting in agreement with states parties would increase the likelihood of cooperation and support on the ground.[18] We also wanted to dissipate fears of a reckless prosecutor while ensuring broader political support heightening the court's legitimacy.[19]

I asked Silvia Fernandez how to obtain states referrals and increase cooperation. She explained that it was not necessary to convince the seventy-eight states that appointed me. If we could convince five or six states parties, they could move the entire network. I learned that states are risk averse; they don't like to take the initiative, but they also don't want to be exposed as opposing a project supported by a majority.

How to convince them? This was my next question. She patiently explained: *We could meet some representatives individually, explain our idea, and seek their support. If they agree, you can make public the request for a referral, and they will support your move. If there is no similar group objecting to the proposal, the other states parties would probably follow.*

Then I asked the following: *What would happen if the ambassadors do not support our move and refuse to be involved in referrals?* She explained the diplomat protocol: *Oh, then you should abandon or at least postpone the project. If you go ahead against the states' opinion, there will be no traction, and our office will be isolated.*

I felt that we had no option other than to follow our mandate and face the risk of being isolated by the lack of states support. *We are a Prosecutor Office; we should not follow political decisions. We should not delegate our legal authority to the ambassadors. Can we just announce our decision and then explain our rationale to the ambassadors to obtain their support?*

She agreed: *We can try, but you would take a considerable risk.*

Since then, we adopted a two-step policy: the office would reach an independent technical decision first, and then we would look for support. Darryl Robinson explained the rationale adopted by the office: "the Prosecutor must be analytically detached, to select situations and cases in a principled manner based on Statute criteria, yet the Prosecutor must also engage with the world, in order to build and maintain cooperation from various actors."[20]

Many commentators did not grasp this dual approach. Phil Clark, who is highly committed to Africa's development and very close to the Rwanda experience, wrote an entire book criticizing our lack of engagement. He considered that the ICC represents "a unique form of foreign intervention in African affairs insofar as it views distance and detachment from the domestic realm as a virtue because it believes, this maintains the Court's neutrality and impartiality."[21]

Following our two-step policy, we analyzed that the alleged crimes committed in Ituri met the legal requirements to open an investigation, and then, we planned how to obtain cooperation and support. After we identified that the DRC situation was under the court's jurisdiction, and to maximize the cooperation needed to investigate, the Office of the Prosecutor would use its *proprio motu* power to invite all the states parties to refer the situation before requesting authorization to act independently.[22]

We decided to inform our decision during the first Assembly of States Parties to be celebrated on September 8, 2003, at the United Nations building in New York. A few days before the assembly, during a conversation at Berkeley University with Martin Shapiro, a leading scholar on "*Law and Society*," and Alejandra Huneus, then a young scholar and now a professor at Wisconsin University, I learned a metaphor that explains our policy.

We discussed the problematic interaction between political actors, prosecutors, and judges in the transitions to democracy in Chile and Argentina. Professor Shapiro said a politician is like the guardian of a yard; he needs a brave junkyard dog to control the place, but the dog should not be so brave that it dares to bite the guardian.

"Your current problem," he said, "is that the ICC Prosecutor is an enormous dog with no guardian. Politicians will always complain about your presence in their yard." This conversation confirmed our idea. I would first stand outside the yard's limits, barking to be invited by the guardian.

The prosecutor's *proprio motu* power provided our office the mandate to intervene independently, and we transformed such authority into a solicitation to be invited. However, we planned to inform states parties that we were prepared to request judicial authorization to open an investigation if the states concerned do not ask us.

Requesting a Referral during the Assembly of States Parties

On September 8, 2003, I was seated in a conference room at the UN building in New York with Prince Zeid, President Kirsch, and Bruno Cathala to address the Assembly of the States Parties for the first time. Almost one hundred states delegates were listening.

I tried to go beyond the formalities and engage the states parties: "I . . . want to use this opportunity to encourage States gathered here to take ownership of the Court. . . . In order to work closely with you I wish to inform you about the alleged crimes committed in Ituri, how we intend to proceed, and how you can best assist in our endeavor."

I described the war crimes and crimes against humanity committed in Ituri. I showed our independent determination: "I stand ready to seek authorization from a Pre-Trial Chamber to start an investigation under my proprio motu powers." I was open about the problems our office was going to face. "The protection of witnesses, gathering of evidence, and arrest of suspects will be extremely difficult without the strong support of national or international forces."

I anticipated what would later become our investigation's strategy in Darfur: "If these forces are not available, the Office of the Prosecutor will need to investigate from outside and rely on international cooperation for the arrest and surrender of the alleged perpetrators."

I then proposed a referral from DRC and suggested an idea that the group of experts already discussed: "Our role could be facilitated by a referral or active support from the DRC. The Court and the territorial State may agree that a consensual division of labor could be an effective approach."[23]

I went further and also requested a collective referral. *"A referral or active support from African and Western countries that have taken a role in the peace process as well as other States Parties would show their commitment to the goal of putting an end to the atrocities in the region."*

I openly presented our plans: "After his swearing-in, my Deputy Prosecutor will be devoted to the analysis of this situation, will begin preparing our investigation plan, and will complete the recruitment of the team. All States Parties can support our work by offering security, police, and investigative teams and giving intelligence and other evidence."[24] I included a specific request to conduct financial investigations.[25]

In any case, I promised: "If the seriousness of the information about the crimes is confirmed and if the national State is unable to deal with the problem, my duty will be to seek authority to initiate the investigation of the International Criminal Court."[26]

The DRC authorities reacted the following day by welcoming our initiative. The Congolese representative expressed his keen interest in "the hope voiced by the Prosecutor that the Court would be able to obtain enough information to proceed with prosecutions and end further impunity, once and for all."[27]

The DRC Referral

The Congo War as a Background

After our announcement in the Assembly of States Parties, the UN special rapporteur on human rights in the DRC, Romanian professor Iulia Matoc, made it clear that she also supported the Prosecutor's decision. "Since the war in the Democratic Republic of the Congo has long become a forgotten war, this decision will ensure that justice is done in the most murderous international conflict since the Second World War."[28]

The Congo Wars (or African War) mentioned by the UN special rapporteur Iulia Matoc was the most devastating armed conflict after World War II, the direct consequence of the 1994 Rwandan genocide, and it was connected with the conflicts in DRC, CAR, and Uganda that we investigated. Escaping from the Rwanda conflict,

> more than a million Rwandan Hutus fled into neighboring Zaire—now known as the Democratic Republic of Congo—and settled in enormous refugee camps only a few miles from the Rwandan border. Most were women and children, but at least 30,000 of them were members of the former Rwandan army and militia groups that had carried out the genocide. With help from Zaire's President Marshal Mobutu Sese Seko they began arming themselves to re-take their country. Because the genocidaires blamed Uganda for their problems, they also formed alliances with Sudan-backed anti-Museveni rebels camped in eastern Zaire. Tensions between Uganda and Rwanda on one side, and Zaire and Sudan on the other had been building for years, and a crescendo was not long in coming.[29]

In 1996 the new government of Rwanda reacted by invading Zaire. Burundi, Uganda, Eritrea, and Angola joined the effort. They supported a militia led by Laurent Desire Kabila, who removed Mobutu Sese Seko from the government in May 1997, ending a thirty-two-year dictatorship.

Ugandan and Rwandan forces remained in DRC following Kabila's invitation and consent.

But the following year, relations deteriorated. Laurent Desire Kabila requested that Rwanda and Uganda withdraw their armies from DRC, triggering the Second Congo War. Laurent Desire Kabila obtained support from Namibia, Zimbabwe, Angola, Libya, Sudan, and Chad, and the conflict became an African war.

In May 2001, Laurent Desire Kabila was killed, and Joseph Kabila, his son, became the new Congolese leader and started to negotiate an end to the war. The main hostilities ended in 2002, but organized violence continued in Ituri and the Kivus, the DRC regions close to Uganda and Rwanda, and very rich in minerals. In April 2002, former warring parties signed the Sun City Agreement adopting a transitional government, an effort led by South African President Thabo Mbeki.[30]

Joseph Kabila was sworn in as transitional president for two years. Slowly the "peace institutions" moved forward. Azarias Ruberwa and Jean-Pierre Bemba, the two main rebel groups' leaders, became two vice presidents. "There were periodically mini-coup attempts, betraying the extreme fragility of the security situation."[31]

But in late November 2003, "South African President Thabo Mbeki organized the fourth Kinshasa-Kigali Peace Agreement review meeting in Pretoria. . . . In Kinshasa, the former foes eyed each other warily but without pulling the trigger."[32] In this context, the ICC was perceived as an institution that could help avoid a return to violence.

Obtaining the Referral

The DRC government sent a letter to our office indicating it was supportive of the office's focus on the DRC. Silvia Fernandez took advantage of that and liaised with the European Union (EU) representative to the Great Lakes Region, who facilitated our contact with key people within the DRC transitional government to discuss the possibility of a referral.

Silvia Fernandez visited Kinshasha and met with President Kabila and the vice presidents, including Azarias Ruberwa and Jean-Pierre Bemba. She felt the tensions between them but also their eagerness to adjust to new peaceful international standards.

On March 3, 2004, the president of the DRC, Joseph Kabila, referred the situation to the prosecutor. He explained that his country was unable to carry out investigations and expressed his government's willingness to cooperate with the court.[33]

The policy adopted in the DRC to invite states referral did not create conflicts and became part of the October 2010 draft policy paper on preliminary examinations. It was challenged in the Ugandan situation.[34]

Article 53 Report and the Opening of an Investigation into DRC

Jurisdiction and Admissibility

Our office already had a team in place to conduct a proper detailed analysis. Our staff produced the first internal and confidential Article 53 report, assessing all information relevant to the jurisdiction and admissibility requirements of the Rome Statute.[35]

The temporal jurisdiction was apparent. The DRC ratified the Rome Statute on April 11, 2002, providing jurisdiction to the ICC from July 1, 2002.

Subject-Matter Jurisdiction: The information gathered from public sources exposed underlined crimes and the contextual elements of crimes against humanity and war crimes. There were indications of the deliberate targeting of civilians on a widespread scale, both numerically and geographically. The crimes appeared to have been committed by groups with sufficient cohesion and organizational ability to carry out operations and systematically pursue predetermined objectives. Regarding war crimes, the "Congo War" had ended, but there was an armed conflict in the Ituri region at least between August 2002 and October 2003.[36]

Admissibility: The UNSC's mission to DRC on June 7 to 16, 2003 reported that "[B]oth in Ituri and in the Democratic Republic of the Congo as a whole, impunity is rampant. . . ."[37] Nevertheless, our office focused its analysis on two aspects: (i) the MLC leader, Jean-Pierre Bemba's investigations against his own troops accused of grave violations of international humanitarian law.

The report concluded that they were not genuine and (ii) the trials conducted by DRC authorities before the Bunia *Tribunaux de grande instance* that although genuine could be said not to deal with crimes under ICC jurisdiction, but only with lesser level crimes.

We also evaluated the creation of the *Commission Vérité et Réconciliation* (CVR) established by the *Accord Global et Inclusive* reached in December 2002.[38] It had a mandate that excluded crimes within the court's jurisdiction, and its activities could not qualify as an "investigation" under Article 17 of the statute.

The Article 53 report considered that there were no national proceedings related to the type of cases we were going to investigate, confirmed the gravity of the crimes committed and no interest of justice reason to suspend the investigation, and recommended opening an investigation into DRC.

We discussed the report at the Ex-Com integrated in those days by Silvia Fernandez, deputy prosecutor Serge Brammertz, and senior trial attorney Christine Chung, representing the Prosecution Division.

On June 21, 2004, the Office of the Prosecutor opened the International Criminal Court's first investigation in DRC, fully supported by the national and international communities.

We overcame the first challenge. No one could now present our office as being "frivolous."

Still, as a consequence of our move, we faced new and more complicated problems: We had to investigate, during an ongoing conflict, different militias that were continuously shifting alliances and changing their leadership.

Cooperation Received

The Office of the Prosecutor engaged different actors to obtain cooperation. I met President Kabila in Kinshasha, and I visited the Hema people in Bunia, Ituri's capital. They were not so sympathetic with our efforts in our first case because Lubanga was one of its leaders, but they did not get backing from NGOs and media. I also visited the Ngiti community in an Ituri village.

I knew that Rwanda had interests in stopping the FDLR activities in DRC, and I met President Kagame in Kigali to obtain cooperation for our cases in the Kivus. I started the conversation by saying: *I know you are not supportive of international justice.* He calmly said, *Well, that is an understatement.* The Rwanda minister of justice visited us at The Hague, he promised to support us, and for a while, I thought that our work could help reduce violence in the Kivu province. Our failure to confirm the charges in the Mbarushimana case affected those efforts.

We also established communication channels with MONUC at the operational and leadership level. The former US ambassador before DRC, William Swing, became the head of MONUC, visited our office at The Hague to explain his plans. We took advantage of the opportunity to request his support to implement arrest warrants. On October 1, 2004, under the UK leadership and at our office's initiative, the MONUC mandate was expanded to include the possibility to implement the arrest warrants. The UN Security Council adopted Resolution 1565, authorizing MONUC "to ensure that those responsible for serious violations of human rights and international humanitarian law are brought to justice."[39]

The UN Department of Peacekeeping and its head, Jean Marie Gueheno, protected our investigators in critical moments. The South African legal advisers at The Hague helped us build a strong relationship with the recently formed African Union. I visited President Mbeki in Pretoria, who introduced me to the AU's first chairperson, former Mali president Alpha Konare.

Later, I visited Mr. Konare in Addis Ababa, and I also briefed the AU Peace and Security Council. The AU legal adviser was in permanent contact with our office.

The UN Security Council supported our ICC arrest warrants, the AU was rising, and South Africa was leading. The EU and the UN Security Council endorsed the efforts to end the commission of massive atrocities in Africa. There was no mention of any ICC "African bias."

The Chamber's Decisions on the DRC Jurisdiction

There were three critical rulings on jurisdiction in the DRC situation involving several chambers. The first relevant rulings on jurisdiction were adopted in Ituri's conflict: the Thomas Lubanga case, a member of the Hema community; and the Germain Katanga case, a member of the Lendu community. The other relevant case, against Calixte Mbarushimana, related to the Hutus militias working in the Kivus.

Thomas Lubanga Case

The armed conflict was still ongoing in the Ituri province in the northeastern part of the DRC, an area rich in natural resources such as gold and diamonds. The fight opposed numerous militias from different ethnicities to protect their people and gain power and territory.

One such group, the Union Patriotique des Congolais (UPC), was established in 2000 and appointed Thomas Lubanga Dyilo as its chairman and the commander in chief of the armed wing of the UPC, the Front Patriotique pour la Libération du Congo.[40] We charged him and Bosco Ntaganda, as the second in the UPC military command, with the war crimes of enlisting and recruiting child soldiers and using them in hostilities.

Pre-Trial Chamber I ruled on the DRC jurisdiction when issued the arrest warrant against Thomas Lubanga Dyilo on February 10, 2006. The chamber was presided over by Judge Claude Jorda, former chief prosecutor at the Paris appeals court and former president of the ICTY. He was trying to import to ICC the French tradition of judges in charge of the investigation.

The chamber was also integrated by Judge Sylvia Steiner, a former prosecutor and judge from Brazil who was involved in the Rome Statute discussions. Judge Akua Kuenyehia is the former dean faculty of law of the University of Ghana and an expert on gender issues.

The chamber decided "that an initial determination on whether the case against Mr. Thomas Lubanga Dyilo falls within the jurisdiction of the Court and is admissible is a prerequisite to the issuance of a warrant of arrest for him."[41]

The chamber found that the crimes described by the charges were committed in the temporal and territorial jurisdiction defined by the referral.[42]

Regarding the admissibility, the chamber was able to assess the specific existence of national proceedings not just related to the situation but more particularly to the case and established an important criterion that became the jurisprudence of the court: "the inaction scenario."

The chamber considered "that it is a condition sine qua non for a case arising from the investigation of a situation to be inadmissible that national proceedings encompass both the person and the conduct which is the subject of the case before the Court." "Accordingly, in the absence of any acting State, the Chamber need not make any analysis of unwillingness or inability."[43]

The chamber tried to innovate on gravity and considered that the threshold under Article 17 (1) (d) of the statute includes as a legal requisite, and not just as a prosecutor policy,[44] that the "Court initiates cases only against the most senior leaders suspected of being the most responsible."[45] The chamber observed that "the activities of the Court must be subordinate to the higher purpose of prevention."

The pre-trial chamber considered that the most responsible focus could not be based on the Office of the Prosecutor policy. It ruled such limitations were not "discretionary for the Prosecution because they are a core component of the gravity threshold provided for in article 17 (1) (d) of the Statute."[46] It concluded that "Mr. Thomas Lubanga Dyilo falls within the category of most senior leaders," but "Mr. Bosco Ntaganda does not fall within the category of the most senior leaders in the DRC situation."

We appealed the refusal to issue an arrest warrant against Bosco Ntaganda, and on July 13, 2006, the appeals chamber reversed the Pre-Trial Chamber I's decision. The appeal chamber was presided over by Judge Navanethem Pillay, a South Africa prominent human rights lawyer, who became a judge of the High Court of South Africa, the president of the ICTR, and later the UN high commissioner for human rights. It was also integrated by Judge Philippe Kirsch, who was the chairman of the Rome Conference; Judge Georghios M. Pikis, former president of the Cyprus Supreme Court; Judge Sang-Hyun Song, a highly respected professor of international law from Korea who was a visiting professor at NYU and Harvard; and Judge Erkki Kourula, a former judge in Finland with vast experience as a diplomat before the Council of Europe and the UN, and the head of the Finnish delegation to the Rome Conference.

They ruled that the construction by the pre-trial chamber had no legal foundation. And accordingly, they decided that the "application of such a flawed test by the Pre-Trial Chamber to the circumstances of the case against Mr. Bosco Ntaganda was necessarily incorrect."[47]

The defendants did not even challenge the Office of the Prosecutor's interpretation of the court's jurisdiction in DRC during the trials.

The trial chamber in charge of the Lubanga case was presided over by Judge Sir Adrian Fulford, a High Court judge member of the Queen's Bench, he later became Lord Justice of Appeals in the British system; Judge Elizabeth Odio Benito, former minister of justice and vice president of Costa Rica, and previously an ICTY judge, who later became the president of the Inter American Court of Human Rights; and Judge René Blattmann, a human rights lawyer and former minister of justice for Bolivia.

In its final judgment in the case against Thomas Lubanga, the chamber ruled: "The personal, temporal, territorial and subject-matter elements that are relevant to the Court's jurisdiction have not altered since the Decision on the Confirmation of the Charges, and the issue has not been raised by the parties or any State before the Trial Chamber."[48]

Germain Katanga Case

In 2007 the Office of the Prosecutor was ready to present charges against Ngiti and Lendu militias' commanders fighting the UPC led by Lubanga. Germain Katanga was a leader of the Force de Résistance Patriotique en Ituri (Patriotic Force of Resistance in Ituri: FRPI) integrated by members of the Ngiti community.[49] Mathieu Ngudjolo Chui was the Front des Nationalistes et Intégrationnistes (FNI)'s leader integrated by the Lendu community.[50] Forces combined by both militias attacked Bogoro, a village controlled by UPC.

On July 2, 2007, Pre-Trial Chamber I made an initial determination of the case's admissibility and issued a warrant of arrest regarding Germain Katanga. Judge Akua Kuenyehia was the presiding judge. The chamber was also integrated by Judge Anita Ušacka, a former judge of the constitutional court of the Republic of Latvia, and Judge Sylvia Steiner.

The Pre-Trial Chamber I ruled that the Katanga case was admissible before the ICC. It decided that some proceedings "against Germain Katanga in the Democratic Republic of the Congo do not encompass the same conduct, which is the subject of the Prosecution Application."[51]

Congolese authorities surrendered Katanga to the ICC on October 17, 2007.

In June 2009, Trial Chamber II rejected a Katanga request and confirmed that his case was admissible before the ICC. The presiding judge was Bruno Cotte, who had a distinguished judicial carrier in France, culminating as a Cour de Cassation member. The chamber was also integrated by Judge Fatoumata Dembele Diarra, a former Judge in Mali and the ICTY; and Judge Hans-Peter Kaul, a former German diplomat, head of the Germany delegation during the Rome Conference. They considered that DRC itself expressed, "its unwillingness to prosecute Germain Katanga in the case that is before the Court."[52]

The appeal chamber was presided over by Judge Daniel David Ntanda Nsereko, a very wise person with an extensive carrier as a criminal lawyer in Uganda and international professor. Judge Sang-Hyun Song; Judge Erkki Kourula; Judge Ekaterina Trendafilova, a former deputy district attorney at the Sofia District Court, and Bulgaria's criminal justice professor; and Judge Joyce Aluoch, a former judge of the High Court of Kenya, were the other members. They decided that under Article 17 (1) (d) of the statute, the Katanga case was admissible because of DRC inaction.[53]

The appeal chamber clarified that

> Under Article 17 (1) (a) and (b) of the Statute, the question of unwillingness or inability has to be considered only (1) when there are, at the time of the proceedings in respect of an admissibility challenge, domestic investigations or prosecutions that could render the case inadmissible before the Court, or (2) when there have been such investigations and the State having jurisdiction has decided not to prosecute the person concerned.[54]

It concluded that "Inaction on the part of a State having jurisdiction (that is, the fact that a State is not investigating or prosecuting, or has not done so) renders a case admissible before the Court."[55]

Callixte Mbarushimana Case

The Rwanda genocidaires fled to the Kivu provinces in the Democratic Republic of the Congo. These exiled forces organized themselves into political and military groups designed to oppose the new Rwandan government.

One of these groups was the *Forces Démocratiques pour la Liberation du Rwanda* (FDLR) and Callixte Mbarushimana was executive secretary. I pushed our office to show a different form of criminality. In my opinion, Mbarushimana's contribution to the crimes committed in the Kivus was a media campaign from Europe inciting attacks on the civilian populations in the Kivu provinces throughout 2009. I was trying to expose his supportive role from abroad, expanding the focus of the Prosecution cases.

On September 28, 2010, Pre-Trial Chamber I was presided over by Judge Cuno Tarfusser, with an extensive carrier in Italy, reaching the position of chief prosecutor of the Bolzano District Court.

Judge Sylvia Steiner and Judge Sanji Mmasenono Monageng, former chairperson of the African Commission on Human and Peoples' Rights, and former High Court judge in the Republic of Gambia and then the Kingdom of Swaziland, considered that the Mbarushimana case was admissible and issued a warrant of arrest against him.

On October 11, 2010, Mbarushimana was arrested in Paris by the French gendarmerie. They were patiently waiting for the best opportunity to do it. On November 3, 2010, his surrender to the ICC was approved by the Paris court of appeals and validated by the *Cour de cassation* on January 3, 2011. He was transferred to The Hague Detention Centre on January 25, 2011.

Mbarushimana challenged ICC jurisdiction, arguing that the crimes charged were not part of the situation referred to by the DRC government. They were committed after the referral and outside Ituri, the region mentioned by the Office of the Prosecutor in its letter to the government.

On October 26, 2011, the pre-trial chamber rejected Mbarushimana's argument. The judges considered that "Crimes committed after the referral can fall within the jurisdiction of the Court when sufficiently linked to that particular situation of crisis."[56] Such a link can stretch over several years; accordingly, it cannot be required that the person targeted by the prosecutor's investigation be active throughout the relevant time frame.

The crimes allegedly perpetrated by FDLR forces, which form the basis of the charges against Mr. Mbarushimana, "are indeed inextricably linked to the situation of crisis in the DRC which has been under the constant examination by, and a continuing source of deep concern for the United Nations since at least the early 2000s." Besides, the chamber noted that the referral made explicit reference to the DRC country as a whole.

The charges against Mbarushimana were not confirmed, and he was released.

Notes

1. In October 2007, the OTP changed from using the term "communications" to using the phrase "information regarding alleged crimes," consistent with the terminology in the Rome Statute. However, because the term "communications" was used throughout the time period of this case, it will be used in this chapter.
2. Office of the Prosecutor of the ICC, *Communications received between July 2002 and 8 July 2003*, ICC (July 16, 2003), https://www.icc-cpi.int/NR/rdonlyres/B080A3DD-7C69-4BC9-AE25-0D2C271A9A63/277502/16_july__english.pdf.
3. Office of the Prosecutor of the ICC, Press Release: Communications Received between July 2002 and 8 July 2003, ICC (July 16, 2003).
4. Xabier Agirre, Antonio Cassese, Rolf Einar Fife, Hakan Friman, Christopher Hall, John T. Holms, Jann Kleffner, Hector Olasolo, Norul H Rashid, Darryl Robinson, Elizabeth Wilmhurst, and Andreas Zimmermann.
5. In April 2003, the then director of common services of the International Criminal Court (ICC), Mr. Bruno Cathala, approved Morten Bergsmo's suggestion and created an expert consultation process on "complementarity in practice." They met on May 28, 2003. After my arrival we called for a second meeting to participate in an "informal expert consultation on complementarity in practice" and to prepare a reflection paper on the potential legal, policy, and management challenges that are likely to confront the OTP as a consequence of the complementarity regime of the statute. Xavier Aguirre, Antonio Cassese et al, *Informal Expert Paper: The Principle of Complementarity in Practice*, ICC (2003), https://www.icc-cpi.int/RelatedRecords/CR2009_02250.PDF.
6. "Guiding principles: Two guiding principles should inform the OTP approach to complementarity:

    Partnership: the relationship with States genuinely carrying out proceedings should be constructive. The OTP can encourage and assist national efforts and arrive at consensual divisions of labour in appropriate cases.
    Vigilance: the OTP must gather information in order to verify that national proceedings are carried out genuinely, and be poised to take follow-up steps, leading if necessary to an exercise of jurisdiction.
    Impact: The principle of complementarity can magnify the effectiveness of the ICC beyond what it could achieve through its own prosecutions, as it prompts a network of States to carry out proceedings. The ICC can do this through encouragement and cooperation, through the prospect of exercising jurisdiction, and through standard-setting." *Id.*

7. U.N. SCOR 58th Sess., 4784 mtg., U.N. Doc S/PV.4784 (July 7, 2003).

8. Human Rights Watch, *Ituri: Covered in Blood. Ethnically Targeted Violence in Northeastern DR Congo 15*(11) (A) (July 2003).

9. *Id.*

10. I was assisted by a volunteer, Ines Selwood, a young communication expert who had worked with me in Argentina and was visiting the court.

11. Office of the Prosecutor of the ICC, Press Release: Communications Received between July 2002 and 8 July 2003, ICC (July 16, 2003).

12. *Id.*

13. *Id.*

14. *Id.*

15. *See* U.N. SCOR 58th Sess., 4784 mtg. 9, 26, U.N. Doc S/PV.4784 (July 7, 2003).

16. U.N. SCOR 58th Sess., 4784 mtg. p. 27, U.N. Doc S/PV.4784 (July 7, 2003).

17. *Id.* at 28.

18. Office of the Prosecutor of the ICC, *Report on the Activities Performed during the First Three Years (June 2003–June 2006)* 7 (Sept. 12, 2006), https://www.icc-cpi.int/NR/rdonlyres/D76A5D89-FB64-47A9-9821-725747378AB2/143680/OTP_3yearreport20060914_English.pdf.

19. Paola Gaeta, *Is the Practice of "Self Referrals" a Sound Start for the ICC?*, 2 J. OF INT'L CRIM. J. 949, 950–51 (2004).

20. Darryl Robinson, *The Controversy over Territorial State Referrals and Reflections on ICL Discourse*, 9(2) J. INT'L CRIM. JUST. 355, 368 (2011).

21. PHIL CLARK, DISTANT JUSTICE: THE IMPACT OF THE INTERNATIONAL CRIMINAL COURT ON AFRICAN POLITICS 444–46 (Kindle ed. 2018).

22. Rod Rastan, *The Responsibility to Enforce—Connecting Justice with Unity*, in THE EMERGING PRACTICE OF THE INTERNATIONAL CRIMINAL COURT 163, 174 (Carsten Stahn & Göran Sluiter eds., 2009) ("For both the DRC and Uganda, it is uncertain whether such referrals would have been forthcoming without the availability of an independent triggering mechanism."); *See also* Hakan Friman, *The International Criminal Court: Investigations into Crimes Committed in the DRC and Uganda*, 13 AFR. SECURITY REV. 19, 20 (2004) note 5, at 20 ("While sticks may be useful, and the prosecutor's *proprio motu* powers constitute an important tool, carrots are probably faster and more reliable.").

23. "National authorities with the assistance of the international community could implement appropriate mechanisms to deal with other individuals responsible." Office of the Prosecutor, *Report to the Second Assembly of States Parties to the Rome Statute of the International Criminal Court*, ICC (Sept. 8, 2003), http://legal.un.org/icc/asp/2ndsession/ocampo_statement_8sep(e).pdf. Such criterion suggested by the expert group that prepared the paper "Complementarity in Practice" and included in our policy paper was called a policy of "burden-sharing." This concept has been challenged by Padraig McAuliffe in Padraig McAuliffe, *From Watchdog to Workhorse: Explaining the Emergence of the ICC's Burden-Sharing Policy as an Example of Creeping Cosmopolitanism*, 13 CHINESE J. OF INT'L L. 259 (2014).

24. "In coming weeks, the Office of the Prosecutor will send letters to all States Parties and other countries particularly concerned, informing them that we are analyzing the information regarding Ituri, and inviting them to cooperate." Office of the Prosecutor, *Report to the Second Assembly of States Parties to the Rome Statute of the International Criminal Court*, ICC (Sept. 8, 2003), http://legal.un.org/icc/asp/2ndsession/ocampo_statement_8sep(e).pdf

25. "[F]or example for the purchase of arms, may well provide evidence proving the commission of atrocities." *Id.*

26. *Id.*

27. Statement of Katuala Kaba-Sashala. Press Release, Assembly of States Parties of the International Criminal Court, States parties to International Criminal Court Elect Serge Brammertz of Belgium Deputy Prosecutor, U.N. Press Release L/3048 (Sept. 9, 2003).

28. *The Special Rapporteur welcomes the decision by the Prosecutor of the ICC to make the Democratic Republic of the Congo the first State to be the subject of his investigations.* Iulia Motoc (Special Rapporteur of the Commission of Human Rights), Interim report on the situation for human rights in the Democratic Republic of Congo ¶ 56, U.N. Doc. A/58/534 (Oct. 24, 2003).

29. HELEN EPSTEIN, ANOTHER FINE MESS: AMERICA, UGANDA, AND THE WAR ON TERROR 27–33 (Kindle ed. 2017).

30. See a description of the process in GERARD PRUNIER, AFRICA'S WORLD WAR: CONGO, THE RWANDAN GENOCIDE, AND THE MAKING OF A CONTINENTAL CATASTROPHE 301 (Kindle ed. 2008).

31. "Elections stopped being an abstraction and the population as well as the politicians began to factor them into their calculations. Belief was helping to create fact, and the ghost of the transition began to gain substance." *Id.* at 303.

32. "Trust was in limited supply and everybody was looking over their shoulder . . . The military commanders were rebels in government areas and government rebels in former rebel territories; they had to be flanked by commanders of the opposite camp to keep tabs on them. *Id.* at 301.

33. The Prosecutor v. Thomas Lubanga Dyilo, ICC-01/04-01/06-39-AnxB1-tENG, AnnexB1: Submission of Redacted Documents (Mar. 17, 2006), https://www.icc-cpi.int/RelatedRecords/CR2007_04360.PDF.

34. *Preliminary examination policy (draft): Where the Office of the Prosecutor has decided independently, using its proprio motu powers to trigger the preliminary examination phase, that there is a reasonable basis to proceed with opening an investigation into a situation, and before requesting authorization to the Pre-Trial Chamber, the Office may inform relevant State(s) of its determination and offer them the option to refer the situation to the Court with the aim inter alia of increasing the prospects of cooperation. If the State(s) concerned elects not to refer the situation, the Office remains prepared at all times to proceed proprio motu . . . 82. Pursuant to the principle of independence, the policy of inviting referrals is without prejudice to the case selection and prosecutorial strategy of the Office.* In November 2013, Fatou Bensouda as chief prosecutor published a different and more comprehensive final Policy Paper on Preliminary

Examinations Office of the Prosecutor of the ICC, without mentioning the policy to invite referrals. *Policy Paper on Preliminary Examinations*, ICC (Nov. 2013), https://www.icc-cpi.int/iccdocs/otp/otp-policy_paper_preliminary_examinations_2013-eng.pdf.

35. The Article 53 report is confidential and should not be disclosed in accordance with Rule 81(1).
36. Rome Statute to the International Criminal Court, Art. 8.
37. Rep. of the S.C. Mission to Central Africa, 7 to 16 June 2003, ¶ 28, U.N. Doc. S/2003/653 (June 17, 2003).
38. Accord Global et Inclusif sur la Transition en République Démocratique du Congo, Dec. 17, 2002, clause V.
39. Press Release, Security Council extends Democratic Republic of Congo mission until 31 March 2005, authorizes additional 5,900 troops, police, U.N. Press Release SC/8203 (Oct. 1, 2004).
40. The Prosecutor v. Thomas Lubanga Dyilo, INTERNATIONAL CRIMES DATA BASE, http://www.internationalcrimesdatabase.org/Case/814 (last visited Jan 9, 2021).
41. Prosecutor v. Thomas Lubanga Dyilo, ICC-01/04-01/06, Decision on the Prosecutor's Application for a warrant of arrest. Article 58, ¶20 (Feb. 10, 2006).
42. The chamber took into consideration that the situation was referred to the prosecutor on March 3, 2004, by the president of the DRC, that the prosecution states that it had sent letters of notification to the states parties and other states which within the terms of such provision could exercise jurisdiction over the crimes concerned; and that, according to the Prosecution, no information pursuant to Article 18 (2) of the statute was received. Prosecutor v. Thomas Lubanga Dyilo, ICC-01/04-01/06, Decision on the Prosecutor's Application for a warrant of arrest. Article 58, ¶22 (Feb. 10, 2006), https://www.legal-tools.org/doc/af6679/pdf/.
43. The chamber observed that "two warrants of arrest by the competent DRC authorities were issued against Thomas Lubanga Dyilo in March 2005 for several crimes, some possibly within the jurisdiction of the Court, committed in connection with military attacks from May 2003 onwards and during the so-called Ndoki incident in February 2005."

    The chamber observes that the warrants of arrest issued by the competent DRC authorities against Mr. Thomas Lubanga Dyilo contain no reference to his alleged criminal responsibility for the alleged UPC/FPLC's policy/practice of enlisting into the FPLC, conscripting into the FPLC and using to participate actively in hostilities children under the age of fifteen between July 2002 and December 2003. As a result, in the chamber's view, the DRC cannot be considered to be acting in relation to the specific case before the court. Prosecutor v. Thomas Lubanga Dyilo, ICC-01/04-01/06, Decision on the Prosecutor's Application for a warrant of arrest. Article 58, ¶38–39 (Feb. 10, 2006), https://www.legal-tools.org/doc/af6679/pdf/.
44. "The Chamber notes that the Prosecution's Policy Paper of September 2003 comes to the following conclusion: the Office of the Prosecutor should focus its investigative and prosecutorial efforts and resources on those who bear the greatest responsibility." Prosecutor v. Thomas Lubanga Dyilo, ICC-01/04-01/06, Decision on the Prosecutor's

Application for a warrant of arrest. Article 58, ¶61 (Feb. 10, 2006), https://www.legal-tools.org/doc/af6679/pdf/.

45. "In this regard, the Chamber considers that the additional gravity threshold provided for in article 17 (1) (d) of the Statute is intended to ensure that the Court initiates cases only against the most senior leaders suspected of being the most responsible for the crimes within the jurisdiction of the Court allegedly committed in any given situation under investigation. In the Chamber's opinion, only by concentrating on this type of individual can the deterrent effects of the activities of the Court be maximised because other senior leaders in similar circumstances will know that solely by doing what they can to prevent the systematic or large-scale commission of crimes within the jurisdiction of the Court can they be sure that they will not be prosecuted by the Court." The pre-trial chamber recalled that the United Nations Security Council resolution 1534 of March 26, 2004, says inter alia: "Calls on each Tribunal, in reviewing and confirming any new indictments, to ensure that any such indictments concentrate on the most senior leaders suspected of being most responsible for crimes within the jurisdiction of the relevant Tribunal as set out in resolution 1503 (2003)." Prosecutor v. Thomas Lubanga Dyilo, ICC-01/04-01/06, Decision on the Prosecutor's Application for a warrant of arrest. Article 58, ¶50–55 (Feb. 10, 2006), https://www.legal-tools.org/doc/af6679/pdf/.

46. In conclusion, the chamber considers that any case arising from an investigation before the court will meet the gravity threshold provided for in article 17 (1) (d) of the statute if the following three questions can be answered affirmatively: (i) Is the conduct which is the object of a case systematic or large-scale (due consideration should also be given to the social alarm caused to the international community by the relevant type of conduct)?; (ii) Considering the position of the relevant person in the state entity, organization, or armed group to which he belongs, can it be considered that such person falls within the category of most senior leaders of the situation under investigation?; and (iii) Does the relevant person fall within the category of most senior leaders suspected of being most responsible, considering (1) the role played by the relevant person through acts or omissions when the state entities, organizations, or armed groups to which he belongs commit systematic or large-scale crimes within the jurisdiction of the court; and (2) the role played by such state entities, organizations, or armed groups in the overall commission of crimes within the jurisdiction of the court in the relevant situation? Prosecutor v. Thomas Lubanga Dyilo, ICC-01/04-01/06, Decision on the Prosecutor's Application for a warrant of arrest. Article 58, ¶52 (Feb. 10, 2006), https://www.legal-tools.org/doc/af6679/pdf/.

47. Situation in the Democratic Republic of the Congo, ICC-01/04, Judgment on the Prosecutor's appeal against the decision of Pre-Trial Chamber I entitled "Decision on the Prosecutor's Application for Warrants of Arrest, Article 58." (July 13, 2006), https://www.icc-cpi.int/CourtRecords/CR2006_01807.PDF.

48. Prosecutor v. Thomas Lubanga Dyilo, ICC-01/04-01/06, Summary of the "Judgment pursuant to Article 74 of the Statute," ¶ 3 (Mar. 14, 2012), https://www.icc-cpi.int/CourtRecords/CR2012_03947.PDF

49. The Prosecutor v. Germain Katanga, INTERNATIONAL CRIMES DATA BASE, http://inte rnationalcrimesdatabase.org/Case/3260 (last visited Jan. 9, 2021).

50. The Prosecutor v. Mathieu Ngudjolo, INTERNATIONAL CRIMES DATA BASE http:// www.internationalcrimesdatabase.org/Case/873/Ngudjolo   (last   visited   Jan. 14, 2021).

51. Prosecutor v. Germain Katanga, ICC-01/04-01/07, Warrant of arrest for Germain Katanga (July 2, 2007), https://www.icc-cpi.int/CourtRecords/CR2007_04166.PDF.

52. Prosecutor v. Germain Katanga and Mathieu Ngudjolo Chui, ICC-01/04-01/07, Reasons for the Oral Decision on the Motion Challenging the Admissibility of the Case, (June 16, 2009), https://www.icc-cpi.int/CourtRecords/CR2009_05171.pdf.

53. Prosecutor v. Germain Katanga and Mathieu Ngudjolo Chui, ICC-01/04-01/07 OA 8, Judgment on the Appeal of Mr. Germain Katanga against the Oral Decision of Trial Chamber II of 12 June 2009 on the Admissibility of the Case (Sept. 25, 2009), https:// www.icc-cpi.int/CourtRecords/CR2009_06998.PDF.

54. *Id.* at ¶ 1.

55. *Id.* at ¶ 2.

56. Prosecutor v. Callixte Mbarushimana, ICC-01/04-01/10, Decision on the "Defence Challenge to the Jurisdiction of the Court" (Oct. 26, 2011), https://www.legal-tools. org/doc/864f9b/pdf/.

7

The Uganda Preliminary Examination

Opening an Investigation in Uganda

This chapter analyzes the decisions adopted by the Office of the Prosecutor and the Ugandan government to open an investigation in Uganda confirming the possibility to adopt *jus ad Curiam* resolutions in agreement with states interests.

It presents the distinction between "situation" and "case," the meaning of the "interest of the victims" under Article 53(1)(c), and the consolidation of the policy to invite states to refer their own situations to the ICC.

It describes the information obtained during the *preliminary examination* about crimes against humanity and war crimes committed by the Lord Resistance Army (LRA) since July 2002. Through a conversation with Uganda's lawyers, the office obtained a referral under confidentiality focused exclusively on LRA crimes, a militia led by Joseph Kony.

The prosecution clarified to the Ugandan authorities that the referral included the entire situation of Northern Uganda and that the office would select the cases. However, we were unable to disclose the referral to the chambers, and therefore we could not use it. A confidential conversation with President Museveni in London solved the problem, and he announced the referral in a press conference with my presence.

The chapter also explains the office's conclusion that the Uganda situation fulfilled all the elements required by the statute. Still, the prosecution legal actions received a new criticism based on non-legal narratives: the opposition to justice and the perception of partiality by civil society actors. Traditional and religious Acholi leaders supported by humanitarian NGOs and some states opposed any criminal investigation. Other critics assumed a non-legally required obligation: that impartiality requires investigations and prosecutions to be conducted simultaneously toward both sides of the political divide.

Phuong Pham and Patrick Vinck, who led the Evaluation and Implementation Science at the Harvard Humanitarian Initiative (HHI),

War and Justice in the 21st Century. Luis Moreno Ocampo, Oxford University Press. © Oxford University Press 2022.
DOI: 10.1093/oso/9780197628973.003.0008

developed "population-based data representing the spectrum of attitudes and opinions of those most affected by the violence."[1]

Their study shows the complexity of the communities affected and the variety of opinions. More than half of those interviewed in Northern Uganda chose "peace with trials and punishment." Still, as on many other occasions, a relevant part of the affected population opposed the prosecution's intervention.[2]

The office transformed its experiences into a policy: understanding the ideas and even contradictions of the victims and their representatives should not divert the prosecution from pursuing its legal mandate. Our 2004 *jus ad Curiam* decision in Uganda was reviewed by the judges and confirmed eleven years later.

Uganda's Preliminary Examination

The Timely HRW Report

On July 15, 2003, one day before our first press conference, Human Rights Watch (HRW) produced a very comprehensive report on the LRA's brutal crimes in Uganda. "Since June 2002, the LRA has abducted approximately 8,400 children, resumed its despicable practice of mutilating people it believes to be affiliated with the government, and targeted religious leaders, aid providers, and other civilians."[3]

LRA's abduction threat made children fear for their safety creating the "night commuters" phenomena. "Each night, thousands of children pour into Gulu, Kitgum, and Pader towns (Acholiland) from surrounding areas, hoping to avoid abduction. They seek refuge on verandahs, in the bus park, on church grounds, and in local factories before returning home again each morning."[4]

Exposing the novelty of the international criminal justice approach and the Acholi influence on the HRW vision of the problem in 2003, the report did not request creating a UN Commission of Enquiry or the ICC intervention into the crimes exposed. The 2003's HRW report asked the LRA to stop the attacks, abductions, and killings but did not call to investigate its crimes and disrupt the group's criminal activities.

HRW treated LRA as a permanent and legitimate actor, and it asked for its support and cooperation to "create a conducive environment for the proper functioning of an internationally led human rights monitoring body on northern Uganda, based in Uganda."[5]

The report limited its demands to the UN Secretary-General to "[a]ppoint a special representative for the abducted children of northern Uganda to conduct 'shuttle diplomacy' . . . with the aim of securing the release into safety of all those abducted by the LRA as children, and to seek an end to future abductions."[6]

HRW blamed Uganda's government for failing to control the LRA's atrocities and requested exclusively to "End impunity for human rights violations by government security and armed organizations."[7]

I did not mention the Uganda situation in my briefing to the journalists on July 16, but I started to read more about the problem. I was fascinated by an older article written by Elizabeth Rubin in the *New Yorker* in March 1998 entitled *"Our Children Are Killing Us."*[8]

She described a unique phenomenon: the LRA was an army of abducted children attacking its own community. Elizabeth Rubin was trying to find an answer to an intolerable question: "What it meant for an entire society to live under the threat of having its children abducted and either killed or turned into killers?"

I was impressed that after so much information, and so many years, nothing changed. The LRA had abducted the girls at St. Mary School three different times.[9] Seven years had passed after the last girl's abduction, and the Northern Uganda situation was even worse.[10]

We opened a preliminary examination to evaluate the Uganda situation without making a public announcement.

Uganda's Lawyers' Meeting and the Discussion about a Referral

In June 1999, the DRC had sued Uganda and Rwanda before the International Court of Justice, alleging "acts of armed aggression."[11] As a consequence, Uganda was worried about our plans to open a DRC investigation.

On October 20, 2003, during a meeting at the UN, the representative of Uganda welcomed "the Prosecutor's announcement at the ASP" regarding DRC and observed that it was "a good indication that the Court is indeed in motion and there is no turning back." However, the representative of Uganda, concerned about a case at the ICJ, expressed her hope that the prosecutor "will take all necessary measures to cross-check on all communications forwarded to him."[12]

Uganda lawyers in the ICJ case asked for a meeting with me. I received Paul Reichler, a senior international US lawyer who had represented Nicaragua in its lawsuit against the United States; and Payam Akhavan, former legal adviser to the prosecutor of the ICTY who at the time was a fellow at Yale University.

During the meeting, they presented the argument that Uganda personnel was not involved in DRC crimes. They explained that Uganda withdrew its soldiers from the DRC even before it ratified the statute. Consequently, no Ugandan soldier engaged in the Ituri conflict after the Rome Statute came into force. In any case, they offered access to all the information they had presented before the ICJ.

We had received no information regarding crimes committed by Ugandans in the DRC during our preliminary examination, but we thanked them for their offer in any case. For us, the conflict in Northern Uganda was ranked immediately after Colombia and DRC in terms of gravity. The amnesty blocked the possibility of conducting national proceedings, so it appeared that the situation was admissible.

I asked them about Uganda's views on the problem. We explored the option of receiving a referral from the Uganda government. They told me that they would ask the government for its position.[13]

A Confidential Referral from Uganda

We did not hear from the lawyers again. On December 16, 2003, Lucian Tibaruha, the then Ugandan Solicitor General, visited our office and delivered a letter from Ugandan president Yoweri Museveni, referring the situation concerning the Lord's Resistance Army (LRA) to the ICC.

Uganda's solicitor general explained that we had to maintain the referral confidential until the Ugandan Parliament could change the amnesty law enacted in 2000; otherwise, Joseph Kony could return to Uganda, surrender, and automatically receive amnesty.

Suddenly, we could potentially start investigations in Uganda with state authorities' support and smoothly launch the entire ICC operations, but there were two problems that we had to manage: (1) The referral was confidential. We could not use it. (2) The referral tried to restrict our investigation to LRA's activities, excluding the possibility of investigating alleged crimes committed by government forces.

We faced the second problem by developing the first interpretation of the meaning of "situation" and "case." During the preliminary examination we had to identify a "situation," a space defined in terms of temporal and territorial parameters, under the court's jurisdiction.

During the following phase of the investigation, the office had to identify "cases" defined by Pre-Trial Chamber I as entailing "specific incidents during which one or more crimes within the jurisdiction of the Court seem to have been committed by one or more identified suspects."[14]

"The concept of a situation has broader parameters than that of a case. As negotiations during the drafting history reveal, the term was intended to frame in objective terms the theatre of investigations, thereby rejecting the idea that a referring body could limit the focus of the Prosecutor's activities by reference to particular conduct, suspect, or party."[15]

Considering that Article 14(1) of the Rome Statute provides for the referral of a "situation" rather than the referral of specific cases or suspects, we informed the government of Uganda that, in compliance with our obligations of impartiality, we would interpret the referral to include all crimes committed in Northern Uganda.

The Ugandan government granted amnesty to those who had, since January 26, 1986, engaged in "war or armed rebellion against the government" of Uganda.[16] Under the terms of the act, no prosecution can be pursued "for any crime committed in the cause of the war or armed rebellion."

The amnesty was blocking the possibility of conducting national prosecutions. It could also allow Kony to surrender and obtain immunity for his crimes, but it was not an obstacle for our intervention.[17]

Under international law, national amnesties are not an obstacle to the prosecution of international crimes before international courts. The statute provided no reason to consider that a national amnesty was a legal obstacle for ICC intervention.[18]

However, we noted that the amnesty resulted from a political agreement reached in 1986 between President Museveni and the Acholi, an ethnic group based in the North of Uganda to end the conflict between them.

Yoweri Museveni, then the leader of a rebel group based in the south of Uganda, became Uganda's president removing from power General Tito Okello, an Acholi.[19] Museveni considered that the Acholi were Okello supporters and promoted their marginalization.[20] Alice Lakwena, a spiritual leader, commanded the Acholi armed opposition against Museveni in the early days, but she changed her mind and went into exile in Kenya.

Joseph Kony, another Acholi, took over her role in 1987, claiming to be under instructions from the Holy Spirit. Combining spiritual elements with traditional insurgency to defend the Acholi from Museveni, the LRA became "the de facto representative of the Acholi ethnic community."[21] The Acholi leaders had to accept that Kony was resisting the actions of an external enemy such as Museveni and framed the problem as a civil war.

Paradoxically, Kony did not attack the Ugandan government forces; instead, he directed most of the LRA attacks against civilians, particularly his own Acholi tribe.[22] Kony realized that children were malleable, easily intimidated, eager to please. He abducted more than 20,000 of them and transformed them into soldiers.

President Museveni was "refusing to recognize the LRA as a movement with political motives," considered Kony an insurgent, and was requesting his surrender. Acholi leaders from different faiths created the Acholi Religious Leaders' Peace Initiative (ARLPI) in 1997, aiming to find a political agreement between Kony and the government. For them, it was the only solution to end hostilities in the region. Kony was also attacking them, but they could not challenge him without severe risk to their life. Furthermore, he was a fellow Acholi and was purportedly fighting on their behalf.

In December 1999, proponents of peace talks won an important battle when, after years of lobbying by religious leaders from northern Uganda, Parliament adopted an Amnesty Act offering pardon to all Ugandans formerly or currently engaged in acts of rebellion against the Ugandan Government since 1986. Parliament did not accept the President's proposal to exclude certain groups of people from the amnesty.[23]

In 2002, Barney Afako, a young and brilliant Acholi lawyer, explained: "Among the Acholi of Northern Uganda the bitter experience of unending conflict has generated a remarkable commitment to reconciliation and a peaceful settlement of the conflict rather than calling for retribution of serious abuses."[24]

The Acholi were interested in the amnesty, and the government wanted to maintain an agreement that facilitated the end of the country's rebellions. It accepted some negotiations for peace in different moments, including January 1994[25] and December 1999.[26]

Museveni was trained as a rebel Marxist, but he partnered with the United States and supported the *War on Terror* as a president. Consequently, in December 2001, the United States designated the LRA as a terrorist group[27] helping Uganda negotiate an agreement with the government of Sudan to chase Kony.

Sudan was trying to avoid being identified as harboring terrorist groups by the Bush administration. The agreement allowed Uganda's army, the Ugandan People's Defence Force (UPDF), to launch Operation Iron Fist, a military campaign intended to wipe out the LRA by attacking its southern Sudanese sanctuaries. But Operation Iron Fist intensified the conflict in Northern Uganda.

The LRA evaded the UPDF in Sudan and moved back into Uganda in June 2002, where it has stepped up its abduction, killing, looting, and destruction aimed at civilians and their property.[28] The LRA "spread the conflict to the Ugandan regions of Lango and Teso."[29]

"At the conflict's peak, 1.84 million people (90–95 percent of the population in the three Acholi districts) lived in camps for internally displaced persons in 'appalling' humanitarian circumstances."[30]

President Museveni Lifted the Confidentiality of the Referral

After receiving the referral, we accepted an invitation to have a confidential meeting with President Museveni during his official visit to London at the end of January 2004. Our goal was to convince him to lift the confidentiality of the referral.

In the *jus ad Curiam* phase, we had to interact with government representatives being aware that they have their own interests and different legal options. Payam Akhavan explained in 2005 that

> For Uganda, the referral was an attempt to engage an otherwise aloof international community by transforming the prosecution of the LRA leaders into a litmus test for the much-celebrated promise of global justice." "Given the absence of any vital national interest, influential states have not been inclined either to pressure Sudan to stop harboring the LRA or to help government forces confront the insurgents. Instead, the burden was placed

on Uganda to negotiate a peaceful settlement with a ruthless, cult-like insurgency[31]

A few hours before my meeting with President Museveni, our office met members of the UK Ministry of Foreign Affairs, informing them of my planned encounter in London.

During the conversation, our office realized that the UK staff had no previous information about the referral.

The UK's International Development area informally expressed that our intervention could interfere with the necessary negotiation with the LRA to reach a ceasefire.

That evening I met President Museveni. His schedule the following day included a meeting with Prime Minister Blair and his cabinet members. I had reports stating that the United Kingdom was offering financial assistance to Uganda to fight terrorism in Africa.

The United Kingdom was a global player in the *jus ad Curiam* phase, following its own vision and interests and supporting at the same time its humanitarian projects, the ICC, and the *War on Terror*. I had no idea how the different agendas pursued by the United Kingdom combined. President Museveni was playing a role in Somalia in the *War on Terror*. After talking to the UK government, he could cancel the referral during the following day or keep it confidential. During the *jus ad Curiam* phase, all those options were legally open to him.

We met in a private meeting room at the Inter-Continental London Park Lane Hotel. President Museveni was seated in a big chair. At his right, his minister of defense Amama Mbabazi was sitting in a similar chair, and they offered me the third chair in front of them.

President Museveni was very cordial and spoke a few Portuguese words, a language he learned in Mozambique, where he had trained as a guerrilla leader. After some small talk, President Museveni explained their efforts to end the conflict.

He recognized that our office would analyze allegations against his troops but was denying any wrongdoing. Eventually, he said that if his forces committed any crime, Uganda would prosecute them. Finally, he went straight to the point; he turned to Minister Mbabazi and said, "I believe we should go public with the referral." Easy, I thought. We have the referral. But Minister Mbabazi opposed the idea: "First, we should modify the amnesty law. If not, it will be a contradiction, and we will have problems. We need some time, probably a few months."

President Museveni listened to his trusted Minister Mbabazi, who had been with him since the beginning of the rebellion. There will be no referral, I thought. The Parliament might not change the amnesty. "Can we exclude Kony and the LRA leaders from the amnesty law?," asked the president.

"Yes, we can. We are discussing the option with the members of the Parliament. I think it will be possible to exclude LRA leaders, but it will take some months," answered the minister.[32]

Observing the discussion between them was like watching the final points of an even tie break in a tennis match. One second it seemed like we had a referral, the next like we'd lost it. I knew my risk. The following day after meeting Blair, the president could decide to cancel the entire project. Even if he did not, the Parliament could disagree with removing the LRA's leaders from the amnesty, and the referral would stay confidential.

The president foresaw the Acholi resistance without mentioning: *It will be a complicated process.* The minister agreed, but he insisted that it would be necessary.

Suddenly, the president turned to me and asked, "If I do a press conference tomorrow announcing the referral, will you appear with me?"

I had ten seconds to decide. I knew the perception of being manipulated by the president would increase if I attended a press conference with him, but it was only a perception problem. As an international prosecutor, I had a duty to interact with national authorities. Our office had already reached the preliminary conclusion to open an investigation into the Uganda situation. We could obtain cooperation and launch the entire court activities dissipating sovereign fears. Making the referral public was my chance to consolidate a smooth ICC beginning.

So, I made my decision: "Of course, Mr. President. I will be there."

On January 29, 2004, I was seated with President Museveni at a small press conference in London, making a public announcement of the referral received in December. We did not promote the event, and there were a small number of journalists, but no pictures and no videos were taken.

I don't know what would have happened if I refused to be at the press conference. But Uganda Parliament took more than two years to amend the Amnesty Act; it did it in April 2006, and the trigger was the issuance of the ICC arrest warrants.[33]

The Criticism of the International Criminal Justice Intervention

The Interests of the Victims

The Rome Statute Article 53(1)(c) imposes a specific obligation on the prosecutor to consider the interests of victims before starting an investigation or prosecution. Consequently, we had to understand various arguments exposed by actors supporting or rejecting the initiative to include criminal justice in the Ugandan conflict. The Uganda referral announcement opened the door for active cooperation from Uganda to our investigations and support from states parties.[34]

But, different from the DRC situation, it also created conflicts with various constituencies.

We were applying a very innovative international law for the first time, challenging at the same time the frame of different groups: local leaders, peace negotiators, humanitarian workers, and legal experts.

They selected their analytical frameworks according to their varied interests, sometimes in contradiction among themselves and many times in opposition to our statutory mandate. The disagreement with our intervention in Uganda had two main opposing arguments:

(a) The Acholi Religious Leaders' Peace Initiative (ARLPI), some states, international NGOs providing humanitarian assistance, and some scholars opposed international criminal justice intervention in Uganda to allow a potential negotiation.

The argument was that "peace must come before justice. . . the Acholi people should be allowed to respond to the legacy of past atrocities in their own way and employ means that resonate and accord with local traditions."[35]

"Some have also faulted the Prosecutor for announcing the referral in the company of President Museveni."[36]The only solution for them was a political negotiation.

(b) On the other side, some NGOs and academics supported international criminal justice intervention in Uganda. However, they were not discussing with those opposing our intervention. Instead, they criticized how we were implementing our justice mandate and considered that accepting a referral and sharing a press conference with President Museveni affected our impartiality and provided a signal of impunity for state forces.

I explained our rationale to different actors. I met the Acholi paramount chief and other *traditional leaders* in London. I also spoke to Catholic and Christian priests living in Northern Uganda personally and by phone, explaining our mission and goals. I realized that none of them could talk publicly in favor of our justice initiative without the risk of being attacked by the LRA.

I encouraged some of them to keep speaking openly against us as a unique way to protect themselves, but I wanted to be sure they understood our mandate.

In February 2004, I took advantage of one of the first regular diplomatic briefings at the seat of the court to clarify that we "will investigate all crimes related to the situation in an impartial way."[37]

In the meantime, Kony's violence continued without provoking international reactions.

On February 21, the LRA attacked the Barlonyo camp for displaced people, killing more than 200 persons. The UN Security Council did not comment. Instead, it reacted in less than one hour to an Al Qaeda bombing in Madrid in March 2004 that caused a similar number of deaths. I wanted to focus the world's attention on how to stop the crimes.

The following month I explained to the Council of Europe's Committee of Legal Advisers on Public International Law: "In our approach to selecting situations, we are carefully staying within the center of our mandate."[38] We also made a distinction between the role of a national or international prosecutor. As the ICC prosecutor, I intended to pursue constructive relations with states during the *jus ad Curiam* phase.

I mentioned the possibility of receiving referrals, discussing modalities of cooperation, and prospects to exercise proceedings themselves. In these conversations, we never discussed who should be indicted, a *jus in Curiae* topic.[39] I ended by mentioning President Museven's public pledge "to cooperate with the ICC if it investigates his army's alleged involvement in war crimes."[40]

The Opposition to International Criminal Justice

The Religious and Traditional Leaders
In April 2004, ARLPI expressed specific concerns against our intervention: "The ICC intervention will block the provision of an alternative exit strategy to the LRA as a whole and individuals within it, and this will certainly put the lives of the captives with the rebels at risk."[41] ARLPI was worried about the Acholi victims within the LRA ranks.

The States Parties Involved in Peace Negotiations
The United Kingdom was not the only country supporting peace negotiations between Kony and the Museveni government. In May 2004, the ambassador from a Scandinavian country highly supportive of the court, who was leading the Ministry of Foreign Affairs African Department, came to my office asking to stop our intervention in Uganda.

In the ambassador's expert view, an investigation into the massive abduction of children organized by Joseph Kony would only perpetuate his crimes.

The legal adviser of such a country had an important role during the Rome Conference, considerable influence in the network of foreign affairs legal advisers, and a strong position on legal matters. Regardless, the MFA legal adviser could not agree on a consistent policy with his national colleagues in charge of Africa and those promoting negotiations to end conflicts. His colleagues had difficulties grasping the new framework established by the Rome Statute.

The ambassador considered that the Ugandan army could not defeat Kony and, if indicted, Kony would retaliate against civilians. He also asked me who would execute an eventual arrest warrant against Kony and sarcastically questioned, *Where is your army?*

The ambassador's expert opinion was that negotiation was the only way to stop Kony's crimes.

I acknowledged the interest and dedication of his country. I explained that under Article 53(1)(c) of the statute, the prosecutor could decide not to initiate an investigation if it is not in the interest of justice. Therefore, I invited him to present evidence supporting the arguments he had made. I felt very proud of my straight answer and the wisdom of the Rome Statute.

In response, the ambassador was not very diplomatic; he laughed and said, "Evidence? You have no idea what a peace process is. A peace process is a fragile mechanism; it is a small light at the end of a tunnel. It is just hope. I cannot provide evidence."

Then he re-evaluated his answer and said, "Do you need evidence? Let me present my evidence: I am trying to talk with Kony—I am calling him, and he is not taking my call. That is my evidence." I thanked the diplomat and did not encourage him to present his evidence in a more formal setting.

The Humanitarian, Christian, and Ugandan Scholar Groups

International religious and humanitarian organizations working in the region were against our intervention. In 2004, Tim Allen, a British anthropologist with vast experience in Northern Uganda, was asked to assess the implications of Uganda's referral by Save the Children, and he concluded:

> I was immediately struck by a consensus among aid workers that the ICC intervention was likely to be unhelpful. Their views were reiterated by almost all the urban-based "opinion leaders" I interviewed, including human rights activists and Christian clergy. "Justice," one local human rights activist told me, does not just come from the "briefcase of the white man" and cannot be established by international decree. It has to be locally grounded to have meaning.[42]
>
> He explained: At the time, the case for local—or more accurately— Acholi justice tended to focus on just one ritual, mato oput (drinking the bitter root). It was maintained that this was the ancient rite that allows for reconciliation with compensation rather than revenge. Aid funds had been made available to support mato oput rituals, and a council of "traditional chiefs" or rwodi was being created to perform them.[43]

Allen quoted the survey conducted by Phuong Pham and Patrick Vinck showing that 2,500 randomly selected adults in Gulu, Pader, and Kitgum Districts were asked, "What is Justice?" and 31 percent answered "trials," 18 percent "reconciliation," and just 7 percent mentioned "traditional justice."[44]

The report shows that food and security were the priorities. Still, when the communities affected by LRA were asked how they wanted to deal with the LRA, respondents fell along a spectrum. Most of them favored punishment (trial, imprisonment, killing, 66 percent) to deal with LRA. Most respondents (76 percent) said that UPDF members should be held accountable for their crimes.[45]

The Criticism of Our Implementation of International Criminal Justice

Some experts and NGOs expressed a different set of criticisms related to the proper way to implement our legal mandate and mentioned the lack of impartiality allegedly exposed by my joint press conference[46] and the referral's limited scope.[47]

They proposed that our office keep a distance from heads of state that could be eventual suspects. They considered that my direct interaction with President Museveni and the referral text could affect my impartiality perception.

Darryl Robinson explained the complexity of combining two different legal frames, international and criminal law.

> As a matter of international law, a territorial state is a lawful authority in the territory whose cooperation is required to carry out meaningful operations on its soil. As a matter of criminal law, those authorities are also potential targets of investigation. Combining these strands, in international criminal law, territorial states are both lawful authorities whose cooperation is valuable and also objects of analysis and investigation.[48]

The supporters of international criminal justice did not want to debate with the humanitarian and Christian NGOs that opposed our intervention; they aimed to influence and transform our approach. HRW adjusted its 2003 position proposing a political agreement. In 2004 it started to demand justice and assumed the ICC Office of the Prosecutor's obligation to investigate the Ugandan troops and the LRA's crimes simultaneously. HRW presented as a duty what it is just one of many possible tactics by the prosecutor.[49]

"Human Rights Watch has documented many shocking abuses by the LRA in Uganda," said Richard Dicker, director of the International Justice program at HRW. "But the ICC prosecutor cannot ignore the crimes that Ugandan government troops allegedly have committed."[50] HRW was trying to avoid the perception of a partial Office of the Prosecutor.

Still, its early criticism of our *jus ad Curiam* decision aimed to influence our resolutions during the following *jus in Curiae* phase. Without intention, HRW criticism promoted the narrative of lack of impartiality alleged by the Acholi community.

I thought the criticism was premature. We were in the *jus ad Curiam* phase, and aligning the state position with our mandate was very helpful. Additionally, even President Museveni recognized that we would identify the suspects and the incidents without any limitation. More importantly, the discussion diverted the attention from the difficult task of investigating and stopping the LRA's crimes.

The 2003 HRW report did not analyze if the allegations against Uganda's security forces constituted war crimes or crimes against humanity and recognized the existence of some national proceedings that could make such investigations inadmissible.[51]

The criticism of bias in favor of the Uganda's president reappeared during our bi-annual meeting with civil society organizations. I was less patient with the global NGOs based in New York than those living in Gulu. In my opinion, I was receiving unfounded criticism constituting an improper attempt to influence our decisions affecting the cooperation needed to stop the crimes.

I challenged the NGOs that criticized my meeting with President Museveni, explaining that I had to deal with heads of states as an international prosecutor. It was part of my mandate to obtain information as well as their cooperation.

"I could understand that you don't like Museveni, but I have no option. He is the Uganda President." I went further: "Can you make a list of the leaders I can meet? Can I meet Prime Minister Berlusconi, who is indicted for corruption? or President Bush? If I can only meet the Prime Minister of Sweden or Norway, I will not be able to do my job."

I ended, "You were fighting at Rome for the Prosecutor's independence, and you won. It was a crucial fight, creating a completely different kind of international organization, but as a consequence, I am independent, even from you." My attitude did not increase my popularity with HRW.

As an example of the complexities of international dynamics, during the review conference in Kampala in 2010, the same NGO members criticizing our meeting with President Museveni were having dinner at the presidential palace and shaking hands with him.

The Criticism of the Territorial State Referral Policy

We implemented our policy to invite states referral for the first time in DRC. But its implementation in Uganda generated significant criticism and the labeling of "self-referrals."

One of the most prolific writers on this theme was William Schabas, who affirmed that such a policy had no basis in the Rome Statute and its diplomatic negotiations. He labeled it as a "flawed sophomoric experiments," which "distort[s] the proper role of the Court."[52]

Similarly, an influential article by Mahnoush Arsanjani and W. Michael Reisman expressed that our interpretations were departing from the text of the statute. They warned that states might seek to co-opt or use the ICC to pursue adversaries or resolve internal political problems.[53]

Those comments ignored the legal text, the drafting history and assumed without any reason that the Office of the Prosecutor compromised its impartiality. In a paper published in 2011, Darryl Robinson clarified the confusion.

He said, the "critiques assert, rather categorically, that there is 'no indication,' 'not a trace' and 'not the slightest hint' in the drafting history that territorial state referrals were ever contemplated. Surprisingly, the cited records establish the opposite . . . the controversy was not whether to allow territorial state referrals; it was whether states parties without a direct interest such as territory should also be allowed to make referrals."[54]

Robinson shows that the opposite interpretation "to preclude self-referrals would require that we read" words that are not in the statute.[55] Article 14(1) establishes, "A State Party may refer to the Prosecutor a situation in which one or more crimes within the jurisdiction of the Court appear to have been committed requesting the Prosecutor to investigate the situation."

Professor Schabas also presented a policy objection: "when a State is actively engaged in initiation of the process, there is potential for manipulation. In effect, the state quite predictably uses the international institution to pursue its enemies."[56] Professor Schabas argued that self-referrals entail an "implied compact with governments" or a "degree of complicity" between the state and the Office of the Prosecutor.

To be sure, political authorities made *jus ad Curiam* decisions motivated by their own interests. It happened after World War II, during the Balkans and Rwanda conflicts, and at the Rome Conference. DRC and Uganda's leaders followed their interests when they referred their situations to our office.

The US National Security Strategy set out by President Obama in 2010 presented self-interest as an explicit policy: "[W]e are supporting the ICC's prosecution of those cases that advance US interests and values."[57]

However, as "the International Court of Justice (ICJ) has noted, the motives of a state or body of states in triggering a legal process are legally irrelevant."[58]

States or Security Council referrals are adopted following political views, but such a circumstance does not affect "the validity of the referral."[59]

The distinction between *jus ad Curiam* and *jus in Curiae* helps to analyze the problem. The *jus in Curiae* decisions, including the value of the evidence obtained, the charges, and identifying the incidents and the suspects, should not involve political actors. However, by design, during the *jus ad Curiam* decisions, the Office of the Prosecutor must interact with states authorities.[60]

Robinson highlighted how the wrong external comments could affect the Office of the Prosecutor legitimacy: "the prospect of improper understandings attached to territorial state referrals has graduated in the literature from speculation to presumed fact." Now commentators are assuming "the impropriety that they purport to prove."[61] More than eight commentators followed Professor Schabas's mistaken analysis.

Triggering the Jurisdiction of the Court in Uganda

The Decision to Open an Investigation in the Light of the Facts

In June 2004, the Office of the Prosecutor's Executive Committee received the internal Article 53 report assessing the Uganda situation and considering that the referral included all crimes committed in Northern Uganda since July 1, 2002.[62] There was a reasonable basis to believe that crimes against humanity and war crimes during an armed conflict between the Uganda government and LRA were committed.

Kony's criminal intentions were easy to prove; he publicly called to commit crimes against humanity, justifying his decision to target and punish the Acholi people for their alleged collaboration with Uganda's government. Although there was some information to indicate that elements within Sudan may have provided support and supplies to the LRA, there was no confrontation between the two national armies. Therefore, it was an internal conflict.

The absolute majority of these crimes appeared to have been committed by LRA members. However, the report found that some war crimes were allegedly committed by the Uganda People's Defence Force (UPDF) within the temporal jurisdiction of the ICC,

Uganda had the institutions to conduct judicial proceedings. We found a few criminal investigations against members of Uganda's army in Gulu civil courts. Still, due to the amnesty law, the referral indicated that Uganda did not initiate and did not intend to conduct criminal proceedings against the "LRA."

In terms of gravity, we found that between July 2002 and June 2004, the LRA was allegedly responsible for more than 1,800 murders, at least 2,600 abductions, and approximately 400 instances of torture. LRA committed the gravest crimes in Northern Uganda since July 1, 2002.

During the preliminary examination phase, the information gathered did not provide a basis to consider that the UPDF alleged crimes reached the level of gravity required for potential cases to be admissible under Article 17. In any case, we continued monitoring them and the existence of national proceedings.

In terms of "interest of justice," in June 2004, there was no information about any negotiation to end the conflict. Consequently, it was unnecessary to decide whether a peace process constituted a reason to suspend the opening of an investigation.

We still exercised caution, taking into consideration our meeting with the Scandinavian ambassador. We delayed for another month the beginning of the Uganda investigation. On July 29, 2004, the Office of the Prosecutor decided to open an investigation into the situation in Northern Uganda.

The Interest of the Victims

Since February 2004, the office conducted twenty-five field missions to meet with local and international stakeholders to understand the context and the victim's interests. During the following months, we met NGOs and experts that supported international criminal justice but challenged our decisions on accepting a referral and selecting LRA's crimes. During the investigations, we refined our understanding of the "interest of the victims" and made efforts to harmonize our position with the communities affected.

In April 2005, we held a meeting with an expanded list of delegates and leaders from communities affected by Kony's attacks, including the Acholi, Lango, Teso, and Madi areas; and Mirjam Blaak, Uganda's ambassador before the Netherlands. The first day of the meeting was very complicated.

The Lango, Teso, and Madi communities perceived Kony as a foreigner. Those communities and the Acholi also distrusted the Ugandan government and were afraid of LRA. Many considered that our judicial mandate could exacerbate violence.

The following day, we focused the discussions on the ICC's and the community leaders' respective contributions in pursuit of the common goal of ending violence. We explained that the office had been in touch with the government of Sudan, and we were discussing an agreement to enforce the arrest warrant in their territory.

Finally, we reached some consensus around Sudan's role in protecting the LRA and the possibility to combine traditional justice mechanisms with the office's policy to pursue only those most responsible.

All the parties issued a joint statement appealing to the government of Sudan "to continue cooperating with the Government of Uganda, the ICC, international actors, and all stakeholders in an effort to bring peace to Uganda."[63]

The consensus was short-lived. It ended as soon as they were back in Uganda. But it was beneficial to understand their views.

The Office of the UN High Commissioner for Human Rights studied the victims' perceptions in Northern Uganda, confirming that the respondent victims considered both amnesty and prosecution necessary responses to harm.[64]

The office concluded that respecting the *victims'* interest implies a duty to be mindful of divergent views without affecting the prosecution's respect for its legal mandate. "The Office will give due consideration to the different views of victims, their communities, and the broader societies in which it may be required to act."[65]

The ICC Jurisdiction in Uganda as Not Controversial

The Court's Assessment on Admissibility

During the second part of 2004, we had to develop our security protocols to conduct investigations in Northern Uganda while the LRA was very active. Our team of lawyers and investigators integrating people from Tanzania, Nigeria, Portugal, the United States, United Kingdom, France, and New Zealand had to invent formulas to blend in the region and keep a low profile.

The office was able to conduct an in-depth and efficient investigation in only nine months. On May 6, 2005, we requested to Pre-Trial

Chamber II to issue an arrest warrant against Joseph Kony and his four top commanders.

In July 2005, Pre-Trial Chamber II decided to issue all the arrest warrants requested. The chamber was presided by Judge Tuiloma Neroni Slade, a former prosecutor and attorney general from Samoa, who represented his country at the Rome Conference and later became Samoa's UN, Permanent Representative.

Judge Fatoumata Dembele Diarra and Judge Mauro Politti, a former prosecutor and judge from Italy, and a member of his country delegation at the Rome Conference, integrated the chamber.

The judges considered, "without prejudice to subsequent determination, the case against Joseph Kony, Vincent Otti, Raska Lukwiya, Okot Odhiambo, and Dominic Ongwen falls within the jurisdiction of the Court and appears to be admissible."[66]

Ten years later, in January 2015, Dominic Ongwen appeared before the ICC, but he did not challenge the court's jurisdiction. The pre-trial chamber was presided over by Judge Cuno Tarfusser. Judge Marc Perrin de Brichambaut, a French judge with extensive international experience, also integrated the chamber.[67] The third member was Judge Chang-ho Chung, an experienced South Korean judge. He previously served as a United Nations International Judge in the Extraordinary Chambers in Cambodia's courts from 2011 to 2015.

The judges decided, ". . . in accordance with article 19 of the Statute, the Chamber is satisfied that the Court has jurisdiction over the present case."[68]

Multiple Frames of Analysis

At the beginning of our work, we took a *jus ad Curiam* decision that different judges reviewed at various times and confirmed eleven years later. But the analysis of our legal choices exposed the other frameworks used by the experts:

(a) HRW considered that the prosecution must investigate at the same time all the sides of the conflict to be impartial.

(b) Experts like Phil Clark did not appreciate "the ICC' s model of 'neutral and impartial' justice."[69] He did not analyze our legal framework and made no distinctions: for him, ICC was "the latest in a long line of international actors that have intervened in Africa, including European colonial powers, the World Bank and International Monetary Fund."[70]

(c) Sara Nouwen did not provide evidence of our partiality. Still, she alleged that we took the political decision to be on the Museveni side and used international law's uncertainty to cover our intentions.[71] Similarly, Professor Schabas considered that "the Prosecutor does make political choices," although he recognized that his comment is based "upon intuition rather than evidence."[72]

These commentators reached three different conclusions exposing the application of multiple non-legal frameworks. According to those commentators, the Office of the Prosecutor impartiality implies (a) a duty to investigate all the sides simultaneously, (b) an imperialistic approach, or (c) a political cover-up. Their competing narratives affect the desirable consensus of the international community of experts.

As indicated by a bright PhD candidate, Sophie T. Rosenberg, "the political vision of impartiality dictates that the Prosecutor should remain politically neutral by ensuring its actions do not appear to favor one side of the domestic balance of power."[73] But legal impartiality "does not require the Prosecutor to consciously avoid influencing the domestic balance of power."[74]

Notes

1. They were supported by Marieke Wierda, from the International Center for Transitional Justice; Eric Stover, faculty director of the Human Rights Center, University of California at Berkeley; and Adrian di Giovanni, from the International Development Research Centre, Canada. PHUONG PHAM ET AL, FORGOTTEN VOICES: A POPULATION-BASED SURVEY OF ATTITUDES ABOUT PEACE AND JUSTICE IN NORTHERN UGANDA (2005).

2. The Harvard Humanitarian Initiative used the "population-based data" model to understand victims' interests in more than fifteen situations. Patrick Vinck et al., *Exposure to War Crimes and Implications for Peace Building in Northern Uganda*, 298 JAMA, 543, 543 (2007).

3. Hum. Rts. Watch, *Abducted and Abused* (July 15, 2003).

4. *Id.*

5. *Id.*

6. *Id.*

7. *The report emphasized that the* "Ugandan Legal Institutions Including the Police, the Judiciary, and the Uganda Human Rights Commission" *have to* "Ensure that the treason and anti-terrorism provisions of the Ugandan Penal Code are not applied to any person without a thorough investigation and are not used to detain persons (especially if they are political opposition members) against whom there is little or no evidence." *Id.*

8. Elizabeth Rubin, *Our Children Are Killing Us*, New Yorker (Mar. 23, 1998), https://www.newyorker.com/magazine/1998/03/23/our-children-are-killing-us.

9. *Id.*

10. The Lord's Resistance Army established a routine of attacking schools throughout the 1990s and continued to do so after its return from Sudan in 2002. Many schools have been closed or displaced, and many families are reluctant to send their children to school, for fear of abduction. Hum. Rts. Watch, *Abducted and Abused* (July 15, 2003).

11. The DRC sought reparation for acts of intentional destruction and looting and the restitution of national property and resources appropriated for the benefit of Uganda and Rwanda. Armed Activities in the Territory of Congo (Democratic Republic of the Congo v. Uganda), ICJ (last visited Apr. 14, 2020), https://www.icj-cij.org/en/case/116.

12. "[A]nd not rely on unsubstantiated or uncorroborated information forwarded to him . . . part of which may be as a result of overzealous individuals who want to settle old scores or grievances." *See, e.g.*, Statement of the Representative of Uganda, Sixth Comm., Summary record of the 10th mtg., agenda item 154, U.N. GAOR 58th Sess. U/N. Doc. A/C.6/58/SR.10 (Nov. 30, 2005).

13. Phil Clark spoke with an official in the MoD who explained, "The President's Office contacted us about communications received from the [ICC] Prosecutor. The Court wanted to discuss what a referral from our side would . . . mean for both parties. . . . We didn't go looking for that—it came from them. In all truth, it was a blessing because we'd tried everything against the LRA—[peace] talks, military operations, amnesties. We needed a new approach and here was something new, something unexpected." Phill Clark, Distant Justice: The Impact of the International Criminal Court on African Politics 73 (Kindle ed. 2018). *See also* Sarah M. H. Nouwen, Complementarity in the Line Fire: The Catalyst Effect of the International Criminal Court in Sudan and Uganda (Kindle ed., Cambridge Series in Law and Society, 2013).

14. Rod Rastan, *What Is the "Case" for the Purpose of the Rome Statute?*, 19 Crim. L. Forum 435, 435 (2008)

15. *Id.*

16. Amnesty Act (2000), Part II, Section 3 (1).

17. Paul Seils & Marieke Wierda, *The International Criminal Court and Conflict Mediation*, International Center for Transitional Justice (June 2005), https://www.ictj.org/sites/default/files/ICTJ-Global-ICC-Mediation-2005-English.pdf.

18. In her 1999 analysis of the statute, Ruth Wedgood presented that the Rome Statute, "skirted the question of amnesties" as the first question. Ruth Wedgwood, *The International Criminal Court: An American View*, 10 Eur. J. of Int'l L., 93, 97 (1999).

19. SARAH M. H. NOUWEN, COMPLEMENTARITY IN THE LINE FIRE: THE CATALYST EFFECT OF THE INTERNATIONAL CRIMINAL COURT IN SUDAN AND UGANDA 125–26 (Kindle ed., Cambridge Series in Law and Society, 2013).

20. *Id.*

21. Anthony Vinci, *Existential Motivations in the Lord's Resistance Army's Continuing Conflict*, 30 (4) STUDIES IN CONFLICT & TERRORISM 337, 348 (2007) as quoted by David Lanz, *The ICC's Intervention in Northern Uganda: Beyond the Simplicity of Peace vs. Justice*, RELIEF WEB https://reliefweb.int/sites/reliefweb.int/files/resources/EC662 15A0071F156C12573910051D06D-Full_Report.pdf, (last visited Apr. 24, 2020).

22. *Democratic Republic of Congo: The Conflict in Focus*, CONCILIATION RESOURCES, https://www.c-r.org/where-we-work/east-and-central-africa/history-lords-resista nce-army-conflict (last visited Apr. 15, 2020).

23. SARAH M. H. NOUWEN, COMPLEMENTARITY IN THE LINE FIRE: THE CATALYST EFFECT OF THE INTERNATIONAL CRIMINAL COURT IN SUDAN AND UGANDA 127–28 (Kindle ed., Cambridge Series in Law and Society, 2013).

24. Barney Afako, *Reconciliation and Justice: "Mato oput" and the Amnesty Act*, 11 ACCORD 64, 64 (2002).

25. Betty Bigombe, then minister of state for the Pacification of Northern Uganda, met with Kony to negotiate a settlement.

26. 1996–1997: The Acholi Diaspora organization Kacoke Madit and the Catholic peace organization Sant'Edigio also organized talks between the LRA secretary for External Affairs and Mobilization, James Obita, and the government of Uganda. 1998–2002: Carter Centre. 2002–2003: Acholi Religious Leaders' Peace Initiative (ARLPI).

27. Philip T. Reeker, deputy spokesman, Statement on the Designation of 39 Organizations on the USA Patriot Act as a Terrorist Exclusion List in Washington DC (Dec. 6, 2001).

28. Hum. Rts. Watch, *Abducted and Abused* (July 15, 2003).

29. SARAH M. H. NOUWEN, COMPLEMENTARITY IN THE LINE FIRE: THE CATALYST EFFECT OF THE INTERNATIONAL CRIMINAL COURT IN SUDAN AND UGANDA 129 (Kindle ed., Cambridge Series, 2013).

30. *Id.* at 126–29.

31. Payam Akhavan, *The Lord's Resistance Army Case: Uganda's Submission of the First State Referral to the International Criminal Court*, 99 AM. J. OF INT'L L. 403, 404 (2005).

32. Sara Nouwen said that "in December 2003, when due to its confidentiality the referral was not yet known to the Ugandan Parliament, the executive gazetted an Amendment Bill to exclude 'leaders of rebellion' as beneficiaries of the amnesty." *Id.* at 211.

33. In April 2006, parliament passed the Amnesty Amendment Bill (2003), PHIL CLARK, DISTANT JUSTICE: THE IMPACT OF THE INTERNATIONAL CRIMINAL COURT ON AFRICAN POLITICS 221 (Kindle ed. Cambridge University Press).

34. The policy of inviting referrals "has met with widespread approval from the ninety-eight states parties to the Rome Statute, which is vital for the Office of the Prosecutor's ongoing efforts to build up a viable support network for the investigations and effective cooperation on judicial assistance." Hans-Peter Kaul, *Construction Site for More*

Justice: The International Criminal Court after Two Years, 99 AM. J. OF INT'L L. 370, 374 (2005).

35. PHUONG PHAM ET AL, FORGOTTEN VOICES: A POPULATION-BASED SURVEY OF ATTITUDES ABOUT PEACE AND JUSTICE IN NORTHERN UGANDA (2005).

36. *Id.*

37. "I can confirm that the scope of the referral will be interpreted in accordance with the principles underlying the Statute. I will investigate all crimes related to the situation in an impartial way. I will continue to receive information from any source on crimes within the jurisdiction of the Court." Luis Moreno Ocampo, Chief Prosecutor of the International Criminal Court, Statement to Diplomatic Corps in The Hague (Feb. 12, 2004).

38. "In their letter the Ugandan government referred the 'situation concerning the Lord's Resistance Army.' We explained to them that the scope of the referral would be interpreted following the principles underlying the Rome Statute." Luis Moreno-Ocampo, Chief Prosecutor of the International Criminal Court, Remarks at the 27th meeting of the Committee of Legal Advisers on Public International Law (CADHI) held in Strasburg, (Mar. 18 & 19, 2004).

39. *Id.*

40. "I am ready to be investigated for war crimes...(ellipsis as published) and if any of our people were involved in any crimes, we will give him up to be tried by the ICC,"... "And in any case, if such cases are brought to our attention, we will try them ourselves," Museveni said." *Id.*

41. *Position Paper on the ICC*, ARLPI (Apr. 30, 2004).

42. Tim Allen, *War and Justice in Northern Uganda: an Assessment of the International Criminal Court's Intervention*, Special Report Crises States Programme, Development Studies Institute, London School of Economics, (Jan. 1, 2005). *See* Martha Minow, *Do Alternative Justice Mechanisms Deserve Recognition in International Criminal Law: Truth Commissions, Amnesties, and Complementarity at the International Criminal Court*, 60 HARV. INT'L L.J. 1 (2019).

43. Tim Allen, *The International Criminal Court and the Invention of Traditional Justice in Northern Uganda*, 107 POLITIQUE AFRICAINE 147, 149 (2005).

44. A follow-up study was carried out in 2007, based on interviews with 2,875 people. When asked which mechanisms would be most appropriate to deal with those LRA and UPDF responsible for violations of human rights, equal numbers mentioned the ICC (29 percent) and the Ugandan national Court system (28 percent). Twenty percent said the amnesty commission. Only 3 percent mentioned traditional ceremonies. Simon Simonse, Willemijn Verkoren & Gerd Junne, *NGO Involvement in the Juba Peace Talks: The Role and Dilemmas of IKV Pax Christi, in* THE LORD'S RESISTANCE ARMY: MYTH AND REALITY 318 (Tim Allen & Koen Vlassenroot eds., 2010).

45. PHUONG PHAM ET AL, FORGOTTEN VOICES: A POPULATION-BASED SURVEY OF ATTITUDES ABOUT PEACE AND JUSTICE IN NORTHERN UGANDA (2005).

46. "Another issue was the impact of the announcement of the referral by means of a joint press conference by the Office of the Prosecutor and President Yoweri Museveni. This

caused the perception that the Prosecutor was being manipulated by the government, which is itself party to the conflict."

Paul Seils & Marieke Wierda, *The International Criminal Court and Conflict Mediation*, INTERNATIONAL CENTER FOR TRANSITIONAL JUSTICE (June, 2005), https://www.ictj.org/sites/default/files/ICTJ-Global-ICC-Mediation-2005-English.pdf.

47. "[B]y referring only the crimes of the rebel side to the Prosecutor, President Museveni blocks an investigation into any allegations against the conduct of his own UPDF [Ugandan People's Defence Forces] forces in Northern Uganda." Chidi Anslem Odinkalu, *Uganda: Museveni Has Been Clever, Will ICC Be Wise?*, THE VANGUARD (Feb. 6, 2004), http://allafrica.com/stories/200402060623.html.

48. Darryl Robinson, *The Controversy over Territorial State Referrals and Reflections on ICL Discourse*, 9 J. INT'L CRIM. JUST. 355, 368 (2011).

49. The idea is still presented as a measure of impartiality: Tiemesen proposed to use "a relatively objective measure of impartiality—the degree to which the Court's prosecutorial strategy holds both sides of a conflict accountable for what are verifiable atrocities." Alana Tiemessen, *The International Criminal Court and the Politics of Prosecutions*, 18 INT'L J. OF HUM. RTS 444, 445 (2014).

50. *ICC: Investigate All Sides in Uganda*, HUM. RGTS. WATCH (Feb. 4, 2004, 07:00 PM), https://www.hrw.org/news/2004/02/04/icc-investigate-all-sides-uganda.

51. "Although the Ugandan government has an obligation to intervene to end such abuses, government forces themselves have been responsible for human rights violations, including cases of torture and rape, summary execution, and arbitrary detention of suspects. Government investigators have pursued some cases of abuse by UPDF soldiers, but prosecutions have languished and wrongdoers continue to enjoy virtual impunity." Hum. Rts. Watch, *Abducted and Abused* (July 15, 2003).

52. William Schabas, *Complementarity in Practice: Some Uncomplimentary Thoughts*, 19 CRIMINAL L. FORUM 5 (2009).

53. Darryl Robinson, *The Controversy over Territorial State Referrals and Reflections on ICL Discourse*, 9 J. INT'L CRIM. JUST. 355, 367(2011).

54. *Id.* at 363.

55. *Id.* at 360.

56. *Id.* at 367.

57. THE WHITE HOUSE, UNITED STATES NATIONAL SECURITY STRATEGY (May 2010),

58. Darryl Robinson, *The Controversy over Territorial State Referrals and Reflections on ICL Discourse*, 9 J. INT'L CRIM. JUST. 355, 367 (2011).

59. "A state may have any number of obvious or hidden motivations when it issues a referral concerning its territory, just as it may when referring a situation on other state's territory (e.g., embarrassing an enemy, appeasing an interest group, etc.) Similarly, Security Council members may have geostrategic, domestic, and reputational considerations in mind when referring situations." *Id.* at 368. *See also* Vladimir Tochilovsky, *Objectivity of the ICC Preliminary Examinations*, *in* QUALITY CONTROL IN PRELIMINARY EXAMINATION: VOL. 2 395 (Morten Bergsmo & Carsten Stahn eds., 2018).

60. *Id.* at 369.

61. Thus, in the most recent article, Muller and Stegmiller assert as a simple matter of fact that self-referrals "will often be accompanied and burdened by 'understandings' between The Hague and the referring state that can taint the subsequent proceedings." *Id.*

62. Office of the Prosecutor, *Report on the Activities Performed during the First Three Years (June 2003–June 2006)*, ICC (Sept. 12, 2006), https://www.icc-cpi.int/NR/rdonly res/D76A5D89-FB64-47A9-9821-725747378AB2/143680/OTP_3yearreport20060 914_English.pdf.

63. *Joint Statement by ICC Chief Prosecutor and the visiting Delegation of Lango, Acholi, Iteso and Madi Community Leaders from Northern Uganda*, ICC (Apr. 16, 2005), https://www.icc-cpi.int/Pages/item.aspx?name=joint%20statement%20by%20 icc%20chief%20prosecutor%20and%20the%20visiting%20delegation%20of%20la ngo%20ach.

64. The United Nations Office of the High Commissioner for Human Rights conducted a qualitative research study "over six months from January to June 2007." UN Office of the High Comm. for Hum. Rts, *Making Peace Our Own: Victims' Perceptions of Accountability, Reconciliation and Transitional Justice in Northern Uganda* (Aug. 2007).

65. Office of the Prosecutor, *Policy Paper on the Interests of Justice*, ICC (Sept. 2007), https://www.icc-cpi.int/NR/rdonlyres/772C95C9-F54D-4321-BF09-73422BB23 528/143640/ICCOTPInterestsOfJustice.pdf.

66. Situation in Uganda, ICC-02/04-01/05-1-US-Exp 12-07-2005 2/1, Pre-Trial Camber II (July 8, 2005), https://www.icc-cpi.int/CourtRecords/CR2006_01019.PDF.

67. He was legal adviser to the French Foreign Ministry, served as secretary-general of the Organisation for Security and Cooperation in Europe (OSCE) from 2005 to 2011, and had taught extensively international law in Sciences-Po in Paris.

68. "The Prosecutor charges Dominic Ongwen with crimes against humanity under article 7 and war crimes under article 8 of the Statute (jurisdiction ratione materiae) committed on the territory of the Uganda (jurisdiction ratione loci) between 1 July 2002 and 31 December 2005 (jurisdiction ratione temporis, see ICC-02/04-01/15-3-Conf-AnxB), and which fall within the parameters of the situation referred by Uganda to the Prosecutor (ICC-02/04-01/15-3-Conf-AnxA and ICC-02/04-1)." Prosecutor v. Dominic Ongwen, ICC-02/04-01/15, Pre-Trial Chamber II Decision on the confirmation of charges against Dominic Ongwen (Mar. 26, 2016), https://www. icc-cpi.int/CourtRecords/CR2016_02331.PDF.

69. Phill Clark, Distant Justice: The Impact of the International Criminal Court on African Politics 4 (Kindle ed. 2018).

70. *Id.* at 422–26.

71. Sarah M. H. Nouwen, Complementarity in the Line Fire: The Catalyst Effect of the International Criminal Court in Sudan and Uganda 33 (Kindle ed., Cambridge Series in Law and Society, 2013). *See also* Sarah M. Nouwen & Wouter G. Werner, *Doing Justice to the Political: The International Criminal Court in Uganda and Sudan*, 21 EJIL, 491 (2010).

72. "The thesis in this article is that the Prosecutor does, in fact, make political choices. He does not seriously consider for prosecution all admissible situations that fall within the jurisdiction of the Court." William A. Schabas, *Victor's Justice: Selecting "Situations" at the International Criminal Court*, 43 (3) JOHN MARSHALL L. REV. 535, 549 (2010). And Rod Rastan considered that the charge of "politicised selectivity (not a light charge)" was based as Schabas recognized "upon intuition rather than evidence." Rod Rastan, *Comment on Victor's Justice & The Viability of Ex Ante Standards*, 43 (3) JOHN MARSHALL L. REV. 569, 575 (2010).

73. Sophie T. Rosenberg, *The International Criminal Court in Cote d'Ivoire. Impartiality at Stake?*, 15 J. INT'L CRIMINAL JUST. 471 (2017).

74. *Id.*

8

The Office of the Prosecutor Policy
on "Interest of Justice"

The chapter presents the Office of the Prosecutor interpretation of Article 53 1(c) and 2(c), establishing its authority "not to proceed" with an investigation if the prosecution is not in "the interests of justice."

Our understanding was adopted from the beginning of my tenure, refined by our practice in Darfur, Colombia, particularly Uganda, and formalized into a specific policy in September 2007: Under the Rome Statute, the broader matter of international peace and security is not the office's responsibility; it falls within other institutions' mandates, including states and the UN Security Council.

During the Rome Conference in 1998, states perceived the tension between negotiations to end a conflict and the duty to prosecute. They adopted Article 16, providing authority to the UN Security Council to suspend investigations. Still, they could not find a common position regarding the Office of the Prosecutor authority to stop investigations.

"Views on the matter clashed sharply, as many participants felt very strongly that prosecution is the sole appropriate response (and indeed an obligatory response), whereas others felt very strongly that alternative mechanisms were acceptable . . . Thus, the drafters turned to the faithful and familiar friend of diplomats, ambiguity."[1]

States delegated the solution to the problem to the Office of the Prosecutor without providing a detailed frame. Ambiguity facilitated the Rome Statute's adoption, but it also promoted demands to the prosecutor to adjust to political demands.

States representatives privately demanded to the Office of the Prosecutor to adjust to their preferences. The ambassador who tried to stop the Uganda investigation's opening by saying that Kony was not taking his phone calls is just an example. We had similar experiences in other situations. An event that happened in January 2007, while preparing to present our first case in the Darfur situation, is even more descriptive.

War and Justice in the 21st Century. Luis Moreno Ocampo, Oxford University Press. © Oxford University Press 2022.
DOI: 10.1093/oso/9780197628973.003.0009

Our jurisdiction division (JCCD) received a phone call from an embassy's legal adviser at The Hague. She said, "We learned that you are preparing a case in Darfur against a minister. We believe you must go higher in the hierarchy. A minister is not enough." Our officer thanked the legal adviser for her interest and did not comment on the substance.

The same day, during the afternoon, the same legal adviser called again. She said, "I am very sorry, but I sent a cable to my capital including our conversation, and I received new instructions: my country considers that it is not a good time to present a case in Darfur. Our opinion is that you should stop your request."

The example shows how political priorities change in just hours and could not be considered by the Office of the Prosecutor. Adjusting to the political preferences violates the Office of the Prosecutor's duty to be independent[2] and impartial.[3]

Juan Mendez, who in those days was the president of the International Center for Transitional Justice (ICTJ) and Special Advisor on the Prevention of Genocide to the UN Secretary-General, described the role of a criminal justice system and its interrelation with a political process:

> For justice to have a preventive effect, the most important condition is that justice has to follow its own rules, especially to allow the operation of the law without interference and not subject to political considerations. Paradoxically, justice contributes to peace and prevention when it is not conceived as an instrument to either.[4]

Part 1 of this chapter presents the background and the public discussion on our draft policy. It also describes the impact of the ICC's arrest warrants against LRA's top commanders, contributing to remove the militia from Uganda and Sudan. The "Juba talks" opened at the LRA's initiative, created the possibility to reach an agreement to end the conflict. The negotiation triggered conflictive demands on our office: to facilitate the talks requesting the arrest warrants' removal following the "interest of justice"[5] or, the opposite view encouraging the office to be very active publicly demanding immediate compliance with the arrest warrants.

Part 2 exposes the adoption in September 2007 of the Prosecutor's Policy on the "interest of justice." We understood the importance of limiting our authority to strict judicial matters. We elucidated the distinction between the "interest of justice" and "the interest of peace," respecting the political actors' authority and their responsibility, including the UN Security Council on matters of international peace.[6]

We were ready to respect any UN Security Council decision to suspend our investigations following Article 16. Furthermore, in the situations referred by the council, we adopted a policy to inform the council in advance of the issuance of arrest warrants. Our policy paper made transparent that the Office of the Prosecutor's mandate did not include participating in political negotiations. However, there are still political actors, negotiators, and experts demanding that the prosecutor adjusts to political negotiations.

Part 1: Background of "The Interest of Justice Clause"

Gilbert Bitti participated in the statute discussions from 1995 until 1998. He explained that the first informal proposal was made by the United Kingdom delegation to empower the prosecutor *not* to file an indictment when it was *not* in *the interests of justice*.[7]

The goal was to provide "wide discretion on the part of the prosecutor to decide not to investigate comparable to that in (some) domestic systems." An example invoked was "if the suspected offender was very old or very ill." But the project also included the discretion to refuse to prosecute even though a prima face case against an accused has been established if "there were good reasons to conclude that a prosecution would be counter-productive."

The difference between civil and common law traditions elicited lengthy and challenging negotiations about the "interests of justice" at the Rome Conference. The UK proposal was consistent with the common law tradition to provide discretion to prosecutors to select the incidents and the suspects following the *opportunity principle*. In England and Wales, the Code for Crown Prosecutors establishes a public interest test that prosecutors should consider.[8]

Neither the US law nor the US courts have found a duty to prosecute. "If anything, one of the distinctive features of US law is that prosecutors have almost unlimited discretion not to prosecute."[9]

In the civil law model, prosecutors usually are not free to choose incidents or suspects. In Italy, for instance, the legality principle or principle of mandatory prosecution requires that the prosecutor file charges whenever there is sufficient evidence to do so.[10] In recent decades, the opportunity principle was partially introduced in civil law traditions like Germany and Latin America.[11]

An agreement on Article 53 of the Statute was only reached in the last week of the conference. Even so, a footnote was attached "some delegations expressed concern regarding the reference to the interests of justice."

Some concerns were "that (powerful) States may push the Prosecutor, by threatening, for example, not to cooperate with the Court, to use the 'interests of justice' criterion in order not to start an investigation or a prosecution for the purposes of protecting their own nationals."[12] The argument was used in 2019 by the pre-trial chamber to refuse authorization to the prosecutor to open an investigation in Afghanistan.

The statute drafting history further reveals that the "interests of justice" criterion was exclusively designed as a negative determination with a significant consequence.[13] The statute allowed the prosecutor to submit a request for the opening of an investigation without submitting any material on the "interest of justice," *in* "contrast with the jurisdiction and admissibility criteria where the Prosecutor must make positive determinations."[14]

Preparing the Policy in the Interest of Justice

The Guidelines of the Rome Statute

During the public hearings at the Peace Palace after my swearing in, we received recommendations to develop a "clear criteria according to which decisions to take no further action are taken 'in the interests of justice.'"[15] Since then, the prosecution had looked closely into the interaction between peace negotiations and criminal investigations and started to prepare a formal policy.

Without using the labels, we found a fundamental difference between the *jus ad Curiam* and *jus in Curiae* phases.

We considered that the Office of the Prosecutor's discretion is very limited during the *jus ad Curiam* phase. Instead, the prosecutor's discretion is bigger in selecting incidents and suspects.

At the end of a *preliminary examination,* there are two mandatory options: the prosecution should abstain from intervening when national institutions conduct genuine proceedings. Alternatively, the prosecution must trigger the court's intervention to ensure the "end of impunity" if the situation fulfills all of the Article 53 requirements.

Both different mandates were presented in the policy paper adopted in September 2003. We made clear that "The Prosecutor can proceed only where States fail to act or are not "genuinely" investigating or prosecuting." The policy paper also explained that "the ICC must fill the gap created by States' failure to satisfy their duty to investigate and the Office of the Prosecutor will need to exercise its investigative powers with firmness and efficiency."

Fabricio Guariglia, in charge of the Prosecution Division, and Emeric Rogier, responsible for the preliminary examination process for more than a decade, considered this: The statute has set clear criteria governing the process, and once these criteria are met, the duty of the prosecutor is to proceed.[16]

The policy paper explains our choices in selecting suspects between a massive number of perpetrators during the *jus ad Curiae* phase: "as a general rule, the Office of the Prosecutor should focus its investigative and prosecutorial efforts and resources on those who bear the greatest responsibility, such as the leaders of the State or organization allegedly responsible for those crimes." The collection of evidence defined the incidents and specific targets.

During my tenure, we devoted time and efforts to refine the Office of the Prosecutor policy in *the interest of justice.*

My First Meeting with Mediators

As part of our reflection, I participated in a confidential meeting at the UN headquarters in New York in 2004 to discuss the "Guidelines for UN representatives on certain aspects of negotiations for conflict resolutions." UN Secretary-General Kofi Annan adopted them confidentially in 1999, and UN experts debated their impact and renewal.[17]

Following the "Joinet Principles,"[18] the guidelines advised UN mediators to reject peace agreements that provide amnesties for atrocity crimes, highlighting states' legal obligations to end impunity for serious crimes.[19]

Alvaro de Soto, one of the top UN negotiators, led the 2004 discussion. The question presented was the following: Should the guidelines be updated?

One of the participating mediators gave his experience candidly at the beginning of the meeting: "These guidelines are so strict that put UN mediators out of business. I ignore them. As soon I start my conversations with the leaders involved in the conflict, I accept that an amnesty should be established. The focus of mediation is on the future."

I forced myself to remain silent. A small group of NGO representatives was in the room, and I imagined they would confront the mediator.

A few minutes later, when a representative of an international human rights NGO took the floor, she ignored the guidelines' lack of implementation. Instead, she proposed new constraints: "The guidelines were correct in 1999, but now they have to be adjusted to include gender issues and the rights of the children," she said without even mentioning the mediator's comments.

Idealism is a vital part of human rights movements and fits well with the diplomatic approach. Years later, an ambassador explained to me: *"at the UN, when we discuss principles, we do not discuss facts. When we discuss the facts, we don't discuss principles."* Diplomats need to reach agreements on different topics, and that model helps them manage conflicts with their colleagues.

During the discussions led by de Soto, I learned about the mediators' mindset and the lack of harmonization between the general principles and their enforcement. Before the meeting ended, I made my point on the specificity of my role as the ICC prosecutor, the need for mediators to learn about the court's jurisdiction in the situations where the negotiation is conducted, and the irrelevance of amnesties before international courts.

I had the impression that the meeting was informative, but it would not force the UN mediators to respect the guidelines' limits. I was wrong: three years later, the same "Guidelines" defined the UN role in the negotiations with Joseph Kony.

The Background of the Situation in Uganda

The Efforts to Negotiate with Joseph Kony

The analysis of the Uganda situation exposed the enormous difficulties to mediate a conflict and stop the violence. The LRA consistently used peace negotiations to recover from difficult circumstances and to obtain support. For instance, the 1994 peace negotiation was used by Kony to ally with Sudan's government against Museveni, the common enemy. The LRA became a *proxy force* in the conflict between North and South of Sudan.[20]

There were many new unsuccessful mediation efforts, including one led by the Carter Center between 1998 and 2002.[21] In 2003 the Acholi

Religious Leader Peace Initiative (ARLPI) obtained a ceasefire to facilitate negotiations. The truce was overridden by Kony when he killed his own representative.[22]

A few weeks later, in June 2003, the LRA attacked the Catholic Church clergy in retaliation for their role in the negotiation.[23]

HRW explained Kony's strategy combining negotiations, collecting resources and weapons, and attacking the Acholi in the internally displaced persons (IDP) camps.[24]

In May 2002, the Kacoke Madit,[25] the Acholi community in the diaspora, recognized that the LRA had no interest in peace. Joseph Kony's "position and leadership in the bush will be difficult, if not impossible, to sustain should he return to civilian life after a peace settlement, and it may therefore be unlikely that he should choose to do so."[26]

In February 2004, while the Office of the Prosecutor was conducting a preliminary examination of the Uganda situation, Betty Bigombe was in her house in Washington, DC. She had met with Joseph Kony in January 1994 to negotiate a settlement as the Minister of State for the Pacification of Northern Uganda. Ten years later, she saw the news about the Barlonyo attack and decided to *participate in the events.*

She requested a leave of absence from her job at the World Bank and, using her savings, traveled to Northern Uganda to start a new negotiation. There she found support from her community and some foreign states. In July 2004, we learned about Bigombe's efforts and established permanent communication with her.

On November 15, 2004, Bigombe succeeded in brokering a limited ceasefire between the LRA and the government of Uganda, which was subsequently extended for forty-seven days.

During that period, top LRA Political Commissar Sam Kolo met with Ugandan traditional, religious, and local government leaders as Kony's envoy.

A bishop involved in the negotiation later told me that one of the LRA's leaders said to him, "I don't understand what we are doing here. Normally, after ten minutes, we kill everybody." We were informed that a permanent ceasefire would be signed on December 30, 2004.

We continued our investigations during the entire peace process. A bishop who was against the LRA agreement suggested we go to his village to obtain evidence. I was very proud of our investigators' ability to maintain a low profile; we had already finished collecting testimonies in his village, and the bishop was not aware of it.

Bigombe 2004's negotiations forced us to reassess the "interest of justice" established by Article 53(2)(c), the norm to be eventually applied in the LRA case because the Uganda investigation was already opened. Should the Office of the Prosecutor suspend the Uganda investigations to facilitate Bigombe negotiation?

Already we had adopted the policy to keep investigating, but we were reassessing our answer to the question. In any case, the 2004 negotiation collapsed. Kony ordered the killing of Kolo, leading to his defection from the LRA, and refused to appear at the signing ceremony. Although another ceasefire began in February, it never picked up momentum.

The Legal Interpretation

On November 30 and December 1, 2004, we presented our deliberations during our biannual consultation with NGOs. We circulated a "Consultation Proposal on the Interests of Justice," asking for feedback. We presented ideas received by the office and our preliminary interpretation of the meaning of the phrase "in the interests of justice" included in the Rome Statute. We invited opinions on our policy.[27]

HRW *presented an in-depth* legal analysis of Article 16 describing the Office of the Prosecutor as "*a judicial, non-political organ, with no political legitimation.*" It concluded that "it is the Security Council, not the prosecutor, who is empowered to act, taking into account issues such as international peace and security."[28]

Amnesty International alerted that a policy to suspend investigations to facilitate political negotiations "would open the Court to permanent blackmail by warring factions implicated in crimes under international law."[29]

The International Federation for Human Rights (FIDH) presented its arguments supporting a similar line: "To invoke political negotiations not to investigate would thus go against the spirit and the letter of the Rome Statute."[30]

In a much more nuanced opinion, the ICTJ, inspired by the South African truth commission experience,[31] identified the relevant issue as "the interplay between negotiation efforts and the activities of the ICC which may be proceeding on parallel tracks."[32]

The ICTJ admitted the deferral of trials that directly contributed to increased political instability until such risk had significantly receded.[33] In agreement with HRW, it presented the UN Security Council as the proper forum. "Should mediators strongly feel that an investigation was likely to have serious negative consequences, it may be appropriate for them to make their concerns known to the Council and to suggest a deferral."[34]

The ICTJ also recalled that "the obligations assumed by states under the ICC Statute reinforce the position that certain kinds of amnesties are simply not negotiable." Therefore, negotiators must be clear "that the matter is essentially out of their control and to concentrate less on the issue of amnesty and more on the question of what other measures that address past abuses may be appropriate." The ICTJ emphasized that it would be up to the court and not the state to determine if alternatives were acceptable.[35]

We agreed with most of the legal points discussed. The issue was not about the convenience or the opportunity to negotiate. In our opinion, our mandate did not include the authority to manage political negotiations.

The Issuance of the Arrest Warrants and the Agreement with Sudan to Enforce Them

While our investigation obtained the necessary evidence, Bigombe's negotiation had ended. By May 2005, she "was holed up at the Acholi Inn in Gulu, with the LRA refusing to take her calls and the prospects for peace seemingly dashed."[36]

We continued consulting with the local communities to consider their interests, but when we requested arrest warrants against the five top LRA commanders, there was no negotiation process. In any case, I talked by phone with Betty Bigombe to inform her that we were planning to request arrest warrants soon. We engaged with the negotiator maintaining our judicial mandate.

We had lengthy discussions at the office on how we should react if the LRA retaliated against the victims due to our actions. We concluded that we should protect all our witnesses, considering the possibility that the LRA would commit more crimes. Simultaneously, we could not stop our investigations for fears of retaliation, allowing the criminal to blackmail us. We had to prepare our decisions carefully, act firmly, and afterward maximize the support for the court's decisions.

The Request of the Arrest Warrants Against the LRA's Commanders

Requesting the Arrest Warrants

On May 6, 2005, less than ten months after the beginning of the investigation, the office submitted a sealed request for warrants of arrest for alleged crimes against humanity and war crimes against the most responsible LRA's commanders.

We requested arrest warrants against Joseph Kony (founder and top commander of the LRA), Vincent Otti (then LRA vice-chairman and second-in-command), Raska Lukwiya (then LRA army commander), Okot Odhiambo (then LRA deputy army commander), and Dominic Ongwen (then an LRA brigade commander). The last three were also victims of the LRA. They had been abducted and transformed into militiamen.

Our office selected six incidents, including the Barlonyo attack, focusing the investigation on crimes committed between July 2002 and 2004. On July 8, 2005, the Pre-Trial Chamber II issued the warrants of arrest and, at our request, kept them confidential until October 13, 2005 out of concern for the safety of victims and witnesses.

The Agreement with Sudan to Enforce the Arrest Warrants

A combination of circumstances forced the LRA to leave its safe haven in Sudan and move to Garamba Park in DRC. On January 9, 2005, the Comprehensive Peace Agreement (CPA) between the government of Sudan and the rebel group, Sudan People's Liberation Movement (SPLM), ended one of the longest civil wars in the world, creating "international pressure on Khartoum to ensure greater stability around the Sudan—Uganda border."[37]

The CPA requested to remove the LRA.[38] Consequently, Sudan granted Uganda "unprecedented permission to hunt Kony anywhere in the south for a month." Suddenly, the LRA was chased by Uganda and the SPLM in agreement with the Sudanese government.[39]

The Office of the Prosecutor's mandate includes galvanizing national and international efforts to implement arrest warrants. Following such obligation, I had a meeting in The Hague with the then Sudan's minister of foreign affairs, opening a dialogue between our offices.

The government of Sudan discussed with our office its involvement in the Northern Uganda conflict. It denied any connection with the LRA, agreed to prosecute any Sudanese individual involved in the LRA's crimes, and to execute arrest warrants if issued. We had no evidence to present a case against Sudanese individuals involved in the LRA's crimes and the agreement helped us implement our mandate: Sudan, a non-state party with no obligation to enforce arrest warrants, was assuming a commitment. In furtherance of this goal, in October 2005, the office signed a formal agreement with Sudan to execute the LRA arrest warrants.

The steady military losses and the defection of some LRA commanders, coupled with the limitation of Sudanese support following the CPA signature and the agreement with our office, had significantly weakened the LRA. It lost its rear military bases and its training sites within Uganda.

Kony was debilitated, and he went back to his negotiation tactic. In the fall of 2005, LRA envoys[40] requested Pax Christi[41] to explore possibilities for a political solution to the conflict. The NGO engaged the vice president of South Sudan, Riek Machar, who became the chief mediator, providing his support and advice in the peace process.[42]

In November 2005, Vincent Otti led part of LRA to cross into eastern DRC jungles and set up camp in the Garamba National Park.

President Museveni, frustrated by the lack of international support to use military forces to arrest Kony, embraced the negotiation process. On July 5, 2006, he pledged to grant Kony total amnesty "despite the International Criminal Court indictments if he responds positively to the talks with the government in Juba, southern Sudan, and abandons terrorism."[43]

He explained that the "noble cause of trying Kony before the ICC had been betrayed by the failure of the United Nations, which set up the court, to arrest him, despite knowing his location in DR Congo's Garamba National Park."[44]

The Relationship with Mediators and the Humanitarian Organizations

The Peace Negotiations from the Humanitarians' Point of View

Patrick Corrigan's op-ed demanding the end of the ICC investigation summarized many commentators' perceptions.

Because immediate civilian protection has the concrete result of saving thousands of lives, the "Responsibility to Protect" civilians should be considered a more fundamental norm than that of accountability through international law. The Rome Statute . . . grants the Prosecutor the ability to withdraw ICC investigations in the event that they do not serve "the interests of justice". . . . The ICC prosecutor must now make the right decision and seize the moment for long-delayed peace and justice in northern Uganda.[45]

In 2006 Patrick Corrigan was a young and idealist student who believed that starting a negotiation process would imply the protection of civilians. In 2007 the Centre for Humanitarian Dialogue produced a report, "Charting the Roads to Peace," analyzing peace negotiations' data from 1920–2005.

The report found that most mediation failed (between 50 percent and 60 percent) to reach an agreement, and "43% of negotiated settlements relapsed into conflict within five years."[46] While a negotiation could be necessary, it is not a guarantee of civilians' protection. Besides, talks with Kony consistently increased violence.

Still, ten years later, many continue arguing that "situating the protection of civilians and punishment of perpetrators in a 'protection first, punishment later' temporal sequence is critical to facilitate international efforts to protect civilians in northern Uganda."[47]

A paper by David Lanz, a young scholar from *the* Fletcher School of Law and Diplomacy, presented the problem very clearly:

While the pressure generated by the ICC indictments was instrumental to bringing the LRA to the negotiating table in the first place, they now potentially constitute a major stumbling block to the successful conclusion of peace negotiations, especially considering that LRA cadres are primarily motivated by their own survival and safety.[48]

He proposed two possible solutions: a *deferral from the UN Security Council (Art. 16)* or—*preferably*—*via the ICC Prosecutor's own decision that withdrawal is "in the interest of justice."*[49]

We consistently refused demands to cancel our investigation and request the arrest warrants removal to facilitate the negotiations. Those demands were proposing to expand the specific mandate of the ICC Office of the

Prosecutor well beyond its core and, at the same time, were neglecting the role played by national and international political authorities, including the UN Security Council.

We followed a different approach: parallel tracks respecting each of our legal mandates. "The Office will seek to work constructively with and respect the mandates of those engaged in other areas but will pursue its own judicial mandate independently."[50]

We wanted to focus on our justice mandate, to show a firm line while at the same time respecting the roles of the other actors, in particular political leaders and humanitarian workers.

We avoided confronting President Museveni's statements publicly as much as possible, especially at the beginning of the process. According to Bosco, Mirjam Blaak, the Uganda ambassador, perceived our "reticence as constructive."[51] But he also indicated that within the Court were some "officials seethed about the weakness of the Ugandan commitment."[52]

I explored the rationale of other actors on a trip to New York. Jonathan Fanton, the President of the MacArthur Foundation, organized a confidential meeting with the humanitarian NGOs working in Uganda to increase our mutual understanding. The New York meeting helped appreciate humanitarian organizations' concerns to be our witnesses and therefore be targeted by the LRA.

Our efforts to reach the local communities created fears of "giving the impression of a great deal of cooperation between aid organizations and the ICC."[53] They considered themselves independent and neutral and legitimately feared being called upon as witnesses in trials when disclosing information that could ultimately impair their access to victims. We agreed that our office would not call humanitarian workers to be witnesses. That was already our policy, but they did not know it.

The Open Society Institute, Justice initiative project, organized a one-day seminar with Ugandan lawyers and experts in its headquarters. The idea was that they were ready to support justice efforts. Still, I found that all of them were involved in projects with the Acholi leaders and considered that our intervention affected the peace initiative.

At my office in The Hague, I received a Swiss ambassador leading a Juba negotiation team. He considered that a settlement's chance should be the only priority and requested that we remove the arrest warrants. The conversation was unpleasant and ended with a strong disagreement.

I learned that after the end of the Juba talks, Switzerland did an in-depth review of the process and adjusted its negotiation strategy, adopting a very comprehensive approach that included a justice component.

Meeting Mediators in Oslo

My participation at the end of June 2006 at the Oslo Forum provided me with a better understanding of the peace negotiators' mindset.[54] I met a small but very influential group of negotiators, including some who had attended the UN meeting led by Alvaro de Soto.

They were mediating the same conflicts that our office was investigating. I found that for mediators, the legal limits were an uncomfortable novelty. They perceived judicial constraints as an unrealistic idea. For mediators, negotiation was the priority. The title of my intervention during the 2006 Oslo retreat suggested the mediators' positions prioritizing negotiations. It was this: *Do criminal indictments help or hinder peace talks?*

Snyder and Vinjamuri had argued that international prosecutions could discourage pragmatic bargaining between warring parties and block the use of amnesty that could usher in peace.[55] But their work was published in 2003 before the ICC Office of the Prosecutor became operational.

I knew their paper, and I tried to be pragmatic in my Oslo meeting. I presented to the mediators some possible advantages of the ICC's existence: using our investigations to understand better the parties involved in the conversations and obtain leverage in their negotiation efforts.

But the senior mediators perceived their role as neutral, they were not advising a party, and some considered that my proposal could affect their impartiality. Besides, most of the mediators who talked to me assumed they were dealing with criminals. Their preference was to ignore the previous crimes to reach an agreement and concentrate on stopping violence. The ICC focuses on the leader's responsibility for the crimes committed was a new factor that was disturbing their work.

During the last day of the retreat, while drinking coffee with a group of mediators, I understood that I should not try to explain to the mediators how to negotiate. I adjusted and tried a more straightforward and limited argument: *This is the law. Whether you like it or not, it is the law. You should respect it in any new negotiation.* They did not like my argument, but it was clear.

The Nuremberg Declaration on Peace and Justice

We were able to engage with the mediators again during a large international conference held in Nuremberg from June 25 to 27, 2007, co-hosted by Germany, Jordan, and Finland. The venue was the historic courtroom 600 of the Nuremberg palace, a perfect place to discuss "Building a Future on Peace and Justice."

The Centre for Humanitarian Dialogue, the Oslo forum's co-sponsor, chaired a workshop at the conference entitled "Negotiating Justice" and invited many mediators to be present.

I had the chance to inaugurate the conference with the German foreign minister, Frank-Walter Steinmeier. I learned from my experience in Oslo and focused my comments on a primary point: any peace negotiation must respect the Rome Statute framework and the International Criminal Court's judicial decisions.

"Asking the Prosecution to use its discretionary powers to adjust to the situations on the ground, to indict or withdraw indictments according to short term political goals" constitutes an interference with justice.

I challenged the states to propose a comprehensive legal solution that ensured that any conflict resolution initiative is compatible with the Rome Statute. "International justice, national justice, search for the truth, peace negotiations can and must work together; they are not alternative ways to achieve a goal; they can be integrated into one comprehensive solution."

I explained that in Uganda, the court had issued arrest warrants only against five individuals; other national mechanisms can help the other combatants, those who wanted to give up arms and rejoin their families, and those who did not bear the greatest responsibility.

Without denying the *immense challenges for political leaders, I recalled that the enforcement of court's decisions was national states' responsibility.*[56] I took advantage of talking in the same place where the Nazi leaders were convicted and ended with the idea of the law protecting individuals worldwide as a realistic position.

"This law was built upon the lessons of decades of massive violence and atrocities when the international community failed, failed to protect Jewish, Russians, members of different communities in Europe and the Balkans, Tutsis, Arabs."

During the following three days, the mediators were exposed to justice NGOs and legal expert views. It was clear that there was a new legal frame that should be respected. One year later, the conference's discussions were transformed into the "Nuremberg Declaration on Peace and Justice."[57] Among its recommendations, it stated that mediators' "commitment to the core principles of the international legal order has to be beyond doubt."

The Mediator Mindset Evolution

In 2009, Priscilla Hayner prepared a document for the Centre for Humanitarian Dialogue, "Negotiating Justice: Guidance for Mediators." She recognized, "There is confusion about the role of international justice in the context of national peace processes, and there is a general lack of sufficient and clear information on available policy options."[58]

Still, in 2018, Priscilla wrote an entire book entitled *The Peacemaker's Paradox*, expressing the frustrations of some actors for my decisions as ICC prosecutor and considering that "The relatively new factor of an independent international prosecutor can be destabilizing to peace efforts."[59]

She quoted Anthony Dworkin's argument that the "ICC and other courts are often burdened with a political role in contexts of conflict that extends far beyond their capacities."[60] The main point of our policy that we had no authority in the political negotiations was not analyzed. The missing part is the states and UN Security Council's role in harmonizing the interaction between the different frames while all the actors respecting the new legal framework adopted by the Rome Statute.

The mediators' understanding of the legal requirements evolved: Norway and the Center for Humanitarian Dialogue played a vital role in the peace negotiations between Colombia; and the FARC, which scrupulously respected the Rome Statute framework. Fatou Bensouda, the ICC's chief prosecutor, intervened at the Oslo retreats 2015 and 2016.

Comments on a new Policy Paper on Interest of Justice Draft

We made public a new draft of our policy, emphasizing that our role was to enforce the legal limits. The political actors were responsible of reaching a substantial agreement respecting the legal framework.

In September 2006, FIDH supported that "*Article 16 is the only provision that allows for some kind of political interference in the judicial matters of the*

Court."[61] On November 28, 2006, the International Crisis Group made a similar point: *If a policy decision needs to be made to give primacy to peace . . . it should be made by the institution with political and conflict resolution mandate, namely the UN Security Council.*[62]

At the beginning of 2007, ICTJ organized a meeting in Cape Town[63] with around twenty experts representing states, international organizations, and NGOs that allowed our office to consolidate its experience.

Part 2: The Official Adoption of the Policy

From Policy to Reality

By September 2007, there were ongoing negotiations between the LRA and Uganda, between Darfur rebel groups and the Sudanese government. At the same time, Colombia was trying to demobilize old Marxist guerrilla movements. In this context, the Office of the Prosecutor publicly defined the scope of its discretion based on the "interest of justice."

First, we followed Juan Mendez's opinion and considered that the exercise of the prosecutor's discretion not to proceed is exceptional and that there is a presumption in favor of investigation or prosecution.

Second, the criteria for its exercise will naturally be guided by the objects and purposes of the statute—namely, ending impunity to contribute to the prevention of the most serious crimes of concern to the international community.

Third, there is a difference between the concepts of the *interest of justice* and the *interest of peace*. The broader matter of international peace and security is not the office's responsibility; it falls within other institutions' mandate. The statute recognizes a role for the UN Security Council to defer ICC action where it considers it necessary to maintain international peace and security.

To keep our independence but harmonizing it with the *jus ad Curiam* authority of the UN Security Council to suspend our investigations under Article 16 of the Rome Statute, the Office of the Prosecutor adopted a policy of informing the council in advance of its decisions to request arrest warrants or summons to appear.

I thought that alerting the council in advance would allow the council members to discuss the application of Article 16. I wanted to make our office predictable in all respects and bridge the gap with the diplomatic community by allowing the UN Security Council to exercise its authority to suspend our investigations to conduct negotiations if it wanted to do so.

In December 2006, we implemented for the first time the policy of informing the council in advance of the prosecution's decision to request arrest warrants or summons to appear against Ahmed Haroun, a Sudanese minister and militia leader.

During my briefing in December 2007, I warned the UN Security Council that we were planning to request new arrest warrants against the person that instructed and protected Minister Haroun.[64]

In June 2008, during the following briefing, I announced to the council my decision to present two new cases. In July 2008, I requested arrest warrants against President Bashir.

A few months later, I visited New York and met one ambassador who asked—*Prosecutor, how can you request an arrest warrant against a head of state without informing us in advance?*

Ambassador, I announced all of you officially during my last two meetings at the UN Security Council.

You said that you said that—he recognized—*but we did not believe you would do it.*

For a while, I repeated the diplomat's comment during my lectures, provoking laughs in the audience, but I now realize that he was expressing a different protocol.

I thought that announcing our intentions in advance would provide time for the Security Council to adjust to the Rome Statute's newly imposed legal limits. The council could plan political strategies to support the judges' ruling or consider an Article 16 decision.

However, for some UN Security Council members, my announcement was seen as part of the diplomatic tradition of consultation. Consequently, they assumed that I was only exploring the idea of indicting President Al Bashir and would not act before they had provided their formal or informal consent. They misunderstood my pronouncement, ignoring the independent judicial mandate of my office. Diplomats and negotiators must know precisely the judicial process.

Chapter 20 presents how the announcement of the request for arrest warrants in the Libya situation improved states representatives' ability to foresee the ICC actions. Paul Seils, who led the Situation Analysis at the ICC

Office of the Prosecutor,[65] said that the policy paper *removed the risk of ambiguity in the ICC "Peace versus Justice" debate.*[66]

Patryck Labuda, a dedicated scholar, considered: "The Rome Statute's 'interests of justice' clause generated much debate before and after Rome, but it had essentially disappeared from view after 2007 when the Prosecutor issued a policy paper on that topic."[67]

Still, world experts continue suggesting that the prosecutor make a decision that exceeds her legal mandate. For instance, in 2013, Robert Mnookin analyzed the office policy on the interest of justice:

> In suggesting that wisdom requires that the prosecutor ignore the more extreme rhetoric found in the policy paper—the rhetoric suggesting that peacemaking is never relevant to the exercise of prosecutorial discretion under the Rome Statute—I might be accused of endorsing a degree of hypocrisy: allowing the prosecutor to say one thing but do another. But as Rochefoucauld once said, "Hypocrisy is the homage vice pays to virtue."[68]

Even Dianne Orentlicher, who in 1991 wrote a seminal paper defining the "Duty to prosecute,"[69] revisited her position in 2014.[70] "[I]f asked whether I would insist on prosecutions if doing so would block a peace agreement that would end human carnage, I would respond (as I always have), 'Of course not!' Still, I would resist changing the normative default rule of international law."

Taking into consideration our office's decision in the Kony case, she suggested: "to maintain the principle affirming the broad trend in international law supporting criminal accountability for those who bear principal responsibility for atrocious crimes, while, insisting on the importance of local agency in fashioning and implementing policies of justice."[71]

The Revision at the ICC

On October 21, 2008, the pre-trial chamber made the *proprio motu* decision to initiate proceedings under Article 19(1) of the statute to analyze the admissibility of the cases against the LRA's leaders.[72]

Contrary to our strategy to isolate the judges from the political debate, the chamber ruled on an issue under a political negotiation without any party request. The judges have absolute power in the courtroom, and, in my view, they should not be involved in a political debate. The prosecutor must preserve the judges' authority and interact with the other actors.

> The key to the growing prominence of prosecutors, both in the United States and elsewhere, lies in the prosecutor's preeminent ability to bridge organizational and conceptual divides in criminal justice. Above all else, prosecutors are mediating figures, straddling the frontiers between adversarial and inquisitorial justice, between the police and the courts, and between law and discretion.[73]

In our submission to the chamber, we informed that we had not identified "any national proceeding related to the case." We considered that the case's admissibility was not affected by Uganda's ongoing attempts at negotiations with the Lord's Resistance Army or by the Agreement on Accountability and Reconciliation. On this basis, we concluded that the case remained admissible.

The chamber ruled that the signing of the agreement, respectively in June 2007 and February 2008, "made it necessary and appropriate for the Chamber to exercise its powers under Article 19(1)."[74]

> The purpose of the Proceedings remains limited to dispelling uncertainty as to who has ultimate authority to determine the admissibility of the Case: it is for the Court, and not for Uganda, to make such determination. The Chamber determined that at that stage, the Case was admissible under article 17 of the Statute.[75]

The ruling was in the abstract and had no impact.

The discussion on the interest of justice in the Uganda situation was not a *jus in Curiae* matter related to the suspects' responsibility. It was a *jus ad Curiam* debate about the convenience of international criminal justice intervention.

Before a decision affecting the case's admissibility or interfering with the judicial proceedings, the judges had no role in such a conversation. The political negotiation's main actors were local leaders, NGOs, states, the UN Security Council, and international organizations. The *interest of justice* policy's application is further discussed in Chapter 9 about Uganda, Chapter 14 in Colombia, and Chapter 20 in Libya.

Notes

1. Darryl Robinson, *Serving the Interests of Justice: Amnesties, Truth Commissions and the International Criminal Court*, 14 EUR. J. INT'L L. 481, 483 (2003).
2. "Several countries in Europe, Latin America, and elsewhere consider prosecutors as impartial officials who have to look equally for inculpatory and exculpatory elements of proof; have to document all their procedural activity and do not consider the elements of proof that they gather as elements of the prosecutor, but rather of the state's impartial investigation; do not consider that they lose if the defendant is acquitted; and may even appeal a conviction in favor of the defendant." In contrast the "adversarial systems tend to consider the prosecutor as a party that is opposed to the defense." Maximo Langer & David Alan Sklansky, *Epilogue Prosecutors and Democracy— Themes and Counterthemes, in* PROSECUTORS AND DEMOCRACY: A CROSS-NATIONAL STUDY (ASCL STUDIES IN COMPARATIVE LAW) 300, 315 (Maximo Langer & David Alan Sklansky eds., Kindle ed. 2017).
3. Article 67 (2) of the Rome Statute.
4. Juan Mendez, *Justice and Prevention, in* THE INTERNATIONAL CRIMINAL COURT AND COMPLEMENTARITY: FROM THEORY TO PRACTICE 33, 36 (Kindle ed. 2011).
5. Article 53 (2) (c) of the Rome Statute.
6. Regulation 29(4), Regulations of the Office of the Prosecutor. Prosecutor v. Germain Katanga and Mathieu Ngudjolo Chui, ICC-01/04-01/07 OA 8, Judgment on the Appeal of Mr. Germain Katanga against the Oral Decision of Trial Chamber II of 12 June 2009 on the Admissibility of the Case, ¶ 56 (Sept. 25, 2009), https://www.icc-cpi.int/CourtRecords/CR2009_06998.PDF.
7. During the first session of the Preparatory Committee (March 25–April 12, 1996), which was established by UN GA Resolution 50/46. UK delegation proposed a modification of Article 26(4) of the ILC Draft Statute. Gilbert Bitti, *The Interests of Justice— Where Does That Come From? Part I*, EJIL: TALK! BLOG (Aug. 13, 2019), https://www.ejiltalk.org/the-interests-of-justice-where-does-that-come-from-part-i/; and Gilbert Bitti, *The Interests of Justice—Where Does That Come From? Part II*, EJIL: TALK! BLOG (Aug. 14, 2019), https://www.ejiltalk.org/the-interests-of-justice-where-does-that-come-from-part-ii/.
8. Maximo Langer & David Alan Sklansky, *Epilogue Prosecutors and Democracy— Themes and Counterthemes, in* PROSECUTORS AND DEMOCRACY: A CROSS-NATIONAL STUDY (ASCL STUDIES IN COMPARATIVE LAW) 300, 316–19 (Maximo Langer & David Alan Sklansky eds., Kindle ed. 2017).
9. *Id.* at 315.
10. *Id.* at 316–19.
11. In Germany, "The prosecution service is by law governed by the principle of legality meaning that there is a duty to investigate whenever there are allegations of a crime committed." Shawn Boynw, *German Prosecutors and the Rechtsstaat. Id.* at 138, 169
12. Gilbert Bitti, *The Interests of Justice—Where Does That Come From? Part II*, EJIL: TALK! BLOG (Aug. 14, 2019), https://www.ejiltalk.org/the-interests-of-justice-where-does-that-come-from-part-ii/.

13. *Id.*
14. "The fact that the Prosecutor does not have to justify in any way his or her decision to investigate or to prosecute with regard to the 'interests of justice' criterion stands in sharp contrast with the requirement to provide reasons when he or she reaches a negative determination on this criterion, as provided for in rules 105(3) and (5) and 106(2) of the Rules of Procedure and Evidence (the 'Rules')." *Id.*
15. Office of the Prosecutor, *Summary of recommendations received during the first Public Hearing of the Office of the Prosecutor, convened from 17–18 June 2003 at The Hague*, ICC, https://www.icc-cpi.int/iccdocs/otp/ph1_conclusions.pdf (last visited May 17, 2020).
16. Fabricio Guariglia & Emeric Rogier, *The Selection of Situations and Cases by the OTP of the ICC, in* THE LAW AND PRACTICE OF THE INTERNATIONAL CRIMINAL COURT (Carsten Stahn ed., Kindle ed. 2015).
17. *Guidelines for U.N. representatives in certain aspects of negotiations for conflict resolution*, 2006 JURIDICAL Y.B., ST/LEG/SER.C/44.
18. The Joinet Principles are set of principles based on the question of the impunity of perpetrators of human rights violations (civil and political), formulated by Louis Joinet at the requirement of the Sub-Commission on Prevention of Discrimination and Protection of Minorities. Comm. on Human Rights, Rep. of prepared by Mr. Joinet pursuant to Sub-Commission decision 1996/119, U.N. Doc. E/CN.4/Sub.2/ 1997/20/Rev.1(Oct. 2, 1997).
19. Paul Seils, *ICC's Intolerance of Impunity Does Not Make It and Enemy of Peace*, ICTJ (Nov 12, 2014), https://www.ictj.org/news/icc-impunity.
20. During this period, Kony was also negotiating arrangements with the government of Sudan via the Equatoria Defence Force (EDF). SARAH M. H. NOUWEN, COMPLEMENTARITY IN THE LINE FIRE: THE CATALYST EFFECT OF THE INTERNATIONAL CRIMINAL COURT IN SUDAN AND UGANDA 128–29 (Kindle ed., Cambridge Series in Law and Society, 2013).
21. The goal was to broker a peace agreement between the government of Sudan/LRA and the government of Uganda/the Sudan People's Liberation Army (SPLA).
22. ARLPI held a few meetings with LRA commanders during 2003 and succeeded in facilitating an exchange of letters between the government of Uganda and Joseph Kony, who announced a unilateral ceasefire on March 2. A few days later, President Museveni called for a limited ceasefire with the LRA for the areas in which the LRA should assemble to hold peace talks with the government-appointed peace team, headed by his younger brother Lt. Gen. Salim Saleh. On March 9, 2003, James Opoka, the former aide to Kiiza Besigye, was reportedly executed on the orders of Joseph Kony. "According to news reports, Kony suspected him of establishing a political wing inside the LRA without Kony's consent." Hum. Rts. Watch, *Abducted and Abused* (July 15, 2003).
23. Kony ordered that " 'Catholic missions must be destroyed, priests and missionaries killed in cold blood and nuns beaten." *Id.*
24. "[O]ne of the peace negotiators from the ARLPI noted that there was an enormous change in the LRA's attitude towards negotiations between July and September 2002.

Whereas in July 2002 there was a military stalemate and the LRA seemed to be interested in peace talks, by September the LRA had acquired new military equipment and was unwilling to negotiate seriously. *Id.*

25. In 1996–97 Kacoke Madit and the Catholic peace organization Sant'Edigio organized talks between the LRA secretary for external affairs and mobilization, James Obita, and the government of Uganda. Although this process succeeded in bringing the state minister for foreign affairs Amama Mbabazi together with Obita, the talks broke down and Obita was later briefly imprisoned by the LRA.

26. Conciliation Resources, *Learning from Past Experiences to Inform Future Efforts: The Conflict in Northern Uganda May*, CONCILIATION RESOURCES, https://rc-services-assets.s3.eu-west-1.amazonaws.com/s3fs-public/Learningfromthepast_200 205_ENG.pdf.

27. Some of the papers presented can be found on the website of ICC Now: http://iccnow. org/?mod=interestofjustice.

28. *See* Henry Lovat interesting criticism: Henry Lovat, *Delineating the Interests of Justice*, 35 DENVER J. OF INT'L L. & POLICY 275 (2007).

29. Amnesty Int'l, *Open letter to the Chief Prosecutor of the International Criminal Court: Comments on the concept of the interests of justice* AI Index: IOR 40/023/2005 (June 17, 2005).

30. (The report was presented in French. Translation by the author) Fed. Int'l des Ligues des Droits de l'Home, *Reflexions Sur La Notion "Intérêts De La Justice," Au Terme De L'article 53 Du Statut De Rome* (June 20, 2005).

31. Alex Boraine, founder of the ICTJ had observed in 2000 that "[i]t is to be hoped ... that when the International Criminal Court comes into being, it will not, either by definition or by approach, discourage attempts by national states to come to terms with their past. ... It would be regrettable if the only approach to gross human rights violations comes in the form of trials and punishment." Darryl Robinson, *Serving the Interests of Justice: Amnesties, Truth Commissions and the International Criminal Court*, 14 EU. J. OF INT'L L. 481, 482 (2003)(quoting A. Boraine, A country Unmasked: South Africa's Truth and Reconciliation Commission (2000)).

32. Paul Seils & Marieke Wierda, *The International Criminal Court and Conflict Mediation*, INT'L CENTER FOR TRANSITIONAL JUST. (June 2005), https://www.ictj.org/ sites/default/files/ICTJ-Global-ICC-Mediation-2005-English.pdf.

33. *Id.*

34. *Id.*

35. *Id.*

36. "The CPA pushed the LRA toward peace talks by forcing the Sudanese government to halt its support for the LRA, dispersing the LRA from its bases and incentivising the newly autonomous government of southern Sudan to deal with 'foreign forces' including the LRA." PHIL CLARK, DISTANT JUSTICE: THE IMPACT OF THE INTERNATIONAL CRIMINAL COURT ON AFRICAN POLITICS 208 (Kindle ed. 2018).

37. *Id.* at 212–14.

38. "The CPA has a provision in the Security Agreement that all foreign groups must be forced out of Sudan. The late leader of Southern Sudan, Dr. John Garang, had the LRA

and foreign terrorist groups in mind when he insisted on this provision." TED DAGE, CONG. RESEARCH SERV., RL33701 UGANDA: CURRENT CONDITIONS AND THE CRISIS IN NORTH UGANDA 7 (Apr. 29, 2011). In July 2005, Garang "emphasized that a continuing LRA presence represented an unacceptable threat to the people and government of South Sudan, and they would have to leave." Ronald R. Atkinson, *"The Realists in Juba"? An Analysis of the Juba Peace Talks, in* THE LORD'S RESISTANCE ARMY: MYTH AND REALITY 208 (Tim Allen & Koen Vlassenroot eds., Kindle ed., 2012).

39. C. Bryson Hull, *Southern Sudanese Long for Capture of Uganda Rebel,* GLOBAL POL'Y FORUM (Oct. 26, 2005), https://www.globalpolicy.org/component/content/article/165/29580.html.

40. "Only when one of Pax Christi's earlier contacts confirmed that the leadership had sent a group on a peace mission did Pax Christi engage."Simon Siomnese et al., *NGO Involvement in the Juba Peace Talks: The Role and Dilemmas of IKV Pax Christi, in* THE LORD'S RESISTANCE ARMY: MYTH AND REALITY 229 (Tim Allen & Koen Vlassenroot eds., Kindle ed., 2012).

41. Pax Christi was founded in Europe in 1945 as a reconciliation movement bringing together French and Germans after World War II. It is a global catholic movement that works to establish peace, respect for human rights and justice and reconciliation, counting with 120 member organizations active in more than fifty countries worldwide.

42. These talks eventually led to meetings between the LRA's number two, Vincent Otti, and the vice president of South Sudan, Riek Machar, in April 2006; between Kony and Machar in May. Pax Christi, *Pax Christi: Breakthrough in Peace Talks in Northern Uganda,* RELIEF WEB (Aug. 26, 2006), https://reliefweb.int/report/uganda/pax-christi-breakthrough-peace-talks-northern-uganda.

43. Integrated Regional Information Networks, *LRA Leader Must Be Arrested, ICC Insists,* GLOBAL POL'Y FORUM (July 5, 2006), https://archive.globalpolicy.org/intljustice/wanted/2006/0703iccinsists.htm.

44. *Id.*

45. Patrick Corrigan, *Why the ICC Must Stop Impeding Juba Process,* GLOBAL POL'Y FORUM (July 27, 2007), https://archive.globalpolicy.org/intljustice/icc/investigations/uganda/2007/0727iccimpeding.htm

46. Centre for Humanitarian Dialogue, Charting the Roads to Peace, Facts, Figures and Trends in Conflict Resolution, 2007.

47. Raymond Kwun Sun Lau, *Protection First, Justice Later?, in* CIVILIAN PROTECTION IN THE TWENTY-FIRST CENTURY: GOVERNANCE AND RESPONSIBILITY IN A FRAGMENTED WORLD (Cecilia Jacob & Alistar D. B. Cook eds., 1st ed., 2016).

48. David Lanz, *The ICC's Intervention in Northern Uganda: Beyond the Simplicity of Peace vs. Justice,* RELIEF WEB (May 1, 2007), https://reliefweb.int/sites/reliefweb.int/files/resources/EC66215A0071F156C12573910051D06D-Full_Report.pdf.

49. *Id.*

50. Office of the Prosecutor of the ICC, *Policy Paper on the Interests of Justice,* ICC (Sept. 2007), https://www.icc-cpi.int/NR/rdonlyres/772C95C9-F54D-4321-BF09-73422BB23528/143640/ICCOTPInterestsOfJustice.pdf.

51. Mirjam Blaak said, "If the court had been hammering on us and saying that what we were doing was illegal, that would have complicated matters and there would have been less confidence in the process." DAVID BOSCO, ROUGH JUSTICE: THE INTERNATIONAL CRIMINAL COURT IN A WORLD OF POWER POLITICS 130 (Kindle ed., 2014).

52. "One journalist noted, 'Court officials are privately furious, not only because they risk seeing their historic first case reduced to farce, but because they launched the inquiry at the request of the Ugandan government, which is now accusing the ICC of neo-colonialism.'" *Id.* at 129.

53. Raymond Kwun Sun Lau, *Protection First, Justice Later?*, *in* CIVILIAN PROTECTION IN THE TWENTY-FIRST CENTURY: GOVERNANCE AND RESPONSIBILITY IN A FRAGMENTED WORLD (Cecilia Jacob & Alistar D. B. Cook eds., 1st ed., 2016).

54. The Oslo Forum is a series of retreats for international conflict mediators. It is co-hosted by the Royal Norwegian Ministry of Foreign Affairs and the Centre for Humanitarian Dialogue and provides a discreet and informal space to reflect on current mediation practice.

55. Jack Snyder & Leslie Vinjamuri, *Trials and Errors: Principle and Pragmatism in Strategies of International Justice*, 28 INT'L SECURITY 5–44 (2003).

56. KAI AMBOS ET AL., BUILDING A FUTURE ON PEACE AND JUSTICE: STUDIES ON TRANSITIONAL JUSTICE, PEACE AND DEVELOPMENT: THE NUREMBERG DECLARATION ON PEACE AND JUSTICE (2008).

57. Permanent Representatives of Finland, Germany and Jordan, Letter dated June 13 from the Permanent Representatives of Finland, Germany, and Jordan to the U.N. addressed to the Secretary General, Annex at 5, U.N. Doc. A/62/885 (June 19, 2008).

58. PRISCILLA HAYNER, NEGOTIATING JUSTICE: GUIDANCE FOR MEDIATORS (Center for Humanitarian Dialogue report, 2009).

59. PRISCILLA HAYNER, THE PEACEMAKER'S PARADOX 6–7 (Kindle ed., 2018).

60. Anthony Dworkin, International Justice and the Prevention of Atrocity, European Council on Foreign Relations, Oct. 2014. PRISCILLA HAYNER, THE PEACEMAKER'S PARADOX 125 (Kindle ed., 2018).

61. It concluded, "only the Security Council can request the suspension of investigations or prosecutions for political reasons such as diplomatic negotiations or peace processes." Fed. Int'l des Ligues des Droits de l'Home, *Comments on the Office of the Prosecutor's draft policy paper on "The interest of justice"* (Sept. 14, 2006).

62. Nick Grono, *The Role of the International Criminal Court in African Peace Processes*, INT'L CRISIS GRP. (Nov. 28, 2006), https://www.crisisgroup.org/africa/horn-africa/sudan/role-international-criminal-court-peace-processes-0.

63. I am very thankful for Louis Bickford's initiative.

64. We said: "Haroun's presence in the Ministry of Humanitarian Affairs and the other high-profile responsibilities he is being given by the Government of Sudan signals official tolerance or even active support for his crimes. Government of Sudan officials have decided . . . to protect and promote Ahmad Haroun" Prosecutor of the International Criminal Court, *Sixth Report to the Security Council pursuant to UNSC*

Res. 1593 (2005), ICC (Dec. 5, 2007), https://www.icc-cpi.int/NR/rdonlyres/19A83 943-DF47-4DC0-9EB1-1A84CF862290/281540/ProsecutorsReportUNSCDec0 7EN.pdf.

65. He was also the chief of the Rule of Law and Democracy Unit at the United Nations Office of the High Commissioner for Human Rights in Geneva, and vice president of the International Center for Transitional Justice in New York.

66. It "put an end to confusion and indeterminacy by making it clear that, in effect, once an ICC investigation has been started, there would be very little prospect of stopping it. . . ." That message was nothing but consistent with Joinet in 1997 or with Kofi Annan in 1998. Pauls Seils, *ICC's Intolerance of Impunity Does Not Make It an Enemy of Peace*, INT'L CTR. FOR TRANSITIONAL JUST. (Nov. 17, 2014), https://www.ictj.org/news/icc-impunity.

67. Patryk I. Labuda, *A Neo-Colonial Court for Weak States? Not Quite. Making Sense of the International Criminal Court's Afghanistan Decision*, EJIL: TALK! BLOG (Apr. 13, 2019), https://www.ejiltalk.org/a-neo-colonial-court-for-weak-states-not-quite-mak ing-sense-of-the-international-criminal-courts-afghanistan-decision/.

68. Robert H. Mnookin, *Rethinking the Tension between Peace and Justice: The International Criminal Prosecutor as Diplomat*, *in* THE FIRST GLOBAL PROSECUTOR: PROMISE AND CONSTRAINTS (LAW, MEANING AND VIOLENCE) 69, 90 (Martha Minow, C. Core True-Frost et al. eds., Kindle ed., 2015)(ebook).

69. Dianne Orentlicher is a law professor and U.N. Expert. Dianne Orentlicher, *Settling Accounts: The Duty to Prosecute Human Rights Violations of a Prior Regime*, 100 YALE L.J. 2537 (1991).

70. Diane Orentlicher, *"Settling Accounts" Revisited: Reconciling Global Norms with Local Agency*, 1 INT'L J. OF TRANSITIONAL JUST. 10, 14–21 (2007).

71. "I took very much to heart the entreaties of colleagues from Argentina and other countries that had been reckoning with crimes of their recent past, some of whom had played leading roles in national efforts to mount prosecutions. These colleagues wanted me to understand, above all, that they would have been better equipped to confront the inevitable military backlash against prosecutions if international law stood firmly in their court—if, i.e., they could credibly invoke a mandate for their work in international law. Some of the strongest claims in my article were, in fact, prompted by their views. As I write, this issue looms large in the context of the ICC Prosecutor's indictment of five members of the notoriously savage Ugandan rebel group, the Lord's Resistance Army (LRA), including its leader, Joseph Kony. . . . [M]any of my African colleagues are disposed to regard with suspicion claims of African exceptionalism when it comes to international norms concerning justice." Diane Orentlicher, *"Settling Accounts" Revisited: Reconciling Global Norms with Local Agency*, 1 INT'L J. OF TRANSITIONAL JUST. 10, 14–21 (2007).

72. The Prosecutor v. Joseph Kony, Vincent Otti, Okot Odhiambo, Dominic Ongwen, ICC-02/04-1/05, Decision on the admissibility of the case under article 19 (1) of the Statute (Mar. 10, 2009), https://www.icc-cpi.int/CourtRecords/CR2009_01678.PDF.

73. Jordan A. Sklansky, *The Nature and Function of Prosecutorial Power*, 106 J. CRIMINAL L. & CRIMINOLOGY 473, 473 (2016).

74. The Prosecutor v. Joseph Kony, Vincent Otti, Okot Odhiambo, Dominic Ongwen, ICC-02/04-1/05, Decision on the admissibility of the case under article 19 (1) of the Statute (Mar. 10, 2009), https://www.icc-cpi.int/CourtRecords/CR2009_01 678.PDF.

75. *Id.*

9

The ICC Shadow in the Uganda Situation

Arrest Warrants, Juba Talks, and the Intervention of Invisible Children

This chapter presents the first international efforts to implement ICC arrest warrants and how Kony launched, in parallel, a negotiation process to manage the pressure against his group. Different actors played under the "shadow" of the ICC's decisions. It was impossible to create a substantial operation to arrest the LRA's leaders, and Kony never signed the agreement prepared during the "Juba talks."

However, the negotiation succeeds differently, and a group of young activists from San Diego promoted efforts to arrest Kony. The chapter proposes to evaluate the ICC's impact on the LRA's disruption as a part of the activities performed by different actors with conflicting agendas.

For the first time, concerned states and the UN discussed implementing the ICC's arrest warrants. The UN Security Council tasked the UN peacekeeper forces in the DRC and Sudan to contribute to the ICC arrest warrants' enforcement. The frustration of the collective approach to arrest LRA leaders facilitated the opening of the negotiations in Juba.

The chapter presents the "Juba talks" initiated at Kony's initiative and describes the political negotiations with the LRA, involving states, the UN secretary-general, and the African Union (AU). These institutions have the mandate and legal resources to harmonize judicial and political activities. The UN Security Council was also following the Juba talks closely, establishing an agenda that requested peace and justice.[1]

The final agreement reached at Juba had very complex and interesting aspects, including designing a national transitional justice system.[2] Still, Kony never signed it. As in previous occasions, Kony used the negotiation process to obtain resources, attacked his own representatives (in this case, he ordered the killing of Vincent Otti, the LRA's deputy commander), and strengthened his militia by abducting more children, but this time in the

War and Justice in the 21st Century. Luis Moreno Ocampo, Oxford University Press. © Oxford University Press 2022. DOI: 10.1093/oso/9780197628973.003.0010

DRC and the Central African Republic. There were no more LRA crimes in Uganda, but since 2007, the group terrorized other communities.

Despite that, the Juba negotiation succeeded in creating a multiparty understanding between South Sudan, Uganda, and the DRC, allowing a new interaction between the communities in Northern Uganda and the Ugandan government. Moreover, part of the *Juba talks'* success was that they achieved definite marginalization of the LRA in Uganda.

A group of young activists from San Diego, Invisible Children, decided to participate in the events lobbying the US Congress to adopt a law to ensure US efforts to arrest Kony. In legal terms, they overcame the Ugandan's deficit of representation. They were able to expose Kony's crimes globally and connected the victims with US authorities.

Invisible Children created a global demand for justice through a video called "Kony 2012," calling for his arrest. It became the most viral video, reaching more than one hundred million viewers in a few days. Invisible Children also coordinated the African Union (AU), Uganda, and the Central African Republic efforts and put pressure to implement the US commitment to arrest Joseph Kony. It created a collective action to chase Kony, which drastically reduced the LRA activities in DRC and the Central African Republic.[3] The LRA was severely degraded, but at the time of this writing, Kony is still at large, hidden in Sudan.

Part 1: Arrest Warrants

The Critical Role of the UN in Sudan, Uganda, and the DRC

Harvard Law School dean Martha Minow introduced me to the "shadow of the law" metaphor. Decades ago, Professor Robert Mnookin argued that most divorce cases never reach the courts; they are solved under the "shadow of the law." Many other couples and lawyers later use judges' rulings on specific cases to resolve their disputes.[4] The metaphor illustrates how other actors consider the ruling of the courts to define their own behavior.

As in any court, the judges make the final decisions based on the evidence and the law. Unlike any other court, the ICC's decision impacts the citizens and the institutions of more than 120 states and beyond. States, international organizations, NGOs, and local leaders participated in the events that followed the ICC arrest warrants' issuance against LRA's commanders. All of them, including Joseph Kony, took into consideration the ICC *shadow*. Since the two "Congo wars," the UN Security Council was deeply involved in the North/South Sudan conflict and the "Great Lakes region peace process."

As mentioned, on October 1, 2004, under the United Kingdom leadership and at our office's initiative, the UN Security Council expanded the MONUC mandate to include the possibility to implement arrest warrants.

The lack of resources to implement its mandate affected MONUC's ability to cooperate efficiently with any arrests. The UN Secretary-General Kofi Annan reminded the council that "the newly approved ceiling of 16,700 in total falls well below the figure" that he recommended. Thus, he expressed that MONUC will have "to review the scope of the support it can provide for the peace process."[5]

The UN Security Council Resolution 1649, December 2005, confirmed MONUC's mandate to cooperate to "bring such perpetrators to justice."[6] But there were no additional resources added.

Still, in January 2006, the Museveni administration opposed the inclusion of Northern Uganda in the council's discussions.[7] On January 27, 2006, the situation changed. After a crucial meeting that included fourteen Foreign Affairs' Ministers[8], the UN Security Council adopted resolution 1653, condemning armed groups' activities, including the LRA, in the Great Lakes region. It demanded the governments of Uganda, the DRC, and Burundi to "take measures to prevent the use of their respective territories in support of activities of armed groups."[9]

The council also turned to the secretary-general in search of recommendations on how best to support such efforts.[10] During the meeting, Uganda's minister of foreign affairs, Sam Kutesa, demanded support from the UN to execute the warrants.[11] Canada, the group of friends of the Great Lakes region leader,[12] together with the Netherlands[13] and Norway, members of the Uganda "Core Group,"[14] emphasized the International Criminal Court's arrest warrants' importance.

On March 20, 2006, a follow-up meeting was organized by the UN at a ministerial level to discuss an action plan to address the crisis in Northern Uganda with the Ugandan government and a group of donor countries, including the United States, the United Kingdom, Norway, the Netherlands, and Canada.[15]

Ten leading nongovernmental agencies, most of them with a humanitarian mandate, were also involved. Justice and implementing the arrest warrants were not part of their agenda. They called on the international community to urge the Ugandan government to resolve the conflict peacefully and protect the two million internally displaced people.[16]

A few days later, on March 24, 2006, the council unanimously adopted Resolution 1663 (2006), strongly condemning the activities of armed groups such as the LRA in Sudan and urging UNMIS to make full use of its current mandate and capabilities.[17] The council requested recommendations from the secretary-general on how to address the LRA's problem more effectively, including the role of UNMIS.[18]

Uganda Demands Help to Arrest Kony

On April 19, 2006, the council discussed implementing the International Criminal Court's arrest warrants for the first time.[19] Sam Kutesa, the minister of foreign affairs of Uganda, briefed the council on a national plan that included five thematic issues[20] and the establishment of a small regional security group to deal with the LRA.[21]

Amama Mbabazi, then minister of defence of Uganda, alerted that "LRA is slowly rebuilding its capacity" abducting children in Southern Sudan and the Democratic Republic of the Congo, creating the risk of another Congo war.

Mbabazi requested combined efforts "to disarm, capture or arrest the indicted LRA terrorist leaders and hand them over to the International Criminal Court in The Hague."[22] On May 4, 2006, President Museveni confirmed the approach "[Through] working with the Sudan government, SPLA, Congo government and MONUC, we want to capture Kony and a few of his associates and hand them over to The Hague so as to end impunity."[23]

The Role of UNMIS and MONUC to Execute ICC Arrest Warrants

The expected "Report of the Secretary-General pursuant to resolutions 1653 (2006) and 1663 (2006)" was presented on June 29, 2006. It concluded: "While recognizing the threat posed by LRA, I should like to reiterate that, since UNMIS and MONUC already have challenging tasks to perform in their respective areas of responsibility, they should channel their capacities and resources primarily to address those challenges."[24]

It described the limited UNMIS mandate to support "the parties in the implementation of the Comprehensive Peace Agreement." Still, it took note that "In resolution 1663 (2006), the Council urged UNMIS to "make full use of its current mandate and capabilities against LRA." And it also recognized: "While the Sudan is not a State party to the Rome Statute, it has signed a memorandum of understanding with the International Criminal Court pledging to hand over the indicted LRA leaders to The Hague."

The report proposed a reduced role in arresting LRA's leaders for MONUC and UNMIS "Dealing with the regional implications of LRA activities lies within the area of national responsibility of the Governments in the region. UNMIS and MONUC can provide assistance, within their existing mandates and capabilities, but should not be seen as an alternative to authorities in the LRA-affected region in the maintenance of law and order."[25]

It also explained that to conduct operations against LRA, UNMIS would require: "... an enhanced configuration of forces and more robust assets, specialized equipment and real-time intelligence."

The report informed that "MONUC is aware of its mandate to detain the LRA leaders who have been indicted by the International Criminal Court, and would seek to do so if it came across them while carrying out its mandated duties."

The report mentioned the incident involving MONUC peacekeepers, considering that "[a]part from its deadly attack on MONUC personnel . . . LRA appears to be inactive in the eastern Democratic Republic of the Congo."

I read that line as a criticism of the active use of MONUC forces to implement arrest warrants. UN Department of Political Affairs and Peace-Building suggested that if MONUC remained passive, the LRA would not attack it.

Kony's proposal to negotiate derailed the support for the efforts to arrest. The report mentioned: "recent contacts between the Government of Southern Sudan and Messrs. Kony and Otti, with the apparent knowledge of the Government of Uganda, suggest the possibility of a negotiated solution with LRA."[26]

Following such vision, the report mentioned the negotiation as the primary strategy, including the possibility of appointing "a senior-level envoy to help the Government of Uganda deal with the situation created by the LRA activities."[27]

In response to the report, Uganda sent a letter to the council expressing its frustration: "It would appear that the task of dealing with LRA is being left largely to the Governments of the region. We feel that the United Nations should be a real partner and not just an observer. The situation in which LRA is just enjoying a holiday in the Garamba National Park as it were, regrouping and recruiting, is certainly unacceptable. The Security Council, which is primarily responsible for the maintenance of world peace and security, must be a key player in arresting those criminals."[28]

Part 2: Negotiations in Juba

The Juba Process

The Beginning of a New Peace Process

As mentioned in the previous chapter, in the fall of 2005, LRA requested Pax Christi[29] to explore possibilities for a political solution to the conflict. The vice president of South Sudan, Riek Machar, became involved.

By February 2006, a formal agreement was reached: the LRA would stop hostilities in the South of Sudan and start a peace process. At the same time, the government of the South of Sudan acknowledged that the LRA had a legitimate cause, that Uganda had not been sufficiently committed to resolving the conflict, and "made assurances that they would support the withdrawal of the warrants issued in October 2005 against the top LRA leaders by the International Criminal Court."[30]

The United States disagreed and presented its pragmatic policy; it expected Uganda "to cooperate in arresting ICC-indicted individuals," noting that "Uganda is a signatory to the Rome Statute, but the United States is not."[31]

Our office already considered that peace negotiations and justice were not sequential, rather two different parallel processes. Our limited comment was that: "The governments of Uganda, Sudan, and the Democratic Republic of Congo are obligated to give effect to the arrest warrants, and we are confident that they will honor their joint commitment to do so."[32] We were not part of the negotiations, but we refused to interfere with the peace process.

Raising Hopes and Promises

The Juba talks were formally opened on July 14, 2006, and raised hopes for ending the conflict. For the first time, an outside mediator "with vested interests in helping navigate an end to the conflict"[33] led the negotiations. There were confidence-building meetings with Acholi leaders and the signing of a cessation of hostilities renewed several times.[34]

President Museveni set up three phone lines for Kony and Otti and personally spoke with them several times. Uganda's government even facilitated a trip to reunite Kony with his mother after twenty years of separation.[35]

The Juba talks were structured around five main discussion points. However, each party had its own agenda: "From the outset, foremost among the LRA's demands was the withdrawal of the ICC arrest warrants against its commanders."[36] On September 6, 2006, Vincent Otti stated the ICC was the LRA's main concern: "No rebel will come out unless the ICC revokes the indictments," he told Kampala's KFM radio by satellite phone.[37]

Our office kept its noninterference policy at this critical moment and refused to comment: "We have made statements in the past; they still stand."[38]

A few weeks later, Vincent Otti further explained that the ICC indictments are the "only obstacle" to the talks' success. With arrest warrants still valid, Otti said, signing a peace agreement "would not be a correct" decision.[39]

On October 9, 2006, an LRA's spokesperson presented this demand as a matter of trust: "We want a guarantee, that nobody is going to pounce, jumping on them immediately after we have signed a treaty when they no longer have arms. But we all want peace to return to northern Uganda, and as a good gesture, we need the ICC to say, well, if that be the case, then we drop this case."[40]

The Charles Taylor Precedent

According to the BBC, the LRA commanders were worried that justice would eventually catch up with them, as was the case with former Liberian leader Charles Taylor.[41] In an interview conducted on June 12, 2006, Kony was reading an old *Newsweek* and Charles Taylor was on the cover: Taylor was about to be extradited to stand trial in The Hague at the Special Court on Sierra Leone. The journalist interviewing him said that the extradition "*seemed puzzling to Kony.*"[42]

A week later, on June 20, 2006, Jendayi Frazer, assistant secretary for African Affairs, compared Kony's situation with that of Charles Taylor.[43]

To dissipate the LRA's fears, Vice President Machar confirmed that "The President of Uganda has informed us that he will not do a Charles Taylor way on Kony (sic) and the other commanders."[44]

Juba Talks Progress

On September 13, 2006, the International Crisis Group released an assessment on the situation in Uganda, indicating that "the peace talks in Juba have made surprising progress and . . . offer the best chance to end a twenty-year civil war."[45]

It suggested that if a deal had to be made to bring peace, "the least worst option might be an asylum for the indicted commanders in a country not party to the Rome Statute, conditioned on their full compliance with the peace agreement."[46]

It also mentioned that the process "nearly torpedoed" after Raska Lukwiya, the LRA's top commander after Kony and Otti and an ICC's indictee, was killed by the Ugandan army in August 12. Instead, a new agreement on the cessation of hostilities was signed.[47]

The Roles of the UN Secretary-General and the Security Council in the Juba Process

Improvements in the Light of Juba Talks

Among the different actors taking part in the events, it was then UN under-secretary-general for humanitarian affairs Jan Egeland. On November 12, 2006, he traveled to the Sudan/Congo border to meet Kony to discuss captive women and children's release.[48] Egeland was very respectful of our judicial mandate and was trying to comply with the UN policy to "avoid any direct contacts with indicted-leaders unless such contacts are strictly necessary to carry out their mandated activities, and not beyond."[49] He called me before his trip to find a proper way to interact with Kony. We agreed that a meeting with Kony to alleviate the victims' situation was part of his mandate. However, Egeland's request did not succeed "because of Kony's denial of kidnapping or holding people against their will."[50]

On November 16, 2006, the UN Security Council formally included the Juba negotiation in its agenda. It issued a presidential statement calling on all talks' parties to commit fully to a further long-term and peaceful solution. The council stressed the importance of both parties respecting the cessation of hostilities, signed on August 29, and renewed on November 1.[51]

It also demanded the Lord's Resistance Army release all women, children, and other non-combatants immediately, following its resolution 1621 (2005) on children and armed conflict.[52] Supporting the justice intervention, the council invited the UN members "to ensure that those responsible for serious violations of human rights and international humanitarian law would be brought to justice."[53]

Two weeks later, on November 30, 2006, the UN secretary-general decided to offer his good offices to the region's countries and appointed Joaquim Chissano, former president of Mozambique, as his special envoy for the LRA-affected areas.

Chissano was highly respected; he practiced meditation, studied in Paris, and also fought for Mozambique's independence, becoming the minister of foreign affairs of the first independent government. He was elected president on three different occasions. In 2005 he decided not to run for another election. Additionally, he had been the chairman of the African Union in 2003.

In 1992 Chissano had led a peace agreement with a rebel group in Mozambique that concluded in a blanket amnesty. Instead, UN Secretary-General Kofi Annan instructed him as the special envoy to liaise with the International Criminal Court highlighting the independent judicial process to address the problem.[54] We received him at The Hague, and our offices were always in contact.

Before Chissano's appointment, the UN Office of Legal Affairs produced a note clarifying the UN special envoy's legal limits with the LRA's leaders.[55] It was based on the 1999 guidelines discussed in the meeting led by de Soto in 2004.

A month later, on September 25, 2006, an interoffice memorandum relating to the "United Nations position on peace and justice in post-conflict societies" was issued.[56] It established four points:

1. *There is no sustainable peace without justice—although they can be sequenced in time.*
2. *The United Nations does not recognize any amnesty for genocide, crimes against humanity, war crimes, and other serious violations of international humanitarian law.*
3. *While the ICC is independent of the United Nations, the United Nations supports the Court and avoids any action likely to undermine its authority.*
4. *Contacts between United Nations representatives and persons indicted by international criminal jurisdictions holding positions of authority in their respective countries should be limited to what is strictly required for carrying out United Nations mandated activities.*[57]

Such legal frame was respected by the special envoy and by the council decisions.[58]

The Role of Chissano

In the meantime, "the LRA delegation grew increasingly disenchanted with what they perceived as the ineffectiveness, volatile personal style and lack of even-handedness of the lead mediator" Riek Machar. By late 2006, the LRA had lost trust in South Sudan's government, "both to ensure security and provide fair and impartial mediation."[59]

On January 9, 2007, during a ceremony at Juba to commemorate the second anniversary of the Comprehensive Peace Agreement (CPA), two statements triggered the LRA's reaction. Salva Kiir, president of South Sudan, said, "he was losing patience with the LRA over delays in the talks," and Al-Bashir, president of Sudan, added: "We are prepared to constitute a joint force to eliminate the LRA. We do not want them. If we cannot find a peaceful solution to the LRA conflict, then we must pursue a military solution."[60]

On the day that talks were to resume, the LRA delegation head, Martin Ojul, announced that the LRA would not go back to Juba, given the statements made by Kiir and Bashir and security considerations.[61]

The LRA demanded replacing Machar as the chief mediator and a change of venue for the talks[62], insisting that it would not return to Juba, threatening the cessation of the hostilities agreement that would expire on February 28, 2007.[63]

The efforts of UN Special Envoy Chissano paved the way to solve the problem. He met with Kony along the Congo/Sudan border at the beginning of March to search for a compromise. Minister Rugunda, the government negotiator, accompanied him on the second visit and talked face to face with Kony for the first time. Acholi leaders, meeting in Juba at the beginning of the month, called for the talks to resume and proposed reforms to strengthen the peace process.[64]

By early 2007, most LRA fighters had left Northern Uganda, enabling some of the more than one million displaced to leave the camps. *Roads throughout the conflict area became accessible into the night, resulting in greater security and mobility. Humanitarian workers could travel without army escorts and improved the delivery of aid and services to camps. Apart from this, more land was being opened up for the impoverished people to farm.*[65]

On March 22, 2007, under South Africa's leadership, the council was briefed by Joachim Chissano and issued a presidential statement confirming the special envoy's important achievements.

The council welcomed the meeting between Uganda's government and the Lord's Resistance Army on March 11, with community representatives present, and the progress made toward a resumption of talks.[66] It "reiterated that those responsible for serious violations of human rights and international humanitarian law must be brought to justice, and urged that the peace process be concluded expeditiously."[67]

Pax Christi Netherlands opened a back channel to facilitate the negotiation.[68] The result was that the parties extended the cessation of the hostilities agreement from April through June.[69] According to David Bosco, in early 2007, "a draft agreement circulated among the negotiators in Juba that included a call for an Article 16 resolution," which entails a deferral of the investigation for a year.[70] Bosco considered that *"for the court, the Juba process was an ominous sign that even supportive states might not back the institution when it mattered most."*[71] He missed that Article 16 is part of the Rome Statute system.

Sara Nouwen made the point neglected by Bosco, explaining that the ICC, particularly the arrest warrants and the principle of complementarity, "helped to put the issue of accountability firmly on the Juba negotiating table—a first in the many negotiations between the GoU and rebel movements."[72]

The Juba talks were under the ICC *shadow*. "Seemingly aware of the complementarity principle, Kony argued that '[t]he ICC should leave Uganda to handle the issue of accountability since Uganda has a functional justice system with jails in Luzira, Lugore, etc.'"[73]

An agreement on comprehensive solutions to the conflict was reached on May 2, 2007, and on reconciliation and accountability on June 29. The second identified "a combination of local and national justice mechanisms—already in place or to be instituted—to promote reconciliation and address issues of accountability for wrongs committed by both rebel and state actors (with hints that this combination of mechanisms might satisfy the ICC)."[74]

Following the agreements, "rebel elements in southern Sudan moved to the LRA's jungle hideout near Garamba National Park in Congo in May and June, thus expanding the peace process's major achievement: more security for millions of civilians in northern Uganda and southern Sudan."[75]

Part 3: The End of the Juba Process

The Failure of the Negotiations and Military Pressure

The Juba talks created conflicts between the two LRA top leaders. In October 2007, Vincent Otti, LRA's second-in-command, was killed on Kony's orders.[76] The commanders considered loyal to Otti were either killed or defected.[77] The LRA denied Otti's death for two months, insisting that he was alive and under house arrest—accused of being a government spy.[78]

Two persons abducted as children and already indicted became the second and third in command: Okot Odhiambo and Dominic Ongwen. Some deserters said the reason for Kony's order was Otti's enthusiasm for peace talks.[79]

On November 13, 2007, Joaquim Chissano was visiting the UN in New York. He explained to a group of journalists the complexities of the negotiations: "Achieving an alternative form of justice rather than submitting to the International Criminal Court process was a 'delicate but not impossible' prospect in negotiations."[80]

When asked about the rumors concerning the relationship between the top two LRA leaders, Mr. Chissano said, "there was no point in speculating. If Mr. Otti had died or indeed been killed, the possible effect would merely be a weakening of the LRA negotiating position."[81]

In January 2008, Kony confirmed Otti's killing, considered it an internal matter, and affirmed "what happened to Otti and others" would not derail the ongoing peace talks in Juba.[82] Kony said that he was waiting to sign the final peace agreement before local and international observers and then return to his home village in Odek, northeast of Gulu town.[83]

Just the week before the negotiations commenced, Kony fired the LRA's delegation's chief and three other members. He believed they were too close to Otti.[84]

"Under the delegation's new head, David Matsanga, the Juba talks resumed in January 2008 after a six-month hiatus. Within weeks, in early February, appendices to the major agenda items 2 and 3 were negotiated, as was a permanent ceasefire and—the talks' final agenda item—an agreement on disarmament, demobilization, and reintegration (DDR) of the rebel fighters. Suddenly, a final peace agreement looked imminent."[85]

On February 19, the Ugandan government and Lord's Resistance Army (LRA) rebels ended a landmark agreement.[86]

On February 23, 2008, Minister Rugunda, representing the government of Uganda, and LRA's representative David Matsanga signed a Permanent Ceasefire Agreement in Juba. Rugunda said that Uganda's government has never seen any danger emanating from ICC as a stumbling block and reiterated that a Ugandan court would be in charge of LRA cases.[87]

David Matsanga said Joseph Kony had "blessed the signing and extended greetings to all the parties and the mediators by satellite phone from his hideout location in Riikwang a few minutes before signing ceremony takes off."[88]

Our office received information that the LRA "began a mass abduction campaign at the same time of the agreement," taking hundreds of civilians from the Central African Republic, Sudan, and the DRC back to their base in Garamba. It was giving them military training.[89] A member of the Office of the Prosecutor discussed the matter with a member of Chissano's team, but they considered that it was the time to discuss peace, no crimes.

In March 2008, an LRA delegation went to the ICC seat at The Hague. The court issued a statement informing that it would not be discussing specifics of the case.[90] The LRA delegates met members of the registry to discuss "procedural issues."[91] Our office refused to meet the rebel envoys and, we briefly commented, "The arrest warrants issued by the court remain in effect and have to be executed." I also expressed my concern at recent attacks committed by the LRA rebels in the Central African Republic.[92]

On April 10, after many delays, Kony was to have added his signature. Instead of signing and in confusing circumstances, he appointed James Obita "as new head of the rebel delegation and invited leaders and elders from northern Uganda for a meeting in South Sudan in early May to discuss the contested issues of restorative and retributive justice."[93]

On May 13, however, after four days of waiting, the assembled leaders who had come to meet the rebel leader issued a communiqué that lamented his failure to show up. They commended the patience and efforts of chief mediator Riek Machar (who had waited with the group), urged Kony to sign the peace agreement, and continued commitment to peace.

Then, on May 25, the news was released that Kony had finally rejected signing any peace agreement, "saying that he would rather die in the bush than turn himself over to the [Government of Uganda] or ICC and 'be hanged.' "[94]

"Still, efforts to keep the process alive continued. Chissano publicly continued to hold out hope." In October, "after two months more had passed with no apparent progress, President Salva Kiir signaled an end to South Sudan's open-ended commitment to the Juba talks."[95]

"In northern Uganda, meanwhile, even with the uncertainty caused by the often halting nature of the Juba talks, a transition on the ground from war to peace was underway . . . The roads were busy as people traveled freely, without fear. The relative peace . . . remained fragile, but it was real and palpable. Peace was returning to northern Uganda."[96]

At the same time, the situation for the rebels in Garamba was also changing. On June 6, 2008, BBC published that Lord's Resistance Army "is forcibly recruiting fresh fighters and acquiring new arms in neighboring countries."[97]

DRC's President Kabila informed the UN Security Council during a visit to Kinshasa of the importance of pursuing a military option. He added that the Democratic Republic of the Congo had initiated contacts with the governments of Uganda and Southern Sudan in that regard. MONUC stressed that it was still limited in its capacity to deal with the LRA issue.[98]

"In July/August 2008, the DRC army began deploying along two sides of the forest . . . the LRA in September began attacking both Congolese and nearby South Sudanese civilians, while sometimes engaging FARDC and SPLA troops as well."[99]

"As these developments were unfolding in the DRC, a two-day meeting of 'stakeholders' in the 'Juba dialogue' was held in Kampala in early November. Machar and Chissano issued a joint communiqué giving Kony a November 30 deadline to sign the Final Peace Agreement. Kony signaled a willingness to do so, and the DRC announced that it would cease military operations against the LRA to facilitate the signature. Museveni and other GoU spokesmen reiterated several times that once Kony appended his signature, they would request that the ICC defer or 'lift' their warrants."

"Over 29/30 November, a large contingent of Ugandan and international delegates gathered and waited at the designated LRA assembly point in Ri-Kwangba. Kony once more failed to show up. For almost all concerned, the Juba peace process had reached a dead end."

"On Sunday, 14 December, the UPDF began bombing LRA camps in Garamba. . . . the LRA managed to elude and thwart UPDF efforts against them while also launching retaliatory attacks against civilian soft targets."[100]

On December 22, 2008, the UN Security Council issued a presidential statement strongly condemning the repeated failure of Joseph Kony to sign the Final Peace Agreement.

"Recalling that the International Criminal Court had issued arrest warrants for certain LRA leaders, the Council reaffirmed that ending impunity was essential for a society recovering from conflict to come to terms with past abuses and to prevent their recurrence."[101]

A few days later, the LRA killed at least eighty people on December 25, 2008. Batande village's residents gathered for Christmas lunch after the morning church service when LRA members surrounded them, tied them up with rope or rubber strips from bicycle tires, and killed them with blows to the head. When the killing ended, the LRA combatants ate the Christmas feast the villagers had prepared and then slept among the dead bodies before continuing on their trail of destruction and death. LRA combatants attacked another twelve villages on December 26, 27, and 28.[102]

With the UNSC agreement, the secretary-general suspended the special envoy's mandate as of June 2009. LRA continued its attacks. In December 2009, troops under Dominic Ongwen's command killed at least 345 civilians and abducted another 250 in the Makombo area of Northeastern Congo.

Kony 2012

Since 2004 Invisible Children was following what happened in Northern Uganda, supporting humanitarian efforts, and producing films to mobilize US youth. In April 2007, nearly 70,000 Americans participated in an event organized by Invisible Children to draw attention to the displacement disaster in Northern Uganda.[103]

They were filming a documentary about the Juba talks, and in 2006 Bob Bayley, one of the three founders, interviewed me in my hotel in New York. Bobby was friendly and informal, but he thought that our office was blocking the agreement. He wanted to present me as the "stumbling block" of the negotiation in the film in preparation.

I told them that I was not interfering with the negotiation, and I went beyond my official lines. I said that the Juba talks would fail, Kony would attack again, and it would be very painful.

In November 2008, Invisible Children's crew was waiting for Joseph Kony at the designated LRA assembly point in Ri-Kwangba, the Democratic Republic of Congo. Kony's signature would be the end of their movie and their four-year journey to end LRA's attacks. They waited in vain. Despite their frustration, they started to discuss what to do.

Invisible Children realized that the ICC arrest warrants were not the stumbling block: rather the solution to Kony's problem. Exposing unique flexibility, Invisible Children changed course and it decided to organize a campaign to implement the ICC arrest warrants.

Together with Enough Project and Resolve Uganda, Invisible Children promoted the adoption of the "Lord's Resistance Army Disarmament and

Northern Uganda Recovery Act of 2009." Invisible Children organized rock concerts in support of the campaign, set up discussions with our office, the African Union, the governments of Uganda and DRC, the US Congress members, and even stood in front of a senator's office who was blocking the adoption of the legislation for a week.

The US Congress passed the project with broad bipartisan support on May 12, 2010. The law stated that, in the continued absence of a negotiated solution, it was US policy to support efforts "to protect civilians from the Lord's Resistance Army, to apprehend or remove Joseph Kony and his top commanders from the battlefield . . . and to disarm and demobilize the remaining LRA fighters."[104]

The law also required President Obama to develop a comprehensive, multilateral strategy to protect civilians in central Africa from LRA attacks and take steps to stop the rebel group's violence permanently. Furthermore, it calls on the United States to increase humanitarian assistance to countries currently affected by LRA violence and support economic recovery and transitional justice efforts in Uganda.[105]

President Obama signed the bill into law on May 24, 2010, during a White House ceremony that included Congress's members and the three organizations' representatives.[106]

Since 2008, the United States had provided support to Ugandan-led military operations to capture or kill LRA commanders, later integrated into an African Union "Regional Task Force" against the LRA. The Obama administration expanded US support for these operations in 2011 by deploying US military advisers to the field.[107]

Invisible Children's leaders promoted the use of radio antennae to disseminate early warnings and alert isolated villages in DRC's remote areas about the LRA's attacks. They attended the hearing on the closing arguments in the trial against Thomas Lubanga and considered there was not enough world attention because Lubanga was not known outside the DRC.

Invisible Children decided to transform Joseph Kony into the most well-known criminal in the world. They carefully crafted a thirty-minute video to launch through the internet. "Rapidly shared through social network sites, Kony 2012 soon earned the title of fastest spreading online video ever produced."[108]

"Kony 2012" reached over one hundred million views in just six days. More than 90 percent of the viewers agreed with its message. Invisible Children created the collective effort to arrest Joseph Kony, which the UN

Security Council could not achieve. Still, the success triggered criticism that ignored the previous complex work of Invisible Children and many actors in the conflict.[109]

The combination of the "Lord's Resistance Army Disarmament and Northern Uganda Recovery Act of 2009" and *Kony 2012* changed the LRA operations. In April 2013, Secretary of State John Kerry offered up to $5 million for information leading to the arrests, transfer, or conviction of three top LRA leaders sought by the ICC: Kony, Odhiambo, and Ongwen. Secretary Kerry said, "the last piece of legislation I passed as a Senator is one of the first I'm now ready to deploy on an issue we care about deeply."[110]

The State Department affirmed that the reward offer would contribute to the objective of ending impunity and promoting justice, "a key pillar" of the administration's Atrocity Prevention Initiative and National Security Strategy.[111]

Odhiambo was killed in 2013. In January 2015, the Seleka armed group in the Northern Central African Republic captured Dominic Ongwen.[112] Seleka fighters deliver him to US troops and allegedly requested the reward.[113] Ongwen was transferred to the custody of AU forces on January 14, 2015,[114] and a few days later to the ICC.[115]

The UN Security Council members welcomed the arrival of Dominic Ongwen from the Central African Republic to the International Criminal Court on January 20, 2015.[116] On January 26, 2015, Dominic Ongwen appeared before the ICC. He said, "I was born in 1975. I was abducted in 1988, and I was taken to the bush when I was 14 years old up 'til now."[117]

In March 2016, the pre-trial chamber confirmed the charges against Ongwen. Judge Cuno Tarfusser integrated it as the presiding judge, Judge Marc Perrin de Brichambaut, and Judge Chang-ho Chung. No one challenged the Office of the Prosecutor's *jus ad Curiam* decision adopted twelve years before.

The pre-trial chamber considered: "in accordance with article 19 of the Statute, the Chamber is satisfied that the Court has jurisdiction over the present case."[118]

In early 2017, Uganda and the United States stopped their military operations against the LRA. There were fears that this would *"allow Kony to rebuild the combatant force, which had reduced in size by at least 75% since 2008 in part due to low morale and waves of defections. Kony did indeed give orders in early 2018 to forcibly recruit new members, leading to the abduction of more than 40 children and youth in the following months."*[119]

In any case, civilian killings by LRA have decreased markedly,[120] and the number of people displaced as a direct result of LRA attacks or out of fear of coming under attack by the LRA has also reportedly declined. The numbers went "from 1,200 in 2009 to fewer than 20 in 2014 to 7 in 2019."[121]

In 2019 Kony lived in Kafia Kingi, a contested enclave on Sudan, South Sudan, and the Central African Republic's borders. According to defectors, the LRA at the end of 2019 was made up of a few dozen people, including Kony's sons Salim and Ali.[122] With little or no direction from their leader, other LRA commanders continued in 2019 to roam remote regions of Eastern CAR and Northern Democratic Republic of Congo (DRC), where they looted and abducted from small farming communities to survive.[123]

At the moment of writing this book, Kony is the only fugitive of the cases opened in state parties' jurisdiction during my term. The ICC contributed to the prevention of the crimes. Kony is still escaping from the ICC, but the LRA is disrupted.

Notes

1. In a presidential statement the council demanded *"that those responsible for serious violations of human rights and international humanitarian law must be brought to justice, and urg[ed] that the peace process be concluded expeditiously."* U.N. President of the S.C., Presidential Statement dated Mar. 22, 2007, U.N. Doc. S/PRST/2007/6 (Mar. 22, 2007).

2. (a) A cessation of hostilities agreement in August 2006 and a subsequent agreement on a monitoring mechanism and addendum; (b) the agreement and annex on accountability and reconciliation, which establishes the legal framework for accountability and reconciliation mechanisms in the promotion of peace with justice in Uganda (February 2008); (c) the agreement and implementation protocol on comprehensive solutions, which covers the strategic issues of rehabilitation, recovery and development of Northern Uganda (February 2008); (d) the agreement on a permanent ceasefire (February 2008); and (e) the agreement on disarmament, demobilization, repatriation, and reintegration.

3. Noam Cohen, *A Video Campaign and the Power of Simplicity*, N.Y. TIMES (Mar. 11, 2012), https://www.nytimes.com/2012/03/12/business/media/kony-2012-video-illustrates-the-power-of-simplicity.html.

4. Robert H. Mnookin & Lewis Kornhauser, *Bargaining in the Shadow of the Law: The Case of Divorce*, 88 YALE L.J. 950 (1979).

5. U.N. SCOR, 59th Sess., 5048th mtg., U.N. Doc. S/PV.5048 (Oct. 1, 2004).

6. S.C. Res. 1649 ¶ 18, S/RES/1649 (2005) (Dec. 21, 2005).

7. "Any call for the situation in northern Uganda to be put on the agenda of the Security Council is therefore unjustified." Chargé d'affaires a.i. of the Permanent Mission of

Uganda to the U.N., Letter dated Jan. 16, 2006 from the Chargé d'affairs a.i. of the Permanent Mission of Uganda to the U.N. addressed to the President of the Security Council, U.N. Doc. S/2006/29 (Jan. 19, 2006). *See also* Sandrine Perrot, *Northern Uganda: A "Forgotten Conflict," Again? The Impact of the Internationalization of the Resolution Process, in* THE LORD'S RESISTANCE ARMY: MYTH AND REALITY 187, 193 (Tim Allen & Koen Vlassenroot eds., Kindle ed. 2012).

8. The meeting included the presence of fourteen Foreign Affairs' ministers.

9. *Id.*

10. *Id.*

11. *Id.*

12. The group of friends and special envoys included representatives of the European Commission, the African Union, and twenty-seven countries: Austria, Belgium, Canada, China, Denmark, Finland, France, Gabon, Germany, Greece, Holy Seat, Ireland, Italy, Japan, Kuwait, Luxembourg, the Netherlands, Nigeria, Norway, Portugal, Russia, South Africa, Spain, Sweden, Switzerland, the United Kingdom, the United States of America.

13. The Netherlands Special Envoy to the Great Lakes Region said: "we hope that the International Criminal Court's arrest warrants concerning five leaders of the LRA will be effectively executed as soon as possible, also in the light of their preventive impact on further atrocities." U.N. SCOR 61st Sess., 5359 mtg, U.N. Doc. S/PV.5359 (Resumption 1) (Jan. 27, 2006).

14. "Informal groups may be specifically formed to address specific crises and have pro-liferated in recent decades along with the number of armed conflicts and the UN's involvement in them. As Jochen Prantl stresses, . . . [they] are 'diplomatic devices op-erating with no formal mandate from the Security Council or the General Assembly.'" Monica Herz, *Formal and Informal Group, in* THE OXFORD HANDBOOK ON THE UNITED NATIONS (Thomas G. Weiss & Sam Dawsed eds., 2nd ed., Oxford University Press, 2018). *A Uganda core group* was constituted in 2004 by the United Kingdom, Norway and the Netherlands. They were later joined by Ireland, Germany, Sweden and Canada. Sandrine Perrot, *Northern Uganda: A "Forgotten Conflict," Again? The Impact of the Internationalization of the Resolution Process, in* THE LORD'S RESISTANCE ARMY: MYTH AND REALITY 187, 191 (Tim Allen & Koen Vlassenroot eds., Kindle ed. 2012). It included observers to the talks like Kenya, Mozambique, Tanzania, and a very active South Africa Richard Dicker, *Trading Justice for Peace in Uganda Won't Work*, HUM. RTS. WATCH (May 2, 2007, 8:00 PM), https://www.hrw.org/news/2007/05/02/trading-justice-peace-uganda-wont-work#.

15. "It was agreed that dealing with LRA as a regional threat would remove the fear among IDPs and allow for a faster return and resettlement as well as post-conflict re-construction in Northern Uganda." Permanent Representative of Uganda to the U.N., Letter Dated Apr. 24, 2006. addressed to the President of the Security Council, U.N. Doc. S/2006/271 (Apr. 28, 2006).

16. Oxfam's statement did not include the need to do justice. *High-Level Meeting Must Lead to Immediate Improvements for Two Million Displaced People in Northern*

Uganda, OXFAM NEW ZEALAND (Mar. 21, 2006), https://www.oxfam.org.nz/news-media/media-releases/high-level-meeting-must-lead-to-immediate-improvements-for-two-million-displaced-people-in-northern-uganda/.

17. S.C. Res. 1663, ¶ 7, U.N. Doc. S/RES/1663 (Mar. 24, 2006).

18. *Id.*

19. U.N. SCOR 61st Sess., 5415 mtg., U.N. Doc. S/PV.5415 (Apr. 19, 2006).

20. The *cessation of hostilities and regional security; the enhancement of protection of the civilian population; increased humanitarian assistance to internally displaced persons; peacebuilding and reconciliation; and the return and resettlement of internally displaced persons. Id.*

21. The security group was to focus on "a joint regional military mechanism involving Uganda, the Democratic Republic of the Congo and the Sudan as well as the [MONUC and the UNMIS] to disarm the LRA based in southern Sudan and in Garamba National Park in the Democratic Republic of the Congo; facilitating and cooperation with the International Criminal Court to execute the warrants of arrest against the LRA leadership; and consolidation and promotion of dialogue between the Government of Uganda and middle-level LRA commanders to ensure a peaceful resolution of the conflict in northern Uganda." *Id.*

22. He suggested reaching agreements "to ensure that the LRA terrorists are disarmed and the indicted leaders arrested." He also suggested including countries with military power like France or Australia. Expanding on the regional security group mentioned by the minister of foreign affairs, Mbabazi described how to establish international security cooperation U.N. SCOR 61st Sess., 5415 mtg., U.N. Doc. S/PV.5415 (Apr. 19, 2006).

23. Integrated Regional Information Networks, *Call for Regional Effort to Tackle LRA*, GLOBAL POL'Y FORUM (May 9, 2006), https://www.globalpolicy.org/component/content/article/207/39821.html.

24. Security Council, Report of the Secretary-General pursuant to resolutions 1653 (2006) and 1663 (2006), ¶ 51, S/2006/478 (June 29, 2006).

25. U.N. Secretary General, Report pursuant to resolutions 1653 (2006) and 1663 (2006), ¶ 52, U.N. Doc. S/2006/478 (June 29, 2006).

26. The Secretary General "suggest the possibility of a negotiated solution with LRA." U.N. Secretary General, Report pursuant to resolutions 1653 (2006) and 1663 (2006), ¶ 32, 36, S/2006/478 (June 29, 2006).

27. *However, such contacts also raise the issues of impunity and the responsibility of the Southern Sudanese authorities to apprehend the individuals indicted by the Court.* Secretary-General, Report pursuant to resolutions 1653 (2006) and 1663 (2006), ¶ 50 S/2006/478 (June 29, 2006).

28. Permanent Representative of Uganda to the U.N., Letter dated July 20, 2006, addressed to the President of the Security Council, U.N. Doc. S/2006/558 (July 20, 2006).

29. Pax Christi was founded in Europe in 1945 as a reconciliation movement bringing together French and Germans after World War II. It is a global catholic movement that works to establish peace, respect for human rights and justice and reconciliation,

counting with 120 member Organizations active in more than fifty countries worldwide.

30. Ronald R. Atkinson, *"The Realists in Juba"? An Analysis of the Juba Peace Talks*, in THE LORD'S RESISTANCE ARMY: MYTH AND REALITY 205, 210–11 (Tim Allen & Koen Vlassenroot eds., Kindle ed. 2012).

31. TNH, *Uganda: We Respect Gov't Decisions, but Those Who Committed Atrocities Should Account—US*, RELIEF WEB (July 6, 2006), https://reliefweb.int/report/uga nda/uganda-we-respect-govt-decision-those-who-committed-atrocities-should-account-us.

32. Integrated Regional Information Networks, *LRA Leader Must Be Arrested, ICC Insists*, GLOBAL POL'Y FORUM (July 5, 2006), https://www.globalpolicy.org/compon ent/content/article/165/29603.html.

33. Ronald R. Atkinson, *"The Realists in Juba"? An Analysis of the Juba Peace Talks*, in THE LORD'S RESISTANCE ARMY: MYTH AND REALITY 2005, 214 (Tim Allen & Koen Vlassenroot eds., Kindle ed. 2012).

34. "The first confidence-building meeting took place at the end of July 2006." Apart from this, on November 14, an Acholi delegation including a government representative went to a remote area near Ri-Kwangba to meet with Joseph Kony and Vincent Otti. Int'l Crisis Grp., *Northern Uganda: Seizing the Opportunity for Peace Africa Report N° 124* (Apr. 26, 2007).

35. *Id.*

36. "*[A] cessation to hostilities; comprehensive political solutions to the conflict; account-ability and reconciliation; DDR; and a permanent ceasefire.*" PHIL CLARK, DISTANT JUSTICE: THE IMPACT OF THE INTERNATIONAL CRIMINAL COURT ON AFRICAN POLITICS 214–15 (Kindle ed. 2018).

37. *Ugandan Rebels in Amnesty Demand*, BBC NEWS (Sept. 6, 2006, 4:43 PM), http://news.bbc.co.uk/2/hi/africa/5320254.stm.

38. *Id.*

39. Esti Tambay, *Uganda: LRA Reiterates Demand for Warrants Withdrawal*, COALITION FOR THE ICC, http://iccnow.org/index.php?mod=newsdetail&news=1930 (quoting The Monitor (Uganda), "Kony Rebels Refuse to Sign Peace Deal," Oct. 10, 2006, http://allafrica.com/stories/200610091534.htm).

40. Joah Fisher, *Uganda LRA Want Warrants Dropped*, BBC NEWS (Oct. 9, 2006, 2:11 AM), http://news.bbc.co.uk/2/hi/africa/6032453.stm.

41. *Id.*

42. Mareike Schomerus, *"A Terrorist Is Not a Person Like Me": An Interview with Joseph Kony*, in THE LORD'S RESISTANCE ARMY: MYTH AND REALITY 113, 113–14 (Tim Allen & Koen Vlassenroot eds., Kindle ed. 2012).

43. Frazer stressed the importance of the indictments as part of a process of accounta-bility, but the priority was to push Kony "out of the bush." Jendayi Frazer, US Assistant Secretary for African Affairs, "Engaging the Horn of Africa" Press Roundtable, Windsor Victoria Hotel, Entebbe, Uganda (June 20, 2006).

44. "Speaking about the guarantees, the South Sudan Vice President and chief mediator Dr Riek Machar, told the government negotiators led by the Internal Affairs Minister,

Dr Ruhakana Rugunda, at his office yesterday, that President Museveni had already communicated his commitment to the government of South Sudan." Grace Matsiko et al., *I Cannot Betray Kony Museveni*, GLOBAL POL'Y FORUM (Aug. 16, 2006), https://www.globalpolicy.org/component/content/article/165/29608.html.

45. Int'l Crisis Grp., *Policy Briefing: Peace in Norther Uganda?* (Sept. 12, 2006).

46. *Id.*

47. *Id.*

48. Jeffrey Gettleman, *U.N. Envoy Meets with Ugandan Rebel*, N.Y. TIMES (Nov. 13, 2006), https://www.nytimes.com/2006/11/13/world/africa/13uganda.html. *Jungle Boos for Peace Process*, NEW HUMANITARIAN (Nov. 17, 2006), https://www.thenewhumanitarian.org/fr/node/228385.

49. *Guidelines for U.N. representatives in certain aspects of negotiations for conflict resolution*, 2006 Juridical Y.B., ST/LEG/SER.C/44.

50. Raymond Kwun Sun Lau, *Protection First, Justice Later?*, *in* CIVILIAN PROTECTION IN THE TWENTY-FIRST CENTURY: GOVERNANCE AND RESPONSIBILITY IN A FRAGMENTED WORLD (Cecilia Jacob & Alistar D. B. Cook eds., 1st ed. 2016).

51. Press Release, Security Council, Security Council Presidential Statement Demands Release of Women, Children by Lord's Resistance Army, Expeditious Conclusion of Peace Process, U.N. Press Release SC/8869 (Nov. 16, 2006).

52. *Id.*

53. *Id.*

54. Security Council, Letter dated Nov. 30, 2006 from the Secretary General to the President of the Security Council, U.N. Doc. S/2006/930 (Dec. 1, 2006).

55. The note accepted that "direct contacts with the five indicated leaders may be required. They should, however, be limited to what is strictly required for carrying out his mandate The presence of the Special Envoy in any ceremonial or similar occasions should be avoided." *Note to the Under-Secretary-General for Political Affairs regarding guidance on activities of the Special Envoy in [Rebel Group]-affected areas*, 2006 Juridical Y.B., ST/LEG/SER.C/44.

56. *Interoffice memorandum relating to the United Nations position on peace and justice in post-conflict societies*, 2006 Juridical Y.B., ST/LEG/SER.C/44.

57. *Id.*

58. On December 20, 2006, the UN Security Council issued a Presidential Statement congratulating eleven African leaders who participated in the International Conference's second summit on the Great Lakes Region in Nairobi. The representative of the Russian Federation perceived "*The Council was playing an active role in the peacebuilding process.*" Press Release, Security Council, In Presidential Statement, Security Council Congratulates Great Lakes Region Leaders on Signing of Security Pact, U.N. Press Release SC/8917 (Dec. 20, 2006).

59. Ronald R. Atkinson, *"The Realists in Juba"? An Analysis of the Juba Peace Talks*, *in* THE LORD'S RESISTANCE ARMY: MYTH AND REALITY 205, 217 (Tim Allen & Koen Vlassenroot eds., Kindle ed. 2012) (quoting "Al-Bashir wants Ugandan rebels out of Sudan, *Sudan Tribune*, Jan. 11, 2007).

60. *Id.* at 215.

61. *Id.*
62. Int'l Crisis Grp., *Northern Uganda: Seizing the Opportunity for Peace Africa Report N°
    124* (Apr. 26, 2007).
63. *Id.*
64. *Id.*
65. *Id.*
66. Press Release, Security Council, Security Council Stresses Support for Negotiated
    Settlement Between Government of Uganda, Lord's Resistance Army, U.N. Press
    Release SC/8976 (Mar. 22, 2007).
67. *Id.*
68. Int'l Crisis Grp., *Northern Uganda: Seizing the Opportunity for Peace Africa Report N°
    124* (Apr. 26, 2007).
69. "While this moves the LRA further from northern Uganda and reduces the immediate
    threat to civilians, it also gives the rebels an opportunity to regroup in a single location
    and potentially strengthen their military posture. To alleviate Ugandan government
    concerns on this score, eight AU monitors from Kenya, South Africa, Tanzania and
    Mozambique are to join the monitoring team full-time at Ri-Kwangba." *Id.*
70. DAVID BOSCO, ROUGH JUSTICE: THE INTERNATIONAL CRIMINAL COURT IN A WORLD
    OF POWER POLITICS 130 (Kindle ed. 2014).
71. *Id.* at 131.
72. SARAH M. H. NOUWEN, COMPLEMENTARITY IN THE LINE FIRE: THE CATALYST
    EFFECT OF THE INTERNATIONAL CRIMINAL COURT IN SUDAN AND UGANDA 160–62
    (Kindle ed. Cambridge Series in Law and Society, 2013).
73. "Complementarity became the axis of the Juba peace talks and put accounta-
    bility firmly on the agenda. Subsequently, complementarity has had several other
    effects, such as the preparations for a Ugandan War Crimes Court; the review of
    the International Criminal Court Bill in the light of possible domestic proceed-
    ings and increased attention for compliance with so-called international standards
    in domestic proceedings." Sarah Nouwen, *Complementarity in Uganda Domestic
    Diversity or International Imposition?*, THE INTERNATIONAL CRIMINAL COURT AND
    COMPLEMENTARITY: FROM THEORY TO PRACTICE 1150 (Carsten Stahn & Mohamed
    M. El Zeidy eds., Kindle ed. 2011).
74. Ronald R. Atkinson, *"The realists in Juba"? An analysis of the Juba peace talks, in*
    THE LORD'S RESISTANCE ARMY: MYTH AND REALITY 205, 219 (Tim Allen & Koen
    Vlassenroot eds., Kindle ed. 2012).
75. Int'l Crisis Grp., *Policy Briefing: Northern Uganda Peace Process: The Need to Maintain
    Momentum* (Sept. 14, 2007).
76. *Otti "Executed by Ugan Rebels,"* BBC NEWS (Dec. 21, 2007, 4:01 PM), http://news.bbc.
    co.uk/2/hi/africa/7156284.stm.
77. Rob Crilly, *Lord's Resistance Army Used Truce to Rearm and Spread Dear in Uganda,*
    THE TIMES (Dec. 16, 2008, 12:00 AM), https://www.thetimes.co.uk/article/lords-res
    istance-army-uses-truce-to-rearm-and-spread-fear-in-uganda-splng3lvpqr.
78. Rebel Death May Hurt Uganda Talks, BBC News (Jan. 25, 2008, 10:24 AM), http://
    news.bbc.co.uk/2/hi/africa/7208562.stm.

79. Francis Kwera, *Deputy of Uganda's Rebel LRA Executed: Deserter*, REUTERS (Nov. 30, 2007, 3:32 PM), https://www.reuters.com/article/us-uganda-rebels/deputy-of-ugan das-rebel-lra-executed-deserter-idUSL3055222220071130.

80. *Press Conference by Special Envoy for Areas Affected by Lord's Resistance Army on Peace Talks Between Ugandan Government, Rebel Group*, U.N. (Nov. 13, 2007), https://www. un.org/press/en/2007/071113_Chissano.doc.htm.

81. *Id.*

82. *Uganda: LRA Allegedly Confirms Otti's Death; Status of Peace Talks; Related News and Opinions*, ICCNOW (Jan. 23, 2008), http://iccnow.org/?mod=newsdetail&news= 2485 (quoting Kony dares Museveni on Vincent Otti death, by Samuel O. Egadu & John P'lajur (The Monitor), Jan. 23, 2008, http://www.monitor.co.ug/artman/publ ish/news/kony_dares_Museveni_on_Vincent_Otti_death.shtml).

83. He also said that he discussed the agreement with his representatives on the third point of the agenda, accountability and reconciliation, and dismissed claims that he was recruiting youths. *Uganda: LRA Allegedly Confirms Otti's death; Status of Peace Talks; Related News and Opinions*, ICCNOW (Jan. 23, 2008), http://iccnow. org/?mod=newsdetail&news=2485 (quoting Kony dares Museveni on Vincent Otti death, by Samuel O. Egadu & John P'lajur (The Monitor), Jan. 23, 2008, http://www. monitor.co.ug/artman/publish/news/kony_dares_Museveni_on_Vincent_Otti_de ath.shtml).

84. David Smock, *Uganda/Lord's Resistance Army Peace Negotiations: An Update From Juba*, U.S. INST. FOR PEACE (Feb. 2008), https://www.usip.org/sites/default/files/PB-Uganda-Lord.PDF.

85. Ronal R. Atkinson, *"Th Realists in Juba"? An Analysis of the Juba Peace Talks*, in THE LORD'S RESISTANCE ARMY: MYTH AND REALITY 205, 219–22 (Tim Allen & Koen Vlassenroot eds., Kindle ed. 2012).

86. *Ugandans Reach War Crimes Accord*, BBC NEWS (Feb. 19, 2008, 6:09 PM), http:// news.bbc.co.uk/2/hi/africa/7252774.stm.

87. Isaac Vuni, *Uganda, Rebel LRA Signs Permanent Ceasefire Agreement in Juba*, SUDAN TRIBUNE (Feb. 24, 2008), https://www.sudantribune.com/spip.php?article26110.

88. *Id.*

89. Matthew Brubacher, *The ICC Investigation of the Lord's Resistance Army: An Insider's View*, in TIM ALLEN, THE LORD'S RESISTANCE ARMY: MYTH AND REALITY 262, 262 (Tim Allen & Koen Vlassenroot eds., Kindle ed. 2012).

90. "As a neutral organ that facilitates fair trial, the registry does not engage in substantive discussions with any of the parties on the merits of cases before the court," the statement said. Press Release, International Criminal Court, ICC—ICC Registry officials meet with Lord's Resistance Army delegation, ICCC Press Release (Mar. 10, 2008).

91. They were "related to the legal representation of those accused before the ICC, as well as procedure and time limits for the filing of documentation and materials with the registry." *Id.*

92. ICC Rejects Uganda Rebel Overture, BBC NEWS (Mar. 5, 2008), http://news.bbc. co.uk/2/hi/africa/7277577.stm.

93. Ronald R. Atkinson, *"The Realists in Juba"? An Analysis of the Juba Peace Talks*, in THE LORD'S RESISTANCE ARMY: MYTH AND REALITY 205, 219–22 (Tim Allen & Koen Vlassenroot eds., Kindle ed. 2012).

94. *Id.*

95. *Id.*

96. *Id.*

97. *Ugandan Rebels "Prepare for War,"* BBC NEWS (June 6, 2008, 5:06 PM), http://news.bbc.co.uk/2/hi/africa/7440790.stm.

98. Rep. of the S.C. mission to Djibouti (on Somalia), the Sudan, Chad, the Democratic Republic of the Congo and Côte d'Ivoire, 31 May to 10 June 2008, at 29, U.N. Doc. S/2008/460.

99. Ronald R. Atkinson, *"The Realists in Juba"? An Analysis of the Juba Peace Talks*, in THE LORD'S RESISTANCE ARMY: MYTH AND REALITY 205, 219–22 (Tim Allen & Koen Vlassenroot eds., Kindle ed. 2012).

100. *Id.*

101. "The Council expressed its appreciation for the efforts undertaken by Joaquim Chissano and agreed with his recommendation that the peace efforts should continue." Press Release, Security Council, Security Council Strongly Condemns Attacks By Lord's Resistance Army In Democratic Republic Of Congo, Southern Sudan, U.N. Press Release SC/9555 (Dec. 22, 2008).

102. *DR Congo: LRA Slaughters 620 in "Christmas Massacres" Protection Urgently Needed as Killings Continue*, HUM; RTS. WATCH (Jan. 17, 2009), https://www.hrw.org/news/2009/01/17/dr-congo-lra-slaughters-620-christmas-massacres.

103. "There is a growing movement led by the youth of America to not only spread awareness of this conflict, but to generate the pressure necessary for our leaders to help end it," said Jason Russell, Invisible Children's Director. US *Congressmen Urge Bush to Support Ugandan Peace Talks*, SUDAN TRIBUNE (July 10, 2007), https://www.sudantribune.com/spip.php?article22773.

104. Press Release: New Law Gives President Obama Mandate to Help End LRA's Violence and Child Abductions in Central Africa, ENOUGH PROJECT (May 25, 2010), https://enoughproject.org/press-releases/press-release-new-law-gives-president-obama-mandate-help-end-lras-violence-and-child-abductions.

105. *Id.*

106. *Id.*

107. ALEXIS ARIEFF ET AL., CONG. RESEARCH SERVICE, R42094 THE LORD'S RESISTANCE ARMY: THE U.S. RESPONSE (Sept. 28, 2015).

108. Johannes Von Engelhardt & Jeroen Jansz, *Challenging Humanitarian Communication: An Empirical Exploration of Kony 2012*, 76 INT'L COMM. GAZETTE 464, 464 (2014).

109. "Drawing on Mutua's (2001) framework of savages, victims and saviours, this article analyses the Kony 2012 phenomenon to illustrate how a digital campaign can validate and reproduce subjectivities and structures of domination rather than stimulate sustainable reform-based change." Nerida Chazal & Adam Pocrnic, *Kony 2012: Intervention Narratives and the Saviour Subject*, 5 INT'L J. FOR CRIME, JUST. & SOC. DEMOCRACY 98, 99 (2016).

110. He also established a similar reward to another ICC fugitive: Sylvestre Mudacumura, the military commander the Democratic Forces for the Liberation of Rwanda (FDLR) that was involved in the Rwanda genocide. John Kerry, *More Work to Bring War Criminals to Justice*, HUFFINGTON POST (Apr. 3, 2013, 11:28 AM), https://www. huffpost.com/entry/war-crimes-rewards-program_b_3007049.

111. ALEXIS ARIEFF ET AL, CONG. RESEARCH SERVICE, R42094 THE LORD'S RESISTANCE ARMY: THE U.S. RESPONSE 12 (Sept. 28, 2015).

112. Jeffrey Gettleman, *Senior Rebel from Uganda to Be Moved to the Hague*, N.Y. TIMES (Jan. 13, 2015), https://www.nytimes.com/2015/01/14/world/africa/ugandan-rebel-commander-to-be-tried-at-international-criminal-court.html?action=click&mod ule=RelatedCoverage&pgtype=Article&region=Footer.

113. Rebel leaders with Seleka, a Muslim rebel movement in the Central African Republic, have said they captured Ongwen in battle and want the bounty for handing him over to the US military. The US government has condemned Seleka in the past for killing civilians and bringing turmoil to the country, so it would be awkward for Washington to pay off the group. Pentagon officials acknowledged that US forces took custody of Ongwen from the rebels. Craig Whitlock, *Detention of African Warlords Raises Legal Questions for Pentagon*, WASHINGTON POST (Jan. 13, 2015), https://www.washingtonpost.com/world/national-security/detention-of-warlord-raises-legal-questions-for-pentagon/2015/01/13/3839c43e-9b4b-11e4-96cc-e85 8eba91ced_story.html.

114. *ICC: LRA Transfer Advances Chance for Justice*, HUM. RTS. WATCH (Jan. 20, 2015, 5:43 PM), https://www.hrw.org/news/2015/01/20/icc-lra-transfer-advances-cha nce-justice.

115. ALEXIS AIEFF ET AL., CONG. RESEARCH SERVICE, R42094 THE LORD'S RESISTANCE ARMY: THE U.S. RESPONSE (Sept. 28, 2015).

116. U.N. Press Release, Security Council Press Statement on Transfer of Dominic Ongwen to International Criminal Court, Security Council Press Statement SC/ 11744-AFR/3055-L/3241 (Jan. 20, 2015).

117. Prosecutor v. Dominic Ongwen, ICC-02/04-01/05, Transcript of the Initial Appearance Hearing of Mr. Ongwen (Jan. 26, 2015).

118. Prosecutor v. Dominic Ongwen, ICC-02/04-01/15, Decision on the confirmation of charges against Dominic Ongwen ¶ 2 (Mar. 23, 2016), https://www.icc-cpi.int/ CourtRecords/CR2016_02331.PDF.

119. Paul Ronan & Kristof Titeca, *Kony's Rebels Remain a Threat, but They're Also Selling Honey to Get By*, AFRICAN ARGUMENTS (Mar. 10, 2020), https://africanarguments. org/2020/03/10/joseph-kony-lra-rebels-threat-selling-honey/.

120. *Mapping Violence in Central Africa*, CRISIS TRACKER, https://crisistracker.org (last visited May 18, 2020).

121. ALEXIS AIEFF ET AL., CONG. RESEARCH SERVICE, R42094 THE LORD'S RESISTANCE ARMY: THE U.S. RESPONSE 3 (Sept. 28, 2015).

122. Paul Ronan & Kristof Titeca, *Kony's Rebels Remain a Threat, but They're Also Selling Honey to Get By*, AFRICAN ARGUMENTS (Mar. 10, 2020), https://africanarguments. org/2020/03/10/joseph-kony-lra-rebels-threat-selling-honey/.

123. *Id.*

10

The Role of NGOs Referring the Central African Republic Situation

The Rome Statute innovation on *jus ad Curiam* provides new possibilities for smaller and weaker actors to achieve their goals. David Bosco affirmed: "The evidence of the court's first decade does not disturb the broad insight that international organizations often serve as vehicles for major-power influence."[1] I agree with Bosco that big powers can take advantage of international institutions, and the book presents different examples. However, the Rome Statute could also be "an enabling device"[2] for smaller states and even individual citizens. Article 15 of the statute establishes that "non-governmental organizations or other reliable sources" could provide information to the Office of the Prosecutor to initiate an investigation. The law defines who are the people entitled *to participate in the events* and the scope of their authority.

The FIDH (International Federation for Human Rights), an international human rights NGO established in 1922 integrating 192 organizations from 117 countries, took advantage of the Rome Statute's new framework. In 2003 it presented information to our office about crimes committed in the Central African Republic (CAR).

Goungaye Wanfiyo, president of the Ligue Centrafricaine des Droits de l'Homme (LCDH), a FIDH local affiliate, went further. He convinced General François Bozizé, who led the October 2002 coup d'état and became the president of CAR in March 2003, to refer the situation to the ICC.

In December 2004, president Bozizé, represented by Goungaye Wanfiyo, referred the Central African Republic situation to the ICC for crimes falling within the Rome Statute jurisdiction throughout the CAR territory since July 1, 2002. The CAR's referral suggested, "to open an investigation into this situation with a view to determining whether the former president Ange Felix Patasee, Mr. Jean-Pierre Bemba [and others] can be accused."

Jean-Pierre Bemba, a Congolese militia leader, deployed forces to CAR to protect Patassé's government from General Bozizé's rebel forces. Allegedly members of Bemba's militia committed a massive rape campaign against

War and Justice in the 21st Century. Luis Moreno Ocampo, Oxford University Press. © Oxford University Press 2022.
DOI: 10.1093/oso/9780197628973.003.0011

the population suspected of supporting the rebellion. The Office of the Prosecutor started a preliminary examination to decide if an investigation should be opened. We had to assess the alleged crimes, some local proceedings, and new crimes committed by different actors. There were national proceedings pending before the Court of Cassation.

The NGOs became impatient and mobilized President Bozizé and the pretrial chamber to expedite the opening of an ICC investigation. In November 2006, Pre-Trial Chamber III, presided by Judge Sylvia Steiner and integrated by Judge Hans-Peter Kaul and Judge Ekaterina Trendafilova, took a proactive role. It requested our office to provide a "report containing information on the current status of the preliminary examination of the CAR situation, including an estimate of when the preliminary examination of the CAR situation will be concluded."

We considered that the pre-trial chamber has no authority before the Office of the Prosecutor concludes the preliminary examination. The statute "grants to the Prosecutor the prerogative to determine when to initiate an investigation."[3] And the chamber can eventually review the decision not to investigate based on the "interest of justice."

In May 2007, the office opened an investigation for crimes committed in the CAR.

In May 2008, Pre-Trial Chamber I issued an arrest warrant against Jean-Pierre Bemba Gombo. Belgium implemented it immediately and surrendered Mr. Bemba to the ICC. Mr. Bemba formally challenged the case's admissibility. In June and October 2010, the trial and appeal chamber analyzed the national proceedings conducted and unanimously ruled that the case was admissible.

The Referral

On October 25, 2002, General François Bozizé, the former army chief of staff of the CAR armed forces, started a rebellion to remove President Ange-Félix Patassé. To protect his authority, President Patassé mobilized the remaining CAR national armed forces and requested assistance from Jean-Pierre Bemba, leader of a Congolese militia called the "Mouvement de Libération du Congo" (MLC).

On October 26, 2002, Bemba deployed his forces to the CAR to support President Patassé and fight against Bozizé's rebel troops.

In exchange for MLC troops' provision, Bemba received the benefit of securing the CAR as MLC's strategic rear base, deterring potential attacks from Kabila's DRC government against his forces through the CAR route.

Once the MLC troops established control over former rebel-held territories, they sought to punish perceived rebel sympathizers. They systematically targeted the civilian population by conducting house-to-house searches, killing many civilians, massively raping and looting.

Until April 2003, Bemba's militias systematically raped men, women, and children in their homes, forced people to watch rapes of family members in public locations, including streets and squares. Many of the women victims of rapes and gang rapes contracted HIV and became pregnant due to these rapes. Civilians that were killed included those who tried to prevent or resist rapes, attacks, or lootings.[4]

The CAR situation was the clearest example of gender crimes to punish a community I witnessed during my tenure. It also included something unique: the deliberate rape of the local leaders in front of their community, all of them men.

I was trying to understand the perpetrators' rationale. I discussed the issue with Catharine McKinnon, a leading scholar and activist on gender issues that was my special adviser: *Why are they targeting the community leaders to be raped? Why did they choose to rape these men and not to kill them?* She considered that *they were trying to mistreat the men so badly that they treated them as a woman.*

On March 15, General Bozizé took control of Bangui and proclaimed himself president. Former president Patassé went into exile, and Bemba's men crossed the Oubangi River in haste to return to the Democratic Republic of Congo.[5] A few months later, on June 30, 2003, as part of the peace process resulting from the Pretoria Agreement, Jean-Pierre Bemba was appointed vice president of the DRC transitional government.[6]

The CAR's NGOs "were well aware that the Rome Statute had come into force on July 1, 2002," they were conscious of CAR institutions' weaknesses, and they took the initiative to request the ICC intervention.[7]

Even before my appointment, in February 2003, FIDH formally sent to the ICC its report on "War Crimes in the CAR," which contained numerous testimonies and evidence concerning crimes falling within ICC jurisdiction perpetrated during the armed conflict between the loyalists and General Bozizé from October 2002 until March 2003.[8]

We opened a preliminary examination to analyze the CAR situation. Unlike in Northern Uganda, CAR's victims and NGO leaders were trying to engage the ICC. Goungaye Wanfiyo, president of the Ligue Centrafricaine des Droits de l'Homme (LCDH), affiliated to FIDH, understood the legal system created by the Rome Statute and perceived an opportunity to strengthen their chances to prevent and punish the crimes.

Wanfiyo planned to obtain a state referral taking advantage of the official narrative. President Bozizé had said to CAR people, "it is me who fought against the Banyamulenge, the Congolese, here is your savior."[9] Goungaye Wanfiyo considered that Bozizé could obtain political advantages by referring to the ICC the CAR situation.[10] He started a campaign to achieve that goal and met different CAR officials.[11]

In February 2004, FIDH sent to the Office of the Prosecutor a second report entitled "What Justice for the Victims of War Crimes?" This report provided more details about the crimes, and it also explained the state of domestic judicial proceedings against some of the alleged criminals.[12]

Goungaye Wanfiyo's strategy succeeded, and the CAR's Council of Ministers offered him to be state counsel to present the CAR situation to the ICC. As an NGO leader, he did not like to work for the government, but he accepted the position to ensure the ICC's intervention.[13]

On January 7, 2005, our office received a letter signed by Goungaye Wanfiyo as the counsel authorized by the CAR president to refer "*the situation of crimes falling within the jurisdiction of the Court committed anywhere on the territory of the Central African Republic since July 1, 2002, the date of entry into force of the Rome Statute.*"

FIDH supported the move but alerted that there was a political goal behind it:

[T]he referral comes only a few days before the presidential and legislative elections scheduled for February 2005, the timing thus being very opportune for the President. However, FIDH considers that the ICC involvement in the CAR situation is essential to bring effective independent justice that respects victims as well as the right of suspects to have a fair trial.[14]

FIDH also denounced extrajudicial executions carried out with at least the inferred agreement of the highest state authorities, under the pretext of fighting crime and insecurity. It urged our office "to immediately open an investigation on the international crimes committed in CAR since July 1, 2002, by the former loyalist forces of Patassé and by the former rebel troops of General Bozizé."[15]

Preliminary Examination: The Admissibility of the Situation

Bemba Internal Proceedings

During the preliminary examination phase, we evaluated that the CAR situation was under the ICC's temporal, territorial, and material jurisdiction, but we found some obstacles regarding complementarity.

At the end of the year 2002, Bemba was well aware of the risk of being prosecuted for the crimes committed in CAR. He decided to open a trial against twenty-seven suspects of the MLC forces and made declarations that "he had arrested eight soldiers for crimes committed in the CAR" and that "'he expected an investigation to be initiated between Chad and the CAR.'"[16]

Mr. Bemba wrote a letter, dated February 20, 2003, to the then FIDH president, Mr. Sidiki Kaba, explaining his efforts to do justice and offering to work with the FIDH.[17] He stated that he had ordered the establishment of a commission of inquiry to verify allegations, identifying those implicated, and had put them at the disposal of an MLC's military justice system. He referred to his correspondence with General Cissé and the MLC's intention to work with an international commission of inquiry, complaining that the FIDH had not contacted the MLC to obtain information.

On February 26, 2003, the president of the FIDH, Mr. Kaba, replied, noting that the MLC had prosecuted some individuals accused of pillaging but "expressed serious reservations as to the legitimacy, impartiality, and independence of those proceedings." He informed Mr. Bemba that, in light of its mandate, the FIDH had formally seized the International Criminal Court with the matter on February 13, 2003, and "encouraged Mr. Bemba to transmit the information at his disposal to the ICC."[18]

Our office collected information about the different MLC investigations and found that they did not address commanders' responsibility, did not question suspects about murder, and did not pursue reports of rape; they were primarily focused on pillages. In any case, Mr. Bemba had been preparing his legal defense since 2002.

CAR National Investigations

Besides, we also had to evaluate the existence of national proceedings. The public prosecutor of Bangui Regional Court (Procureur de la République près le Tribunal de Grande Instance de Bangui) launched in 2003 a criminal investigation against former president Patassé, Bemba, and others; and a final decision was still pending before the Court of Cassation.

On August 28, 2004, the public prosecutor of Bangui Regional Court concluded that there "was insufficient evidence that Mr. Bemba either participated in the crimes perpetrated by his troops or that he was aware of how the troops were used on the ground." And he recommended termination of the proceedings against Mr. Bemba.

On September 16, 2004, the senior investigating judge (Doyen des Judges d'Instruction près le Tribunal de Grande Instance de Bangui) concluded that Mr. Bemba's prosecution was barred by diplomatic immunity, taking into consideration his status as DRC's vice president. Besides, in the operative part of the order, the senior investigating judge dismissed the charges against Mr. Bemba and other persons due to insufficient evidence.

The principal public prosecutor's office represented by the "Avocat Général" appealed, affirming that Mr. Bemba's complicity in his troops' crimes had been indisputably established and that it was not possible to permit the charges against him to be dismissed.

On December 11, 2004, Mr. Goungaye Wanfiyo, acting as counsel on behalf of President Bozizé, sent a letter to the Bangui Court of Appeal. The letter proposed severing the proceedings and referring to the ICC the crimes of rape, murder, destruction of movable and immovable property, and pillaging. It was suggested that if the ICC prosecutor initiated an investigation, it would be conducted using means not available to the CAR.[19]

On December 16, 2004, the court of appeal of Bangui ruled that the charges against Mr. Bemba and other persons must be upheld. It decided that the "blood crimes" (crimes de sang) for which Mr. Bemba and other persons stood accused constituted war crimes, should be severed from the economic crimes, and should be submitted to the competent authorities to be referred to the ICC.

The CAR prosecutor appealed to the Court of Cassation (Chambre Criminelle de la Cour de Cassation), the national's highest court.

In November 2005, members of our office visited Bangui to carry out an in-depth assessment of those proceedings. Also, as part of the evaluation of the interests of justice, during the visit, our office listened to victims' views and considered their interests. We received explicit confirmation that many of the CAR victims were awaiting the ICC's involvement to see justice done.

Finally, in April 2006, the Court of Cassation ruled that "there can be no doubt that the Central African judicial services are unable genuinely to investigate or prosecute" in the proceedings against Mr. Patassé, Mr. Bemba, and others. The CAR judiciary was powerless concerning them, a situation which the Court of Cassation concluded was a "de facto embodiment of their impunity."

Faced with these conclusions, the Cour de Cassation decided that *Recourse to international cooperation is the only means to prevent impunity in this case.*[20] It also found that in referring these individuals, including Mr. Bemba, to the ICC, the court of appeal of Bangui had "applied the law in due fashion."[21] The CAR's court observed that the ICC is the forum to try perpetrators of the most serious crimes if states are genuinely unable to try them.[22]

The Pre-Trial Chamber Intervention during the Preliminary Examination Phase

FIDH reiterated in numerous public comments the Office of the Prosecutor's duty to respond as quickly as possible to the Central African victims' demand for justice. It stated that many of whom were to die, having contracted HIV during the events of 2002–2003.[23] *FIDH strongly denounced the delay taken by the Office of the Prosecutor in the preliminary analysis of CAR's situation. This analysis was excessively lengthy in comparison to the time that passed between the referral and the decision to open an investigation into the situations in Uganda, the Democratic Republic of Congo, and Darfur.*[24]

Antoine Bernard, then FIDH's chief executive officer, actively participated in our biannual meeting with NGOs and insisted in his elegant and friendly way to open a CAR investigation.

On September 27, 2006, a letter signed by Goungaye Wanfiyo representing the CAR government requested formally to the pre-trial chamber that the ICC prosecutor provide information "on the alleged failure to decide, within a reasonable time, whether or not to initiate an investigation." He also requested to take measures to preserve evidence and to protect the victims.[25]

The pre-trial chamber, integrated by Presiding Judge Sylvia Steiner, Judge Hans-Peter Kaul, and Judge Ekaterina Trendafilova, accepted the request. It considered that the preliminary examination of a situation "must be completed within a reasonable time from the reception of a referral by a State Party . . . regardless of its complexity."[26]

The chamber mentioned "that the preliminary examinations of the situations in the Democratic Republic of the Congo and Northern Uganda were completed within two to six months" (in fact, they took eleven and twelve months, respectively). The judges considered "that almost two years have passed since the Prosecutor received the referral of the Government of the Central African Republic."

They added, "that after the filing of the CAR Request on September 27, 2006, no information on the status of his ongoing preliminary examination of the CAR situation has been given by the Prosecutor to the Government of the Central African Republic."[27]

The pre-trial chamber ordered us to provide the chamber and the government of the CAR:

no later than December 15, 2006, with a report containing information on the current status of the preliminary examination of the CAR situation, including an estimate of when the preliminary examination of the CAR situation will be concluded and when a decision pursuant to Article 53 (1) of the Statute will be taken.[28]

We discussed how to react. In our view, the ruling was affecting the division of competences between our office and pre-trial chambers. It also expanded the rights of states who have referred situations to the court. We had to respect the chamber's decision, but at the same time, we considered that it was infringing on our mandate. We filed on the time indicated by the chamber, stating:

The Rome Statute, in Article 53 (1), grants to the Prosecutor the prerogative to determine when to initiate an investigation. The Pre-Trial Chamber's supervisory role, under Article 53 (3), only applies to the review of a decision under Article 53 (1) and (2) by the Prosecutor not to proceed with an investigation or a prosecution. The OTP submits that to date, no decision under Article 53 (1) has been made and that accordingly, there is no exercise of prosecutorial discretion susceptible to judicial review by the Chamber. The OTP is nonetheless including in this submission a description of the current status of the preliminary examination of the CAR situation.[29]

We noted that, pursuant to Rule 105 (1), *the Office of the Prosecutor's duty* "is confined to promptly informing in writing the referring State of a decision not to initiate an investigation under Article 53 (1)" and, to that date, no decision had been made under Article 53 (1). Accordingly, the duty enshrined in Rule 105 had not arisen.[30]

We committed to deciding on Article 53 (1) as expeditiously as possible, noting that no provision in the statute or the rules establishes a definitive time period to complete the preliminary examination. We submitted that "this was a deliberate legislative decision that provides the required flexibility to adjust the parameters of the assessment or analysis phase to the specific features of each particular situation. That choice, and the discretion that it provides, should remain undisturbed."[31]

The chamber requested the OTP to estimate when the preliminary examination would be concluded and when a decision under Article 53 (1) would be made. However, we informed that, as I had indicated in my statement to the Assembly of State Parties, we hoped that a decision could be made in the near future, but a more specific estimate was not possible at that time.[32]

Opening the Investigation

Our preliminary examination was delayed because we had received information about new crimes allegedly committed by government security forces in the northwest of CAR from 2005 to 2007. We learned that

> Abuses . . . diminished since most of the elite Presidential Guard (GP) forces, which committed the most serious abuses, were withdrawn from the region in mid-2007, in response to international concern. Taking the place of the GP in the north were Central African Armed Forces (FACA) units, with well-trained commanders installed in a deliberate effort to address indiscipline.[33]

We were assessing the scope of the investigation to be opened, taking into consideration information affirming that the government had "taken some steps to counter impunity in CAR by prosecuting individual members of the CAR security forces found to be responsible for crimes such as theft and assault, but for the most part the CAR government turned a blind eye to abuses committed by its forces."[34]

On April 12, 2007, rebels integrated into a group called UFDR, and the government of CAR signed a peace agreement to end hostilities. The UFDR agreed to sequester its men in an army cantonment, from where they would eventually be reintegrated into the national army.

In return, the government considered UFDR as a political party, accepting its contribution as it does not resort to violence. A law would be passed extending amnesty to former UFDR fighters, and a joint committee would be set up to monitor the peace process, the draft said.[35]

On May 22, 2007, we announced opening an investigation in the CAR focusing on the most serious crimes. They were mainly committed during a peak of violence in 2002–2006. We also announced that the Office of the Prosecutor would continue to monitor closely allegations of crimes committed since the end of 2005.

I visited Bangui in January 2008 to explain our case to the victims. I also met President Bozizé and warned him about the possibility of investigating the allegations of new crimes committed by his troops. In June 2008, our office sent a letter to President Bozizé noting that acts of violence committed in the north of the country would require sustained attention.[36]

On June 21, 2008, CAR's government and three rebel groups signed a comprehensive peace agreement that included an amnesty.[37] The tension between impunity and ceasefire also appeared in the CAR situation. On August 1, 2008, President Bozizé sent a letter to the UN Secretary-General requesting the adoption of a UN Security Council Resolution under Article 16. The goal was to "ensure that the authorities of the CAR remain competent over the acts covering the periods comprised by the amnesty laws' that had been adopted based on Article 2 of the Comprehensive Peace Agreement."[38]

The office had an impact on the president's decision. *According to Bozizé's correspondence, the request was prompted by a communication from the prosecutor of the ICC informing him that the Office of the Prosecutor was focusing special attention on ongoing acts of violence taking place in the north of the CAR.*[39]

Even though Article 2 of the Accord Global excludes amnesty for crimes under the ICC jurisdiction, the CAR government claimed that an eventual implementation of the prosecutor's letter would endanger the peace agreement's respect and implementation. The CAR government considered that ICC activities constituted a threat to its discretion in prosecuting individuals for Rome Statute crimes.[40]

Jus in Curiae: The Court Rulings

Jean-Pierre Bemba was defeated in the 2006 DRC's national elections by his rival, incumbent President Joseph Kabila, but he was elected DRC senator on January 19, 2007. In March 2007, Bemba refused to integrate its militia into the DRC regular army, and a military confrontation started in Kinshasa. After two hundred deaths, Bemba took refuge at the South African embassy, and on April 11, 2007, he left DRC for Portugal.

Our office was preparing the cooperation needed from Portugal to implement the eventual arrest warrants in the CAR case. Still, a few weeks before we submitted our request, Bemba moved to Belgium.

I was worried that Bemba's friends could protect him, but Belgium implemented the court's arrest warrant immediately and surrendered Jean-Pierre Bemba to the seat of the court.

On June 15, 2009, Pre-Trial Chamber II accepted that the case was admissible, confirmed most of the charges, changed the mode of liability, and committed Mr. Bemba to trial. Judge Ekaterina Trendafilova was the presiding judge, and Judge Hans-Peter Kaul and Judge Cuno Tarfusser were the other two chamber members.

In February 2010, Mr. Bemba challenged the admissibility of the case. On June 24, 2010, Trial Chamber III, integrated by Presiding Judge Adrian Fulford, Judge Elizabeth Odio Benito, and Judge Joyce Aluoch, decided that the case against Jean-Pierre Bemba was admissible.

The trial chamber confirmed that the absence of national investigations made unnecessary the analysis of ability or willingness. It stated,

> "*The final result of those national proceedings, when coupled with the CAR's reference of the case to the ICC, is that . . . there has been no previous decision on the merits by a competent court." The State decided to prosecute Mr. Bemba; the Senior Investigating Judge's dismissal was overturned on appeal, and there was a near simultaneous referral of the case to the relevant authorities at the ICC under Article 14 of the Statute; no trial of the conduct has taken place, and instead the entire criminal proceedings against the accused are being prosecuted before this Court, because of the State's domestic inability to conduct this trial. It follows the case is admissible.*[41]

On October 19, 2010, the appeal chamber integrated by Presiding Judge Anita Usacka, Judge Sang-Hyun Song, Judge Akua Kuenyehia, Judge Erkki

Kourula, and Judge Daniel David Ntanda Nsereko confirmed the decision. "When a Trial Chamber is presented with the question of whether the outcome of domestic judicial proceedings was a decision not to prosecute in terms of Article 17 (1) (b) of the Statute, the Trial Chamber should accept prima facie the validity and effect of the decisions of domestic courts, unless presented with compelling evidence indicating otherwise."[42] The appeals chamber also declined to consider "the question of unwillingness or inability" because "there were no domestic investigations or prosecutions against the Appellant."[43]

On March 21, 2016, Trial Chamber III, with the positive vote of Judge Sylvia Steiner, Judge Joyce Aluoch, and Judge Kuniko Ozaki, found Jean-Pierre Bemba Gombo guilty under Article 28(a) of the statute, as a military commander of murder and rape as crimes against humanity and war crimes and pillaging as a war crime.

On June 8, 2018, the appeal chamber, with the vote of Judge Christine Van den Wyngaert, Judge Chile Eboe-Osuji, and Judge Howard Morrison, reversed the conviction and acquitted Mr. Bemba of all the charges brought against him. Judge Sanji Mmasenono Monageng and Judge Piotr Hofmański voted in dissent to confirm the trial chamber conviction.

Notes

1. David Bosco, Rough Justice 187 (Kindle ed. 2014).
2. Martti Koskenniemi, From Apology to Utopia, The Structure of International Legal Argument 614 (2005).
3. Situation in Central African Republic, ICC-01/05, Prosecution's Report Pursuant to Pre-Trial Chamber Ill's 30 November 2006 Decision Requesting Information on the Status of the Preliminary Examination of the Situation in the Central African Republic ¶ 1 (Dec. 15, 2006), https://www.icc-cpi.int/CourtRecords/CR2007_03777.PDF.
4. Prosecutor v. Jean-Pierre Bemba Gombo, ICC-01/05-01/08, Public Redacted Version of the Amended Document containing the charges filed on 30 March 2009 ¶ 39 (Mar. 30, 2009), https://www.icc-cpi.int/RelatedRecords/CR2009_02181.PDF.
5. Karine Bonneau et al., FIDH and the Situation in the Central African Republic before the International Criminal Court: The Case of Jean-Pierre Bemba Gombo 5 (Antoine Bernard ed., 2008).
6. *Id.* at 12.
7. Marlies Glasius described Central African Republic institutional weakness; "in 2007, International Crisis Group commented that 'failed state' was not an accurate label for

the CAR, since it assumes that there have in the past been adequate state structures. Instead, it reached for the label 'phantom state' to describe the lack of any meaningful institutional capacity." Marlies Glasius, *A Problem, Not a Solution Complementarity in the Central African Republic and Democratic Republic of the Congo, in* THE INTERNATIONAL CRIMINAL COURT AND COMPLEMENTARITY: FROM THEORY TO PRACTICE 1204, 1206 (Carsten Stahn & Mohamed M. El Zeidy eds., Kindle ed. 2011).

8. KARINE BONNEAU ET AL., FIDH AND THE SITUATION IN THE CENTRAL AFRICAN REPUBLIC BEFORE THE INTERNATIONAL CRIMINAL COURT: THE CASE OF JEAN-PIERRE BEMBA GOMBO 14 (Antoine Bernard ed., 2008).

9. Marlies Glasius, *A Problem, Not a Solution Complementarity in the Central African Republic and Democratic Republic of the Congo, in* THE INTERNATIONAL CRIMINAL COURT AND COMPLEMENTARITY: FROM THEORY TO PRACTICE 1204, 1210 (Carsten Stahn & Mohamed M. El Zeidy eds., Kindle ed. 2011).

10. *Id.*

11. KARINE BONNEAU ET AL., FIDH AND THE SITUATION IN THE CENTRAL AFRICAN REPUBLIC BEFORE THE INTERNATIONAL CRIMINAL COURT: THE CASE OF JEAN-PIERRE BEMBA GOMBO 13 (Antoine Bernard ed., 2008).

12. *Id.* at 12.

13. Marlies Glasius, *A Problem, Not a Solution Complementarity in the Central African Republic and Democratic Republic of the Congo, in* THE INTERNATIONAL CRIMINAL COURT AND COMPLEMENTARITY: FROM THEORY TO PRACTICE 1204, 1210 (Carsten Stahn & Mohamed M. El Zeidy eds., Kindle ed. 2011).

14. FIDH, *The Central African Republic Triggers the ICC Jurisdiction: FIDH calls for the Prosecutor to Open an Investigation,* INT'L FED. FOR HUMAN RTS. (Jan. 3, 2005), https://www.fidh.org/en/region/Africa/THE-CENTRAL-AFRICAN-REPUBLIC.

15. *Id.*

16. Prosecutor v. Jean-Pierre Bemba Gombo, ICC-01/05-01/08A, Judgment on the appeal of Mr. Jean-Pierre Bemba Gombo against Trial Chamber III's "Judgment pursuant to Article 74 of the Statute" ¶ 126 (June 8, 2018), https://www.icc-cpi.int/Court Records/CR2018_02984.PDF.

17. *Id.* at ¶ 127.

18. *Id.*

19. Prosecutor v. Jean-Pierre Bemba Gombo, ICC-01/05-01/08, Decision on the Admissibility and Abuse of Process Challenges ¶ 11 (June 24, 2010), https://www.icc-cpi.int/CourtRecords/CR2010_04399.PDF.

20. KARINE BONNEAU ET AL., FIDH AND THE SITUATION IN THE CENTRAL AFRICAN REPUBLIC BEFORE THE INTERNATIONAL CRIMINAL COURT: THE CASE OF JEAN-PIERRE BEMBA GOMBO 13 (Antoine Bernard ed., 2008).

21. Prosecutor v. Jean-Pierre Bemba Gombo, ICC-01/05-01/08 OA 3, Corrigendum to Judgment on the appeal of Mr. Jean-Pierre Bemba Gombo against the decision of Trial Chamber III of 24 June 2010 entitled "Decision on the Admissibility and Abuse of Process Challenges" ¶ 45 (Oct. 19, 2010), https://www.legal-tools.org/doc/37e559/pdf/.

22. The Prosecutor v. Jean-Pierre Bemba Gombo, ICC-01/05-01/08, Decision on the Admissibility and Abuse of Process Challenges ¶ 18 (June 24, 2010), https://www.icc-cpi.int/CourtRecords/CR2010_04399.PDF.

23. Karine Bonneau et al., FIDH and the Situation in the Central African Republic before the International Criminal Court: The Case of Jean-Pierre Bemba Gombo 14 (Antoine Bernard ed., 2008).

24. *Id.*

25. It is not clear if Goungaye Wanfiyo was acting in accordance with his instructions. See Situation in the Central African Republic, ICC-Ol/OS, Submission by the Registrar of a communication informing the termination of the mandate of Maître Nganatouwna Goungaye Wanfiyo (Aug. 20, 2007), https://www.icc-cpi.int/CourtRecords/CR2007_03781.PDF.

26. Situation in Central African Republic, ICC-01/05, Decision Requesting Information on the Status of the Preliminary Examination of the Situation in the Central African Republic, at 4 (Nov. 30, 2006) https://www.icc-cpi.int/CourtRecords/CR2007_03 776.PDF.

27. *Id.*

28. *Id.* at 5.

29. Situation in Central African Republic, ICC-01/05, Prosecution's Report Pursuant to Pre-Trial Chamber Ill's 30 November 2006 Decision Requesting Information on the Status of the Preliminary Examination of the Situation in the Central African Republic ¶ 1 (Dec. 15, 2006), https://www.icc-cpi.int/CourtRecords/CR2007_03 777.PDF.

30. *Id.* at ¶ 10.

31. *Id.*

32. *Id.* at ¶ 20.

33. *Central African Republic (CAR) Events of 2008*, Hum. Rts. Watch, https://www.hrw.org/world-report/2009/country-chapters/central-african-republic (last visited July 1, 2020).

34. *Id.*

35. *CAR Signs Peace Deal with Rebels*, Al Jazeera (Apr. 13, 2007), https://www.aljazeera.com/news/africa/2007/04/2008525141354666960.html.

36. *Central African Republic (CAR) Events of 2008*, Hum. Rts. Watch, https://www.hrw.org/world-report/2009/country-chapters/central-african-republic (last visited July 1, 2020).

37. Deborah Ruiz Verduzco, *The Relationship between the ICC and the United Nations Security Council, in* The Law and Practice of the International Criminal Court 4559, 5043 (Carsten Stahn ed., Kindle ed. 2015).

38. *Id.*

39. *Id.* at 5045.

40. *Id.* at 5051.

41. "i) a case (that) is being investigated or prosecuted by (the) State with jurisdiction over it" (Article 17(l)(a))—there is no current investigation or prosecution in the CAR; ii) a case where the state "decided not to prosecute the person concerned" (Article 17(l)(b) of the statute) because the state decided the accused should be prosecuted by the International Criminal Court; or (iii) a case where the person concerned "has already been tried for conduct which is the subject of the complaint" (Article

17(l)(c) of the statute)—Finally, the case satisfies the gravity test (Article 17(l)(d) of the statute). Prosecutor v. Jean-Pierrre Bemba Gombo, ICC-01/05-01/08, Decision on the Admissibility and Abuse of Process Challenges ¶ 261 (June 24, 2010), https://www.icc-cpi.int/CourtRecords/CR2010_04399.PDF.

42. Prosecutor v. Jean-Pierre Bemba Gombo, ICC-01/05-01/08 OA 3, Corrigendum to Judgment on the appeal of Mr. Jean-Pierre Bemba Gombo against the decision of Trial Chamber III of 24 June 2010 entitled "Decision on the Admissibility and Abuse of Process Challenges" ¶ 1 (Oct. 19, 2010), https://www.legal-tools.org/doc/37e559/pdf/.

43. *Id.* at ¶108.

11

The Office of the Prosecutor Using Its *Proprio Motu* Authority in Kenya

Kenya's 2008 post-election violence produced more than 1,000 deaths and the forced displacement of 350,000 persons in a few weeks. It was a different type of conflict than DRC, Uganda, or CAR. Massive violence was used to transform the outcome of the political elections. The distinction between *jus ad Curiam* and *jus in Curiae* helps distinguish the ICC intervention in Kenya's situation.

Everything went well during the *jus ad Curiam* phase. It was led by Kofi Annan representing the AU, carrying out a very successful mediation stopping the violence and forcing a unique political agreement. After the deal, Kofi Annan continued participating in Kenya, promoting the constitution's reform, supporting the efforts to investigate the crimes committed and integrating the ICC in the international, regional, and national political scenario. It was a privilege for me to interact with him during the preliminary examination. His authority, his skills, and his dignity helped Kenya to overcome the crisis.

Civil society in Kenya was very active, and national commissions conducted serious investigations providing the Office of the Prosecutor with factual information.

The Kenya investigation was triggered for the first time using the prosecutor's proprio motu powers. Dissipating the reservations during the Rome Conference, everyone agreed with the independent ICC intervention, including Kenya's president and prime minister, the AU, the EU, and the United States.

The first part of the following *jus in Curiae* phase also worked well. The six suspects, including Uhuru Kenyatta, then deputy prime minister; Francis Muthaura, then a powerful secretary-general of the cabinet; and William Ruto, then a leader of the opposition, appeared voluntarily before the International Criminal Court.

War and Justice in the 21st Century. Luis Moreno Ocampo, Oxford University Press. © Oxford University Press 2022.
DOI: 10.1093/oso/9780197628973.003.0012

Kenya challenged the cases' admissibility. Pre-trial and appeal chambers issued groundbreaking decisions on complementarity, confirming the Office of the Prosecutor position. The ICC chambers consolidated the jurisprudence on "inactivity" without analyzing "inability" or "unwillingness" and confirmed the prosecution decisions on jurisdiction.

The suspects appeared voluntarily, and the pre-trial chamber confirmed the charges against four of them.

Kenyatta and Ruto, leaders of the opposite camps in 2008, created a ticket for the 2013 election. An important opposing candidate died when his helicopter crashed. Mr. Kenyata and Mr. Ruto became Kenya's president and vice president after an almost peaceful election in 2013. After their election, they continued appearing before the court, and Kenya remains a Rome Statute' state party. A divided UN Security Council rejected the application of Article 16, and the Assembly of States Parties amended the rules to facilitate the trials.

The witnesses disappeared or recanted their testimonies, and finally, the cases were vacated. President Kenyatta obtained support from the United Kingdom and the United States for his role in the counterterrorism efforts. The Rome Statute was fully implemented and the ICC made some contribution to the prevention of violence, but there was no justice for the victims.

2007 Post-Electoral Violence in Kenya

In the 2007 election, the leading contenders were the incumbent President Mwai Kibaki, supported this time by his former adversary, Uhuru Kenyatta; and Raila Odinga, a Luo supported by William Ruto, a Kalenjin that in the past supported Kenyatta. While the actual voting was mostly peaceful, the tensions heightened with the delay in tallying the votes.

On December 28, 2007, the Kenyan media unofficially announced that Raila Odinga, leading the Orange Democratic Movement (ODM), a coalition of Luo and Kalenjin ethnic groups, got 50.5 percent support. The incumbent President Mwai Kibaki, Party of National Unity (PNU), representing the majority Kikuyu ethnic group, obtained just 42.6 percent.[1]

However, on December 30, 2007, the Kenyan Electoral Commission chairman officially declared Kibaki as the winner for a tiny margin of 2 percent.[2] Within minutes of the commission's declaration of Kibaki as the victor, "tribe-based rioting and violence, primarily directed against Kikuyus [Kibaki and Kenyatta tribe] broke out across Kenya, and the government suspended live television coverage for some days."

On January 6, adding to the explosive atmosphere, Raila Odinga vowed to go ahead with a rally of one million people to be held on January 8, despite the government's insistence that the rallies would be illegal. African leaders like South Africa's Archbishop, Desmond Tutu, and four former African presidents tried to promote dialogue by visiting Kenya on January 2 and 8.[3] They supported John Kufour, Ghana president and chair of the African Union, who arrived in Kenya on January 8. They visited the communities affected by the still ongoing violence.

Mindful of the mediation process, Odinga canceled the rallies planned for January 8 but refused to meet Kibaki.[4] On January 9, President Kufuor met separately with Kibaki and Odinga and managed to get them to agree to a team of African leaders who would come and help broker a solution. The African Union established the AU Panel of Eminent Personalities[5] and appointed former UN secretary-general Kofi Annan to lead it.[6]

The international efforts were focused on stopping the crimes and avoiding a new Rwanda. France, the United States, and the UN requested the end of violence.[7] French Foreign Minister Bernard Kouchner stated: "It is said that it is an ethnic battle. Yes, without a doubt, in Africa, it is often that. But it is also a battle for democracy."[8] Jendayi Frazer, the top US diplomat for Africa, visited Kenya at the end of January and stated that some of the violence had been ethnic cleansing intended to drive people from their homes.[9]

In March, Human Rights Watch produced a report concluding that the Kenyan government and opposition leaders had helped finance and organize violence.[10] On January 25, Odinga responded that the people had been acting spontaneously.[11] Both were right. There was a planned campaign that triggered spontaneous demonstrations.

The Office of the Prosecutor's Preliminary Examination in Kenya (2008)

Kenya ratified the Rome Statute and has provided jurisdiction to the ICC since June 1, 2005. Showing the ICC "shadow," justice was part of the discussion from the beginning of the crisis. Since January 2008, the Office of the Prosecutor has received communications requesting our intervention, including from the ODM members.[12] At the beginning of February, the Office of the Prosecutor formally opened a preliminary examination and made our first public statement highlighting our impartiality.[13]

Kenya was different from our previous situations. Militias had committed the most serious crimes in the DRC, Uganda, and the Central African Republic. Instead, in Kenya, the suspects were top political leaders from the most significant political parties using violence to obtain authority.

The first issue of our analysis was about the subject matter jurisdiction. There was no armed conflict in Kenya, so the question was this: Were crimes against humanity committed? Was the violence planned? Was it "widespread or systematic" as required by the statute?

The International Intervention to Control the Violence (2008)

As the UN secretary-general, Kofi Annan had been deeply involved in the adoption of the Rome Statute. He had opened the Rome Conference and had interrupted his visit to Argentina on July 17, 1998, to arrive on time to participate in the closing ceremony.

As the AU mediator, Kofi Annan tried to show that peace and justice worked hand in hand. He accepted the position to lead the AU panel under one condition: exclusivity. He demanded President Kufour that AU Panel "efforts would be the only process involved to prevent the parties from indulging in 'mediation shopping.' "

Annan ensured that the AU, the EU, France, the United Kingdom, the United States, and the UN also respect his exclusivity. Annan had witnessed many times how "faction leaders gamed the situation, seizing on and switching between the opportunities presented by alternative mediators and negotiating plans, dragging out the process in their favor and at the expense of peace."[14] He became the only mediator of the conflict.[15]

This exclusivity was tested as soon as Annan arrived in Kenya. Members of the Kibaki government were against any internationalization of the process. They held power and did not want to change the status quo. They tried to include a different mediator, one who was close to them: Yoweri Museveni, the Ugandan president.[16]

Museveni called Kofi Annan the same day of his arrival in Kenya, saying that his plan had, in principle, been agreed by both the government and the opposition. Annan perceived Museveni's intervention as an attempt to present him endorsing the Kibaki's plan.[17] Consequently, Annan made his excuses to President Museveni, stating that he still had to call all the parties.[18]

On January 24, Annan organized a first personal meeting between Kibaki and Odinga since the crisis began. They agreed to create two negotiating teams and launch the Kenyan National Dialogue and Reconciliation process five days later. The negotiation started on January 29. In this context, Annan had to manage attempts to derail the process.[19]

During the peace talks, violence continued in Kenya. Between January 24 and 27, several buildings were set on fire in Nakuru, and at least fifty-five people were killed. By January 28, the ODM chairperson Henry Kosgei accused the government of facilitating the killing in Nakuru by imposing a curfew, which he said was used "to keep some groups indoors to be killed."[20]Mugabe Were, an ODM member of Parliament, was shot and killed in Nairobi. Renewed protests and violence followed his death.

Annan met Kenyan NGOs, churches, businesspeople, and other civil society actors, promising them that any decision between the parties would be made public. He fully understood the risks of failure and committed himself to stay in Kenya until the "job was done."

The United States and the AU were supporting Annan. President George W. Bush made strong statements in support of the mediation efforts.[21] The US secretary of state Condoleezza Rice arrived in Kenya on February 18 and met with Kibaki, Odinga, and Annan. She emphasized the importance of reaching a settlement, saying that one should have already been in place.[22] However, she also said that the United States was not trying to "*dictate a solution to Kenyans.*"[23]

After complex negotiations, and while violence continued unabated, Annan forced a final meeting between Kibaki and Odinga. The teams representing both leaders reached agreements on different substantial issues and power-sharing. Kibaki would remain the president. An executive position of prime minister would be created, which would be occupied by Odinga. But there were significant disputes about the scope of the powers of the prime minister.

Annan suspended the discussion on February 26, saying that they had "not broken down" but that the leaders needed to "become directly engaged in these talks."[24] They had to resolve the last problems. The president of Tanzania, Jakaya Kikwete, the new chairperson of the AU, joined the meeting, and after five hours of discussion, they announced the deal. Different from other situations like Darfur or DRC, the warriors were not involved. It was an agreement between the country's top political leaders.

On February 28, 2008, under the AU supervision, the parties signed the Agreement on the Principles of Partnership of the Coalition Government.[25] The agreement aimed to "implement a coherent and far-reaching reform agenda, to address the fundamental root causes of recurrent conflict, and to create a better, more secure, more prosperous Kenya for all." Contrary to many other mediation efforts, Annan continued working in Kenya, implementing the agreement obtained. He promoted the discussion on a new constitution and its enactment.[26]

The Annan agreement on the constitution's reforms was rooted in years of political struggles. In 2002, Kibaki and Odinga promised to adopt a new constitution establishing a fair distribution of land and power for the different ethnic groups. The actors' background shows the peculiar Kenya dynamics combining constitutional reforms, ethnic loyalties, and changing political alliances.[27] Kofi Annan's intervention allowed them to implement peacefully the constitutional changes discussed by Kenyan leaders for ten years.

The Commission of Inquiry into the Post-Election Violence (CIPEV)

On March 6, 2008, our office requested information from selected sources, including the government of Kenya, the Kenyan National Commission of Human Rights (KNCHR), and the ODM. We were collecting the information needed to decide on the preliminary examination. Our request pushed Kenyan authorities to discuss their primary obligation to investigate the crimes.

The National Accord and Reconciliation Act, agenda IV, included the imperative to end impunity. President Kibaki and Prime Minister Odinga agreed to establish a Commission of Inquiry into the Post-Election Violence (CIPEV).[28] The CIPEV was established on May 23, 2008, and was commonly called the "Waki Commission" after its chief, Judge Philip Waki.[29] It had the mandate to investigate the facts and circumstances related to acts of violence that followed the elections and recommend measures to bring justice to those responsible for the violence and eradicate impunity.[30]

During this process, in August 2008, the Kenyan National Commission of Human Rights issued its own report concluding that "the violence was characterized by widespread or systematic ethnically-targeted killings of people, looting and destruction of property belonging to communities aligned with PNU by ODM aligned supporters; and counter-attacks similarly intent on killing people and destroying property owned by ODM aligned communities."[31]

In a few months, the CIPEV collected two hundred testimonies and other evidence[32] and concluded that the post-election violence resulted in 1,133 deaths attributing 405 to the police forces. A total of 3,561 people suffered injuries, and 117,216 private properties (including residential houses, commercial premises, and vehicles, farm produce) were destroyed.

The CIPEV report documented gang and individual rapes, including ethnically driven and horrendous female and male genital mutilation. Approximately 350,000 persons were displaced from their residence or business. The CIPEV report established the systematic character of the crimes and was very useful to understand the reasons for the lack of genuine criminal investigations.

The commission found political interferences coming typically "in the form of orders from above."[33] It reported that both sides of the dispute had encouraged and funded attacks against opponents and recommended institutional and legal reforms as well as the establishment of a Special Tribunal for Kenya to seek accountability against persons bearing the greatest responsibility for crimes, particularly crimes against humanity.

The CIPEV took advantage of Kofi Annan's role and the ICC's existence to pressure the new government. It established a timetable for implementing crucial judicial and legal reforms toward forming the recommended special tribunal. The CIPEV clarified that if such measures were not implemented, the ICC's prosecutor should receive a sealed list of alleged perpetrators provided to Kofi Annan.

The Project of a Kenyan Special Tribunal (2009)

The Kenyan civil society and Annan played a critical role in promoting justice for the victims and challenged politicians' interests. Two days after the CIPEV delivered its report, Annan visited Kenya and called on the government to follow the recommendations.[34]

The ODM parliamentary group reacted to the CIPEV report by making the national sovereignty argument. It announced that ODM would "resist and stop any rendition or surrender of Kenya citizens to a tribunal outside its territory as the national jurisdiction and national systems have no collapsed."[35]

President Kibaki was subtler. He stated publicly: "I am aware that many Kenyans require justice for past injustices but let us also keep in mind that although the truth will set us free—justice must be tempered with forgiveness for reconciliation to take root." He proposed: "let us prepare as a nation to consider restitution and forgiveness complementing truth and justice in order to give our nation a fresh start. I want to call upon all Kenyans to forgive one another."[36]

Annan made a strong statement emphasizing that impunity should not be perpetuated and that perpetrators of post-election violence should be prosecuted even: "if it would harm the Coalition Government."[37] Politicians started to change their narratives.

Contrary to the criterion adopted by the CIPEV, the report produced by the Kenya National Commission of Human Rights (KNHRC) issued in 2008 contained an annex with the list of suspects, including Kenyatta and Ruto. William Ruto, mentioned as a leader of the violence by the KNHRC report, started to criticize Odinga's support for the CIPEV report and threatened to leave the ODM. Henry Kosgey, ODM chairman, also criticized the CIPEV report.[38]

The Kenyan's Special Tribunal

On December 16, 2008, just one day before the deadline established by the CIPEV, President Kibaki and Prime Minister Odinga agreed to implement the report's recommendations, including the establishment of a Special Tribunal.[39] But there were not enough votes in the parliament to approve the project.

The opposition to the Special Tribunal came from a peculiar coalition of parliamentarians. Some of them were promoting impunity, and others were supporting justice before the ICC.

Some parliamentarians in favor of justice like Gitobu Imanyara boycotted the Special Tribunal project, considering that its architecture was deliberately flawed, allowing for manipulations.[40] Parliamentarians promoting impunity also opposed the Special Tribunal; they assumed that the ICC would be inefficient and coined the phrase "don't be vague, let go to The Hague."[41]

On the other side, some of those supporting the Special Tribunal creation were also aiming for impunity. They thought that a Special Tribunal, even with international judges, would be easier to manipulate. One of them explained that the Special Tribunal members would be "our employees, and we shall control them. We cannot control The Hague."[42]

On February 18, 2009, and On June 11, 2009, Annan extended the deadline established by CIPEV to provide the information to the ICC and gave the Kenyan government until the end of August 2009 to establish a tribunal to try the leaders of the 2007 post-election violence. In a private conversation, Kofi Annan alerted me that Kenyan political leaders will try to take advantage of me to circumvent his deadline. He advised me to protocolize whatever promise they would made.

The First Meeting with a Kenyan Delegation at The Hague

On July 3, 2009, a delegation of the Kenyan government led by Mutula Kilonzo, minister of Justice and Constitutional Affairs; Hon. James Orengo, minister of Lands' and Attorney General Amos Wako, came to our office in The Hague. One of my assistants heard the attorney general's conversation with his staff in the corridor of my own office, debating the best way to control my decisions.

In our formal meeting, the delegation explained to us that impunity was not an option. The Kenyans talked about their plans to do justice and requested additional time to carry out their efforts before opening our investigation. We had no valid reason to deny the request; it was our first meeting with Kenyan authorities, and my duty was to respect genuine national efforts.

Following Kofi Annan's advice and avoiding empty promises, I suggested that we sign a document clarifying our shared understanding, including that Kenya would refer the situation to the ICC if their efforts failed. Kenya's representatives requested time to discuss between them, and after half an hour, they agreed with our proposal. We signed a document establishing that before September 2009:

(a) The government of Kenya would provide a report on the current status of investigations and prosecutions arising out of the post-election violence and any other information requested by the prosecution of the ICC to perform its preliminary examinations.

(b) The Government of Kenya would provide information on measures put in place to ensure the safety of victims and witnesses pending the initiation and completion of suitable judicial proceedings.

(c) The Government of Kenya would inform us on modalities for conducting national investigations and prosecutions of those responsible for the 2007 violence through a special tribunal or other judicial mechanism adopted by the Kenyan Parliament with clear benchmarks over the next 12 months.

(d) In the alternative, if there is no parliamentarian agreement, following the Kenyan commitment to end impunity of the most responsible of the most serious crimes, the Government of Kenya would refer the situation to the prosecutor in accordance with article 14 of the Rome Statute.[43]

After their visit to The Hague, the Kenyan delegation informed Kofi Annan that they had reached an agreement with the ICC to set up a local justice mechanism in due time. The Kenyan government perceived this as a success, rendering the deadline given by the CIPEV moot. Complying with the agreed minutes and in response to the Office of the Prosecutor's request, the Kenyan attorney general Amos Wako sent two reports to our office on July 13, 2009.[44]

On July 14, 2009, Minister of Justice Kilonzo proposed a new version of the Constitution of Kenya Amendment Bill and the Special Tribunal Bill, tightening some of the original bills' loopholes.[45] Considering the Kenyan government's agreement to provide information to the prosecution, Annan decided to hand over the CIPEV envelope identifying the suspects to our office without waiting for the end-of-August deadline.

On July 16, we received the sealed envelope and six boxes containing documents and supporting material compiled by CIPEV. We opened the sealed envelope at an Ex Com meeting, examined its content, and resealed it. We never opened again and made a public statement clarifying that the list was not binding to us.

Meanwhile, and in a low-profile model, Kenyatta and Ruto had started to ally. On July 24, 2009, *Africa Confidential* published that "there are other veiled hints of a new KK (Kikuyu-Kalenjin) alliance between Ruto and Finance Minister Kenyatta in anticipation of the 2012 election."[46] On July 30, 2009, the Kenya Cabinet had a meeting to discuss Kilonzo's proposal. William Ruto and Uhuru Kenyatta presented as an alternative a revision of the Truth, Justice, and Reconciliation Commission, which became the preferred course of action.

The cabinet promised to make the Truth, Justice, and Reconciliation Commission more representative and effective.[47] It used strong language: "reaffirmed its commitment to the rule of law, and in particular in its commitment to the ICC" *and* resolved "to undertake accelerated and far-reaching reforms in the judiciary, police and investigative arms of Government to enable them investigate and prosecute" post-election violence locally.

The option of setting up a Special Tribunal had not received enough support and, according to Justice Minister Mutula Kilonzo, had not even been discussed. Sixty civil society organizations wrote an open letter to the president and prime Minister accusing them of a "collective conspiracy to protect suspects responsible of horrendous atrocities." In August, Gitobu Imanyara, as an individual member of Parliament, took the initiative to draft a second bill to establish a Special Tribunal, considering that it would enjoy support from a majority of MPs.[48]

The Article 53 Report (2009)

The CIPEV and the KNCHR reports provided a factual basis for our preliminary examination to identify that the attacks were both widespread and systematic, with thousands of victims.[49] Additionally, we were able to collect information about sexual violence in many forms during the post-election violence.[50]

We estimated that more than nine hundred documented acts of rape and other forms of sexual violence had been committed and found a significant underreporting in the occurrence of sexual violence. Our crime pattern analysis showed two main violence peaks: from December 30, 2007, to January 5, 2008; and between January 21 and 28, 2008. We concluded that there was a reasonable basis to believe that crimes against humanity under the ICC's temporal and territorial jurisdiction were committed.

The Office of the Prosecutor Article 53 report found no national proceedings against those most responsible for the crimes committed. Attorney General Wako's reports confirmed that there had only been a limited number of proceedings for less serious offenses committed during the post-electoral violence.[51] It was consistent with the CIPEV analysis on the political interference of Kenya's investigation.

The Article 53 report also evaluated that the gravity requirement was present. It took into consideration the scale, with thousands of killings and hundreds of thousand people forcibly displaced, the nature that included violent crimes and rapes to displace people from their ancestral lands, the manner exposing orders from leaders, and the impact on the country's stability.

The report included the comments received on September 17 and 18, 2009, during a roundtable discussion in our office with the Kenyan civil society's main actors.[52] It concluded that crimes against humanity might have been committed in Kenya. It also considered that there were no domestic proceedings against those bearing the greatest responsibility, the crimes were of sufficient gravity, and there were no "interest of justice" reasons to stop the investigations. Accordingly, we decided to start an investigation and offer the Kenyan government the opportunity to refer its situation.

The First *Proprio Motu* Investigation (2009–2010)

After our detached decision, the next step was to engage all the stakeholders, particularly the Kenya government, to promote cooperation. Kenya's institutional system was working. In September 2009[53] and in November 2009,[54] Kenyatta and Ruto asked the High Court of Kenya to remove their names from the Kenya National Commission of Human Rights report. The high court rejected both petitions for different reasons.

The failure to create a judicial organ to deal with the violence triggered the agreement signed in our office with the Kenyan delegation. Point *d)* of the document stated: *if there is no parliamentarian agreement . . . the Government of Kenya would refer the situation to the Prosecutor.*[55] At the beginning of October 2009, before opening an investigation, we requested a meeting with President Kibaki and Prime Minister Odinga. We followed our policy of inviting the national authorities to refer their situation and the agreement signed with Kenya.

On November 5, 2009, I visited Kenya for the first time. My presence at the airport had an unexpected impact. Workers managing the luggage or providing indications to the pilots stopped their work to greet me. It confirmed the enormous expectations that Kenyans had of our work. On November 5, 2009, Kenyan President Mwai Kibaki and Prime Minister Raila Odinga received me in the president's office in Nairobi. Secretary-General Francis Muthaura was also in the room.

I explained to them that we had concluded that crimes against humanity might have been committed in Kenya, and our legal duty was to proceed with an investigation. I explained the different ways to trigger the ICC jurisdiction, namely a referral from the Kenyan government or an independent decision of the prosecutor according to Article 15 of the Rome Statute.

Prime Minister Odinga was very open, explaining all their efforts to control violence and investigate the crimes. President Kibaki was quiet, listening. I invited them to refer the situation and informed them that, if not, I would request a pre-trial chamber authorization.

President Kibaki said he could not refer the situation because I would end up prosecuting members of the government.[56] But he said that the government would fulfill its duties of cooperation and support our decision. I told him that I fully respected his views. Still, it would be important to announce together my independent decision to request to open an investigation and the government's commitment to respect the Rome Statute. I reminded them of the Kenyan delegation's commitment in point (d) of the agreement signed in my office and the importance of showing that we were not in a conflict.

They asked me for some time to discuss between them. I spent the following half hour discussing with Minister of Justice Kilonzo the possible text to make the announcement. The president and the prime minister agreed to make a joint announcement, and the three of us appeared before dozens of journalists at the garden of the presidential building.

In a joint press conference flanked by Kenya's president and Kenya's prime minister, I announced our decision to use for the first time our *proprio motu* authority to request authorization to proceed with an investigation into the situation of the Republic of Kenya.

No one in Rome predicted such a possibility. There was no agreement, but there was no open opposition.

Our office was able to move ahead without creating *an antagonistic relationship* with the national government.[57] The president and prime minister issued a joint statement in which they recalled their constructive meeting with the prosecutor. They respected the principles, and affirmed their commitment to establish a local judicial mechanism to deal with the perpetrators of the post-election violence and cooperate with the ICC within the Rome Statute framework and the Kenyan International Crimes Act.

The Gitobu Imanyara project was going to be debated on November 11, 2009, but the parliament speaker suspended the bill's debate due to the lack of a quorum. On December 2, 2009, a parliamentary debate to discuss the bill ended prematurely due to a lack of quorum. Only three MPs contributed to the debate.

On November 26, 2009, we filed a request to the Pre-Trial Chamber II of the ICC to obtain authorization to start an investigation in Kenya's situation. Our application explained the arguments discussed in our Article 53 report describing the crimes' widespread and systematic nature.

The office emphasized the numerous incidents of sexual violence, including rape of men and women, sexual mutilation, and other forms of sexual violence such as gang rapes by groups of men, which were prevalent to grab land.[58] The attacks were committed "to pressure people to leave their homes, to retaliate against them for having voted for the wrong candidate, tribe or party and in tandem with that to dominate, humiliate and degrade them and their communities."[59]

Pre-Trial Chamber Decision to Authorize an Investigation into Kenya

On February 18, the Pre-Trial Chamber II requested clarifications about: (1) the connections between the acts of violence and a state's policy or one or more organizations; and (2) specific information about incidents to be investigated, possible targets, and domestic investigations.[60]

On March 3, 2010, we identified senior political and business leaders associated with the main political parties who organized, enticed, or financed attacks against the civilian population.

The filing asserted that those senior leaders were guided by the political objectives of retaining or gaining power. They utilized their personal, government, business, and tribal networks to commit crimes. Additionally, the information indicated that individuals associated with the ruling PNU might have used the means and apparatus of the Kenya Police Service to commit crimes. We clarified that there were no judicial proceedings against them.

We attached two confidential, ex parte annexes: he first describing the most serious criminal incidents that appear to have resulted from an organizational policy, and the second a preliminary list of twenty political and business leaders from both parties who appeared to be the most responsible.[61]

On March 31, 2010, Pre-Trial Chamber II, by the vote of Judge Ekaterina Trendafilova, presiding judge and Judge Cuno Tarfusser, granted our request and expanded the timeframe from June 1, 2005, until the day of our presentation November 26, 2009.[62] The two judges followed the precedent in the case against Katanga and Ngudjolo Chui that required that crimes should:

[B]e conducted in furtherance of a common policy involving public or private resources. Such a policy may be made either by groups of persons who govern a specific territory or by any organization with the capability to commit a widespread or systematic attack against a civilian population. The policy need not be explicitly defined by the organizational group. Indeed, an attack which is planned, directed or organized—as opposed to spontaneous or isolated acts of violence—will satisfy this criterion.[63]

Judge Hans Peter Kaul dissented. He considered that article 7(2)(a) of the statute required that those "organizations" should partake some state characteristics.[64] He read article 7(2)(a) of the statute as excluding non-state groups, "such as groups of organized crime, a mob, groups of (armed) civilians or criminal gangs."

Interestingly, Judge Kaul's dissent "accept[s] that some of the violence appears to have been organized and planned in advance." He recognized "that some local leaders, some local businessmen, some local politicians, some religious leaders, some journalists at local vernacular radio stations, some chiefs of communities and some civic and parliamentary aspirants were involved in the preparation of the violence." Despite this, he ultimately considered that there was no "'organization' behind the violent acts which may have established a policy to attack the civilian population," as defined by the Rome Statute.

The Identification of the Suspects and the Summons to Appear (2010)

From May 8–12, 2010, I visited Kenya to meet with Kenya's post-election violence victims. The five-day visit included meetings with all Kenyan society segments, notably with civil society and women's groups; the business community; religious leaders; and media, including community, local and regional radio stations. During my visit, we organized a town hall meeting to explain our plans to the local communities, which was recorded and presented by all the Kenyan TV channels as a one-hour special program. We publicly invited the victims to send representations to the pre-trial chamber.

To protect the witnesses and their family members, we followed our Darfur approach and conducted investigations outside of Kenya. The prosecution conducted ninety-two missions to sixteen countries. We received a lot of information about threats to potential witnesses. We requested the Registry's Victim and Witness Unit to relocate witnesses. The process was complicated. We had no authority to decide who should be protected, and our investigation depended on the registry's decisions.

We aimed to present all the cases together before the next election programmed to 2012. In less than one year, we collected the necessary evidence proving some of the most serious incidents and identified the persons most responsible. The first case alleged that since December 2006, MP William Ruto and ODM chairman Henry Kosgey began preparing a plan to attack the Rift Valley's Kikuyu groups perceived as supporters of the Party of National Unity (PNU). Joshua Arap Sang used his radio program to collect allies and provide signals to members of the plan on when and where to attack. They coordinated a series of actors and institutions to establish a network, using it to implement an organizational policy to commit crimes. They aimed to gain regional and national power.[65] The network conducted the operations planned after the election results were announced.

The second case presented the Kikuyu pro-Kibaki response. It alleged that Ambassador Francis Kirimi Muthaura, head of the civil service and secretary of the cabinet; Uhuru Muigai Kenyatta, who became deputy prime minister; and Mohamed Hussein Ali, then chief of police, developed and implemented a plan to attack ethnic groups perceived as ODM supporters.[66]

We discussed with the joint team and Ex Com how to proceed and concluded that a summon to appear could be more successful than arrest warrants. The suspects were top political leaders, they had the interest to avoid be fugitives, and we wanted to provide them incentives to cooperate with the court. Besides, a summons to appear is a personal decision of the individual, not requiring a government decision.

The office also concluded that there was a possibility of a return to violence. The president and the prime minister had the responsibility to manage the ICC decision's impact within Kenya. On December 1, 2010, I traveled to Nairobi to inform President Kibaki and Prime Minister Odinga of the suspects' names. It was a short meeting. I informed them that we would publicly request in a couple of weeks a summon to appear. They have to be prepared to manage any violent reaction. President Kibaki was shocked that Francis Muthaura, his secretary-general, a person very close to him who had an office in the same building, would be indicted. I had to repeat his name.

On December 15, the Office of the Prosecutor requested the PTC to issue summons to appear against the six individuals mentioned. I publicly announced that if they fail to turn up or attempt to hinder the investigation—for example, by intimidating witnesses—we would request arrest warrants.[67]President Kibaki issued a statement appealing for calm. He said the ICC process had only just begun and that until it had been completed, any other calls for action to be taken against the six would be "against the rules of natural justice."

President Kibaki expressed that he was "fully committed to the establishment of a local tribunal."[68] The government informed that it was beefing up security countrywide to forestall any violent reactions that may follow the announcement.[69] The parliament interrupted its business to debate a motion urging the government to pull out the ICC process.[70]

BBC East Africa correspondent Will Ross commented that there had "been a degree of panic among some members of the usually untouchable political elite." He considered that *"most Kenyans feel these prosecutions are vital to undermine the deeply rooted culture of impunity."* And the critical question now is "whether those accused will hand themselves over or be shielded by politicians and evade justice."[71]Pre-Trial Chamber II reviewed the evidence and, after requesting further information relating to the first case, issued summons to appear for all the six suspects on March 8, 2011.[72]

Kenya's Challenge of the ICC's Jurisdiction

Kenya's government did not challenge the ICC intervention until the judges confirmed our request. A few days later, on March 30, 2011, Kenya's government implemented a December cabinet decision and filed a legal challenge to the cases' admissibility under Article 19 of the statute.

Kenya claimed that it would carry out its own investigations into the post-election violence. The government acknowledged that no national proceedings were currently underway against the six individuals named suspects by the ICC. However, it explained that its strategy was to follow a "bottom-up" approach by concentrating its initial investigations and prosecutions on lower-level perpetrators first before moving on to higher-level suspects.[73]

On May 30, 2011, the pre-trial chamber rejected the Kenyan government's challenge. The chamber welcomed the government's judicial reforms and the willingness to investigate the post-election violence. But the judges considered that the Kenyan government's ongoing investigations were focused on lower-level perpetrators, as the challenge acknowledged.

On that basis, the chamber concluded that the Kenyan government's inactivity concerning the investigation or prosecution of these six individuals rendered the two cases admissible.[74] The decision neither analyzed the "willingness" nor the Kenyan state's institutional capacity; instead, it strictly focused on the existence of similar national proceedings.

On June 6, 2011, the Kenyan Government filed an appeal against the pre-trial chamber's decision.[75] It argued that the chamber must make its determination "with a full understanding of the fundamental and far-reaching constitutional and judicial reforms" both recently enacted and anticipated, as well as "the investigative processes that are currently underway."

Kenya submitted that the new constitution adopted in August 2010 strengthens "fair trial rights and procedural guarantees" in the criminal justice system and "empowers Kenyan national courts to deal with the cases currently before the Court, without needing to pass legislation establishing a special tribunal."

Further, their application argued that the adoption of reforms such as the appointment of a new chief justice and High Court judges also "meant that Kenya is able to conduct national criminal proceedings for all crimes arising from the post-election violence."

The appeal chamber welcomed the express will of the government of Kenya to investigate the case. But it found only one investigative activity related to *"a file [that] was opened against one of the six suspects on account of witness statements taken by the [investigative] team."* Kenya did not provide the chamber with any information about these statements' time or content. "The Government of Kenya also state[d] that it [had] instructed the 'team of investigators to carry out exhaustive investigations,'" but it did not "explain or show the Chamber any concrete step that has been or is being currently undertaken in this respect."[76]

As a result, "in the absence of information, which substantiates Government of Kenya's challenge that there are ongoing investigations against the three suspects ... the Chamber consider[ed] that there remain[ed] a situation of inactivity" and rejected the appeal.[77]

The Confirmation of Charges and the Security of the Witnesses

The accused accepted to present voluntarily before the court, and the initial appearance hearing took place on April 7, 2011. The confirmation of charges hearing was held during September 2011 in all the suspects' presence. Interestingly, none of them challenged the admissibility of the cases adducing the existence of similar national proceedings.[78]

We had collected information alleging that Ruto was threatening the witnesses. In a confidential hearing in the presence of Mr. Ruto, we requested his arrest. A warrant against him could had been implemented immediately. The pre-trial chamber asked to disclose the information sources to Mr. Ruto's lawyers. We refused, considering that such disclosure would put the sources in danger, and the pre-trial chamber rejected our request.

On January 23, 2012, the judges declined to confirm the charges against Mr. Ali and confirmed the charges against Mr. Muthaura and Mr. Kenyatta and committed them to trial. The same day, the judges declined to confirm the charges against Mr. Kosgey, confirmed the charges against Mr. Ruto and Mr. Sang, and committed them to trial.

The Political Alliance Kenyatta-Ruto and the Outcome of the Judicial Proceedings

Uhuru Kenyatta and William Ruto renewed their political alliance and became candidates as president and vice president. They had a significant contender. In November 2011, George Saitoti announced he would stand for the presidency in future elections.[79]

Saitoti was a Masai with Kikuyu ancestors and was perceived as a strong candidate for the 2013 elections.[80] He was an economist and mathematician educated in the United States and United Kingdom, Kenya's vice president between 1989 and 2002, and, at that moment, a powerful security minister. He was the government's face on security matters, including Kenya's decision to send troops to Somalia in 2011.[81]

In June 2012, George Saitoti was killed when the police helicopter he was riding in plunged into a forest west of Nairobi. Kenyan officials said they did not know the crash's cause, though there was no evidence that it resulted from a terrorist attack or foul play.[82]

Kenyatta and Ruto were elected president and vice president in a mostly peaceful 2013 election. Kenya obtained the AU support and requested the adoption of an Article 16 UN Security Council Resolution suspending the proceedings invoking its role in the war against terrorism in Somalia.[83] On November 15, 2013, the UN Security Council discussed the matter. Seven council members voted in favor of the text (Azerbaijan, China, Morocco, Pakistan, Russia, Rwanda, Togo). The United States and the seven states parties abstained (Argentina, Australia, France, Guatemala, Luxembourg, Republic of Korea, United Kingdom). The draft was, therefore, not adopted.[84]

Russia said African countries had presented compelling arguments at a critical time for Kenya, whose military was playing a key role in Somalia. It also stated that the application of Article 16 would have increased the credibility of the international system of justice among African countries, showing its readiness to address "complicated and ambiguous" situations.

China was in favor of adopting an Article 16 decision; it considered that Kenya played a long-standing role in the fight against terrorism and bolstering peace and security in Africa. The United States considered that the issue should be addressed in the court and by the Assembly of States Parties.

Rwanda's representative stressed, "Let it be written in history that the Council failed Kenya and Africa on this issue." He considered that the decisions "undermined the principle of sovereign equality and confirmed the long-held view that international mechanisms were manipulated to serve select interests." Article 16 had never been meant to be used by an African State; it appeared to be a tool used by Western powers to "protect their own," he added. Ethiopia stated that the matter was not simply a Kenyan one but an African one.

On November 21, 2013, during the Assembly of States Parties, a special segment was organized as requested by the African Union: "Indictment of sitting Heads of State and Government and its consequences on peace and stability and reconciliation."[85]

As a result, on November 27, 2013, the Assembly of States Parties amended the Rules of Procedure and Evidence accepting the presence of accused through the use of video technology, excusing the presence of the accused during part of the trial, in particular when the accused has to fulfill extraordinary public duties.[86]

President Kenyatta and Vice President Ruto continued appearing before the court, and Kenya remains a Rome Statute' state party. Witnesses disappeared, and many recanted their testimonies.

On March 18, 2013, the charges against Francis Kirimi Muthaura were withdrawn.

On December 5, 2014, prosecutor Fatou Bensouda filed a notice to withdraw charges against Mr. Kenyatta. She explained, "the severe challenges my Office has faced in our investigation of Mr. Kenyatta." Including that:

- several people who may have provided important evidence regarding Mr. Kenyatta's actions have died, while others were too terrified to testify for the prosecution;
- key witnesses who provided evidence in this case later withdrew or changed their accounts, in particular, witnesses who subsequently alleged that they had lied to my office about having been personally present at crucial meetings; and
- the Kenyan Government's non-compliance compromised the prosecution's ability to thoroughly investigate the charges, as recently confirmed by the Trial Chamber.[87]

On April 5, 2016, Trial Chamber V(A), by the majority vote of Presiding Judge Chile Eboe-Osuji, and Judge Robert Fremr, denied prosecution requests for legal re-characterization and vacated the charges against William Ruto and Joshua Arap Sang without prejudice to their prosecution afresh in the future.[88] Judge Chile Eboe-Osuji was:

[S]atisfied that the evidence presented by the Prosecution had amply demonstrated the incidence of witness interference at a disturbing scale . . . While the full breadth of the interference is yet unknown—and may never be known—I am satisfied (with the fullest confidence) that the extent of the evidence of interference is enough to make acquittal of the accused grossly unjust.[89] "The incidence of interference was bolstered and accentuated by an atmosphere of intimidation," including "voices from the executive and legislative branches of the Government."[90]

He also wrote: *"Conviction in every criminal case is never the hallmark of success—or 'performance indicator,' to borrow a fashionable phrase—for a court of law." "The same general consideration goes for the purpose of prosecution."*[91]

Judge Herrera Carbucchi voted in dissent. In her views, "the charges against both accused should not be vacated in the present case."[92]

On March 13, 2015, Trial Chamber V(B), noting the prosecution's withdrawal of charges against Mr. Kenyatta, decided to terminate the proceedings in this case and to vacate the summons to appear against him.[93]

The Influence of the War on Terrorism on Those Who Participate in the Events

In September 2013, a terrorist attack in a shopping mall in Nairobi that killed four British citizens was attributed to the Somali-based militant group al-Shabaab. UK Prime Minister Cameron had a phone conversation with President Uhuru Kenyatta and offered the Kenyan authorities "every assistance."[94]

Two months after the ICC vacated the proceedings against Kenyatta, President Obama visited Nairobi. He made clear that "part of why he'd held off on a visit until now was "deep concerns" over the violence that followed the 2008 elections here, and which made Kenyatta the first sitting leader of a country to appear before the International Criminal Court."

The agenda included battling al-Shabaab, and Kenya's role in counterterrorism, including funding and training.[95]

President Kenyatta said there was "very close cooperation" with the United States, and "the fight against terror will be central."[96]

Notes

1. Brian Kennedy, *Kenya: Early Results Give Raila Odinga Lead*, ALL AFRICA (Dec. 28, 2007), http://allafrica.com/stories/200712280783.html.
2. On December 30, 2007, the election commission declared the incumbent President Mwai Kibaki as the winner, with 4,584,721 votes compared with 4,352,993 for Mr. Raila Odinga—a spread of about 2 percent.
3. Benjamin Mkapa (Tanzania), Joaquim Chissano (Mozambique), Ketumile Masire (Botswana) and Kenneth Kaunda (Zambia).
4. *Kenya Opposition Cancels Protests*, BBC NEWS, http://news.bbc.co.uk/2/hi/africa/7174670.stm (last updated Jan. 7, 2008).

5. Also integrated by Graça Machel, former Mozambique's minister of education and wife of Nelson Mandela and Benjamin Mkapa, former president of Tanzania.

6. KOFI ANNAN, INTERVENTIONS: A LIFE IN WAR AND PEACE 190 (Kindle ed. 2012).

7. US Secretary of State Condoleezza Rice was calling both sides to end the violence, and Ban Ki-moon, the UN secretary-general, was "concerned with the deteriorating humanitarian situation, as large numbers of people have been displaced by the violence." Jeffrey Gettleman, *Disputed Vote Plunges Kenya Into Bloodshed*, N.Y. TIMES (Dec. 31, 2007), http://www.nytimes.com/2008/01/03/world/africa/03kenya.html.

8. *France's Kouchner Believes Kenyan Vote Rigged*, REUTERS (Jan. 4, 2008), http://mobile.reuters.com/article/idUSL0444796820080104?irpc=932.

9. Jeffrey Gettleman, *Disputed Vote Plunges Kenya Into Bloodshed*, N.Y. TIMES (Dec. 31, 2007), http://www.nytimes.com/2008/01/31/world/africa/31kenya.html.

10. Hum. Rts. Watch, *Ballots to Bullets: Organized Political Violence and Kenya's Crisis of Governance*, Volume 20, No. 1 (A) (Mar. 2008).

11. Elizabeth A. Kennedy, *Fighting Erupts In Western Kenyan Town*, FOX NEWS (Jan. 25, 2008), https://www.foxnews.com/printer_friendly_wires/2008Jan25/0,4675,KenyaElectionViolence,00.html.

12. LIONEL NICHOLS, THE INTERNATIONAL CRIMINAL COURT AND THE END OF IMPUNITY IN KENYA (Kindle ed. 2015).

13. Office of the Prosecutor, *OTP Statement in Relation to Events in Kenya*, ICC (Feb. 5, 2008), https://www.icc-cpi.int/NR/rdonlyres/1BB89202-16AE-4D95-ABBB-4597C416045D/0/ICCOTPST20080205ENG.pdf.

14. KOFI ANNAN, INTERVENTIONS: A LIFE IN WAR AND PEACE 189 (Kindle ed. 2012).

15. *Id.* at 191.

16. *Id.*

17. In accordance with Museveni's press secretary on January 23, Kibaki and Odinga met separately with Ugandan President Yoweri Museveni and an agreement was reached in principle to establish a judicial commission that would investigate the accusations of vote rigging; however, the two sides disagreed as to whether the government alone should appoint the members of the commission. Museveni was also said to have proposed a power-sharing deal, which was rejected by the government on the grounds that it was unwilling to share power with the ODM due to the latter's alleged responsibility for the killing of innocent people. Emmanuel Gyezaho & Grace Matsiko, *Kenya: Museveni Proposes Power Sharing Deal to Raila, Kibaki*, ALL AFRICA (Jan. 24, 2008), https://allafrica.com/stories/200801231038.html.

18. KOFI ANNAN, INTERVENTIONS: A LIFE IN WAR AND PEACE 191 (Kindle ed. 2012).

19. Members of the government changed the layout of the negotiation room, putting the special presidential chair in the middle. Annan refused the change explaining that: "this is not a presidential meeting." It was not a protocol detail; Annan had to be in the middle and chair the meeting to ensure the neutrality of the process and to keep Odinga in the negotiations. Francis Muthaura and Uhuru Kenyatta, who later were indicted for their role in the violence, were the members of the government who were insisting on keeping the presidential chair. In the end, Kibaki kept his chair on the side and Annan was in the middle chairing the meeting. KOFI ANNAN, INTERVENTIONS: A LIFE IN WAR AND PEACE 193 (Kindle ed. 2012).

20. *Kibaki Facing Genocide Claims*, OGIEK (Jan. 28, 2008), http://www.ogiek.org/news-2/news-post-08-01-677-1.htm

21. On February 14 President Bush said, "There must be an immediate halt to violence." This was Mr. Bush's toughest language to date about the crisis in Kenya, in a speech intended to preview his Africa trip. "There must be justice for the victims of abuse and there must be a full return to democracy." Sheryl Gay Stolberg, *Turmoil in Africa Alters Focus of Bush's 5-Nation Tour*, N.Y. TIMES (Feb. 15, 2008), http://www.nytimes.com/2008/02/15/world/africa/15prexy.html.

22. Secretary of State Condoleezza Rice visited Kenya on February 18. She met the leaders of rival political factions and said afterward that while their differences were "not unbridgeable," the two sides must move much faster to accept a power-sharing deal that would lead to a coalition government. Sheryl Gay Stolberg & Jeffrey Gettleman, *Rice, in Nairobi, Offers Incentives to End Violence*, N.Y. TIMES (Feb. 19, 2008), http://www.nytimes.com/2008/02/19/world/africa/19kenya.html.

23. *Rice Calls for Kenya Power-Sharing*, AL JAZEERA (Feb. 18, 2008), https://www.aljazeera.com/news/africa/2008/02/2008525115657555560.html.

24. *Annan Frustrated by Kenya Talks*, BBC NEWS (Feb. 25, 2008), http://news.bbc.co.uk/2/hi/africa/7263359.stm

25. Michelle D. Gavin, *Policy Options Paper—Kenya*, COUNCIL ON FOREIGN RELATIONS (Mar. 13, 2008), available at https://cdn.cfr.org/sites/default/files/pdf/2008/03/Kenya_POP.pdf).

26. On August 4, 2010, the Kenyan public voted to accept a new draft constitution, with 67 percent of Kenyans approving the referendum. The constitution devolves power to local governments, provides the Kenyan people with a bill of rights, and paves the way for land reform. Under the new constitution, the electoral commission is considered independent and beyond presidential control. *The Crisis in Kenya*, INT'L COAL. FOR THE RESPONSIBILITY TO PROTECT, http://www.responsibilitytoprotect.org/index.php/crises/crisis-in-kenya (last visited July 3, 2020).

27. Since independence, Kikuyu was the president. Jomo Kenyatta, the father of the independence, was replaced by Daniel Moi, who after twenty-four years in power agreed to leave his position and promoted Uhuru Kenyatta, Jomo's son, as the candidate for the ruling KANU Party in the 2002 elections.

   The contender in 2002 was Mwa Kibaki, a Kikuyu that was a minister under Jomo Kenyatta and Daniel Moi presidencies, and the vice president between 1978–1988, but moved to the opposition and he had lost the 1992 and 1997 elections. Raila Odinga, a Luo and the son of the first Kenyan vice president, for years was confronting Daniel Moi's authoritarian government. Odinga was in jail different times, went into exile, obtained the third position in the 1997 election after Moi and Kibaki but suddenly in 2001 accepted a ministerial position in the Moi government and joined KANU. Moi's decision to handpick Uhuru Kenyatta as the presidential candidate for the 2002 election created discontent and Odinga led a massive exit from KANU. He created a party and made an alliance with Kibaki who promised to appoint him as a prime minister and that half of the cabinet positions would be for Odinga's followers.

The 2002 elections were considered fair and free. Kibaki was supported by Odinga and obtained 63 percent of the votes, defeating Uhuru Kenyatta. The problem started later when Kibaki proposed a new constitution that was perceived to consolidate presidential powers and weaken regional governments, contrary to the pre-election draft. The alleged "betrayal" produced a split within the cabinet. Odinga and the former KANU that followed him campaigned against the adoption of the new constitution. Leaders of different ethnic groups, including William Ruto, a Kalenjin that made his political carrier in KANU, joined the alliance against Kibaki's constitution. In the 2005 referendum the project was rejected by 57 percent of the votes.

28. Two other commissions were created: The Independent Review Commission (IREC or Kriegler Commission) and the Truth, Justice and Reconciliation Commission.

29. The members of the commission as appointed were its chair, Mr. Justice Philip Waki a judge of Kenya's Court of Appeal; and two commissioners, Mr. Gavin McFadyen and Mr. Pascal Kambale, nationals of New Zealand and the Democratic Republic of Congo respectively.

30. The CIPEV mandate was to (a) investigate the facts and circumstances related to acts of violence that followed the elections; (b) investigate the actions or omissions of state security agencies during the course of the violence; (c) recommend measures to prevent future violence; (d) recommend measures to bring justice to those responsible for the violence and eradicate impunity. KENYA: COMMISSION OF INQUIRY INTO THE POST ELECTION VIOLENCE (CIPEV), FINAL REPORT, KEN-OTP-0001-0364 to KEN-OTP-0001-0892, vii (2008).

31. KENYA NATIONAL COMMISSION ON HUMAN RIGHTS, ON THE BRINK OF THE PRECIPICE: A HUMAN RIGHTS ACCOUNT OF KENYA'S POST 2007 ELECTION VIOLENCE 7 (Aug. 2008).

32. "There are 4773 pages of recorded sworn testimony from 156 witnesses and 144 other witnesses who submitted depositions and recorded statements. There are nine volumes of exhibits running into more than 3500 pages and we had at our disposal, in terms of our terms of reference, official reports of previous investigations, investigations from other institutions or organizations and research material from our own researchers and investigators." *Id.* at vii.

33. "Politicians rely on their supporters to enforce immunity while their supporters, who are the handmaidens of the violence, get protection from the political god fathers." *Id.* at 457.

34. SERENA K. SHARMA, THE RESPONSIBILITY TO PROTECT AND THE INTERNATIONAL CRIMINAL COURT 87 (Kindle ed. 2016).

35. *Id.* at 97.

36. *Id.* at 86.

37. *Id.*

38. *Waki: Row over Ruto Threat to Quit ODM*, NATION (Nov. 16, 2008), http://www.nation.co.ke/news/-/1056/491782/-/view/printVersion/-/nqjvgqz/-/index.html   (last updated July 3, 2020).

39. SERENA K. SHARMA, THE RESPONSIBILITY TO PROTECT AND THE INTERNATIONAL CRIMINAL COURT 87 (Kindle ed. 2016).

40. Peter Opiyo & Isaac Ongiri, *The Standard, Kibaki, Raila Final Pitch for Local Tribunal*, STANDARD MEDIA (Feb. 9, 2009), https://www.standardmedia.co.ke/article/1144006 190/kibaki-raila-final-pitch-for-local-tribunal.

41. SERENA K. SHARMA, THE RESPONSIBILITY TO PROTECT AND THE INTERNATIONAL CRIMINAL COURT 88 (Kindle ed. 2016).

42. John Michuki, Kenya National Assembly, February 4, 2009.

43. Office of the Prosecutor, *Agreed Minutes of the Meeting between Prosecutor Moreno-Ocampo and the Delegation of the Kenyan Government*, ICC (July 3, 2009), https:// www.icc-cpi.int/NR/rdonlyres/1CEB4FAD-DFA7-4DC5-B22D-E828322D9764/280 560/20090703AgreedMinutesofMeetingProsecutorKenyanDele.pdf.

44. One was on the Review of Post-Election Violence related in Western, Nyanza, Central, Rift Valley, Eastern, Coast, and Nairobi Provinces, February 2009. The second was a Status Report on the Operationalization of the Witness Protection Program.

45. SERENA K. SHARMA, THE RESPONSIBILITY TO PROTECT AND THE INTERNATIONAL CRIMINAL COURT 89 (Kindle ed. 2016).

46. Africa Confidential, *Kofi Annan Puts Kenyan Politicians on the Spot*, HUMAN RTS. HOUSES (July 24, 2009), https://humanrightshouse.org/articles/kofi-annan-puts-ken yan-politicians-on-the-spot/.

47. SERENA K. SHARMA, THE RESPONSIBILITY TO PROTECT AND THE INTERNATIONAL CRIMINAL COURT 89/90 (Kindle ed. 2016).

48. Martin Mutua & David Ochami, *Waki: MPs Push for "Third" Option*, THE STANDARD, (Feb. 16, 2009), https://www.standardmedia.co.ke/article/1144006747/waki-mps-push-for-third-option.

49. Situation in the Republic of Kenya, ICC-01/09, Request for authorisation of an investigation pursuant to Article 15 ¶ 56 (Nov. 26, 2009), https://www.icc-cpi.int/Court Records/CR2009_08645.PDF.

50. "The Nairobi Women's Hospital received 524 cases of rape between 27 December 2007 and 31 March 2008. During that same period, partner hospitals of the Nairobi Women's Hospital received 286 cases of sexual violence, and the Kenyatta National Hospital responded to another 184 cases. These figures are indicative of the increase in sexual assaults during the post-election violence." Situation in the Republic of Kenya, ICC-01/09, Request for authorisation of an investigation pursuant to Article 15 ¶ 66 (Nov. 26, 2009), https://www.icc-cpi.int/CourtRecords/CR2009_08645.PDF.

51. According to the Report in Western, Nyanza, Central, Rift Valley, Eastern East and Nairobi Provinces, "156 cases were opened in relation to minor offences such as 'malicious damage,' 'theft,' 'house breaking,' 'bond to keep peace,' 'publishing false rumor,' and other criminal offences, such as 'possession of offensive weapon,' 'robbery with violence' or 'assaulting police officer.'" Among the most prominent cases, the four accused who were charged for arsoning the Kiambaa Church in which seventeen to thirty-five persons were burned alive on January 1, 2008, in Eldoret, were acquitted for lack of evidence as a result of "shoddy police investigations." Situation in the Republic of Kenya, ICC-01/09, Request for authorisation of an investigation pursuant to Article 15 ¶ 54 (Nov. 26, 2009), https://www.icc-cpi.int/CourtRecords/CR2009_08 645.PDF.

52. Participants included: members of the Kenyan Section of the International Commission of Jurists (ICJ); the Kenya National Commission on Human Rights (KNCHR); the Kenya Human Rights Commission (KHRC); International Center for Policy and Conflict (ICPC) and the Kenyan office for the International Center for Transitional Justice (ICTJ). All them traveled to The Hague to explain their position concerning the incidents. Press Release, Office of the Prosecutor, ICC Prosecutor: Kenya Can Be an Example to the World Office of the Prosecutor, ICC (Sept. 18, 2009).

53. <Republic v. Kenya National Commission on Humans Rights Ex-Parte Uhuru Muigai Kenyatta, (2010) e.K.L.R. (H.C.K.) (Kenya).

54. *Id.*

55. Office of the Prosecutor, *Agreed Minutes of the meeting between Prosecutor Moreno-Ocampo and the delegation of the Kenyan Government*, ICC (July 3, 2009), https://www.icc-cpi.int/NR/rdonlyres/1CEB4FAD-DFA7-4DC5-B22D-E828322D9764/280560/20090703AgreedMinutesofMeetingProsecutorKenyanDele.pdf.

56. A Reuter journalist explained the point if Kibaki and Odinga "are now seen to be the ones giving up former party allies accused of mobilizing deadly ethnic militias, the coalition could fall apart and tribal violence could flare." David Clarke, *REFILE-ICC Prosecutor to Meet Kenyan Leaders over Trials*, REUTERS (Nov. 4, 2009, 8:28 PM), http://www.reuters.com/article/idUSL4559240.

57. Robert Cryer, *Darfur: Complementarity as the Drafters Intended?*, in THE INTERNATIONAL CRIMINAL COURT AND COMPLEMENTARITY: FROM THEORY TO PRACTICE 1097, 1097 (Carsten Stahn & Mohamed M. El Zeidy eds., Kindle ed. 2011).

58. Situation in the Republic of Kenya, ICC-01/09, Request for authorisation of an investigation pursuant to Article 15 ¶ 96–99 (Nov. 26, 2009), https://www.icc-cpi.int/CourtRecords/CR2009_08645.PDF.

59. COMMISSION OF INQUIRY INTO THE POST ELECTION VIOLENCE (CIPEV), FINAL REPORT 252, KEN-OTP-0001-0364 to KEN-OTP-0001-0892 (Oct. 16, 2008).

60. *ICC Judges Request Clarification and Additional Information with Regard to the Situation in Kenya*, RELIEF WEB (Feb. 19, 2010), http://reliefweb.int/report/kenya/icc-judges-request-clarification-and-additional-information-regard-situation-kenya.

61. For both applications to the pre-trial chamber, we relied on a selected number of reliable and publicly available reports on alleged crimes committed during the post-election violence in Kenya, including the reports published by: the Commission of Inquiry into Post-Election Violence; the Kenyan National Commission on Human Rights (KNCHR); the Office of the High Commissioner for Human Rights; UNICEF, UNFPA, UNIFEM, and Christian Children's Fund; the UN Special Rapporteur on extrajudicial, summary or arbitrary executions; the Oscar Foundation; the Federation of Women Lawyers (FIDA-K); Centre for Rights Education and Awareness (CREAW); Human Rights Watch; and the International Crisis Group.

62. Press Release, ICC, ICC judges grant the prosecutor's request to launch an investigation on crimes against humanity with regard to the situation in Kenya, ICC Press Release (Mar. 31, 2010).

63. Situation in the Republic of Kenya, ICC-01/09, Decision Pursuant to Article 15 of the Rome Statute on the Authorization of an Investigation into the Situation in the Republic of Kenya, ¶ 84 (Mar. 31, 2010), https://www.icc-cpi.int/CourtRecords/CR2010_02409.PDF.

64. "These characteristics could involve the following: (a) a collectivity of persons; (b) which was established and acts for a common purpose; (c) over a prolonged period of time; (d) which is under responsible command or adopted a certain degree of hierarchical structure, including, as a minimum, some kind of policy level; (e) with the capacity to impose the policy on its members and to sanction them; and (f) which has the capacity and means available to attack any civilian population on a large scale." Situation in the Republic of Kenya, ICC-01/09, Decision Pursuant to Article 15 of the Rome Statute on the Authorization of an Investigation into the Situation in the Republic of Kenya, ¶ 51 (Mar. 31, 2010), https://www.icc-cpi.int/CourtRecords/CR2010_02409.PDF.

65. Situation in the Republic of Kenya, ICC-01/09, Prosecutor's Application Pursuant to Article 58 as to William Samoei Ruto, Henry Kiprono Kosgey and Joshua Arap Sang ¶ 1 (Dec. 15, 2010), https://www.icc-cpi.int/CourtRecords/CR2010_11225.PDF.

66. *Id.*

67. *Kenya Election Violence: ICC Names Suspects*, BBC (Dec. 15, 2010), https://www.bbc.com/news/world-africa-11996652.

68. *Id.*

69. *Will ICC Bring Justice or Violence to Kenya?*, BBC (Dec. 15, 2010), https://www.bbc.com/news/world-africa-12002571

70. *Id.*

71. *Kenya Election Violence: ICC Names Suspects*, BBC (Dec. 15, 2010), https://www.bbc.com/news/world-africa-11996652.

72. Prosecutor v. William Samoei Ruto, Henry Kiprono Kosgey and Joshua Arap Sang, ICC-01/09-01/11, Decision on the Prosecutor's Application for Summons to Appear for William Samoei Ruto, Henry Kiprono Kosgey and Joshua Arap Sang (Mar. 8, 2011), https://www.icc-cpi.int/CourtRecords/CR2011_02585.PDF. Prosecutor v. Uhuru Muigai Kenyatta, ICC-01/09-02/11, Decision on the Prosecutor's Application for Summonses to Appear for Francis Kirimi Muthuara, Uhuru Muigai Kenyatta and Mohammed Hussein Ali (Mar. 8, 2011), https://www.icc-cpi.int/CourtRecords/CR2011_02586.PDF.

73. Prosecutor v. William Samoei Ruto, Henry Kiprono Kosgey, Joshua Arap Sang and Prosecutor v. Francis Kirimi Muthaura, Uhuru Muigai Kenyatta And Mohammed Hussein Ali, ICC-01/09-01/11-19 and ICC-01/09-02/11-26, Application on Behalf of the Government of the Republic Of Kenya Pursuant to Article 19 of the ICC Statute ¶ 71 (Mar 31, 2011), https://www.icc-cpi.int/CourtRecords/CR2011_03107.PDF.

74. On the "inaction" prong of the complementarity test in the Rome Statute, *see also* KAI AMBOS, TREATISE ON INTERNATIONAL CRIMINAL LAW. VOL III: INTERNATIONAL CRIMINAL PROCEDURE 296–301 (1st ed., 2016).

75. The Prosecutor v. William Samoei Ruto, Henry Kiprono Kosgey and Joshua Arap Sang, ICC-01/09-01/11, Appeal of the Government of Kenya against the "Decision

on the Application by the Government of Kenya Challenging the Admissibility of the Case Pursuant to Article 19(2)(b) of the Statute" (June 6, 2011), https://www.icc-cpi.int/CourtRecords/CR2011_07027.PDF. Prosecutor v. Francis Kirimi Muthaura, Uhuru Muigai Kenyatta and Mohammed Hussein Ali, 01/09-02/11-104, Appeal of the Government of Kenya against the "Decision on the Application by the Government of Kenya Challenging the Admissibility of the Case Pursuant to Article 19(2)(b) of the Statute" (June 6, 2011), https://www.icc-cpi.int/CourtRecords/CR2011_07029.PDF.

76. Prosecutor v. Uhuru Muigai Kenyatta, ICC-01/09-02/11-96, Decision on the Application by the Government of Kenya Challenging the Admissibility of the Case Pursuant to Article 19(2)(b) of the Statute (May 30, 2011), https://www.icc-cpi.int/pages/record.aspx?uri=1078823.

    For a critical assessment of the ICC's case law on Kenya, *see* Thomas Abel Hansen, *A Critical Review of the ICC's Recent Practice Concerning Admissibility Challenges and Complementarity*, 13 MELBOURNE J. INT'L L. 217 (2012).

77. Judgment on the appeal of the Republic of Kenya against the decision of Pre-Trial Chamber II of May 30, 2011 entitled "Decision on the Application by the Government of Kenya Challenging the Admissibility of the Case Pursuant to Article 19(2)(b) of the Statute," https://www.icc-cpi.int/sites/default/files/CourtRecords/CR2011_13 814.PDF.

78. Prosecutor v. William Samoei Ruto, Henry Kiprono Kosgey and Joshua Arap Sang, ICC-01/09-01/11, Decision on the Confirmation of Charges Pursuant to Article 61(7)(a) and (b) of the Rome Statute (Jan. 23, 2012), https://www.icc-cpi.int/Court Records/CR2012_01004.PDF

79. *Kenyan Minister George Saitoti Killed in Helicopter Crash*, BBC (June 10, 2012), https://www.bbc.com/news/world-africa-18384861

80. Associated Press, *Kenyan Minister Killed in Crash*, GUARDIAN (June 10, 2012, 6:22 PM), https://www.theguardian.com/world/2012/jun/10/kenyan-minister-dies-hel icopter-crash.

81. *Id.*

82. Jeffrey Gettleman, *Kenyan Government Official Killed in Air Crash*, N.Y. TIMES (June 10, 2012), https://www.nytimes.com/2012/06/11/world/africa/kenyan-government-official-killed-in-helicopter-crash.html.

83. S.C.O.R., Identical letters dated 21 October 2013 from the Permanent Representative of Kenya to the United Nations addressed to the Secretary-General and the President of the Security Council, U.N. Doc S/2-13/624 (Oct. 22, 2013).

84. S.C.O.R., 68th Sess., 7060th mtg., U.N. Doc S/PV.7060 Provisional (Nov. 15, 2013).

85. ICC Assembly of States parties, 12th Sess. Special segment as requested by the African Union: "Indictment of sitting Heads of State and Government and its consequences on peace and stability and reconciliation", ICC Doc. ICC-ASP/12/61 (Nov. 27, 2013).

86. Resolution ICC-ASP/12/Res.7, ICC Doc ICC-ASP/12/20 (Nov. 27, 2012).

87. Office of the Prosecutor, *Statement of the Prosecutor of the International Criminal Court, Fatou Bensouda, on the withdrawal of charges against Mr. Uhuru Muigai Kenyatta*, ICC (Dec. 4, 2014), https://www.icc-cpi.int/Pages/item.aspx?name=otp-statement-05-12-2014-2.

88. Prosecutor v. William Samoei Ruto and Joshua Arap Sang, ICC-01/09-01/11, Decision on Defence Applications for Judgments of Acquittal (Apr. 5, 2016), https://www.icc-cpi.int/CourtRecords/CR2016_04384.PDF.

89. *Id.*

90. *Id.*

91. Quoting Canadian Supreme Court, Judge Chile Eboe-Osuji described the role of the Prosecutor to lay before the Judges "credible evidence relevant to what is alleged to be a crime." "The hallmark of success for a court of law is, quite simply, to do justice.... Justice was served when the Prosecutor saw a substantial reason (based on the required level of evidence at that stage) to believe that the charges against Mr. Ruto, Mr. Sang, and Mr. Kosgey had to be brought to the Pre-Trial Chamber for investigation, review, and confirmation; and having so found, robustly pursued confirmation of charges against them. Justice was amply served when (without fear or favour) the Prosecutor and her staff robustly mounted their case against Mr. Ruto and Mr. Sang before this Trial Chamber—in the face of irregularities (not of the Prosecution's making) that are discussed elsewhere in these reasons." *Id.*

92. *Id.*

93. *Case Information Sheet: Situation in the Republic of Kenya*, ICC, https://www.icc-cpi.int/CaseInformationSheets/kenyattaEng.pdf (last updated Mar. 13, 2015).

94. Press Association, *Nairobi Terror Attack: David Cameron Heads Back to No 10*, THE GUARDIAN (Sept. 23, 8:51 AM), https://www.theguardian.com/world/2013/sep/23/nairobi-terror-attack-david-cameron-no-10.

95. Edward-Isaac Dovere, *When Obama met Kenyatta*, POLITICO (July 25, 2015, 2:26 PM), https://www.politico.com/story/2015/07/when-barack-obama-met-kenyatta-120623.

96. David Smith, *Obama's Kenya Agenda Both Personal and Political as Focus Turns to Terrorism*, GUARDIAN (July 24, 2015, 8:02 PM), https://www.theguardian.com/us-news/2015/jul/24/kenya-obama-family-nairobi-security.

12

The Preliminary Examinations Decisions Not to Open an Investigation

Venezuela, Iraq, and Palestine

This chapter presents three Office of the Prosecutor *jus ad Curiam*'s decisions considering that the statute requirements to open an investigation were not fulfilled: two in 2006, Venezuela, and about UK personnel in Iraq, and Palestine in 2012.

We decided that the information available in 2006 did not provide a reasonable basis to believe that a crime against humanity was committed in Venezuela.

We understood that the willful killings allegedly committed by UK personnel in Iraq did not reach the specific gravity threshold established by Article 8(1). Besides, national proceedings had been initiated concerning each of the relevant incidents.

Regarding Palestine, the preliminary examination focused on the Article 12 requirement that a "state" must accept ICC jurisdiction. We considered that the UN General Assembly recognized Palestine as an "observer," not a "Non-member State." After a transparent and thorough review process, we concluded that the prosecutor has no authority to redefine such status and rejected the request.

After the end of my tenure, different actors provided new information regarding Venezuela and UK personnel in Iraq. Under Article 15(6), the prosecutor could, at any moment, reopen a preliminary examination "regarding the same situation in the light of new facts or evidence."

The Organization of American States (OAS) collected information from many sources, and a panel of three experts concluded that crimes against humanity were committed in Venezuela. Six countries and Venezuela itself referred the situation to the ICC. The prosecution received new information about alleged crimes committed by UK personal in Iraq. Chief Prosecutor Bensouda reopened preliminary examinations in both situations.

War and Justice in the 21st Century. Luis Moreno Ocampo, Oxford University Press. © Oxford University Press 2022.
DOI: 10.1093/oso/9780197628973.003.0013

The UN General Assembly adjusted the status of Palestine in 2012; it became a state party in 2015 and referred its own situation to the ICC in 2018. On January 22, 2020, and before opening an investigation, the prosecution requested a ruling under Art. 19 (3) asking the court to confirm that the "territory" over which the ICC may exercise its jurisdiction comprises the Occupied Palestinian Territory, including the West Bank, East Jerusalem, and Gaza.[1]

Some states parties filled observations proposing that Palestine is not a state, even they previously accepted Palestine as a state party of the Rome Statute.

Venezuela

Under President Hugo Chavez, Venezuela ratified the Rome Statute on June 7, 2002, and became the first South American state party. Until the end of 2005, the Office of the Prosecutor received twelve communications exposing alleged crimes committed in Venezuela. Some of them concerned incidents during the short-lived coup against President Chavez in April 2002 before the ICC temporal jurisdiction.

A group of Spanish and Venezuelan lawyers representing victims killed or wounded allegedly by government forces during a peaceful demonstration in front of the presidential palace in Caracas on April 11, 2002 triggered a case in Spain.[2] Spanish law recognizes the concept of universal jurisdiction for criminal offenses and codifies international crimes in its domestic statutes.[3] Judge Fernando Andreu of the Spanish "Audiencia Nacional" decided to defer prosecution of the case brought against Hugo Chavez, president of Venezuela, to the International Criminal Court.[4]

In our analysis, we concluded that these *events occurred prior to the court's temporal jurisdiction and cannot be considered the basis for any investigation under the statute.*

The other communications received put forward allegations that crimes against humanity had been committed against the political opponents by the Venezuelan government forces, *including 45 victims of murder, 39 to 44 of imprisonment, 42 of torture, and larger numbers of victims of persecution.* The office considered *The available information did not provide a reasonable basis to believe that the requirement of a widespread or systematic attack against any civilian population had been satisfied.*[5]

On February 9, 2006, the office concluded that the statute requirements to seek authorization to initiate an investigation in Venezuela's situation have not been satisfied. The office informed that such a conclusion could be reconsidered in the light of new facts or evidence. After the end of my tenure, many further communications were received from Venezuela, exposing a different picture.

The Participation of the OAS Secretary-General in the Events

Luis Almagro, the Organization of American States (OAS) secretary-general, created a new formula to *participate in the events*: On September 14, 2017, he appointed a Panel of Independent International Experts to analyze whether crimes against humanity may have been committed in Venezuela.[6]

The OAS requested written information from many sources and organized public hearings during September, October, and November 2017 at its headquarters in Washington to collect testimonies. The process unveiled a pattern: the Venezuelan Regime using the judicial system to persecute political opposition members.[7]

In the OAS headquarters, on September 15, 2017, General Heber García Plaza, a former minister from Maduro's government, explained that having control over the judges constitutes a policy.[8] General García Plaza testified that a national strategy, called "Plan Zamora," was adopted, defining the United States, Colombia, and "political dissidents" as the enemy. As in Darfur, citizens became an enemy and a target for military plans approved by the government. The massive incarceration was the primary strategy of the persecution.[9]

In February 2018, the Office of the Prosecutor decided to open a preliminary examination for crimes allegedly committed in Venezuela since at least April 2017 in the context of demonstrations and related political unrest. On May 29, 2018, the OAS panel of experts presented its report concluding that there were reasons to believe that crimes against humanity have been committed in Venezuela since at least February 12, 2014. It recommended the following: The Secretary-General of the OAS submits the report and the evidence to the ICC's Office of the Prosecutor and invites States Parties to the Rome Statute to refer Venezuela's situation to the ICC.[10]

Based on the OAS information, in September 2018, six states parties (Colombia, Canada, Paraguay, Argentina, Peru, and Chile) produced the first collective referral under the Rome Statute. They requested the ICC Prosecutor "to initiate an investigation on crimes against humanity allegedly committed in the territory of Venezuela since 12 February 2014."[11]

In February 2020, Venezuelan leader Nicolas Maduro also asked the ICC prosecutor to investigate crimes against humanity committed against the Venezuelan people since at least 2014. He indicated that the crimes were the "result of the application of unlawful coercive measures adopted unilaterally by the government of the United States of America."[12] The Office of the Prosecutor could initiate an investigation in Venezuela supported by all sides.

UK Personnel Involved in Alleged Crimes in Iraq

Until the end of 2005, the Office of the Prosecutor received over 240 communications concerning Iraq's situation. Many of them were related to the armed conflict's legality, but the ICC could not exercise jurisdiction on aggression's crime in those days.

Some communications on alleged war crimes committed by UK personnel operating in Iraq triggered a preliminary examination. The available information established that a considerable number of civilians died or were injured during UK military operations in Iraq but did not indicate intentional attacks on a civilian population.

International humanitarian law and the Rome Statute permit killing in some circumstances. A crime occurs if there is an intentional attack directed against civilians (principle of distinction) (Article8(2)(b)(i)). It also happens if an attack is launched on a military objective in the knowledge that the incidental civilian injuries would be excessive concerning the anticipated military advantage (principle of proportionality) (Article 8(2)(b)(iv)).[13]

The office invited the United Kingdom to provide additional information concerning selected allegations and received a detailed response. It also invited institutions representing victims to report any incident that might constitute war crimes allegedly committed by UK troops.

The prosecution concluded that there was a reasonable basis to believe that an estimated four to twelve victims of willful killing and a limited number of victims of inhuman treatment. The office found that national proceedings had been initiated concerning each of the relevant incidents.

Besides, even where the subject-matter jurisdiction is satisfied, Article 8(1) requests a specific gravity threshold for war crimes. It states that "the Court shall have jurisdiction in respect of war crimes in particular when committed as part of a plan or policy or as part of a large-scale commission of such crimes." Such a threshold is not an element of the crime but rather a criterion on jurisdiction. The office did not find a pattern of *a large-scale commission* of crimes nor evidence of plans, and it concluded that the situation did not reach the "gravity" required by Article 8 (1).

On February 9, 2006, the Office of the Prosecutor concluded, under Article 15(6) of the Rome Statute, that the statute requirements to seek authorization to initiate an investigation in the situation in Iraq have not been satisfied. It alerted that such a conclusion could be reconsidered in the light of new facts or evidence.

New Information on Alleged Crimes Committed by UK Personnel in Iraq

In January 2014, the European Center for Constitutional and Human Rights (ECCHR), a Berlin-based human rights group, and Public Interest Lawyers (PIL), a British law firm, submitted new information to the ICC's Office of the Prosecutor. They requested investigations on alleged UK personnel crimes in Iraq between 2003 and 2008.[14]

British foreign secretary William Hague said Britain's willingness to investigate the allegations meant action by the ICC was unnecessary. "The British armed forces uphold high standards ... so we reject any allegations of systematic abuse. But where there are substantiated allegations of things going wrong, these things have been or are being investigated."[15]

A preliminary examination was reopened in May 2014 and closed on December 14, 2020.

The 2009 Palestine Request

Accepting the ICC's Jurisdiction

On December 27, 2008, Israel launched a large-scale air campaign in the Gaza Strip, the first phase of what was called Operation Cast Lead to stop the ongoing rocket fire from Palestinian armed groups into Israel.[16] Gaza was not under the ICC's jurisdiction, and consequently, we were not following the conflict in our office in The Hague.

We were swamped working in different situations: preparing our opening statement in our first trial, the case against Thomas Lubanga, and our witnesses' questions. Besides, the pre-trial chamber was in the process of reviewing our request for arrest warrants against President Omar Al Bashir, and we had to be ready to galvanize support for arrest efforts. We were also conducting very complex security and diplomatic operations to ensure the rebel leaders' appearance who led the attack against the UN/AU peacekeepers basis in Haskanita, Darfur. We were preparing the confirmation of charges hearing in the case against Jean Pierre Bemba and reviewing the alleged crimes committed in Kenya during the post-electoral violence.

On January 22, 2009, Israel declared a unilateral ceasefire, and twelve hours later, Hamas announced a one-week ceasefire. The same day and without providing any advance notice, the minister of justice of the Palestinian National Authority, Professor Ali Khashan, visited ICC's offices in The Hague and lodged an ad hoc declaration accepting the ICC jurisdiction under Article 12(3) of the Rome Statute.[17]

The registry's personnel debated for a few hours whether they had to analyze the substance of the declaration, particularly the representation of the government of Palestine alleged by the then Minister of Justice Ali Khashan and the international community recognition of the existence of a state of Palestine. The registry consulted our office, and an agreement was reached. Accordingly, the registrar of the Court, Ms. Silvana Arbia, informed the Palestinian Authority that: "The Court has not made any determination on the applicability of Article 12(3) to this particular communication. A conclusive determination on its applicability would have to be made by the judges at an appropriate moment."

Suddenly, without any preparation, we became involved in the Palestine/Israel conflict. Together with my legal advisers and the person in charge of the jurisdiction analysis section, I received Minister Khassan, the ambassador of Palestine to the Netherlands, and his legal advisor in my office on the twelfth floor. I wanted to listen carefully to the minister.

The minister was still concerned by the discussions with the registry. He explained how problematic it was for him to convince the Palestinian Authority to make the declaration accepting jurisdiction. Minister Khassan described how he discussed with his colleagues at the Palestinian Authority the idea to request the ICC's intervention since 2008.

The Palestinian Authority agreed with his proposal subject to obtaining the support of the Arab League. Minister Khassan had several meetings in Cairo to achieve an impossible mission: to convince representatives of the member of the Arab League, including Sudan, to support the Palestinian move to approach the ICC.

At that precise moment, the Office of the Prosecutor requested the issuance of arrest warrants for genocide against the president of Sudan, a member of the Arab League. Remarkably, Minister Khassan obtained the full support of the Arab League, he led the presentation at the court, and suddenly he was facing the risk that his request could be rejected immediately in The Hague.

He asked me to consider how seriously a rejection could impact the court's relation with the Arab world. Dozens of Palestinians from different parts of Europe were waiting for him at a small hotel near our building.

My style was to be direct, an unusual strategy in the diplomatic world. I told Minister Khashan that I could understand the Palestinians' demand for justice and the importance of his efforts, but I could not guarantee success. My promise was to be impartial and to respect the Rome Statute. And on this aspect, I added that it was not clear that the Palestinian Authority could be considered a "state" as required by the Rome Statute.

The minister surprised me, and instead of making a political demand, he presented a legal argument. He was well prepared and recognized the complexity of the issue of Palestinian statehood. Instead of requesting a prompt decision from the prosecutor's office, he asked for a fair process to present the Palestinian Authority's arguments.

Minister Khashan said that in 1989 the UN General Assembly adopted a resolution acknowledging the proclamation of the "state" of Palestine. One hundred four states voted for this resolution; forty-four abstained, only the United States and Israel voted against it. He was not requesting the prosecutor's office a decision on Palestinian statehood but merely the opportunity and the time to present arguments to determine whether Palestine can pass criminal jurisdiction to us.

How should I respond? In January 2009, I had no clarity on the legal aspects surrounding the Palestinian request. Still, it was clear to us that part of our duty as the Office of the Prosecutor was to offer a fair process to present arguments to all the parties interested without prejudice of our final decision.

By Rule 49(2) of the Rules of Procedure and Evidence, those who provided information to the Office of the Prosecutor may submit additional material to the Office of the Prosecutor. Any citizen or organization could send communications to trigger our activities, and, in our practice, we received oral arguments from those senders on many occasions. I promised the minister that the Palestinian Authority would have the opportunity to present its views extensively.

That decision was challenged during the following years. It was my duty to ignore political interests and exclusively to consider the most plausible legal interpretation. Still, I realized that even taking the time to analyze the problem could create conflicts. Mark Ellis, the executive director of the International Bar Association, suggested that the Office of the Prosecutor should immediately clarify that the ICC does not have jurisdiction over crimes committed in the Gaza conflict. He was troubled with the possibility of "raising] unrealistic expectations that the ICC has jurisdiction to investigate alleged crimes committed in Gaza. It does not."[18]

The Scope of the Palestinian Preliminary Examination

The world was discussing the attacks against civilians, but we had to focus on the legal aspects. Article12(3) requires that a "state" accept the exercise of jurisdiction by the court, and there was uncertainty about the "statehood" of the Palestinian National Authority in 2009. As is usual in the matters before the ICC, there were contradictory political and legal views on the meaning of the Rome Statute and the office's work.

A spokesman for the Israeli Foreign Ministry dismissed the Palestinian move as "a good propaganda stunt." He stated that since "The ICC charter is adhered to by sovereign states, and the Palestinian Authority has not yet been recognized as one, so it cannot be a member."[19] Additionally, Israeli officials said that "Hamas has appropriated Gaza and doesn't recognize PA authority." They added, "If the residents of Gaza do not recognize the jurisdiction of the PA, how can the PA bring a case of alleged war crimes committed in Gaza jurisdiction?"[20]

At the same time, victims and NGOs were sending us communications about the suffering of the Palestinian people and demanding justice. Carsten Stahn exposed the dilemma "to reject the declaration would reduce the legitimacy of the Court in the eyes of many states who supported Palestinian statehood." He concluded that "The Prosecutor was being asked to determine the status of Schrödinger's cat, and would be damned if he went one way and damned if he went the other."[21]

We had internal meetings to discuss the scope of our preliminary examination. We considered that the exclusive focus should be whether the Palestinian Authority could be regarded as a "state" under Article 12(3). If we had a positive answer, we would have the authority to examine the alleged crimes committed. Our duty to respect the Palestinian Authority's right to present its arguments allowed us to reach a proper interpretation of our mandate.

The Role of the Arab League

Immediately after the visit of Minister Khassan, on January 26, 2009, the secretary-general of the League of Arab States, Amr Musa, wrote a letter to our office supporting the Palestinian request. I had known Ambassador Musa since 2005. I made periodic visits to Cairo visiting Arab League headquarters to keep the Arab countries informed about the evolution of our investigations in Darfur.

In February, and for the first time in its history, the Arab League created an Independent Fact-Finding Committee headed by Professor John Dugard (South African)[22] to investigate the crimes. The same month the minister of justice, Mr. Ali Khashan, came back to the office with the Palestinian National Authority's minister of foreign affairs, Mr. Riad al-Maliki, confirming the decision to accept jurisdiction. For the first time, the Arab League and the Palestinian Authority made the political decision to rely on a criminal justice system to manage the conflict with Israel.

The Arab League had a different relationship with us in other cases. In March 2009, after the court's decision to issue arrest warrants against Omar Al Bashir, the Arab League declared that it "confirm[ed] our solidarity with Sudan and reject the decision of the Pre-Trial Chamber to the International Criminal Court regarding the President of Sudan, Omar Hassan Ahmed Al-Bashir."[23]

Furthermore, Syria declared that "We will discuss their fabricated accusations against Sudan when those who committed atrocities and massacres in Palestine, Lebanon, and Iraq are arrested and brought before the court facing the same charges, which are not fabricated but proven and documented."[24]

On May 9, Secretary-General Musa submitted to our office the report "No Safe Place" produced by the Arab League Fact-Finding Committee. The committee found that the IDF was responsible for the crime of indiscriminate and disproportionate attacks on civilians.[25] The committee also found that the IDF was responsible for committing crimes against humanity but not genocide.

Remarkable, the committee also concluded that Palestinian militants who fired rockets into Israel committed the war crime of indiscriminate and disproportionate attacks on civilians.[26] The Committee recommended that the League of Arab States endorse Palestine's declaration accepting the International Criminal Court's jurisdiction and request the UN General Assembly support Palestine's declaration.

Consultation Process on the Legal Interpretation of Article 12(3)

We carefully reviewed the Fact-Finding Committee report and decided to visit the Arab League headquarters in Cairo on July 4, 2009, to meet with the secretariat members and clarify our preliminary examination's limited focus. The issue of *statehood* was a precondition of a more in-depth analysis that could include the matters explored by the Arab League's Fact-Finding Committee.

On August 6, 2009, the office wrote to the Embassy of Israel in The Netherlands, informing it that the preliminary examination was opened and its focus. We offered Israel the possibility to submit any relevant information and our availability for further meetings.

On August 14, 2009, the office received from the embassy a copy of the government of Israel's public report on Operation Cast Lead. The document referenced "multiple IDF investigations into allegations made by various groups of violations of the law."

Israel's Embassy responded specifically to our letter on September 7, 2009, thanking us for informing them of the preliminary examination opening. It was a diplomatic but short answer. Israel's letter said that we did not need more information because the case was obvious: Palestine was not a state.

On October 15–16, 2009, Dr. Khashan, accompanied by a delegation from the Palestinian National Authority and advised by Oxford University Professor Vaughan Lowe, visited the court and presented a preliminary report comprising legal arguments in support of the declaration lodged. The delegation also indicated that they would submit a further comprehensive report in 2010 concerning ICC's jurisdiction acceptance. Immediately, the office met with a high-level Arab League Secretariat delegation and all the Fact-Finding Committee members in The Hague.

I kept receiving several Palestinian and Israeli non-governmental organizations, sometimes supported by eminent professors, presenting their views on the issue of jurisdiction.

I had the opportunity to explain our position to Harvard Emeritus Professor Alan Dershowitz. He has strong views about Israel's self-defense rights and understood the need to offer a fair process to the Palestinian Authority.

We took advantage of the biannual meetings with NGOs at the seat of the court, and on October 20, 2010,[27] we organized a special session to discuss Palestine's statehood. It attracted experts and NGOs with different and contradictory views.[28]

The Arguments Relating to the Palestinian Statehood

Some argued that the term "State" is subject to variable defining characteristics under public international law and lacks an unambiguous or "ordinary" meaning. Consequently, it should be interpreted in a manner that will enable the treaty to fulfill its objectives of "ending impunity."

On the contrary, others argued that the express wording of Article 12(3) under the rules of treaty interpretation limits the acceptance of the court's jurisdiction to a "state" following the term's ordinary meaning. They noted that the statute gives no particular meaning to the word "state," adding that there is no basis for inferring that Article 12(3) includes entities that do not qualify as states under public international law.

The UN Security Council

In parallel to our activities, the UN Security Council and the UN Human Rights Council were making autonomous decisions per their specific legal mandates. As soon as the conflict started, Egypt and Saudi Arabia led the efforts to adopt a UN Security Council Resolution.

After difficult negotiations, on January 8, 2009, the UN Security Council, in the presence of several ministers of foreign affairs, adopted Resolution 1860 by fourteen votes and the US abstention.

The council did not use its power under Chapter VII. The resolution was limited to "*Stress[ing]* the urgency of and *call[ing] for* an immediate, durable and fully respected ceasefire, leading to the full withdrawal of Israeli forces from Gaza" and "*Condemn[ing]* all violence and hostilities directed against civilians and all acts of terrorism."[29]

The UN Human Rights Council and the Goldstone Report

On January 3, 2009, the Organisation of the Islamic Conference's executive committee asked the United Nations Human Rights Council (UNHRC) to send a fact-finding mission to Gaza. The lack of veto power produced a different language than the one used by the UN Security Council Resolution.

On January 12, the General Assembly adopted Resolution S-9/1, defining the mission as: "to investigate all violations of international human rights law and international humanitarian law by the occupying Power, Israel, against the Palestinian people."[30]

Many criticized the UN Human Rights Council commission's biased mandate, including former UN High Commissioner for Human Rights Mary Robinson. She refused to head the mission, stating that it was "guided not by human rights but by politics." Richard Goldstone initially refused the appointment for the same reason, calling the mandate "biased" and "uneven-handed."[31]

However, on April 3, 2009, following Goldstone's advice, the president of the Human Rights Council adjusted the mandate "to investigate all violations of international human rights law and international humanitarian law that might have been committed." Goldstone felt that he had a moral duty to accept the new offer and lead the UN Fact-Finding Mission in the Gaza Conflict.[32]

Findings of the Goldstone Report

The "Goldstone report" was presented on September 25, 2009, and concluded that what occurred in just over three weeks at the end of 2008 and the beginning of 2009 was a deliberately disproportionate attack designed to punish, humiliate and terrorize a civilian population, radically diminish its local economic capacity both to work and to provide for itself, and to force upon it an ever-increasing *sense of* dependency and vulnerability.[33]

The Goldstone Report recommended that the UN Security Council refer Gaza's situation to the International Criminal Court unless both parties conducted credible and independent investigations into possible crimes within six months. Regarding the Palestine acceptance of the ICC jurisdiction, it recommended that the Office of the Prosecutor "should make the required legal determination as expeditiously as possible."[34]

Endorsing the report, the High Commissioner for Human Rights, Navi Pillay, said that "holding war criminals accountable and respect for human rights are not obstacles to peace but, rather the preconditions on which trust and, ultimately, a durable peace can be built."[35]

"Human Rights Watch called on the ICC prosecutor to make a prompt legal determination on the Palestinian National Authority request, consistent with the ICC's mandate to end impunity."[36]

The Analysis of the Office of the Prosecutor

The consultation process helped our office to perceive the complexities of our decision. As in many legal discussions, there were arguments to support different conclusions, but we firmly believed that we should neither impose an extralegal criterion nor stretch the norms' meaning.

We perceived the need for a consistent interpretation of the term "*state*" for Article 12(1) and (3). Looking for precedents, the Office of the Prosecutor's team found that the UN secretary-general had been facing similar challenges. We understood that the UN secretary-general's practice could guide our analysis.

We consulted the Summary of Practice of the Secretary-General as Depositary of Multilateral Treaties (ST/LEG/7/Rev.1) as well as the Vienna Convention on the Law of Treaties to ascertain the process that is followed where the status of an entity seeking to accede to a particular multilateral treaty is in question.[37]

Paragraph 81 of the summary refers to treaties, as the Rome Statute, with an "all States formula." In such situations, the Practice Summary notes that the secretary-general

> would not wish to determine, on his own initiative, the highly political and controversial question of whether or not the areas whose status was unclear were States. Such a determination, he believed, would fall outside his competence. He therefore stated that when the 'any State' or 'all States' formula was adopted, he would be able to implement it only if the General Assembly provided him with the complete list of the States coming within the formula.[38]

Paragraph 82 of the same document states:

> This practice of the Secretary-General became fully established and was clearly set out in the understanding adopted by the General Assembly without objection at its 2202nd plenary meeting, on 14 December 1973, whereby 'the Secretary-General, in discharging his functions as a depositary of a convention with an 'all States' clause, will follow the practice of the Assembly in implementing such a clause and, whenever advisable, will request the opinion of the Assembly before receiving a signature or an instrument of ratification or accession.'"[39]

We asked Patricia O'Brien, UN under-secretary-general for legal affairs, for information on

> *the process that would ordinarily be followed to resolve whether an entity has the status of a "State" in order to ratify the Rome Statute.*

Her answer was that

> *the Secretary-General's consistent position and practice has been that it rests with the General Assembly of the United Nations to determine whether a certain territory or entity, whose status as a State is controversial or not clear, falls within the "all States" formula and that if he were to receive an instrument of consent to be bound from any such territory or entity, he would follow the General Assembly's directives on the matter.*

Patricia O'Brien graciously declined to refer specifically to the Rome Statute. Still, she further noted that the General Assembly's practice in this regard is reflected in various General Assembly resolutions which, in different contexts, provide "*unequivocal indications of whether a particular territory or entity is a state. Such resolutions have in turn guided the Secretary-General as to which States are included in the 'all States' formula.*"[40]

We considered that the statute was adopted under the UN General Assembly's auspices, but the Assembly of States Parties became responsible for the subsequent treaty acts. For instance, the Assembly of States Parties adopts the Rules of Procedure and Evidence and could amend the statute. It also settles disputes between states parties.[41] The Assembly has a Credentials Committee, which will be involved in any discussion whether an entity is a state.

We concluded that the question of who can qualify as a state party for Article 12(1) should be decided in a first instance by the UN secretary-general in consultation with the General Assembly. Finally, it should also be a matter that falls within the Assembly of States Parties' prerogative.

The Interaction with Hamas, USA, and Israel

The Office of the Prosecutor *jus ad Curiam* analysis expanded the ICC "shadow." During the last year of the preliminary examination process, Hamas, the United States, and Israel interacted with our office.

In 2011, a professor with an informal connection to Hamas approached the Office of the Prosecutor. He explained that Hamas would not make peace with Israel, but it was ready for a truce and even to investigate its allegations against Hamas's members involved in crimes. He requested more information about the complementarity system.

Wikileaks exposed the impact of the Goldstone Report and the pending decisions of the ICC Prosecutor. It reported a meeting on January 27, 2010, in Tel Aviv between a US delegation headed by Michael Posner, the assistant secretary for Democracy, Human Rights, and Labor, with senior Israeli officials.

Posner explained: "A review of the IDF's investigations, along with an examination of lessons learned and best practices in asymmetrical warfare, would be a more compelling narrative internationally than a limited report focusing only on the cases highlighted in the Goldstone Report."[42]

Israel officers expressed their concern that a response to the Goldstone Report might "not be adequate—or happen quickly enough—to slow progress toward action by ICC prosecutor Luis Moreno-Ocampo." The Israel deputy attorney general "asked Posner's advice on whether the Israelis should meet with Moreno-Ocampo. Posner said that there could be benefits to their talking to him."[43]

In February 2010, a different Wikileaks cable reports that "IDF Military Advocate General Mandelblit . . . warned that PA pursuit of Israel through the ICC would be viewed as war by the GOI."[44] He also stated, "No decision had been made regarding an independent commission to review the IDF investigations." Mandelblit perceived a "lack of political and popular will to initiate such an inquiry at this time."[45]

The United States presented their opinion to our office but following a political approach rather than a legal one. A member of the US government I knew for decades came to The Hague and asked me to close the preliminary examination requested by the Palestinian Authority immediately. When I asked why I should do that, she said: "Because that is what the US wants." I noted her opinions and told her that I understood she was representing her government, but I had legal duties that I intended to respect. I assumed that such a US approach worked in some cases, and, therefore, she was expecting an affirmative answer.

In a subsequent meeting in New York, I met one of the highest authorities on foreign relations in the US government. She also asked me to stop Palestine's preliminary examination. I responded that I was following the preliminary examination procedure, an answer which was met by her silence.

Since I had nothing to add, I also remained silent and stared back at her. For about three minutes, we stared at each other without a word. At the time, my international cooperation adviser, who had a long diplomatic career, told me that he had never been in a meeting with more tension.

Despite their initial objections, I was invited for dinner at the Israeli ambassador's residence in The Hague with the Israeli government members. After that informal meeting, the Office of the Prosecutor had direct contact with Israel's officers, and we could listen to their views. The Israeli decision to engage with the Office of the Prosecutor could have been the result of Posner's advice. Still, it was also influenced by a series of lectures in Israel of Philippe Kirsch, the former-ICC president, a highly respected diplomat, and international lawyer. He explained the process followed by the court and promoted a decision to contact our office.

The Office of the Prosecutor Decision in 2012: Palestine Is Not a "State"

In July 2011, Palestine confirmed to the office that it had submitted its principal arguments. The briefing process was exhausted. Israel and Palestine provided their views, and on April 3, 2012, the Office of the Prosecutor of the International Criminal Court issued its decision.

We explained that "The jurisdiction of the Court is not based on the principle of universal jurisdiction: it requires that the United Nations Security Council (article 13(b)) or a 'State' (article 12) provide jurisdiction."

"The issue that arises, therefore, is who defines what is a 'State' for the purpose of article 12 of the Statute? In accordance with article 125, the Rome Statute is open to accession by 'all States,' and any State seeking to become a Party to the Statute must deposit an instrument of accession with the Secretary-General of the United Nations. In instances where it is controversial or unclear whether an applicant constitutes a 'State,' it is the practice of the Secretary-General to follow or seek the General Assembly's directives on the matter. This is reflected in General Assembly resolutions which provide indications of whether an applicant is a 'State.'"

"The current status granted to Palestine by the United Nations General Assembly is that of 'observer,' not as a 'Non-member State.' The Office understands that on 23 September 2011, Palestine submitted an application for admission to the United Nations as a Member State in accordance with article 4(2) of the United Nations Charter, but the Security Council has not yet made a recommendation in this regard. While this process has no direct link with the declaration lodged by Palestine, it informs the current legal status of Palestine for the interpretation and application of article 12."

"The Rome Statute provides no authority for the Office of the Prosecutor to adopt a method to define the term 'State' under article 12(3) which would be at variance with that established for the purpose of article 12(1)."

"The Office could in the future consider allegations of crimes committed in Palestine, should competent organs of the United Nations or eventually the Assembly of States Parties resolve the legal issue relevant to an assessment of article 12 or should the Security Council, in accordance with article 13(b), make a referral providing jurisdiction"[46]

Decisions After the End of My Tenure

In July 2012, following Palestine's membership in UNESCO, the UN Office of Legal Affairs confirmed the Office of the Prosecutor criterion. It decided that Palestine could not participate in a conference via the "all States" formula since the General Assembly had only treated Palestine at that point as "a sui generis entity."

On November 29, 2012, the situation changed. The UN General Assembly voting by an overwhelming majority—138 in favor to 9 against (Canada, Czech Republic, Israel, Marshall Islands, Micronesia (the Federated States of), Nauru, Panama, Palau, United States), with 41 abstentions—accorded Palestine non-Member Observer State status in the United Nations. It also "established that Palestine was eligible to accede to treaties applying the 'all States' formula to determine membership." With their newly recognized status in their pocket, the Palestinians engaged in substantive peace talks with Israel.

On July 24, 2015, Secretary of State John Kerry chaired a special session of the UN General Assembly. He praised Israeli and Palestinian leaders for their "courageous decision to try to return to final-status talks." However, one year later, the process collapsed. In 2014 and 2015, the Swiss government accepted the Palestine accession for the Geneva Conventions and their three additional protocols.

On January 1, 2015, the government of Palestine lodged a declaration under Article 12(3) of the Rome Statute accepting the jurisdiction of the court over alleged crimes committed "in the occupied Palestinian territory, including East Jerusalem, since June 13, 2014."./

On January 2, 2015, the government of Palestine acceded to the Rome Statute by depositing its instrument of accession with the UN secretary-general with a date of entry into force starting on April 1, 2015.

Following the negotiations conducted to obtain the UN General Assembly declaration conferring the status of "state," Palestine reduced drastically its request to investigate the past. In 2009, Palestine attempted to accept the ICC's jurisdiction dating back to July 1, 2002. Instead, in 2015 it reduced the court intervention's scope to cover only the incidents that happened since

June 13, 2014. Palestine declined to request investigations for what happened for twelve years.

After Palestine's ratification, on January 6, 2015, the UN secretary-general acting as the "depositary" and following the UN General Assembly's decision accepted Palestine as a state that ratified the statute.[47]

The following day, the president of the Assembly of States Parties to the Rome Statute, the Senegalese Minister Sidiki Kaba, reached a similar conclusion and welcomed the state of Palestine's deposit of the instruments of accession to the Rome Statute.[48]

On January 16, 2015, ICC Prosecutor Fatou Bensouda opened a preliminary examination into the situation in Palestine.

On April 1, 2015, the ICC welcomed Palestine as the 123rd state party to its founding Rome Statute in a ceremony held at the court's seat in The Hague in The Netherlands. Judge Kuniko Ozaki, the ICC's second vice president, stated, "As the Rome Statute today enters into force for the State of Palestine, Palestine acquires all the rights as well as responsibilities that come with being a State Party to the Statute. These are substantive commitments, which cannot be taken lightly."

The "State of Palestine" was accepted by the Assembly of the States Parties Credentials Committee during the 2015 Assembly of States Parties. Canada was the only state party that objected to "Palestinian statehood and accession to the Rome Statute."[49] Palestine became a member of the Assembly of States Parties Bureau in 2016.

On May 22, 2018, Palestine referred the situation in the state of Palestine to the Prosecutor.

On January 22, 2020, and before opening an investigation, the prosecution requested a ruling under Art. 19(3). Prosecutor Bensouda asked the court to confirm that the "territory" over which the ICC may exercise its jurisdiction comprises the Occupied Palestinian Territory, including the West Bank, East Jerusalem, and Gaza.[50]

On January 28, 2020, the pre-trial chamber, considering the complexity and novelty of the prosecutor's request, invited states, organizations, and persons to submit observations on the question of jurisdiction.[51]

The Czech Republic, Austria, Australia, Hungary, Germany, Brazil, and Uganda presented their observations considering that Palestine had not fulfilled all statehood criteria under international law. Most of them accepted that they did not object to the acceptance of Palestine as a state party of the Rome Statute. Still, they understood that such an accession could not substitute the missing elements of statehood.[52] The League of Arab States and the Organization of the Islamic Cooperation filled in support of Palestine's position.

Notes

1. Situation in the State of Palestine, ICC-01/18, Prosecution request pursuant to article 19(3) for a ruling on the Court's territorial jurisdiction in Palestine (Jan. 22, 2020), https://www.icc-cpi.int/CourtRecords/CR2020_00161.PDF.
2. Elizabeth Boburg, *Spain Sends the Case Brought Against Venezuelan President Hugo Chavez to the International Criminal Court*, VCRISIS (Nov. 21, 2003), http://www.vcrisis.com/print.php?content=letters/200311210100.
3. Eva Golinger-Moncada, *Why The Case Against Chávez Will Not Be Heard in The Hague*, VENEZUELANALYSIS (Nov. 17, 2003, 11:50 AM), https://venezuelanalysis.com/analysis/225.
4. Elizabeth Boburg, *Spain Sends the Case Brought Against Venezuelan President Hugo Chavez to the International Criminal Court*, VCRISIS (Nov. 21, 2003), http://www.vcrisis.com/print.php?content=letters/200311210100.
5. Office of the Prosecutor, *Response to Communications Received Concerning Venezuela*, ICC (Feb. 9, 2020), https://www.icc-cpi.int/venezuela/Documents/OTP_letter_to_senders_re_Venezuela_9_February_2006.pdf.
6. The panel was integrated by the former secretary-general of the Inter American Human Rights Commission Santiago Cantón (Argentina), the former Canada's Attorney General Irwin Cotler (Canada), and a retired judge of the Inter American Human Rights Court, Manuel Ventura Robles (Costa Rica), produced a Report of the General Secretariat of the Organization of American States and the Panel of Independent International Experts on the Possible Commission of Crimes Against Humanity in Venezuela, OAS official Records OEA/Ser.D/XV.19 (May 29, 2018).
7. The case against Leopoldo Lopez, one of the opposition's prominent leaders, is a good example. Franklin Nieves, a former Venezuelan prosecutor, declared that his superiors coerced him to request Leopoldo Lopez's arrest. Ralenis Tovar, a former judge in Caracas, detailed how she was also coerced into signing arrest warrants for Leopoldo López and three others in February 2014. Judge Tovar explained that as was usual, the coercion began with informal contacts, including a phone call from her superior, the president of the Superior Tribunal of Justice, Gladys Gutiérrez, instructing her to comply with an earlier phone instruction. Judge Tovar described how military and security personnel had taken over the court offices when she arrived and forced her to sign four arrest warrants, including one against Leopoldo López. She tried to refuse, and they threatened her: "You want to be like another Judge Afiuni?" a judge detained in 2009, tortured, and raped for not following the instructions of the Executive. Judge Tovar also said that President Maduro announced on national media that a court had issued an arrest for Lopez, two hours before she finally signed it. Later

Tovar submitted her resignation, fled, and requested asylum in Canada. Commission of Crimes Against Humanity in Venezuela, OAS official Records OEA/Ser.D/XV.19 (May 29, 2018), at 44.

8. He said, "It's the National Executive who orders the opening and closing of the judicial proceedings," and that is President Maduro's wife "Cilia Flores, who personally manages the Superior Tribunal of Justice." *Id.* at 30.

9. *Id.*

10. *Id.* at 449.

11. *Preliminary Examinations—Venezuela I*, ICC, https://www.icc-cpi.int/venezuela (last visited July 13, 2020).

12. *Id.*

13. Article 8(2)(b)(iv) draws on the principles in Article 51(5)(b) of the Protocol additional to the Geneva Conventions of August 12, 1949, and relating to the protection of victims of international armed conflicts (Protocol I), *opened for signature* Dec. 7, 1977, 1125 U.N.T.S. 3, but restricts the criminal prohibition to cases that are "clearly" excessive.

14. Estelle Shirbon, *Campaigners Ask ICC to Investigate Alleged UK War Crimes in Iraq*, REUTERS (Jan 12, 2014, 10:25 AM), https://www.reuters.com/article/us-britain-iraq-icc/campaigners-ask-icc-to-investigate-alleged-uk-war-crimes-in-iraq-idUSBR EA0B08T20140112.

15. *Id.*

16. Rep. of the U.N. Fact-Finding Mission on the Gaza Conflict, 12th Sess., Agenda item 7, U.N. Doc. A/HRC/12/48 (Sept. 25, 2009).

17. The declaration states that "The Government of Palestine hereby recognizes the jurisdiction of the Court for the purpose of identifying, prosecuting and judging the authors and accomplices of crimes committed on the territory of Palestine since 1 July 2002." Office of the Prosecutor, *Visit of the Minister of Justice of the Palestinian National Authority, Mr. Ali Khashan, to the ICC (22 January 2009)*, ICC (Feb. 6, 2009), https://www.icc-cpi.int/NR/rdonlyres/979C2995-9D3A-4E0D-8192-105395DC6 F9A/280603/ICCOTP20090122Palestinerev1.pdf.

18. He explained that during the 1998 Rome diplomatic conference, "Palestine was given observer status, consistent with its observer status at the UN General Assembly; it was not designated a [state] potential signatory." He concluded that "It is imperative that the ICC stays within its jurisdictional boundaries. If the Court were to expand these boundaries unilaterally, it would be a paradigm shift in international law that would be seen as political and reckless."

19. Sebastian Rotella, *International Criminal Court to Consider Gaza Investigation*, L.A. TIMES (Feb. 5, 2009), http://articles.latimes.com/2009/feb/05/world/fg-court-palest inians5.

20. *Id.*

21. Robert Cryer, *The ICC and Its Relationship to Non-States Parties*, in THE LAW AND PRACTICE OF THE INTERNATIONAL CRIMINAL COURT 277 (Carsen Stahn ed., Kindle ed. 2015).

22. It was also integrated by Judge Finn Lynghjem (Norwegian), Solicitor Raelene Sharp (rapporteur, Australian), Professor and forensic expert Francisco Corte-Real

(Portuguese), Professor Paul de Waart (Dutch), and Advocate Gonzalo Boye (Chilean/German).

23. Coalition for the International Criminal Court, *Excerpts from the Arab League Summit 2009 Statements Doha, Qatar 30–31 March 2009*, ICC Now, http://www.icc now.org/documents/Arab_League_Summit_2009_-_SummaryFV.pdf (last visited July 14, 2020).

24. *Id.*

25. "In reaching this conclusion the Committee had regard to the number of civilians killed and wounded and to the extent of the destruction to civilian property. It rejected Israel's determination of who is a civilian. Members of the Hamas civil government responsible for administering the affairs of Gaza are not combatants as claimed by Israel. Nor are members of the police force responsible for maintaining law and order and controlling traffic." League of the Arab States [LAS], Report of the Independent Fact-Finding Committee on Gaza: No Safe Place (Apr. 30, 2009).

26. "The Committee found that Palestinian militants who fired rockets indiscriminately into Israel which killed four civilians and wounded 182 committed the war crime of killing, wounding and terrorizing civilians." *Id.*

27. Office of the Prosecutor, Weekly Briefing 19–25 October 2010, Issue 60, ICC (Oct. 2010).

28. Experts that briefed the Office of the Prosecutor: John Quigley; Daniel Benoliel and Ronen Perry; David Davenport, Kenneth Anderson, Samuel Estreicher, Eugene Kontorovich, Julian G. Ku, and Abraham D. Sofaer; Alain Pellet; Errol Mendes; Malcolm Shaw; and Yaël Ronen. The office also received submissions by the European Centre for Law and Justice; the International Association of Jewish Lawyers and Jurists; Al Haq; the Jerusalem Center for Public Affairs; the European Centre for Law and Justice; and NGO Monitor.

29. S.C. Res. 1890, para. 1, 5, U.N. Doc. S/RES/1860 (Jan. 8, 2009).

30. Human Rights Council Res. S 9/1, The grave violations of human rights in the Occupied Palestinian Territory, particularly due to the recent Israeli military attacks against the occupied Gaza Strip, 9th Special Sess., Jan. 9–12, 2009, U.N. Doc. A/HRC/S-9/L.1, para. 14 (Jan. 12, 2009).

31. Rep. of the Hum. Rts. Council (A/64/53/Add.1), U.N. GAOR 64th Sess., 37 mtg. (Nov. 4, 2009). Richard Goldstone, *My Mandate on Gaza Was Even-Handed, My Loyalty Is to Justice*, GUARDIAN (May 5, 2020, 3:31 PM), https://www.theguardian.com/commentisfree/2010/may/05/richard-goldstone-united-nations.

32. The other three appointed members were Professor Christine Chinkin, Professor of International Law at the London School of Economics and Political Science, who was a member of the high-level fact-finding mission to Beit Hanoun (2008); Ms. Hina Jilani, Advocate of the Supreme Court of Pakistan and former Special Representative of the Secretary-General on the situation of human rights defenders, who was a member of the International Commission of Inquiry on Darfur (2004); and Colonel Desmond Travers, a former Officer in Ireland's Defence Forces and member of the Board of Directors of the Institute for International Criminal Investigations.

33. Rep. of the U.N. Fact-Finding Mission on the Gaza Conflict, ¶ 1893, 12th Sess., Agenda item 7, U.N. Doc. A/HRC/12/48 (Sept. 25, 2009).

34. *Id.*

35. Shlomo Shamir & News Agencies, *UN Human Rights Chief Endorses Goldstone Gaza Report,* HAARETZ (Oct. 14, 2009), https://www.haaretz.com/1.5260303.

36. *Israel/Gaza: Implement Goldstone Recommendations on Gaza,* HUM. RTS. WATCH (Sept. 16, 2009, 4:33 PM), https://www.hrw.org/news/2009/09/16/israel/gaza-implement-goldstone-recommendations-gaza.

37. TREATY SECTION OF THE OFFICE OF LEGAL AFFAIRS, SUMMARY OF PRACTICE OF THE SECRETARY-GENERAL AS DEPOSITARY OF MULTILATERAL TREATIES, U.N. Doc. ST/LEG/7/Rev.1, U.N. Sales No. E.94.V.15(1999).

38. *Id.*

39. *Id.*

40. *See* Annexed correspondence between the Prosecutor and the UN Legal Counsel of May 13, 2011, May 30, 2011.

41. *See, e.g.,* Articles 51, 112, 119, and 121, ICC Statute.

42. *A/S Posner Discusses Goldstone Report with Senior Israeli Officials,* WIKILEAKS (Jan. 27, 2010, 9:33 AM), https://wikileaks.org/plusd/cables/10TELAVIV183_a.html.

43. *Id.*

44. *IDF MAG Mandelblit on IDF Investigations into Operation Cast Lead,* WIKILEAKS (Feb. 23, 2010, 7:09 AM), https://wikileaks.org/plusd/cables/10TELAVIV4, 17_a.html.

45. *Id.*

46. Mohamed M. El Zeidy, *Ad Hoc Declarations of Acceptance of Jurisdiction, in* THE LAW AND PRACTICE OF THE INTERNATIONAL CRIMINAL COURT 9662 (Carsten Stahn ed., Kindle ed. 2015).

47. U.N. Secretary General, Communication on the Accession of State of Palestine to the Rome Statute of the International Criminal Court, (Jan. 6, 2015), https://treaties.un.org/doc/Publication/CN/2015/CN.13.2015-Eng.pdf.

48. Minister Sidiki Kaba, President of the Assembly of States Parties to the Rome Statute of the ICC, Speech at the Welcoming ceremony for a new State Party (Apr. 1, 2015).

49. See the *Report of the Credentials Committee* and *Statement by Canada in explanation of position after the adoption of resolution ICC-ASP/14/Res.4 at the 12 plenary meeting of the Assembly, on 26 November 2015* in Assembly of States Parties to the Rome Statute of the International Criminal Court, 14th Session, 18–26 Nov. 2015, ICC-ASP/14/20.

50. Situation in the State of Palestine, ICC-01/18, Prosecution request pursuant to article 19(3) for a ruling on the Court's territorial jurisdiction in Palestine (Jan. 22, 2020), https://www.icc-cpi.int/CourtRecords/CR2020_00161.PDF.

51. Situation in the State of Palestine, ICC-01/18, Order setting the procedure and the schedule for the submission of observations (Jan. 28, 2020), https://www.icc-cpi.int/CourtRecords/CR2020_00217.PDF.

52. Situation in the State of Palestine, ICC-01/18, Submission of Observations Pursuant to Rule 103 (Mar. 12, 2020), https://legal-tools.org/doc/7qm3y8/pdf/.

13

Preliminary Examinations in Honduras, Nigeria, Korea, Georgia, and Guinea

The Office of the Prosecutor conducted another seven preliminary examinations in the jurisdiction of the states parties during my tenure.

This chapter presents the preliminary examinations conducted in Honduras, Korea, Nigeria, Georgia, and Guinea. The following chapter portrays the preliminary examination conducted in Colombia, recognizing its complexity, and highlighting the preliminary examination's impact without opening an investigation. Chapter 17 depicts the jurisdictional and admissibility analysis of the Afghanistan situation.

The geographical dispersions and the variety of the circumstances described help to perceive the functioning of the autonomous criminal justice system established by the Rome Statute. Except for North Korea, all the states involved cooperated with the Office of the Prosecutor. The Rome Statute was a constraint for different actors in Georgia and Nigeria and played a suggestive preventive role in Honduras and Guinea.

Honduras

Honduras deposited its ratification instrument to the Rome Statute on September 1, 2002, and provided jurisdiction to the ICC from the same day.

On June 28, 2009, President Manuel Zelaya of Honduras *was ousted by the army, capping months of tensions over his efforts to lift presidential term limits.*[1] It was the first military coup in Central America since the end of the Cold War. The same day, the president of the Congress, Roberto Micheletti, was appointed president of Honduras by the Congress, and a State of Emergency was declared.

Thousands of persons marched against or in favor of the removal. Around five thousand people were unlawfully arrested during the relevant period, usually for a short time (from forty-five minutes to twenty-four hours).

War and Justice in the 21st Century. Luis Moreno Ocampo, Oxford University Press. © Oxford University Press 2022.
DOI: 10.1093/oso/9780197628973.003.0014

Twenty civilians were killed, of which eight were alleged victims of *selective murders* (*asesinatos selectivos*) and twelve were of alleged disproportionate shootings in the context of demonstrations and checkpoints.

The Organization of American States issued a statement calling for Mr. Zelaya's return and said it would not recognize any other government. President Obama called on Honduran officials "to respect democratic norms, the rule of law, and the tenets of the Inter-American Democratic charter."[2]

After negotiations to form a government of unity broke down, an agreement was reached, and general elections were held in November 2009. Porfirio Lobo was elected president and granted a general amnesty for certain crimes committed in the post-coup period (excluding crimes against humanity and serious human rights violations).

A national Truth and Reconciliation Commission (TRC) (*Comisión de la Verdad y la Reconciliación*) was established to clarify the events of June 28, 2009.

The office had received seventeen communications concerning Honduras, including one from former President Zelaya on August 21, 2009. In November 2010, the office opened a preliminary examination evaluating the material jurisdiction based on the information obtained by the TRC, the Inter-American Commission of Human Rights, and the Office of the High Commissioner for Human Rights.

The TRC published its findings in July 2011, concluding that a crime of persecution as a crime against humanity under the Rome Statute was committed.

I received in my office NGO delegations requesting our intervention and providing information. The government was cooperating, and the office visited Honduras in 2009 and 2011, meeting the attorney general and other relevant authorities. During my term, we assessed the material jurisdiction.

In October 2015, the Office of the Prosecutor decided to close this preliminary examination.[3]

Republic of Korea

On November 23, 2010, the Democratic People's Republic of Korea's (North Korea) artillery hit Yeonpyeong Island in the Republic of Korea (South Korea). It killed two civilians and two militaries, injured sixty-six people (fifty civilians and sixteen militaries), and destroyed army and civilian facilities on a large scale. The incident was one of the most serious since the end of the Korean War in 1953.[4]

North Korea's supreme military command blamed a previous South Korean military exercise as a provocation: "it is our military's traditional response to quell provocative actions with a merciless thunderbolt."[5]

"South Korean president, Lee Myung-bak, met his top military in an underground bunker in Seoul and ordered the air force to strike North Korean missile bases if there is any further provocation."[6]

Major powers expressed concern. President Obama "was woken just before 4 am by his national security adviser, Tom Donilon, to be informed of the attack, issued a statement condemning it and planned to speak to the South Korean president."[7]

Russian Foreign Minister Sergei Lavrov was also worried; he said, "It is necessary to immediately end all strikes. There is a colossal danger which must be avoided. Tensions in the region are growing."[8]

"China, the impoverished North's only powerful ally, was careful to avoid taking sides, calling on both Koreas to 'do more to contribute to peace.'"[9]

South Korea deposited its ratification instrument to the Rome Statute on November 13, 2002, providing jurisdiction to the ICC from February 1, 2003, onward. The office received several communications alleging that the shelling amounted to war crimes under Article 8 of the Rome Statute.

Subsequent allegations emerged concerning the *Cheonan*'s sinking, a South Korean warship hit by a torpedo allegedly fired from a North Korean submarine on March 26, 2010, which resulted in the death of forty-six persons.

We announced the opening of a preliminary examination on December 6, 2010. The office reviewed a communication sent by two law students from Seoul, and I made it public that these young persons could trigger the ICC process.

In those days, I was in New York briefing the UN Security Council on Darfur, and a Chinese delegation approached us. China was worried. It wanted to know if an arrest warrant against the North Korean leader was already issued. Chinese representatives explained that such a decision could destabilize the country. We explained the scope of the preliminary examination process without providing any comment on the final decision.

We started to evaluate if the shelling constituted a war crime during an international conflict. North and South Korea were technically still at war;

the Armistice Agreement of 1953 is merely a ceasefire agreement. The parties are yet to negotiate the peace agreement expected to conclude the 1950–1953 conflict formally.

Besides, the "resort to armed force between States" in the form of the alleged launching of a torpedo into the *Cheonan* or the launching of shells into Yeonpyeong could create an international armed conflict under customary international law.

South Korea was pleased that the office took the initiative without involving it and extensively answered our information requests. North Korea did not answer the office's request for information sent in April 2012.

On February 2014, the Commission of Inquiry on Human Rights in the Democratic People's Republic of Korea established by the Human Rights Council produced its report.[10] It concluded that crimes against humanity had been committed in that country pursuant to policies established at the highest level of the state. They were "not mere excesses of the State; they are essential components of a political system." The Commission recommended that the Security Council should refer the situation in the Democratic People's Republic of Korea to the International Criminal Court.

But the council did not take action and the Office of the Prosecutor had to take into consideration exclusively the actions in South Korea *territory. Consequently, after the end of my tenure, in June 2014, the Office of the Prosecutor decided it, "currently lacks a reasonable basis to believe that either incident constitutes a crime within the jurisdiction of the Court"* and closed the preliminary examination.[11]

Nigeria

Nigeria deposited its ratification instrument to the Rome Statute on September 27, 2001, providing jurisdiction to the ICC from July 1, 2002, onward. The preliminary examination of the situation in Nigeria was made public on November 18, 2010.[12]

The office started to analyze a massive number of killing and rapes unevenly distributed over time and place due to inter-communal, sectarian, and political violence. The vast majority of the killings were committed in the Middle-Belt states in Central and Northern Nigeria in major assaults along ethnic/sectarian lines by mobs or youth groups. A lesser number of persons died in the oil-rich Niger Delta region as violence among ethnically based gangs and militant groups like the Movement for the Emancipation of the Niger Delta (MEND) and between them and federal forces.[13]

The office aimed to determine whether these attacks were carried out in a coordinated and organized manner constituting crimes against humanity.

On April 21, 2011, the Office of the Prosecutor expressed public concerns about the outbreak of violence in the National Assembly and presidential elections of April 2011. In response, on June 7, 2011, the Nigerian authorities informed the office that a twenty-two member panel was set up to investigate 2011 pre- and post-election violence in Akwa Ibom State and other parts of the country.

In August 2013, the Office of the Prosecutor determined that the information obtained was not sufficient to prove under the standard required by the ICC jurisdiction. Instead, the office had reasons to believe that crimes against humanity, namely murder and persecution, could be attributed to Boko Haram. Therefore, Chief Prosecutor Fatou Bensouda decided that the preliminary examination of those crimes in Nigeria's situation should advance to phase three (admissibility).[14]

Georgia

The South Ossetia and Abkhazia Conflict

On August 8, 2008, a conflict started between Georgia, Russia, and regional authorities in South Ossetia and Abkhazia, a pro-Russian region that won de facto autonomy from Georgia in the early 1990s.

At the beginning of the conflict, the *New York Times* reported that "The fighting that had sharply escalated when Georgian forces tried to retake the capital" of South Ossetia.[15]

Prime Minister Vladimir V. Putin left the Olympics in China and arrived immediately in the region. He said that dozens of people had been killed in South Ossetia and hundreds wounded, and tens of thousands were reported to be fleeing.[16] Russia sent warships to land ground troops in the disputed territory of Abkhazia and broadened its bombing campaign across Georgia.[17]

Just a few months before, in April 2008, Russia had promoted UN Security Resolution 1808 (2008). It reaffirmed the council's commitment *to the sovereignty, independence, and territorial integrity of Georgia within its internationally recognized borders. It supported a settlement of the Georgian-Abkhaz conflict only by peaceful means and within the framework of the Security Council resolutions.*[18]

Prime Minister Putin made clear that, after the incidents, his policy changed. He viewed Georgian claims over the breakaway regions as invalid and expressed that Russia had no intention of withdrawing.[19]

Russian officials considered that ties to the United States had encouraged Georgia's president, Mikheil Saakashvili, into sparking the conflict. President Saakashvili was considered a close US ally who had sought NATO membership for Georgia and made national unification a centerpiece of his agenda.[20]

President Saakashvili declared that Georgia was in a state of war, accused Russia of a "well-planned invasion"[21] to seize ports and an oil pipeline, and overthrow his government.[22] The United States and other Western nations, joined by NATO, condemned the violence and demanded a ceasefire. Secretary of State Condoleezza Rice went a step further, calling on Russia to withdraw its forces.[23]

On November 6, 2008, the *New York Times* informed its readers that a confidential report produced by "an international team working under the mandate of the Organization for Security and Cooperation in Europe, or O.S.C.E" presented Georgia's possible aggression. The O.S.C.E report was presented to states representatives in August and in October and called "into question the longstanding Georgian assertion that it was acting defensively against separatist and Russian aggression."[24]

Instead, the report suggested that Georgia "attacked the isolated separatist capital of Tskhinvali [a city considered South Ossetia capital] on Aug. 7 with indiscriminate artillery and rocket fire, exposing civilians, Russian peacekeepers and unarmed monitors to harm."[25]

On November 12, 2008, the *New York Times* published Russia's and Georgia's comments on its publication. Vitaly Churkin, the then Russia's UN, Permanent Representative, said that the war "was started by the Georgians under a false pretext on the night of Aug. 7. Civilians and Russian peacekeepers were attacked."[26]He added, "The attack on the peacekeepers provided the legal ground for us to act in self-defense under the United Nations Charter. The attack on civilians gave us no other option but to interfere."[27]

Ambassador Churkin denounced a media "vicious 'Russian aggression' campaign," and he highlighted that the report "was withheld from the O.S.C.E. member states."[28]The Russian representative concluded: "Georgia President Saakashvili violated four years of promises he had been giving to us, to the people of Georgia, Abkhazia, and South Ossetia and, we were told, to the American administration, that he would never use force to resolve the conflicts between Georgia and South Ossetia and Abkhazia."[29] Vasil Sikharulidze, ambassador of Georgia, did not deny the allegations but said, "Only Georgia has relentlessly called since August for an international investigation into the war's origins." "The world would benefit from a transparent, international investigation, rather than piecemeal reports based on incomplete evidence."[30]

A ceasefire agreement between Georgia and the Russian Federation, mediated by the French president Nicolas Sarkozy, acting on behalf of the European Union, was reached on August 12, 2008. Still, alleged crimes continued to be committed after that.[31]

The presidents of Georgia and Russia signed a ceasefire agreement in August 2008.[32]

International Legal and Political Efforts to Mediate in the Conflict

Human Rights Watch established that the Saakashvili administration used nationalistic rhetoric to dismiss civil society's pressure for accountability, questioning NGOs' allegiances and undermining their credibility. *"[T]he government 'demonized' the NGO sector and accused civil society of 'backing Russia.' Those who worked on cases involving allegations of abuse by Georgian servicemen were considered 'traitors,' while those attempting to cooperate with Russia's investigation were labeled 'enemies of the state.'"*[33]

Georgia explored different legal venues to impose its narrative of it being a victim of Russian aggression. In August 2008, the Georgian government filed an interstate complaint before the International Court of Justice seeking a declaration that Russia violated its obligations under the International Convention on the Elimination of Racial Discrimination (ICERD) and asked for compensation. In April 2011, the ICJ dismissed the complaint because it lacked jurisdiction. Georgian authorities did not try to negotiate with Russia before lodging their complaint.

In February 2009, Georgia lodged a formal complaint before the European Court of Human Rights (ECHR) in Strasbourg. It alleged that Russia allowed indiscriminate and disproportionate attacks against civilians and their property in Abkhazia; and South Ossetia, by Russian military forces and the separatist forces under their control.

Western leaders did not include in their agenda the issue of accountability for the crimes committed in Georgia. The EU's 2007–2013 strategy for Georgia identified criminal justice reform as a priority. Still, it did not focus on building ties with the ICC or supporting national investigations through technical assistance.[34]

Professor John Gaddis explained the relation between the 2008 conflict and the Cold War: "The story begins with President George H. W. Bush's assurances to Mikhail Gorbachev in 1990, echoed by West German Chancellor Helmut Kohl, that if the Soviet Union would accept a reunified Germany's membership in the NATO alliance, its expansion would go no further."[35]

Besides those promises, on April 21, 1993, in a meeting at the White House with then Polish president Lech Walesa and the Czech president Vaclav Havel, President Clinton, without previous plans, accepted to expand NATO to include the Czech Republic, Poland, and Hungary.[36]

Gaddis said that from that moment, *NATO expansion became US policy.* The idea was presented in a meeting at Yale on September 24, 1998, by President Clinton's team.

A Yale professor asked *whether NATO expansion might not cause difficulties with the Russians, perhaps undermining President Yeltsin's efforts to democratize the country.* There was a moment of shocked silence. Then one of the briefers exclaimed: "Good God! We'd never thought of that!"[37]

In any case, the policy continued. George W. Bush "had presided over the incorporation into the [NATO] alliance of seven additional states—Estonia, Latvia, Lithuania, Slovakia, Slovenia, Romania, and Bulgaria—and was pushing for its further expansion to include Ukraine and Georgia."[38] Gaddis believed that Georgia's Russian reaction was a strategic intervention aiming to stop NATO from continuing expansion.[39]

The Preliminary Examination of the Office of the Prosecutor

The Office of the Prosecutor was aware of the possible risk of being used by the different sides and implemented its impartial mandate in this complex political environment.

Georgia deposited its ratification instrument to the Rome Statute on September 5, 2003, providing jurisdiction to the ICC from December 1, 2003, onward. The Office of the Prosecutor received 3,830 communications concerning the Georgian situation. They represented more than 50 percent of the total of 7,500 communications collected during my entire tenure regarding all the situations.

The Russian prosecutor's office assisted South Ossetia residents in preparing complaints.[40] We also received a comprehensive report, "August Ruins," produced by Georgia's NGOs.[41]

According to Article 5(2), the Office of the Prosecutor could not exercise jurisdiction on the crime of aggression that allegedly triggered the Russian intervention.

The office found a reasonable basis to believe that the war crimes of pillaging, destroying civilian property, and inflicting acts of torture and the crime against humanity of forcible transfer were committed. The office was evaluating who was responsible for the attack against Russian peacekeepers.

Regarding complementarity, Georgia and Russia conducted national investigations, although they did not cooperate because they severed all diplomatic ties. Instead, both collaborated with the ICC Office of the Prosecutor.

The Investigative Committee of the Russian Federation conducted the investigations. Members of the Office of the Prosecutor visited Russia in 2010 and 2011 to assess the national investigations' scope and progress. Russia respected our impartiality and did not present any political argument.

The Russian ambassador at The Hague and the legal adviser invited me to lunch to confirm the preliminary examination's legal parameters. Ambassador Churkin never mentioned the Georgia conflict during our meetings in New York related to Darfur and Libya.

The chief prosecutor of Georgia opened an investigation into allegations of genocide and humanitarian law violations in armed conflict, followed by a second investigation into looting as a war crime. The genocide investigation was soon dropped as being "manifestly ill-founded." Our office visited Georgia in 2008 and 2010, and I received in The Hague Georgia's officers and NGOs.

In September 2011, the Office of the Prosecutor requested a written update on the progress (or lack thereof) of their respective investigation to both governments.

On October 18, 2011, the Russian Embassy replied to the ICC Office of the Prosecutor that "the Georgian side has refused to provide legal assistance in relation to the criminal case." It indicated that "senior officials of foreign states including those of Georgia enjoy immunity from the criminal jurisdiction of the Russian Federation."[42]

Informally the Russian officers said that the evidence collected showed that President Saakashvili was personally involved in the orders to attack Russian peacekeepers. They could not proceed because he had immunity before Russian authorities. However, they said that Georgia's president declined his immunity before the ICC and our office could present charges against him.

On December 12, 2011, the Georgian government provided the Office of the Prosecutor with an updated report, expressing it was "mindful of its international obligation to investigate and prosecute grave crimes that concern the international community as a whole and resorts to its best efforts to comply with those commitments."

After my departure, in the October 2012 parliamentary elections, the opposition defeated President Saakashvili's political party and formed a new government. In March 2015, the new Georgian government informed the ICC that further investigative progress was not possible. On October 13, 2015, ICC prosecutor Fatou Bensouda sought approval from the court's judges to open an investigation in Georgia.

Guinea

Guinea deposited its ratification instrument to the Rome Statute on July 14, 2003, providing jurisdiction to the ICC from October 1, 2003, onward. In December 2008, after the death of President Lansana Conte, who had ruled Guinea since 1984, Captain Moussa Dadis Camara led a group of army officers who seized power in a military coup promising to fight corruption and alleviated poverty.

Camara became the head of state and established a military junta, the *Conseil National pour la Démocratie et le Développement* (CNDD). He made promises. He would not be a candidate, and the CNDD would transfer power after holding presidential and parliamentary elections. However, subsequent statements suggested that he might run, which led to protests by opposition and civil society groups.

In mid-August 2009, the president declined to rule out his candidacy in the 2010 presidential elections. The police gathered intelligence that the opposition was planning to organize a demonstration on September 28.[43] That day, Independence Day of Guinea, the president telephoned very early in the morning the organizer of the protest, Sidya Touré, a former prime minister, to demand the postponement of the planned demonstration and to choose another date and venue.[44]

However, around fifty thousand demonstrators were already outside the capital's largest stadium, carrying placards reading "Down with the army in power."

Upon the arrival of opposition leader Jean-Marie Doré, tear gas was fired into the stadium, and red berets descended from their vehicles and sprayed the crowd with gunfire. Demonstrators seeking to escape were killed by red berets and gendarmes positioned around the stadium. Others were stabbed or beaten inside the stadium and then also systematically robbed by the security forces.

At least 156 persons were killed or disappeared, and no less than 109 women were victims of rape and other forms of sexual violence.[45] Women were taken by red berets from the stadium and the Ratoma Medical Center and held as sex slaves for several days in different locations.[46] France, the United States, the European Union, the Economic Community of West African States (ECOWAS), the African Union, and the United Nations—harshly denounced the September 28 violence in Guinea.

Regional organizations took the lead to contain violence. ECOWAS and the European Union imposed arms embargos; EU, the United States, and the African Union travel bans and asset freezes of CNDD members; EU and France withdrew or canceled economic and military assistance.[47] On October 2, the ECOWAS named President Blaise Compaoré of Burkina Faso to mediate the crisis.[48] The ICC's preliminary examination of the situation in Guinea was announced on October 14, 2009.

On October 20, 2009, the minister of foreign affairs of the Republic of Guinea visited our office, met with deputy prosecutor Fatou Bensouda, and indicated that the Guinean authorities were willing and able to conduct a criminal investigation.[49]

Burkina Faso's President Compaoré had a leading role in the control of the situation. In November 2009, he organized a meeting in Burkina Faso with members of Guinea's military government and its political opponents as part of regional mediation to end the crisis.[50] The same month, the first mission of the ICC Office of the Prosecutor visited Conakry.

The UN established an International Commission of Inquiry that traveled to Guinea on November 25, 2009, to investigate the massacre.[51]The commissioners interviewed 687 witnesses and government members, including President Camara and his presidential guard chief, Lieutenant Abubakar "Toumba" Diakite.[52]

On December 3, 2009, Diakite shot President Camara and explained that the junta leader planned to blame him for the stadium's massacre.[53] President Camara was wounded and spent one month recovering in a Moroccan military hospital.[54] In December, the UN Secretary-General presented the UN Commission of Enquiry report to the UN Security Council. It detailed the crimes, identified the perpetrators, and concluded that the incidents constituted crimes against humanity.[55]

Guinean leaders were afraid that ICC issued arrest warrants against them and looked for options. President Compaoré convinced Camara to meet at Ouagadougou, the Burkina Faso capital, and to stay there. On January 12, 2015, they discussed the power-sharing agreement proposed by ECOWAS.[56]A few days later, on January 15, the Ouagadougou Declaration was adopted. It provided a national unity government led by a civilian prime minister designated by the opposition and the holding of elections within six months.

The accord also committed the transitional head of state, members of the CNDD, the prime minister, members of the unity government, and the security forces not to stand in the election.[57]On January 21, Jean-Marie Doré took office as a new prime minister, and a unity government was established on February 15.

The following day, the UN Security Council issued a presidential statement welcoming the new transitional government's appointment.[58] The council urged the national authorities to prevent any further violence and emphasized the state's responsibility to comply with their obligations to *end impunity*.[59]The national investigation was formally opened on February 8, 2010, before the deputy prosecutor's first visit to Conakry.

The Office of the Prosecutor Preliminary Examination

As part of our preliminary examination process, deputy prosecutor Fatou Bensouda went to Conakry on February 18, 2010, visiting the national stadium and the hospital. She explained that "the Guinean authorities have the primary responsibility of looking into the alleged crimes that fall within the jurisdiction of the ICC."[60]

The office found a reasonable basis to believe that crimes against humanity were committed in Conakry since September 29, 2009. They included murder, enslavement, imprisonment, torture, rape, other forms of sexual violence, enforced disappearances of persons, and other inhuman acts.

The Office of the Prosecutor conducted additional missions to Guinea to follow up on the national investigations. We strengthened the national commitment to deter the commission of new crimes during the election period. Human Rights Watch found that "[d]iscipline within and civilian control over the security forces have since 2010 progressively improved."[61] The new president mentioned the importance of improving Guinea's international reputation by avoiding an ICC investigation.[62]

The preliminary examination continued. National authorities charged former President Camara in 2015, and his presidential guard chief, Lieutenant Abubakar "Toumba" Diakite, was arrested in Senegal and extradited to Guinea in 2017. Different than in the Georgia situation, the ICC preliminary examination process was a piece of a broader intervention. ECOWAS and President Compaoré, the United State, EU, and AU initiatives; local and international NGOs; and other key players' engagement supported the efforts to stop violence and do justice for the stadium incidents.[63]

Notes

1. Elizabeth Malkin *Honduran President Is Ousted in Coup*, N.Y. TIMES (June 28, 2009), https://www.nytimes.com/2009/06/29/world/americas/29honduras.html.
2. *Id.*
3. Office of the Prosecutor, *Situation in Honduras Article 5 Report*, ICC (Oct. 28, 2015), https://www.icc-cpi.int/iccdocs/otp/SAS-HON-Article_5_Report-Oct2015-ENG.PDF.
4. Tania Branigan & Ewen MacAskill, *North Korea: A Deadly Attack, a Counter Strike—Now Koreans Hold Their Breath*, GUARDIAN (Nov. 23, 2020, 8:23 PM), https://www.theguardian.com/world/2010/nov/23/north-south-korea-crisis-conflict.
5. *North Korean Artillery Hits South Korean Island*, BBC NEWS (Nov. 23, 2010), https://www.bbc.com/news/world-asia-pacific-11818005.
6. Tania Branigan & Ewen MacAskill, *North Korea: A Deadly Attack, a Counter Strike—Now Koreans Hold Their Breath*, GUARDIAN (Nov. 23, 2020, 8:23 PM), https://www.theguardian.com/world/2010/nov/23/north-south-korea-crisis-conflict.

7. *Id.*

8. *Russia Sees "Colossal Danger" of Korea Escalation*, REUTERS (Nov. 23, 2010, 7:31 AM) https://www.reuters.com/article/korea-north-russia-lavrov/russia-sees-colossal-danger-of-korea-escalation-idUSLDE6AM0U520101123.

9. *Peter Apps, World Edgy on Korea, Russia Sees "Colossal Danger,"* REUTERS (Nov. 23, 2010, 10:22 AM) https://www.reuters.com/article/us-korea-north-reaction/world-edgy-on-korea-russia-sees-colossal-danger-idUSTRE6AM2YO20101123.

10. Report of the Commission of Inquiry on Human Rights in the Democratic People's Republic of Korea https://www.ohchr.org/en/hr-bodies/hrc/co-idprk/reportofthe-commissionof-inquiry-dprk

11. Office of the Prosecutor, *Situation in the Republic of Kora: Article 5 Report*, ICC (June 23, 2014), https://www.icc-cpi.int/iccdocs/otp/SAS-KOR-Article-5-Public-Report-ENG-05Jun2014.pdf.

12. In the period from November 10, 2005, through November 9, 2011, the Office has received thirty-eight Article 15 communications in relation to the situation in Nigeria, out of which seventeen were manifestly outside the jurisdiction of the Court; eight were found to warrant further analysis; and thirteen communications were included in the preliminary examination.

13. *Timeline—Conflict in Nigeria's Oil Delta*, REUTERS (Nov. 8, 2010, 12:35 PM), https://www.reuters.com/article/nigeria-delta-mend-idAFLDE6A71LX20101108.

14. Office of the Prosecutor, *Situation in Nigeria: Article 5 Report*, ICC (Aug. 5, 2013), https://www.icc-cpi.int/iccdocs/PIDS/docs/SAS%20-%20NGA%20-%20Public%20version%20Article%205%20Report%20-%2005%20August%202013.PDF.

15. Anne Barnard, *Georgia and Russia Nearing All-Out War*, N.Y. TIMES (Aug. 9, 2008), https://www.nytimes.com/2008/08/10/world/europe/10georgia.html.

16. *Id.*

17. *Id.*

18. Press Release, Security Council, Security Council Extends Mandate of Georgia Observer Mission Until 15 October, Unanimously Adopting Resolution 1808 (2008), U.N. Press Release SC/9299 (Apr. 15, 2008).

19. Mr. Putin said: "There is almost no way we can imagine a return to the status quo," Anne Barnard, *Georgia and Russia Nearing All-Out War*, N.Y. TIMES (Aug. 2008), https://www.nytimes.com/2008/08/10/world/europe/10georgia.html.

20. Michael Schwirtz et al., *Russia and Georgia Clash Over Separatist Region*, N.Y. TIMES (Aug. 8, 2008), https://www.nytimes.com/2008/08/09/world/europe/09georgia.html.

21. *Id.*

22. Anne Barnard, *Georgia and Russia Nearing All-Out War*, N.Y. TIMES (Aug. 9, 2008), https://www.nytimes.com/2008/08/10/world/europe/10georgia.html.

23. Michael Schwirtz et al., *Russia and Georgia Clash Over Separatist Region*, N.Y. TIMES (Aug. 8, 2008), https://www.nytimes.com/2008/08/09/world/europe/09georgia.html.

24. C. J. Chivers & Ellen Barry, *Georgia Claims on Russia War Called Into Question*, N.Y. TIMES (Nov. 6, 2008), https://www.nytimes.com/2008/11/07/world/europe/07georgia.html.

25. *Id.*

26. Ambassador Vasil Sikharulidze, *Published Letter to the Editor: The August War: The Russian and Georgian Versions*, N.Y. TIMES (Nov. 12, 2008), https://www.nytimes.com/2008/11/13/opinion/l13caucasus.html.

27. *Id.*

28. *Id.*

29. *Id.*

30. *Id.*

31. Office of the Prosecutor, *Report on Preliminary Examination Activities*, ICC (Dec. 13, 2011), https://www.icc-cpi.int/NR/rdonlyres/63682F4E-49C8-445D-8C13-F310A4F3AEC2/284116/OTPReportonPreliminaryExaminations13December2011.pdf.

32. Situation in Georgia, ICC-01/15, ¶ 15, Decision on the Prosecutor's request for authorization of an investigation, (Jan. 27, 2016), https://www.icc-cpi.int/CourtRecords/CR2016_00608.PDF.

33. HUMAN RIGHTS WATCH, PRESSURE POINT: THE ICC'S IMPACT ON NATIONAL JUSTICE LESSONS FROM COLOMBIA, GEORGIA, GUINEA, AND THE UNITED KINGDOM 74–75 (2018) (citations omitted).

34. *Id.* at 79.

35. John Lewis Gaddis, What Is Grand Strategy? Karl Von Der Heyden Distinguished Lecture at 4 (Feb. 26, 2009), transcript available at https://indianstrategicknowledgeonline.com/web/grandstrategypaper.pdf.

36. *Id.*

37. *Id.* at 3.

38. *Id.* at 4.

39. *Id.*

40. On August 12, 2008, the prosecutor general of the Russian Federation, Yury Chaika, announced that he had created "a special brigade of prosecutors that would provide legal assistance in preparing appeals and complaints to the European Court of Human Rights and the Hague International Criminal Court." *Up In Flames*, HUM. RTS. WATCH (Jan. 23, 2009), https://www.hrw.org/report/2009/01/23/flames/humanitarian-law-violations-and-civilian-victims-conflict-over-south.

41. GEORGIAN YOUNG LAWYERS' ASSOCIATION ET AL., AUGUST RUINS (2008).

42. Office of the Prosecutor, *Report on Preliminary Examination Activities*, ICC (Dec. 13, 2011), https://www.icc-cpi.int/NR/rdonlyres/63682F4E-49C8-445D-8C13-F310A4F3AEC2/284116/OTPReportonPreliminaryExaminations13December2011.pdf.

43. U.N.S.C., Letter dated 18 December 2009 addressed to the President of the Security Council by the Secretary General, U.N. Doc. S/2009/693, ¶ 50 (Dec. 18, 2009).

44. *Id.*

45. *Id.*

46. *Id.*

47. *Bloody Monday*, HUM. RTS. WATCH (Dec. 17, 2009), https://www.hrw.org/report/2009/12/17/bloody-monday/september-28-massacre-and-rapes-security-forces-guinea.

48. Int'l Crisis Group, *Guinea: Military Rule Must End,* Africa Briefing No. 66, at 3(Oct. 16, 2009).

49. Press Release, Office of the Prosecutor, Guinea Minister visits the ICC—Prosecutor Requests Information on National Investigations into 28 September Violence, ICC (Oct. 21, 2009).

50. Scott Stearns, *West African Mediator to Meet Rivals in Guinea Political Crisis*, VOA NEWS (Nov. 18, 2009, 1:04 PM), https://www.voanews.com/archive/west-african-mediator-meet-rivals-guinea-political-crisis.

51. U.N.S.C., Letter dated 18 December 2009 addressed to the President of the Security Council by the Secretary General, U.N. Doc. S/2009/693, ¶62 (Dec. 18, 2009).

52. *Id.*

53. Associated Press, *Guinea Aide Admits Shooting Moussa Dadis Camara*, GUARDIAN (Dec. 16, 2009, 3:15 PM), https://www.theguardian.com/world/2009/dec/16/guinea-aide-shoot-camara.

54. Scott Stearns, *Guinea Military Leader Meets with Regional Mediator*, VOA NEWS (Jan. 13, 2010, 7:00 PM), https://www.voanews.com/africa/guinea-military-leader-meets-regional-mediator.

55. U.N.S.C., Letter dated 18 December 2009 addressed to the President of the Security Council by the Secretary General, U.N. Doc. S/2009/693, ¶62 (Dec. 18, 2009)

56. Scott Stearns, *Guinea Military Leader Meets with Regional Mediator*, VOA NEWS (Jan. 13, 2010, 7:00 PM), https://www.voanews.com/africa/guinea-military-leader-meets-regional-mediator.

57. Press Release, Security Council, Security Council Issues Presidential Statement Welcoming Appointment of Transitional Government in Guinea, U.N. Press Release SC/9863 (Feb. 16, 2010).

58. *Id.*

59. *Id.*

60. *ICC Deputy Prosecutor in Guinea for September Killing Probe*, VOA NEWS (Feb. 18, 2010, 7:00 PM), https://www.voanews.com/africa/icc-deputy-prosecutor-guinea-september-killing-probe.

61. HUMAN RIGHTS WATCH, PRESSURE POINT: THE ICC'S IMPACT ON NATIONAL JUSTICE LESSONS FROM COLOMBIA, GEORGIA, GUINEA, AND THE UNITED KINGDOM 95 (2018) (citations omitted).

62. *Id.*

63. Including the Office of the UN Special Representative of the Secretary-General for Sexual Violence in Conflict, the Team of Experts for Rule of Law/Sexual Violence in Conflict ("Team of Experts") within that office, the UN Peacebuilding Commission, and the Office of the High Commissioner for Human Rights, which maintained an office in Conakry.

14

Jus ad Curiam Decisions in Colombia

Colombia is a functional democracy, and still, it had endured the lengthiest armed conflict in the Western Hemisphere. It presented a unique challenge to the Office of the Prosecutor: different groups committing crimes against humanity,[1] while there were thousands of judicial investigations.

For decades, Colombia was treating guerrilla groups as political movements, and "periodic truces, ceasefires, and attempts to reach a negotiated settlement have punctuated" the conflict.[2]

Violent groups included Marxist guerrillas like the Revolutionary Armed Forces of Colombia (*Fuerzas Armadas Revolucionarias de Colombia, Ejército del Pueblo,* "FARC") and the National Liberation Army (*Ejército de Liberación Nacional,* "ELN"). Paramilitaries were fighting them, primarily the United Self-Defence Forces of Colombia (*Autodefensas Unidas de Colombia,* "AUC"). The illegal drug traffic was crossing in different ways all those groups and promoting other organized crime groups. The Colombian Armed Forces were also involved in massacres of civilians.

President Pastrana's failure to negotiate a peace agreement with FARC that included an amnesty opened a space for a new Colombian attitude. The ratification of the Rome Statute during the last months of Pastrana's administration created a new framework that his successor had to respect.

After ratifying the Rome Statute, Colombia found a new method to negotiate with paramilitaries and guerrillas, integrating peace and justice.

The ICC Office of the Prosecutor's preliminary examination influenced Colombia's decision makers, including the president, members of Congress, NGOs, the army, and judges.

President Uribe negotiated the paramilitaries forces' demobilization; their leaders were willing to surrender to avoid extradition to the United States. The Uribe administration proposals were considered very lenient, and the opposition demanded to view the paramilitaries as criminals and punish them.

War and Justice in the 21st Century. Luis Moreno Ocampo, Oxford University Press. © Oxford University Press 2022. DOI: 10.1093/oso/9780197628973.003.0015

The ICC intervention framing the facts as crimes against humanity provided leverage to those demands and influenced Congress and the Constitutional Court decisions that established the rules. Their decisions transformed violence management, defining a new legal frame for agreements with illegal groups compatible with the Rome Statute. Colombia became the best example of "positive complementarity."

Luis Carlos Restrepo, President Uribe's high commissioner for peace, explained to me: "ICC intervention is doing my job with the paramilitaries very difficult, but it facilitates enormously the negotiation with FARC. Now they are no more a political option; they are criminals."

The Justice and Peace Law created a new paradigm combining demobilization with an alternative punishment. It also provided truth and reparations to the victims. According to official numbers, a total of 31,671 members of paramilitary groups were demobilized by August 2006.[3] Most of the leaders were removed, imprisoned in Colombia, or extradited to the United States. There was an estimation that half of the paramilitaries demobilized returned to drugs illegal activities. Still, more than 15,000 paramilitaries were effectively demobilized.

Besides, until August 2011, 59 senators, 48 members of the House of Representatives, 33 governors, 252 mayors, and 84 local authorities were the subject of investigations following paramilitaries' statements during the Justice and Peace Law proceedings. Further, 40 politicians, after allegations of conspiracy and murder committed in collusion with paramilitaries, were convicted in 16 court decisions.[4]

Under President Uribe and President Santos, the armed forces captured or killed senior guerrilla leaders, released hostages, and removed FARC's and ELN's ability to conduct guerrilla operations in the big cities. The majority of guerrilla leaders were convicted, most of them in absentia. The ICC Office of the Prosecutor intervention influenced President Uribe's administration to open investigations against hundreds of army officers involved in "false positives."

After the end of my tenure, Colombia produced an even more complex peace agreement with the FARC considering the Rome Statute requirements. President Santos received the Nobel Peace Prize for his leadership in signing a deal with FARC. Since the peace agreement with FARC, Colombia faced new challenges controlling massive violence fueled by the multibillion illegal drug business.

Colombia's Decades of Violence without Punishment

Colombia combines an elite committed with the rule of law and a history of massive violence. Since 1964 some Colombians aiming for social equality followed the Cuban model to obtain power and created guerrilla movements. For forty years, Colombia's government was proposing amnesties to facilitate negotiations with them.

In August 1984, President Belisario Betancur's administration signed a ten-month truce with the M-19 revolutionary movement; however, in November 1985, an M-19 commando group seized the Palace of Justice in central Bogotá and abducted all its occupants. Alfonso Reyes, the Supreme Court's president, requested to manage the crises through dialogue.

The army ignored Justice Reyes's demand and launched a military operation to recover the place. After more than twenty-four hours of fighting, flames consumed much of the building, and over a hundred citizens lost their lives, including Alfonso Reyes and most of the Supreme Court judges. Few guerrilla members and civilians who survived were arrested by the army and disappeared.

Between the smoke, it was still possible to read on top of the Justice Palace's front door the words of Colombia's founding father, Francisco de Paula Santander: "Colombians, arms have given you independence, but laws will give you freedom." Like many South American countries, including Peru, Venezuela, Chile, Uruguay, and Argentina, Colombia's revolution in the nineteenth century against Spain, the colonial empire, was fueled by enlightenment ideals. Two centuries later, those principles still had a relevant group of supporters.

In any case, after the Palace of Justice's attack, negotiations without punishment continued in Colombia. President Virgilio Barco (1986–1990) reached an agreement with the M-19 itself, which broke ranks with other guerrilla groups, and abandoned the armed struggle in exchange for amnesty and guarantees of participation in the political process.[5]

The Gaviria administration (1990–1994) followed President Barco's model in its successful negotiations with several small guerrilla groups, which laid down their arms and obtained representation in the constituent assembly. It was not possible to reach an agreement with FARC and ELN.[6]

Gaviria's successor, President Ernesto Samper (1994–1998), sought a resumption of peace negotiations. Guerrillas, branded as *bandits* by the Gaviria government, were once again legitimized as negotiating partners. But the

FARC demanded the demilitarization of an area in Southern Colombia as a precondition for negotiations.[7] In December 1997, Congress adopted Law 418 to "facilitate the dialogue" and agreements with illegal armed organizations that the government recognized had "political character."[8]

Following such a vision, NGOs and the German and Colombia Episcopal Conference promoted meetings with Marxist guerrillas in Germany, including union labor leaders, businesspersons, the Nobel Prize in Literature recipient Gabriel García Márquez, Colombia's general prosecutor, and a German prosecutor.[9]

In this context, Andrés Pastrana was elected president in July 1998 on a platform of peace negotiations. *He saw peace as a prerequisite for drug control and drugs as a social problem.*[10] After a few months, President Pastrana visited Washington to meet President Clinton, promising to "inaugurate a new era in relations between Colombia and the United States."[11]

In November 1998, as a goodwill gesture to the FARC, Pastrana granted the group a demilitarized zone of 42,000 square kilometers—an area the size of Switzerland—in the southern department of Caquetá, accepting FARC demands to conduct the negotiations on Colombia's soil.

Following the previous agreements' path, Pastrana treated FARC as a political movement. Talks began in San Vicente del Caguán, a town within the demilitarized zone (*zona de despeje*), in January 1999. Pastrana traveled to the area to open the negotiations.[12]

The FARC continued military operations while the talks were proceeding, and Pastrana had to manage divisions in his cabinet. Backed by the army's high command, the minister of defense opposed Pastrana's decision to extend the *zona de despeje* indefinitely and resigned in May 1999.[13]

In February 2000, Human Rights Watch exposed evidence of "continuing close ties between the Colombian Army and paramilitary groups responsible for gross human rights violations."[14]

In August 2000, President Pastrana achieved a critical part of his plan: the US Congress approved $1.018 million as the US contribution to what has become known as Plan Colombia. President Clinton and a group of congresspersons visited Colombia to show support for Pastrana's actions.[15]

Colombia exposed some counterinsurgency strategy problems. In 2000, the US Congress recognized the Colombian police efforts but was worried about the army's relations with the paramilitaries.[16] Interestingly, in 1962 a top-level US Special Warfare team from Fort Bragg suggested promoting proxy forces and establishing connections with paramilitary groups.[17]

The Committee on International Relations organized a public hearing on the topic in September 2000. Representative Gary Ackerman recognized the connection between guerrillas and illegal drug traffic. "... *in Colombia, the counternarcotic strategy is, by necessity, counterinsurgency strategy.*" The goal was "to punish the drug traffickers and their guerrilla allies for stopping the flow of narcotics and arresting the traffickers and, with luck, drive the guerrillas to the negotiating table."[18]

Invited to Congress's hearing, Michael Shifter, representing the Inter-American Dialogue, identified Colombia's biggest problem. It was "rampant lawlessness and insecurity. Seventy percent of the world's kidnappings take place in Colombia. US policy should be designed fundamentally to help Colombians address their urgent security crisis. The government cannot now protect its citizens."[19]

FARC also complained about security; it suspended the negotiation in November 2000 to protest the alleged government failure to combat the paramilitary groups. *The government did not negotiate with Paramilitaries, and the guerrillas have insisted on their exclusion of any peace conversation. Still, at the same time, they argue that, for their safety, they cannot demobilize as long as the paramilitaries were not also demobilized.*[20]

In April 2001, the EU members, representatives of other twenty countries, and international organizations met in Bogotá to support the Colombia peace process. They demanded President Pastrana to exert more efforts to control paramilitary groups.[21] The United States designated FARC and ELN as terrorist organizations in 1997. It went further on September 10, 2001, including the United Self-Defense Forces of Colombia, commonly known as the AUC, *Paramilitaries* as a Foreign Terrorist Organization.[22]

In October 2001, Human Rights Watch produced a report labeling the paramilitaries as the Colombian Army "Sixth Division" while recognizing that the authorities, including top generals, publicly denounce paramilitary groups and that "Increasingly, paramilitary fighters are arrested."[23]

But the paramilitary was not the only problem.

The FARC took advantage of the negotiations to recruit and train new members and committed attacks in major metropolitan areas, particularly kidnappings. As security conditions worsened, public opinion turned against peace negotiations.[24]

European diplomacy had made enormous efforts in brokering the peace process. Consequently, it was refusing to accept the frustration of the negotiation.[25] Finally, on December 27, 2001, the EU Council included

FARC in the list of terrorist groups.[26] President Pastrana ended the peace negotiations in February 2002 when FARC abducted Colombian Senator Jorge Gechem Turbay. Three days later, senator and presidential candidate Ingrid Betancourt, who holds dual French–Colombian citizenship, was also abducted.

The Process to Ratify the Rome Statute

Social demands were calling for a different approach, and Colombia adopted the duty to prosecute serious crimes between 2001/2002. It was not an exclusive Rome Statute obligation.

In March 2001, the Inter-American Court of Human Rights handed down an influential ruling in Barrios Altos v. Peru, which seemingly "outlawed" the use of amnesties for atrocity crimes.[27] The judgment also further developed the doctrine that states violate the American Convention on Human Rights not only when they directly commit atrocity crimes but also when they fail to prosecute atrocity crimes.[28]

In May 2001, a group of senators took the initiative to promote the Rome Statute's ratification.[29] On December 27, 2001, the Congress of Colombia produced a constitutional reform including as a new Article 93 of the Constitution the authorization to ratify the Rome Statute, clarifying that the differences with Colombian constitutional guarantees were accepted.[30] Some of such differences included "immunities, life sentences, no prescription" and the application of the principle "*ne bis in idem.*"[31]

In December 2001, President Pastrana embraced the idea officially and requested Congress approve the Rome Statute. Three months later, and after ending the FARC's peace negotiation, the president asked Congress to treat the Rome Statute's adoption under an urgent procedure. Both chambers expedited the treatment, and on June 5, 2002, Law 742/2002 was enacted.[32]

The constitutional court subjected the law to a previous judicial review following the Colombia legal system. The minister of foreign affairs, justice, defense, NGOs, and citizens participated in the judicial debate supporting the ratification.[33] The Colombian general prosecutor considered that the Rome Statute would be "an important preventative mechanism for the different actors of the armed conflict."[34]

The Colombian constitutional court made a thorough review of the statute. It clarified that *state sovereignty exists to protect citizens,* not to hide criminals, and considered that the "complementarity" principle created a framework that respects Colombia's sovereignty.

The constitutional court also highlighted Article 22 of the Colombian Constitution, establishing that "Peace is a right and a duty whose compliance is mandatory." It considered that political crimes could receive national amnesties, but "Final stop" laws impeding the access to justice, blank amnesties, self-amnesties, or any other mechanism frustrating victims' rights to a judicial remedy are in violation of international law. Accordingly, on July 30, 2002, the constitutional court ruled that the Rome Statute was compatible with the national constitution.

On August 5, 2002, just two days before the end of Andres Pastrana's presidency, Colombia deposited its instrument of ratification to the Rome Statute, providing jurisdiction to the ICC since November 2002.

Guillermo Fernandez de Soto, Pastrana's foreign affairs minister, included a declaration according to Article 124 of the Rome Statute delaying the ICC jurisdiction concerning war crimes for seven years. The government adopted a new strategy to control armed groups' crimes: end violence or face the ICC.

President Alvaro Uribe

Alvaro Uribe Velez, a former state governor, won the 1998 election as an independent candidate and promised to double the armed forces' size to control territory lost to the FARC. Uribe had personal experience as a victim of political violence; guerrillas killed his father in 1983, and the FARC nearly succeeded in assassinating him with a bomb during the electoral campaign. During Uribe's inauguration on August 7, 2002, mortar shells fell in an area close to the Congress, where Uribe was, and killed at least fourteen people and wounded forty.[35]

President Uribe received from Pastrana a complex legacy: full national and international support to improve security after the failure of the peace negotiations with the FARC, the Rome Statute legal framework, and US assistance to improve the army. A week before his inauguration, President Bush signed legislation expanding American military support to enhance Colombia's fight against the rebel movement.[36]

President Uribe promised not to engage in peace negotiations without a ceasefire and to oppose a demilitarized zone. In September and November 2002, FARC and paramilitary leaders, including Carlos Castaño, were indicted in the United States on drug-trafficking charges. Privately, Castaño expressed fears that the United States could bomb his camp.[37] Suggesting the influence of such a US decision, just a month later, in December 2002, the paramilitaries declared a unilateral ceasefire accepting Uribe's conditions and proposed to initiate peace talks.

Demobilization of Paramilitaries

The Pact of Santa Fé de Ralito signed on July 15, 2003, formalized the negotiations, and paramilitary leaders agreed to demobilize fully by the end of 2005.[38]

In December 2004, the Inter-American Commission of Human Rights recommended adopting a legal framework for the demobilization of illegal armed groups consistent with the state's international obligations in the areas of truth, justice, and reparation for victims of the conflict.[39] The UN high commissioner for Human Rights and Amnesty International were also demanding more decisive actions.[40]

The Justice and Peace Law

The executive prepared the first draft of a law to facilitate the paramilitaries' demobilization, but it found resistance in the Congress. The Colombian society was developing a consciousness that the perpetrators of gross human rights violations cannot be the object of amnesties or pardons, as in previous peace processes.[41]

Luis Carlos Restrepo, the Colombian high commissioner for peace, understood the new context and explained to paramilitary leaders that they had to pay some time in jail to block the ICC intervention in their cases.[42]

It was in this context that we had the first contact with Colombian authorities. Guillermo Fernandez de Soto, Pastrana's minister of foreign affairs, became Colombia's ambassador at The Hague and, in 2004, invited me to an informal dinner. In those initial years, we keep confidential the opening of a preliminary examination to avoid conflicts with the states under analysis. Later we concluded that the office should make formal and public announcements to maximize the Office of the prosecutor's preventive impact.

Ambassador Fernandez de Soto was concerned that the Office of the Prosecutor was asking for information about Colombia's situation. He wanted to avoid the opening of an ICC prosecution and explained to me the enormous efforts the government was making to control violence. He explored the possibility of establishing a relationship with the Office of the Prosecutor and insisting that President Uribe's military efforts would always respect the Rome Statute limits.

On March 2, 2005, the Office of the Prosecutor sent a letter to the government of Colombia asking for information about crimes against humanity allegedly committed by guerrillas, paramilitaries, army and security officers, and the project to demobilize the paramilitaries.[43] In those days, Congress was debating a new version of the Justice and Peace Law, including Senator Pardo and Congressperson Gina Parody's recommendations. Without our involvement, the legislators discussed our letter.

The Office of the Prosecutor letter was presented during the Parliament committee discussion by Senator Darío Martínez, commenting that the suspension for seven years of the ICC jurisdiction for war crimes did not stop the possibility of investigating crimes against humanity committed by the paramilitaries. "We are approving a law against the international standards," said Senator Martinez.[44] On the spot, the senator requested clarifications from the minister of interior, Sabas Pretelt de la Vega, who participated in the debate. The minister confirmed the reception of the letter.[45]

A public letter by Carlos Isaac Náder, the Supreme Court's president, to Congress confirmed the Rome Statute's influence. In May 2005, Justice Náder wrote that the Justice and Peace Law project did not allow effective justice intervention against crimes against humanity. Justice Náder stated that the ICC prosecutor could review the Colombian judges' reasons not to investigate."[46]

Debates in the Colombian parliament also exposed the Rome Statute influence. Congress member Gina Parody talked about the necessity to respect international standards to avoid future ICC interventions. Congressman Luis Fernando Velasco and Senators Darío Martínez, Germán Vargas Lleras, and Hernán Andrade also discussed the issue.[47]

The "peace and justice law" (Law 975 of 2005) was finally adopted in July 2005 to facilitate the negotiation with the *organized armed groups outside the Law*. It did not require establishing the "*political character*" of the organizations and specifically included members of *guerrilla and self-defense groups* [Paramilitaries] as beneficiaries.

The law offered individuals significantly reduced prison sentences—between five and eight years—in exchange for their "contribution to the attainment of national peace, collaboration with the justice system, reparation for the victims, and the person's adequate re-socialization."[48] "The Law generated massive controversy because some people saw it as a hidden way to grant impunity for the paramilitary groups' crimes.[49]

A constitutional court decision in May 2006 transformed some aspects of the law. The court held that Justice and Peace Law was part of a transitional justice model respecting the constitution. The Justice and Peace Law is not granting amnesty or pardon because neither prevents ongoing criminal prosecutions from continuing nor eliminates penalties. In this regard, the court said, "the law does not establish the extinction of the criminal action." However, it declared some parts of the law unconstitutional and conditioned the interpretation of others.[50]

The court established the beneficiaries' duty to provide full, truthful confessions regarding their participation in crimes, the money illegally obtained, and the criminal apparatus. It also declared that alternative punishment mechanisms were constitutional because they did not disproportionately affect the victims' rights to truth, justice, reparation, and non-repetition. The decision also clarifies the definition of paramilitarism as an ordinary crime.[51]

According to official numbers, a total of 31,671 members of paramilitary groups demobilized by August 2006.[52]

War and Negotiations with FARC

Weakening FARC

Under President Uribe, there were an intense military confrontation with the FARC and, at the same time, frustrated attempts to negotiate the release of hostages. After pushing the FARC out of densely populated areas and regaining control of road arteries and other strategic infrastructure, the security forces focused on attacking traditional FARC strongholds.[53]

The FARC suffered heavy blows at the hands of security forces, including capturing or killing senior and mid-rank officers and losing strategic areas. Still, the guerrilla group kept remote regions' control. It also retained dozens of high-level prisoners as the Colombian/French Ingrid Betancourt, three

U.S. citizens, Governor Guillermo Gaviria, and former Defense Minister Gilberto Echeverri.[54]

The FARC offered to release all its hostages in exchange for all FARC guerrilla prisoners, provided that the government changed its policy and hold negotiations in an agreed-upon demilitarized zone inside Colombia. On May 5, 2003, Colombian soldiers approached a FARC camp in Antioquia in a rescue attempt authorized by President Uribe. As soon as the guerrillas heard helicopters coming, they executed their ten hostages, including Guillermo Gaviria and Gilberto Echeverri.[55]

In August 2003, the FARC and the ELN released a joint note calling Uribe an "enemy of peace" and making a pledge to never engage in talks with his government.[56] Instead, the FARC proposed negotiations to release its high-level hostages to different parties, including France, the United States, Switzerland, Norway, the Colombian Catholic Church, and the UN.[57]

There were various attempts to establish a negotiation, but in April 2005, James Lemoyne, who since 2001 was leading the UN mediation effort in Colombia, ended his work. He could not gain significant ground with either the Uribe administration or the FARC after the collapse of the 1998–2002 peace talks. An effort, suggested by Kofi Annan after a FARC appeal, failed in early 2005 as the parties could not settle on their negotiation terms.[58]

First Visit to Colombia

Impunity Was No Longer an Option

On May 28, 2006, President Uribe won the reelection with 62 percent of the votes. In 2007, our office considered that since 2002 crimes against humanity, including killings, forcible displacement, the kidnapping of civilians, and sexual violence, were committed in Colombia by all armed groups, including the government of Colombia forces.

Paramilitary groups allegedly committed the majority of killings under the ICC jurisdiction, followed by FARC and ELN. The government was prosecuting all of them but not making a systematic effort to investigate the military forces' alleged crimes. The paramilitaries demobilized identified their political connections, and the Colombian Supreme Court was leading an effort to investigate what was called "the parapolitic."

Our crime pattern analysis showed three main phases of the commission of crimes against humanity.

First, and following the collapse of peace negotiations with FARC in 2001, there was a peak of violence from 2002 to 2003 attributed to paramilitary and guerrilla offensives, producing large massacres (115 in 2002) and other crimes.

Second, between 2003 and 2006, there was a sharp decrease in crimes resulting from the weakening of the guerrillas, demobilization of paramilitaries, and increased international pressure (including a non-coordinated combination of the United States, EU, Switzerland, Norway, UN, OAS human rights system, NGOs and the ICC).

The third phase, after 2006, exposed a relative increase of crimes related to the aftermath of the paramilitary demobilization (fragmentation, repositioning of new smaller groups) and continuing guerrilla crimes.

Between 2002 and 2008, military units conducted "false positives" operations. National Army brigades across Colombia were abducting primarily young men or lured them to remote locations under pretenses—such as promises of work—killed them and placed weapons on their bodies, presenting them as guerrilla members. Colombian officers reported them as enemy combatants killed in action.[59] The officers received monetary compensations and alleviated the pressure from superiors to show "positive" results and boost body counts in their war against guerrillas.

I visited Colombia in October 2007. We wanted to contribute to the prevention of these crimes while monitoring Colombia's justice efforts. I had the opportunity to join a special session in Bogotá of the Inter-American Court of Human Rights. I had a long meeting with the NGOs, the prosecutor, the Supreme Court, the High Commissioner for Peace, and President Uribe.

The NGOs presented cases never solved, the victims' suffering, the contradictions, government failures, and the lack of protection for marginal groups, like the Afro Colombian communities and the peasants in remote areas.

NGOs supported the process of *free version* declarations and the investigations triggered by the Justice and Peace Law, and some of them insisting that we should open an investigation. I tried to be very clear that we had to respect complementarity, and our policy was to focus on those "who bear the greatest responsibility."

I had a fascinating meeting with Luis Carlos Restrepo, high commissioner for peace, a mediator who understood how to use the Rome Statute to negotiate peace agreements. He described his challenges and how the ICC was transforming the public discussion about violence, consolidating a new approach: paramilitaries, FARC, and ELN were criminals.

I visited the Colombian general prosecutor's office and discussed how to implement the Justice and Peace Law with him and his team. His office had more than 20,000 officers, seventy times bigger than our own office. I explained to investigators and prosecutors the criteria we developed to investigate the organizations' leaders involved in the crimes' commission.

In a separate meeting, the Supreme Court judges described their challenges and commitment to fulfilling their problematic mission.

President Uribe received me with some of his ministers, but he commanded the conversation. He exposed an in-depth knowledge of what was happening in his government. He explored the possibility of ending the suspension of the ICC jurisdiction for war crimes.[60] I told him that it was a sovereign Colombia decision; we had nothing to comment on that. My feeling was that President Uribe wanted to use the ICC threat to put pressure on the FARC.

President Uribe also explained to me the adoption of the Justice and Peace Law, his commitment to support the efforts to investigate the crimes committed, including the "Parapolitica," and requested that the Colombian authorities should be responsible for carrying out the process.

I ratified our respect for the complementarity principle and recognized that many paramilitary and guerrilla leaders were already convicted or under prosecution. It was also clear that the evidence about the parapolitica was just emerging, and the Colombian authorities would need time to process it. But "false positives" were committed since 2002, and there was almost no conviction on the cases.

President Uribe checked the information with his collaborators and said: "Let us do it; Colombia will investigate those cases." That commitment was probably the most important outcome of my first visit.

Colombia's Office of the Prosecutor focused on those crimes. In a report produced in 2018, Human Rights Watch found that "false positives" investigations began in 2007 and resulted in first convictions around 2009. Since then, Colombian authorities have made significant progress in prosecuting the army members responsible for "false positive" killings.[61]

Similarly, in March 2011, the UN OHCHR stated in its annual report that a "drastic reduction in the number of persons presented as killed in combat while under the custody of the Army, known as 'false positives,' was consolidated."[62]

At the end of my visit in 2007, I publicly summarized the Office of the Prosecutor's position. I explained that the Justice and Peace Law's final version could become a world example to manage conflicts, but its implementation was challenging. I also reminded Colombians that national amnesties for war crimes and crimes against humanity would not stop the ICC's intervention.[63]

The Conflict with FARC, the Role of Venezuela, and Operation Jaque

It is impossible to describe the magnitude of what happened during the following six months in these short pages. FARC retained seven hundred persons as prisoners and insisted that Uribe demilitarize an area as a condition to reach a hostage deal.

In November 2007, Venezuelan President Hugo Chávez tried to mediate with the FARC to release some hostages. But Uribe was angered by Chávez's handling of the delicate negotiations and ended Chávez's involvement. Chávez accused Uribe of disrespecting him, saying, "As long as President Uribe is president of Colombia, I won't have any kind of relationship with him or with the government of Colombia."[64]

But President Chávez was involved in a deal with FARC to liberate two hostages. In January 2008, Clara Rojas, Ingrid Betancourt's vice presidential candidate captured in February 2002, and former Colombian Congresswoman Consuelo Gonzalez, abducted in September 2001, were released. Armed guerrillas escorted the women to a clearing where they were picked up by Venezuelan helicopters that bore International Red Cross insignia.[65] President Chávez received them in his presidential palace, and they appeared together on television as a band played the anthems of Venezuela and Colombia.

President Uribe recognized President Chávez's mediating role but mentioned the names of hostages still held by the rebel group.[66] Without saying, both leaders were debating the FARC's legal status: criminals or freedom fighters?

President Chávez moved forward and called Europe to remove from its list of terrorist organizations the FARC and the ELN. He argued, "I say this even though somebody might be bothered by it: the FARC and the ELN are not terrorist groups. They are armies, real armies . . . that occupy a space in Colombia." He added that the two "insurgent forces" have a goal, "a project," that is, "Bolivarian," and that "we respect." Chávez said his nation is committed to bringing peace in Colombia, a task that means "we must continue to work at the various levels" with FARC and ELN.[67]

However, videos showing FARC hostages in the jungle triggered widespread reactions. On February 4, 2008, hundreds of thousands of Colombians took to the streets across the country in a massive protest against FARC guerrillas and their kidnapping of hostages held for years in hidden jungle camps.[68] A few weeks later, four former Congress members were released by FARC after over six years in captivity. President Chávez reportedly brokered their release.[69]

In March 2008, Colombian planes bombed a FARC camp inside Ecuador, killing Raul Reyes and twenty-six others, among them an Ecuadorean citizen.[70] Reyes was the first member of the FARC secretariat to be killed. Uribe said documents seized at the camp from Reyes's computer show that the FARC had given money to Correa's 2006 presidential campaign in Ecuador. President Chávez had planned to provide the rebels with $300 million. The raid bolstered Uribe's popularity at home to a record 82 percent, although most Latin American countries condemned the Ecuador's sovereignty violation.[71]

Venezuela and Ecuador cut diplomatic ties, and sent troops to the Colombian border in a show of force.[72] Colombia insisted that the UN Charter provided the right to attack its enemies in self-defense.

On March 4, 2008, President Uribe said that his government would denounce President Chávez before the ICC for aiding and abetting FARC.[73] President Chávez vowed war if Colombia pursued its fight with the FARC into Venezuela.[74]

The regional group managed the conflict. On March 8, 2008, President Chávez and Ecuador's President Correa accepted the public apologies of President Uribe and publicly shacked hands in an OAS meeting in the Dominican Republic, ending the dispute between the three countries.[75] There is a pending case before the Inter-American Commission for Human Rights.[76]

In the meantime, FARC had new problems.[77] On March 26, 2008, Manuel Marulanda, the FARC's legendary head, died of a heart attack.[78] A FARC's top-level field commander, known by the alias Karina, surrendered in May.[79]

In July 2008, a carefully planned military "Operation Jaque" freed Ingrid Betancourt, three US defense contractors, and eleven Colombian police and Army officers without a shot being fired or a drop of blood spilled.[80] The FARC commander in charge of the prisoners said that he had to present his hostages to the new FARC chief Alfonso Cano, putting them aboard a helicopter allegedly run by a humanitarian organization. The helicopter belonged to the Colombian Army, and the crew was a special services unit that subdued the rebels in the air without firing a shot. Uribe's approval ratings in Colombia shot to 91 percent.[81]

My Second Visit to Colombia

The Office of the Prosecutor was trying to identify a network of FARC supporters working *abroad*. It sent letters to Colombia's neighbors, other states, and international and regional organizations requesting information about any assistance provided by such a network to the commission of crimes that potentially fall within the court's jurisdiction.[82]

We learned about an arrest in Spain at Colombia's request supporting a FARC-supporting group in Switzerland. We asked Berna authorities about their investigations of these affairs, which could be crimes under our jurisdiction or at least the national crime of money laundering.[83] I perceived the potential impact of a central authority collecting global information.

To prepare for our second visit, we sent a letter to Colombia requesting information about the investigations against crimes committed by leaders of the different groups and the proceedings against the army's members. We also asked about the political leaders supporting violent groups and how to ensure that the paramilitary leaders extradited to the United States would cooperate with the Justice and Peace Law.[84] Our request for an arrest warrant against President Bashir received a lot of attention in Colombia, increasing the interest in our planned visit.[85]

On August 15, 2008, President Uribe himself made a public clarification; if the paramilitaries did not cooperate under the Justice and Peace Law, they would remain under the ordinary justice system without any privilege.[86] In the following days, the Colombian prosecutor reminded US authorities that the extradition did not suspend Justice and Peace Law's application and requested assistance to receive confessions and testimonies.[87]

Salvatore Mancuso, one of the top paramilitaries, was one of the few persons extradited that continued cooperating. He described from Washington some of the massacres and provided names of army officers involved. Mancuso told how they bribed the head of the Administrative Security Department (DAS) to obtain information.[88] He said that he sent a letter to the ICC Office of the Prosecutor asking special attention to the denouncing cases.[89]

We arrived in Colombia on August 25, 2008. The same day President Uribe made declarations welcoming our visit and said that the extradition of the paramilitary leaders to the United States would not produce impunity.[90]

We participated in a seminar with most of the judges and prosecutors involved in the Justice and Peace Law. Vice President Francisco Santos and the minister of justice inaugurated the meeting. The general prosecutor explained that following the paramilitaries confessions, the Colombian Office of the Prosecutor unveiled 1,300 mass graves, and more than 3,500 families received the perpetrators' free version statements accepting responsibility.

The next day with the prosecutor and the chief of police, I visited one of those mass graves. The forensic work required many security forces, prosecutors, and anthropologists, showing the complementarity model's advantage.[91]

During specific meetings, I tried to explain our methods to the Colombian judiciary members: how we investigate the groups that commit the crimes, prove the planning, and the leaders' responsibility. In this sense, I highlighted the unique opportunity to receive information from the paramilitaries about the relation with political actors that supported the commission of crimes.

The next day all the newspapers presented President Uribe in the front pages denouncing a plot against him, including the Supreme Court's involvement and the intention to prosecute him before the ICC.[92]

In the morning, I visited the Supreme Court, which described their efforts to investigate the paramilitaries' information. The same day I had lunch with the president and some of his ministers. President Uribe explained the military and judicial efforts, including new investigations on the *false positives*, and ensured me that the extradited persons would be available.

I took note of all the efforts he mentioned and asked very directly: President, why do you need to confront the Supreme Court? He believed some Supreme Court judges had a personal interest in his case. President Uribe knew them from the university, and he was sure that there was an ideological component in their actions. After lunch, one of the ministries thanked me for my effort, saying that they could not convince the president to avoid public comments.

On this trip, I met Maria Angela Holguin, Vice President Francisco Santos's adviser on foreign affairs in those days. She explained that Colombia did not like to increase its public exposure to justice at the international level as a policy. I insisted that Colombia was the best example of positive complementarity. A state party with a long experience managing violence while considering its legal obligations.

She explained something that I did not realize before: *It is not a sounding policy to present our efforts. It is never enough. If we announce that we will do 10, the international community demands 20. If we commit 20, they said it is not enough; you should do 40. Colombia would never be recognized for its efforts because there are always aspects that could be improved.* She understood the complex international dynamic.

Some efforts to investigate army officers continued. In October 2008, President Uribe removed three generals from service, four colonels, as well as over twenty more officers for an "inexcusable lack of diligence on the part of officers in the rigorous investigation of alleged irregularities in their jurisdiction."[93]

In a 2008 survey carried out in four regional departments, the vast majority of affected communities supported criminal processes; 89 percent believed that guerrillas should be tried and sentenced, and 88 percent believed the same about paramilitaries. National prosecutors continued to be the most trusted option for criminal justice proceedings (62 percent), followed by the president (47 percent) and international justice (38 percent).[94]

In 2009 the suspension of the jurisdiction for war crimes ended. The office started to analyze whether so-called successor paramilitary groups or new illegal armed groups could qualify as organized armed groups, parties to the armed conflict. The government of Colombia refers to these groups as criminal bands (*bandas criminales* or BACRIM) and does not consider them as parties to the armed conflict.[95]

Relations between Colombia and Venezuela deteriorated even more. New information obtained from FARC leaders' computers suggested a collaboration between the guerrillas and high-ranking military and intelligence officials in Mr. Chávez's government. Members of the FARC arranged weapons deals and even obtained identity cards to move with ease on Venezuelan soil.[96] Uribe was very popular and won a referendum allowing him to reform the constitution to run for the third period, but in February 2010, the constitutional court rejected such a possibility.[97]

Uribe accepted the court's decision and supported Juan Manuel Santos, his former minister of defense, who promised to ensure Uribe's "legacy of security and progress is not lost."[98] In the June election second round, Juan Manuel Santos obtained 69 percent of the votes and defeated Antanas Mockus, a creative former mayor of Bogotá. On July 22, 2010, Colombia presented evidence showing 1,500 Colombian guerrillas hiding in Venezuela. President Chávez cut diplomatic ties with Colombia.[99]

President Juan Manuel Santos

A New Leader in the Peace Process

On August 7, 2010, President Santos started his term and said that mending relations with neighbors Ecuador and Venezuela would be one of his government's main priorities. He also declared that a dialogue with the guerrillas would only go ahead if the rebels laid down their arms and stopped their kidnapping, intimidation, extortion, and drug-dealing campaign.[100] On August 10, President Santos and President Chávez met to repair diplomatic relations in a city in the Colombian Caribe just three days later.[101]

A few weeks after his inauguration, I received an invitation to meet the new president for the first time. He received me informally at his home, his wife stayed a few minutes with us, and then she let us alone. He enjoyed more than 80 percent of popularity in those days, and he mentioned: "I am worried because from here I only can go down." He did not give me any detail, but he was interested in the relation between a peace agreement and the ICC role.

I repeated to him the general policy. The Office of the Prosecutor will monitor the existence of national proceedings against those considered who bore the greatest responsibility and expressed my opinion that international justice would not be an obstacle to peace in Colombia. We did not discuss any project, but I had the impression that a new plan was coming.

Military operations continued under President Santos. In September 2010, "Mono Jojoy," FARC number two and leader of the military operations was killed.[102] And in November 2011, FARC's top leader, Alfonso Cano, was killed.[103]

President Santos's Address to the Assembly of the States Parties

Angela Holguin became the new Colombian minister of foreign affairs and organized President Santos's presence as a keynote speaker during the following Assembly of States Parties celebrated on December 6, 2010, in New York.

President Santos proclaimed his determination to fight impunity in Colombia, supporting the ICC and the complementary criminal justice system created by the Rome Statute. He expressly recognized: "Colombia is the first country to have achieved the demobilization of illegal armed groups without having defeated them, without offering impunity, without offering an amnesty. The Justice and Peace Law is an innovative scheme that achieves justice without preventing peace and seeks peace without impunity.[104]

He mentioned that "More than 4,000 people are being investigated under this special procedure; the paramilitary leaders are in jail," highlighting the importance of reaching a judicial truth.[105]

> *Today, more than 400 politicians at all levels—Congress members, governors, mayors, assemblymen, councilmen, are being prosecuted for collaborating with illegal armed groups.*
>
> *And we have paid particular attention to the behavior of our Military and Police. It is the obedience of the Law that distinguishes a soldier from a criminal. As of September of this year, there were 737 active investigations and 298 convictions ... We elevated the following practice to military doctrine: to promote demobilizations over captures and captures over combat deaths.*

President Santos announced an ambitious project to *repair the victims of heinous crimes*, including *land restitution.* He recognized President Uribe's work: *The security indicators of the last eight years are telling: murders have dropped by 45 percent, massacres by 78 percent, and kidnappings by 91 percent.*

President Santos was very clear about the Rome Statute model: *international criminal justice and national justice ... are part of the system created by the Statute of Rome, where the leading role lies with the States and, secondarily, with the International Criminal Court,*

FARC peace negotiation and the Office of the Prosecutor influence.

Three days after the end of my tenure, a new phase started in Colombia: negotiation with FARC. The Office of the Prosecutor's preliminary examination continued to play a critical role, and I became a witness of some critical moments.

The Agreement with FARC

On June 19, 2012, the "Legal Framework for Peace" bill (Marco jurídico para la Paz) was approved by the Colombian Senate, establishing the legal foundations of a new agreement with the FARC that included the duty to do justice for the crimes.

The bill introduced transitory Articles 66 and 67 to the Constitution. It established a transitional justice strategy that included prioritization and selecting cases against the most responsible for crimes against humanity or war crimes.

I witnessed the complexity of the FARC agreement developed by the Santos administration, supported by Cuba and Norway, and the impact of ICC Prosecutor Bensouda's actions. During the following years, Sergio Jaramillo, as commissioner for peace and former Vice President Humberto De La Calle, as the chief negotiator, led the discussion with FARC.

Colombia implemented a comprehensive strategy including legal reforms, meetings of victims with FARC in Havana, and a presidential election to consolidate President Santos's legitimacy to sign the agreement. The transparency of the process was unique; the media exposed all the points under discussion.

In November 2012, the Office of the Prosecutor published an interim report on Colombia stating that: "subject to the appropriate execution of sentences of those convicted. . . those who appear to bear the greatest responsibility within FARC and ELN for the most serious crimes have already been the subject of genuine national proceedings."[106]

The report did not require more investigations as Colombia was proposing except for the "false positive." It recognized that "A large number of investigations have been initiated into the killings of civilians in false-positive cases. Yet, the existing proceedings have largely failed to focus on the persons who might bear the greatest responsibility for the commission of these crimes."[107]

In November 2012, ICC Prosecutor Fatou Bensouda stated that she considered the FARC leaders had already been investigated and convicted but required a genuine implementation of these decisions. In May 2015, the ICC

Deputy Prosecutor added that an alternative punishment, including transitional justice measures designed to end armed conflicts, could be compatible with the Rome Statute's principles. He quoted as examples requiring the convicted person to participate in the process of establishing the truth about crimes, demobilization, and a guarantee of non-repetition.

I visited Colombia a few times to participate as an expert in some seminars allowing me to understand the enormous efforts that many Colombians were making. My son Francisco supported the work of Sri Sri Ravi Shankar, an Indian spiritual leader teaching meditation and nonviolence, and participated in some meetings with FARC in Havana. He was training them in meditation and discussing Gandhi's ideals. During these experiences, FARC leaders requested my son to organize a meeting with me.

I spent a weekend in a conference room at the Hotel Nacional in Havana, discussing the ICC's role with FARC leaders. While they accepted that crimes against humanity could not be amnestied, they refused to accept a punishment, which they considered an unnecessary humiliation. They still had 8,000 soldiers, and they were not surrendering but making a voluntary agreement. I warned them that they could also be prosecuted in the United States for money laundering. They were taxing drug traffickers. That was new for them.

It was a fascinating meeting, but I left Havana with no hopes.

A month later, I was again in Bogotá in a meeting with the top Colombian generals when the president called me to ask for my thoughts on an agreed text on the issue of punishment. I had the chance to read the draft establishing an alternative punishment mechanism with the minister of justice, Yesid Reyes, the son of the murdered Supreme Court President Alfonso Reyes. Many Colombians are resiliently using the law to obtain freedom.

To my surprise, the FARC had accepted an alternative punishment: to demobilize, to abandon their weapons, to help to remove mines, to provide information and reparations to the victims, and a restriction of liberty to a confined area. There they would work for the communities for up to eight years. It was less than the paramilitaries received but much more than I was expecting, and crucially it was within the parameters defined by Prosecutor Bensouda.

In March 2016, I was invited again to visit Havana. I met FARC and Colombia delegation leaders separately, trying to reach a final agreement, and wanted to establish international protection for the agreement. Both sides were tired and stressed, like a runner in the last kilometer of a marathon.

It was the moment, they all had to make final concessions and trust in each other. We explored the possibility of obtaining a UN Security Council resolution recognizing the agreement made. A version of the idea was subsequently included in the final text to provide reliable international legal protection to both sides.

The 2016 Agreement with FARC

In a unique Colombia magic realism, the following events succeeded in less than ten days.

(a) On September 26, 2016, Monday, top FARC leader Rodrigo Londoño, a.k.a. Timochenko, and President Santos signed a historic agreement. It was a beautiful ceremony in Cartagena's main square, with Beethoven music and a group of women singing popular songs, in the presence of sixteen heads of State, more than forty Ministers of Foreign Affairs, the UN Secretary-General Ban Ki-moon, the President of the World Bank and the Director of the International Monetary Fund.

Still, Colombians had to vote in a referendum to approve the agreement, but the expectation was a Yes victory by a wide double-digit margin.[108]

(b) On October 2, 2016, the NO won the referendum for a narrow majority of 50.2 percent to 49.8 percent.
(c) On October 4, 2016, Tuesday, President Santos tweeted that he invited his predecessors "to dialogue . . . in a constructive spirit."[109]
(d) On October 5, 2016, Wednesday, President Santos and former President Uribe, leader of the NO, met for the first time in six years to resolve differences.
(e) On October 7, 2016, Friday, the Nobel Committee awarded the Peace Prize to President Santos.
The search for an agreement with former President Uribe ended. And Colombia stays divided for the following years.

In any case, President Santos and FARC leader Timochenko signed a new accord in November 2016 despite objections that derailed the original deal.[110]

A transitional justice mechanism was established: the Special Jurisdiction for Peace.

Ivan Duque, supported by Uribe, was elected president in August 2018. He promised to modify (though not abolish) the FARC agreement.[111] More than 700 community leaders were killed from the beginning of 2016 to June 2019. *Most of those murders took place in regions that the FARC had controlled but abandoned when it disarmed.*[112]

The United States requested the extradition of a senior FARC leader for drug traffic. In August 2019, Ivan Márquez, FARC leader of the negotiation, announced that a "new phase of the armed struggle" was beginning and re-took arms, followed by some of FARC's former members.[113] Still, more than 5,000 former FARC members demobilized after the 2016 peace agreement.[114]

The Office of the Prosecutor 2019 Report on Preliminary Examination indicated that the Colombian authorities had made progress in conducting national proceedings.

Notes

1. According to the government of Colombia's Presidential Human Rights Program, the number of civilians killed over the period 2003–2010 amounts to 3,166, including killings of Indigenous persons, trade unionists, teachers, local authorities and civilians killed in massacres. Non-governmental sources estimate that approximately 6,040 civilians have been killed in the context of the armed conflict from 2003 until 2009. *Base de datos sobre Conflicto Armado Colombiano*, CENTRO DE RECURSOS PARA EL ANÁLISIS DE CONFLICTOS, http://www.cerac.org.co/es/recursos/datosconflictoscolom bia/ (last visited July 3, 2012). Office of the Prosecutor, *Situation in Colombia Interim Report*, ICC (Nov. 14, 2012), https://www.icc-cpi.int/NR/rdonlyres/3D3055BD-16E2-4C83-BA85-35BCFD2A7922/285102/OTPCOLOMBIAPublicInterimReportNovem ber2012.pdf.

2. ANGEL RABASA & PETER CHALK, COLOMBIAN LABYRINTH 71 (Online ed. 2001).

3. Nelson Camilo Sánchez León, *Acceptance of International Criminal Justice: Country Study on Colombia, in* AFTER NUREMBERG. EXPLORING MULTIPLE DIMENSIONS OF THE ACCEPTANCE OF INTERNATIONAL CRIMINAL JUSTICE (Susanne Buckeley-Zistel, Friederike Mieth, & Marjana Papa eds., 2016).

4. Office of the Prosecutor, *Report on Preliminary Examination Activities (2011)*, ICC (Dec. 13, 2011), https://www.icc-cpi.int/NR/rdonlyres/63682F4E-49C8-445D-8C13-F310A4F3AEC2/284116/OTPReportonPreliminaryExaminations13December2 011.pdf.

5. ANGEL RABASA & PETER CHALK, COLOMBIAN LABYRINTH 72 (Online ed., 2001).

6. The People's Liberation Army (EPL), the Quintín Lame Group, and the Revolutionary Workers' Party (PRT). *Id.*

7. *Id.* at 73.

8. Ley 418 de diciembre 26 de 1997 [Colom.].

9. Redacción el Tiempo, *Comienza el Proceso Más Solido de Paz*, EL TIEMPO (July 1, 1998), https://www.eltiempo.com/archivo/documento/MAM-816790.

10. VIRGINIA MARIE BOUVIER, COLOMBIA BUILDING PEACE IN A TIME OF WAR (Kindle ed. 2009).

11. *Remarks by President Clinton and President Andres Pastrana of Colombia at Arrival Ceremony*, WHITE HOUSE (Oct. 28, 1998), https://clintonwhitehouse4.archives.gov/textonly/WH/New/html/19981028-12229.html.

12. Diana Jean Schemo, *Colombia Installs New President Who Plans to Talk to Rebels*, N.Y. TIMES (Aug. 8, 1998), https://www.nytimes.com/1998/08/08/world/colombia-insta lls-new-president-who-plans-to-talk-to-rebels.html.

13. *Id.*

14. Hum. Rts. Watch, COLOMBIA: The Ties That Bind: Colombia and Military-Paramilitary Links (Vol. 12, No. 1 (B) (2000).

15. Marc Lacey, *Clinton Defends Colombia Outlay*, N.Y. TIMES (Aug. 31, 2000), https://www.nytimes.com/2000/08/31/world/clinton-defends-colombia-outlay.html.

16. On August 22, President Clinton waived the remaining six conditions even as American officials admitted that Colombia's military maintained ties to paramilitary groups, had failed to suspend or prosecute implicated officers, and refused to enforce civilian jurisdiction over human rights crimes. "You don't hold up the major objective to achieve the minor," said a spokesperson for the office of White House adviser and drug czar Gen. (Ret.) Barry McCaffrey. Implementing Plan Colombia: The US Role, Hearing of the H.R. Before the Subcomm. on the Western Hemisphere of the Comm. on Int'l Relations of the H.R., 106th Cong. 188 (2000).

17. The idea presented in 1962 was to create proxy forces to eliminate communists "in the event the Colombian internal security system deteriorates further." Headquarters, US Army Special Warfare School, "Subject: Visit to Colombia, South America, by a team from Special Warfare Center, Fort Bragg, North Carolina, 26 February 1962." Kennedy Library, Box 319, National Security Files, Special Group; Fort Bragg Team; Visit to Colombia; 3/62. As quoted *in* MICHAEL McCLINTOCK, INSTRUMENTS OF STATECRAFT 222 (Kindle ed. 1992). HUMAN RIGHTS WATCH, COLOMBIA'S KILLER NETWORKS (1996).

18. Implementing Plan Colombia: The U.S. Role, Hearing of the H.R. Before the Subcomm. on the Western Hemisphere of the Comm. on Int'l Relations of the H.R., 106th Cong. 188 (2000).

19. *Id.*

20. ANGEL RABASA & PETER CHALK, COLOMBIAN LABYRINTH 77 (Online ed. 2001).

21. Juan Carlos Iragorri, *UE Pide Políticas Contra Paras*, EL TIEMPO (Abr. 30, 2001), https://www.eltiempo.com/archivo/documento/MAM-536195.

22. Colin L. Powell, *Designation of the AUC As a Foreign Terrorist Organization*, U.S. DEP'T OF STATE (Sept. 10. 2001), https://2001-2009.state.gov/secretary/former/pow ell/remarks/2001/4852.htm.

23. HUMAN RIGHTS WATCH, THE "SIXTH DIVISION" MILITARY-PARAMILITARY TIES AND U.S. POLICY IN COLOMBIA (2001).

24. THOMAS CAROTHERS, ANDREW O'DONOHUE, DEMOCRACIES DIVIDED 157 (Kindle ed. 2019).

25. Joaquín Roy, Europe: Neither Plan Colombia, nor Peace Process—From Good Intentions to High Frustrations (Miami Eur. Un. Cent., Working Paper Vol. 2, No. 7, 2002), available at https://eulacfoundation.org/en/system/files/Europa%20Neit her%20Plan%20Colombia%2C%20nor%20Peace%20Process%20-%20From%20G ood%20Intentions%20to%20High%20Frustrations.pdf.

26. Council Decision 2016/1711, art. 1, 2016, O.J. (LI 259/3).

27. Courtney Hillebrecht & Alexandra Huneeus, with Sandra Borda, The Judicialization of Peace, 59 HARVARD INT'L L.J. 279, 282 (2018).

28. Id.

29. Senators Jimmy Chamorro Cruz, Luis Elmer Arenas Parra, Nicolás Dieb Maloof Cuse, Francisco Rojas Birry, Alfonso Lizarazo Sánchez, Javier Cáceres Leal, Gustavo Guerra Lemoine, Gentil Escobar, Guillermo Ocampo Ospina, Carlos Eduardo Gómez Sierra. Corte Constitucional [C.C.] [Constitutional Court], Sala Plena, julio 30 2002, Sentencia C-578/02, Gaceta de la Corte Constitucional [G.C.C.] (Colom.)

30. Acto Legislativo Numero 2 de 31 diciembre de 2001 [Colom.].

31. Corte Constitucional [C.C.] [Constitutional Court], Sala Plena, julio 30 2002, Sentencia C-578/02, Gaceta de la Corte Constitucional [G.C.C.] (Colom.).

32. Ley 742 de 5 de junio de 2002 [Colom.].

33. Gustavo Gallon, the Director and founder of the Colombian Commission of Jurists, quoted the Velazquez Rodriguez case decided by the Inter American Human Rights Court, connecting such a decision with the Rome Statute.

34. Corte Constitucional [C.C.] [Constitutional Court], Sala Plena, julio 30 2002, Sentencia C-578/02, Gaceta de la Corte Constitucional [G.C.C.] (Colom.).

35. Juan Forero, Explosions Rattle Colombian Capital During Inaugural, N.Y. TIMES (Aug. 8, 2002), https://www.nytimes.com/2002/08/08/world/explosions-rattle-colombian-capital-during-inaugural.html.

36. Id.

37. Id.

38. Acuerdo de Santa Fe de Ralito Para Contribuir a la Paz de Colombia, July 15, 2003.

39. IACHR Report on the Process of Demobilization in Colombia, OEA/Ser.L/V/II.120 Doc. 60, (Dec.13, 2004).

40. See Report by the United Nations High Commissioner for Human Rights on the human rights situation in Colombia, E/CN.4/2005/10 (Feb. 28, 2005); and Press Release—Colombia: Justice and Peace Law Guarantees Impunity, AMNESTY INT'L (Apr. 26, 2005) https://www.amnesty.org.uk/press-releases/colombia-justice-and-peace-law-guarantees-impunity.

41. Jorge Enrique Gómez Pardo, The Content of Colombian Justice and Peace Law Accomplishes the International Criminal Court Standards, 1 DEBATE INTERAMERICANO 129 (2009).

42. Bibiana Mercado Rivera, CPI Tiene las grabaciones de Ralito, EL TIEMPO (Abr. 3, 2005, 12:00 AM), https://www.eltiempo.com/archivo/documento/MAM-1626547.

43. Office of the Prosecutor, *Situation in Colombia Interim Report*, ICC (Nov. 14, 2012), https://www.icc-cpi.int/NR/rdonlyres/3D3055BD-16E2-4C83-BA85-35BCFD2A7 922/285102/OTPCOLOMBIAPublicInterimReportNovember2012.pdf

44. Redacción el Tiempo, *Corte Penal Pide Cuentas a Colombia*, EL TIEMPO (Mar. 31, 2005, 12:00 AM), https://www.eltiempo.com/archivo/documento/MAM-1631764.

45. *Id.*

46. Redacción el Tiempo, *Paras deben ser procesados por justicia ordinaria: Corte Suprema*, EL TIEMPO (May 7, 2005, 12:00 AM), https://www.eltiempo.com/archivo/documento/MAM-1672937.

47. Jorge Enrique Gómez Pardo, *The Content of Colombian Justice and Peace Law Accomplishes the International Criminal Court Standards*, 1 DEBATE INTERAMERICANO 129 (2009).

48. Alejandro Gómez Velásquez, *The Constitutional Framework for Transitional Justice in Colombia*, 14 OPIN. JURID. UNIV. MEDELLÍN 21 (2015).

49. *Id.*

50. Corte Constitucional [C.C.] [Constitutional Court], Sala Plena, marzo 29, 2000, Sentencia C-370/06, Gaceta de la Corte Constitucional [G.C.C.] (Colom.) y Corte Constitucional [C.C.] [Constitutional Court], Sala Plena, julio 25, 2006, Sentencia C-575/06, Gaceta de la Corte Constitucional [G.C.C.] (Colom.). Alejandro Gómez Velásquez, *The Constitutional Framework for Transitional Justice in Colombia*, 14 OPIN JURID. UNIV. MEDELLÍN 21 (2015).

51. Alejandro Gómez Velásquez, *The Constitutional Framework for Transitional Justice in Colombia*, 14 OPIN JURID. UNIV. MEDELLÍN 21 (2015).

52. Nelson Camilo Sánchez León, *Acceptance of International Criminal Justice: Country Study on Colombia*, in AFTER NUREMBERG. EXPLORING MULTIPLE DIMENSIONS OF THE ACCEPTANCE OF INTERNATIONAL CRIMINAL JUSTICE (Susanne Buckeley-Zistel, Friederike Mieth, & Marjana Papa eds., 2016).

53. Int'l Crisis Group. Ending Colombia's Farc Conflict: Dealing the Right Card Latin America Report N°30 (Mar. 26, 2009).

54. THOMAS CAROTHERS & ANDREW O'DONOHUE, DEMOCRACIES DIVIDED 158 (Kindled ed., Brookings Institution Press, 2019).

55. *Colombia Project*, CENTER FOR INT'L POL'Y, https://web.archive.org/web/2010061 3074559/http://ciponline.org/colombia/farc.htm (last visited Jan. 31, 2021).

56. *Id.*   https://web.archive.org/web/20100613074559/http://ciponline.org/colombia/farc.htm (last visited Jan. 31, 2021).

57. *Id.*

58. *Id.*

59. *Pressure Point: The ICC's Impact on National Justice*, HUM. RTS. WATCH (May 3, 2018), https://www.hrw.org/report/2018/05/03/pressure-point-iccs-impact-national-just ice/lessons-colombia-georgia-guinea-and.

60. After the meeting President Uribe mentioned to the press the possibility of removing the legal obstacle to investigating war crimes. Redacción El Tiempo, *Gobierno quiere que Corte Penal Internacional (CPI) juzgue a criminales de guerra colombianos*, EL TIEMPO (Oct. 18, 2007, 12:00 AM), https://www.eltiempo.com/archivo/documento/CMS-3772834.

61. *Pressure Point: The ICC's Impact on National Justice*, Hum. Rts. Watch (May 3, 2018), https://www.hrw.org/report/2018/05/03/pressure-point-iccs-impact-national-just ice/lessons-colombia-georgia-guinea-and.

62. Office of the Prosecutor, *Situation in Colombia Interim Report*, ICC (Nov. 14, 2012), https://www.icc-cpi.int/NR/rdonlyres/3D3055BD-16E2-4C83-BA85-35BCFD2A7 922/285102/OTPCOLOMBIAPublicInterimReportNovember2012.pdf.

63. Press Release, ICC Prosecutor Visits Colombia, Office of the Prosecutor Press Release ICC-OTP-20080821-PR347 (Aug. 21, 2008), https://www.icc-cpi.int/Pages/item. aspx?name=icc%20prosecutor%20visits%20colombia.

64. Juan Forero, *Venezuela's Chavez Breaks Ties with Colombia*, NPR (Nov 29, 2007, 6:00 AM), https://www.npr.org/templates/story/story.php?storyId=16727300.

65. Renee Montagne & Juan Forero, *FARC Frees Hostages in Deal Brokered by Chavez*, NPR (Jan. 11, 2008), https://www.npr.org/templates/story/story.php?storyId= 18021246.

66. Simon Romero, *Colombian Rebels Free 2 Hostages*, N.Y. Times (Jan. 11, 2008), https:// www.nytimes.com/2008/01/11/world/americas/11colombia.html.

67. *Chavez: Take FARC Off Terror List*, CNN (Jan. 11, 2008, 2:08 AM), http://www.cnn. com/2008/WORLD/americas/01/11/chavez.farc/.

68. Patrick Markey, *Colombians Take to Streets in Huge Anti-FARC March*, Reuters (Feb. 4, 2008, 9:42 PM), https://www.reuters.com/article/us-colombia-hostages/colombi ans-take-to-streets-in-huge-anti-farc-march-idUSN0459656620080205.

69. *FARC Releases Four More Hostages*, Amnesty Int'l (Feb. 28, 2008, 12:00 AM), https://www.amnesty.org/en/latest/news/2008/02/farc-releases-four-more-hosta ges-20080228/.

70. Jeremy McDermott, *How President Alvaro Uribe Changed Colombia*, BBC News (Aug. 4, 2010), https://www.bbc.com/news/world-latin-america-10841425.

71. Hugh Bronstein, *Colombia Says Ecuadorean Killed in Anti-Rebel Raid*, Reuters (Mar. 23, 2008, 11:43 PM) https://www.reuters.com/article/us-colombia-ecuador-idUSN2 329811420080324.

72. Simon Romero, *Settling of Crisis Makes Winners of Andes Nations, While Rebels Lose Ground*, NY. Times (Mar. 9, 2008), https://www.nytimes.com/2008/03/09/world/ americas/09iht-09colombia.10832563.html.

73. Redacción el Tiempo, *Por "patrocinio de genocidas," Colombia denunciará a Hugo Chávez ante la Corte Penal Internacional*, El Tiempo (Mar. 4, 2008, 12:00 AM), https://www.eltiempo.com/archivo/documento/CMS-3985482.

74. Simon Romero, *Settling of Crisis Makes Winners of Andes Nations, While Rebels Lose Ground*, N.Y. Times (Mar. 9, 2008), https://www.nytimes.com/2008/03/09/world/ americas/09colombia.html.

75. Simon Romero & Jeffrey C. McKinley, *Crisis Over Colombian Raid Ends in Handshakes*, N.Y. Times (Mar. 8, 2008), https://www.nytimes.com/2008/03/08/ world/americas/08colombia.html?action=click&module=RelatedCoverage&pgt ype=Article&region=Footer.

76. Aisalla Molina v. Ecuador, Case IP-02, Inter-Am. Comm'n H.R., Report No. 112/10, OEA/Ser.L/V/II.140 Doc. 10 (2010).

77. Simon Romero & Jeffrey C. McKinley, *Crisis Over Colombian Raid Ends in Handshakes*, N.Y. TIMES (Mar. 8, 2008), https://www.nytimes.com/2008/03/08/world/americas/08colombia.html?action=click&module=RelatedCoverage&pgtype=Article&region=Footer.

78. *Id.*

79. Chris Kraul, *15 Hostages Freed as FARC Is Fooled in Cunning Operation*, L.A. TIMES (July 3, 2008, 12:00 AM), https://www.latimes.com/world/la-fg-hostages3-2008jul03-story.html.

80. Sibylla Brodzinsky & Caroline Davies, *Colombia Hostage Rescue: The Audacious Plot That Freed World's Most Famous Captive*, GUARDIAN (July 6, 2008, 00:01 AM), https://www.theguardian.com/world/2008/jul/06/colombia.

81. On November 2011, President Juan Manuel Santos dissolved the DAS, after its former head, Jorge Noguera, was sentenced to jail for 25 years for collaborating with paramilitary death squads. *Colombia's Uribe Calls Off Vote*, BBC NEWS (July 18, 2008, 10:59 PM), http://news.bbc.co.uk/2/hi/americas/7514877.stm.

82. Press Release, ICC Prosecutor Visits Colombia, Office of the Prosecutor, Press Release, ICC -OTP-20080821-PR347 (Aug. 21, 2008).

83. Redacción el Tiempo, *Corte Penal Internacional pide investigar red de las Farc en Suiza*, EL TIMEPO (Sept. 3, 2008, 12:00 AM), https://www.eltiempo.com/archivo/documento/CMS-4498363.

84. Press Release, ICC Prosecutor Visits Colombia, Office of the Prosecutor, Press Release, ICC -OTP-20080821-PR347 (Aug. 21, 2008).

85. Redacción el Timepo, *Fiscal de CPI pide arresto del presidente de Sudán*, EL TIEMPO (July 15, 2008, 12:00 AM), https://www.eltiempo.com/archivo/documento/MAM-3014992.

86. Redacción El Tiempo, *"Impunidad" no habrá, dice Uribe a dudas de Corte Penal Internacional sobre ex "paras" extraditados*, EL TIEMPO (Aug. 15, 2008, 12:00 AM), https://www.eltiempo.com/archivo/documento/CMS-4450195.

87. *Id.*

88. *Colombia President Scraps Spy Agency after Scandals*, BBC NEWS (Nov 1, 2011), https://www.bbc.com/news/world-latin-america-15533091.

89. Redacción el Tiempo, *Mancuso comprometió a nueve oficiales en audiencia*, EL TIEMPO (Nov. 19, 2008), https://www.eltiempo.com/archivo/documento/CMS-4675011.

90. Redacción El Tiempo, *"Aquí no hay nada qué ocultar," dijo Álvaro Uribe ante visita de fiscal de Corte Penal Internacional*, EL TIEMPO (Aug. 25, 2008, 12:00 AM), https://www.eltiempo.com/archivo/documento/CMS-4465838.

91. Redacción el Tiempo, *A verificar si Colombia investiga y juzga a criminales vino fiscal de Corte Penal Internaciona*, EL TIEMPO (Aug. 25, 2008, 12:00 AM), https://www.eltiempo.com/archivo/documento/CMS-4465892.

92. *Presidente Uribe dice que será difícil que sus enemigos lo lleven ante la CPI*, COLOMBIA (Aug. 26, 2008), https://www.colombia.com/actualidad/autonoticias/nacionales/2008/08/26/detallenoticia33824.asp.

93. Office of the Prosecutor, *Situation in Colombia Interim Report*, ICC (Nov. 14, 2012), https://www.icc-cpi.int/NR/rdonlyres/3D3055BD-16E2-4C83-BA85-35BCFD2A7 922/285102/OTPCOLOMBIAPublicInterimReportNovember2012.pdf.

94. Amanda Lyons & Michael Reed-Hurtado, *ICTJ Briefing: Colombia: Impact of the Rome Statute and the International Criminal Court*, ICTJ (2010), available at https://www.legal-tools.org/doc/17ec15/pdf/.

95. Office of the Prosecutor, *Situation in Colombia Interim Report*, ICC (Nov. 14, 2012), https://www.icc-cpi.int/NR/rdonlyres/3D3055BD-16E2-4C83-BA85-35BCFD2A7 922/285102/OTPCOLOMBIAPublicInterimReportNovember2012.pdf.

96. Simon Romero, *Venezuela Still Aids Colombia Rebels, New Material Shows*, N.Y. TIMES (Aug. 2, 2009), https://www.nytimes.com/2009/08/03/world/americas/03ve nez.html .

97. Patrick Markey & Andrew Cawthorne, *Colombia's Uribe Blocked from Re-election*, REUTERS (Feb. 26, 2010, 9:22 PM), https://www.reuters.com/article/us-colombia-uribe/colombias-uribe-blocked-from-re-election-idUSTRE61P5PX20100227.

98. *Colombian Judges Deny Alvaro Uribe Third Term Poll*, BBC NEWS (Feb. 27, 2010, 4:222 AM), http://news.bbc.co.uk/2/mobile/americas/8539784.stm#sa-link_locat ion=more-story-3&intlink_from_url=https%3A%2F%2Fwww.bbc.com%2Fn ews%2F10360979&intlink_ts=1595014619479&story_slot=1-sa.

99. Reuters, *Chávez Cuts Ties With Colombia*, N.Y. TIMES (July 22, 2010), https://www. nytimes.com/2010/07/23/world/americas/23venez.html.

100. *Juan Manuel Santos Sworn In as Colombian President*, BBC NEWS (Aug. 8, 2010, 2:21AM), https://www.bbc.co.uk/news/world-latin-america-10904788

101. Simon Romero, *Leaders Repair Colombia-Venezuela Ties*, N.Y. TIMES (Aug. 10, 2010), https://www.nytimes.com/2010/08/11/world/americas/11venez.html.

102. *Colombian Army Kills Top Farc Rebel Leader Mono Jojoy*, BBC NEWS (Sept. 23, 2010), https://www.bbc.com/news/world-latin-america-11399914.

103. *Top Farc Rebel Leader Alfonso Cano Killed in Colombia*, BBC NEWS (Nov 5, 2011), https://www.bbc.com/news/world-15604456

104. Juan Manuel Santos, President of Colombia, Remarks at the 9th Session of the Assembly of States Parties to the Rome Statute of the International Criminal Court, (Dec. 6, 2010).

105. *Through public hearings with the demobilized, we are reaching a judicial truth that would not otherwise have been possible: 44,000 crimes have been confessed, of which 18,000 were homicides. More than 2,800 graves, with more than 3,400 corpses, have been located and exhumed, and 1,100 bodies have been identified and delivered to their families.* Juan Manuel Santos, President of Colombia, Remarks at the 9th Session of the Assembly of States Parties to the Rome Statute of the International Criminal Court (Dec. 6, 2010).

106. Office of the Prosecutor, *Situation in Colombia Interim Report*, ICC (Nov. 14, 2012), https://www.icc-cpi.int/NR/rdonlyres/3D3055BD-16E2-4C83-BA85-35BCFD2A7 922/285102/OTPCOLOMBIAPublicInterimReportNovember2012.pdf.

107. *Id.*

108. Nicholas Casey, *Colombia Signs Peace Agreement With FARC After 5 Decades of War*, N.Y. TIMES (Sept. 26, 2016), https://www.nytimes.com/2016/09/27/world/ameri cas/colombia-farc-peace-agreement.html.

109. *Santos Will Meet Uribe and Pastrana to Talk FARC Peace*, DW (Oct. 5, 2016), https://www.dw.com/en/santos-will-meet-uribe-and-pastrana-to-talk-farc-peace/a-35958255.

110. Sibylla Brodzinsky, *Colombia Signs Historic Peace Deal with Farc*, GUARDIAN (Nov. 24, 19:45), https://www.theguardian.com/world/2016/nov/24/colombia-signs-histo ric-peace-deal-with-farc-rebels.

111. *Juan Arredondo, The Slow Death of Colombia's Peace Movement*, ATLANTIC (Dec. 30, 2019), https://www.theatlantic.com/international/archive/2019/12/colombia-peace-farc/604078/.

112. *Id.*

113. *Colombia ex-Farc rebel Iván Márquez Issues Call to Arms*, BBC NEWS (Aug. 29, 2019), https://www.bbc.com/news/world-latin-america-49508411.

114. Kanneth Roth, *Colombia Events of 2019*, HUM. RTS. WATCH, https://www.hrw.org/world-report/2020/country-chapters/colombia# (last visited Jan. 31, 2021).

SECOND PART

Jus ad Curiam and Jus ad Bellum Decisions Adopted by the UN Security Council, the US, and Côte d'Ivoire

15

Jus ad Curiam and *Jus ad Bellum* Decisions
in the Iraq Situation

The chapter analyzes the *jus ad Curiam* and *jus ad Bellum* decisions adopted by the US Congress and the UN Security Council in Iraq. It presents some of the consequences of choosing war over justice.

Saddam Hussein was considered a "friendly" force while combating Iran, but his decision to invade Kuwait in August 1990 transformed him into an *enemy.* The UN Security Council Resolutions on Iraq adopted in 1990 and 1991 were a reaffirmation of the international commitment to stop aggressive wars.

In November of 1998, the US Congress promoted a *jus ad Curiam* decision to create an international criminal tribunal to investigate Saddam Hussein. By 2002, the United States alleged that Saddam Hussein had chemical weapons and would supply them to terrorist groups. Instead of investigating Saddam Hussein as a criminal, the Bush administration announced its intention to intervene militarily in Iraq and remove him from power. The Congress supported the President.

In 2003, the Bush administration failed to obtain UN Security Council's support to use military forces against Iraq. However, the United States circumvented the express UN Security Council rejection and made a *jus ad Bellum* decision supported by the United Kingdom. A coalition also integrated by Australia, Denmark, and other Rome states parties invaded Iraq territory. Saddam Hussein did not have a chemical weapons arsenal, but neither national nor international institutions stopped the military intervention.

The chapter also discusses the second phase of the Iraq conflict: the emergence of an insurgency fueled by the US occupation. The United States decided to remove most Sunni from Iraq's government, particularly from the army and security forces. They were considered a critical part of the

War and Justice in the 21st Century. Luis Moreno Ocampo, Oxford University Press. © Oxford University Press 2022.
DOI: 10.1093/oso/9780197628973.003.0016

"enemy." The United States supported Shia community members, the same religious group that governs Iran, to rule Iraq. Paradoxically, the United States strengthened Iran—one of the United States' "three axes of evil"—influence on Iraq.

The US national institutions, including Congress, the Judiciary, the media, and people voting in the elections, were able to influence some of the *jus in Bello* decisions, particularly the use of "torture" to obtain information. But the *jus ad Bellum* decision adopted on the wrong basis was maintained for decades. The US Congress did not revoke the authorization to intervene. After its initial opposition to the US military intervention in 2003, the UN Security Council adjusted to the post-invasion situation, focused on humanitarian assistance, and ended up recognizing the occupation.

The Abu Ghraib scandal exposed the lack of international or national legal protection for Iraqis under occupation. Multiple legal systems were interacting, and the *jus ad Bellum* decision imposed the US rules of engagement and excluded the Iraq legal protection to its citizens. COIN, a new US counterinsurgency concept developed in 2006, was tested in Iraq in 2007; it had a short-term impact in reducing violence but did not eliminate the insurgency. The US rules of engagement allowed the possibility to use lethal military force in a country that was not at war with the United States. A video leaked by soldier Manning showing a US Apache helicopter shooting people in a Baghdad square confirmed that the United States, the occupying force, did not protect Iraqis from US operations.[1]

The military intervention in Iraq produced thousands of killings and millions displaced and favored the Islamic state's (ISIS) appearance. Former members of the Hussein regime defeated in the conventional war became insurgents, were involved in creating the Islamic state (ISIS) in Iraq, and later in Syria receiving Sunni support. ISIS perpetrated genocide against Yazidi and Christian minorities in Iraq. It also spread violence into Syria and other places, destabilized the entire region, and contributed to the biggest refugee crisis in humanity's history.

This chapter and the following Chapter 16 suggest that the direct US military intervention in Iraq and then in Syria, exposing its personnel to criminal investigations, prevented UN Security Council from referring those situations to the ICC. The depletion of the US Armed Forces foreclosed the possibility of impartial investigations. States parties should be aware of that impact on their efforts to promote international criminal justice.

Jus ad Bellum and Jus in Bello Decisions in Iraq

Saddam Hussein as a Close Friend to the United States

In his State of the Union speech in January 2002, President Bush announced a different phase in the war on terror identifying North Korea, Iran, and Iraq as the axis of evil.[2] President Bush highlighted that Saddam Hussein "had been hiding a biological weapons program that included anthrax and botulinum toxin" and "forced the UN weapons inspectors to leave the country."[3] The decision to focus on Iraq did not have a relation with the September 11 Al Qaeda attack. Already in November 2001, the Joint Intelligence Committee (JIC) assessed that Iraq had played no role in the 9/11 attacks and that practical cooperation between Iraq and Al Qaeda was "unlikely."[4]

Saddam Hussein Was a US Friend

Until 1990, Saddam Hussein was a friend against Iran, the US enemy, and his crimes against Iraqi citizens were denied. In 1988, after clear evidence that Saddam Hussein used chemical weapons against Iran and gassed and executed some 100,000 Kurds, the United States doubled its credits to Iraq.[5] In 1990 a congressional delegation visited Iraq and declared Hussein "a leader with whom the United States could work."[6] Secretary of State George Shultz considered the US' friendly strategy regarding Iraq "a limited form of balance-of-power policy."[7]

On July 25, 1990, Saddam Hussein was ready to invade Kuwait. He met with the US ambassador to Baghdad, April Glaspie, who told him: "[W]e have no opinion on the Arab-Arab conflicts, like your border disagreement with Kuwait." She encouraged Saddam Hussein to use diplomatic methods and to find a solution quickly.[8]

As tested in Munich in 1939, when the United Kingdom and France tried to appease Hitler, Saddam Hussein perceived negotiations as a green light for his military plans. A week later, Iraq invaded Kuwait, marking the end of Saddam Hussein's friendship with the United States.

An Efficient UN Security Council When There Is Consensus

Saddam Hussein's actions provided an opportunity for the Security Council members to collaborate. On November 29, 1990, Resolution 678/90 authorized it to "use all necessary means" to free Kuwait. There were twelve positive votes, including the Soviet Union. China abstained, and Yemen and Cuba voted negatively. There was no discussion on sovereignty. Kuwait's ambassador had requested the intervention of the Security Council to protect his country. The Soviet Foreign Minister Shevardnadze stated: "The fact that today we respond to these challenges in a different way than we did yesterday is extremely important. We give preference to the law, to acts based on the UN Charter."[9]

A military coalition led by the United States defeated Iraq troops in Kuwait, but it had no Security Council mandate to oust Hussein and did not march to Baghdad. Hussein's regime survived, but the council established a series of measures, including disclosing and dismantling Iraq weapons of mass destruction programs.[10]

After the end of the Gulf War and in agreement with Shevardnadze, President George H. W. Bush stated: "[w]e can see a new world coming into view. A world where there is the very real prospect of a new world order."[11] But he did not propose a new legal architecture.

Colin Powell, the Armed Forces' chief of staff during the conflict, explained that continuing the war and invading Iraq after the Gulf War had no purpose. *It would require deploying major occupation forces for years and a very expensive American pro-consulship in Baghdad.* He concluded: "Fortunately for America, reasonable people at the time thought not. They still do."[12] By 2003, the US administration had forgotten such a lesson.

Treating Hussein as a Criminal

During the war, the idea to prosecute the Iraqi leader was mentioned. "In October 1990, President George H.W. Bush, with the image of Iraqi despot Saddam Hussein as Hitler in mind, had twice threatened Saddam with another Nuremberg."[13]

After winning the war and pushing Iraqi forces back within their borders, the idea of a *jus ad Curiam* decision organizing a justice system to investigate Saddam's crimes was proposed again. During its summit in Luxembourg in April 1991, the European Community proposed to the UN secretary-general, to establish an international court to hold Saddam Hussein "personally responsible for genocide and war crimes."[14]

By October 1998, the US Congress adopted a *jus ad Curiam* decision, not a *jus ad Bellum*, to deal with Iraq's situation. Congress proposed to create an International War Crimes Tribunal for Iraq: "the Congress urges the President to call upon the United Nations to establish an international criminal tribunal for the purpose of indicting, prosecuting, and imprisoning Saddam Hussein and other Iraqi officials who are responsible for crimes against humanity, genocide, and other criminal violations of international law."[15] Congress made very clear that "Nothing in this Act shall be construed to authorize . . . the use of US Armed Forces."[16]

The idea did not flourish. The Rome Statute had been adopted four months earlier, but there were no serious attempts to use it in Iraq. In the years to come, Hussein's regime conflicts with the Gulf countries, Israel, and Kurds, Shias, and other national groups did not disappear.

President Bush *Jus ad Bellum* Decision

In November 2001, President George W. Bush invoked the previous *jus ad Curiam* decision adopted by Congress to adopt a *jus ad Bellum* decision on Iraq. He explained that the regime change in Iraq was a strategy already adopted by the US Congress in 1998 at President Clinton's request without mentioning that Congress expressly rejected using the US Armed Forces.[17] President Bush explained his war approach as part of his diplomacy: "My first choice was to use diplomacy. Two months after 9/11, I asked Don Rumsfeld to review the existing battle plans for Iraq. We needed to develop the coercive half of coercive diplomacy."[18]

President Bush tried to redefine the UN Charter concept of self-defense and explained his "pre-emptive action" strategy: "The lesson of 9/11 was that if we waited for a danger to fully materialize, we would have waited too long."[19] Condoleeza Rice made the point very clear: "We don't want the smoking gun to be a mushroom cloud."[20]

UN Security Council Controlling the Bush Administration Plans to Intervene in Iraq

In September 2002 and following an agreement with the United Kingdom, President Bush addressed the UN General Assembly proposing to use the military to enforce the UN Security Resolutions adopted in 1990 ordering Saddam Hussein's regime's disarmament. He challenged the other members of the council to respond to Iraq's noncompliance, asking: "Are Security Council resolutions to be honored and enforced, or cast aside without consequence? Will, the United Nations, serve the purpose of its founding, or will it be irrelevant?"[21] He was very open to act unilaterally if needed.[22]

The following month the US Congress supported President Bush by adopting a *jus ad Bellum* decision passing the "Authorization for Use of Military Force Against Iraq Resolution of 2002" (October 16, 2002).[23] The goals were to defend the United States' national security against Iraq's continuing threat and enforce all relevant UN Security Council resolutions regarding Iraq. The congressional decision received bipartisan support and assumed that "Iraq had large stockpiles of chemical weapons and a large-scale biological weapons programs."[24]

On November 8, 2002, the UN Security Council Resolution 1441[25] was adopted by consensus demanding Iraq's compliance with previous resolutions related to disarmament and establishing an ultimatum. The US permanent representative, John Negroponte, stated the council decided "to afford Iraq a final opportunity to comply."[26]

The French, Russian, and Chinese representatives expressed their support to the resolution despite their opposition to any military intervention.[27] The United Kingdom perceived the resolution as a significant success for its strategy to influence President Bush's plans.

Following President Bush's instructions in February 2003, US Secretary of State Colin Powell tried to convince the council to authorize military intervention. He presented satellite photographs, audio intercepts, and intelligence information during a ministerial-level meeting of the UN Security Council to prove that Iraq was still engaged in the production of weapons of mass destruction.[28]

Powell did not convince the other UN Security Council permanent members. "To what extent did the nature and scope of the threat justify the recourse to force?," asked France's minister of foreign affairs and suggested that the answer, "obviously, required a collective responsibility on the part of the world community."[29] Russia and China also opposed the initiative.

On February 24, 2003, the United States, the United Kingdom, and Spain[30] circulated a draft resolution calling on the Security Council to declare Iraq in material breach of its obligations to disclose its programs and authorize military action against Iraq. President Bush was personally making calls to Mexico and Chile's presidents to obtain their support.[31] The majority of the council members opposed the initiative. There was no need for a French veto. The draft resolution did not receive enough support from nine council members and was not adopted.[32]

In the meantime, the Blair government insisted on providing legal foundations for an Iraq intervention. For months, British Foreign Office experts led by Elizabeth Wilmshurst, the UK Foreign Office deputy legal adviser, discussed the legality of the military intervention in Iraq. They considered that an invasion would be contrary to international law in the absence of a new Security Council resolution.

On March 2, Lord Goldsmith, the United Kingdom's attorney general, produced a lengthy legal opinion arguing that a case could be made for war without a second resolution. He warned, however, that it could be seriously open to legal challenge. The political decision was made, and on March 13, the United Kingdom's attorney general informed the UK ministers that war without a second UN resolution was legal.

On March 17, 2003, Ambassador John Negroponte withdrew the second resolution at the UN. The United States ignored the rejection of the council's majority and decided to bypass the UN Security Council adopting Lord Goldsmith's arguments. It considered that in 2002 Iraq was in "material breach" of the ceasefire conditions *"reviving"* the prior authorization to use force. Consequently, an Iraq intervention in 2003 was a collective defense exercise already authorized by the UN Security Council Resolution 678 adopted in 1990.[33]

That night, President Bush addressed the nation from the White House. "The United Nations Security Council has not lived up to its responsibilities, so we will rise to ours. . . . Saddam Hussein and his sons must leave Iraq within forty-eight hours. Their refusal to do so will result in military conflict, commenced at a time of our choosing."[34]

In the same week, Elizabeth Wilmshurst interviewed me for the ICC Chief Prosecutor position, the military intervention led by the United States started in Iraq, and she resigned.[35]

On March 20, 2003, the United States sent a letter (S/2003/351) to the council notifying it that coalition forces had "commenced military operations in Iraq." According to the letter, the "actions being taken are authorized under existing Council resolutions, including its resolutions 678 (1990) and 687 (1991)."[36]

On March 26 and 27, 2003, the Security Council met, in response to requests from the League of the Arab States and the Non-Aligned Movement, protesting for the military intervention in Iraq. Sixty-eight UN member states participated in the debate, but a divided council could not adopt a formal decision.[37]

The Iraq Military Intervention

The "coalition of the willing" participating in Iraq's 2003 intervention took a few weeks to defeat the Iraq army.

On May 1, 2003, President Bush made a speech from the Lincoln, a military air carrier, announcing "Major combat operations in Iraq have ended. . . . The transition from dictatorship to democracy will take time, but it is worth every effort. Our coalition will stay until our work is done. Then we will leave, and we will leave behind a free Iraq."[38]

The conventional war was successful, Saddam Hussein's regime ended, and the international coalition led by the United States controlled the Iraq territory. However, the *jus ad Bellum* decision to intervene militarily lost legitimacy when it was found, contrary to the Bush administration's assertion, that Iraq did not possess an active stockpile of chemical weapons.

The 2006 US National Defense Strategy recognized "that pre-war intelligence estimates of Iraqi WMD stockpiles were wrong . . . We must learn from this experience if we are to counter successfully the very real threat of proliferation."[39] Still, the 2002 Congress *jus ad Bellum* decision was never reviewed.

The UN Security Council could not control the jus ad Bellum decision adopted by the United States and United Kingdom.

The UN Security Council could not confront the United States and United Kingdom, two permanent members with veto power. It accepted their intervention in Iraq as a fact, considered them occupying forces, and moved forward, focusing on its humanitarian assistance efforts.

Ten days after the beginning of the Iraq intervention, the UN Security Council adopted unanimously Resolution 1473 (2003). It gave Secretary-General Kofi Annan more authority to administer the "oil-for-food" program's humanitarian assistance.

The US representative welcomed the council's strong support for the text. The Russian and Syrian ambassadors stressed that such consent was not intended to legitimize the military intervention without the council's authorization. Russia highlighted that under the Fourth Geneva Convention, the occupying power was responsible for meeting civilians' humanitarian needs.

Similarly, but less confrontative, French Permanent Representative De La Sabliere considered it important that the Iraqi people received the necessary food and medicine. He highlighted that the text recalled the principles of international law and international humanitarian law.

In April, the council expanded the authorization to facilitate humanitarian assistance, and in May 2003, the council moved a step forward. It decided to lift the trade and financial sanctions on Iraq, extended the "oil-for-food" program for six months, and requested the appointment of a special representative of the UN Secretary-General.[40]

The Authority (the occupying Powers under unified command) and the special representative of the UN Secretary-General will be responsible until the people of Iraq elected a government internationally recognized.[41]

Kofi Annan agreed to appoint a special representative to coordinate the post-conflict processes in Iraq. "Whatever differences there have been in the recent past, we now have a new basis on which to work." He defined the goal to be "that the people of Iraq form a free and representative Government of their own choice."[42]

A few days later, Annan appointed Sergio Vieira de Mello as his special representative. Sergio called me to insist on his commitment to work together. He was confident of achieving quick results and that Iraqis would perceive the difference between the UN personnel and occupying forces.

On July 22, 2003, Sergio Vieira de Mello briefed the council for the first time. He was accompanied by three members of the new Governing Council of Iraq. He highlighted the relevance of a millennial Iraq civilization and made clear that he was working to achieve *as soon as possible the full restoration of Iraq's full sovereignty.*"[43]

Sergio knew that his life was at risk. He told the council: "There have been virtually daily attacks on coalition forces." He was a true believer in the UN's impartial role. "Our security continues to rely significantly on the reputation of the United Nations."[44] But the UN's reputation did not protect Sergio: he and twenty-two colleagues were killed just two months later in Baghdad.

UN participation ended up providing legitimacy to the occupation. The *jus ad Bellum* decision adopted by the United States and the United Kingdom based on wrong assumptions and opposed by the council majority was consolidated.

Two months after the attack against the UN, on October 16, 2003, Council Resolution 1511 adopted unanimously, recognized the Coalition Provisional Authority "until an internationally recognized, representative government established by the people of Iraq is sworn in and assumes the responsibilities of the Authority."[45]

Since then, the UN Security Council has extended the Coalition Provisional Authority's mandate at the Iraqi government's request. But in late 2007, Iraq's Prime Minister Maliki asked the Security Council to extend the mandate "for the last time."[46]

Consequently, to protect its personnel from the Iraq justice system, the United States needed a Status of Force Agreement (SOFA) before the end of 2008 and had to embark on a complex negotiation with the Iraq provisional government.[47]

The Transition from Iraq's Dictatorship

The Aftermath

Iraq's post-invasion situation was more complicated than the US plans envisioned. Iraq's insurgency was fueled by the US provisional government decisions to dismantle Saddam Hussein's intelligence, security, and armed forces, and the official Baath Party.

Paul Bremmer III, a US diplomat, arrived in Baghdad on May 12, 2003, and became the supreme authority in Iraq. Four days later, and following the Department of Defense instructions, he issued Order 1, "De-Baathification of Iraqi Society," excluding from public office all the Baath "senior party members" and all the "three highest levels of management positions."[48]

Following a war approach, instead of analyzing individuals' responsibilities, Sunnis public officers were considered *enemies* to be removed. Members of the Shia community, the same religious group that controls Iran, took control of the Governing Council of Iraq and made sectarian decisions, further marginalizing Sunnis.

As a consequence, the Sunni insurgency continued escalating. Bremmer recognized, "The implementation is where I went wrong . . . The mistake I made was turning it over to the Governing Council. I should have turned it over instead to a judicial body of some kind."[49] A justice mechanism could have been more effective.

In his memoirs, President Bush recognized that the Sunnis' removal was a counterproductive measure: "Many Sunnis took them as a signal they would have no place in Iraq's future. This was especially dangerous in the case of the army. Thousands of armed men had just been told they were not wanted.

Instead of signing up for the new military, many joined the insurgency."[50] Some of Hussein's dismissed officers became involved in Al Qaeda's establishment in Iraq that later became ISIS.

Jus in Bello in Iraq

The Abu Ghraib scandal exposing US forces' misbehavior was another factor that promoted insurgency. A Carr Center study considered that the mistreatment of detainees was "the single most important motivating factor" in persuading foreign jihadists to join the war.[51] It mentioned 250 people arrested in Saudi Arabia attempting to leave the country to join extremist groups.[52] It also signaled twenty-six martyrdom videos in which the suicide bombers quote torture at Abu Ghraib as the motivation for their attacks.[53]

General McChrystal acknowledged, "The thing that hurt us more than anything else in the war in Iraq was Abu Ghraib." He continued: "The Iraqi people . . . felt it was proof positive that the Americans were doing exactly what Saddam Hussein had done—that it was proof [that] everything they thought bad about the Americans was true."[54]

Senator McCain reached a similar conclusion in 2008 when he asked a captured senior Al Qaeda leader what had allowed the group to establish a foothold in Iraq. "Two things," the prisoner replied, according to a State Department cable. "The chaos after the success of the initial invasion, and the greatest recruiting tool: Abu Ghraib."[55]

The Abu Ghraib scandal coincided with Saddam Hussein's capture in December 2003. He was finally prosecuted before Iraq's national courts for crimes committed in July 1982 in the Shia town of Dujail, where he ordered the execution of 148 residents for attacking his motorcade. He was convicted and hanged in December 2006. Another case against him for genocide against Iraqi Kurds allegedly committed at the end of the 1980s did not finish.[56] Both cases could have been prosecuted in 1991.

The Adoption of COIN

The counterinsurgency phase of the Iraq conflict became more and more challenging. There was an increasing number of deaths of civilians and combatants and rising tensions between Iraqi communities.

The only new strategy was counterinsurgency (COIN), developed in 2006 by the US Army and Marines, led by General David Petraeus and Marine General James Mattis. They were frustrated by "the poor management of the situation in Iraq post-invasion.... The core to their message was that this was an essentially political undertaking. The military role was to gain popular support for the government."[57]

The counterinsurgency (COIN) manual adopted considers that "Soldiers and Marines are expected to be nation builders as well as warriors. They must be able to facilitate establishing local governance and the rule of law."[58]

The manual was inspired by David Galula, a French colonel with experience in Algeria's colonial war.[59] A film called *The Battle of Algiers*, released in 1966, exposed how the French occupation of Argelia fueled the national insurgency. But the United States still considered itself as a liberation force and did not grasp the lesson of other colonial interventions.

The US Change on Iraq

In 2006 the US democracy made a judgment on the Iraq War. "The Democrats, by now almost unanimously critical of the war, won a sweeping victory."[60] A report promoted by Congress "recommended that the American military switch from fighting the insurgency to training Iraqi troops to do this and that all American combat forces be withdrawn by the first quarter of 2008."[61]

At the beginning of 2007, President Bush changed the military strategy but not in Congress's direction. Instead, he increased the number of US soldiers in Iraq, replaced the secretary of defense, and made General David Petraeus the commander of American forces in Iraq, with a mandate to implement a policy of counterinsurgency (COIN).[62]

Under the Petraeus command, "the troops made common cause with local tribal militias, helped provide security to the people living in the region, drove out the terrorist interlopers, and brought a semblance of peace to what had been the most violent part of the country."[63] "The increase in troop strength and the new strategy the troops carried out also received a distinctive title—"the surge"—and the surge achieved its principal goal: the violence in the capital and the western part of the country dropped sharply."[64]

The Apache Helicopter Shooting in Baghdad

In any case, the difficulties of defending the local population were exposed by a Baghdad incident during the "surge." On July 12, 2007, Saleh Mutasher, an Iraq citizen, was driving his car to visit his brother; his two young children were with him. Saleh Mutasher saw a bleeding man crawling on the street and stopped the vehicle to help him. With the assistance of a person walking in the neighborhood, Saleh Mutasher carried the wounded man into his car to go to the hospital.

Saeed Chmagh, the bleeding man, worked for Reuter and was injured a few minutes before by US soldiers shooting from an Apache military helicopter. The US soldiers confused Saeed Chmag with an *enemy combatant* terrorist. The US soldiers followed the rules and did not shoot against Chmag when he crawled on the street because he had no weapons. However, the soldiers mistakenly assumed that because Saleh Mutasher was trying to help Saeed Chmagh, he was also an *enemy combatant* trying to recover weapons and wounded comrades.

The Apache helicopter crew requested permission to engage to stop what it considered an enemy military operation of recovering weapons, received authorization from their authorities, and opened fire. Saleh Mutasher and Saeed Chmagh were killed. Saleh's children were severely wounded and were rescued and evacuated to a hospital by US soldiers arriving at the scene a few minutes later.

When a member of the Apache crew saw the wounded Saleh's daughter in the arms of the US soldier, he realized the impact of their intervention and commented: "Well, it's their fault for bringing their kids to a battle."[65] The US soldier believed that he was operating on a battlefield *abroad* in denial that Baghdad was *home* for Saleh Mutasher.[66]

The US legal system did not protect civilians attacked by US troops in foreign countries. The Coalition Provisional Authority issued Order 17, establishing "that all personnel of the multinational force (MNF) and the CPA, and all International Consultants, are immune from Iraqi legal process, and are subject to the exclusive jurisdiction of their 'Sending States.'"[67] Consequently, US soldiers operating in Iraq were under US exclusive jurisdiction, and Iraq criminal law did not protect civilians affected by US soldiers in Iraq. The victims had no rights before US troops.

The United States conducted a military investigation and concluded that the Apache helicopter intervention followed the rules of engagement. After the insistent demands from Reuter, the video's leaked by Private Manning, and the Apache helicopter video's exposure by Wikileaks, the United States recognized the mistake and authorized to pay compensation to Saleh Mutasher's family.[68]

The US soldiers in the helicopter were not charged. The video shows that the soldiers made a mistake. They assumed that the victims were enemy combatants who could be killed according to the law of war. Under the US rules of engagement, the Apache soldiers did not commit a war crime. Still, they killed for no reason Iraqi civilians.

Jack Goldsmith published a fascinating book presenting how the US constitutional system provides forms of control that "preserve the framers' original idea of a balanced constitution with an executive branch that, despite its enormous power, remains legally and politically accountable to law and to the American people."[69]

In my view, the crucial problem is not about the limited ability of the national institutions to control *jus in Bello* decisions. Instead, there is no real control of the *jus ad Bellum* decisions. They were adopted in 2001 and 2002 by Congress without temporal limits. There are no institutions or enough citizen interest to protect aliens living in foreign countries victims of such *jus ad Bellum* decisions.

After the shooting in Baghdad, the Apache helicopter's personnel returned to their base for dinner on time to watch President Bush's press conference, which had begun in Washington just a few minutes before. "Our top priority is to help the Iraqis protect their population," President Bush was saying.[70]

Satar Mustashar, Saleh's brother, had a different perception of the US role in Iraq. He was interviewed by a Dutch filmmaker a year later and concluded: "If I ever see an American, I will kill him and drink his blood, that will give me comfort."[71] He was one of the Iraqis that President Bush aimed to protect, and he was transformed into an enemy.

The Consequences of the *Jus ad Bellum* Decision

The insurgency grew. "The de-Baathification law promulgated by L. Paul Bremer, Iraq's American ruler in 2003, has long been identified as one of the contributors to the original insurgency."[72] Former Saddam regime officers were involved in developing the Islamic state and became the leaders of its most crucial sectors: security, military, and finance.[73] They also have brought the smuggling networks designed to avoid sanctions in the 1990s, facilitating the Islamic state's illicit oil trade.[74]

The Iraq War was expanded to Syria. Between January and March 2011, a conflict started in Syria that "soon became a sectarian war, with the majority Sunnis fighting to overthrow" Assad, a Shia supported by Iran.[75]

Notes

1. *U.S. Security Agreements and Iraq*, COUNCIL ON FOREIGN RELATIONS (DEC. 23, 2008), https://www.cfr.org/backgrounder/us-security-agreements-and-iraq.
2. George W. Bush, 43rd President of the United States of America, State of the Union Address at the United States Capitol (Jan. 29, 2002).
3. GEORGE W. BUSH, DECISION POINTS 227 (Kindle ed. 2010).
4. The Report of the Iraq Inquiry Executive Summary, Report of a Committee of Privy Counsellors, Ordered by the House of Commons to be printed on 6 July 2016. Jemima Kiss, *Reuters Staff Killed in Iran*, GUARDIAN (July 12, 2007, 5:37 PM), https://www.theguardian.com/media/2007/jul/12/reuters.pressandpublishing.
5. Between 1983 and 1988, the United States had supplied Iraq with more than $500 million per year in credits to purchase American farm products under a program called the Commodity Credit Corporation (CCC). The program hiked annual CCC credits above $1 billion." SAMANTHA POWER, A PROBLEM FROM HELL 3870 (Kindle ed. 2013).
6. *Id.*
7. "The United States was aghast at the prospect of Iraqi oil reserves falling into the Ayatollah Khomeini's hands; it feared that radical Islam would destabilize the pro-American governments in Saudi Arabia and the Gulf emirates. Thus, with each Iranian battlefield victory, the United States inched closer to Iraq." *Id.*
8. *Confrontation in the Gulf Excerpts from Iraqi Document on Meetings with U.S. Envoy*, NY TIMES (Sept. 23, 1990), https://www.nytimes.com/1990/09/23/world/confrontation-in-the-gulf-excerpts-from-iraqi-document-on-meeting-with-us-envoy.html?pagewanted=7&src=pm/.
9. DAVID BOSCO, FIVE TO RULE THEM ALL 162 (1st. ed. 2009).
10. S.C. Res. 687, U.N. Doc S/RES/687 (Apr. 3, 1991).
11. "A world where the United Nations, freed from Cold War stalemate, is poised to fulfill the historic vision of its founders. A world in which freedom and respect for human rights find a home among nations." DAVID BOSCO, FIVE TO RULE THEM ALL 165 (1st. ed. 2009).
12. Colin L. Powell, *U.S. Forces: Challenges Ahead*, Winter 1992/1993 FOREIGN AFFAIRS (1993).
13. GARY JONATHAN BASS, STAY THE HAND OF VENGEANCE 206 (Kindle ed., Princeton Studies in International History and Politics, 2000).
14. "My twelve Community colleagues have asked me to address myself to you, so that you examine the question of personal responsibility of the Iraqi leaders in the tragedy

that is unfolding, in particular on the basis notably of the Convention to Prevent Genocide, and the possibility of trying them before an international court." PIERRE HAZAN, JUSTICE IN A TIME OF WAR: THE TRUE STORY BEHIND THE INTERNATIONAL CRIMINAL TRIBUNAL FOR THE FORMER YUGOSLAVIA 287 (Kindle ed., James Thomas Snyder trans., 2004).

15. Iraq Liberation Act of 1998, H.R. Rep. 4655-338, 105th Congress § 6 (1998).
16. Rule of Construction. "Nothing in this Act shall be construed to authorize or otherwise speak to the use of United States Armed Forces (except as provided in section 4(a)(2)) in carrying out this Act." *Iraq Liberation Act of 1998, H.R. Rep. 4655-338*, 105th Congress § 8 (1998).
17. GEORGE W. BUSH, DECISION POINTS 227–28 (Kindle ed. 2010).
18. *Id.* at 229.
19. *Id.* at 229.
20. CONDOLEEZA RICE, NO HIGHER HONOR 198 (Kindle ed. 2011).
21. GEORGE W. BUSH, DECISION POINTS 239 (Kindle ed., 2010).
22. "The Security Council resolutions will be enforced—the just demands of peace and security will be met—or action will be unavoidable. And a regime that has lost its legitimacy will also lose its power." George W. Bush, 43rd President of the United States of America, Remarks at the United Nations General Assembly (Sept. 12, 2002). *See* comment in *Mr Bush Lays Out His Case*, THE ECONOMIST (Sept. 12, 2002), https://www.economist.com/united-states/2002/09/12/mr-bush-lays-out-his-case. CONDOLEEZA RICE, NO HIGHER HONOR 183 (Kindle ed. 2011).
23. *Authorization for use of military force, H.J. Res. 114–243*, 107th Cong. (2002).
24. The Senate passed the resolution 77 to 23. The House passed it 296 to 133. President Bush commented that "Both margins were larger than those of the votes for the Gulf War. The resolution garnered votes from prominent Democrats, including Senators Hillary Clinton, Joe Biden, John Kerry, John Edwards, and Harry Reid." GEORGE W. BUSH, DECISION POINTS 241 (Kindle ed. 2010).
25. S.C. Res. 1441, U.N. Doc. S/RES/1441 (Nov. 8, 2002).
26. U.N. SCOR, 57th Sess., 4644th mtg., at U.N. Doc. S/PV.4644 (Nov. 2, 2002).
27. U.N. SCOR, 57th Sess., 4644th mtg., at U.N. Doc. S/PV.4644 (Nov. 2, 2002).
28. Secretary Powell concluded that "clearly, Saddam Hussein and his regime will stop at nothing until something stops him." Press Release, Security Council, Briefing Security Council, US Secretary of State Powell Presents Evidence of Iraq's Failure to Disarm, U.N. Press Release SC/7658 (Feb. 5, 2003).
29. Press Release, Security Council, Briefing Security Council, US Secretary of State Powell Presents Evidence of Iraq's Failure to Disarm, U.N. Press Release SC/7658 (Feb. 5, 2003).
30. Ashifa Kassam, *Spanish ex-Prime Minister Defends Decision to Back Iraq War*, GUARDIAN (Nov. 2, 2015, 2:38 PM), https://www.theguardian.com/world/2015/nov/02/spain-ex-premier-jose-maria-aznar-iraq-war.
31. GEORGE W. BUSH, DECISION POINTS 246 (Kindle ed. 2010).

32. Press Release, Security Council, Briefing Security Council, US Secretary of State Powell Presents Evidence of Iraq's Failure to Disarm, U.N. Press Release SC/7658 (Feb. 5, 2003).

33. Sean D. Murphy, *Assessing the Legality of Invading Iraq*, 92 GEORGETOWN L.J. 173, 179 (2004).

34. George W. Bush, 43rd President of the United States of America, Remarks by the President in Address to the Nation, The Cross Hall (Mar. 17, 2003).

35. NEIL MACKAY, THE WAR ON TRUTH 226 (1st ed. 2006).

36. THE UNITED NATIONS SECURITY COUNCIL—ITS ROLE IN THE IRAQ CRISIS: A BRIEF OVERVIEW, CONG. RESEARCH SERV. RS21323 6 (May 16, 2003).

37. *Id.*

38. *Bush Makes Historic Speech Aboard Warship*, CNN (May 2, 2003, 01:48), http://edit ion.cnn.com/2003/US/05/01/bush.transcript/.

39. THE WHITE HOUSE, 2006 THE NATIONAL SECURITY STRATEGY OF THE UNITED STATES OF AMERICA (Mar. 16, 2006).

40. Press Release, Security Council Lifts Sanctions on Iraq, Approves UN Role, Calls for Appointment of Secretary-General's Special Representative, U.N. Press Release SC/7765 (May 22, 2003).

41. *Id.*

42. U.N. SCOR 48th Sess., 4761st mtg., at 12, U.N. Doc. S/PV.4761 (May 22, 2003).

43. U.N. SCOR 48th Sess., 4791st mtg., at 3, U.N. Doc. S/PV.4791 (July 22, 2003).

44. "As the Council will be aware, security in Iraq remains tenuous. Too many are losing their lives, on an almost daily basis. It is imperative that security, law and order be restored throughout Iraq as soon as possible. The United Nations presence in Iraq remains vulnerable to any who would seek to target our Organization, as recent events in Mosul—described in the Secretary-General's report—illustrate." *Id.* at 5.

45. U.N. SCOR 48th Sess., 4791st mtg., at 5, U.N. Doc. S/PV.4844 (July 22, 2003).

46. Greg Bruno, *U.S. Security Agreements and Iraq*, COUNCIL ON FOREIGN RELATIONS (Dec. 23, 2008), https://www.cfr.org/backgrounder/us-security-agreements-and-iraq.

47. Greg Bruno, *U.S. Security Agreements and Iraq*, COUNCIL ON FOREIGN RELATIONS (Dec. 23, 2008), https://www.cfr.org/backgrounder/us-security-agreements-and-iraq.

48. MIRANDA SISSONS & ABDULRAZZAQ AL-SAIEDI, A BITTER LEGACY: LESSONS OF DE-BAATHIFI CATION IN IRAQ 11 (2013), https://www.ictj.org/sites/default/files/ICTJ-Report-Iraq-De-Baathification-2013-ENG.pdf.

49. Bremmer explained "that the Baath Party had been one of the primary instruments of Saddam's control and tyranny over the Iraqi people for decades. Saddam Hussein himself openly acknowledged that he modeled the Baath Party on the Nazi Party because he admired the way in which Hitler was able to use the Nazi Party to control the German people. Just as in our occupation of Germany we had passed what were called "de-Nazification decrees" and prosecuted senior Nazi officials, the model for the de-Baathification was to look back at that de-Nazification." L. Paul Bremer, *Key*

Controversies and Missteps of the Postwar Period, PBS (OCT. 17, 2006), https://www.
pbs.org/wgbh/pages/frontline/yeariniraq/analysis/fuel.html#2.

50. GEORGE W. BUSH, DECISION POINTS 259 (Kindle ed. 2010).

51. Douglas A. Johnson, Alberto Mora, & Averell Schmidt, *The Strategic Costs of Torture*,
FOREIGN AFFAIRS, ttps://www.foreignaffairs.com/articles/united-states/strategic-
costs-torture (last visited June 11, 2020).

52. In 2009, a Saudi official echoed when "he concurred with the Obama administration's
decision not to release any more photos of Abu Ghraib, alleging that when the scandal
first broke, Saudi authorities arrested 250 people attempting to leave the country to
join extremist groups." *Id.*

53. *Id.*

54. "According to State Department cables . . . the mistreatment of detainees at Abu
Ghraib and Guantánamo Bay was 'the single most important motivating factor' in
persuading foreign jihadists to join the war." *Id.*

55. *id.*

56. CNN Ed. Research, *Saddam Hussein Trial Fast Facts*, CNN, https://www.cnn.com/
2013/10/30/world/meast/saddam-hussein-trial-fast-facts/index.html (last updated
Mar. 16, 2020 9:03).

57. *Conrad Crane, a professor at the US Army's Strategic Studies Institute, coordinated the
exercise.* LAWRENCE FREEDMAN, THE FUTURE OF WAR 194–95 (Kindle ed. 2017).

58. The U.S. Army and Marine Corps Counterinsurgency Field Manual developed under
the direction of General Petraeus was adopted in 2006. U.S. Army Field Manual No.
3-24 Marine Corps Warfighting Publication No. 3-33.5

59. DAVID GALULA, PACIFICATION IN ALGERIA, 1956–1958 (1st 1963). "To confine
soldiers to purely military functions while urgent and vital tasks have to be done,
and nobody else is available to undertake them, would be senseless. The soldier must
then be prepared to become . . . a social worker, a civil engineer, a schoolteacher, a
nurse, a boy scout." DAVID GALULA, COUNTERINSURGENCY WARFARE: THEORY
AND PRACTICE 62 (New ed. 2006). Argentina's generals also prepared a counter insurgency plan following the concepts developed by four French colonels that spent
time between 1956 and 1960 in the Argentina Military School. The plan was secretly
implemented in 1976 and it was exposed during the "Trial of the Juntas" in 1985.

60. MICHAEL MANDELBAUM, MISSION FAILURE 233–34 (Kindle ed. 2016).

61. *Id.*

62. *Id.* at 235–36.

63. *Id.* at 235–36.

64. *Id.* at 236.

65. DAVID FINKEL, THE GOOD SOLDIERS 1707 (Kindle ed. 2009).

66. *Id.*

67. CPA Order 17, Status of the Coalition Provisional Authority, MNF—Iraq, Certain
Missions and Personnel in Iraq,6 established that all personnel of the multinational
force (MNF) and the CPA, and all International Consultants, are immune from Iraqi
legal process, and are subject to the exclusive jurisdiction of their "Sending States." R.

CHUCK MASON, CON. RESEARCH SERV. R40011, U.S.-IRAQ WITHDRAWAL/STATUS OF FORCES AGREEMENT: ISSUES FOR CONGRESSIONAL OVERSIGHT 2 (2009).

68. DAVID FINKEL, THE GOOD SOLDIERS (Kindle ed. 2009).

69. JACK GOLDSMITH, POWER AND CONSTRAINT: THE ACCOUNTABLE PRESIDENCY AFTER 9/11 xvi (Kindle ed. 2012).

70. DAVID FINKEL, THE GOOD SOLDIERS 1750 (Kindle ed. 2009).

71. PERMISSION TO ENGAGE (Henneke Hagen for VPRO Backlight, VARA, 2011) is a documentary film by Suchen Tan.

72. Liz Sly, *The Hidden Hand Behind the Islamic State Militants? Saddam Hussein's*, WASH. POST (Apr. 4, 2015), https://www.washingtonpost.com/world/middle_east/the-hidden-hand-behind-the-islamic-state-militants-saddam-husseins/2015/04/04/aa976 76c-cc32-11e4-8730-4f473416e759_story.html .

73. Isabel Coles & Ned Parker, *How Saddam's Men Help Islamic State Rule*, REUTERS (Dec. 22, 2015, 10:00 AM), https://www.reuters.com/investigates/special-report/mideast-crisis-iraq-islamicstate/.

74. Liz Sly, *The Hidden Hand Behind the Islamic State Militants? Saddam Hussein's*, WASH. POST (Apr. 4, 2015), https://www.washingtonpost.com/world/middle_east/the-hidden-hand-behind-the-islamic-state-militants-saddam-husseins/2015/04/04/aa976 76c-cc32-11e4-8730-4f473416e759_story.html. *See also* Deborah Amos, *How the Islamic State Smuggles Oil to Fund Its Campaign*, NPR (Sept. 9, 2014 3:42 AM), https://www.npr.org/sections/parallels/2014/09/09/346844240/how-the-islamic-state-smuggles-oil-to-fund-its-campaign.

75. MICHAEL MANDELBAUM, MISSION FAILURE 305–06 (Kindle ed., 2016).

16

The UN Security Council Resolution Referring the Darfur Situation to the ICC

In 2003, our office did not even analyze the crimes allegedly committed in the Darfur situation. It was out of our jurisdiction: Sudan has never been a state party to the Rome Statute. The UN Security Council was the only institution with the authority to provide jurisdiction in Darfur to the ICC.

Still, there was no expectation that the council would achieve a constructive relationship with the court in those days. The American Service Patriot Act forbade any US support for the ICC, and the Bush administration was campaigning against the court. China considered that the ICC intervention could affect Sudan's stability. Both countries had reasons to veto a Darfur referral.

However, in March 2005, the UN Security Council made a *jus ad Curiam* decision and referred the Darfur situation to the ICC. There was not a single decision maker. As Tolstoy said, *the people who participate in the events* made the difference.

A variety of activists, motivated for different reasons, created a US demand to control what was considered a genocide. Kofi Annan and other UN authorities were also active and transformed the US complaints about genocide into international action.

The plight of the Darfuris was initially heard by evangelists protecting Christians in the South of Sudan and by members of the Jewish community concerned about genocide. They and journalists like Nicholas Kristoff, human rights leaders such as John Prendergast, celebrities like Don Cheadle, and students and public officers mobilized by Samantha Power's book *A Problem from Hell* created a US constituency demanding to stop a genocide.

They influenced national leaders as Secretary of State Colin Powell. He labeled the crimes as genocide and, following a new interpretation of the Genocide Convention, demanded establishing a UN Commission of Enquiry.

War and Justice in the 21st Century. Luis Moreno Ocampo, Oxford University Press. © Oxford University Press 2022.
DOI: 10.1093/oso/9780197628973.003.0017

States at the UN Security Council had the option to select between multiple legal systems following their interests. Nine of them were states parties of the Rome Statute committed to doing justice for atrocity crimes. The "ICC-9," as US cables began referring to the group, changed the council's dynamic.[1]

France's UN permanent representative at New York, Ambassador Jean-Marc de la Sablière, led the "ICC-9," and the Bush administration was forced to accept the resolution. Council members had the discretion to include international criminal justice in Darfur or not. States parties' leadership at the council imposed the Rome Statute model.

The *jus ad Curiam*'s decisions on Darfur included a second part: the Office of the Prosecutor's decision triggering the court's jurisdiction. The ICC prosecutor filters the decisions adopted by the political actors. The Office of the Prosecutor opened a preliminary examination and received the information about the crimes committed collected by the UN Commission of Enquiry.

We started an interaction with many actors to obtain cooperation, including Sudan's government, to check the existence of relevant national proceedings. In June 2005, we concluded the preliminary examination process, and we opened an investigation in Darfur.

To respect the UN Security Council's authority to suspend our investigations, we announced in advance our intentions to request the first arrest warrants during our official briefings at the UN headquarters in New York in December 2006. We did the same in December 2007 and June 2008.

How the UN Security Council Moved from Preventing ICC Interventions to Referring the Darfur Situation?

Building Momentum

For decades, US evangelists were protecting the Christian communities living in the South of Sudan from an Islamic regime. President George W. Bush had promised to place religious persecution and atrocities by the Sudan regime at the forefront of his foreign policy agenda. He appointed John Danforth, an Episcopal minister and former senator from Missouri, as his special envoy.

In September 2001, Samantha Power wrote a long piece in *The Atlantic*, criticizing the US decisions that facilitated the Rwanda genocide, affirming that they "cast the darkest shadow over the Clinton Administration's foreign-policy record." She reminded that later the same President Clinton criticized his own administration's policies: "Never again, must we be shy in the face of evidence."[2]

President Bush received a memo summarizing *The Atlantic* article and "wrote in firm letters in the margin of the memo: 'NOT ON MY WATCH.' While he was commander in chief, he was saying, genocide would not recur."[3]

In July 2002, Danforth helped reach an agreement between Sudan's government and the rebel Sudan People's Liberation Movement/Army (SPLM/A) to end the Sudanese civil war.[4]

In early 2003, while the Sudan North/South negotiations were progressing, a conflict in the region of Darfur erupted.[5] Rebel groups attacked government installations demanding wealth-sharing agreements like those arranged to solve the North–South conflict.

The Sudanese government had problems controlling the Darfur rebellion, and negotiations started, but it objected strenuously to any suggestion that Darfur be included in the North–South's negotiation. The regime saw the SPLM/A's interest in Darfur as a sign of bad faith and an attempt to broaden the talks' agenda to advance its political project of the "New Sudan."[6]

However, in March and April 2003, rebels attacked the airport's military section in El Fashir, destroying several military aircraft on the ground, killing many soldiers, and even abducting the Sudanese Air Force top commander.[7]

President Al Bashir changed his strategy and publicly instructed the army to quell the rebellion in two weeks and not "bring back any prisoners or wounded."[8] He "didn't want any villages or prisoners, only scorched earth."[9] The Bashir regime used "Janjaweed" local militias to complement the Sudan armed forces. It launched a brutal series of attacks against civilians in the towns and villages mainly inhabited by the Fur, Masalit, and Zaghawa ethnic groups perceived as rebel supporters.

International Concerns

On December 5, 2003, UN Undersecretary-General for Humanitarian Affairs Jan Egeland asserted that Darfur "has quickly become one of the worst humanitarian crises in the world." A few days later, UN Secretary-General Kofi Annan stated that he was alarmed by the human rights violations and lack of humanitarian access in Darfur. Both of them continued denouncing the attacks in Darfur during the following months and made presentations to the UN Security Council.[10]

In April 2004, UN Secretary-General Kofi Annan took advantage of the commemoration of the tenth anniversary of the Rwanda Genocide to present to the Commission on Human Rights in Geneva an "Action Plan to Prevent Genocide." Annan included a somber warning that reports on the situation in Darfur left him "with a deep sense of foreboding." He presented Darfur as the test to prevent a Genocide and the UN Security Council as the authority to protect humanity. He proposed five steps, including "military action" as the last resource.[11]

The US Reaction in Darfur

A peculiar coalition was pushing for action. In April 2004, Congressman Frank Wolf, republican and evangelist, quoting Samantha Power, introduced a draft resolution "condemning the Government of Sudan for its involvement in attacks against innocent civilians in the impoverished Darfur."[12]

The same month, Samantha Power compared the international community's inactivity to stop the genocide in Rwanda with the situation in Darfur. "Again, the United States and its allies are bystanders to slaughter, seemingly no more prepared to prevent genocide than they were a decade ago."[13] She influenced the creation of STAND, Students Take Action Now for Darfur, reaching more than 750 chapters on college campuses across the United States.[14]

Samantha Power's book, "A Problem from Hell," proposed that to move the US government to act against genocide, "there needs to be a politically salient constituency of citizens raising its voice."[15] Such a proposal became an article of faith within the Darfur advocacy community. However, the United States was a staunch opponent of the ICC "and the 'embryonic constituency of citizen advocates for Darfur' was too busy with its own organization to enter into the debate over who should deal with justice."[16]

The US Ambassador to the UN Commission on Human Rights, Richard Williamson, presented in Geneva on April 23, 2004, a report entitled "Ethnic Cleansing in Darfur." But a resolution jointly drafted by the UN Commission members belonging to Africa (including Sudan's delegate) and Europe limited itself to "express concern" over human rights violations in Sudan. It did not qualify them as international crimes or making any mention of Genocide.[17]

A week later, news about the Abu Ghraib torture scandal dominated the news. Sudan, which was reelected to the UN Commission on Human Rights for a three-year term, stated that the United States, "while shedding crocodile tears over the situation in Darfur . . . is turning a blind eye to the atrocities committed by the American forces against the innocent civilian population in Iraq."[18]

The State Department planned an investigation on Darfur.[19] Lorne Craner, assistant secretary for Democracy, Human Rights and Labor; and Pierre-Richard Prosper, US ambassador-at-large for war crimes, took the lead.[20] They created a team integrating people with NGOs' investigatory experience[21] and others with regional knowledge to conduct systematic research of the Darfuris who had fled across the border into Chad.[22]

Meanwhile, the media started to pick the issue. In March, Nicholas Kristoff denounced in the *New York Times*, "The government of Sudan is engaging in genocide against three large African tribes in its Darfur region here."[23]

In April, Samantha Power published an op-ed entitled "Remember Rwanda, but Take Action in Sudan," suggesting that "outside powers cannot wait for confirmation of genocide before they act." She mentioned the efforts of "the Clinton administration in 1994 . . . to avoid using the term 'genocide' . . . because it could commit the United States 'to actually do something.'" She proposed mobilizing the UN to send 10,000 peacekeepers and to refer the situation to the ICC.[24]

In April and May, the UN Security Council reacted to the Darfur crises by issuing a presidential statement that requires unanimity, calling for a cease-fire first, and disarming the Janjaweed militias without qualifying the crimes committed. In June 2004, similar to what transpired ten years before with Rwanda, the State Department considered that to use the term *"genocide,"* the factual circumstances should be known.[25]

At the end of June, UN Secretary-General Kofi Annan and US Secretary of State Colin Powell did separate visits to internally displaced persons (IDP) camps in Darfur.[26] Following such visits, the State Department implemented the plan designed by Craner and Prosper.

Qualifying Darfur Crimes as Genocide

Declaring Genocide

On July 22, 2004, both chambers of the US Congress adopted unanimous resolutions condemning the continuing atrocities in the Darfur region of

Western Sudan as "genocide" and asking the president to act in conjunction with the international community to stop the violence.[27]

In a joint press conference, UN Secretary-General Kofi Annan and US Secretary of State Colin Powell called on the international community to pressure the government of Sudan to honor its promises vis-à-vis Darfur.[28] A week later, on July 30, 2004, the UN Security Council passed Resolution 1556, with China and Pakistan abstaining, giving the government of Sudan thirty days to disarm the Janjaweed under the threat of considering economic and military sanctions.[29]

The State Department produced its report called "Documenting Atrocities in Darfur."[30] The following day, Secretary Powell convened a conference call with his main collaborators and went through the facts and law.

Powell and his advisers noted that villages of people considered Africans were being destroyed, and neighboring Arab villages were not. Men were killed, women raped, and water polluted. There was deliberate targeting of some ethnic groups.[31] Sudan was preventing medicines and humanitarian assistance despite persistent international calls for access to internally displaced people's camps.[32]

The question was this: "If the Government of Sudan was not committing genocide, then 'what else are they trying to do?'"[33] To Powell, the conclusion was clear, and he just informed President Bush that he would make public his assessment. The president instructed Condoleezza Rice to tell all the principals of the various government agencies that Powell would be making a genocide determination.[34]

In a testimony before the Senate Foreign Relations Committee on September 9, 2004, Powell announced: "genocide has been committed in Darfur and that the Government of Sudan and the Janjaweed bear responsibility—and that genocide may still be occurring."[35] Then, Powell clarified a new US legal position: "no new action is dictated by this determination."

He avoided Clinton administration embarrassment following the legal interpretation adopted by William Taft IV, the State Department's legal adviser, "A determination that genocide has occurred in Darfur would have no legal—as opposed to moral, political, or policy—consequences for the United States."[36]

Article I of the Genocide Convention places an obligation on those who have joined, like Sudan and the United States, to "undertake to prevent and to punish" genocide. Taft explained that the US State Department had rejected an "expansive reading" of such a norm. Parties of the Genocide Convention are not obliged to "take particular measures to 'prevent' genocide in areas outside their territory."[37]

The Obama administration later followed that interpretation. The United States transferred the responsibility and requested the UN Security Council "to initiate a full investigation."[38]

The UN Commission of Inquiry

On September 18, 2004, the UN Security Council adopted Resolution 1564 by a vote of eleven members in favor, none against, with four abstentions from Algeria, China, Pakistan, and Russia. It called on the secretary-general to "establish an international commission of inquiry, to . . . investigate reports of human rights violations in Darfur, and determine whether acts of genocide had occurred there."[39]

In October 2004, Kofi Annan appointed the members of the UN Commission of Inquiry and the Office of the UN High Commissioner for Human Rights headed by Louise Arbour, former ICTY prosecutor provided support. The former president of the ICTY, Antonio Cassese, became the chairperson.[40]

The UN Commission of Inquiry's report, released on January 31, 2005, established that the government of Sudan and the *Janjaweed* were responsible for serious violations of international human rights and humanitarian law amounting to war crimes and crimes against humanity. However, it also concluded that "the Sudan's Government has not pursued a policy of genocide."

The report stated that "the crucial element of genocidal intent appears to be missing, at least as far as the central Government authorities are concerned."[41]

The next day, global headlines condensed the detailed report into a single message: "Sudan's Darfur Crimes Not Genocide."[42] The government of Sudan celebrated such a decision as a triumph. However, the critical aspect of the report was the definition of a way forward: "The Commission strongly recommends that the Security Council immediately refer the situation of Darfur to the International Criminal Court."

Speaking from Brussels after a meeting between EU foreign ministers that followed the release of the UN Commission's report, the EU Foreign Affairs Chief Javier Solana said that those responsible for the violence in Darfur should face war crimes charges at the ICC.

Condoleeza Rice, New Secretary of State and the ICC-9 Leadership

European countries were committed to seeing the recently created International Criminal Court take to investigate Darfur, but the question was how to overcome the US opposition to the ICC.

The debate started at the beginning of January, even before the UN Commission of Inquiry report was formally presented. Upon learning that Cassese was to recommend a referral to the ICC, Jack Danforth, the US permanent representative before the UN, turned to Washington, exploring his mandate's limits.

> Danforth was informed by French Ambassador de la Sablière that France would, in fact, take up Cassese's recommendation. Danforth asked Rice for some direction: should the US seek to A) block the ICC referral all together, or B) simply carve out US exemption (that is, insert language into the resolution that would grant immunity to any Americans that might be somehow be caught up in the investigation.) Danforth recommended the later course, saying that doing so would make life easier for everyone.[43]

The appointment of Condoleeza Rice as the new Secretary of State transformed the Bush administration approach. President Bush requested her to rebuild transatlantic relations, and she announced a trip to Europe the day she took office. Darfur, in particular the question of who should do justice in Darfur, was Rice's first test case for transatlantic relations.

Rice tasked Pierre Prosper, the ambassador-at-large for war crimes, with finding an alternative to the ICC. Prosper met in New York with Security Council representatives from Tanzania, Benin, and the United Kingdom to try without success to sell them on an alternative: an AU and UN ad hoc "Sudan tribunal" using the infrastructure of the International Criminal Tribunal for Rwanda in Tanzania. "Prosper played to the Security Council representatives from Tanzania and Benin as Africans, asking, 'Is this the message that we want to send to the African continent, that whenever there's a problem . . . justice has to be exported to The Hague? We say no.'"[44] As an internal document circulated from Prosper's War Crimes Office explained, "We do not want to be confronted with a decision on whether to veto an ICC resolution in the Security Council."[45]

I was visiting Harvard in January 2005 for a few days. I had lunch with two Harvard law professors, Jack Goldsmith, the former Bush administration's Assistant Attorney General; and Ryan Goodman, human rights and humanitarian law professor. We discussed the ICC functions and the Darfur problem. A few weeks later, Jack wrote an op-ed in the *Washington Post* explaining, the United States had proposed at Rome that the UN Security Council should trigger the ICC, and Darfur was offering a possibility to implement such a principle.[46]

He anticipated, "Opposition by China and Russia would be harder to overcome but would at least make clear to the world that those two powerful nations are even more opposed to the ICC than the United States."

Goldsmith also made his realist point: "Critics would decry this approach as a double standard for Security Council members, who can protect themselves by vetoing a referral. But this double standard is woven into the fabric of international politics and is the relatively small price the international system pays for the political accountability and support that only the big powers, acting through the Security Council, can provide."[47]

He recognized that the ICC was already a reality "up and running." The Security Council had presupposed its authority in 2002 and 2003, invoking Article 16. And he made a financial point that Congress would appreciate: The United States "can, for a change, enjoy the fruits of international justice without having to pay for it."

In the end, he recommended that "The Bush administration should play the difficult hand likely to be dealt it by the Cassese commission to its own political advantage. A more moderate stance toward the ICC could be a more effective one."[48]

France Leadership and the ICC-9

Around the same time, the French Ambassador Jean-Marc de la Sablière held his own informal meetings to get support in Paris. He believed that France could push the United States on the Darfur referral.[49]

Nine of the fifteen members of the UN Security Council were also members of the Rome Statute and committed to doing justice for atrocity crimes. The "ICC-9," as US cables began referring to the group, changed the council's dynamic.[50]

France's draft obtained additional support: Russia, the Philippines, and Japan were also on-board. De La Sablière had more than the eight votes needed to adopt a resolution, and his only concern was to overcome the United States' veto. Accordingly, France had drafted a resolution that would grant immunity to US citizens[51] to "put Americans in a position where they would have to oppose something reasonable—and endorse impunity."[52]

Rice called her counterpart in Paris to try and get a delay but was told it was de la Sablière's call to make. Ambassador de la Sablière cornered the United States into presenting an alternative or resorting to its veto power.

The next afternoon was tense. The American Service Protection Act (ASPA) limited the US flexibility but its draft went too far in protecting any personnel from a nonstate party. The US proposal "would have excluded not just Americans from jurisdiction of the court but every Sudanese national as well."[53] De la Sablière told the US delegate that he would not forward the draft to Paris for approval.[54]

The same evening, the United States had adjusted the language of the draft resolution. the United States asked instead for an "exclusive jurisdiction" provision, specifying that citizens of a state outside Sudan that was not a party to the ICC would remain under the exclusive jurisdiction of their own courts regarding any alleged crimes. Such a language followed the precedent established by the previous UN Security Council Resolution 1497, adopted on August 1, 2003, related to Liberia's UN stabilization force.

France had abstained from such a resolution on Liberia because the jurisdiction language undermined the cause of international justice. Now the United States was asking for this very same language on the Darfur referral. France was in a diplomatic bind—unable to move forward without the United States' support but unwilling to give the United States what it requested to abstain from vetoing the resolution. When the UN Security Council members met the following day, Ambassador de la Sablière asked for a twenty-four-hour delay on the vote.[55]

The French decided they would vote for the resolution, but they couldn't sponsor it; de la Sablière asked the UK representative, Emyr Jones Parry, to sponsor the resolution on the condition that there would be no changes.[56] As the United Kingdom had no prior record of refusing exclusive jurisdiction language, its delegate stepped up.[57] Prosper recalls that even once the British took over the resolution, the United States was pushing for language changes.[58]

The Adoption of the Referral

At 10:35 p.m. on Thursday, March 31, 2005, UN Security Council Resolution 1593, referring Darfur to the ICC, was passed with eleven votes for none against, and four abstentions—Algeria, Brazil, China, and the United States[59]

Following the vote, US Ambassador Anne Woods Patterson explained that she did not oppose the resolution because the language protecting the United States and other contributing States was precedent setting. She was pleased that the resolution recognized that the United Nations would bear none of the expenses incurred in connection with the referral.[60]

Ambassador Wan Guangya of China expressed his concerns: "Like the rest of the international community, China deplored deeply the violations of international humanitarian law and human rights law and believed that the perpetrators must be brought to justice." China made an enormous effort to harmonize its position. It "preferred a trial in Sudanese courts, did not favor the referral to the International Criminal Court without the consent of the Sudanese Government and had found it difficult to endorse the Council authorization of that referral."[61]

Algeria abstained because it perceived that the AU should handle the matter. The Security Council's president, Ronaldo Mota Sardenberg of Brazil, said his country was in favor of the resolution but had been unable to join those who had voted in favor due to the exemption of jurisdiction adopted at the insistence of the United States. Months later, in a private conversation, he explained me that he had to go to Brasilia to explain to a group of young diplomats fully committed to the Rome Statute that his vote was not in opposition to the ICC but rather against the concessions to the United States.

Denmark; the Philippines; Greece; Tanzania; and Romania, part of the ICC-9, expressed their concerns about the text adopted to please the United States but voted in favor. The Tanzanian ambassador hoped that the international community would not abandon the people of Sudan, particularly those in Darfur, and said that every new delay in adopting the resolution represented a failure to serve the interests of justice.[62]

Ambassador Andrey Denisov of Russia presented the consistent Russian position in favor of international justice, which Jack Goldsmith did not grasp in his article. He said that the Security Council members "had reaffirmed that the struggle against impunity was one of the elements of long-term stability in Darfur. All those responsible for grave crimes must be punished, as pointed out in the report of the Commission of Inquiry." He added that the resolution would promote an "effective solution to the fight against impunity."[63]

The council invited the representative of Sudan to present its views. Ambassador Elfatih Mohamed Ahmed Erwa said, "the ICC was intended for developing and weak countries and was a tool to exercise cultural superiority." He concluded: "The Council was continuing to use a policy of double standards and sending the message that exemptions were only for major powers."

At a press briefing the following day, the Under-Secretary of State Nicholas Burns provided Secretary Rice's vision of the abstention decision.

> I think that what the Secretary has been able to achieve here is indicative of the improved working relations that we have under her tenure with Europe in general and with other members of the Security Council. I think you all know she's been to Europe twice since she became Secretary of State.[64]

Just a few weeks later, the CIA showed how to use the UN Security Council as leverage to support the war on terror: it flew in a private jet, "Salah Abdallah Gosh, the head of Sudan's intelligence agency, to Washington, DC, to discuss anti-terror policies, despite the fact that Gosh is thought by some to be heavily implicated in the genocide in Darfur."[65] Deputy Secretary of State Robert Zoellick included the war on terror and democracy as the Bush administration's main goals in Sudan.[66] Each actor followed its interests and decided the legal system to be applied.

The Darfur Preliminary Examination

Deciding to Trigger the Court's Jurisdiction

The UN Security Council referral did not affect or reduce the Office of the Prosecutor's obligation to decide whether the court's jurisdiction should be triggered.[67] The prosecutor filters the decisions adopted by the political actors, including the UN Security Council.

We immediately opened a *preliminary examination* process. I traveled to New York to receive from the hands of Kofi Annan a sealed envelope with the name of the individuals identified as suspects by the UN Commission of Inquiry. We opened the envelope at our office, read it, sealed it again, and never reopened it. Under the Rome Statute, we had to make an independent decision based on the information collected.

The UN Commission of Inquiry had collected documents and interviewed victims and members of the Sudanese government. While I was in New York, one of our investigators traveled to Geneva in the ICC's van and returned with more than 2,500 items, including documentation, video footage, and interview transcripts. The van arrived in The Hague very late at night. He had no access to the building, and to ensure the chain of custody, he slept in the van on top of six boxes containing the documents. That was the commitment of the office members.

We found in the boxes coming from Geneva a sealed envelopment with US intelligence. We gave instructions, and our office called the US embassy in The Hague: "We found something that belongs to you. You should send someone to pick it." The US embassy's legal adviser had to request a permit to visit our premises. She received the envelope still sealed. It was the first official meeting between the United States and our office. For us, it was a simple decision following our rules, but David Bosco wrote that this gesture increased the United States' respect for our office.[68]

In the Darfur situation, the temporal and geographic jurisdiction did not present problems, so we immediately started to analyze the eventual commission of crimes, including genocide. However, the most complicated question was the existence of national proceedings. Unlike in Uganda and DRC, Sudan's government was affirming that it was investigating Darfur crimes.

To undertake the preliminary examination, our office needed to receive information, and we worked to obtain the political support required to receive such information. States parties of the Rome Statute have a duty to cooperate, but their top authorities' understanding could increase or reduce their efforts.

Many African countries received displaced people from Darfur. We needed their assistance to obtain information about the national proceedings in Sudan and, in particular, their cooperation for our future investigations.

In April 2005, the then-deputy prosecutor, Fatou Bensouda, met with African Union (AU) officials in the Ethiopian capital of Addis Ababa to negotiate a cooperative relationship between the ICC and the AU and to establish the modalities of that relationship concerning the Darfur referral.[69] The following month, I met with President Obasanjo, president of Nigeria; and the AU chairman, in Abuja, to continue building the cooperative arrangement.

Most Arab countries are nonparties and had no obligation to cooperate with the ICC. We established a good relationship with the Arab League, Qatar, and Egypt to obtain assistance.

Meeting the Sudanese Authorities

We were able to establish a relationship with the Sudanese government itself to analyze their proceedings. In April and May 2005, we had meetings in The Netherlands and Switzerland with a Sudanese minister's delegation.

The first meeting was in an Amsterdam hotel. The Sudanese delegation was integrated by a minister; a Supreme Court judge; and an expert on negotiations who, to present his country good intentions, gave us a bag of Sudan's oranges describing their quality. The conversation started tense but gradually became less stressful and more technical, as we discussed details of the Rome Statute and the processes carried out in Sudan.[70]

After a few hours, the minister in charge was direct. He said: "Prosecutor, we respect your mandate, but we cannot allow you to present a case against a Sudanese individual before the ICC."

I was impressed by his openness: "Thank you for your frankness, Minister. With the same sincerity, I must tell you that my mandate is to do a case if you fail to act. I will fulfill my duties. Maybe the best option for you is to allow us to present a case. Then you adjust to the international legal framework and organize a mechanism to control crimes and punish those responsible. That could be a way to move ahead."

"Oh, there is a win-win," said the negotiation expert, but the minister remained silent.

The meeting ended well. The Sudanese authorities were committed to cooperate during the preliminary examination phase, providing details of the alleged national proceedings, and coordinating a follow-up encounter. When they were leaving, they told me that in Sudan, the tradition to say goodbye is to kiss and asked if they can do it.

Against the permanent advice of the members of my office, I tried to make a joke. I explained that they could kiss all the delegation members but not Gavin, a British national working in the Jurisdiction, Complementarity, and Cooperation Division (JCCD).

In our office, we established rules to protect minorities. We realized the British do not like spontaneous affection. They need some warning. The office

adopted a protocol requiring a week advanced notice to kiss or hug British per-
sons. So, you could not kiss Gavin today, but now he is informed, and you could
do it in the next meeting.

It was one of the few occasions that my improper comments played well.
Sudan is a former British colony. I did not know if they liked the idea that we
considered British people part of a minority or agreed with my politically
incorrect comment, but they celebrated my joke. After that, we met regularly in Geneva, and kissing and hugging Gavin became the icebreaker of our
encounters.

During the following months, the Sudanese government provided information about its national proceedings and allowed us to visit Khartoum and
interview the judges and prosecutors in charge. The meetings helped us understand the complexities of the Sudanese political system, confirm that the
national proceedings were not related to the Darfur crimes, and improve our
assessment of the security situation.

The Article 53 (1) Report

In a few months, our office was able to produce a thorough Article 53 report.

The UN Commission of Inquiry and even a Sudanese National
Commission of Inquiry had concluded that national forces and its militias
allies committed crimes against humanity.

We also confirmed the existence of an armed conflict in Darfur.

We noted that the Sudanese government's position was that the areas
in which crimes allegedly took place had a significant presence of enemy
combatants. Information from the UN supported this assertion in some
instances. Since at least February 2003, fighting began between rebel groups
(initially the "Justice and Equality Movement" (JEM) and the "Sudan
Liberation Army" (SLA) and government forces and militias allied with
them). We obtained proofs about the war crimes' contextual element required by the statute.

While observing that the UN Commission had decided it did not have the
information to conclude that genocide had taken place in Darfur, our report
concluded that the allegations of genocide would be further investigated.

The office analyzed the existence of national proceedings.[71] We found
that proceedings within the regular Sudanese justice system presented by

the government of Sudan as investigations of army officers or Janjaweed militia for crimes committed in Darfur were for crimes unrelated to the Darfur conflict.

Concerning special courts, which were three-person security courts established under the Special Courts Act of Sudan, our office found that their proceedings were exclusively against alleged members of armed opposition groups.

Finally, our office studied the Committees Against Rape's work, which had been established by a ministerial order in 2004 to investigate, but not to prosecute, the crime of rape against women. The Rape Committees had concluded that there was a very low incidence of rape in Darfur. This conclusion stood in contrast to evidence from a range of sources that had documented significant numbers of conflict-related rapes in the Darfur region.

In terms of gravity, the UN had estimated in those days that at least 180,000 people had died as a result of the crisis and that over 2 million had been displaced either internally or as refugees. Furthermore, the determination by the UNSC that the situation in Darfur represented a threat to international peace and security provided further acknowledgment of the gravity of the situation.

The report found no reason to consider that an investigation would affect the interests of justice. On June 1, 2005, following the internal Article 53 Report, the Office of the Prosecutor decided to initiate an investigation concerning Darfur's crimes since February 2003.

Respecting the Council Authority under Article 16

Diplomacy and Justice

In December 2006, we implemented for the first time the policy of informing the council in advance of the prosecution's decision to request arrest warrants or summons to appear. Our report to the UN Security Council said, "The Office is seeking to finalize the preparation of the submission to the Judges by February 2007."[72]

We were ready to present our first case in the Darfur situation. The following day the Chinese ambassador in New York requested a meeting with me. He was the most skillful diplomat I ever met. He started thanking me for my immediate positive answer to meet him, emphasizing that our office always provided whatever information China needed.

Then the ambassador said: "You are always very open to us, and therefore we considered you a friend. Consequently, when you said that you would identify a Sudanese officer to be prosecuted, our delegation said nothing against you. Friends never—*he emphasized*—never criticize a friend. But friends always tell the truth to their friends, which is why I requested to meet you. China considers that stability is the way to protect human rights, and we are worried that your action could be counterproductive."

His manners were so elegant, his voice so gentle, that I found myself thanking him for a subtle intrusion in my independent mandate during the *jus in Curiae* phase. In any case we proceeded with our request.

One year later, during my briefing in December 2007, I warned the UN Security Council that we were planning to request new arrest warrants. We said, "Government of Sudan officials have decided . . . to protect and promote [Minister] Ahmad Haroun" and that the Office of the Prosecutor would proceed against the person that instructed and protected the minister.[73]

I confirmed my decision in my briefing to the council in June 2008. My announcement triggered a series of political reactions exposing states' reluctance to confront a head of state.

In the following years, I learned that the agreement between the UN Security Council members to adopt a *jus ad Curiam* decision did not include support for the subsequent implementation of the *jus in Curiae* decisions, particularly the arrest warrants' enforcement. Any new resolution would require new agreements to do justice for Darfur victims, which was impossible.

Notes

1. REBECCA HAMILTON, FIGHTING FOR DARFUR 58–59 (Kindle ed. 2011).
2. Samantha Power, *Bystanders to Genocide*, ATLANTIC (Sept., 2001), https://www.thea tlantic.com/magazine/archive/2001/09/bystanders-to-genocide/304571/.
3. SAMANTHA POWER, A PROBLEM FROM HELL 10424 (Kindle ed. 2013).
4. The government of Sudan and SPLM/A agreed to "continue negotiations on the outstanding issues of power-sharing, wealth-sharing, human rights and a ceasefire." *Machakos Protocol*, U.N. PEACEMAKER, https://peacemaker.un.org/sudan-macha kos-protocol2002 (last visited May 7, 2020).
5. Hum. Rts. Watch, *Darfur Destroyed* (May 2004).

6. JULIE FLINT & ALEX DE WAAL, DARFUR: A NEW HISTORY OF A LONG WAR 88–91 (2nd ed., 2008).

7. The Sudan Liberation Movement/Army and the Justice and Equality Movement (JEM) began organizing themselves in the course of 2001 and 2002 in opposition to the Khartoum government. The vast majority of the members of the two rebel movements came from essentially three tribes: the Fur, the Massalit and the Zaghawa. Report of the Int'l Comm. of Inquiry on Darfur to the U.N. Secretary-General Pursuant to S.C. Res. 1564 of 18 Sept. 2004, ¶ 62 (Jan. 25, 2004).

8. Situation in Darfur, Sudan, ICC-02/05-152, Summary of the Prosecutor's Application under Article 58, Pre-Trial Chamber I ¶ 53 (July 14, 2008), https://www.icc-cpi.int/CourtRecords/CR2008_03987.PDF.

9. Id.

10. Chronology: The Darfur Crisis, in GENOCIDE IN DARFUR: INVESTIGATING THE ATROCITIES IN THE SUDAN xx (Samuel Totten & Eric Marjusen eds., 2006).

11. "First, preventing armed conflict. Second, protection of civilians in armed conflict. Third, ending impunity. Fourth, early and clear warning. He informed the creation of a new post of Special Adviser on the Prevention of Genocide. Fifth, he proposed "the need for swift and decisive action when, despite all our efforts, we learn that genocide is happening, or about to happen." "By 'action' in such situations I mean a continuum of steps, which may include military action." Kofi Annan, UN Secretary General, Address to the Commission on Human Rights (Apr. 7, 2004).

12. More than ever, Ms. Power's book reminds all of us, especially those in public service, of the unique power and responsibility of our voice in confronting evil and our moral responsibility to speak out." Letter: Congressman Wolf Introduces Bill Condemning Sudan, FREE REPUBLIC (Apr. 21, 2004, 12:51 AM), http://www.freerepublic.com/focus/f-news/1121546/posts.

13. Samantha Power, Remember Rwanda, but Take Action in Sudan, N.Y. TIMES (Apr. 6, 2004), http://www.nytimes.com/2004/04/06/opinion/remember-rwanda-but-take-action-in-sudan.html?_r=0.

14. REBECCA HAMILTON, FIGHTING FOR DARFUR 55 (Kindle ed. 2011).

15. Id. at 49.

16. Id. at 55.

17. Id. at 35–36.

18. Id. at 35–36 (quoting Colum Lynch, U.S. Protests Sudan's Election to Human Rights Panel, WASH. POST (May 5, 2004).

19. Prosper commented that the instructions were "let's just get the facts, let's call it what it is, and let's deal with it." Stephen A. Kostas, Making the Determination of Genocide in Darfur, in GENOCIDE IN DARFUR: INVESTIGATING THE ATROCITIES IN THE SUDAN 117 (Samuel Totten & Eric Markusen eds., 2006).

20. Craner recounts that, from the beginning of his tenure as assistant secretary, he had standing instructions that "there was not going to be another Rwanda." The scar of Rwanda on the State Department was genuine, according to Craner. Id. at 114. He was influenced by Samantha Power's book A Problem from Hell: America and the Age of Genocide. "I started thinking that if we could put the information authoritatively

in front of people then no one would be able to deny it,' recalls Craner." REBECCA HAMILTON, FIGHTING FOR DARFUR 30–31 (Kindle ed. 2011)(ebook) (quoting Lorne Craner, interview with Rebeca Hamilton, Mar. 23, 2007).

21. "There was initially some opposition within his bureau and the rest of the state Department to putting NGOs in such a prominent role. . . . Craner, who had himself served as the president of an NGO, viewed them as the best available option." Stephen A. Kostas, *Making the Determination of Genocide in Darfur, in* GENOCIDE IN DARFUR: INVESTIGATING THE ATROCITIES IN THE SUDAN 120 (Samuel Totten & Eric Markusen eds., 2006).

22. "[Powell, [Under-Secretary of State] Grossman and [Deputy Secretary of State] Armitage all said to us, 'Don't filter the information—write what you think is true— just tell it like it is,' recalls Craner." REBECCA HAMILTON, FIGHTING FOR DARFUR 30–31 (Kindle ed. 2011). "Both Craner and Prosper shared the objective of determining whether genocide had been committed and emphasized its persuasive rhetorical significance." Stephen A. Kostas, *Making the Determination of Genocide in Darfur, in* GENOCIDE IN DARFUR: INVESTIGATING THE ATROCITIES IN THE SUDAN 117–19 (Samuel Totten & Eric Markusen eds., 2006).

23. REBECCA HAMILTON, FIGHTING FOR DARFUR 31 (Kindle ed., 2011).

24. Samantha Power, *Remember Rwanda, but Take Action in Sudan,* N.Y. TIMES (Apr. 6, 2004), http://www.nytimes.com/2004/04/06/opinion/remember-rwanda-but-take-action-in-sudan.html?_r=0.

25. At the time, the head of US AID Andrew Natsios was providing details about the human costs of the conflict, and the state department possessed sufficient satellite imagery and external reporting to conclude there were "indicators of genocide." Stephen A. Kostas, *Making the Determination of Genocide in Darfur, in* GENOCIDE IN DARFUR: INVESTIGATING THE ATROCITIES IN THE SUDAN 114 (Samuel Totten & Eric Markusen eds., 2006).

26. "According to Prosper, Powell was 'appalled by what he saw and what was hidden from him [on his visit], and he just really dug into the issue.'" *Id.* at 119–20.

27. CATHINKA VIK, MORAL RESPONSIBILITY, STATECRAFT AND HUMANITARIAN INTERVENTION 83 (1st ed., 2015). *See* Declaring Genocide in Darfur, Sudan, H. Con. Res. 467, 108th Cong. (2004).

28. *Chronology: The Darfur Crisis, in* GENOCIDE IN DARFUR: INVESTIGATING THE ATROCITIES IN THE SUDAN xxvii (Samuel Totten & Eric Markusen eds., 2006).

29. S.C. Res. 1556, ¶ 6, U.N. Doc S/RES/1556 (July 30, 2004).

30. "In the State Department's Bureau for International Organization Affairs, some were concerned that finding genocide would trigger a referral to the International Criminal Court (ICC), a move seen to contribute to the court's legitimacy, against which the Bush administration had steadfastly fought" But ."The Darfur genocide inquiry was viewed positively by the leadership in the state Department, . . . everyone as taking a 'let the chips fall where they may' approach to the genocide inquiry and determination, the ICC was a distant consideration, many steps down the line." Stephen A. Kostas, *Making the Determination of Genocide in Darfur, in* GENOCIDE IN DARFUR: INVESTIGATING THE ATROCITIES IN THE SUDAN 121 (Samuel Totten & Eric Markusen eds., 2006).

31. *Id.*
32. *Id.*
33. Powell and Prosper looked at the coordination and collaboration between the government of Sudan and the *Janjaweed*. "The Government of Sudan 'had knowledge across the board. Let's *pretend* that it wasn't coordinated. They knew what was going on and not only did they do nothing to stop it, they intentionally obstructed assistance that would have bettered the situation. so, when you have knowledge, you take no steps to stop it, and then, when people are trying to help, you block the assistance, what else could you want other than for these people to die or to be destroyed.'" *Id.* at 122.
34. "I never asked the president, 'Do I have permission to do this?,'" says Powell. "I just said that this was what I was going to do." REBECCA HAMILTON, FIGHTING FOR DARFUR 37–38 (Kindle ed. 2011).?
35. Congressional Testimony by then-Secretary of State Colin Powell, September 9, 2004. He stated that: "We believe the evidence corroborates the specific intent of the perpetrators to destroy 'a group in whole or in part,' the words of the Convention. This intent may be inferred from their deliberate conduct. We believe other elements of the convention have been met as well." Colin L. Powell, Secretary of State of the United States of America, Testimony Before de Senate Foreign Relations Committee (Sept. 9, 2004).
36. Rebecca Hamilton, *Inside Colin Powell Decision to Declare Genocide in Darfur,* ATLANTIC (Aug. 2011), https://www.theatlantic.com/international/archive/2011/08/inside-colin-powells-decision-to-declare-genocide-in darfur/243560/.
37. Rebecca Hamilton, *Inside Colin Powell decision to Declare Genocide in Darfur,* ATLANTIC (Aug. 2011), https://www.theatlantic.com/international/archive/2011/08/inside-colin-powells-decision-to-declare-genocide-in darfur/243560/.
38. *Appendices: The Crisis in Darfur, in* GENOCIDE IN DARFUR: INVESTIGATING THE ATROCITIES IN THE SUDAN 266 (Samuel Totten & Eric Markusen eds., 2006).
39. S.C. Res. 1564, ¶12, U.N. Doc. S/RES/1564 (Sept. 18, 2004).
40. Mohamed Fayek, Hina Jilani, Dumisa Ntsebeza, and Therese Striggner-Scott were the other members of the commission.
41. Report of the Int'l Comm. of Inquiry on Darfur to the U.N. Secretary General Pursuant to S.C. Res. 1564 of 18 Sept. 2004 (Jan. 25, 2004).
42. REBECCA HAMILTON, FIGHTING FOR DARFUR 59 (Kindle ed. 2011).
43. Scott Paul, *From Mark Goldberg on Sudan and the International Criminal Court,* WASHINGTON NOTE (Aug. 2, 2007), https://washingtonnote.com/from_mark_goldb/.
44. REBECCA HAMILTON, FIGHTING FOR DARFUR 58 (Kindle ed. 2011).
45. *Id.*
46. Jack Goldsmith, *Support War Crimes Trials for Darfur,* WASH. POST, Jan. 24, 2005, A15.
47. *Id.*
48. *Id.*
49. DAVID BOSCO, ROUGH JUSTICE: THE INTERNATIONAL CRIMINAL COURT IN A WORLD OF POWER POLITICS 109 (Kindle ed. 2014).

50. Rebecca Hamilton, Fighting for Darfur 58–59 (Kindle ed. 2011).

51. Maggie Farley, *U.N. to Send 10,700 Peacekeepers to Sudan*, L.A. Times, Mar. 25, 2005, A3.

52. David Bosco, Rough Justice: The International Criminal Court in a World of Power Politics 109–110 (Kindle ed. 2014).

53. Rebecca Hamilton, Fighting for Darfur 58 (Kindle ed. 2011). See endnote 1?

54. *Id.*

55. *Id.* at 66–67.

56. *Id.* at 66–67.

57. *Id.* at 66–67.

58. *Id.* at 66–67.

59. Press Release, Security Council, Security Council Refers Situation in Darfur, Sudan, to Prosecutor of International Criminal Court, U.N. Press Release SC/8351 (Mar. 31, 2005).

60. Ann W. Patterson, Ambassador Acting US Representative to the United Nations, Explanation of Vote on the Sudan Accountability Resolution in the Security Council (Mar. 31, 2005).

61. Press Release, Security Council, Security Council Refers Situation in Darfur, Sudan, to Prosecutor of International Criminal Court, U.N. Press Release SC/8351 (Mar. 31, 2005).

62. *Id.*

63. *Id.*

64. Rebecca Hamilton, Fighting for Darfur 66–68 (Kindle ed. 2011).

65. *Chronology: The Darfur Crisis, in* Genocide in Darfur: Investigating the Atrocities in the Sudan xxxvi (Samuel Totten & Eric Markusen eds., 2006).

66. Andrew S. Natsios, *Moving Beyond the Sense of Alarm, in* Genocide in Darfur: Investigating the Atrocities in the Sudan 27 (Samuel Totten & Eric Markusen eds., 2006).

67. Jens David Ohlin suggested that the prosecutor's authority to trigger the court's jurisdiction was constrained by the UN Security Council: "Chapter VII authority in making a referral, such referrals are mandatory and binding expressions of international law, and in so doing the Security Council constricts the prosecutorial discretion that the ICC prosecutor otherwise enjoys under the Rome Statute in cases initiated proprio motu or by referral from state parties." *The Emerging Practice of the International Criminal Court*, edited by Carsten Stahn & Göran Sluiter

68. David Bosco, Rough Justice: The International Criminal Court in a World of Power Politics 114 (Kindle ed. 2014).

69. Prosecutor of the International Criminal Court, *First Report to the Security Council Pursuant to UNSC Res. 1593 (2005)* (June 29, 2005), https://www.icc-cpi.int/NR/rdonlyres/CC6D24F9-473F-4A4F-896B-01A2B5A8A59A/0/ICC_Darfur_UNSC_Report_290605_EN.pdf.

70. *Id.*

71. *See* the Reports of the Prosecutor of the International Criminal Court to the UNSC pursuant to UNSC Res. 1593 (2005) dated 29 June 2005, 13 December 2005, 14 June

2006, 14 December 2006, 7 June 2007, 5 December 2007, 5 June 2008, 3 December 2008, 5 June 2009, 3 December 2009, 17 June 2010, 10 December 2010, 8 June 2011, and 15 December 2011.

72. Prosecutor of the International Criminal Court, *Fourth Report to the Security Council Pursuant to UNSC Res. 1593 (2005)* (Dec. 14, 2006), https://www.icc-cpi.int/NR/ rdonlyres/8903D205-6272-4498-8E83-258F9C99611A/0/OTP_ReportUNSC4Dar fur_English.pdf.

73. Prosecutor of the International Criminal Court, *Sixth Report to the Security Council Pursuant to UNSC Res. 1593 (2005)* (Dec. 5, 2007), https://www.icc-cpi.int/NR/ rdonlyres/19A83943-DF47-4DC0-9EB1-1A84CF862290/281540/ProsecutorsRe portUNSCDec07EN.pdf.

17

President Obama's *Jus ad Bellum* and *Jus in Bello* Decisions in Iraq and Afghanistan

This chapter describes the *jus ad Bellum* decisions adopted by President Obama and its implementation. American Civil Liberty Union and Professor Jack Goldsmith considered that President Obama's embracing of the War on Terror paradigm created a *new normal*. Killing those labeled as "*enemy combatants*" in sovereign countries that were not at war with the United States became the new accepted norm.

In 2001, President Bush had to improvise a reaction to the Al Qaeda attack. He neglected the law enforcement approach to face international terrorism, promoted a particular *jus ad Bellum* decision, launched "the War on Terror" and invaded Afghanistan.

In 2003, President Bush ignored Congress's previous *jus ad Curiam* decision to create an international court to investigate Saddam Hussein. He made a new *jus ad Bellum* decision to intervene in Iraq against the UN Security Council's will.

In 2009, President Obama had the opportunity to end the US occupation in Afghanistan and to consider international terrorism again as a law enforcement problem.

But President Obama concluded that the Authorization to use Military Force issued by Congress in 2001 remained valid. He tried to refine the US military approach in Afghanistan, but the military counterinsurgency strategy (COIN) applied in Iraq during the "surge" by General Petraeus was his only alternative.[1] No one suggested President Obama create a robust law enforcement intervention specially designed to face a non-government criminal network infiltrated in Pakistan.

For months, Obama and his top political and military advisers had lengthy discussions on military strategies, but the plans approved neither stabilized Afghanistan nor ended the insurgency. After a few years, President Obama abandoned COIN and replaced it with a simple attrition tactic focused on killing "enemies." President Obama applied the policy of targeted killings

War and Justice in the 21st Century. Luis Moreno Ocampo, Oxford University Press. © Oxford University Press 2022. DOI: 10.1093/oso/9780197628973.003.0018

even more vigorously than President Bush.[2] He authorized lethal operations in Pakistan, Syria, Iraq, Yemen, Somalia, Djibouti, and the Horn of Africa to engage terrorist groups "around the world" and "on the high-seas."[3] President Obama expanded

> [T]he Bush administration practice of targeting and killing enemy suspects in Pakistan and other places outside a traditional battlefield and inside countries with which the United States is not at war . . . It ramped up drone attacks quite a bit, using them more frequently during Obama's first year than Bush had in the previous seven combined.[4]

Harold Koh, then legal adviser of the State Department, provided the Obama administration legal reasoning: "as a matter of international law, the United States is in an armed conflict with Al Qaeda, as well as the Taliban and associated forces, in response to the horrific 9/11 attacks, and may use force consistent with its inherent right to self-defense under international law."[5]

The Due Process Clause of the Fifth Amendment denies the US government the authority to deprive any person of his life, liberty, or even property, without due process of law.[6] The War on Terror created an almost permanent and worldwide exception to the Due Process Clause.

Koh considered that the United States "has the authority under international law, and the responsibility to its citizens, to use force, including lethal force, to defend itself, including by targeting persons" and it "is not required to provide targets with legal process before the state may use lethal force."[7]

Rose Brooks, who worked at the Pentagon between 2009 and 2011, described the interaction with other states' legal systems. "When it comes to issues of sovereignty, US officials have repeatedly stated that they only use force inside the borders of a sovereign state when that state either consents to the use of force or is 'unwilling and unable' to take 'appropriate action' to address the threat itself."[8]

Paradoxically, the US military actions in Pakistan and Afghanistan increased the popular support to the insurgency. The epistemic community is neither alerting the problem nor providing alternative strategies.[9]

President Obama continued the pragmatic US approach regarding the ICC, supporting its interventions in different countries, particularly Kenya and Uganda but opposing any investigations against US personnel. As the following chapter describes, the War on Terror promoted efforts to protect US personnel involved in tortures and abductions.

The problem is not about leadership but rather about global legal designs based on national authorities' decisions. Barack Obama, the first US Afro-American president, worked for all US citizens but not for humanity. He is brilliant, committed to public service, and was entirely dedicated to his national mission. Still, his decisions consolidated the worst trend in the world history regarding people forcibly displaced.

Obama's Presidency

In July 2008, even before his nomination as the candidate for the Democratic Party was confirmed, Senator Barak Obama was considered a global change's leader. He stood before more than 200,000 cheering admirers in Berlin, affirming that the world was facing "dangers that cannot be contained within the borders of a country or by the distance of an ocean."[10]

But he did not propose to adopt a new international system to deal efficiently with a global network of terrorists, and he did not mention the possibility to enforce arrest warrants for genocide in Darfur. Obama's solutions were national and included war, not international criminal justice. He considered Al Qaeda members as enemies to be defeated and called to win the war in Afghanistan.[11]

Obama criticized some of the *jus in Bello* practices adopted by President Bush: he demanded to ban the use of torture, close the CIA "black sites," and dismantle Guantanamo.[12] Barak Obama also challenged the wisdom of the *jus ad Bellum* decision to intervene in Iraq, "*a country that had absolutely nothing to do with the 9/11 attacks.*"[13] He called Iraq a "dumb war."[14] He proposed, "America must shift its defense resources from Iraq to Afghanistan."[15]

Making war was not President Obama's only security policy. As a candidate, Obama was proposing "five goals essential to making America safer: ending the war in Iraq responsibly; finishing the fight against al Qaeda and the Taliban; securing all nuclear weapons and materials from terrorists and rogue states; achieving true energy security; and rebuilding our alliances to meet the challenges of the 21st century."[16]

Barak Obama, as president, had to deal with many complex challenges. According to Richard Haas, who was part of the Bush administration and a top expert on US international relations,[17] Obama received "a recession, a massive deficit, debt, a stretched and exhausted military, two wars, and a world marked by pronounced anti-Americanism."[18]

President Obama had to face the challenges mentioned by Haas and at the same time had to maintain good relations with both parties at the Congress to fulfill his promise that "a quality and affordable health care would not be a privilege, but a right."[19]

Obama's *Jus in Bello* Strategy in Afghanistan

The Afghans: Partners or Victims?

Even before the beginning of his tenure, President Obama was trying hard to refine his military strategy for Afghanistan and defeat Al Qaeda. He asked Vice President-elect Joe Biden to go to Pakistan and Afghanistan before the inauguration. "This should be a bipartisan effort," Obama said, and a Republican senator, Lindsey Graham, was included in the delegation.[20]

Since the 1980s, and with US acceptance, Pakistan armed and funded the Taliban to act "as a counterbalance to their regional rival, India."[21] Vice President Biden understood Pakistan's resistance to support US efforts against the Taliban.

> "What Pakistan doesn't want, as a matter of faith, is a unified Afghan government that is led by a Pashtun sympathetic to India" like Karzai. So, for Pakistan, supporting the Taliban "is a hedge against that." "But our policy is designed to strengthen a Karzai government and to wipe out the Taliban." "Essentially, American policy reinforces Pakistani hedging in a self-defeating cycle, causing Pakistan to aid the Afghan insurgency that the U.S. is trying to beat."[22]

After visiting Pakistan, Biden and Graham went to Kabul and met President Karzai. They complained about corruption and the lack of good governance, including allegations against Karzai's brother. President Karzai changed the topic: "There's only one issue that troubles us," Karzai said, "and that's civilian casualties. We need to work together on this."

Neither Biden nor Graham were able to grasp the problem identified by President Karzai. "We're doing everything we can to minimize civilian casualties," Biden answered to Karzai. "In a war, they can't all be avoided. You know that."

It would help, he added, if Karzai didn't hold news conferences denouncing the United States every time there were allegations of civilian casualties. "You need to come to us. We will find the facts each time, but what we have to avoid is immediate public statements that don't reflect the facts." Senator Graham, an Air Force Reserve lawyer, jumped in. *"Our rules of engagement are very sensitive to civilian casualties,"* he said. And dismissing the law enforcement paradigm clarified: "We're not going to ask our troops to become cops."

"It's not a criticism," the Afghan president said. "It's letting you know there's a problem."—"But let's deal with that problem in private instead of press conferences," Biden said.

Karzai's tone sharpened. Civilian casualties were a public matter. "The Americans seemed to believe the death of, say, 30 Afghan villagers was insignificant."—"This has gone on for too long," Karzai said. "The Afghan people must be partners, not victims."[23]

A similar problem was discussed simultaneously in Washington by the Pakistan ambassador before the United States and Richard Holbrooke, the new US special envoy before Pakistan and Afghanistan. The Pakistani ambassador was complaining about the civilian casualties produced by US drone attacks. The practice increased Pakistanis opposition to the United States.

Holbrooke said that "he understood Pakistan's need to protest the drone strikes since the government could not afford to be seen as complicit. But the protests should not fuel uncontrollable anti-Americanism."[24]

John Tirman wrote an entire book analyzing the problem, *One of the most remarkable aspects of American wars is how little we discuss the victims who are not Americans.*[25]

Instead of controlling international terrorism, the drones' attacks were increasing the popular support for the insurgencies. As a matter of law, torture is illegal, and killing an enemy combatant in a war could be considered legal.[26] Still, a *War on Terror* focused on killing the insurgents should be questioned as a matter of policy.

In those days, two US experts that worked in Afghanistan and Iraq highlighted the problem. They explained in a *New York Times* op-ed that the strikes "did kill individual militants who were the targets," but "public anger over the American show of force solidified the power of extremists." Every one of the "dead noncombatants represent an alienated family, a new desire for revenge, and more recruits for a militant movement that has grown exponentially even as drone strikes have increased."[27]

Similarly, General McChrystal considered, "Killing and capturing the insurgents is not the primary goal, and it may often be counterproductive, causing destruction that creates backlash among the population and fuels their support for the insurgency."[28]

McChrystal was primarily referring to the duty of revenge by tribe, friends, and family. As mentioned, General McChrystal labeled this paradoxical impact of the military operations against terrorism as the "insurgent math."[29]

McChrystal's perception was confirmed by a report about "The effect of civilian casualties in Afghanistan and Iraq"[30] produced in July 2010 by the National Bureau of Economic Research (NBER). The NBER report was assembled by researchers from Princeton, Stanford, and the London School of Economics. It was facilitated by Col. Joseph Felter, who had worked in Afghanistan. It concluded that "In Afghanistan, we find strong evidence that local exposure to civilian casualties caused by international forces leads to increased insurgent violence over the long-run, what we term the 'revenge' effect."[31]

The NBER report considered: "The data are consistent with the claim that civilian casualties are affecting future violence through increased recruitment into insurgent groups after a civilian casualty incident. Local exposure to violence from ISAF appears to be the primary driver of this effect."[32]

Radha Iyengar, a researcher from the London School of Economics and one of the NBER researchers, said: "It doesn't matter if the coalition is responsible for the killing." Paradoxically "... greater violence against coalition forces followed civilian casualty incidents whether the deaths were caused by ISAF or by the Taliban." "From what we heard from company commanders, the villagers say, 'If you weren't here, the Taliban wouldn't be blowing things up.'" Either way, Afghan villagers blame foreign forces, and such sentiments bolster the insurgents.[33]

A different study confirmed Radha Iyengar's observation: "when Western forces inflicted harm, their support went down, and that of the Taliban went up. The reverse, however, was not the case. Taliban violence made little difference either way. The Taliban had a 'home team discount' and were more likely to be forgiven."[34]

Piazza and Choi also support General McChrystal's personal experience and NBER report, using data on international military interventions for 125 to 182 countries from 1970 to 2005. The research sustains that states experience more terrorism after they are subject to military interventions.[35]

John Tirman described the phenomenon as "the US military was battling an insurgency that was to some important degree one of its own making, and the methods of battling it only intensified that very response of resistance."[36]

There is not an epistemic community providing alternative strategies.

US political leaders with vast experience as Biden and Holbrooke could not present a new strategy. Army officers as General Petraeus and McChrystal perceived the problem and proposed to minimize civilian casualties adopting COIN. They realized that the killing strategy was fueling popular support for the insurgency. But COIN's success required good governance, an alliance with an efficient national state, something that the Afghan warlords could not provide. In the end, neither COIN nor the classic military strategy protected civilians in Afghanistan.

War in Afghanistan, Not in Pakistan

As soon he took office, President Obama convinced a trusted CIA expert, Bruce Riedel, to review the Afghanistan policy. In a few days, he received a new concept: the focus must shift to Pakistan and away from Afghanistan. The mission should be targeting Al Qaeda and not the Taliban.[37]

Why did the Obama administration want to expand the war in Afghanistan when it knew that Al Qaeda was in Pakistan? The Taliban government was committing crimes against the Afghan citizens, but it had no policy to attack the United States. From a US security point of view, the Taliban were not a priority. Instead of focusing on arresting bin Laden and those who committed the crimes on 9/11, Afghanistan's invasion distorted the goal. President Obama inherited the problem, received military advice to do COIN and no other options, and decided to maintain the course.

A Law Enforcement Option

The military strategy monopolized the discussion on Afghanistan. Instead, political, legal, and law enforcement activities faced anarchism, the terrorism of the era between 1878 and 1934.[38]

During Obama's first months in office, the most senior national security team led by the president himself met many times for two or three hours to discuss the strategy.

At the beginning of the process, the president asked: "Is there anybody who thinks we ought to leave Afghanistan?" No one said anything. "Okay," he said, "now that we've dispensed with that, let's get on."[39] The president did not ask how to return to the law enforcement strategy, and his team did not even imagine such a possibility.

During the Cuban missile crisis Abram Chayes, as the Secretary of State's Legal Advisor, was in the situation room to find strategic solutions using the UN and the OAS legal frameworks. In 2009, there were not law enforcement minds in the strategic discussion. No one evaluated whether a new and specific international justice mechanism could help to control global terrorism.[40]

The United States could have been inspired by its own national experience at the beginning of the twentieth century when it adjusted its institutions to deal with new threats. During the nineteenth century, there was no federal criminal justice system; the authorities of "cities, counties, and states" enforced criminal law at *home*.

In 1908, Charles Bonaparte, Theodore Roosevelt's Attorney General, created a small force of special agents that later became the Federal Bureau of Investigations (FBI). The goal was to face new forms of criminality that could not be controlled by the local or states authorities, like transporting "women over state lines for immoral purposes." The FBI jurisdiction expanded to deal with "the gangster era" and a "resurgent white supremacy movement."[41]

A book published in 2002 comparing the UK and US counterinsurgencies campaigns in Malaya and Vietnam found that the British abandoned the classic military attrition strategy and, because of its traditional role as a colonial police force, slowly evolved to a successful integrated approach.[42]

The author, Lieutenant Colonel John Nagl, was on the writing team that produced the US Army/Marine Corps Counterinsurgency Field Manual, but the idea to integrate the military operations with a judicial system was not included. International criminal justice is a blind spot for US experts.

I spent six years at Harvard trying to open a discussion on developing options to deal with international terrorism, and I failed. Experts work in "echo chambers." I took advantage of my students' background and organize a small group integrated by a New York police officer, a major from the US military intelligence with experience in Afghanistan; and a young prosecutor, to explore options.

One possible idea coming from our discussions is to blend the military and the law enforcement model by creating a new "Special Anti-terrorist

Criminal Justice System." The goal should be to disrupt the terrorist organizations focusing on the leaders, violent individuals, and financial contributions.

The system could integrate some of the following characteristics: (a) a Global Bureau of Investigations (GBI) against terrorism to investigate and control international terrorist groups. Some personnel could work in Afghanistan, but analysts and leaders should be based outside to provide complete protection; (b) strong cooperation between the relevant intelligence and police services on a case-by-case basis, something already happening on the ground; (c) establishing some special courts, following the US Foreign Intelligence Surveillance Court model, with the ability to order coercive measures, including freezing assets; (d) the possibility of arresting a suspect for a limited number of years using intelligence information without disclosure as happens during grand jury investigations; (e) to implement the arrest through an independent and robust enforcement arm, combining special forces dedicated to that task.

Like the US Federal Courts, a group of special international courts against terrorism could be developed to provide fair trials. In 2017, the EU Council established the European Public Prosecutor presenting cases before a network of national courts.[43]

The investigations should include a vital money tracking component. Financial investigations are a crucial part of any effort to disrupt a criminal organization and are missing in the War on Terror. The United States neglected the countries financing terrorism as soon they supported the US War on Terror, appeared as US allies, and helped fund UN programs to control terrorism financing.

The "Special Anti-terrorist Criminal Justice System" could be an exclusive US exercise in agreement with different national governments. Or better, the UN Security Council could also adopt part of it. As Chapter 22 shows, Russia and China supported the effort to control international terrorism.

The "Special Anti-terrorist Criminal Justice System" could be sustained in time; overcome political changes as happened in Afghanistan' and, exported to investigate Al Qaeda in Pakistan, and other terrorist groups operating worldwide, including in Yemen, Syria, Libya, and Somalia. More importantly, the system could protect the Muslim population in its vast majority against Islamic terrorism.

President Obama did not receive plans to focus exclusively on the control of international terrorism. The twenty-first century did not produce a grand strategy to harmonize global efforts to deal with international terrorism.

Expanding the Number of Troops in Afghanistan

President Obama made efforts to review the military plans from the beginning of his tenure. Bob Woodward wrote a fascinating book, *Obama's War*, describing the administration's internal discussions in detail. It shows President Obama's enormous efforts to create a consistent strategy and the mismatch between political goals and military operations.

The military plans and superior commands should be analyzed in detail because they are the most relevant legal systems for US personnel and aliens living in countries considered by the United States "unwilling or unable" to control international terrorism.

When President Obama took office in January 2009, General David Petraeus, who led the adoption of COIN, was already in charge of the central command responsible for Afghanistan and Iraq. He aimed to repeat the success of the "surge" and demanded to implement a request for 30,000 more troops that the Bush administration had not acted on.[44]

"President Obama asked for clarification. 'Do you have to have all of this now?' No one answered before Vice President Biden nearly erupted. 'We have not thought through our strategic goals!' he complained. Everyone should agree to a strategy before the president ordered up more troops."[45]

The army reduced its request to 17,000 more troops. The president was frustrated that he had to commit those numbers before the Riedel review was completed.[46] At the end of March, President Obama, surrounded by General Petraeus and his National Security team, announced a "comprehensive, new strategy for Afghanistan and Pakistan."

President Obama mentioned the risk of the return of the Taliban for the people of Afghanistan, showing his empathy with them: "For the Afghan people, a return to Taliban rule would condemn their country to brutal governance, international isolation, a paralyzed economy, and the denial of basic human rights to the Afghan people—especially women and girls."[47]

Beyond those words and following Riedel's advice, at that initial moment, President Obama did not include "defeating" the Taliban in the mission. "I want the American people to understand that we have a clear and focused goal: to disrupt, dismantle, and defeat al Qaeda in Pakistan and Afghanistan and to prevent their return to either country in the future."[48]

A few weeks later, Secretary of Defense Gates made a significant move. He appointed General McChrystal, very close to Petraeus and a firm believer in COIN, as the new Afghanistan commander.[49] Secretary Gates also modified the goal, transforming the mission from "disrupt" the Taliban into "defeat" them.[50]

"Disrupt" means to increase the enemy's vulnerability and "defeat" to produce the loss of the enemy's physical means or the will to fight. *This single verb reinterpreted the whole Riedel review, broadening the narrow intention of defeating al Qaeda to include the Afghan Taliban.*[51]

General Lute, who was in the National Security Council, realized the relevance of the change. Before approval, he discussed it with the head of the National Security Council, General James Jones, who, as a military officer, understood the difference between "disrupt" and "defeat." But General Jones distrusted senior White House political advisers and considered that "defeat" would get "the military to take full ownership of the strategy." General Lute also presented the problem to National Security's deputy Tom Donilon, who would not discuss the wording; he had a political view as a former member of the Clinton administration and made a political decision. He knew the importance of keeping the secretary of defense on board and "was okay because Gates was making the bid."

General Lute was worried, but as a military officer, he followed his superiors' instructions, and the change was approved.[52] After months of deliberations, the primary efforts would be spent not in Pakistan against Al Qaeda rather in Afghanistan to "defeat" the Taliban.

Following the COIN doctrine,[53] McChrystal produced a final evaluation that baldly said, "Almost every aspect of our collective effort . . . has lagged a growing insurgency" "The status quo will lead to failure . . ."[54] and that was going to happen in the next twelve months.[55]

The Secretary of Defense Robert Gates and the top military leaders[56] presented COIN to President Obama as the only option, with three different numbers of US personnel deployed.[57] Petraeus supported the increase of troops in the media, infuriating President Obama.[58] Obama advisers considered that "The president is being screwed by the senior uniformed military."[59]

Obama's Deliberation on the Afghanistan Strategy

The absence of a feasible Pakistan plan and a reliable partner in the Afghanistan government affected the COIN strategy.[60] The McChrystal report defined as a crucial factor for victory an "Afghan state . . . .that fulfilled the needs of its people and thus preempted or co-opted the insurgents' appeal."[61]

Admiral Mike Mullen, chairman of the Joint Chiefs of Staff, alerted "that no strategy will work as long as pervasive corruption . . . continue to characterize governance in Afghanistan."[62] During the discussion, he recognized, "Governance is at least the same threat, if not the greater threat, than the Taliban themselves."

General Karl W. Eikenberry, the military commander in Afghanistan during Bush time and later President Obama's ambassador to Kabul was not a COIN supporter.[63] He asked a relevant question about the policy: *Was it simply to prevent Afghanistan from being a safe haven for Al Qaeda? Or was it to turn Afghanistan into another Denmark?*[64] General Eikenberry was right that COIN is just a military component of a broader institutional and political effort, but he was not ready to propose an alternative.

Vice President Biden asked a fundamental question: "If the government's a criminal syndicate a year from now, how will troops make a difference?"[65] Secretary of State Clinton said the dilemma was which should come first— more troops or better governance? "Preventing collapse requires more troops, but that doesn't guarantee progress."[66] CIA Director Leon Panetta summarized: "We can't leave, and we can't accept the status quo."[67]

After a long carrier at the CIA, since 2009, John Brennan became a presidential adviser on counterterrorism. He went back to the fundamental problem: "There are very few al Qaeda in Afghanistan." He alerted that Al Qaeda was planning to go "to places like Yemen and Somalia . . . . And al Qaeda is taking advantage of these ungoverned spaces where there is little or no US troop presence. His worry was the rest of the world."[68]

President Obama realized that the plan's core goal was not clear and explained the difference between "defeat" and "disrupt," a problem that General Lute had anticipated and was neglected. "What Stan [McChrystal] concluded," Obama said, "is in terms of the Taliban, using the word 'defeat' is probably overambitious. Disrupt the Taliban, control their momentum, keep them from establishing a platform that can be used, destabilizing efforts."[69]

General Lute was right, but President Obama got the point too late and changed nothing.

As Leon Panetta said, "No Democratic president can go against military advice, especially if he asked for it." His recommendation was, "So just do it. Do what they say."[70]

The distinction between defeating Al Qaeda in Pakistan and an effort to defeat the Taliban was never transformed into a new operational concept.[71] There was no plan B to discuss and the COIN strategy in Afghanistan was approved.

The Announcement of Afghanistan's Obama Strategy

On December 1, 2009, President Obama presented his plan resulting from months of internal debates in West Point, a military academia in New York state. He invoked the 2001 congressional authorization, the NATO support, reminding that the "UN Security Council endorsed the use of all necessary steps to respond to the 9/11 attacks" and recognizing that *al Qaeda's leadership* adopted Pakistan *as a safe haven.*[72]

He described his March decision: *I set a goal that was narrowly defined as disrupting, dismantling, and defeating al Qaeda and its extremist allies.*[73] And then, Obama took the responsibility of the new effort going in a different direction: *to send an additional 30,000 US troops to Afghanistan. After 18 months, our troops will begin to come home.*[74]

President Obama also warned Pakistan: "We cannot tolerate a safe haven for terrorists whose location is known and whose intentions are clear." And he confirmed that the War on Terror had not a specific battlefield. "Where al Qaeda and its allies attempt to establish a foothold—whether in Somalia or Yemen or elsewhere—they must be confronted by growing pressure and strong partnerships."[75]

He obtained support from different sides, including the Republicans and European allies. Nato's chief, Anders Fogh Rasmussen, says, "this is not just America's war . . . what is happening in Afghanistan poses a clear and present danger to the citizens of all our countries."[76]

The Nobel Peace Prize and President Obama's Global Vision

On October 9, 2009, the Norwegian Nobel Committee decided to award the Nobel Peace Prize to President Obama,[77] endorsing his appeal that "Now is the time for all of us to take our share of responsibility for a global response to global challenges."[78]

On December 10, 2009, a few days after his West Point speech, President Obama received the prize in Oslo. He did not propose a new global institutional architecture. On the contrary, President Obama started his Nobel lecture presenting his national role. He reminded everyone that he was "the Commander-in-Chief of the military of a nation in the midst of two wars."[79] "We must begin by acknowledging the hard truth: We will not eradicate violent conflict in our lifetimes. There will be times when nations—acting individually or in concert—will find the use of force not only necessary but morally justified." He equated Germany's Nazi government with Al Qaeda, a criminal organization. *Evil does exist in the world. A nonviolent movement could not have halted Hitler's armies. Negotiations cannot convince al Qaeda's leaders to lay down their arms.*[80]

President Obama invoked Gandhi and Martin Luther King's names but did not propose to follow their vision: "as a head of state sworn to protect and defend my nation, I cannot be guided by their examples alone." President Obama provided a moral basis to his realist assumptions.

> But the world must remember that it was not simply international institutions—not just treaties and declarations—that brought stability to a post-World War II world. Whatever mistakes we have made, the plain fact is this: The United States of America has helped underwrite global security for more than six decades with the blood of our citizens and the strength of our arms.[81]

He proposed to "direct our effort to the task that President Kennedy called for long ago." "Let us focus," he said, "on a more practical, more attainable peace, based not on a sudden revolution in human nature but on a gradual evolution in human institutions." President Obama asked a rhetorical question: *What might this evolution look like? What might these practical steps be?* And he retained the concept of killing *enemies* abroad, proposing a very open approach on *jus ad Bellum* and a restrictive but classic one on *jus in Bello*.

President Obama affirmed: "I—like any head of state—reserve the right to act unilaterally if necessary, to defend my nation. Nevertheless, I am convinced that adhering to standards, international standards strengthen those who do, and isolates and weakens those who don't."[82] President Obama did not propose a global institutional solution. He did not mention the new International Criminal Court's existence or the possibility to face terrorists as criminals. President Obama ignored the UN Charter limitation of self-defense, went back to Grotius concepts, and recommended unilateral decisions to use military forces against international wrongdoers: "And this becomes particularly important when the purpose of military action extends beyond self-defense or the defense of one nation against an aggressor. More and more, we all confront difficult questions about how to prevent the slaughter of civilians by their own government, or to stop a civil war whose violence and suffering can engulf an entire region. I believe that force can be justified on humanitarian grounds."

President Obama forgot the global model presented by Theodore Roosevelt in his own Nobel Peace lecture a century before and the new world order defined by the Kellogg–Briand Pact.

Change of Plans

In June 2010, a *Rolling Stone* article created a scandal that transformed the Afghanistan plans. The discussion was not about COIN, or a new strategy focused on Pakistan, rather about the Obama presidential authority. The article presented General McChrystal saying to his men that Obama's strategy review was "painful" and some of his aides were criticizing Biden, Holbrooke, and Eikenberry, precisely those who opposed the COIN strategy.[83]

On June 23, President Obama accepted McChrystal's resignation and replaced him with his boss, General David Petraeus. The change of the central concept of the operation, from disrupt to defeat, basically Secretary Gates's insubordination to the instruction received, was tolerated but a few personal comments considered unacceptable. Public opinion was wrongly focused on a personal characteristic, not on a substantial problem.

After a year, the COIN strategy became unpopular: "Obama believes the military can do enormous things," said Benjamin J. Rhodes, the deputy national security adviser. "It can win wars and stabilize conflicts. But a military can't create a political culture or build a society."[84] President Obama did not like the COIN approach because "what you're purchasing is responsibility for Afghanistan over the long term."[85] But there was no other strategy.

President Obama reduced the number of soldiers to 10,000 "to carry out a singular, ruthless mission of killing suspected terrorists and keeping the country from spiraling out of control . . . as part of a broader counterterrorism policy from Central Asia to North Africa."[86] A *New Yorker* report said that John Brennan frequently met with President Obama, helping to orchestrate a vast expansion of the targeted-killing program and shape the various "kill lists."[87]

Brennan considered that the conflict was endless: "That's why using terminology like 'success,' like 'victory' and 'win,' complicates our task."[88] He also challenged the military approach: "The counterterrorist program will continue regardless of the decision on any of these military options."[89] He was appointed CIA director in March 2013. The new tactic was to conduct an attrition operation, transfer the responsibilities to the national authorities, and eventually leave Afghanistan.

In May 2013, President Obama promised: ". . . to take strikes against high-value Al Qaeda targets, but also against forces that are massing to support attacks on coalition forces."[90] The Taliban were attacking US troops, and they continued to be the main enemy in Afghanistan.

The US military operation continued in Afghanistan alongside the NATO-led ISAF mission until the end of December 2014, when both combat missions officially concluded and were replaced by new tasks focused primarily on training, advising, and assisting the Afghanistan National Security Forces. In any case, US troops also continued conducting targeted killings.

Many human rights groups criticized these attacks as illegal assassinations or 'extrajudicial killings,' and some accused the Obama administration of war crimes. But the administration has been unmoved. '[V]ery frankly, it's the only game in town in terms of confronting and trying to disrupt the al Qaeda leadership,' said CIA Director Leon Panetta.[91]

For years, the *War on Terror* produced civilian casualties that promoted support to the insurgency.

The United States has bombed at least eight wedding parties between 2001 and 2013, six in Afghanistan, one in Iraq, and one in Yemen.[92] After implementing the new Obama strategy to transfer responsibilities to Afghan authorities, a US attack on the Doctors Without Borders hospital in the city of Kunduz on October 3, 2015, killed forty-two civilians and wounded hundreds. *The Defense Department's internal investigation concluded that the attack was "unintentional." Sixteen US personnel were disciplined, but no criminal charges were filed.*[93]

The Pentagon reported that 466 Iraqi civilians had died as a result of coalition airstrikes. Stephen Walt quoted *a detailed and rigorous investigation by the New York Times* that challenged the Pentagon numbers and multiplied the numbers of civilian deaths.[94] But 446 Iraqi civilians killed are enough to explain the reaction against US military operations.

On February 11, 2015, President Obama asked Congress to authorize military force against yet another enemy—the Islamic State this time— while affirming at the same time, *"I do not believe America's interests are served by endless war, or by remaining on a perpetual war footing."*[95] Still, no options were developed, and the War on Terror became the *forever war.*

The New Normal

In July 2010, the American Civil Liberty Union raised its voice against President Obama's policy and evaluated that:

> [O]n a range of issues including accountability for torture, detention of terrorism suspects, and use of lethal force against civilians, there is a very real danger that the Obama administration will enshrine permanently within the law policies and practices that were widely considered extreme and unlawful during the Bush administration. There is a real danger, in other words, that the Obama administration will preside over the creation of a "new normal."[96]

Jack Goldsmith, in 2012, agreed with the ACLU and explained that the strategy to confront terrorism as a war and not as a crime created the "new normal."[97] The qualification as war provided the United States with legal authority to kill whoever the United States consider an enemy combatant.

Goldsmith, who has a unique academic and government practice, wrote a book explaining: "Two presidential administrations with starkly different views about executive power and proper counterterrorism tactics ended up in approximately the same place because forces more powerful than the aims and inclinations of the presidents and their aides were at work."[98] Goldsmith provided an insight that explains the "new normal": "The continuity between the two administrations also reflects a persistence in the interests and outlook of the national security leadership and especially of the national security bureaucracy." Obama kept the Bush's defense secretary (Robert Gates) and many of those working in the area.[99]

"Even when there is a departure from this pattern at the top, as when intelligence novice Leon Panetta took over the CIA, the underlying bureaucracy, with its administration-transcendent expertise and perspective, persists."[100] John Rizzo was a lawyer with more than thirty years of experience at the CIA that requested the opinion on the enhanced interrogation technique, "seeking maximum legal protection for its officers."[101] He became the CIA's general counsel under Panetta.

"Every new administration comes in with new ideas about how to reform the national security agencies," said John Rizzo, "Each one realizes when they get inside that their options are much more limited by reality than they believed."[102]

As Goldsmith, Stephen Walt is attributing the lack of change to a US foreign policy elite operating "in a system that rewards conformity, penalizes dissent, and encourages its members to remain within the prevailing consensus."[103]

The broad epistemic community of experts and scholars fails to propose alternative solutions to manage international violence's new challenges. Decision makers have to improvise their options.

Notes

1. *See also* U.S. Dep't of the Army, The U.S. Army/Marine Corps Counterinsurgency Field Manual (2007).
2. Jack Goldsmith, Power and Constraint: The Accountable Presidency After 9/11 13–15 (Kindle ed. 2012). *See Civilian Casualties & Collateral Damage*, Lawfare, https://www.lawfareblog.com/civilian-casualties-collateral-damage (last visited Mar. 10, 2020).
3. The President of the United States, Report on the Legal and Policy Frameworks Guiding the United States' Use of Military Force and Related National Security Operations (2016).
4. Jack Goldsmith, Power and Constraint: The Accountable Presidency After 9/11 13–15 (Kindle ed. 2012). *See Civilian Casualties & Collateral Damage*, Lawfare, https://www.lawfareblog.com/civilian-casualties-collateral-damage (last visited Mar. 10, 2020).
5. Harold Hongju Koh, *Keynote Address: The Obama Administration and International Law*, 104 Am. Soc'y Int'l L. Proc. 207, 218 (2010).
6. Owen Fiss, A War Like No Other: The Constitution in a Time of Terror 267 (Kindle ed., 2015).
7. Harold Hongju Koh, *Keynote Address: The Obama Administration and International Law*, 104 Am. Soc'y Int'l L. Proc. 207, 219 (2010).
8. Rosa Brooks, How Everything Became War and the Military Became Everything: Tales from the Pentagon 285 (Kindle ed. 2016).

9. Brett Stephens, Fareed Zakaria et al., Has Obama Made the World a More Dangerous Place? The Munk Debate on America Foreign Policy (Munk Debates) (Kindle ed. 2015).

10. *Obama's Speech in Berlin*, N.Y. Times (July 24, 2008), https://www.nytimes.com/2008/07/24/us/politics/24text-obama.html.

11. Id.

12. Helene Cooper et al., *On the Issues: Iraq and Afghanistan*, N.Y. Times (May 23, 2012), https://www.nytimes.com/elections/2008/president/issues/iraq.html.

13. Matthew Yglesias, *The Lost Opportunity*, Atlantic (July 15, 2008), https://www.theatlantic.com/politics/archive/2008/07/the-lost-opportunity/49293/.

14. Mark Landler, *The Afghan War and the Evolution of Obama*, N.Y. Times (Jan. 1, 2007), https://www.nytimes.com/2017/01/01/world/asia/obama-afghanistan-war.html.

15. Helene Cooper et al., *On the Issues: Iraq and Afghanistan*, N.Y. Times (May 23, 2012), https://www.nytimes.com/elections/2008/president/issues/iraq.html.

16. Matthew Yglesias, *The Lost Opportunity*, Atlantic (July 15, 2008), https://www.theatlantic.com/politics/archive/2008/07/the-lost-opportunity/49293/.

17. He was director of policy planning for the Department of State during the first years of the George W. Bush administration and since 2002 the president of the Council on Foreign Relations.

18. Richard N. Haas, War of Necessity, War of Choice: A Memoir of Two Iraq Wars 270 (Kindle ed. 2009).

19. *Improving Health for All Americans*, White House, https://obamawhitehouse.archives.gov/the-record/health-care (last visited Jan. 20, 2021).

20. Bob Woodward, Obama's Wars 62 (Kindle ed. 2010).

21. Ronan Farrow, War on Peace: The End of Diplomacy and the Decline of American Influence 28 (Kindle ed. 2018.

22. Bob Woodward, Obama's Wars 163 (Kindle ed. 2010).

23. *Id.* at 68–69.

24. *Id.* at 87.

25. John Tirman, The Deaths of Others 3 (Kindle ed. 2013).

26. Owen Fiss, A War Like No Other: The Constitution in a Time of Terror 267 (Kindle ed. 2015).

27. David Kilcullen & Andrew McDonald Exum, *Death from Above, Outrage Down Below*, N.Y. Times (May 6, 2009), https://www.nytimes.com/2009/05/17/opinion/17exum.html.

28. Ganesh Sitarama, *Counterinsurgency, the War on Terror, and the Laws of War*, 95 Va. L. Rev. 1745, 1747 (2009).

29. Stanley McChrystal, *Gen. MacChrystal's Speech on Afghanistan*, Real Clear Politics (Oct. 1, 2009), https://www.realclearpolitics.com/articles/2009/10/01/gen_mcchrystals_address_on_afghanistan_98537.html.

30. Luke N. Condra et al., *The Effect of Civilian Casualties in Afghanistan and Iraq* (Nat'l Bureau of Econ. Research, Working Paper 16152, 2011).

31. Id.

32. The data analyzed by the team involved 2,118 incidents that resulted in 4,077 civilians killed between January 2009 and March 2010.

33. Bob Dreyfuss, *How the US War in Afghanistan Fueled the Taliban Insurgency*, THE NATION (Sept. 18, 2013), https://www.thenation.com/article/archive/how-us-war-afghanistan-fueled-taliban-insurgency/.

34. LAWRENCE FREEDMAN, THE FUTURE OF WAR 207 (Kindle ed. 2017)(quoting Jason Lyall, Graeme Blair, & Kosuke Imai, *Explaining Support for Combatants during Wartime: A Survey Experiment in Afghanistan*, AM. POL. SCI. REV. 107(4) (2013).

35. James Piazza & Seung-Whan Choi, *International Military Interventions and Transnational Terrorist Backlash*, 62 INT'L STUD. Q. 686, 686 (2018).

36. JOHN TIRMAN, THE DEATHS OF OTHERS (Kindle ed. 2011).

37. BOB WOODWARD, OBAMA'S WARS 99 (Kindle ed. 2010).

38. "Careful police intelligence work and international police cooperation, together with a more rigorously professional system of protection for monarchs and heads of state, aided in curbing anarchist terrorism, while heavy-handed repression only worsened it." RICHARD BACH JENSEN, THE BATTLE AGAINST ANARCHIST TERRORISM: AN INTERNATIONAL HISTORY, 1878–1934 2 (Kindle ed. 2014).

39. *Id.* at 186.

40. In 2013 *The Atlantic* published an article by Hassan Abbas: "In battling terrorism, physical elimination of the enemy matters but is not decisive. Hitting at the mindset of the terrorist and discrediting the ideas that generate terrorism is the big prize. A law enforcement action that flows out of a 'rule of law' paradigm, involving meticulous investigations and prosecution in courts, is likely to be far more damaging for the ideas that terrorists stand for—it may take longer to deliver, but it will be more sustainable, and the results will be more durable." Hassan Abbas, *How Drones Create More Terrorists*, ATLANTIC (Aug. 23, 2013), https://www.theatlantic.com/internatio nal/archive/2013/08/how-drones-create-more-terrorists/278743/.

41. *FBI History*, FEDERATION OF AMERICAN SCIENTISTS, https://fas.org/irp/agency/doj/fbi/fbi_hist.htm, (last updated June 18, 2003).

42. JOHN NAGL, COUNTERINSURGENCIES LESSONS FROM MALAYA AND VIETNAM: LEARNING TO EAT SOUP WITH A KNIFE 1540 (Kindle ed. 2002).

43. Francesco De Angelis, *The European Public Prosecutor's Office (EPPO)—Past, Present, and Future*, 4 EUCRIM 272, (2019).

44. BOB WOODWARD, OBAMA'S WARS 70 (Kindle ed. 2010).

45. *Id.* at 80–81.

46. *Id.* at 113.

47. Barack Obama, 44th President of the U.S., Remarks by the President on a New Strategy for Afghanistan and Pakistan at Dwight D. Eisenhower Executive Office Building (Mar. 27, 2009).

48. *Id.*

49. BOB WOODWARD, OBAMA'S WARS 119 (Kindle ed. 2010).

50. *By mid-July, General Lute was reading the final pieces of feedback about the 40-page draft of the SIP [Strategic Implementation Plan]. Gates's memo concerned him. The mission in Afghanistan could not be to "disrupt" the Taliban, Gates wrote. This needs to be "defeat." Lute instantly grasped the magnitude of Gates's recommendation, which had been pushed by the Pentagon for months and exhibited the strong influence of*

Petraeus and his COINistas, the true believers in counterinsurgency . . . Defeating the Taliban would take more troops, money, and time than disrupting would. Id. at 145–46.

51. *Id.* at 147.

52. *Id.*

53. "Dave and I had shared an early fascination with irregular wars and the counterinsurgents who had fought them in Indochina and Algeria." GENERAL STANLEY MCCHRYSTAL, MY SHARE OF THE TASK: A MEMOIR 102 (Kindle ed. 2013).

54. BOB WOODWARD, OBAMA'S WARS 176 (Kindle ed. 2010).

55. *Id.* at 161.

56. ROBERT M. GATES, DUTY 364 (Kindle ed. 2014).

57. General Eikenberry "considered that instead of *"broad options,"* the military gave Mr. Obama only "variations" on "the more robust counterinsurgency model." BOB WOODWARD, OBAMA'S WARS 213 (Kindle ed. 2010).

58. "It angered Obama that Petraeus was publicly lobbying and prejudging a presidential decision." *Id.* at 158.

59. *Id.* at 173.

60. U.S. Army Field Manual No. 3-24 Marine Corps Warfighting Publication No. 3-33.5

61. FRED KAPLAN, THE INSURGENTS: DAVID PETRAEUS AND THE PLOT TO CHANGE THE AMERICAN WAY OF WAR 307 (Kindle ed. 2013).

62. ROBERT M. GATES, DUTY 364 (Kindle ed. 2014).

63. He considered that "a counterinsurgency strategy was too ambitious and would edge into nation-building—a massive undertaking that could be a dramatic overreach." BOB WOODWARD, OBAMA'S WARS 218 (Kindle ed. 2010).

64. Marc Landler, *The Afghan War and the Evolution of Obama*, N.Y. TIMES (Jan. 1, 2017), https://www.nytimes.com/2017/01/01/world/asia/obama-afghanistan-war.html.

65. BOB WOODWARD, OBAMA'S WARS 221 (Kindle ed. 2010).

66. *Id.* at 223.

67. ROBERT M. GATES, DUTY 364 (Kindle ed. 2014).

68. *Id.* at 227–28.

69. *Id.* at 229.

70. *Id.* at 247.

71. *Id.* at 168.

72. Barack Obama, 44th President of the U.S., Remarks by the President in Address to the Nation on the Way Forward in Afghanistan and Pakistan (Dec. 1, 2009).

73. *Id.*

74. *Id.*

75. *Id.*

76. Daniel Nasaw & Mark Tran, *Taliban Rejects Obama Plan. World Reaction—Live*, THE GUARDIAN NEWS BLOG (Dec. 2, 2009, 10:58 AM), https://www.theguardian.com/glo bal/blog/2009/dec/02/afghanistan-barack-obama.

77. *Obama represented all the ideals for which the Nobel Committee had worked hard for many decades: a better-organized world with a focus on the UN and multilateral di- plomacy; dialogue and negotiations in almost all situations; the vision of a world free*

from nuclear weapons; strengthening of democracy and human rights; a new climate policy. GEIR LUNDESTAD, THE WORLD'S MOST PRESTIGIOUS PRIZE 161–69 (Kindle ed. 2019).

78. *The Nobel Peace Prize for 2009*, THE NOBEL PRIZE, https://www.nobelprize.org/pri zes/peace/2009/press-release/ (last visited June 11, 2020).

79. "One of these wars is winding down. The other is a conflict that America did not seek; one in which we are joined by 42 other countries—including Norway—in an effort to defend ourselves and all nations from further attacks." Barack Obama, 44th President of the U.S., A Just and Lasting Peace, Nobel Lecture Oslo (Dec. 10, 2009) (transcript available at https://www.nobelprize.org/prizes/peace/2009/ obama/lecture/).

80. *Id.*

81. *Id.*

82. "The service and sacrifice of our men and women in uniform has promoted peace and prosperity from Germany to Korea, and enabled democracy to take hold in places like the Balkans. We have borne this burden not because we seek to impose our will. We have done so out of enlightened self-interest—because we seek a better future for our children and grandchildren, and we believe that their lives will be better if others' children and grandchildren can live in freedom and prosperity." *Id.*

83. BOB WOODWARD, OBAMA'S WARS 372 (Kindle ed. 2010).

84. Marc Landler, *The Afghan War and the Evolution of Obama*, N.Y. TIMES (Jan. 1, 2017), https://www.nytimes.com/2017/01/01/world/asia/obama-afghanistan-war.html.

85. BOB WOODWARD, OBAMA'S WARS 184 (Kindle ed. 2010).?

86. Marc Landler, *The Afghan War and the Evolution of Obama*, N.Y. TIMES (Jan. 1, 2017), https://www.nytimes.com/2017/01/01/world/asia/obama-afghanistan-war.html.

87. Connie Bruck, *The Inside War*, NEW YORKER (June 15, 2015), https://www.newyor ker.com/magazine/2015/06/22/the-inside-war.

88. BOB WOODWARD, OBAMA'S WARS 227 (Kindle ed. 2010).

89. *Id.* at 296.

90. Barack Obama, 44th President of the U.S.A, Remarks at the National Defense University, (May 23, 2017), (transcript available at https://obamawhitehouse.archives. gov/the-press-office/2013/05/23/remarks-president-national-defense-university). *See also* HAROLD HONGJU KOH, THE TRUMP ADMINISTRATION AND INTERNATIONAL LAW 97 (Kindle ed. 2018).

91. JACK GOLDSMITH, POWER AND CONSTRAINT: THE ACCOUNTABLE PRESIDENCY AFTER 9/11 13–15 (Kindle ed. 2012).

92. Tom Engelhardt, *Why Are So Many of Our "Surgical" Strikes Going So Terribly Wrong?*, NATION (Dec. 20, 2013), https://www.thenation.com/article/archive/us-has-bom bed-least-eight-wedding-parties-2001/.

93. STEPHEN M. WALT, THE HELL OF GOOD INTENTIONS 178 (Kindle ed. 2018).

94. *Id.* at 177–78.

95. ROSA BROOKS, HOW EVERYTHING BECAME WAR AND THE MILITARY BECAME EVERYTHING: TALES FROM THE PENTAGON 347–48 (Kindle ed. 2016).

96. *Establishing a New Normal. National Security, Civil Liberties, and Human Rights under the Obama Administration, An 18-Month Review*, AM. CIVIL LIBERTIES UNION (July 2010), https://www.aclu.org/sites/default/files/field_document/Establ ishingNewNormal.pdf.

97. "On the issues of whether terrorism is to be confronted as a war or as a crime, the legal basis for military detention, the discretionary approach to trials and detention, habeas corpus, the legal basis for rendition, state secrets, and surveillance, Obama's position is basically the same as the one that prevailed at the end of the Bush administration." JACK GOLDSMITH, POWER AND CONSTRAINT: THE ACCOUNTABLE PRESIDENCY AFTER 9/11 19–20 (Kindle ed. 2012).

98. *Id.* at 102.

99. Most of Obama's team were part of the decisions adopted during the Bush administration including Robert Gates, the "Chairman of the Joint Chiefs of Staff (Admiral Mike Mullen), his longtime FBI Director (Robert Mueller), his Deputy National Security Advisor for Afghanistan and Iraq (General Douglas Lute), and his head of the National Counterterrorism Center (Michael Leiter). Obama's principal adviser for counterterrorism, John Brennan, was a twenty-five-year intelligence veteran and George Tenet's chief of staff when the CIA established its interrogation program during the Bush years. Admiral Dennis Blair, Obama's first Director of National Intelligence (DNI), replaced another Navy man, Vice Admiral Michael McConnell, Bush's last DNI. And Obama's second DNI, James Clapper, was Bush's last Under Secretary of Defense for Intelligence." *Id.* at 27–28.

100. *Id.* at 27–28.

101. Eric Lichtblau & Scott Shane, *Report Faults 2 Authors of Bush Terror Memos*, N.Y. TIMES (Feb. 19, 2010), https://www.nytimes.com/2010/02/20/us/politics/20justice. html?hpw.

102. JACK GOLDSMITH, POWER AND CONSTRAINT: THE ACCOUNTABLE PRESIDENCY AFTER 9/11 27–28 (Kindle ed. 2012).

103. STEPHEN M. WALT. THE HELL OF GOOD INTENTIONS 69 (Kindle ed. 2018).

18

The ICC Investigation in Afghanistan

This chapter presents one of the consequences of *jus ad Bellum* decisions in Afghanistan and Iraq: they provided incentives to protect the US personnel involved in war crimes and to oppose justice. Already in 1873, Louis Gabriel Gustave Moynier, the Swiss lawyer who cofounded the ICRC, noted that states at war have no interest in punishing crimes committed by their own soldiers, and international courts are required to guarantee the law of war's enforcement.[1] One hundred fifty years in advance, Moynier predicted the US objections to the ICC investigations of Afghanistan's torture.

Afghanistan is a state party of the Rome Statute that provided jurisdiction to the ICC from May 1, 2003, onward. Since 2004, the media unveiled the commission of tortures in Afghanistan under the Bush administration. Consequently, the US Army and the CIA inspector general launched inquiries on the allegations of torture.

Congress conducted investigations and produced two main reports. These inquiries demonstrated significant evidence that US personnel engaged in systematic acts of torture suggesting superior instructions. But neither the Bush nor the Obama administrations investigated those who authorized the crimes. Furthermore, President Trump supported army officers investigated by US justice.

Different crimes under the court's jurisdiction were committed by various parties in Afghanistan, including tortures by US personnel. There were no national investigations against those most responsible for the crimes. Neither a high-ranking member of the executive branch nor a top CIA or US Army officer was ever convicted.

Regarding US investigations of torture, it is possible to distinguish three different moments: first, cover-up and denial; second, minimizing, presenting the facts as isolated incidents originated in a few rogue subordinates that would be punished; and third, forget the past and focus on the future. The first two phases happened during the Bush administration; the Obama presidency developed the third one. The lack of national investigations made the cases admissible before the ICC.

War and Justice in the 21st Century. Luis Moreno Ocampo, Oxford University Press. © Oxford University Press 2022. DOI: 10.1093/oso/9780197628973.003.0019

As mentioned, President Obama immediately banned the use of torture[2] and ordered the closing of CIA "black sites," secret facilities established around the world to interrogate suspects without any external constraint.[3] He also recognized that US personnel committed acts of torture but refused to investigate those who ordered them. President Obama's policy "to look forward as opposed to looking backward" required his administration to protect individuals involved in torture and disappearance.

President Trump stretched the protection policy. When the ICC prosecutor opened the Afghanistan investigation, the Trump administration revoked her visa in April 2019. In September 2020, the US government "designated" the prosecutor and the head of the Jurisdiction Division as if they were terrorists "for having directly engaged in an effort to investigate US personnel."

As already mentioned in Chapter 2, the 2005 National Defense Strategy of the United States noted that "our strength as a nation-state will continue to be challenged by those who employ a strategy of the weak using international fora, judicial processes, and terrorism."[4]

Beyond the different US presidents' personalities, there is a constant: US strategy to address international terrorism is in open confrontation with any independent judicial scrutiny. The War on Terror demands loyalty to the United States as a principal value rather than a commitment to the law. In war, those who support the opponent became part of the "enemy." The conflict is with any judicial investigation, not just with the ICC.

The ICC became the only independent judicial system that can provide rights to Afghan victims. Still, the narrative is not presenting the problem accurately: US personnel tortured, the United States refused to investigate, and it attacked the ICC to cover up the crimes committed.

The US Investigations of Torture

The Uncovering of the Interrogations

The arrest of a senior Al Qaeda operative named Abu Zubaydah in March 2002 who allegedly had information of an imminent attack against the United States triggered the adoption of exceptional interrogation techniques. Even President Bush was involved in their approval. *"I took a look at the list of techniques. There were two that I felt went too far, even if they were legal. I directed the CIA not to use them."*[5]

In December 2007, the *Times* revealed that CIA officers had secretly destroyed the Abu Zubaydah interrogations' videotapes. Michael Hayden, the CIA director, offered information to the Senate Committee, and for months, two Senate staff members reviewed it. These circumstances were the genesis of the Senate 2012 Torture Report.[6]

The attempt to adopt coerced interrogation techniques as a formal policy by the Secretary of Defense found strong opposition in the military forces under his authority. Rumsfeld did not adopt the most abusive policies formally. Still, there was an informal process of "blurring of interrogation techniques used at Guantánamo Bay and in Afghanistan that were applied improperly in Iraq."[7]

Fist: Cover-Up and Denial

"While he was secretary of defense, Mr. Rumsfeld denied many times that torture was a policy of the American government."[8] A Report of the Committee on Armed Services US Senate connected Mr. Rumsfeld's official policies and the events exposed in Abu Ghraib.[9] Still and based on public information, the causal relationship could be *plausibly denied.*

On October 11, 2002, Major General Michael Dunlavey, the commander at Guantánamo Bay, requested authority to use aggressive interrogation techniques. At the end of October 2002, the Joint Chiefs of Staff's chairman solicited the military services' views on the request.[10] There was substantial internal opposition to the proposal.

William Haynes II, the general counsel of the Department of Defense (DoD), realized that "there was a sense by the DoD Leadership that this decision was taking too long." He produced a one-page memo to the secretary, recommending that he approve all but three of the eighteen techniques requested by the Guantánamo Commander.

On December 2, 2002, Secretary Rumsfeld signed Mr. Haynes's recommendation.[11] On January 15, 2003, Navy General Counsel Alberto Mora warned Mr. Haynes that he was going to send a signed memo expressing that interrogatory methods that the secretary of defense had authorized "could rise to the level of torture." The same day, Secretary Rumsfeld signed a memo rescinding authority for the techniques and established a "Working Group" to review them.[12]

For the next few months, senior military and civilian lawyers tried, without success, to have their concerns about the legality of aggressive methods reflected in the Working Group's report.[13] Their arguments were rejected, and John Yoo, a Berkeley professor leading the Department of Justice's Office of Legal Counsel (OLC), issued an opinion based on previous memos accepting the legality of the aggressive methods allowing the official adoption of some but not all of the techniques.[14]

On April 16, 2003, the secretary of defense authorized the use of twenty-four specific interrogation techniques for use at Guantánamo. But he was cautious. The authorization did not include some of the methods accepted in the Working Group report and invited a request for "additional interrogation techniques for a particular detainee" if it was needed.[15]

The rescission of the previous Rumsfeld instruction did not cancel the use of aggressive tactics in Iraq.[16] Between August 31 and September 9, 2003, a commander from Guantánamo led a strategic interrogation's team that visited Baghdad to conduct an "Assessment of DoD Counter-Terrorism Interrogation and Detention Operations in Iraq." They used Guantánamo's "operational procedures and interrogation authorities as baselines for its observations and recommendations."[17]

In late December 2003, the legal situation changed. As the new Assistant Attorney General for the Office of Legal Counsel, Jack Goldsmith notified Mr. Haynes that DoD could no longer rely on Mr. Yoo's memo in determining the lawfulness of interrogation techniques. But at that time, the abuses in Abu Ghraib had already happened. They were committed between November and December 2003 and were reported by a soldier on January 13, 2004.

Major General Antonio Tabuga, who had no connection with the problem, was assigned to investigate the case. On April 4, 2004, Major Gral Tabuga presented his conclusion: "Several US Army Soldiers have committed egregious acts and grave breaches of international law." He also considered that the three intelligence officers in charge "were either directly or indirectly responsible for the abuses at Abu Ghraib" and recommended investigating them.[18]

General Tabuga's confidential report was leaked by the *New Yorker* on April 30, 2004, transforming an internal inquiry into a national and international debate. Rumsfeld had to appear before Congress and apologize.

In July 2004, Goldsmith withdrew another previous OLC memo defining torture and resigned the same day. The War on Terror is demanding to cover the crimes committed by US personnel, loyalty to the political decisions, not to the rule of law.

He explained, "the main reason I resigned was that important people inside the administration had come to question my fortitude for the job and my reliability."[19] Jack Goldsmith is politically conservative, a friend of John Yoo, and he liked to work with the CIA, but he firmly believed in the legal limits.[20]

Second: Minimizing

The abuse of prisoners in Abu Ghraib created a scandal and forced Secretary of Defense Donald Rumsfeld to adopt a new line: to blame low-ranking officers. He announced further inquiries to "Watch how a democracy deals with wrongdoing."[21]

On August 24, 2004, an independent commission headed by former Secretary of Defense James Schlesinger considered that there was "institutional and personal responsibility at higher levels" for Abu Ghraib but cleared Rumsfeld of any direct responsibility.[22] In his investigation into Abu Ghraib, Major General George Fay reported that interrogation techniques developed for GTMO [Guantánamo] became "confused" and were implemented at Abu Ghraib.[23]

The Justice Department announced that it looked into three suspicious deaths of detainees, two in Iraq and one in Afghanistan, and the CIA and contractors' involvement in the deaths.[24]

There were some convictions against low-ranking members of the army for the Abu Ghraib scandal. Some of them received three, eight, and ten years in prison, but most were lightly punished. For instance, an army dog handler was found guilty of aggravated assault and unlawfully using his dog to threaten detainees and sentenced to ninety days hard labor, a reduction of rank, and $600 per month for a year.[25]

Lt. Col. Steven L. Jordan was the only high-ranking intelligence officer charged for the Abu Ghraib events, but on April 28, 2006, he was cleared of all wrongdoing. Janis Karpinski, the brigade commander in charge of all twelve Iraqi detention facilities, including Abu Ghraib, was demoted from brigadier general to colonel. *Karpinski maintained that she and her troops were following interrogation guidelines approved by top brass.*[26]

In 2005 Rumsfeld said, "people have been punished and convicted in a court-martial. So the idea that there's any policy of abuse or policy of torture is false. Flat false."[27]

Third: Forgetting

The Abu Ghraib scandal was a shock but just the tip of the iceberg. On September 6, 2006, Michael Hayden, the CIA director, appeared before the Senate Intelligence Committee and described a network of "black sites": secret facilities where CIA interrogators subjected detainees to "enhanced interrogation techniques."

Afterward, Senator Feinstein wrote to Hayden that his testimony was "extraordinarily problematic." Hayden commented: "This is not CIA's program. This is not the President's program. This is America's program."[28]

Immediately President Bush reacted in the way proposed by Feinstein. He acknowledged the existence of black sites and *announced that 14 individuals were being transferred from Central Intelligence Agency (CIA) custody to DoD custody at Guantánamo.*[29]

Obama's Promises and Their Implementation

During the 2008 campaign, Barack Obama was cautious about investigating the past. He stated: *if crimes have been committed, they should be investigated.* But he also said:

I would not want my first term consumed by what was perceived on the part of Republicans as a partisan witch hunt because I think we've got too many problems we've got to solve. So, this is an area where I would want to exercise judgment -- I would want to find out directly from my Attorney General . . . are there possibilities of genuine crimes as opposed to really bad policies.[30]

As the US president elected in January 2009, Obama "signaled . . . that he was unlikely to authorize a broad inquiry into Bush administration programs." He had "a belief that we need to look forward as opposed to looking backward" and praised the intelligence personnel. "And part of my job," he continued, "is to make sure that, for example, at the CIA, you've got extraordinarily talented people who are working very hard to keep Americans safe. I don't want them to suddenly feel like they've got spend their all their time looking over their shoulders."[31]

On April 16, 2009, due to a long-standing case filed by the American Civil Liberties Union and the Center for Constitutional Rights, the Justice Department released legal memos produced by the Bush administration approving aggressive interrogation tactics.[32]

The *Washington Post* mentioned a "fierce battle within the highest ranks of the Obama White House about the benefits of releasing the information."[33] President Obama made the memos public, but he also issued a statement promising to fight in the future to maintain the confidentiality of classified national security information, appeasing the intelligence community.[34]

President Obama announced at the same time his policy on prosecutions: those who implemented what he considered torture following orders will not be prosecuted and praised the intelligence personnel for protecting America.[35] He made clear his intentions to ignore past crimes to create a bipartisan consensus:

> This is a time for reflection, not retribution. . . . [A]t a time of great challenges and disturbing disunity, nothing will be gained by spending our time and energy laying blame for the past . . . [w]e must resist the forces that divide us, and instead come together on behalf of our common future.[36]

However, in August 2009, the Justice Department's ethics office recommended a re-examination of a Bush administration-era decisions to refrain from prosecuting several cases related to CIA interrogations. Attorney General Eric Holder chose John Durham to head the criminal probe.[37]

In November 2010, the Justice Department said there would be no charges in destroying the Abu Zubaydah videotapes of CIA interrogations.[38] Two years later, on June 30, 2011, Attorney General Holder, following Mr. Durham's advice, announced *a full criminal investigation regarding the death in custody of two individuals.*[39]

More than one year later, on August 30, 2012, Attorney General Holder *announced that no one would be prosecuted for those two cases, eliminating the last possibility that any criminal charges will be brought as a result of the brutal interrogations carried out by the CIA.*[40]

Years later, during a small seminar at Harvard, a member of the Obama administration explained that the Bush administration's leaders that promoted the policies could have been prosecuted. But the Obama administration evaluated the risk of alienating the Republican Party and complicating the relationship with Congress. Considering the political consequences, the decision adopted was to stop all the investigations against high-level ranking personnel.

Instead, the person prosecuted by the Department of Justice during the Obama administration was John C. Kiriakou, a former CIA counterterrorism officer who denounced publicly "that the CIA was torturing its prisoners, that torture was official US government policy." An FBI investigation against Kiriakou started in 2007, had been closed, but the Obama administration reopened it. Kiriakou served twenty-three months in jail.[41]

The Media and Senate Impetus

Even before Obama was appointed the president, on November 20, 2008, the Senate Armed Services Committee approved the final report of the "Inquiry into the Treatment of Detainees In US Custody" with the favorable vote of some members of the Republican Party.[42] The report's executive summary was made public on December 10, 2008, by the committee's chairman Senator Carl Levin and Senator John McCain.

McCain was the Republican candidate defeated by President Obama in the national elections a month before. As a former prisoner of war for five years in Vietnam, he had a strong commitment against torture.[43] The report concluded: "the abuse of detainees at Abu Ghraib in late 2003 was not simply the result of a few soldiers acting on their own" and blamed Secretary of Defense Donald Rumsfeld.[44] Senator McCain said, "These policies are wrong and must never be repeated."[45]

At the beginning of the Obama tenure, Senator Patrick J. Leahy, chairman of the Judiciary Committee, suggested something like a "Truth Commission," a "middle ground to get to the truth of what went on during the last several years, in a way that invites cooperation."[46] His proposal was not adopted.

In March 2009, Senator Feinstein, as the Senate Intelligence Committee's chairperson, transformed the small inquiry focused on the videos' destructions into a full investigation of the CIA program. She was supported at the beginning, the committee voted in favor of it, 14 to 1.[47] Leon Panetta, then head of the CIA, wanted to have some control over the confidential material and proposed a deal: instead of turning over the documents in masse to Senator Feinstein staff, CIA would set up a secure reading room in Virginia, where the papers will be reviewed, and the documents themselves would stay with the CIA.

Panetta said, "I thought it was a sound compromise and a good deal for the agency, so I didn't think to clear it with the White House." But then Obama's chief of staff summoned him to an "ugly" meeting: "The president wants to know who the fuck authorized this release to the committees."[48]

The Congress's support to investigate torture was also diminishing. Six Republicans recused themselves, and after three- and one-half years, in December 2012, the final report was confidential and approved by just one Republican and eight Democrats. *The report examined different cases concluded that the enhanced techniques were far more brutal than the agency had disclosed and were an ineffective means of obtaining accurate information.*[49]

The report also *included an appendix devoted to Hayden, detailing more than thirty misstatements in one session of his testimony. (Hayden argues that the Democrats misinterpreted the intent of his testimony, saying, "I described the norms—how things were supposed to work—and they found the exceptions.")*[50]

The Conflict between the Senate and the CIA during the Obama Presidency

The fact that the decision to *look forward as opposed to looking backward* was adopted by President Obama, who made his campaign on values and denounced the torture practice as a senator, confused many of his followers. President Obama's rationale was that he had to continue the War on Terror, and he needed CIA support.

To release a public version, "Feinstein and several other Democrats on the committee fought strenuously against the CIA—and, unexpectedly, the Obama White House."[51] On January 15, 2013, John Brennan, as the new head of the CIA, escalated the conflict. Brennan officially complained to Feinstein that the Senate staff was hacking into the agency's computer system and obtained the "Panetta review," an internal document analyzing the same activities under investigation by the Senate.

Brennan said that the Senate staffers had printed out copies of the documents and demanded that Feinstein return all of them to the CIA. Two days after the meeting, Feinstein wrote to Brennan, urging him to stop investigating her staff and noting that the CIA's search could have violated constitutional principles of separation of powers.[52]

In late January, the CIA inspector general, David Buckley, learned about the search and told Brennan that he would investigate the CIA's actions. (The agency maintains that Brennan requested the inquiry unprompted.)[53]

The conflict continued. In February, the CIA filed a crimes report with the Department of Justice against a Senate staff member for hacking its system. In early March, articles about the conflict appeared in the press. CIA Director John Brennan denied allegations against the CIA: "I am deeply dismayed that some members of the Senate have decided to make spurious allegations about CIA actions that are wholly unsupported by the facts."[54] "Nothing could be further from the truth."[55]

Feinstein answered on March 11, saying that the CIA. might well have violated the constitutional principle of separation of powers, the Computer Fraud and Abuse Act, and an executive order that prohibits the CIA from conducting domestic searches or surveillance. The crimes report that the CIA had filed with the Department of Justice, she said, was an effort to intimidate her staff.[56] It would be months before Brennan's denial was publicly proved false.

On July 31, 2014, the CIA inspector general, David Buckley, released a summary of findings in the internal investigation he had started in January. He concluded that agency employees had acted improperly in accessing the computers and the e-mail of the committee staff and that the crimes report that the CIA had filed with the Justice Department was based on erroneous information.[57] According to the official's memo, included in the inspector general's report, Brennan informed the White House of each decision he adopted.

As a result, John Brennan apologized to the US Senate intelligence committee leaders, conceding that the agency employees spied on committee staff and reversed months of furious and public denials.[58] In any case, the following day, the president stood by his CIA director. "I have full confidence in John Brennan," Obama said.

He also considered that enhanced interrogation techniques were torture and recognized "we tortured some folks." But at the same time, he declared: "It's important for us not to feel too sanctimonious in retrospect about the tough job that those folks had. A lot of those folks were working hard under enormous pressure and are real patriots."[59]

Senator Feinstein feared that if the report were not released before the Republicans took control of the Senate in January 2015, it never would be. Some of her colleagues believed that the White House was deliberately running out the clock. "Obama participated in the slowdown process."[60]

On Tuesday, December 9, 2014, the report was released, creating a national and international debate.[61]

The Impact of the Senate Report

Brennan responded to the report in a press conference at CIA headquarters in Langley—the first such conference to be televised live. He considered that the report was partial because the Republicans did not support it.[62]

Brennan also contradicted the main conclusion of the committee: "The record simply does not support the study's inference that the agency repeatedly, systematically and intentionally misled others on the effectiveness of the program."[63]

During a White House news conference, the next day, Obama made his most forthright acknowledgment yet of the substance of the report *"these enhanced interrogation techniques . . . were torture, we crossed a line."* But he emphasized his "full confidence" in Brennan: "Keep in mind—John Brennan called for that IG [Inspector General] report, and he's already stood-up a task force to ensure that lessons are learned, and mistakes are resolved."[64]

In fact, the inspector general lost his position. In mid-January 2015, Brennan's task force, composed of three CIA officers and two members from outside the agency, dismissed Inspector General Buckley's conclusion that the officers who searched the Senate computers had acted improperly. The same month, Buckley left the CIA.[65]

American Civil Liberties Union Director Anthony Romero proposed a new way. He considered it clear that President Obama "is not inclined to pursue prosecutions" and therefore "He should therefore take ownership of this decision." Romero called on President Barack Obama to pardon George W. Bush and his administration officials for their role in the torture practice's approval.

If the choice is between a tacit pardon and a formal one, a formal one is better. Pardons would make clear that crimes were committed.[66]

Harold Koh, who was no longer a member of the Obama administration, opposed a pardon.[67] He mentioned that the *New York Times* had invoked the

Freedom of Information Act to request the disclosure of documents from a Justice Department investigation into CIA interrogations, including summaries of interviews with about one hundred witnesses and documents explaining why in the end, no charges were filed. Koh proposed to relaunch prosecutions and accept pending Freedom of Information requests "to get the full story."[68]

But instead of following Koh's advice, the Obama administration urged the court to reject the *New York Times* request.[69] In 2019 a film called *The Torture Report* was released, exposing Senator Feinstein's teamwork.

The International Dimensions

The CIA's kidnapping in Milan of Osama Mustafa Hassan Nasr, known as Abu Omar, is an excellent example of the Obama administration's active protection to those involved in abductions and torture.

Abu Omar, an Egyptian citizen who received political asylum in Italy in 2001, was already under an Italian investigation for his possible involvement with international terrorism.[70] In February 2003, Abu Omar was abducted by CIA operatives in Milan, transported by plane from a US base at the Aviano airport, handed over clandestinely to Egyptian intelligence for interrogation, and was allegedly tortured for seven months.[71]

The Italian investigation confirmed the involvement of CIA operatives, and the subsequent criminal proceedings led to the conviction of twenty-three US officials in absentia. In July 2013, at the request of Italian authorities, police in Panama detained one of them, the former CIA station chief in Milan, Robert Seldon Lady. The Obama administration negotiated with Panamanian authorities, and on July 19, 2013, Robert Lady "was released and was in route to the U.S," State Department spokeswoman said.[72]

In September 2014, Amnesty International produced a report challenging "President Obama's silence on accountability and redress" from an international perspective.[73] Amnesty had no doubt "that this was a program not just of "enhanced interrogation" but also of enforced disappearance."[74]

President Trump went beyond President Obama's protection. He pardoned two army officers charged with war crimes and restored a Navy SEAL officer's rank previously acquitted by a military jury on all but a minor count.[75] At a November 2019 political rally, Trump brought two of them on stage, claiming that he had "stuck up for three great warriors against the deep state."[76]

The three presidents' decisions to cover US officers' crimes consolidated the concept that US personnel are free to commit crimes against aliens in foreign countries. Even US justice investigations against military personnel were affected. Worst yet, the policy affected those trying to control the crimes. People with authority *to participate in the events*, like Senator Feinstein, were marginalized. CIA Inspector General Buckley and Assistant Attorney General Jack Goldsmith had to resign. Major General Tabuga was forced to retire in January 2007. The chapter is an example of the influence of *jus ad Bellum* decisions on *jus ad Curiam*.

The Office of the Prosecutor Preliminary Examination on Afghanistan

Jurisdiction to Open an Examination

Afghanistan deposited its ratification instrument to the statute on February 10, 2003, providing ICC with jurisdiction over crimes committed on its territory or by its nationals from May 1, 2003, onward.

Since 2006 our office has conducted a preliminary examination of alleged crimes under our jurisdiction committed in Afghanistan by different forces, including different Taliban groups, militias from the North Alliance, Afghan National Security Forces, and US personnel.

During my tenure, we were trying to obtain information about the crimes committed in Afghanistan. The Taliban and the North Alliance were loosely composed of militias acting without strong coordination, so it was complicated to identify those most responsible. We did not obtain clear information about the allegations of torture against the US personnel and the command chain. We did not consider that drone attacks could constitute war crimes.[77]

During the preliminary examination phase, we relied on information provided by third parties and looked for it. I met the Afghanistan permanent representative before the UN. He was previously a human rights activist and promised his cooperation, but he warned us that the government was divided and not very efficient.

We sent letters to the Afghanistan ambassador in The Hague to open a cooperation channel, but we received no answer for months. Finally, our officers reached him, but he refused to cooperate, saying that Afghanistan was not a state party.

We gave him details of his country's decision. He promised to investigate the matter. Finally, months later, he called us apologizing and recognizing that, indeed, Afghanistan was a state party of the Rome Statute. Then Minister of Foreign Affairs Abdullah Abdullah, without consultations had signed all the possible treaties connected with human rights to prevent the country from going back to violence. Abdullah Abdullah was then an opposition leader, and there was a reluctance to cooperate with the court.

Our office discussed a new strategy to obtain information from the states parties contributing troops to the International Security Assistance Force (ISAF) in Afghanistan. States parties have a legal duty to cooperate with our office, and they have data that could have helped us know precisely what happened in Afghanistan.

A Carr Center for Human Rights Policy study led by Doug Johnson[78] and Alberto Mora[79] with Averell Schmidt presented some examples of states parties' information. For instance, *Australian, British, Canadian, and New Zealand military lawyers* [all Rome Statute' states parties] *approached Mora, the US Navy General Counsel, at a military conference in Singapore. They "advised him that their countries' cooperation with the United States 'across the range of military, intelligence, and law enforcement activities in the war on terror would continue to decline' so long as Washington persisted in using torture."*[80]

We appreciated the sensitivities of the state parties' involvement in Afghanistan's military efforts and sent them just a draft to consult the text of our request for cooperation. The mere possibility to receive questions created an uproar in some countries that were reluctant to share their information. We received no relevant information.

Since 2009, the UN Assistance Mission to Afghanistan (UNAMA) systematically recorded civilian casualties. However, the information did not provide a reasonable basis to believe that the international military forces intended to target the civilian population. There were not Afghanistan investigations to consider. The Afghan Parliament passed a general amnesty in 2007, which entered into force in 2009, establishing its de jure inability to conduct national proceedings.[81]

The ICC Preliminary Examination Reports on Afghanistan

In December 2011, our office made public for the first time its report on preliminary examinations, informing that it has continued to seek and analyze information from multiple sources on alleged crimes committed by all parties in Afghanistan.

Since 2014, the Office of the Prosecutor Report on Preliminary Examination showed that the Afghanistan situation moved to the admissibility phase, implying that the Office considered that crimes were committed under the Rome Statute jurisdiction.

A member of the Obama administration told me that she was worried because the situation moved from phase 2.3 to 3.1. I admired how the Office of the Prosecutor was progressing, following its rules, making its decisions wholly transparent and predictable.

The Office of the Prosecutor 2017 report established that there was a reasonable basis to believe, at a minimum, crimes under the court's jurisdiction were committed by *(a) members of the Taliban and their affiliated Haqqani Network; (b) by members of the Afghan National Security Forces ("ANSF"), in particular, the National Directorate for Security ("NDS") and the Afghan National Police ("ANP");.(c) by members of the US armed forces on the territory of Afghanistan and members of the CIA in secret detention facilities both in Afghanistan and on the territory of other States Parties, principally in the 2003–2004 period.*[82]

Regarding admissibility, "the status of forces agreements in place between Afghanistan and the US as well as between Afghanistan and ISAF troop-contributing countries, provided for the exclusive exercise of criminal jurisdiction by the authorities of the sending State."[83]

The Office of the Prosecutor clarified that the US "investigations and/or prosecutions appear to have focused on alleged acts committed by direct physical perpetrators and/or their immediate superiors."[84]

However, the report stated that none of the US' investigations examined the responsibility of those who "developed, authorized or bore oversight responsibility for the implementation by members of the US armed forces of the interrogation techniques." The prosecution reached a similar conclusion on those who appeared most responsible for the crimes allegedly committed by the CIA members.[85] The Office of the Prosecutor was following ongoing investigations in Poland, Romania, and Lithuania about *black sites* and continually assessing their progress.

On November 20, 2017, ICC Prosecutor Fatou Bensouda requested the Pre-Trial Chamber III to authorize an investigation into the situation in Afghanistan since July 1, 2002.[86]

The pre-trial chamber, integrated by Presiding Judge Antoine Kesia-Mbe Mindua, Judge Tomoko Akane, and Judge Rosario Salvatore Aitala, rejected the prosecutor's request. It affirmed that "notwithstanding the fact that all the relevant requirements are met as regards both jurisdiction and admissibility, an investigation into the situation in Afghanistan would not serve the interests of justice."[87] The pre-trial chamber concluded that "interests of justice" is an obstacle to open an "investigation not feasible and inevitably doomed to failure."[88]

Such a criterion is not in the statute. The judges were replacing the legal text with their political opinions. The pre-trial chamber evaluated the political landscape "both in Afghanistan and in key States (both parties and non-parties to the Statute), coupled with the complexity and volatility of the political climate still surrounding the Afghan scenario, make it extremely difficult to gauge the prospects of securing meaningful cooperation from relevant authorities for the future."[89] A similar comment could be presented for each of the situations before the ICC. None of them was feasible ex ante.

The pre-trial chamber infringed in the prosecutor role and requested that investigations must focus on crimes that "appear to have more realistic prospects to lead to trials and thus effectively foster the interests of justice."[90]

The decision created controversies, the prosecutor appealed, and many experts requested to present amicus curiae. From December 4 through December 6, 2020, Appeal Chamber Presiding Judge Piotr Hofmański, Judge Howard Morrison, Judge Luz del Carmen Ibáñez Carranza, Judge Solomy Balungi Bossa, and Judge Kimberly Prost heard their arguments.

On March 5, 2020, the appeals chamber reversed the pre-trial chamber decision and authorized the prosecutor to commence an investigation into Afghanistan.[91] The appeals chamber considered that the chambers have no authority to review under Article 15(4) of the statute the concept of "interest of justice." Such analysis is an exclusive Office of the Prosecutor's prerogative in the situations opened using its *proprio motu* power provided by Article 15.

The appeal chamber ruled unanimously that "the Prosecutor is authorized to commence an investigation 'in relation to alleged crimes committed on the territory of Afghanistan in the period since 1 May 2003, as well as other alleged crimes that have a nexus to the armed conflict in Afghanistan and are sufficiently linked to the situation and were committed on the territory of other States Parties in the period since 1 July 2002.' "[92] That aspect of the decision opened the door to include the *black sites* in Romania, Poland, and Lithuania in the investigation.

The US Reaction

The same day of the appeal chamber's ruling, the US State Department made a press statement: "This is a truly breathtaking action by an unaccountable political institution, masquerading as a legal body. It is all the more reckless for this ruling to come just days after the United States signed a historic peace deal on Afghanistan—the best chance for peace in a generation. Indeed, the Afghan government itself pleaded with the ICC to not take this course. But the ICC politicians had other goals. This is yet another reminder of what happens when multilateral bodies lack oversight and responsible leadership and become instead a vehicle for political vendettas."[93]

A few weeks later, on June 11, 2020, President Trump issued an executive order (EO) declaring that efforts by the International Criminal Court to investigate US personnel or personnel of US allies who are also not parties to the Rome Statute "constitutes an unusual and extraordinary threat to the national security and foreign policy of the United States."[94]

In September 2020, following the executive order, the United States "designated" ICC Prosecutor Fatou Bensouda for having directly engaged to investigate US personnel and the ICC's head of the Jurisdiction, Complementarity and Cooperation Division, Phakiso Mochochoko, for having materially assisted Prosecutor Bensouda.[95]

The consequences of being *designated* include, but are not limited to, freezing their assets and blocking any persons, including financial institutions, from conducting transactions with or provide services to the designated individual. Anyone who materially assists the designated individual can themselves be designated.[96]

ICC officers joined a "list of individuals, groups, and entities, such as terrorists and narcotics traffickers designated under programs that are not country-specific. Collectively, such individuals and companies are called 'Specially Designated Nationals.'"[97]

Secretary of State Mike Pompeo announced the measures against ICC officers. He did not mention US responsibility for tortures and claimed to support the international justice concept:

> Today's announcement reflects the American commitment to real justice and accountability. From the Nuremberg and Tokyo trials after World War II to the more recent Yugoslavia, Lebanon, and Rwanda tribunals, the

United States has consistently sought to uphold good and punish evil under international law. We will continue to do so.[98]

Accordingly, international justice should be applied to others but not to the United States intervening in a Rome Statute state party. Charles Kupchan, in a very well-documented book, explained the importance of maintaining the historical roots of US isolationism, and at the same time, considered that "the United States cannot afford to abandon its role as a beacon of republican values and institutions."[99]

Kupchan, as many in the United States, did not perceive that a permanent US War on Terror is affecting international and national values and institutions. Instead, Martha Minnow, former Harvard Law School's dean graphically said during a conference: "The War on Terror's biggest casualty was our values."

On April 2021, the Biden administration lifted the sanctions against ICC personnel. Following the Bosco prediction, Secretary of State Blinker preferred to manage the ICC "through engagement with all stakeholders in the ICC process."[100]

Notes

1. "A treaty was not a law imposed by a superior authority on its subordinates [but] only a contract whose signatories cannot decree penalties against themselves since there would be no one to implement them. The only reasonable guarantee should lie in the creation of international jurisdiction with the necessary power to compel obedience." LOUIS GABRIEL GUSTAVE MOYNIER, ÉTUDE SUR LA CONVENTION DE GENÈVE POUR L'AMÉLIORATION DU SORT DES MILITAIRES BLESSÉS DANS LES ARMÉES EN CAMPAGNE 300 (Librairie de Joël Cherbuliez, 1870), *quotations translated in* I PIERRE BOISSIER, FROM SOLFERINO TO TSUSHIMA: HISTORY OF THE INTERNATIONAL COMMITTEE OF THE RED CROSS 282 (1963) *See* Christopher Keith Hall, *The First Proposal for a Permanent International Criminal Court*, 38 INT'L REV. OF THE RED CROSS 57 (1998). Christopher Keith Hall was a legal adviser for Amnesty International at its International Secretariat in London.
2. "A scaled-back set of harsh methods was approved by the Justice Department and White House in 2007, but they were rarely if ever used before President Obama banned such methods shortly after taking office." Eric Lichtblau & Scott Shane, *Report Faults 2 Authors of Bush Terror Memos*, N.Y. TIMES (Feb. 19, 2010), https://www.nytimes.com/2010/02/20/us/politics/20justice.html?hpw.

3. John Rizzo, CIA General Counsel under Panetta, considers: "President Obama endorsed the use of rendition. Instead of 'renditions,' the term chosen by the Obama people was "short-term transfers." JOHN RIZZO, COMPANY MAN: THIRTY YEARS OF CONTROVERSY AND CRISIS IN THE CIA 260 (Kindle ed. 2014).

4. JACK GOLDSMITH, THE TERROR PRESIDENCY: LAW AND JUDGMENT INSIDE THE BUSH ADMINISTRATION 53 (Kindle ed. 2007).

5. GEORGE W. BUSH, DECISION POINTS 169 (Kindle ed. 2010).

6. Connie Bruck, *The Inside War*, NEW YORKER (June 15, 2015), https://www.newyor ker.com/magazine/2015/06/22/the-inside-war.

7. See Maj. Gen. George R. Fay and Lt. Gen. Anthony R. Jones's report. Eric Schmmit, *The Reach of War: Abu Ghraib Report; Abuses at Prison Tied to Officers in Intelligence*, N.Y. TIMES (Aug. 26, 2004), https://www.nytimes.com/2004/08/26/world/reach-war-abu-ghraib-report-abuses-prison-tied-officers-intelligence.html.

8. Doreen Carvajal, *Groups Tie Rumsfeld to Torture in Complaint*, N.Y. TIMES (Oct. 27, 2007), https://www.nytimes.com/2007/10/27/world/europe/27rumsfeld.html.

9. The report quoted Major General Fay saying that the policy approved by the Secretary of Defense on December 2, 2002, contributed to the use of aggressive interrogation techniques at Abu Ghraib in late 2003. COMM. ON ARMED SERV. U.S. SENATE, 110TH CONG., INQUIRY INTO THE TREATMENT OF DETAINEES IN U.S. CUSTODY xxiv (Comm. Print 2008).

10. *Id.*

11. COMM. ON ARMED SERV. U.S. SENATE, 110TH CONG., INQUIRY INTO THE TREATMENT OF DETAINEES IN U.S. CUSTODY xix (Comm. 2008).

12. *Id.*

13. *Id.*

14. *Id.*

15. "Secretary Rumsfeld's memo said, however, that 'If, in your view, you require additional interrogation techniques for a particular detainee, you should provide me, via the Chairman of the Joint Chiefs of Staff, a written request describing the proposed technique, recommended safeguards, and the rationale for applying it with an identified detainee.'" *Id.*

16. "Despite the Secretary's January 15,2003 rescission of authority to use aggressive techniques, his initial approval continued to influence interrogation policies." *Ibid.*

17. The official title of the Taguba report is "Article 15-6 Investigation of the 800th Military Police Brigade." ANTONIO M. TAGUBA, ARTICLE 15-6 INVESTIGATION OF THE 800TH MILITARY POLICE BRIGADE 8 (2004).

18. *Id.* at 48.

19. JACK GOLDSMITH, THE TERROR PRESIDENCY: LAW AND JUDGMENT INSIDE THE BUSH ADMINISTRATION 161 (Kindle ed. 2007).

20. He mentioned that CIA personnel "were exposed to a buzzsaw of contradictory commands: stay within the confines of the law, even when the law is maddeningly vague, or you will be investigated and severely punished; but be proactive and aggressive and imaginative, push the law to its limit, don't be cautious, and prevent another attack at all costs, or you will also be investigated and punished." *Id.* at 162.

21. David Stout, *Rumsfeld Offers Apology for Abuse of Iraqi Prisoners*, N.Y. TIMES (May 7, 2004), https://www.nytimes.com/2004/05/07/politics/rumsfeld-offers-apology-for-abuse-of-iraqi-prisoners.html.

22. Seymour M. Hersh, *The General's Report*, NEW YORKER (June 18, 2007), https://www.newyorker.com/magazine/2007/06/25/the-generals-report.

23. "For example, Major General Fay said that removal of clothing, while not included in CJTF-Ts SOP, was 'imported' to Abu Ghraib, could be 'traced through Afghanistan and GTMO.'" COMM. ON ARMED SERV. U.S. SENATE, 110TH CONG., INQUIRY INTO THE TREATMENT OF DETAINEES IN U.S. CUSTODY xxiv (Comm. Print 2008).

24. CNN Editorial Research, *Iraq Prison Abuse Scandal Fast Facts*, CNN (last updated Mar. 22, 2020, 8:35 PM), https://www.cnn.com/2013/10/30/world/meast/iraq-prison-abuse-scandal-fast-facts/index.html.

25. *Id.*

26. Samira Simone, *Abu Ghraib Head Finds Vindication in Newly Released Memos*, CNN http://edition.cnn.com/2009/US/04/22/us.torture.karpinski/index.html (last visited June 11, 2020).

27. Doreen Carvajal, *Groups Tie Rumsfeld to Torture in Complaint*, N.Y. TIMES (Oct. 27, 2007), https://www.nytimes.com/2007/10/27/world/europe/27rumsfeld.html.

28. Connie Bruck, *The Inside War*, NEW YORKER (June 15, 2015), https://www.newyorker.com/magazine/2015/06/22/the-inside-war.

29. Periodic Report of the United States of America to the United Nations Committee Against Torture (Third to Fifth periodic report) ¶ 23(Aug. 13, 2013), https://2009-2017.state.gov/j/drl/rls/213055.htm.

30. Will Bunch, *Obama Would Ask His AG to "Immediately Review" Potential of Crimes in Bush White House*, PHILA. INQUIRER (Apr. 14, 2008, 9:47 PM), https://www.inquirer.com/philly/blogs/attytood/Barack_on_torture.html.

31. David Johnston & Charlie Savage, *Obama Reluctant to Look Into Bush Programs*, N.Y. TIMES (Jan 11, 2009), https://www.nytimes.com/2009/01/12/us/politics/12inquire.html.

32. Carrie Johnson & Julie Tate, *New Interrogation Details Emerge as Administration Releases Justice Department Memos*, WASH. POST (Apr. 17, 2009), https://www.washingtonpost.com/wp-dyn/content/article/2009/04/16/AR2009041602768.html?sid=ST2009041602877.

33. *Id.*

34. *The release of these memos "is required by the rule of law." "While I believe strongly in transparency and accountability, I also believe that in a dangerous world, the United States must sometimes carry out intelligence operations and protect information that is classified for purposes of national security. I have already fought for that principle in court and will do so again in the future." "I will always do whatever is necessary to protect the national security of the United States." Statement of President Barack Obama on Release of OLC Memos*, THE WHITE HOUSE PRESIDENT BARACK OBAMA (Apr. 16, 2009), https://obamawhitehouse.archives.gov/realitycheck/the-press-office/statement-president-barack-obama-release-olc-memos.

35. "In releasing these memos, it is our intention to assure those who carried out their duties relying in good faith upon legal advice from the Department of Justice that

they will not be subject to prosecution. The men and women of our intelligence community serve courageously on the front lines of a dangerous world. Their accomplishments are unsung and their names unknown, but because of their sacrifices, every single American is safer. We must protect their identities as vigilantly as they protect our security, and we must provide them with the confidence that they can do their jobs." *Id.*

36. *Id.*

37. Kevin Whitelaw, *CIA Under Scrutiny as Prosecutor Leads Abuse Inquiry*, NPR (Aug. 24, 2009, 9:20 AM), https://www.npr.org/templates/story/story.php?storyId=112166549.

38. Scott Shane, *No Charges Filed on Harsh Tactics Used by the CIA.*, N.Y. TIMES (Aug. 30, 2012), https://www.nytimes.com/2012/08/31/us/holder-rules-out-prosecutions-in-cia-interrogations.html.

39. *Statement of the Attorney General Regarding Investigation into the Interrogation of Certain Detainees*, U.S. DEP'T. OF JUSTICE (June 20, 2011), https://www.justice.gov/opa/pr/statement-attorney-general-regarding-investigation-interrogation-certain-detainees.

40. Scott Shane, *No Charges Filed on Harsh Tactics Used by the CIA.*, N.Y. TIMES (Aug. 30, 2012), https://www.nytimes.com/2012/08/31/us/holder-rules-out-prosecutions-in-cia-interrogations.html.

41. *The FBI began investigating me immediately. A year later, the Justice Department concluded that I had not committed a crime. . . . The CIA asked the new Obama Justice Department to reopen the case against me. It did, and three years later, I was charged with five felonies . . . I agreed to plea to a lesser charge. I served 23 months in prison.* John Kiriakou, *I Went to Prison for Disclosing the CIA's Torture*, WASH. POST (Mar. 16, 2018, 7:00 AM), https://www.washingtonpost.com/outlook/i-went-to-prison-for-disclosing-the-cias-torture-gina-haspel-helped-cover-it-up/2018/03/15/9507884e-27f8-11e8-874b-d517e912f125_story.html.

42. "Committee staff said the full report was approved in a unanimous voice vote by 17 of the panel's 25 members. The panel consists of 13 Democrats and 12 Republicans." David Morgan, *Senate Report Ties Rumsfeld to Abu Ghraib Abuse*, REUTERS (Dec. 11, 2008, 9:48 PM), https://www.reuters.com/article/us-usa-abuse/senate-report-ties-rumsfeld-to-abu-ghraib-abuse-idUSTRE4BA7JV20081211.

43. McCain was a prisoner of war for five years during the Vietnam War and was tortured. John S. McCain, *John McCain, Prisoner of War: A First-Person Account*, U.S. NEWS (Jan 28, 2008, 11:00 AM), https://www.usnews.com/news/articles/2008/01/28/john-mccain-prisoner-of-war-a-first-person-account.

44. "Secretary of Defense Donald Rumsfeld's December 2,2002 authorization of aggressive interrogation techniques and subsequent interrogation policies and plans approved by senior military and civilian officials conveyed the message that physical pressures and degradation were appropriate treatment for detainees in US military custody." COMM. ON ARMED SERV. U.S. SENATE, 110TH CONG., INQUIRY INTO THE TREATMENT OF DETAINEES IN US CUSTODY xxix (Comm. Print 2008).

45. David Morgan, *Senate Report Ties Rumsfeld to Abu Ghraib Abuse*, REUTERS (Dec. 11, 2008, 9:48 PM), https://www.reuters.com/article/us-usa-abuse/senate-report-ties-rumsfeld-to-abu-ghraib-abuse-idUSTRE4BA7JV20081211.

46. Scott Shane, *No Charges Filed on Harsh Tactics Used by the CIA.*, N.Y. TIMES (Aug. 20, 2012), https://www.nytimes.com/2012/08/31/us/holder-rules-out-prosecuti ons-in-cia-interrogations.html; *see also* Patrick Leahy, *Statement At Hearing On*, U.S. SENATOR PATRICK LEAHY OF VERMONT (Mar. 4, 2020), https://www.leahy.senate.gov/ press/statement-at-hearing-on.

47. In December 2007, the *Times* revealed that CIA officers had secretly destroyed videotapes of the Abu Zubaydah interrogations. Hayden offered information to the Senate Committee and for months, two staff members reviewed the cables. That was the genesis of Senator Feinstein's interest on the topic Connie Bruck, *The Inside War*, NEW YORKER (June 15, 2015), https://www.newyorker.com/magazine/2015/06/22/ the-inside-war.

48. LEON PANETTA, WORTHY FIGHTS 233 (Kindle ed. 2014).

49. Connie Bruck, *The Inside War*, NEW YORKER (June 15, 2015), https://www.newyor ker.com/magazine/2015/06/22/the-inside-war.

50. *Id.*

51. *Id.*

52. *Id.*

53. *Id.*

54. *Id.*

55. Jeremy Herb, *Brennan: CIA Hacking Allegations Not True*, THE HILL (Mar. 11, 2014), https://thehill.com/policy/defense/200448-brennan-cia-hacking-allegations-not-true. Adam Serwer, *Can Trump Bring Back Torture?*, ATLANTIC (Jan. 26, 2017), https://www.theatlantic.com/politics/archive/2017/01/trump-torture/514463/.

56. Connie Bruck, *The Inside War*, NEW YORKER (June 15, 2015), https://www.newyor ker.com/magazine/2015/06/22/the-inside-war.

57. *Id.*

58. Brennan acknowledged that an internal investigation had found agency security personnel transgressed a firewall set up on a CIA network, which allowed Senate committee investigators to review agency documents for their landmark inquiry into CIA torture. Spencer Ackerman, *CIA Admits to Spying on Senate Staffers*, GUARDIAN (July 31, 2012, 8:00 PM), https://www.theguardian.com/world/2014/jul/31/cia-admits-spy ing-senate-staffers.

59. Josh Gerstein, *Obama: "We Tortured Some Folks,"* POLITICO, https://www.politico. com/story/2014/08/john-brennan-torture-cia-109654 (last updated Aug. 2, 2014).

60. By early 2014, it had become clear that the White House was reluctant to take sides against the CIA. Brennan had notified Denis McDonough, Obama's chief of staff, while his agents were searching the Senate computers; he also informed the White House counsel before the crimes report was filed with the Department of Justice. Obama halted neither action. Connie Bruck, *The Inside War*, NEW YORKER (June 15, 2015), https://www.newyorker.com/magazine/ 2015/06/22/the-inside-war.

61. Feinstein had to overcome the opposition from Secretary of State John Kerry, a good friend. "He talked about the dangers this would cause around the world, which I saw as right out of the White House playbook—or the CIA playbook," Rockefeller said. Feinstein had heard this argument from McDonough and Brennan many times. *Id.*

62. "Our hope was that [the Senate Committee] would offer an impartial and authoritative assessment of the program . . . Unfortunately, the committee could not agree on a bipartisan way forward. . . . [W]e view the process . . . as flawed." *Transcript: CIA Director John Brennan Addresses Senate's Report on CIA Interrogation Program,* ABC NEWS (Dec. 11, 2014), https://abcnews.go.com/International/transcript-cia-direc tor-john-brennan-senates-report-cia/story?id=27539690.

63. He considered that "The cause and effect relationship between the use of Enhanced Interrogation Techniques (EITs) and useful information subsequently provided by the detainee is, in my view, unknowable." Connie Bruck, *The Inside War,* NEW YORKER (June 15, 2015), https://www.newyorker.com/magazine/2015/06/22/the-inside-war.

64. Paul Lewis, *Obama Admits CIA "Tortured Some Folks" but Stands by Brenan Over Spying,* GUARDIAN (Aug.1, 2014, 11:05 PM), https://www.theguardian.com/world/ 2014/aug/01/obama-cia-torture-some-folks-brennan-spying.

65. Connie Bruck, *The Inside War,* NEW YORKER (June 15, 2015), https://www.newyor ker.com/magazine/2015/06/22/the-inside-war.

66. Anthony D. Romero, *Pardon Bush and Those Who Tortured,* N.Y. TIMES, (Dec. 8, 2014), https://www.nytimes.com/2014/12/09/opinion/pardon-bush-and-those-who-tortured.html.

67. "Americans vigorously protest when other countries offer such blanket amnesties to their government torturers. We should reject such ideas here, too." He proposed to allow relevant CIA officers to speak to Congress, and declassify the rest of the report and that "A bipartisan select committee of Congress should be appointed to hold hearings to get the full story." Harold Hongju Koh, *The Torture Report is Only the First Step,* FOREIGN POLICY (Dec. 12, 2014, 10:30 AM), https://foreignpolicy.com/2014/ 12/12/the-torture-report-is-only-the-first-step/.

68. Charlie Savage, *U.S. Tells Court That Documents from Torture Investigation Should Remain Secret,* N.Y. TIMES (Dec. 10, 2011), https://www.nytimes.com/2014/12/11/us/ politics/us-tells-court-that-documents-from-torture-investigation-should-remain-secret.html.

69. *Id.*

70. Foro it. II Milano, 22 giugno 2005, no. 10838/05 R.G.N.R and no. 1966/05 R.G.GIP (It.) (translation by Alessandro Bygate and Nicole Hazzan, acting on assignment as appointed by the undersigned Deputy Public Prosecutor, Dr. Armando Spataro, available at http://www.statewatch.org/cia/documents/milan-tribunal-19-us-citiz ens-sought.pdf).

71. Foro it. II Milano, 22 giugno 2005, no. 10838/05 R.G.N.R and no. 1966/05 R.G.GIP (It.) (translation by Alessandro Bygate and Nicole Hazzan, acting on assignment as appointed by the undersigned Deputy Public Prosecutor, Dr. Armando Spataro available at http://www.statewatch.org/cia/documents/milan-tribunal-19-us-citizens-sou ght.pdf).

72. *Panama Frees ex-CIA Official Detained in Italy "Rendition" Case*, NBC NEWS (Jul. 19, 2013, 11:16 AM), http://investigations.nbcnews.com/_news/2013/07/19/19562968-panama-frees-ex-cia-official-detained-in-italy-rendition-case?lite.

73. The report mentioned the failure to meet US international human rights obligations after public knowledge for many years and a plea for sympathy for the perpetrators, even as the government blocks remedy for the victims, "'understanding' has become part of an official narrative that is interwoven with impunity. As such, it effectively becomes justification." Victims of human rights violations have the right under international law to effective access to meaningful remedy. Amnesty Int'l, *USA "We Tortured Some Folks,"* AI Index AMR 51/046/2014 (Sept. 2, 2014).

74. AI quoted the European Court of Human Rights finding that Abu Zubaydah was transferred on December 5, 2002, to a secret CIA detention facility located at Stare Kiejkuty in Poland and held there until transfer to "another CIA secret detention facility elsewhere" on September 11, 2003. This marked the first time a European Union member state had been found complicit in the USA's rendition, secret detention, and torture of alleged terrorism suspects. Many other countries, in Europe and elsewhere, were involved over the years. The USA's secret detention and rendition programs relied upon their cooperation. *Id.*

75. Dave Philipps, *Trump Clears Three Service Members in War Crimes Case*, NY TIMES, (Nov. 15, 2019), https://www.nytimes.com/2019/11/15/us/trump-pardons.html.

76. Maggie Haberman, *Trump Brings 2 Officers He Cleared of War Crimes Onstage at Fund-Raiser*, N.Y. TIMES (Dec. 8, 2019), https://www.nytimes.com/2019/12/08/us/politics/trump-war-crimes-pardons.html.

77. For instance, Ryan Goodman considers that "During wartime a critical legal question involves the scope of authority to choose whether to kill or capture enemy combatants." Ryan Goodman quoted an ICRC report: "[I]f a combatant can be put out of action by taking him prisoner, he should not be injured; if he can be put out of action by injury, he should not be killed; and if he can be put out of action by light injury, grave injury should be avoided." ICRC, WEAPONS THAT MAY CAUSE UNNECESSARY SUFFERING OR HAVE INDISCRIMINATE EFFECTS: REPORT ON THE WORK OF EXPERTS (1973). He concluded: "The right to kill and injure in war is not unlimited. The limitations on that right, however, are themselves not unconditional." Ryan Goodman, *The Power to Kill or Capture Enemy Combatants*, 24 EUR. J. OF INT'L L. 819, 852 (2013).

78. Doug Johnson is a human rights expert and activist leading during the 1970s a boycott campaign against Nestle, directing the Centre for Victims of Torture for more than two decades, Carr Center for Human Rights policy director and leading a global project "New tactics for human rights." He has been my friend since 1985.

79. Alberto Mora was the general counsel of the US Navy since 2001 until 2006 and led a brave effort within the Defense Department to oppose the use of torture. *Alberto Mora, Interview*, THE NAT'L SEC. ARCHIVE, THE GEORGE WASH. UNIV. (Sept. 17, 2007), https://nsarchive2.gwu.edu/torturingdemocracy/interviews/alberto_mora.html. Jane Mayer, *The Memo*, NEW YORKER (Feb. 20, 2006), https://www.newyorker.com/magazine/2006/02/27/the-memo.

80. Douglas A. Johnson, Alberto Mora, & Averell Schmidt, *The Strategic Costs of Torture*, FOREIGN AFFAIRS, https://www.foreignaffairs.com/articles/united-states/strategic-costs-torture (last visited June 11, 2020).

81. The "Law on Public Amnesty and National Stability" provides legal immunity to all belligerent parties including "those individuals and groups who are still in opposition to the Islamic State of Afghanistan," without any temporal limitation or any exception for international crimes. Situation in the Islamic Republic of Afghanistan, ICC-02/17-7-Conf-Exp, Request for authorisation of an investigation pursuant to article 15, ¶ 272 (Nov. 20, 2017).

82. Office of the Prosecutor, *Report on Preliminary Examination Activities 2017*, ICC (Dec. 4, 2017), https://www.icc-cpi.int/itemsDocuments/2017-PE-rep/2017-otp-rep-PE_ENG.pdf.

83. *Id.*

84. *Id.*

85. *Id.*

86. *Id.*

87. Situation in the Islamic Republic of Afghanistan, ICC-02/17, Decision Pursuant to Article 15 of the Rome Statute on the Authorisation of an Investigation into the Situation in the Islamic Republic of Afghanistan ¶ 90, (Apr. 12, 2019), https://www.icc-cpi.int/CourtRecords/CR2019_02068.PDF.

88. *Id.*

89. *Id.*

90. *Id.*

91. *Id.*

92. *Id.*

93. Michael R. Pompeo, *ICC Decision on Afghanistan*, U.S. DEP'T OF STATE (Mar. 5, 2020), https://www.state.gov/icc-decision-on-afghanistan/.

94. *Executive Order on Blocking Property of Certain Persons Associated with the International Criminal Court*, THE WHITE HOUSE PRESIDENT DONALD TRUMP (June 11, 2020), https://www.whitehouse.gov/presidential-actions/executive-order-blocking-property-certain-persons-associated-international-criminal-court/.

95. Michael R. Pompeo, *Actions to Protect U.S. Personnel from Illegitimate Investigation by the International Criminal Court*, U.S. DEP'T STATE (Sept. 2, 2020), https://www.state.gov/actions-to-protect-u-s-personnel-from-illegitimate-investigation-by-the-international-criminal-court/.

96. Haley S. Anderson, *Why Them? On the U.S. Sanctions Against Int'l Criminal Court Officials*, JUST SECURITY (Sept. 2, 2020), https://www.justsecurity.org/72275/why-them-on-the-u-s-sanctions-against-intl-criminal-court-officials/.

97. *Specially Designated Nationals and Blocked Persons List (SDN) Human Readable Lists*, U.S. DEP'T TREASURY https://home.treasury.gov/policy-issues/financial-sanctions/specially-designated-nationals-and-blocked-persons-list-sdn-human-readable-lists (last updated Dec. 16, 2020).

98. Michael R. Pompeo, *Actions to Protect U.S. Personnel from Illegitimate Investigation by the International Criminal Court*, U.S. DEP'T STATE (Sept. 2, 2020), https://www.

state.gov/actions-to-protect-u-s-personnel-from-illegitimate-investigation-by-the-international-criminal-court/.

99. CHARLES A. KUPCHAN, ISOLATIONISM 369 (Kindle ed. 2020).

100. *US Lifts Trump-Era Sanctions against ICC Prosecutor*, BBC NEWS (Apr. 2, 2021), https://www.bbc.com/news/world-us-canada-56620915.

19

The Libya *Jus ad Curiam* Decision

For decades Muammar Gaddafi ruled Libya with an iron fist and promoted terrorist acts around the world. As international relations "realists" explain, Gaddafi protected Libya and his own regime through military force and financial resources. He did not foresee that shooting some Libyan demonstrators could prompt a new international legal framework and end his rule.

How was it possible that the UN Security Council took a *jus ad Curiam* decision by consensus and referred the Libya situation to the ICC in just a few days?

As Tolstoy said, people that participated in the event defined the adoption of Resolution 1970, referring Libya to the ICC. Mohamed Bouazizi, a street salesman in Tunisia, burned himself, triggering the Arab Spring. A small demonstration in Benghazi on February 15, 2011, became a Libya rebellion. Ibrahim Dabbashi, Deputy Libyan permanent representative at the UN, defected publicly on February 21, 2011, and requested a referral to the ICC. On February 23, the French UN embassy legal adviser, Beatrice Le Fraper du Hellen, included in the first draft resolution the referral to the court using the wording of the previous Resolution 1593, which referred the Darfur situation to the ICC.

Paradoxically, Gaddafi's enormous power created global consensus against him. The ICC-10, the ten states parties of the Rome Statute in the council in February 2011, facilitated an immediate majority. President Obama was not inclined to involve US troops in the conflict. Still, the draft resolution did not request military forces, and his administration could not oppose a language accepted by the Bush administration.

During the debate, the Libya permanent representative sent a letter to the council insisting on the referral. The United States and Russia, the African Union, represented by South Africa and Lebanon in the name of the Arab League, supported the initiative. India and China adjusted their opposition, and the resolution was adopted unanimously.

War and Justice in the 21st Century. Luis Moreno Ocampo, Oxford University Press. © Oxford University Press 2022. DOI: 10.1093/oso/9780197628973.003.0020

The situation was admissible, and the ICC Office of the Prosecutor took a *jus ad Curiam* decision in a few days. The ICC opened an investigation into the ongoing crimes committed in Libya two weeks after the conflict started.

The Beginning

Everything happened in a short time. In December 2010, Mohamed Bouazizi was selling fruits on the side of a Tunisian's road to make a living, and the local authorities confiscated his produce. He felt humiliated and set himself on fire, unrest broke out, and the police crackdown on the protesters only fueled a national revolt in Tunisia. Bouazizi died on January 4, the revolt spread into cities; and ten days later, President Ben Ali escaped to exile.

Since January 5, 2011, thousands of protesters gathered in Tahrir Square in Cairo protesting against the regime, and on February 11, 2011, the president of Egypt, Hosni Mubarak, resigned. The Arab Spring was in motion.

Gaddafi was following the events. He considered Ben Ali's and Mubarak's passivity the wrong policy. He was willing to kill people rather than to relinquish power.[1] On February 15, 2011, the families of more than 1,200 prisoners killed at the Abu Salim prison in June 1996 held a protest in Benghazi. Under Libyan law, it was a crime to oppose Gaddafi's regime and challenge his authority.[2]

Libyan authorities took limited measures, and they just arrested the lawyer, Fathi Terbil, who was representing the victims. But the families took to the streets to demand his release, and shortly after that, other citizens came to join the demonstration. The Arab Spring started in Libya.

On February 17, 2011, mass demonstrations commenced in Benghazi, Tripoli, and other cities, calling for Gaddafi's regime's end, and security forces responded by opening live fire on demonstrators. These initial killings led to larger demonstrations throughout the country with growing demands by the people of Libya to end the dictatorship and, in response, a systematic and even more violent response from Gaddafi's security forces.

On February 20, government forces opened fire on those attending the funeral of their fellow demonstrators killed during the protests.[3] Television channels like Al Jazeera (owned by Qatar) and Al Arabiya (owned by Saudi Arabia), BBC, CNN, and social media disseminated these images worldwide.

The same day, Saif Al-Islam Gaddafi, considered an informal prime minister, spoke on Libyan state television. He was refusing to recognize the Libyans' demands, blaming the unrest on "foreign agents" and threatening the country with a "civil war" that would be "worse than Iraq and . . . Yugoslavia" and would lead to "thousands of deaths."

During that night, massive demonstrations against Gaddafi took place in Tripoli's different areas after the sunset prayers. Gaddafi's security forces started shooting as soon as they encountered groups of demonstrators walking toward Green Square.[4] The protesters set government buildings on fire.

Gaddafi spoke on Libyan state television from his headquarters in Tripoli. He refused to acknowledge the demonstrators' demands and stated that he did not regret the crimes committed by his security forces. On the contrary, Gaddafi called the protesters "rats," "garbage," and "mercenaries" and threatened "to clean Libya inch by inch, house by house, small street by small street, individual by individual, corner by corner until the country is clean from all garbage and dirt."[5]

Libya's conflict became worldwide news, and people were requesting ICC intervention. On February 23, our office issued a press release making clear that the ICC had no jurisdiction in a state nonparty like Libya.[6]

On February 26, 2011, the UN Security Council was discussing the Libyan situation. I was in the Buenos Aires' airport taking a plane to be back at The Hague after visiting my family for a few days. Following our policy not to spend any resources on situations clearly outside our jurisdiction, I had no specific information about the Libyan conflict or the negotiations in New York. My focus was on the Cote d'Ivoire situation where the authorities had requested our intervention and preparing the closing arguments in our first trial, the Lubanga case.

Muammar Gaddafi

Gaddafi's Policies

For more than forty years, Gaddafi was ruling Libya, and since 1990 he had absolute power over its people and assets. The Decree of Revolutionary Legitimacy of 9 March 1990 expressly established that Gaddafi's instructions were binding and had the force of law even for the General People's Congress and the Executive (People's Committees) or the Central Bank.[7]

At the beginning of his rule, Gaddafi renegotiated the contracts with the international oil companies operating in Libya, which became the first developing country to secure a majority share of its own oil production revenues.[8]

Gaddafi used part of the oil resources to provide free education and health protection to the Libyan citizens, gaining support from national and international audiences that emphasize social justice. At the same time, Gaddafi terrorized his own population to maintain his power, and allegations of atrocities mushroomed against his regime.

Internationally, Gaddafi supported rebellions in Asia, Africa, and Latin America, including sustaining groups like Mandela's ANC, Nicaragua's Sandinistas, IRA (Irish Republic Army) in Northern Ireland, and ETA (Euskadi Ta Askatasuna, or Basque Homeland and Freedom) in Spain. Gaddafi became, for many in the South, an anti-imperialist icon. Nelson Mandela called him "my brother leader" and explained "This man helped us at a time when we were all alone."[9] Mandela was always grateful for his support,[10] and one of his grandsons was named Gadaffi.[11]

On the other side, Gaddafi and the United States had a conflicting relation. The American ambassador was withdrawn from Tripoli in 1972 to protest Libya's support for "international terrorism and subversion against moderate Arab and African governments."[12] In December 1979, the US. government declared Libya, a "state sponsor of terrorism."[13] President Reagan considered that Gaddafi gave support to "terrorist groups around the world," was developing chemical weapons to advance his revolution,[14] and "[t]hrough terrorism . . .he was trying to unify the world of Islam into a single nation of fundamentalists under rigid religious control."[15]

Of "all the problems that have confronted Ronald Reagan as President, none has proved so intractable as terrorism."[16] Even Reagan had to use an iron vest, taking into consideration Gaddafi's plans to assassinate him.[17] The United States had tried different mechanisms: closing embassies,[18] breaking relations,[19] travel bans, prohibiting trade, freezing assets,[20] demanding foreign authorities to establish similar measures[21], and military threats. None of them stopped the Libyan leader.

In 1981 two United States jets shot down two Libyan jets that had fired on them during a naval exercise.[22] The Reagan administration felt the frustration foresaw by Jackson: "The only answer to recalcitrance was impotence or war. Only sanctions which reach individuals can peacefully and effectively be enforced."[23]

A Very Limited *Jus ad Bellum* Decision

In April 1986, Libyan agents were considered responsible for bombing a nightclub in Berlin, wounding 231 persons, including 56 US citizens, and killing a Turkish woman and two U.S. soldiers.[24] On April 15, 1986, President Reagan took a limited *jus ad Bellum* decision in retaliation and authorized military strikes.[25] "I warned that there should be no place on earth where terrorists can rest and train and practice their deadly skills."[26]

France, Spain, and Italy denied the US Air Force overflight rights, complicating the operation.[27] In any case, eighteen US warplanes dropped bombs in Libya, destroying Gaddafi's tent.[28] A Libyan missile shot down an American F-111 over the Gulf of Sidra, killing two US officers. After the limited operation, President Reagan clarified that "the attack was not intended to kill Qaddafi; that would have violated our prohibition against assassination."[29]

Gaddafi, supposedly forewarned by Italian Prime Minister Bettino Craxi, escaped before the attack and survived.[30] He presented the event as a significant victory. Libya installed a sculpture in the shape of an arm and hand squeezing a fighter plane to memorize the incidents.

In those days, some experts in the Middle East were "questioning the utility of military strikes as a weapon against terrorism."[31] The limited US. military operation in Libya created international relations frictions during the 1980s. A visit by the Soviet Union minister of foreign affairs to the United States was canceled, threatening a scheduled summit between Reagan and Gorbachev.[32]

Lieutenant Colonel Oliver North, a decorated Vietnam veteran, was involved in planning the Libya operation as the National Security Council specialist on terrorism.[33] He declared that "the Libyan raid was a chance to begin a new phase in the American counterterrorism struggle—the direct use of military force."[34]

A Very Limited *Jus ad Curiam* Decision Supported by Mandela

Libya continued to be involved in terrorist attacks, and the UN Security Council promoted a *jus ad Curiam* decision. The judicial authorities of

France, the United Kingdom, and the United States concluded that two Libyan officials were involved in the bombings against a Pan Am plane while flying over Lockerbie (1988), resulting in 270 deaths and a French aircraft flying over Niger (1989), causing 171 deaths.

In January 1992, the UN Security Council discussed the possibility to sanction individuals at the international level, a deliberation that exposed the need for an International Criminal Court. The Libyan authorities welcomed a neutral international investigation but affirmed that the UN Security Council had no competence.[35] The US. Representative regretted that there was no institution to investigate the crimes.[36]

Diego Arria, the ambassador of Venezuela, mentioned: "the inability of the General Assembly to take a stand on the establishment of an international criminal tribunal had made it necessary for the Council to act."[37] Two months later, the UN Security Council adopted Resolution 748. It imposed sanctions on Libya until it hands over the two accused of trial, makes compensation to the victims' families, and demonstrates concrete actions renouncing terrorism.[38]

In October 1997, President Mandela broke the UN Security Council's isolation by traveling to Libya by car.[39] Mandela visited the place bombed by the Reagan administration and said, "No country can claim to be the policeman of the world, and no state can dictate to another what it should do."[40] He supported the Organization of African Unity, called for a trial for the two suspects in a neutral third country, and committed to promoting such a solution.[41]

In 1998, after years of diplomatic maneuvering, Libya agreed to hand over the two suspects for trial before a Scottish court sitting in the Netherlands, and the council suspended the sanctions by its Resolution 1192.

In April 1999, Libya surrendered the two Libyan suspects.[42] On January 31, 2001, a Scottish court seated in the Netherlands found Abdelbaset al-Megrahi guilty of murder and sentenced him to a minimum of twenty years imprisonment in Scotland.[43] Al Amin Fhima was found not guilty, and there was no investigation on the link between Gaddafi himself and the bombing. Abdelbaset al-Megrahi was released on compassionate grounds on August 20, 2009.

In November 2010, Mandela received Gaddafi and said that South Africa played a significant part in the Lockerbie case agreement, and he considered it a "highlight" of his presidency.[44]

Gaddafi's Support to the War on Terror

The 2001 *War on Terror* transformed the conflictive relation between the United States and United Kingdom with Libya. *"One of the most pressing imperatives was to create close ties with the intelligence agencies of the Arab world."*[45]

On September 20, 2001, the head of the MI6 had a meeting with Moussa Koussa, then head of the Libyan External Security Organisation (ESO), Gaddafi's notorious overseas intelligence agency that allegedly organized many of Libya's terrorist attacks.[46]

Koussa offered to provide MI-6 with information extracted from men held in Libyan prisons, and both agreed that their countries' counterterrorism experts "should meet to discuss the enemies we both face."[47] Gaddafi regime was persecuting Islamists, and "in the face of the threat from al-Qaida, both were utterly pragmatic."[48]

"By August 2002, relations between Britain and Libya were tentatively restored, with the goal of what Blair would later call the "huge prize" of security co-operation with Libyan intelligence. Gaddafi's son Saif was admitted to the London School of Economics at his second attempt."[49] Blair proposed to lift all the sanctions against Libya if Gaddafi abandoned "his Weapons of Mass Destruction (WMD) program."[50]

"In early 2003, as US and UK forces mustered on the borders of Iraq, Gaddafi was afraid they would target Libya. According to one diplomat, he called the Italian prime minister, Silvio Berlusconi, begging him to 'tell them I will do whatever they want.' "[51] The negotiations included compensating the victims of terrorism. In August 2003, Libya sent a letter to the UN Security Council pledging to cooperate in the international fight against terrorism and pay the families of those killed at Lockerbie.[52]

And on September 12, 2003, the United Nations Security Council lifted decades-old sanctions imposed against Libya after Tripoli agreed to pay up to $10 million each to the Lockerbie victims' families. UK Ambassador Emyr Jones Parry, who presided over the meeting and tabled the resolution, said: *"We look forward to the full re-emergence of Libya into the international community."*[53]

Three months later, US./U.K. officers started to dismantle Libya's "chemical weapons program that was rudimentary and untested, and a nuclear weapons project that was at a surprisingly advanced stage."[54]

On December 19, 2003, Prime Minister Blair and President George W. Bush announced that Libya agreed to dismantle its "Weapons of Mass Destruction" program. President Bush announced the agreement and suggested a connection with the War on Terror.[55] In his memoirs, he presented such a link more explicitly.[56]

Blair explained that "Today's announcement shows that we can fight this menace through more than purely military means. We have never wanted, as our opponents falsely claim, to dominate the world, to wage war on Muslims or Arabs, to interfere with the legitimate rights of sovereign nations."[57] There was no mention of any human rights problem inside Libya.

Prime Minister Blair visited Libya for the first time on March 25, 2004. After being photographed shaking hands with Gaddafi, Blair announced that Libya had "found a common cause, with us, in the fight against extremism and terrorism."[58] Simultaneously, it was announced that Anglo-Dutch oil giant Shell had signed a deal worth up to £550m for gas exploration rights off the Libyan coast.[59]

In May 2006, the United States restored full diplomatic relations with Libya and removed it from the list of countries designated as state sponsors of terrorism.[60] In September 2008, Secretary of State Condoleezza Rice met Gaddafi in Tripoli.[61]

The Denial of Gaddafi's Latest Abuses

Gaddafi's oppression of Libyans, his past terrorist crimes, and new conflicts were ignored. The international community accepted Gaddafi's authoritarian decisions. For instance, in 2006, a Libya's investigation based on untruth testimonies obtained by torture ended with a conviction of "five Bulgarian nurses and a Palestinian doctor for deliberately infecting more than 400 children with H.I.V."[62]

Libya has asked for compensation similar to the amount paid to the Lockerbie victims: $10 million per child. In July 2007, after eight years in prison, the European Union, led by President Sarkozy, made a deal to end the nurses' ordeal.[63]

A different conflict started in July 2008, when Gaddafi's son Hannibal and his wife were arrested for allegedly beating two employees at a hotel in Geneva. Gaddafi immediately retaliated, arresting two Swiss businesspeople for supposed visa irregularities. Libya also imposed trade sanctions on Switzerland, stopped Swiss flights to Tripoli, withdrew more than $5bn from its banks, and cut the crude oil exports that provided half of all country's oil needs.[64]

Switzerland soon dropped the charges against Gaddafi's son, but Libya kept the businessmen under house arrest. Between January and May 2009, a negotiation was conducted to solve the problem.

In July 2009, Gaddafi took advantage of the G8 meeting to raise the idea of dismembering Switzerland with its territory parceled out to neighboring "France, Germany, and Italy."[65]

A month later, the Swiss president, Hans-Rudolf Merz, had to fly to Tripoli to deliver an "official and public apology [for Hannibal's] unjustified and unnecessary arrests."[66]The Libyan government had promised to release the two businessmen,[67] but refused to grant them permission to leave the country.

Switzerland considered different options to manage the hostage problem, including the possibility to send special forces.[68]

In November 2009, Switzerland drew up a blacklist of 188 Libyans, including Gaddafi and his son, who would "for reasons of public and national security" no longer be allowed to enter Switzerland.[69] Following the Schengen agreement, the Swiss decision implied that Gaddafi, and his entourage were not permitted to enter Europe.[70] Gaddafi retaliated, banning the access of all European citizens to Libya.

On February 24, 2010, Gaddafi declared jihad against the "faithless" Swiss. The US. State Department spokesman Philip Crowley questioned his remarks but was forced to make a public apology.[71]

The EU evaluated its options and reacted against Switzerland, forcing it to withdraw the travel ban. Miguel Angel Moratinos, the foreign minister of Spain—in charge of the EU presidency—flew at the end of March to Libya to apologize for the problem on behalf of the EU. "We regret and deplore the trouble and inconvenience caused to those Libyan citizens. We hope that this move will not be repeated in the future," he told Gaddafi.[72]

For decades, Gaddafi manipulated the international community. He relied upon military power and economic interest to impose his will. However, the Libyan deputy representative before the UN, Ambassador Ibrahim Dabbashi, decided to participate in the events and triggered a different process.

Ambassador Dabbashi Triggering the UN Security Council Agenda

Before the Rebellion

Libya replaced Qatar at the council representing the Arab world. At the end of 2008, Amb. Nassir Abdulaziz Al-Nasser, Qatar Permanent representative, invited me to a farewell lunch at a club in New York and introduced me to Ambassador Ibrahim Dabbashi, the UN Deputy permanent representative of Libya. Ambassador Al-Nasser wanted to keep the communication between the Arab members of the council and our office.

Ambassador Dabbashi was very polite and discreet, and he limited his interventions during lunch. We did not have a substantial conversation and he was not present during my visits to the Libyan embassy in preparation of my Security Council briefings on Darfur in 2009 and 2010.

As soon as the rebellion started in Benghazi, Dabbashi decided that it was the moment to talk openly. He discussed with his wife and children how to manage the risk of retaliation against their extended family still living in Libya.

The morning of February 21, 2011, just three days after the beginning of the Libya rebellion, Ambassador Dabbashi called to all the members of the Libyan mission in New York for a meeting. He had planned a press conference to inform that he was no longer representing Gaddafi, asking the international community to refer the situation to the International Criminal Court.

Dabbashi invited his colleagues to join him to defy Gaddafi and stated that he would understand if they declined the invitation because of the dangers for themselves and their families. All the staff at the mission supported Dabbashi, and promised would stand side by side with him as he announced the defection. But they were worried about the permanent representative Ambassador Abdurrahman Mohamed Shalgham, a former minister of foreign affairs with strong personal ties with Gaddafi. Since the conflict started, Amb. Shalgham was not present in the office. Dabbashi assured his colleagues that he would talk to Shalgham before the press conference.

In the afternoon, fifteen minutes before meeting the journalists, Dabbashi called Amb. Shalgham and informed him about the press conference and requested instructions. Shalgham was still evaluating the situation in Libya and was not sure what side to choose. To avoid a conflict, Amb Shalgham told Dabbashi to do whatever he wanted. Dabbashi's smart move allowed him to defect, still respecting the permanent representative's authority and instructions.

Ambassador Dabbashi spoke from the Libyan mission's ground-floor lobby on Manhattan's East Side, under a Gaddafi's giant portrait riding a white horse and surrounded by dozen colleagues who stood behind him. He said, "We find it is impossible to stay silent." "We state clearly that the Libyan mission is a mission for the Libyan people. It is not for the regime."[73]

He added: "We are sure that what is going on now in Libya is crimes against humanity and crimes of war" and requested the intervention of the International Criminal Court, the creation of a "no-fly zone," and the transfer of medical supplies across the borders. Ambassador Dabbashi said he had not seen the permanent representative since Friday, February 18, and did not know his whereabouts or whether he shared the opinion of many in his mission. Asked whether he feared reprisals from Colonel Gaddafi, Mr. Dabbashi said: "Whatever the risk is, it will not be the risk that the Libyan people are facing."[74]

Ambassador Dabbashi led by example. During the following hours, other Libyan diplomats worldwide abandoned the regime, including the Libyan ambassadors to the United States, France, India, UNESCO, and the Arab League. Many of them requested international intervention. More importantly, in Libya, the minister of the interior and veteran loyalist Abdel-Fatah Younes al-Obeidi defected and called on the army to "serve the people and support the revolution and its legitimate demands."[75]

Gaddafi's Minister of Justice, Mustafa Abdel-Jalil, also resigned and became the National Transitional Council leader. Two Libyan pilots defected by landing their Mirage F1 fighter jets on Malta after disobeying orders to attack Benghazi's protesters.

Dabbashi's Move to Put the UN Security Council in Motion

Dabbashi knew that time was essential, the international community's attention span is short, and his goal was to convince the UN Security Council to act immediately and decisively. But as a deputy permanent representative, Dabbashi had no authority to request a Security Council meeting on behalf of Libya, only permanent representatives can make such a request.

To overcome his lack of authority, Ambassador Dabbashi took advantage of the legal rules conferring power. He sent a "note verbale" that requires no signature, informing the UN secretary-general that Ambassador Shalgham, the permanent representative, was not in the New York mission and could not represent Libya before the UN.

The note further stated that in his absence, the deputy representative, Amb. Dabbashi, would be the acting head of the mission and could represent Libya's interests at the UN. Following this, Amb. Dabbashi sent a letter to the UN Security Council, this time signed by himself as the acting representative of Libya, asking for a council meeting on Libya.

The Intervention of Regional Organizations

Simultaneously, on the 21st of February 2011, the Qatari prime minister, Hamad bin Jasim bin Jabr al-Thani, appealed for immediate international action to end the Libyan crackdown and called for an Arab League meeting to discuss the crisis. The following day, the Arab League took an unprecedented decision denouncing the Libyan government's violence[76] and suspending Libya's participation.[77]

On February 23, 2011, the Peace and Security Council of the African Union strongly condemned "the indiscriminate and excessive use of force and lethal weapons against peaceful protestors, in violation of human rights and International Humanitarian Law." The AU called on the Libyan authorities "to ensure the protection and security of the citizens."[78]

The Security Council Meeting of the February 22, 2011

Following Dabbashi's request, the Security Council met in the consultation room on the morning of February 22 to start an entire day discussion on the Libya situation. Seventy-five states requested to participate in the debate, exposing the world's interests.[79]

Amb. Shalgham, Libya's permanent representative, arrived at the UN and told media correspondents that he was against the council's meeting unless it would call for a peaceful settlement. He continued to support Gaddafi, calling him a childhood friend. "I can criticize him, but I cannot attack him." Amb. Shalgham said, "I am still trying to speak to the leader [Gaddafi]. We have to stop attacking Libyans." Asked who was to blame, he answered: "All the regime is responsible. I am one of them—we are all responsible."[80]

At midday, Amb. Shalgam met with Dabbashi and other Libyan diplomats and informed them that he had received instructions from Tripoli to fire everyone at the mission. But he said he would not do so, but they have to manage the situation carefully.

The afternoon meeting was closed for the public. Shalgham stated before the Security Council that the Libyan public prosecutor had begun to investigate the killings and that there had not been any aerial bombardments of demonstrators. He conceded that the country's eastern side had fallen and was no longer under the government's control. He also said he held discussions with senior government members, including the foreign minister, to persuade them to stop the bloodshed.[81]

After the meeting, the president of the Security Council issued a press statement informing that its members "condemned the violence and use of force against civilians" and "deplored the repression against peaceful demonstrators." They "underscored the need to hold to account those responsible for attacks, including by forces under their control, on civilians."[82] Amb. Dabbashi, keeping his independent voice, continued pushing the council. He said that the press statement, "It is not strong enough, but any message to the Libyan government at this stage is good."[83]

The Drafting and the Adoption of the UN Security Council Resolution 1970

The Drafting of the Unwritten Protocol

The UN Security Council's decision-making process follows an unwritten protocol. Usually, France, the United Kingdom, and the United States consult each other on draft resolutions. After, they would include China and Russia in the consultation, and finally, the drafts are passed to non-permanent members of the council.[84]

In the Libyan case, France and the United Kingdom, the only permanent members of the Security Council that are state parties of the Rome Statute, triggered the process to adopt UN SC Resolution 1970. Their legal advisers and permanent representatives, people that participated in the events, defined the outcome.

President Sarkozy's Decision

France has a permanent interest in its relations with its Mediterranean neighbors. Shortly after his election, President Mitterrand gave Ben Ali a grand reception in Paris, and President Chirac declared Ali's Tunisia was "on the road to modernization, democracy, and social harmony."[85]

Nicolas Sarkozy's election campaign in 2007 included the promotion of a trans-Mediterranean union. He paid a visit to Ben Ali in Tunisia in April 2008. In July 2008, he gathered most of the heads of state and government from the forty-three Euro-Mediterranean countries in Paris to create the Union Mediterranean.

When the Arab Spring started, France was not prepared. Ms. Michèle Alliot-Marie, then France's foreign affairs minister, admitted in January 2011 to parliamentarians that France had been caught off-guard by the rapid chain of events in Tunisia and Egypt. On January 11, 2011, she offered Ben Ali the support of "[French] security forces in order to settle security situations of this type."[86] Three days later, Ben Ali requested asylum in Saudi Arabia.

After, President Sarkozy stated that Tunisia's revolt left him with "despair . . . a stifling feeling that we had not taken the right step."[87] He perceived the Libyan crisis as an opportunity to adjust to the new Arab landscape. He appealed to the European Union to impose sanctions on Libya, led the calls for a NATO-imposed no-fly zone to be enforced over Libya to "prevent the use of that country's warplanes against [its] population," and requested to the French mission at New York to draft a robust UN Security Council Resolution.

Prime Minister Cameron

The British prime minister, David Cameron, was also trying to adjust to the Arab Spring. Since February 21, he had been visiting the Middle East in a previously planned tour with "the aim of encouraging political reform, boosting trade and strengthening security ties." Cameron was revisiting Blair's strategy and promoting democracy on his Middle East trade and security agenda.

On February 23, in an interview with Al Jazeera in Doha, Prime Minister Cameron did not immediately endorse President Sarkozy's proposals but presented a road map for the Libyan crisis to achieve similar goals. He suggested to "send a very clear warning to Colonel Gaddafi" and to move ahead "through the UN Security Council." He also said, "I do not think we are at that stage yet [of military actions]. We are at the stage of condemning the actions Colonel Gaddafi has taken against his own people."[88]

The French and U.K. mission at New York worked together to prepare a draft resolution establishing sanctions and including the ICC referral. The French legal adviser at New York, Beatrice Le Frapper du Hellene, was one of the French delegation leaders at Rome in 1998. She replaced Silvia Fernandez at our office as the director of the Jurisdiction, Complementarity and Cooperation Division (JCCD) in 2007. In 2011, as the French legal adviser in the New York mission, she took the opportunity to include a referral to the ICC in a draft resolution as one of the measures to adopt. She had the authority to participate in the events, and she proposed a *jus ad Curiam* decision.

The draft resolution language was a literal copy and paste of the previous Resolution 1593 (2005) that referred the Darfur situation to the ICC, excluded jurisdiction over nationals of non-state parties, and was accepted by the Bush administration. Moreover, it neither requested financial support from the UN nor established a duty of cooperation with the ICC for non-state parties. The United Kingdom passed the draft resolution to the Obama administration on February 24, 2011.

The United States

While Africa, the Arab world, and Europe were building a united front on Libya's situation, the United States was still debating its position. The situation reminded many in the Obama administration of the lack of reaction to the Rwandan genocide. But there were other concerns, Libya was a partner in the *War on Terror*. The Department of Defense did not consider Gaddafi threatening a vital US. national interest, and it was worried about engaging in a new military effort.

Speaking at West Point, the Secretary of Defense Robert Gates stated, "In my opinion, any future defense secretary who advises the president to again send a big American land army into Asia or the Middle East or Africa should have his head examined, as General MacArthur so delicately put it."[89]

However, since the French draft UN SC Resolution proposal did not include military intervention, it was almost impossible for the Obama administration to oppose the language of an ICC referral previously accepted by the Bush administration.

The Consultation of the February 25, 2011, and the Request of Amb. Shalgham

On the morning of February 25, 2011, the United States accepted the resolution's draft language. It continued its internal debate on a no-fly zone while Russia and China received the draft. It was a Friday, the day of prayers for the Muslim community. More than one hundred civilians were killed throughout Tripoli as they were pouring from the mosques. The same day Gaddafi gave another speech in the Green Square of Tripoli, stating that "when it becomes necessary the arsenal will be opened to allow all Libyans to be armed. Libya will become red flame."

In an interview that evening, Saif-Al-Islam Gaddafi made clear that the regime had the will to fight to maintain its power: "Plan A is to live and die in Libya, Plan B is to live and die in Libya, Plan C is to live and die in Libya."

Libya was a UN Human Rights Council member in 2011. On February 25, the council convened its first-ever special session devoted to a situation in its members' territory, established a Commission of Inquiry, and recommended that the General Assembly consider suspending Libya's membership.[90]

That same afternoon, the Security Council was briefed by UN Secretary-General Ban Ki-moon on Libya's situation. He painted an alarming picture: Gaddafi and his son considered Libyan citizens *enemies* and threatened them with war. There were serious allegations of indiscriminate killings, arbitrary arrests, the shooting of peaceful demonstrators, detention, and torture of opposition groups.

The UN secretary-general estimated that more than 1,000 people had been killed and a growing number of displaced persons. He mentioned the Responsibility to Protect commitment and urged the council to take effective action to ensure "real accountability" and "consider concrete action."

Then the Security Council received the permanent representative of Libya, Abdurrahman Mohamed Shalgham. Most of the Security Council ambassadors knew Amb. Shalgham very well as he had represented Libya at the Security Council in 2010, and he was considered a loyal representative of Gaddafi's regime.

However, Amb. Shalgham knew that prominent Gaddafi supporters had abandoned him and had adjusted his position stating, "Libyans are asking for democracy; they are asking for progress; they are asking for freedom, and they are asking for their rights. They demonstrated peacefully. They did not throw a single stone. They were killed."

He compared Gaddafi with Pol Pot and Hitler. He recalled that Colonel Gaddafi exclaimed, "either I rule you, or I kill you." He dismissed the threats to distribute weapons: "Muammar Al-Gaddafi cannot give a single weapon to any person in Libya because they will not be used for him, they will be used against him."

He said, "I regret being in this position. I say to my brother Gaddafi, leave the Libyans alone." And he concluded: "Please, United Nations, save Libya. No to bloodshed. No to the killing of innocents. We want a swift, decisive and courageous resolution."[91]

Ambassador Shalgham's request transformed the debate. His presentation evoked what happened during Kuwait's discussion. There was no intrusion on a sovereign country. The law conferred power to Shalgham, and the still loyal Libyan permanent representative asked the council to intervene.

The United Nations Security Council Unanimous Vote

The non-permanent members of the Security Council received the draft resolution tabled by the United Kingdom after the Libyan permanent representative's appearance. Eight of the ten Security Council non-permanent members were also state parties of the ICC. They had already adopted a commitment "to end the impunity for the most serious crimes to the international community as a whole." Still, they had to find a balance, considering their regional position and Rome Statute's membership.

Germany[92] and Portugal represented the European Union, whose members are all parties to the ICC. The EU had pushed the Human Rights Council to create a Commission of Inquiry, saying that the crimes in Libya "may amount to crimes against humanity." Bosnia-Herzegovina, another state party of the Rome Statute and non-permanent council member aiming to join the EU, followed the same policies.

Colombia and Brazil represented the Latin American and the Caribbean regions. All the South American countries, Mexico, and most of the Central American countries are ICC members. Peru was the first country in the world to sever its diplomatic relations with Libya. Venezuela initially made some statements supporting Gaddafi but became isolated and did not interfere with the region's position in the Security Council.

However, the wording of the draft resolution, repeating the Darfur referral, created problems for Brazil. As a consequence of its commitment to the ICC system, in 2005, Brazil abstained on a similar text, considering it unacceptable to exempt jurisdiction for nationals of non-state parties. It was therefore problematic for it to accept in Libya what it had rejected in the Darfur situation.

South Africa, Nigeria, and Gabon, three states parties to the ICC, were representatives of Africa's Security Council. In a meeting on February 25, the South African Ambassador, Mr. Basso Sango, made a statement clarifying during the discussion on the resolution tabled by the United Kingdom that he would speak in the name of South Africa and the AU. He carefully used the words of the AU communiqué.[93]

Lebanon represented the Arab countries and supported the referral following the strong Arab League position on Libya. Indian ambassador Hardeep Singh Puri had instructions from his capital to oppose any ICC reference in the resolution. Recognizing that council support for some reference to the ICC was substantial, he suggested that the resolution include only the threat of a referral.[94]

The Adoption of the Resolution

During the consultations on the morning of the 26th of February, it was clear that most of the Security Council members supported the resolution, including the ICC referral.[95] However, Portugal and India expressed doubts about its convenience, and they voiced their concerns that the referral could obstruct a future political agreement. France and other representatives countered that Gaddafi would not negotiate, but in the unlikely event that he would, Article 16 could provide a solution.

The discussion was transformed when Amb. Shalgham sent a letter to the Security Council insisting that the ICC referral be included in the resolution. French officials ensured that it was circulated quickly to all council members. South Africa could not ignore a specific request from a fellow African country: Ambassador Baso Sangqu of South Africa stated that the

Libyan people have been calling for an end to the indiscriminate use of force and noted the request of the Libyan delegation.

The ICC-10 showed the normative impact of the Rome Statute. Gabon and Nigeria, the other African states parties, were also supporting the referral.[96] Brazil Ambassador Maria Luiza Ribeiro made reservations on the clause providing immunity to non-state party personnel.[97]

Ambassador Susan Rice highlighted that, for the first time, the Security Council had unanimously referred an egregious human rights situation to the International Criminal Court. She invoked a statement issued by President Obama a few hours before. When a leader's only means of staying in power is to use mass violence against his own people, he has lost the legitimacy to rule and needs to do what is right for his country by leaving now.

Ambassador Vitaly Churkin of Russia stated that he supported the resolution because of his country's deep concern over the situation, its sorrow over the lives lost, and its condemnation of the use of military force against peaceful demonstrators. He noted the League of the Arab States and the African Union's demands, supported a political solution, and opposed forceful interference in Libya's affairs, making the situation worse.

Ambassador Nawaf Salam of Lebanon, a non-state party representing the Arab world, a strong supporter of the ICC intervention, voted in line with the Arab consensus, the African Union, and the Organization of the Islamic Conference. He stressed the importance of reaffirming Libya's territorial unity. After lunchtime, the only two countries that were not in the affirmative were China and India. China expressed the need to consult with the African Union, but South Africa emphasized that it represented the African Union's position.

Ambassador Hardeep Singh Puri used his authority to convince his country to join the consensus and explained in his vote that India hoped that calm and stability were restored without further violence. Noting that five council members were not parties to the Rome Statute, including India, he said he would have preferred a "calibrated and gradual approach" to the issue. However, he noted that several council members, including representatives from Africa and the Middle East, believe that referral to the court would immediately cease violence. The letter from the permanent representative of Libya strengthened this view.

The Chinese ambassador could have abstained but did not like to ruin the consensus and requested time to receive approval from his capital for a positive vote. The meeting was reconvened around 8 p.m. the same day and Ambassador Li Baodong of China stated that the greatest urgency was to cease the violence and resolve the crisis through peaceful means, such as dialogue. Considering the special circumstances in Libya and the Arab and African countries' views, the Chinese delegation voted in favor of the resolution.

The resolution was adopted by consensus.[98]

The council "demanded an end to the violence and decided to refer the situation to the International Criminal Court while imposing an arms embargo on the country and a travel ban and assets freeze on the family of Muammar Al-Qadhafi and certain government officials."[99]

Ambassador Ibrahim Dabbashi welcomed the referral, launched an appeal to all the officers of the Libyan armed forces to renounce their support for Gaddafi. The UN secretary-general, Ban Ki-moon, answering India, said that the referral, "While it cannot, by itself, end the violence and the repression, it is a vital step—a clear expression of the will of a united community of nations."

To confirm the unique momentum, on March 1, 2011, the US. Senate passed a resolution by unanimous consent that "Welcomes the vote of the U.N. Security Council on resolution 1970 referring the situation in Libya to the International Criminal Court (ICC)."[100]

That was the peak of the global consensus to include international justice to protect citizens.

The *Jus ad Curiam* Decision of the Office of the Prosecutor

Triggering the Jurisdiction of the Court

On Sunday, February 27, I arrived at Schiphol Airport from Buenos Aires. In a bar in front of our gate, the TV monitor announced in big letters that the UN Security Council had decided to refer the Libya situation to our office. The UN Commission of Enquiry was not yet established, but just ten days after the beginning of the conflict, the council, by consensus, referred the Libya situation to the ICC.

I used the time between Schiphol Airport and my house at The Hague to absorb the new information. We had to do justice in the ongoing Libyan conflict, and I started to think about our next steps. That afternoon, I called Ex

Com members, and we decided to organize a meeting at 9 a.m. the following day with people from the different divisions. I spent my Sunday afternoon reading as much as possible on the Libyan situation.

On Monday, I arrived at the office very early to be prepared for our crucial meeting. The Libya referral was unexpected, but our office was ready to face the new challenge. We had an operational manual in place, clear policies, and experience with the council, and we had just to decide on specific issues.

The first point to discuss during our meeting was the triggering of the jurisdiction of the court. We did not find any reason to delay a decision. The office had learned from its experience in the Darfur situation that timing was crucial. The international consensus and the UN Security Council's interest to do justice could evaporate within days. Without such alignment with the political actors, the cooperation required to conduct investigations and their impact could be dramatically reduced. Considering the information already available, we instructed the Analysis Section to produce Article 53's report in two days.

The office issued a press statement the same Monday, February 28, explaining that we have to *decide whether an investigation . . . should be opened.* We used the media to show our interest to receive "*footage and images to confirm the alleged crimes and, . . . to Libyan officials and army officers to receive information about the identity of authorities with command and control over the organizations allegedly involved in the crimes.*"

I tried to be predictable: "The Office will act swiftly and impartially. There will be no impunity for leaders involved in the commission of crimes."[101] We aimed to "contribute to the prevention" of future crimes trying to deter Libyan officers from committing crimes.

On March 2, Ex Com discussed an Article 53 report considering that crimes against humanity and possible war crimes (during a non-international armed conflict) may have been committed. There were no national investigations to evaluate. As the Libyan ambassador recognized, the Gaddafi regime treated the rebels as enemies, and there was no prospect of judicial investigations against them.

The gravity of the crimes was evident: the reports mentioned hundreds of victims in a few days, and a more aggressive campaign was progressing against the Libyans. The report considered that there was no *interest of justice* reason to stop or to suspend the investigation. It concluded that an investigation on the Libya situation should be opened.

ExCom decided to open an investigation and prepared the public announcement. We called for a meeting the following day to discuss our next steps.

The Opening of the Investigation

On March 3rd, during a press conference, I announced that the office decided to "open an investigation into alleged crimes against humanity committed in Libya since the 15th of February, as security forces attacked peaceful demonstrators."

We explained: the office will investigate the most responsible people for Libya's most serious crimes in the coming weeks. *The Office will then present its evidence to the Judges, and they will decide on whether or not to issue arrest warrants.* We showed a map indicating the time and place of the major incidents.

Because the media was reporting daily attacks, our office was trying to maximize the preventive impact of its first decision. We aimed to encourage defections, putting on notice those in charge of the troops and obtaining evidence to prove criminal intentions. We stated: *We identified some individuals with formal or de facto authority who commanded and had control over the forces that allegedly committed the crimes. They are – MUAMMAR AL GADDAFI, the chairman of the Revolutionary Command Council, and his inner circle; the Minister of Foreign Affairs; the Head of Regime Security and Military Intelligence; – the Head of Gaddafi's Personal Security; the Head of the Libyan External Security Organization. We hereby put them on notice: if forces under their command commit crimes, they could be held responsible.*

We also put on notice the rebel groups: *We have information that some opposition groups also have weapons. If they commit crimes, their leaders will also be investigated. We will act with impartiality.* We continue inviting people to help us: *Any person can contact our Office to clarify his or her responsibility. We have a mandate to do justice. We will do it.*[102]

Western leaders immediately sought to convert the referral into leverage on the regime. British officials reportedly made concerted efforts to contact senior Libyan officials and warn them of the consequences of a continued crackdown. "People working for this regime should remember that international justice has a long reach and a long memory," said Prime Minister David Cameron.

President Obama reportedly communicated with senior regime officials to warn them against attacking civilians. That message was aired in public as well. "I want to send a very clear message to those who are around Colonel Gaddafi," he said during an Oval Office appearance. "It is their choice to make, how they operate moving forward, and they will be held accountable for whatever violence continues to take place there."[103]

On March 30, one of the persons that we put on notice, the Libyan minister of foreign affairs and former head of the External Security Organisation (ESO), Moussa Koussa, defected. The *Guardian* said: "He fled to the UK in a specially arranged flight organized by the British intelligence services. Koussa's defection will be seen as a vindication of the coalition's efforts to intimidate key members of the regime by warning them that if they do not defect, they will be taken to the international criminal court to face war crimes trials."[104] As mentioned, Koussa had a close relationship with the MI 6, which allegedly facilitated his escape. Our office could not confirm the causal relationship between our decision to open an investigation and his defection.

Notes

1. In an interview published on the February 8, 2011, Gaddafi deplored Mubarak's and Ben Ali's fate and "warned Libyans not to be involved in any acts which will harm security or cause chaos, vowing that their tribes will be held responsible in the event of doing so." *Gaddafi Fears Riots, Says Mubarak Is Poor*, ALBAWABA (Feb. 8, 2011), http://www.albawaba.com/main-headlines/gaddafi-fears-riots-says-mubarak-poor.
2. Situation in the Libyan Arab Jamahiriya, ICC-01/11, Prosecutor's Application Pursuant to Article 58 as to Muammar Mohammed Abu Minyar Gaddafi, Saif Al-Islam Gaddafi and Abdullah Al-Senussi ¶ 4 (May 16, 2011), https://www.icc-cpi.int/CourtRecords/CR2011_06155.PDF.
3. *Id.*
4. *Id.*
5. *Id.*
6. "The decision to do justice in Libya should be taken by the Libyan people. Currently, Libya is not a State Party to the Rome Statute." *Statement by ICC Prosecutor Luis Moreno-Ocampo on Libya*, ICC (Feb. 23, 2011), https://www.icc-cpi.int/Pages/item.aspx?name=statement%20by%20icc%20prosecutor%20luis%20moreno_ocampo%20on%20libya.
7. In addition, "[t]here is no division of power or checks and balances within the system in Libya. Finally, Gaddafi controls the judiciary." Situation in the Libyan Arab Jamahiriya, ICC-01/11, Prosecutor's Application Pursuant to Article 58 as to Muammar Mohammed Abu Minyar Gaddafi, Saif Al-Islam Gaddafi and Abdullah

Al-Senussi ¶ 4 (May 16, 2011), https://www.icc-cpi.int/CourtRecords/CR2011_06155.PDF.

8. Other nations soon followed this precedent, and the 1970s Arab petro-boom began. Martin Asser, *The Muammar Gaddafi story*, BBC News (Oct. 21, 2012), https://www.bbc.com/news/world-africa-12688033.

9. Reuters, *Despite U.N. Ban, Mandela Meets Gaddafi in Libya*, N.Y. Times, Oct. 23, 1997, A3.

10. In 1999, just before stepping down as South Africa's first democratically elected president, Mandela invited Gaddafi to Cape Town. Mandela spoke of "a world where the strong may seek to impose upon the more vulnerable; and where particular nations or groups of nations may still seek to decide the fate of the planet—in such a world respect for multilateralism, moderation of public discourse and a patient search for compromise become even more imperative to save the world from debilitating conflict and enduring inequality." James Kirchick, *South Africa Stands With Qaddafi*, Atlantic (Sept. 6, 2011), https://www.theatlantic.com/international/archive/2011/09/south-africa-stands-with-qaddafi/244584/.

11. Farouk Chothia, *What Does Gaddafi's Death Mean for Africa?*, BBC News (Oct. 21, 2011), https://www.bbc.com/news/world-africa-15392189.

12. John O'Neil, *U.S. Restores Diplomatic Ties to Libya*, N.Y. Times (May 15, 2006), https://www.nytimes.com/2006/05/15/world/middleeast/15cnd-libya.html.

13. Department of State Publication: Background notes series. *Archive: Background Note Libya*, U.S. Dep't State, https://2001-2009.state.gov/r/pa/ei/bgn/5425.htm (last visited June 20, 2020).

14. Ronald Reagan, An American Life: An Enhanced eBook with CBS Video: The Autobiography 10545 (Kindle ed. 2011).

15. *Id.* at 4193–98

16. R. W. Apple Jr., *Fair Warning; Reagan Confronts an Intractable Qaddafi*, N.Y. Times, Apr. 13, 1986, sec. 4, p. 1.

17. Ronald Reagan, An American Life: An Enhanced eBook with CBS Video: The Autobiography 4207–11 (Kindle ed. 2011).

18. "At the end of the Carter Administration, US embassy staff members were withdrawn from Tripoli after a mob attacked and set fire to the embassy in December 1979." Department of State Publication: Background notes series. *Archive: Background Note Libya*, U.S. Dep't State, https://2001-2009.state.gov/r/pa/ei/bgn/5425.htm (last visited June 20, 2020).

19. During the 1980s and 1990s Gaddafi's regime continued supporting terrorist groups and was targeting Libyan dissidents in Britain and across Europe. In 1981 the United States expelled the Libyan embassy from Washington. In 1984, shots fired from the Libyan's embassy in London wounded people demonstrating against Muammar Gaddafi and killed a British police officer. The United Kingdom broke off relations with Gaddafi's government as a result of the incident. Estelle Shirbon, *Man Arrested over 1984 Murder Outside Libyan Embassy in London Is released*, Reuters (May 16, 2017), https://www.reuters.com/article/us-britain-libya/man-arrested-over-1984-murder-outside-libyan-embassy-in-london-is-released-idUSKCN18C20V.

20. Reagan considered different mechanisms to deal with Gaddafi, including travel bans, prohibitions to import oil, and export controls. Department of State Publication: Background notes series. *Archive: Background Note Libya*, U.S. Dep't State, https://2001-2009.state.gov/r/pa/ei/bgn/5425.htm (last visited June 20, 2020).

21. Reagan knew that Gaddafi was constructing a nuclear weapon plant and asked Helmut Kohl, the Germany chancellor, to stop the participation of German companies in such construction. Ronald Reagan, The Reagan Diaries 667 (Douglas Brinkley ed., Kindle ed. 2009).

22. John O'Neil, *U.S. Restores Diplomatic Ties to Libya*, N.Y. Times (May 15, 2006), https://www.nytimes.com/2006/05/15/world/middleeast/15cnd-libya.html.

23. Robert H. Jackson, Chief of Council, *Opening Statement to the Four-Nation International Military Tribunal (IMT) at Nuremberg, in* International Military Tribunal Secretariat of the Tribunal, II Trial of the Major War Criminals Before the International Military Tribunal 98–155 (Official text English ed., 1947).

24. *See* German ambassador's speech at U.N. SCOR 58th sess. 4820th mtg. at 4, U.N. Doc. S/Pv.4820(PARTII) (Provisional) (Sept. 12, 2003). *See also* Natalia Malinarich, *Flashback: The Berlin Disco Bombing*, BBC News (Nov. 13, 2001, 4:01 PM), http://news.bbc.co.uk/2/hi/europe/1653848.stm.

25. Seymour M. Hersh, *Target Qaddafi*, N.Y. Times, Feb.22, 1987, at 17.

26. Bernard Weinraub, *U.S. Jets Hit Terrorist Centers in Libya; Reagan Warns of New Attacks if Needed*, N.Y. Times (Aug. 15, 1986), https://www.nytimes.com/1986/04/15/politics/us-jets-hit-terrorist-centers-in-libya-reagan-warns-of-new-attacks.html.

27. Andrew Glass, *U.S. Planes Bomb Libya, April 15, 1986*, Politico (Apr. 15, 2019), https://www.politico.com/story/2019/04/15/reagan-bomb-libya-april-15-1986-1272788.

28. Seymour M. Hersh, *Target Qaddafi*, N.Y. Times, Feb. 22, 1987, 17.

29. In 1975, a committee chaired by Senator Frank Church (the Church Committee), rejected assassination as an instrument of American policy. President Gerald Ford, Jimmy Carter, and Ronald Reagan issued executive orders implementing such recommendation. Elizabeth B. Bazan, Cong. Research Serv. RS21037 Assassination Ban and E.O. 12333: A Brief Summary 1–2 (2002).

30. Andrew Glass, *U.S. Planes Bomb Libya, April 15, 1986*, Politico (Apr. 15, 2019), https://www.politico.com/story/2019/04/15/reagan-bomb-libya-april-15-1986-1272788.

31. Seymour M. Hersh, *Target Qaddafi*, N.Y. Times, Feb. 22, 1987, 17.

32. Andrew Glass, *U.S. Planes Bomb Libya, April 15, 1986*, Politico (Apr. 15, 2019), https://www.politico.com/story/2019/04/15/reagan-bomb-libya-april-15-1986-1272788.

33. Later, Colonel North was involved in the Iran-contra scandal, funneling proceeding from illegal sale of arms to Iran to illegally finance the contras operations against the Nicaragua Sandinista regime. https://www.britannica.com/event/Iran-Contra-Affair.

34. Seymour M. Hersh, *Target Qaddafi*, N.Y. Times, Feb. 22, 1987, 17.

35. U.N. SCOR 47th sess., 3033rd mtg. at 6, U.N. Doc. S/PV.3033 (Provisional) (Jan. 21, 1992).

36. *Id.*

37. *Id.*

38. The sanctions were expanded in 1993 with the adoption of Security Council Resolution 883. Michael P. Scharf, *Insights Vol. 5, Issue 5: A Preview of the Lockerbie Case*, AM. SOC'Y. INT'L LAW (May 4, 2000), https://www.asil.org/insights/volume/5/issue/5/preview-lockerbie-case.

39. "We cannot be unmoved by the plight of our African brothers and sisters," Mandela said. *Mandela Visit to Libya Gives Kadafi a Boost*, L.A. TIMES, Oct. 23, 1997, 12 AM, https://www.latimes.com/archives/la-xpm-1997-oct-23-mn-45897-story.html.

40. "Those that yesterday were friends of our enemies have the gall today to tell me not to visit my brother Gaddafi. They are advising us to be ungrateful and forget our friends of the past." Linda Housman, *Branded African Icons. Mandela and Gaddafi, "The Saint" versus "The Mad Dog,"* GLOBAL RESEARCH (Jan 5, 2014), https://www.globalr esearch.ca/branded-african-icons-mandela-and-gaddafi-the-saint-versus-the-mad-dog/5363898.

41. Reuters, *Despite U.N. Ban, Mandela Meets Gaddafi in Libya*, N.Y. TIMES, Oct. 23, 1997, A3.

42. Michael P. Scharf, *Insights Vol. 5, Issue 5: A Preview of the Lockerbie Case*, AM. SOC'Y. INT'L LAW (May 4, 2000), https://www.asil.org/insights/volume/5/issue/5/preview-lockerbie-case.

43. *Id.*

44. Iconic, *Nelson Mandela Meets Libyan* leader, Muammar Gaddafi, YOUTUBE (Nov. 9, 2010), https://www.youtube.com/watch?v=umgMDJIpkn0.

45. Ian Cobain, *How Britain Did Gaddafi's Dirty Work*, GUARDIAN (Nov. 9, 2017, 6:00 AM),   https://www.theguardian.com/news/2017/nov/09/how-britain-did-gadda fis-dirty-work-libya

46. The MI5 considered that "Qaddafi was responsible for a series of attacks on Libyan émigrés in Britain, which included three killings at the beginning of the decade." CHRISTOPHER ANDREW, DEFEND THE REALM 689 (Kindle ed. 2009).

47. *Id.*

48. Ian Cobain, *How Britain Did Gaddafi's Dirty Work*, GUARDIAN (Nov. 9, 2017, 6:00 AM),   https://www.theguardian.com/news/2017/nov/09/how-britain-did-gadda fis-dirty-work-libya

49. *Id.*

50. *Id.*

51. *Id.*

52. UK, *US Tell Security Council They Are Ready to See Sanctions Against Libya Lifted*, U.N. NEWS (Aug. 18, 2003), https://news.un.org/en/story/2003/08/77072-uk-us-tell-security-council-they-are-ready-see-sanctions-against-libya-lifted.

53. U.N. SCOR 58th sess. 4820th mtg. at 6, U.N. Doc. S/Pv.4820(PARTII)(Provisional) (Sept. 12, 2003).

54. Ian Cobain, *How Britain Did Gaddafi's Dirty Work*, Guardian (Nov. 9, 2017, 6:00 AM), https://www.theguardian.com/news/2017/nov/09/how-britain-did-gadda fis-dirty-work-libya.

55. *President Bush: Libya Pledges to Dismantle WMD Programs*, The White House President George W. Bush (Dec. 19, 2003, 5:32 PM), https://georgewbush-whi tehouse.archives.gov/news/releases/2003/12/20031219-9.html.

56. "As we hoped, the liberation of Iraq had an impact beyond its borders. Six days after Saddam's capture, Colonel Muammar Qaddafi of Libya—a longtime enemy of America and state sponsor of terror—publicly confessed that he had been developing chemical and nuclear weapons." George W. Bush, Decision Points 267–68 (Kindle ed. 2010).

57. *Full transcript: Blair's Libya statement*, BBC News, http://news.bbc.co.uk/2/hi/uk_n ews/politics/3336073.stm (last updated Dec. 19, 2003).

58. Ian Cobain, *How Britain Did Gaddafi's Dirty Work*, The Guardian (Nov. 9, 2017, 6:00 AM), https://www.theguardian.com/news/2017/nov/09/how-britain-did-gadda fis-dirty-work-libya.

59. In addition to Shell, other British firms like BAE Systems have already begun tapping the opportunities in Libya. *Blair Hails New Libyan Relations*, BBC News, http://news. bbc.co.uk/2/hi/uk_news/politics/3566545.stm (last updated Mar. 25, 2004).

60. John O'Neil, *U.S. Restores Diplomatic Ties to Libya*, N.Y. Times (May 15, 2006), https://www.nytimes.com/2006/05/15/world/middleeast/15cnd-libya.html. *Students Protest at Gaddafi Visit*, BBC News, http://news.bbc.co.uk/2/hi/europe/8095982.stm (last updated June 11, 2009).

61. Helene Cooper, *Isolation Over, Libyan Leader Meets with Rice*, N.Y. Times (Sept. 5, 2008), https://www.nytimes.com/2008/09/06/world/africa/06diplo.html.

62. Craig S. Smith, *Libya Sentences 6 to Die in HIV Case*, N.Y. Times (Dec. 20, 2006), https://www.nytimes.com/2006/12/20/world/middleeast/20libya.html.

63. Libya and the European Union agreed to develop a "full partnership," with the Europeans promising a package of aid to develop Libyan hospitals and other infrastructure. Eleanor Beardsley, *Libya Frees Condemned Medical Workers*, NPR (July 24, 2007, 6:00 AM), https://www.npr.org/templates/story/story.php?storyId=12193699.

64. Ian Black, *Libya Convicts Swiss Pair in Apparent Revenge for Arrest of Gaddafi's Son*, Guardian (Dec. 2, 2009, 2:40 PM), https://www.theguardian.com/world/2009/dec/ 02/swiss-businessmen-sentenced-libya.

65. Patrick Goodenough, *Still Angry Over Treatment of His Son, Gaddafi Wants Switzerland Abolished*, CNS News (Sept. 4, 2009, 4:38 AM), https://cnsnews.com/ news/article/still-angry-over-treatment-his-son-gaddafi-wants-switzerland-abolished.

66. *Libya Convicts Swiss Pair in Apparent Revenge for Arrest of Gaddafi's Son*, Guardian (Dec. 2, 2009), (https://www.theguardian.com/world/2009/dec/02/swiss-business men-sentenced-libya.

67. He added that the public apology was necessary to win pledges by the Libyan prime minister, Al-Baghdadi Ali Al-Mahmoudi, that the two Swiss would be allowed to leave the country by September 1. Federico Bragagnini, *Merz Out on a Limb Over His*

Visit to Libya, Swiss Info (Aug. 21, 2009, 9:06 PM), https://www.swissinfo.ch/eng/merz-out-on-a-limb-over-his-visit-to-libya/72172.

68. Ian Black, *Switzerland Considered Sending Special Forces into Libya to Rescue Citizens*, Guardian (June 21, 2010, 8:03 PM), https://www.theguardian.com/world/2010/jun/21/switzerland-plan-commandos-libya.

69. Daniel Flynn, *Libya and Swiss Close to Ending Visa Dispute: Italy*, Reuters (Feb. 17, 2010, 1:07 PM), https://www.reuters.com/article/us-libya-visas-italy/libya-and-swiss-close-to-ending-visa-dispute-italy-idUSTRE61G3C020100217..

70. Raphael Minder, *Rare Discord Upsets Usual Swiss Calm*, N.Y. Times (Mar 31, 2010), https://www.nytimes.com/2010/04/01/world/europe/01iht-letter.html?searchResultPosition=37

71. "The US State Department spokesman Philip Crowley said that a call for jihad was "lots of words . . . and not necessarily a lot of sense." Gaddafi threatened that there would be "negative repercussions" for American oil companies in Libya. On March 10, both Crowley and the American government offered their apologies to the Libyan dictator. He accepted them and said that Tripoli would resume relations with Washington "in a manner of mutual respect." I should have focused solely on our concern about the term 'jihad,' which has since been clarified by the Libyan government," said the chastened spokesman, P. J. Crowley. "I regret that my comments have become an obstacle to further progress in our bilateral relationship." Ian Black, *Gaddafi Weighs Up Options in Light of Switzerland's No Entry Sign*, Guardian (Mar. 10, 2010, 11:75 AM), https://www.theguardian.com/world/2010/mar/10/libya-switzerland-gaddafi-feud.

72. Ian Black, *Libya Claims Victory in Swiss Row After Visa Ban on Officials Lifted*, Guardian (Mar. 28, 2010, 5:52 PM), https://www.theguardian.com/world/2010/mar/28/libya-switzerland-visa-ban-lifted.

73. Colin Moynihan, *Libya's U.N. Diplomats Break with Qaddafi*, N.Y. Times (Feb. 21, 2011), https://www.nytimes.com/2011/02/22/world/frica/22nations.html. *See also* Colin Moynihan, *Ibrahim Dabbashi's Press Conference*, N.Y. Times (Feb. 21, 2011), https://www.nytimes.com/video/world/africa/100000000653690/libyanrep.html.

74. Colin Moynihan, *Libya's U.N. Diplomats Break with Qaddafi*, N.Y. Times (Feb. 21, 2011), https://www.nytimes.com/2011/02/22/world/frica/22nations.html. *See also* Colin Moynihan, *Ibrahim Dabbashi's Press Conference*, N.Y. Times (Feb. 21, 2011), https://www.nytimes.com/video/world/africa/100000000653690/libyanrep.html.

75. Ian Black, *Libya: Defections Leave Muammar Gaddafi Isolated in Tripoli Bolthole*, Guardian (Deb. 23, 2011, 9:33 PM), https://www.theguardian.com/world/2011/feb/23/muammar-gaddafi-libya-tripoli-uprising.

76. Ola Galal, *Arab League Bars Libya from Meetings, Citing Forces' "Crimes,"* Bloomberg (Feb. 22, 2011, 3:46 PM), https://www.bloomberg.com/news/articles/2011-02-22/arab-league-bars-libya-from-meetings-citing-forces-crimes-.

77. *Arab League Suspends Libya from Future Sessions*, World News Mpelembe (Feb.22, 2011, 5:39 PM), http://world-news.mpelembe.net/home/arableaguesuspendslibyafromfuturesession.

78. Peace and Security Council of the African Union, Communiqué of the 261st mtg., ¶ 2, 3, 5, PSC/PR/COMM(CCLXI) (Feb. 23, 2011), https://www.peaceau.org/uplo ads/psc-communique-on-the-situation-in-libya.pdf.

79. "S.C. Official communiqué of the 6486th (closed) meeting of the Security Council, U.N. Doc. S/PV.6486 (Feb. 22, 2011).

80. Ed Pilkington, *UN Ambassadors Clash Over Condemnation of Gaddafi*, GUARDIAN (Feb. 23, 2011 1:57 AM), https://www.theguardian.com/world/2011/feb/23/un-ambassadors-clash-gaddafi.

81. *Id.*

82. *Id.*

83. *Id.*

84. DAVID BOSCO, ROUGH JUSTICE: THE INTERNATIONAL CRIMINAL COURT IN A WORLD OF POWER POLITICS 179 (Kindle ed. 2014).

85. Katherine Connelly, *Tunisia: Celebrations Spread to Paris, and Why the French Government Shouldn't Be Sleeping Peacefully*, COUNTERFIRE (Jan. 16, 2011), http://www.counterfire.org/index.php/articles/international/9291-tunisia-celebrations-spread-toparis-and-why-the-french-government-shouldnt-be-sleeping-peacefu lly#sthash.8SnOPK5s.dpuf.

86. Roula Khalaf & Scheherazade Daneshkhu, *France Regrets Misjudgment over Ben Ali*, FINANCIAL TIMES (Jan. 18, 2011), https://www.ft.com/content/68bef0c2-232a-11e0-b6a3-00144feab49a.

87. *Sarkozy says France 'Underestimated' Tunisian Anger*, BBC NEWS (Jan. 24, 2011), https://www.bbc.com/news/world-europe-12265740.

88. Nicholas Watts & Patrick Wintour, *Libya No-Fly Zone Call by France Fails to Get David Cameron's Backing*, GUARDIAN (Feb. 23, 2011, 15:55), https://www.theguard ian.com/world/2011/feb/23/libya-nofly-zone-david-cameron.

89. Thom Shanker, *Warning Against Wars Like Iraq and Afghanistan*, N.Y. TIMES (Feb. 25, 2011) https://www.nytimes.com/2011/02/26/world/26gates.html.

90. *International Commission of Inquiry Appointed to Investigate Human Rights Violations in Libya*, RELIEF WEB (Mar. 11, 2011), https://reliefweb.int/report/libya/international-commission-inquiry-appointed-investigate-human-rights-violati ons-libya.

91. S.C.O.R., 66th Sess., 6490th mtg., U.N. Doc S/PV.6490 Provision (Feb. 25, 2011).

92. From the beginning of Libya's crisis, Germany pushed within the European Union for a clear condemnation of the Gaddafi government and argued that the European Union should pressure Gaddafi to stop the violence with one voice. Werner Hoyer, Germany's Deputy Foreign Minister stated: "The European Union should not let itself be blackmailed (by Gaddafi)." Angela Merkel described Gaddafi's speech of the 22nd of February as "very, very frightening," referred to a "declaration of war" by Gaddafi against his own people and called for sanctions against the Gaddafi government. Germany supported the Special Session of the Human Rights Council and co-sponsored the Resolution that recommended the suspension of Libyan membership. The German Foreign Minister, Guido Westerwelle, stated that "if this

violence continues, everyone in Europe will know that this cannot go unanswered." Germany's UN Mission strongly advocated for the ICC referral.

93. Expressing regret and concern about the excessive use of force against civilians by the authorities in Libya. He promised that everything would be done to stop those responsible. http://www.unmultimedia.org/tv/webcast/2011/02/h-e-mr-baso-san gqu-south-africa-on-libyasecurity-council-media-stakeout.html

94. DAVID BOSCO, ROUGH JUSTICE: THE INTERNATIONAL CRIMINAL COURT IN A WORLD OF POWER POLITICS 167 (Kindle ed. 2014).

95. *Id.*

96. Ambassador Joy Ogwu of Nigeria noted that the African Union, the Organization of the Islamic Conference, and the League of Arab States have all condemned the disproportionate use of force against civilians. He also highlighter the importance of the letter from the Permanent Representative of Libya.

97. Brazil expressed its strong reservation to the resolution's operative paragraph 6, and reiterated its firm conviction that initiatives aimed at establishing those exemptions were not helpful to advance the cause of justice and accountability.

98. Ambassador Néstor Osorio of Colombia stated that the resolution sent the "direct and solid message" that the violence in Libya must cease and that those responsible for it must answer for their crimes. Ambassador Jose Filipe Moraes Cabral of Portugal stated that impunity would not be tolerated, and serious crimes would be prosecuted. Bosnia and Herzegovina stood by its position that the perpetrators of such crimes must be held accountable. Gabon reminded the Libyan regime of the consequences of its actions.

99. Press Release, Security Council, In Swift, Decisive Action, Security Council Imposes Tough Measures on Libyan Regime, Adopting Resolution 1970 in Wake of Crackdown on Protesters, SC/10187/REV.1 (Feb. 28, 2011).

100. S. Res. 85, 112th Cong. (2011).

101. "February 28, 2011. 'Information suggests that forces loyal to Colonel Muammar Qadhafi are attacking civilians in Libya,' said Prosecutor Luis Moreno-Ocampo. 'This could constitute crimes against humanity and must stop. The Office will act swiftly and impartially. There will be no impunity for leaders involved in the commission of crimes.'" *Statement by the Office of the Prosecutor on Situation in Libya*, ICC (Feb. 28, 2011), http://www.icc-cpi.int/en_menus/icc/structure%20of%20 the%20court/office%20of%20the%20prosecutor/reports%20and%20statements/ statement/Pages/statementlybia28022011.aspx.

102. *Statement of the Prosecutor on the Opening of the Investigation into the Situation in Libya*, ICC (Mar. 2, 2011) (transcript available at http://www.icc-cpi.int/NR/rdonly res/035C3801-5C8D-4ABC-876B-C7D946B51F22/283045/StatementLibya_03032 011.pdf).

103. DAVID BOSCO, ROUGH JUSTICE: THE INTERNATIONAL CRIMINAL COURT IN A WORLD OF POWER POLITICS 168 (Kindle ed. 2014).

104. Patrick Wintour et al., *Libya: Moussa Koussa, Gaddafi's Foreign Minister, Defects to UK*, GUARDIAN (Mar. 31, 2011, 1:18 AM), https://www.theguardian.com/world/ 2011/mar/31/libya-mousa-kousa-gaddafi-foreign-minister.

20

War and Justice in the Gaddafi Case

After our *jus ad Curiam* decision opening an investigation into Libya, Gaddafi forces were still advancing to Benghazi. To protect civilians, in March 2011, the UN Security Council adopted a *jus ad Bellum* decision. It had substantial differences with the decisions adopted in Afghanistan and Iraq.

First, it was a collective resolution adopted by the UN Security Council. Second, there was political support from the region. The Arab League demanded international intervention. Third, the alleged goal was to protect Libyans following the Responsibility to Protect principle. Fourth, it was implemented by a coalition led by NATO, with other forces, including Sweden and Arab countries like Qatar, Jordan, and Emirates participating in the hostilities. Fifth, following rebel demands, there were no international forces on the ground. Sixth, there was no attempt to conduct a counterinsurgency operation in Libya during the post-conflict.

The Office of the Prosecutor had to investigate ongoing crimes committed in Libya in a highly politically charged scenario. We collected evidence protecting witnesses and investigators and re-evaluated "the interest of justice," confirming that the situation was admissible. We warned the UN Security Council that we were planning to request arrest warrants during our briefing in April and received strong support.

In May, we asked the court to issue arrest warrants against Libya's supreme leader Muammar Gaddafi, his son and informal Prime Minister Saif Gaddafi, and the head of Intelligence Al-Senussi. The pre-trial chamber reviewed the evidence and issued the arrest warrants in June 2011. The court was able to act decisively before the conflict ended.

The Gaddafi regime collapsed. A group of rebels executed Muammar Gaddafi. Al-Sennusi escaped, was arrested in Mauritania, and extradited to Libya, where he was prosecuted. Saif Gaddafi tried to escape, but a Zintan militia arrested him. Libya challenged the admissibility of both cases before the ICC. The court accepted Libya's position in the Al-Sennusi case and rejected it in the case against Saif Al-Islam Gaddafi. For the first time in the history of the court, an admissibility challenge was successful.

War and Justice in the 21st Century. Luis Moreno Ocampo, Oxford University Press. © Oxford University Press 2022.
DOI: 10.1093/oso/9780197628973.003.0021

The Gaddafi regime's end did not create national order. Libyan institutions were not ready to organize a peaceful coexistence. In 2014 a new civil war started, and a separate Congress was established in Tobruk. It provided a general amnesty in 2015, and the Zintan militia released Saif Gaddafi. He challenged his case's admissibility before the ICC, arguing that he was already prosecuted and convicted in absentia for the same crimes.[1] The chambers rejected his arguments because there was not a final judgment of conviction.

The 2011 UN Security Council's *jus ad Curiam* and *jus ad Bellum* decisions were implemented. Still, Libya's national political system could not manage the new conflicts, and new actors committed more crimes.

UN Security Council *Jus ad Bellum* Libya's Decision

The US Senate resolution adopted on March 1, 2011, called Gaddafi to "resign his position" and urged the UN Security Council "to take such further action to protect civilians in Libya from attack, including the possible imposition of a no-fly zone over Libyan territory."[2]

A few days later, President Obama, President Sarkozy, and Prime Minister Cameron demanded that Gaddafi step down.[3] Instead, Gaddafi escalated the attacks. By the beginning of March, Gaddafi forces had recovered from early losses and were marching toward Benghazi, the home of the revolution and main opposition stronghold, and recapturing cities and towns along the way.[4]

Secretary of Defense Robert Gates considered that Benghazi's "capture would lead to a bloodbath. The president . . . was not happy with the options his advisers offered.[5]

Susan Rice, then US permanent representative before the UN, explained the *jus ad Bellum* discussions between the P-3:

> By early March, the British and French had begun to lobby for the international imposition of a no-fly zone over Libya to protect civilians from Qaddafi's forces. In Washington, we agonized over how to respond. There was reluctance to get into a third war, after Afghanistan and Iraq, in yet another Muslim-majority country. Doing nothing, however, pierced the conscience of many of us.[6]

On March 10, Obama's national security adviser, Thomas E. Donilon, "deflected calls for more aggressive action in Libya." He said that the United States "will not, at least for now, put its pilots in harm's way by enforcing a no-flight zone over the country."[7] His comments were consistent with "President Obama . . . policy of restraint . . . an emphasis on pragmatism over idealism . . . his first job is to be the American president."[8]

On March 12, the Arab League paved the way for international military intervention. It requested "that the UN Security Council impose a no-fly zone in Libya . . . and recognized the rebel council as the legitimate representative of the Libyan people."[9] Secretary of State Hillary Clinton was in Paris and considered that decision a "turning point," "The Arab League asked for action against one of its own members."[10]

During those days, we had our investigations on Gaddafi well advanced. I informally explored with France and UK governments the possibility to include in the *jus ad Bellum* debate the authority to execute any ICC arrest warrants. France and the United Kingdom were leading the efforts to get a UN Security Council resolution authorizing a military operation in Libya and were already overwhelmed with the discussions' complexities. They just ignored my informal comments.

Secretary Clinton met in Paris with Mahmoud Jibril, a Libyan political scientist with a PhD from the University of Pittsburgh appointed by the National Transitional Council (NTC) as the prime minister. She found him "to be impressive and polished, especially for the representative of a rebel council on the verge of annihilation."[11]

Secretary Clinton also reported to the White House that President Sarkozy and the UK Secretary of Defense *were prepared to take the lead in any military action.* She estimated that some Arab countries *would even actively participate in combat operations* and that *the rebels would turn out to be credible partners.*[12] Lebanon representing the Arab region in the council was demanding a limited intervention without boots on the ground.

At the end of March 15, after discussing the limitations of a "no-fly zone" and exploring different options, President Obama decided that

> he would favor US military action, but only under several conditions: 1) that Amb Rice could obtain UNSC authorization for a robust mandate to protect civilians; 2) that Hillary Clinton could get the Arab League countries to agree to participate, and 3) that the US role would be limited—it

would launch the attacks, take out Qaddafi's air defenses, and establish air superiority but after that, the Europeans, especially the Brits and French, would have to carry the bulk of the load.[13]

The following day, Amb. Rice asked for the floor as soon as the Security Council meeting started. Following President Obama's decision, she requested more than "a simple no-fly zone." "This would need to be an unfettered mandate to protect civilians, and I don't want any ambiguity about what we intend to do with it. This will be an air war to save innocent lives."[14] Her assistants distributed a US draft to the other fourteen members: the new language would "authorize Member States . . . to take all necessary measures . . . to protect civilians and civilian populated areas."[15]

Susan Rice described the moment: "The Council was dead silent for several seconds after I finished. Lebanon broke the silence and signaled that it was on board with a stronger US text. The United Kingdom followed suit." French Ambassador Gerard Araud was shocked "by the abrupt shift in the U.S. position."[16] *By the end of the day, as my team quietly polled Council members, it seemed we were in striking distance of enough votes.*[17]

"*In the hours before the UN vote was scheduled, with his troops and militia massing just ninety miles south of*" Benghazi, "the Libyan leader took to the radio with a warning to residents: 'We are coming.'" He pledged to go house by house looking for "traitors" and told Libyans to "capture the rats." To the opposition fighters, he said, "We will find you in your closets. We will have no mercy and no pity."[18] Hillary Clinton considered that Gaddafi's statement facilitated the approval of the UN Resolution.[19]

The Libya *jus ad Bellum* discussion was a test for the proposed reform to expand the number of permanent members. In that moment, except Japan, all countries aspiring to be permanent members were part of the UN Security Council: India, Brazil, Germany, and South Africa, the only one that finally voted in favor.[20] But to obtain a South African positive vote, President Obama had to call President Zuma and Amb. Rice had to stake out her counterpart Amb. Sangqu at the entrance to the Security Council.[21]

The final discussion was at 6 p.m. in the UN Headquarters. Alain Juppe, minister for foreign affairs of France, traveled to New York to ensure that France's role, tabling the resolution and pushing for the intervention, was recognized. He believed "this new Arab springtime is good news . . . for all of us," but the will of the Libyan people had been "trampled under the feet of the Qadhafi regime" as *Qadhafi mercilessly attacked his own people.*[22]

The Chinese ambassador who was presiding the session called for a vote: China[23] and Russia[24] decided to abstain without using their veto. Brazil,[25]Germany[26], and India,[27] three candidates to be permanent members, also abstained. The UN Security Council Resolution 1973 (2011) was adopted by a vote of ten in favor to none against, with five abstentions.

The resolution authorized the member states, acting nationally or through regional organizations or arrangements, to take "all necessary measures" to protect civilians under threat of attack in the country while excluding *a foreign occupation force of any form on any part of Libyan territory*.

The council was providing international protection to Libyan citizens, and they were grateful.

The vote was followed by thousands of Libyans gathered in Benghazi's main square, gazing up at jumbo video screens tuned to live coverage of the Security Council . . . The celebrations lasted deep into the night, as people honked their car horns and waved Libya's flag from the pre-Qaddafi era.[28]

"Within hours of that resolution, French warplanes flew the mission's first combat sorties, and cruise missiles from US warships struck Libyan air defense and radar installations."[29] Over the next seventy-two hours, Libya's air defenses were successfully destroyed, and the people of Benghazi were saved from imminent devastation.[30]

For a few days, France was objecting to allowing NATO to coordinate the plans.[31] Agreements were reached, and since March 30, NATO was in charge of coordinating the operations that were executed by sixteen countries, including not NATO members like Sweden, Qatar, Jordan, and the United Arab Emirates.[32]

Planning Libya's Investigations While the Conflict Was Just Evolving

To investigate Libya's situation, we triggered an additional budget to deal with emergencies and appointed a special join team to collect the evidence.[33] Ex Com members and I were personally involved in planning the investigation together with the joint team. We had to develop a collection plan, a cooperation plan, and plans related to administration, security, and communication.

Each day the media published information about new alleged crimes committed in Libya, adding more case hypotheses. The rebels promoted information about massive rapes that had to be corroborated, and some of their activities could constitute war crimes. It was not easy to analyze the hierarchies and the method to commit crimes. Our investigators were willing to take the risk and go to Libya to collect evidence. However, the statute establishes the office's duty to protect any persons connected with our work (*Article 54(3)(f) and Article 68(1)*).

I refused to send investigators to a very unstable Libya to obtain crime base testimonies. We decided to collect evidence without visiting Libya following the tactic we used in Darfur: we searched for those who escaped or defected. We look for insiders outside Libya and obtained documents and films.[34] In a few weeks, we had clarity on Gaddafi's security apparatus structure and decision-making process.

Gaddafi divided all power and responsibilities beneath him, particularly in the security and the military, to ensure that no single person or entity could challenge his authority. We learned that Gaddafi relied on his inner circle, mainly family members, whom he has placed in strategic positions to implement a systematic policy of suppressing any challenge to his authority.

Also, Gaddafi transmitted his orders orally either directly or through the Secretariat or Registry, also known as Information Bureau of the Leader; he did not want to leave any written trace of his actions. He closely follows up on the implementation of his orders.

In the early days of the demonstrations, Gaddafi transmitted orders through his Secretariat to "discipline" civilians who had openly rebelled against the regime by killing them and destroying their property. Our evidence showed that Saif Gaddafi was involved in designing a plan that expressly included lethal force against demonstrators and alleged dissidents.

Further, Al-Senussi, upon Gaddafi's instructions, directed and coordinated the operation of the security forces in Benghazi and expressly ordered the shooting of civilians. Since February 15, security forces had carried out a systematic campaign of arrests and detentions of alleged dissidents following such a plan. As a result, demonstrators, political activists, journalists, and persons who shared information with the media, among others, have been systematically arrested. The whereabouts of many of them were unknown. The arrests and detentions have been followed by systematic torture.

Security forces carried out a cover-up operation to hide the evidence of past crimes and facilitate the commission of future ones. The plot included dozens of attacks on the press since the start of the popular demonstrations.

We prioritized the alleged crimes committed by the states forces because they were much graver than the allegations against rebel groups. We keep collecting evidence about new crimes committed by different sides and exonerating material. Still, we developed a first case hypothesis focused on the initial incidents.

Revisiting the Interest of Justice

Calculating the Following Steps

Our investigations were well advanced, and, at the beginning of April, we were almost ready to request an arrest warrant. Following the policy adopted since the Darfur investigation, we decided to inform the council during our first briefing on Libya scheduled for the beginning of May before presenting our case in court. The council would have the chance to use its Article 16 authority.

In the meantime, we started to explore how to implement an eventual court decision. Mahmoud Jibril, prime minister of the Transitional National Council, visited our office at The Hague. During lunch, we discussed how to use our investigative activities to promote defections to prevent crimes and obtain inside information. He insisted on the concept that no foreign troops should be involved in grounds operations and that the rebels should implement any arrest warrants if the judges decide to issue them.

In an April 14, 2011, letter, the Transitional National Council responded officially to the Office of the Prosecutor: "We are fully committed to supporting the fast implementation of such arrest warrants and expect the international community to cooperate fully."

Brainstorming with the Obama Administration

During those days, I received a call from members of the Obama administration, exploring the timing of our request for arrest warrants and the possibility to keep a space open for an eventual negotiation with Gaddafi. I trusted my interlocutors, and I departed from my reluctance to mention Article 16.

I told them that we were almost ready to proceed, but we were waiting for our UN Security Council briefing. If the council decided to suspend the investigation using Article 16 to facilitate the negotiation, we would fully respect the decision without any negative comment. In the meantime, we considered that there was no reason to delay our request.

They also, in confidence, explained that there was no agreement with Gaddafi. As a consequence, it was problematic for the United States to request an application of Article 16. It was like brainstorming, with no specific request, but I felt that the United States felt uncomfortable that the Office of the Prosecutor could limit its negotiation space.

The office policy considered that the UN Security Council is responsible for ensuring international peace, and our office should not interfere with its mandate. In any case, following that conversation, the office conducted a new assessment of the "interest of justice" under Article 53(2)(c) of the statute.

The office's April 29, 2011, internal report considered that the likelihood of an arrest warrant against Libya's leaders had been foreseen by the UN Security Council when referring the situation to the court. The resolution specifically mentioned the possibility to suspend the investigation per Article 16.

The report said, "As to the question of whether arrest warrants negatively impact mediation efforts, this has not been empirically proven. In some of the Office's previous cases, negotiations appear to have been prompted by the request and issuance of arrest warrants."

"In other cases, the prospect for negotiations was used as an excuse by those who allegedly committed the crimes to regain power or commit new atrocities, and mediation efforts were manipulated by those leaders." The report quoted a few examples:

(a) After the prosecution presented its case against Ahmed Harun and Ali Kushayb in February 2007, an AU/UN negotiation started in April 2007. It did not include a request to respect justice; it failed to achieve progress, and it collapsed in June 2008. A month later, in July 2008, the request to issue an arrest warrant against President Al Bashir produced a new process of negotiation led by UN/AU mediation supported by the Arab League.

(b) In the case of Joseph Kony and the other LRA's leaders, the issuance of arrest warrants led to an agreement between the office and the government of the Sudan to implement them. This contributed to forcing Joseph Kony to leave his safe haven in Southern Sudan and establish a camp in Garamba Park, DRC.

Such a move, local and national leaders' commitment, and the Ugandan army's efforts contributed to ending the massive atrocities affecting Northern Uganda for twenty years. The Juba talks consolidated the end of massive violence in Northern Uganda. Still, they allowed Joseph Kony to regroup, collect money from the international community, buy weapons, and launch massive attacks against the civilian population in the DRC, Central African Republic, and Southern Sudan.

(c) During the Ivory Coast crisis, President Gbagbo reportedly used the AU efforts to negotiate an exit to solidify his position, allegedly distribute weapons between the local population, and fuel the armed conflict.

(d) In the DRC, the evidence collected in the case against members of the FDLR (Forces démocratiques pour la libération du Rwanda) demonstrates that during 2009 the group committed atrocities to force the international community to negotiate. FDLR phone intercepts revealed its leaders' complaints about the "injustice" of not having received a peace offer despite all the atrocities committed. They expressly mentioned some examples, including Jean-Pierre Bemba and the LRA.

Our internal report highlighted that professional negotiators had been urged to adjust to the new limits created by international criminal law during the last years.[35] *Concerns have also been raised concerning difficulties of implementing arrest warrants in Libya. The enforcement of the Court's decisions and, in particular, its arrest warrants remain the responsibility of States. The Court cannot suspend its judicial activities because persons might not be immediately arrested.* The Office of the Prosecutor confirmed that there was no interest of justice reasons to suspend its request for arrest warrants in the Libya situation.

Interacting with NATO

Before briefing the UN Security Council, I visited Brussels' NATO headquarters a couple of times, trying to understand how to harmonize the justice and military operations. I perceived a vast gap between the political actors' broad discretion on *jus ad Bellum* and *jus ad Curiam* and the structured military and judicial process. I wanted to understand the possibilities of harmonizing our different frames.

The 2014's memories of the US Secretary of Defense Robert Gates exposed such a gap. He described the UN Security Council Resolution 1970 without even mentioning the ICC referral.[36] The role of the International Criminal Court was not in his mind.

NATO was different. The ICTY Prosecutor Louise Arbour created huge controversies when she mentioned the possibility of investigating the NATO campaign. The Kosovo bombing investigation was never presented before the judges, but it significantly impacted NATO. Since then, legal training for NATO officers included the possibility to be investigated by international criminal tribunals.

In any case, my conversations with NATO officers in Brussels helped me understand the possibilities and the limits of our cooperation. They were trying to adjust to an unexpected operation that included interacting with the AU, the Arab League, and the ICC Office of the Prosecutor. NATO was responsible for central planning and coordination, but the operations were under the national commanders of the forces involved. NATO officers ensured me that their legal area vetted all the plans.

During my second visit, I warned NATO that we were planning to request arrest warrants in May and asked them if that could negatively impact the military operations. *On the contrary,* was the answer of the NATO leaders, *such a move will boost the Libyan people's morale to resist the attacks, and it could increase defections in the Army.*

Great, in this case, could you help disseminate the indictments' information?
Oh no, it is not our role.
But do you have plans for psychological operations?
Yes, but we never plan operations that are not under the NATO command.

I understood their rationale, realizing the difficulties of coordinating a network of independent international organizations working together but following different standards.

My connection with NATO helped me assist the "International Commission of Inquiry to investigate all alleged violations of international human rights law in the Libyan Arab Jamahiriya" created by the UN Human Rights Council. The commission was presided by Philippe Kirsch, the former ICC president, and we had an excellent interaction. In one of our phone conversations, Philippe mentioned that NATO was not answering the commission's questions, and he had to include that lack of cooperation in his report. I offered him to informally check what the NATO obstacle was.

I learned that NATO considered that International Humanitarian Law ruled their military operations. Consequently, its legal adviser believed that NATO had no relation with a Commission of Inquiry focused on human rights. Philippe sorted out the problem, but the incident confirmed the lack of integration of the legal frames. Each actor was following his own standards.

Briefing the Council

On May 4, 2011, I addressed the UN Security Council for the first time on the Libya situation. I informed the Council:

> In the coming weeks, I will request the judges to issue arrest warrants against three individuals who appear to bear the greatest criminal responsibility for crimes against humanity committed in the territory of Libya since 15 February.[37]

Following our agreement with the NTC, I said, "Should the judges decide to issue arrest warrants, the primary responsibility to execute them will lie with the territorial authorities."[38]

As Bosco said, "none too subtly,"[39] I linked our judicial activities to the stated council goal of protecting civilians: *Arresting those who ordered the commission of crimes will contribute to the protection of civilians in Libya. If those who called crimes are not stopped and arrested, crimes will continue unabated. Judicial activity will deter crimes by removing those who ordered the crimes.*[40]

Following the distinction between planning and operations that I learned in my meetings at NATO, I suggested that the council could request planning of eventual arrest operations to be conducted by the local forces. *Arrests cannot be successfully conducted without serious planning and preparation, which takes time. The international community should take steps now to assist with such practical planning.* No one picked this idea.

After my briefing, the state representatives presented their countries' positions. Several states, including the United Kingdom[41], Germany,[42] Colombia,[43] South Africa,[44] and the United States[45] expressly appreciated our intervention's speed. The Russian ambassador started his intervention, stating. "What the Prosecutor has said today is encouraging." No one mentioned the possibility of invoking Article 16. On the contrary, most of the Council's members fully supported the arrest warrants' request.

The US Ambassador Rice took note of our plans. She stated: "The spectre of ICC prosecution is serious and imminent and should serve as a warning to those around Al-Qadhafi of the perils of continuing to tie their fate to his."

Lebanon "believe[d] that the success of the ICC in those efforts [would] act as a deterrent in the future and serve as a tool to end the era of impunity in Libya. Here, [it] commend[ed] the Prosecutor's comments on the imminent issuance of arrest warrants."[46]

Portugal[47] and France[48]also supported the preventive function of the arrest warrants. The French representative stated that the council took "unanimously an informed decision aimed at ensuring that those mainly responsible for these crimes were prosecuted, judged and imprisoned. The judicial process is underway and must run its course."

Bosnia Herzegovina[49] made similar comments.

Three countries, China,[50] Brazil,[51] and Nigeria[52] suggested that our office adjusts to the diplomatic and political process. On the other side Gabon,[53] Colombia,[54] and India[55] considered that our office should not take into consideration any political factor.

China[56] demanded full respect for the Resolution 1973 limits. Russia[57] went further and affirmed that the international forces could also be involved in crimes and requested investigations on all sides, including rebels and international forces.

The United Kingdom recognized that its personnel was subject to the ICC authority and "supports the Court's mandate to fight impunity, in Libya and elsewhere." Nigeria demanded to investigate the fate of those sub-Saharan Africans detained by the rebels.

South Africa reminded that it was the co-sponsor of Resolution 1970. It requested our office to investigate all the sides of the conflicts, including the international forces, and made a subtle point about the scope of the immunity for non-states parties. South Africa hoped that in less than six months, "the ICC will have issued indictments against those most responsible for the atrocities committed in Libya."[58]

Arrest Warrants

The absence of any comment in the council about Article 16 removed any reason to delay our decision.

The office already gathered direct evidence about Muammar Gaddafi's orders, Saif Al-Islam organizing mercenaries' recruitment, and Al-Sennusi's participation in the attacks against demonstrators. Additionally, the office documented how the three held meetings to plan the operations. We believed that the first case described the attacks on civilians comprehensively while continued investigating new crimes.

On May 16, I announced that we had requested arrest warrants.

The evidence shows that Gaddafi forces attacked Libyan civilians in their homes and in the public space, repressed demonstrations with live ammunition, used heavy artillery against participants in funeral processions, and placed snipers to kill those leaving mosques after the prayers. The evidence shows that such persecution is still ongoing, as I speak today, in the areas under Gaddafi's control.[59]

A month later, on June 27, 2011, the pre-trial chamber issued the three warrants. Judge Sanji Mmasenono Monageng read the decision in Court. Benghazi residents greeted the news with a hail of airborne gunfire and blasts of car horns.

Mustafa Abdel Jalil, the chairman of the NTC, welcomed the move by saying, "justice has been done." He ruled out suggestions that a foreign force would be needed to implement the arrest warrant. "We will do all we can to bring Gaddafi to justice . . . The Libyan people are able to implement this decision."[60]

During those days, I received information from different sources that a plan was discussed at the NTC dividing Libya into two parts led by Benghazi and Tripoli. Saif Gaddafi was the name suggested replacing his father. But a rebel city like Misrata would end under the control of Gaddafi, and its leaders fiercely opposed such agreement. Chairman Jalil also confronted those attempts to negotiate with the regime. "The decision that was made today by the International Criminal Court stops all suggestions of negotiations with or protection for Gaddafi."[61]

Implementing the Arrest Warrants

Worsening Context

As Bosco said, "For a brief moment, power and justice appeared to be working toward one purpose: the enforcement of international law protecting civilians. But, as Gaddafi clung to power, an operation that Western leaders had hoped would quickly tip the balance against the regime turned into a protracted and controversial campaign."[62]

After three months of international military intervention, it was challenging to predict the Libyan conflict's outcome.[63] The rebel militias had organizational problems.[64] In July, the US, French, and UK diplomats were exploring a negotiation with Gaddafi.[65]

Things became worst when on July 28, the top NTC's military leader and former Gaddafi's minister of the interior, Abdel-Fatah Younes al-Obeidi, the one who defected and called on the army to "serve the people," was killed in confusing circumstances.[66] The NTC dissolved its own cabinet "for improper administrative procedures" to appease his tribe.[67]

In August, I went to Brussels. I met a senior member of the European Union, who was very depressed with the situation. He expressed his concerns: *Gaddafi is still very powerful. He has more than 5000 troops protecting him in Tripoli. The rebels would not be able to defeat Gaddafi.*

The following day Tripoli fell, as most of the 5,000 soldiers were just waiting to surrender.[68] No one predicted such an outcome.[69]

The Execution of Gaddafi and the Arrest of Saif Gaddafi and Al-Sennusi

On October 20, Muammar Gaddafi survived a NATO airstrike on his convoy and took refuge in a large drainage pipe with several bodyguards. Gaddafi was captured by rebel forces and killed.

A week later, a person who refused to identify himself contacted our office, invoking to represent Saif Gaddafi, and said that he was exploring how to surrender himself. Our office invited him to do it, but there was no follow-up.

A few weeks later, on November 19, 2011, a Zintan militia captured Saif Al-Islam Gaddafi when he tried to flee to Niger. The following day Libyan authorities made public their intentions to prosecute him in Libya.[70] We decided to go to Tripoli immediately to discuss the matter with the Libyan authorities. We thought that the best option was that the new Libya government invites the ICC judges to conduct the trial in Tripoli.

Deputy Prosecutor Fatou Bensouda and I arrived in Libya on November 22, the new interim government's first day. Everyone welcomed us. The Zintan militia controlled the airport; and the commander, who was previously a travel agent, was telling me stories about his difficult life during the rebellion.

Our Libyan bodyguards were all university students who wanted to go back to their studies. On our trip to the hotel, we passed through Gaddafi military headquarters, and I was impressed by the precision of the bombing. The walls were destroyed, but the sidewalk was intact.

It was a very intense emotional experience. Tripoli was a party; people were celebrating on the streets with flags, and a feeling of freedom was in the air. There were also concerns. A man approached me at the hotel; he said that his ten-year-old son was abducted and raped inside a military tank. He knew the person who did it. He showed me his rifle, saying: *I could kill him, but I want justice. Can you do it?* I could not promise him to present his son's case before the ICC.

After lunch, we were received by Mustafa Abdel Jalil, the chairman of the NTC and the new prime minister. They were very warm, expressing in the name of the Libyan people the thanks for our efforts. They explained that the court's intervention during the rebellion was crucial for the Libyans as it exposed the crimes and the perpetrators. They felt internationally supported in their struggle for justice when they were the victims. But the chairman explained that now as the government, they needed to show that they were able to administer justice in Libya.

I recognized the advantage of doing the trial in Libya. Still, I suggested that the ICC's intervention would protect the new administration from any misperception of bias or an unfair trial. I presented the idea that the government could invite the judges of the court to sit in Tripoli and conduct the ICC trial in Libya.

The chairman was the former minister of justice. He knew the Rome Statute, and instead of talking about political convenience, he made a legal argument. *I understand that under the principle of complementarity, the Libyan justice system has primacy.*

For me, this was the end of any possible discussion. In legal terms, Libya has primacy under the complementarity principle, the cornerstone of the Rome Statute. Hence, I explained to the chairman that Libya had the right to complete the trials independently. Still, they had the parallel duty to implement genuine national proceedings and challenge the cases' admissibility before the ICC chambers. The ICC judges will make the final decision.

The chairman agreed and asked me to receive the Libyan general prosecutor to establish cooperation between our offices. I explained that I could not advise him, but I would be delighted to cooperate, respecting our legal boundaries. A few hours later, I met General Prosecutor Abdelaziz Al Hasadi and discussed the mechanism of cooperation. He was committed to doing justice in Libya, and he led the investigation of the case against Al-Sennusi.

I went back to The Hague, and we had a status conference to provide to the pre-trial chamber further details. Showing the hard post-revolution times, General Prosecutor Abdelaziz Al Hasadi was killed three years later.

The Chambers Decisions

On November 22, 2011, Pre-Trial Chamber I formally terminated the case against Muammar Gaddafi due to his death. On March 17, 2012, Al-Senussi was arrested in Mauritania, and six months later, he was surrendered to Libya. Libya started criminal proceedings against him and Saif Al Gaddafi in absentia.

On April 2, 2013, Libya challenged the admissibility of the case against Al-Senussi and Saif Al Gaddafi, alleging that its national judicial system was actively investigating Mr. Gaddafi and Mr. Al-Senussi for the same conduct under ICC investigation. The new government of Libya and the defendants were litigating before the ICC for the following years.

All the parties were represented by international lawyers with a strong background in the protection of human rights.[71] Al-Senussi and Saif Gaddafi opposed Libya's request. They wanted to be prosecuted by the ICC.

The ICC case against Saif Al- Islam Gaddafi was admissible.

On May 31, 2013, Pre-Trial I rejected "Libya's challenge to the admissibility of the case against Saif Al- Islam Gaddafi." It considered that Libya failed to demonstrate that "the Libyan and the ICC investigations cover the same conduct, and that Libya is able genuinely to investigate Mr. Gaddafi." Furthermore, analyzing the requisites established by Articles 17(l)(a) and (3) of the statute, the chamber concluded that Libya was "unable to secure the transfer of Mr. Gaddafi's custody from his place of detention under the Zintan militia into State authority."[72]

Libya requested a review of the decision, and on May 21, 2014, the appeal chamber confirmed the Pre-Trial Chamber I ruling on admissibility, based on the sameness of the case. It is defined: "To be able to carry out the assessment as to whether the same case is being investigated, it will be necessary for a Chamber to know the contours or parameters of the investigation being carried out both by the Prosecutor and by the State."[73] It did not analyze the arguments about Libya's ability.

The Pre-Trial Chamber I considered that the Libyan investigation against Al-Senussi was focused on "substantially the same conduct as alleged in the proceedings before the Court." The Chamber observed that "contrary to the situation in relation to Mr. Gaddafi, who is not under the control of the State national authorities and for whom attempts to secure legal representation have repeatedly failed, Mr. Al-Senussi is instead imprisoned in Tripoli by the central Government," and Libya submits that "recently, several local lawyers have indicated their willingness to represent Mr. Al-Senussi in the domestic proceedings."

The domestic authorities were undertaking concrete and progressive steps covering the same case. The chamber concluded "the case against Mr. Al-Senussi is therefore inadmissible before the Court under Article 17(1)(a) of the Statute."[74] For the first time in the history of the court, an admissibility challenge was successful.

Al-Senussi wanted to be prosecuted at the ICC, and his defense appealed. It argued that Libya was not investigating the same case, that the decision contradicted the Saif Al-Islam Gaddafi findings, and that Libya was unable to carry out the proceedings against Mr. Al-Senussi.

On July 24, 2014, the appeal chamber confirmed the decision. It considered that the pre-trial chamber finding was not in error; different than in the Saif Al-Islam Gaddafi case, Libya was investigating the same case as the one before the ICC. The appeal chamber also considered that the national proceeding was genuine. [75]

In 2014 a civil war started in Libya, and a different government was established in Tobruk to confront the alleged advance of Islamic groups. In July 2015, the Libyan Court in Tripoli sentenced in absentia Saif Gaddafi to death, but it could not implement such a decision.[76]

In September 2015, the Libyan House of Representatives based in Tobruk adopted Law 6/2015. It provided a "General Amnesty for all Libyans who committed crimes during the period from 15 February 2011 until the promulgation of the Present Law." The law also established that "Criminal proceedings related to such crimes shall be terminated, and sentences handed down shall be revoked."[77] On June 9, 2017, the Zintan militia released Saif Gaddafi "acting on a request from the "interim government" based in Tobruk."[78]

On June 6, 2018, Saif Al-Islam Gaddafi filed a challenge to the admissibility of his case, invoking Articles 17(1)(c) and 20(3) of the statute establishing the *ne bis in idem* principle. He alleged that he had already been tried, convicted, and sentenced by a Libyan court for substantially the same conduct as alleged in the proceedings before the court. He also argued that the Libyan authorities had subsequently granted him an amnesty, based on Law No. 6, and had been released from prison on or around April 12, 2016.

The pre-trial chamber considered that Mr. Gaddafi should still be subject to appeal before the court of cassation, and he has been tried and convicted in absentia. According to Libyan law, once the person convicted in absentia is arrested, his trial should start anew. The judges ruled that Article 20(3) "envisages a prohibition of a second trial when there is a final decision or judgment of acquittal or conviction . . . In other words, what is required is a judgment which acquired a res judicata effect."

On March 9, 2020, the appeals chamber confirmed the pre-trial chamber decision considering that Article 17(1)(c) and Article 20(3) of the statute require a final decision issued by a national jurisdiction to be inadmissible on the basis of these provisions.[79]

Notes

1. There were some media campaigns aiming to propose him as a presidential candidate. A Stanford University center found a Facebook campaign presenting Saif Gaddafi as "president" affirming that he "is very popular in Libya" and "there is no alternative." *Freeman Spogli Institute for International Studies*, STANFORD UNIVERSITY, https://fsi. stanford.edu/research (last visited Jan. 3, 2021). See also SASAPOST Outlet, *Gaddafi's Sons Come Back to Power in Libya?*, 112 UA (Sept. 4, 2020), https://112.internatio

nal/politics/gaddafis-sons-come-back-to-power-in-libya-54428.html. Al Jazeera report, Al Jazeera, *Why Was Saif al-Islam Gaddafi Released from Prison? | Inside Story*, YouTube (June 11, 2017), https://www.youtube.com/watch?v=49pkr5JJNk0.

2. S. Res. 85, 112th Cong. § 7 (2011).

3. On March 4, 2011 Obama said, "Colonel Gadhafi needs to step down from power and leave." News Wires, *"Step Down" Obama Tells Gaddafi*, France 24 (Mar. 4, 2011, 9:47 AM), https://www.france24.com/en/20110304-step-down-says-obama-gaddafi-US-Libya. On March 10, French President Nicolas Sarkozy and British Prime Minister David Cameron said, "Libyan leader Muammar Gaddafi and his ruling clique have lost legitimacy and must step down to end violence in the country." *Sarkozy, Cameron: Gaddafi must step down now*, Reuters (Mar. 10, 2011, 5:47 PM), https://www.reuters.com/article/france-britain-libya/sarkozy-cameron-gaddafi-must-step-down-now-idUSPISAEE74J20110310.

4. Samantha Power, The Education of an Idealist 295 (Kindle ed. 2019).

5. Robert Michael Gates, Duty 518 (Kindle ed. 2014).

6. Susan Rice, Tough Love: My Story of the Things Worth Fighting For 280 (Kindle ed. 2019).

7. Mark Landler & Helen Cooper, *Obama Seeks a Course of Pragmatism in the Middle East*, N.Y. Times (Mar. 10, 2011), https://www.nytimes.com/2011/03/11/world/africa/11policy.html.

8. *Id.*

9. Hillary Rodham Clinton, Hard Choices 367 (Kindle ed. 2014).

10. Richard Leiby & Muhamad Mansour, *Arab League Asks U.N. for No-Fly Zone over Libya*, Wash. Post (Mar 12, 2011), https://www.washingtonpost.com/world/arab-league-asks-un-for-no-fly-zone-over%20libya/2011/03/12/ABoie0R_story.html.

11. Hillary Rodham Clinton, Hard Choices 370 (Kindle ed. 2014).

12. *Id.* at 369–70.

13. Susan Rice, Tough Love: My Story of the Things Worth Fighting For 280–87 (Kindle ed. 2019).

14. *Id.*

15. Samantha Power, The Education of an Idealist 302–04 (Kindle ed. 2019).

16. *Privately*, explained Susan Rice, *I assured Gérard that* "[w]e genuinely favored the more robust mandate as the only approach we thought had merit, if we were going to act." Susan Rice, Tough Love: My Story of the Things Worth Fighting For 280–87 (Kindle ed. 2019).

17. That night . . . Churkin said, "I believe Moscow will abstain on your resolution." *Id.* Russian Foreign Minister Sergey Lavrov said to Hillary Clinton, "I take your point about not seeking another war. But that doesn't mean that you won't get one." He added, "the Russians had no interest in protecting Qaddafi or seeing him slaughter his people . . . we will abstain, and it will pass." Hillary Rodham Clinton, Hard Choices 371–77 (Kindle ed. 2014).

18. Samantha Power, The Education of an Idealist 302–04 (Kindle ed. 2019).

19. Hillary Rodham Clinton, Hard Choices 367–68 (Kindle ed. 2014).

20. Mr. Sangqu (South Africa) insisted on "a lasting political solution." "We believe that by adopting resolution 1973 (2011), which South Africa voted in favour of, the Security Council has responded appropriately to the call of the countries of the region to strengthen the implementation of resolution 1970 (2011), and has acted responsibly to protect and save the lives of defenceless civilians, who are faced with brutal acts of violence carried out by the Libyan authorities." "This is consistent with the African Union Peace and Security Council decision to respect the unity and territorial integrity of Libya and its rejection of any foreign military intervention, whatever its form." U.N. SCOR 66th sess., 6498th mtg. at 9-10 U.N. Doc. S/PV.6498 (Provisional) (Mar. 17, 2011).

21. "With the vote scheduled for late afternoon on Thursday, March 17, President Obama called President Jacob Zuma of South Africa to press for his support. The NSC staff reported to my team that Obama sensed he had gotten a favorable response, but Zuma was not clear. Moreover, in New York we had not heard anything at all from the South African Mission. My staff was chasing them, trying to determine their position, but could not find out even if they had received instructions from Pretoria, much less what they were. That's why I staked out my South African counterpart at the entrance to the Security Council." SUSAN RICE, TOUGH LOVE: MY STORY OF THE THINGS WORTH FIGHTING FOR 280–87 (Kindle ed. 2019).

22. U.N. SCOR 66th sess., 6498th mtg. at 2 U.N. Doc. S/PV.6498 (Provisional) (Mar. 17, 2011). Press Release, Security Council Security Council Approves "No-Fly Zone" over Libya, Authorizing "All Necessary Measures" to Protect Civilians, by Vote of 10 in Favour with 5 Abstentions, U.N. Press Release SC/10200 (Mar. 17, 2011).

23. Security Council President Amb. Li Baodong said, China is always against the use of force in international relations. China attaches great importance to the relevant position by the 22-member Arab League on the establishment of a no-fly zone over Libya. We also attach great importance to the position of African countries and the African Union. In view of this, and considering the special circumstances surrounding the situation in Libya, China abstained from the voting on resolution 1973 (2011). U.N. SCOR 66th sess., 6498th mtg. at 2 U.N. Doc. S/PV.6498 (Provisional) (Mar. 17, 2011).

24. Vitaly Churkin, from the Russian Federation said, "[T]he draft was morphing before our very eyes, transcending the initial concept as stated by the League of Arab States. Provisions were introduced into the text that could potentially open the door to large-scale military intervention." "Responsibility for the inevitable humanitarian consequences of the excessive use of outside force in Libya will fall fair and square on the shoulders of those who might undertake such action. If this comes to pass, then not only the civilian population of Libya but also the cause of upholding peace and security throughout the entire region of North Africa and the Middle East will suffer. Such destabilizing developments must be avoided." U.N. SCOR 66th sess., 6498th mtg. at 2 U.N. Doc. S/PV.6498 (Provisional) (Mar. 17, 2011).

25. Maria Luiza Riberio Viotti from Brazil stated, "We are not convinced that the use of force as provided for in paragraph 4 of the resolution will lead to the realization of our common objective—the immediate end to violence and the protection of civilians." Id. at 6.

26. Peter Wittig "Germany will not contribute to such a military effort with its own forces. Germany therefore decided to abstain in the voting." *Id.* at 5.

27. Manjeev Singh Puri (India): "The Council has today adopted a resolution that authorizes far-reaching measures under Chapter VII of the United Nations Charter, with relatively little credible information on the situation on the ground in Libya." *Id.* at 6.

28. SAMANTHA POWER, THE EDUCATION OF AN IDEALIST 302–04 (Kindle ed. 2019).

29. DAVID BOSCO, ROUGH JUSTICE: THE INTERNATIONAL CRIMINAL COURT IN A WORLD OF POWER POLITICS 168 (Kindle ed. 2014).

30. HILLARY RODHAM CLINTON, HARD CHOICES 367–68 (Kindle ed. 2014).

31. "Turkey and others were drawing the line at a pure no-fly zone with no air-to-ground strikes . . . Sarkozy feared that if NATO ran the mission, we would end up watching as Benghazi burned." The discussion was changing: "Turkey was insisting that 'It's important for the people of Libya. If there is a UN umbrella and under that NATO is doing the operation no one will see this as crusaders or East versus West.'" *Id.*

32. Belgium, Canada, Denmark, France, Greece, Italy, Jordan, Netherlands, Norway, Qatar, Spain, Sweden, Turkey, United Arab Emirates, United Kingdom, and United States have provided air assets and flown sorties in support to the operation. Operation Unified Protector Protection of Civilians and Civilian-Populated Areas & Enforcement of the No-Fly Zone, NATO, https://www.nato.int/nato_static_fl2014/ass ets/pdf/pdf_2011_10/20111005_111005-factsheet_protection_civilians.pdf (last visited June 25, 2020).

33. We added Judge Baltasar Garzon as provisional adviser and Dolores Delgado, an experienced Spanish prosecutor specialized on Jihad criminality, that later became Spain's minister of justice and general prosecutor.

34. In accordance with Regulation 34 a provisional case hypothesis (or hypotheses) identifying the incidents to be investigated and the person or persons who appear to be the most responsible should be established. The incidents should reflect the most serious crimes and the main types of victimization—including sexual and gender violence and violence against children—and which are the most representative of the scale and impact of the crimes. To be able to request an arrest warrant or summons to appear pursuant to Article 58, the office needed to clearly identify the crimes and modes of liability alleged, based on solid factual and evidentiary foundations.

35. "Now that the ICC has been established, mediators should make the international legal position clear to the parties . . . as an independent judicial body, the Court will proceed, . . . and the process of justice will take its course." UN Secretary General, *Enhancing Mediation and its Support Activities,* ¶ 37, U.N. Doc. S/2009/189 (Apr. 8, 2009).

36. The Security Council acted again on February 26, demanding an end to the violence and imposing an arms embargo on the country and a travel ban and assets freeze on Qaddafi, his family, and other government officials. ROBERT MICHAEL GATES, DUTY 511 (Kindle ed. 2014).

37. U.N. SCOR 66th sess., 6528th mtg. at 4, U.N. Doc. S/PV.6528 (Provisional) (May 4, 2011).

38. *Id.*
39. David Bosco, Rough Justice: The International Criminal Court in a World of Power Politics 169 (Kindle ed. 2014).
40. U.N. SCOR 66th sess., 6528th mtg. at 4, U.N. Doc. S/PV.6528 (Provisional) (May 4, 2011).
41. "We are grateful to the Prosecutor for the swift action he has taken to implement resolution 1970 (2011)." *Id.*
42. "The initial swift progress that has been made in the investigation, which the Prosecutor has told us about, is encouraging. We deem it of the highest importance that justice be done as quickly as possible for the victims of the conflict in Libya." *Id.* at 5–6.
43. "[T]he Court and the Prosecutor's Office have been particularly diligent with regard to the practical implementation of resolution 1970 (2011)." *Id.* at 9.
44. "We are particularly impressed by the speed with which the investigations were completed." *Id.* at 11.
45. "My Government welcomes the swift and thorough work of the Prosecutor." *Id.* at 12.
46. "Lebanon emphasizes the importance of holding accountable those responsible for horrific crimes against the Libyan people, who are eager to win their freedom." *Id.* at 12–13.
47. "The International Criminal Court has an important role to play in this regard not only in investigating the most serious crimes and in judging and punishing the perpetrators most responsible, but also in preventing the escalation of violence as a dissuasive instrument for potential perpetrators and sometimes the only source of hope for endangered civilians and communities in conflict zones." *Id.* at 7.
48. "As the Prosecutor explained, the International Criminal Court will prosecute only the leading perpetrators: those who organized, ordered or financed crimes. There is still time for those who were misled into becoming involved in the criminal campaign led by Al-Qadhafi against innocent civilians to dissociate themselves from it. There can be no political or other kind of solidarity with those who order or commit such crimes." *Id.* at 14.
49. "We firmly believe that addressing these crimes and punishing those responsible is, beyond any doubt, the main precondition for reconciliation, sustainable and long-lasting peace and stability. . . . Furthermore, the Prosecutor of the ICC has our full support for his work." *Id.* at 13.
50. "China has always believed that the pursuit of justice should be premised on the core values of safeguarding peace and security and maintaining international peace and harmony. Peaceful dialogue and negotiations are the best way forward toward a political solution to this crisis. We endorse the five- point road map proposed by the African Union. . . . We would like to see the Special Envoy of the Secretary-General, Mr. Al-Khatib, playing a stronger role on the political track. At the same time, we would like to ensure that the International Criminal Court properly assesses the requirements to resolve in crisis in Libya appropriately in its efforts to implement resolution 1970 (2011) and to play a positive and constructive role in promptly restoring peace, security and order in Libya." *Id.* at 10.

51. "As developments in Libya unfold, we hope that the ICC investigations can have an impact on the desired goals—a cease to violence and the restoration of calm. In the post-conflict stage, the ICC's role will continue to be essential in helping to ensure accountability and justice, which are so important to achieving durable peace." *Id.* at 8.

52. "[I]t is important that the activities of the Prosecutor be carefully calibrated to support the ongoing political efforts to find a peaceful solution." *Id.* at 10.

53. "The political efforts under way must not affect the requirements of justice regarding crimes committed against humanity." *Id.* at 8.

54. "The Council also stressed that all those responsible for, or complicit in, attacks against the civilian population, including aerial and naval attacks, must face the consequences of their actions." *Id.* at 9.

55. "The Prosecutor should carry out a thorough and impartial investigation and not be influenced by any non-judicial considerations. All those responsible for committing crimes covered under the Rome Statute should be held accountable, irrespective of which side of the conflict they may belong to and even if they have changed sides. Political considerations should not exonerate anyone from prosecution." *Id.* at 7.

56. "The international community must respect the sovereignty, independence, unity and territorial integrity of Libya. The internal affairs and fate of Libya must be left up to the Libyan people to decide. We are not in favour of any arbitrary interpretation of the Council's resolutions or of any actions going beyond those mandated by the Council." *Id.* at 10.

57. "Unfortunately, it must be noted that actions by the NATO-led coalition forces are also resulting in civilian casualties, as was seen in particular during recent bombings in Tripoli." *Id.* at 9.

58. "Crimes may have been committed by Government and opposition forces alike. To protect the Court's integrity and to ensure that all who were caught in the crossfire of the conflict are protected, all crimes, regardless of the perpetrators, should be considered. Nonetheless, we would recall that the caveat in paragraph 6 is limited to actions established or authorized by the Security Council. Therefore, any actions that fall outside the scope of resolution 1973 (2011) should not benefit from the protection offered by the caveat. It is our sincere hope that, in considering the evidence, the Office of the Prosecutor will also consider any actions that may have been committed in the purported implementation of resolution 1973 (2011)." *Id.* at 11.

59. David Bosco, *Who Can Arrest Gaddafi?*, FOREIGN POL'Y (May 16, 2011), https://foreignpolicy.com/2011/05/16/who-can-arrest-gaddafi/

60. *ICC Issues Gaddafi Arrest Warrant*, AL JAZEERA (June 27, 2011), https://www.aljazeera.com/news/africa/2011/06/20116278148166670.html.

61. *Id.*

62. DAVID BOSCO, ROUGH JUSTICE: THE INTERNATIONAL CRIMINAL COURT IN A WORLD OF POWER POLITICS 169 (Kindle ed. 2014).

63. "There was a moment, around about June or July," recalled Mr. Shapiro, the State Department's Libya policy adviser, "when the situation on the ground seemed to settle into a stalemate and we weren't sure we were winning, or at least winning quickly enough." Jo Becker & Scott Shane, *Hillary Clinton, "Smart Power" and a Dictator's*

Fall, N.Y. Times (Feb. 27, 2016), https://www.nytimes.com/2016/02/28/us/politics/ hillary-clinton-libya.html.

64. "Groups share common goals but are undermined by local rivalries. Orders from the senior regional command are followed arbitrarily... Information flows only partly up and down the chain of command. C. J. Chivers, *Problem With Logistics, Coordination and Rivalries Hamper Libya's Rebels*, N.Y. Times (July 20, 2011), https://www.nytimes. com/2011/07/21/world/africa/21libya.html?searchResultPosition=45.

65. "[D]iplomats from the United States, Britain and France have adopted a new tactic in recent days: offering the besieged leader the opportunity to remain in Libya if he dissolves the government and steps aside." The French minister of Foreign Affairs, Alain Juppé, said that "one of the scenarios" to resolve the conflict in Libya "is that he stays in Libya on one condition, which I repeat: that he very clearly steps aside from Libyan political life." Helene Cooper & John F. Burns, *Plan Would Keep Qaddafi in Libya, but Out of Power*, N.Y. Times (July 27, 2011), https://www.nytimes.com/2011/ 07/28/world/africa/28libya.html?searchResultPosition=46.

66. There were suspicions about his loyalty and he had been summoned for questioning by the judges, he had been "released on his own recognizance," and then an armed gang had killed him. David D. Kirkpatrick, *Death of Rebel Leader Stirs Fears of Tribunal Conflict*, N.Y. Times (July 28, 2011), https://www.nytimes.com/2011/07/29/ world/africa/29libya.html.

67. Mahmoud Jibril was the only member of the cabinet who kept his job Kareem Fahim, *Libyan Rebels Dissolve Cabinet Amid Discord*, N.Y. Times (Aug. 8, 2011), https://www. nytimes.com/2011/08/09/world/africa/09libya.html.

68. For instance, the *Washington Post* informed that Gaddafi soldiers protecting the TV station in Tripoli simply took off their uniforms, lay down their weapons and ran. "Underneath their uniforms, they had civilian clothes, jeans and T-shirts, as though they were expecting this." ; Simon Denyer & Leila Fadel, *Tripoli's Sudden Fall Revealed Rotten Heart of Gaddafi's Regime*, Wash. Post (Aug. 31, 2011), https://www.was hingtonpost.com/world/middle-east/tripolis-sudden-fall-revealed-rotten-heart-of-gaddafis-regime/2011/08/27/gIQABpgssJ_story.html.

69. "[F]ew among the Western countries and their allies anticipated the speed of the de-mise of the Qaddafi government, and they are now scrambling . . . to put together a post-conflict plan for Libya." Steven Erianger, *Rebel's Sudden Success Sends European Backers Scrambling*, N.Y. Times (Aug. 22, 2011), https://www.nytimes.com/2011/08/ 23/world/europe/23europe.html?searchResultPosition=54.

70. Chris Stephen & David Batty, *Saif al-Islam Gaddafi Captured in Libya*, Guardian (Nov. 19, 2011, 12:52 PM), https://www.theguardian.com/world/2011/nov/19/saif-al-islam-gaddafi-captured.

71. Professor James Crawford, the chair of the UN International Law Commission (ILC) working group that produced the Draft Statute in 1994 represented Libya be-fore the court with Ahmed El-Gehani. Philippe Sands and Payam Hakhavan were advising Libya. Saif Gaddafi was represented by John R. W. D. Jones, who was the first head of the Special Court's Defense Office for Sierra Leone and coedited a Rome Statute comment Prof. Antonio Cassese. Al-Senussi was represented by a team of top

international lawyers led by Ben Emmerson and Rodney Dixon and including Amal Alamuddin and Professor William Schabas.

72. The Prosecutor vs. Saif Al-Islam Gaddafi and Abdullah Al-Senussi, ICC-01/11-01/11, Decision on the admissibility of the case against Saif Al-Islam Gaddafi, ¶ 215 (May 31, 2013), https://www.icc-cpi.int/CourtRecords/CR2013_04031.PDF.

73. The Prosecutor vs. Saif Al-Islam Gaddafi and Abdullah Al-Senussi, ICC-01/11-01/11 OA 4, Judgment on the appeal of Libya ¶85 (May 21, 2014) https://www.icc-cpi.int/CourtRecords/CR2014_04273.PDF.

74. The Prosecutor vs. Saif Al-Islam Gaddafi and Abdullah Al-Senussi, ICC-01/11-01/11, Decision on the admissibility of the case against Abdullah Al-Senussi, ¶ 311 (Oct. 11, 2013), https://www.icc-cpi.int/CourtRecords/CR2013_07445.PDF.

75. The Prosecutor vs. Saif Al-Islam Gaddafi and Abdullah Al-Senussi, ICC-01/11-01/11 OA6, Judgment on the appeal of Mr. Abdullah Al-Senussi against the decision of Pre-Trial Chamber I of 11 October (July 24, 2014), https://www.icc-cpi.int/CourtRecords/CR2014_06755.PDF.

76. *Libya Trial: Gaddafi Son Sentenced to Death Over Cries*, BBC News (July 28, 2015), https://www.bbc.com/news/world-africa-33688391.

77. The Prosecutor v. Saif Al-Islam Gaddafi, ICC-01/11-01/11, Public with Confidential Annex I and Public Annexes II and III, https://www.legal-tools.org/doc/2c966c/pdf/.

78. *Gadaffi's Son Saif Freed in Libya*, BBC News (June 11 2017), https://www.bbc.com/news/world-africa-40236808.

79. The Prosecutor v. Saif Al-Islam Gaddafi, ICC-01/11-01/11, Judgment on the appeal of Mr. Saif Al-Islam Gaddafi of 5 April 2019 (Mar. 9, 2020), https://www.icc-cpi.int/CourtRecords/CR2020_00904.PDF (citations omitted).

21

Jus ad Curiam and *Jus ad Bellum* Decisions in *Côte d'Ivoire*

During the 2010 post-election conflict in Côte d'Ivoire, national, regional, and international organizations, including the ICC, adopted *jus ad Curiam* and *jus ad Bellum* decisions. The implementations of such measures helped Côte d'Ivoire to control massive crimes and maintain almost a decade of relative peace.

The first *jus ad Curiam* decision in this situation was adopted under the Laurent Gbagbo presidency in 2003. President Gbagbo was elected in a highly contested election in 2000 that created a conflict in September 2002 between people from the North and the South of the country. There were some political agreements, and an Amnesty Law excluding the Rome Statute crimes was promulgated.[1]

In this context, in October 2003, the ICC received a letter signed by President Gbagbo's minister of foreign affairs, accepting the court's jurisdiction per Article 12 (3). The declaration conferred temporal jurisdiction to the ICC since the events of September 19, 2002, and "for an unspecified period of time."

Since 2003 we have conducted a preliminary examination of the Côte d'Ivoire's situation, collecting information about the different incidents. New political agreements and UN Security Council decisions without a justice component were adopted to control recurrent violence.

After the next elections in Côte d'Ivoire, in November 2010, the Constitutional Council president overturned the Independent Electoral Commission's decision and declared Gbagbo victorious. Riots were protesting what was considered a baseless decision, triggering massive violence. The regional organization, ECOWAS, the AU, and the UN Security Council recognized Alassane Ouattara as the newly elected president.

On December 14, 2010, our office received a letter from elected President Ouattara confirming the continued validity of the previous *jus ad Curiam* decision and committing his country to cooperate fully with the ICC. We

War and Justice in the 21st Century. Luis Moreno Ocampo, Oxford University Press. © Oxford University Press 2022.
DOI: 10.1093/oso/9780197628973.003.0022

continued reviewing information about the 2010 post-electoral incidents in the Côte d'Ivoire's situation. Still, we were not clear if new crimes under our jurisdiction were committed.

African leaders tried to find a political solution, and some were willing to allow Gbagbo a soft exit or even to stay in power.[2] But the regional group ECOWAS remained firm. On March 30, 2011, acting under Chapter VII and at the request of ECOWAS' heads of state, the UN Security Council authorized the UN mission "to use all necessary means to carry out its mandate to protect civilians under imminent threat of physical violence."

The resolution noted the previous national *jus ad Curiam* decision, "the International Criminal Court may decide on its jurisdiction over the situation in Côte d'Ivoire."[3] The new Côte d'Ivoire government supporters and the international forces were able to defeat Gbagbo forces and arrest him.

A UN Commission of Enquiry Report helped us to obtain the information needed. On June 23, 2011, the Office of the Prosecutor requested authorization from the pre-trial chamber to open an investigation.[4] Pre-Trial Chamber III and the appeal chamber discussed different aspects, but finally, the Office of the Prosecution received the authorization requested.

The office obtained three arrest warrants. Former President Gbagbo was surrendered to the court and challenged the jurisdiction of the ICC in his case. The appeal chamber ruled that the case was admissible.

The Côte d'Ivoire *jus ad Curiam* decision was supported by the UN Security Council and implemented by the ICC. ECOWAS, France, and the council made *jus ad Bellum* decisions that were implemented and ended with the Gbagbo regime. Côte d'Ivoire provides the best example of integration between national, regional, and international efforts to control massive violence. Unlike in Libya, the national government's ability to prevent the civil war's reappearance and the commission of crimes against humanity created years without massive crimes.

The Conflict and the Political Negotiations Since the 2002 Election

The violence in 2010 had roots in ten years of conflicts. In October 2000, Laurent Gbagbo won the elections and, supported by southern Christians, demanded respect for the electoral results.[5] His claim was reinforced by another opposition leader, Alassane D. Ouattara, a former prime minister mainly backed by Muslims from the north. Ouattara was barred from running in the 2000 election and insisted on presenting his candidacy during a new and fairer electoral process.[6]

After incumbent President Gen. Robert Guei accepted his defeat, Laurent Gbagbo declared himself president and promised national reconciliation but immediately refused to call for new elections.

A new conflict started, Gbagbo and Ouattara supporters fought with machetes and clubs, and mosques and churches were attacked in clashes that took an ethnic and religious cast.[7]

In March 2001, President Laurent Gbagbo and Alassane Ouattara met and agreed to work toward reconciliation.[8] But on September 19, 2002, a military rebellion left at least 270 people dead and 300 injured in Abidjan. After the security forces regained control of Abidjan, the mutineers turned rebels and moved north.

The country was split into a rebel-held North and government-held South, and spates of violence lasted well into 2004.[9] A ceasefire agreement was signed on October 17, 2002, monitored by France and ECOWAS.[10] In January 2003, a new agreement was reached (the "Linas-Marcoussis Agreement"). Laurent Gbagbo was confirmed as the president and provided a timetable for credible and transparent national elections.[11]

In its Resolution 1479, adopted on May 13, 2003, the UN Security Council set up a UN Operation in Côte d'Ivoire (UNOCI), with the mandate to facilitate the Linas-Marcoussis Agreement and support the military operations of French and ECOWAS troops.[12] The international forces were preventing a total civil war; they were stationed in the ceasefire line separating both sides.

On August 18, 2003, an Amnesty Law was promulgated, excluding crimes defined by "the Rome Statute."[13] In this context, in October 2003, the ICC received a letter signed by President Gbagbo's minister of foreign affairs, accepting the court's jurisdiction per Article 12 (3). The declaration conferred temporal jurisdiction to the ICC since the events of September 19, 2002, and "for an unspecified period of time." Since 2003 we conducted a preliminary examination of the Côte d'Ivoire's situation, collecting information about different violent incidents.[14]

Crimes and the promotion of conflicts between communities continued in Côte d'Ivoire, and the UN Security Council adopted several decisions to control violence. In February 2004, Resolution 1527 (2004) established a peacekeeping operation based on "ECOWAS forces together with French Forces supporting them."[15]

The following UN Security Council Resolution 1528 (2004) mentioned the need "to put an end to impunity," but there was no follow-up.[16] UN Security Council Resolution 1572 (2004), adopted in November 2004, demanded: "that the Ivoirian authorities stop all radio and television broadcasting inciting hatred, intolerance, and violence." But the council did not impose international justice. Instead, it established an arms embargo.[17] And the hatred campaigns continued during the following years.

Political agreement without criminal investigations also continued. UN Security Council Resolution 1600 (2005) adopted on May 4, 2005, "Welcomed the signature in Pretoria" of a political agreement and commended President Thabo Mbeki and the African Union role.[18]

In October 2005, planned elections were shelved as President Gbagbo invoked a law that he says allows him to stay in power.[19] The country remained essentially divided between the North and South, and discrimination against "foreigners" only grew.[20]

The council continued demanded a political solution. Four years later, UN Security Council Resolution 1880 (2009), adopted on July 30, 2009, supported "the Ouagadougou Political Agreement" providing for the holding of presidential elections.[21] Furthermore, Resolution 1933, adopted in June 2010, expresses its "deep concern at the continuing delays in the electoral process."[22]

The 2010 Elections

Counting the Votes

After ten years of negotiations and violence, the presidential election's first round took place on October 31, 2010. Laurent Gbagbo and Alassane Ouattara were front runners. On November 28, the second round was held in a climate of tension and mutual accusations. On December 2, the Independent Electoral Commission chair announced the provisional results of the second round of the presidential elections, declaring that Alassane Ouattara had garnered 54.1 percent of the votes and Laurent Gbagbo 45.9 percent.

Incumbent President Gbagbo refused to acknowledge Ouattara's victory, claiming that intimidation and fraud in the pro-Ouattara north of the country skewed the vote.[23] The Constitutional Council president overturned the Independent Electoral Commission's decision, declaring Gbagbo victorious. Security forces loyal to Laurent Gbagbo, aided by youth militias and Liberian mercenaries, launched attacks against Ouattara's supporters.

Government forces barricaded Ouattara and his camp in the "Golf hotel" under UN peacekeepers' protection. Gbagbo's foreign minister alleged that there were 300 heavily armed *New Forces* soldiers in the hotel. He considered them as "a threat including for President Gbagbo whose residence is five minutes away by boat ... If the [New Forces] soldiers go, the blockade will be lifted."[24]

International and Regional Organizations Role

As soon as the conflict started, the chair of the AU Commission, Jean Ping, requested that former South African President Thabo Mbeki travel to Abidjan to mediate a peaceful outcome to the dispute between the two men. Mbeki— who was the driving force of the 2005 agreement in Pretoria—flew to Côte d'Ivoire on December 4, 2010. He met the two rivals separately but could not change the stance of either man.

On December 7, 2010, fifteen heads-of-state members of ECOWAS[25] recognized Alassane Ouattara as president-elect of Côte d'Ivoire.[26] They endorsed *the results declared by the Independent Electoral Commission and certified by the Special Representative of the Secretary-General of the United Nations in Côte d'Ivoire.*[27] On December 9, 2010, the African Union followed ECOWAS leadership, considered Ouattara the elected president, and suspended the participation of Côte d'Ivoire in all AU activities.[28]

UN Security Council Resolution 1962 (2010), adopted on December 20, 2010, consolidated the regional decisions.[29] Furthermore, acting through a consensus vote, the UN General Assembly recognized Ouattara as president by formally recognizing a team of diplomats sent by him to be the country's official representatives.[30]

The law *conferred power*: Alassane Ouattara was recognized as the new president by different international organizations following their procedures.

The Office of the Prosecutor First Intervention

Additional killings were also reported in the following two weeks, in their vast majority in Abidjan.

On December 14, 2010, the office received a letter from Alassane Ouattara, as newly elected president, confirming the previous declaration's continued validity and committing his country to cooperate fully with the court.

The conflict continued escalating. A significant upsurge of violence occurred between December 16 and 21, 2010, in the pro-Ouattara march on the Ivorian Radio and Television (RTI) premises in Abidjan, ensuing clashes with the pro-Gbagbo security forces.

On December 21, 2010, I made a public statement making public our preliminary examination and clarifying: "I have not yet opened an investigation. But if serious crimes under my jurisdiction are committed, I will do so."

We had information alleging that Charles Blé Goudé, the minister of youth in the Gbagbo government, was promoting violence. He publicly called on a militia that he led, the Young Patriots, to defend the country against foreigners and foreign peacekeepers.

I warned: "For instance, if as a consequence of Mr. Charles Blé Goudé's speeches, there is massive violence, he could be prosecuted." I also specifically mentioned: "if UN forces are attacked, this could be prosecuted as a different crime." I tried to connect our judicial efforts with the political and military initiatives recognizing that *African states play a critical part in finding a solution to the problem. But if no solution can be found and crimes are committed, African states could be willing to refer the case to my Office and provide forces to arrest those who commit the crimes in Côte d'Ivoire.* I concluded: "Violence is not an option. Those leaders who are planning violence will end up in the Hague."[31]

Beyond our and other efforts, the violence escalated again. Pro-Gbagbo groups used force against Ouattara's supporters on several occasions in the neighborhoods of Abidjan and other parts of the country.

The African Conflicting Views on Managing the Conflict

African leaders were trying to find a political solution that included the possibility of an amnesty and a soft exit for Gbagbo.[32] For a while, they did not mention justice. In late December and early January 2011, ECOWAS dispatched two delegations integrated by three presidents from the region (Benin, Cape Verde, and Sierra Leone) to deliver a joint ECOWAS ultimatum to Gbagbo demanding that he step down or would be forced out by military means.[33]

On their second trip, they were joined by Kenyan Prime Minister Raila Odinga, representing the AU. Reports said they offered an amnesty to Laurent Gbagbo if he left office, as well as a guarantee that his financial assets would be secure.[34] Ouattara said after he met with the envoys that the time for dialogue was now "over" and urged Ecowas "to use all the means at its disposal including the use of legitimate force."[35]

The UN Security Council Strengthened Peacekeeper Forces

On January 7, 2011, UN Secretary-General Ban Ki-moon took a decisive step and sent a letter to the council asking to provide the UN mission with adequate capacity to meet the security challenges.[36] The Resolution 1967 adopted on January 19, 2011, showed a different council's attitude than its passivity in 2004 during the Rwanda genocide. In the same week, the council was very active; it also discussed Libya's referral to the ICC.

UNSC Resolution 1967 authorized the deployment of an additional 2,000 troops for UNOCI and the temporary redeployment of three infantry companies and two military helicopters from the United Nations Mission in Liberia (UNMIL).[37] The Council did not mention the role of the ICC but expressed "that those responsible for crimes against United Nations personnel and civilians must be held accountable."[38]

The African Union Role

On January 16, Kenyan Prime Minister Raila Odinga, acting as an AU envoy, went back to Abidjan to meet Laurent Gbagbo, aiming to break the country's political deadlock.[39] Reports said that Odinga reiterated the international community's offer of a graceful exit, including possible exile abroad with a monthly stipend.[40] After that meeting, Laurent Gbagbo rejected Odinga as a mediator.[41]

The head of UNOCI summarized the problem stating that Gbagbo was asking for a power-sharing government, and Ouattara saying he will only discuss such a possibility after taking complete control of the country.[42]

On January 18, the army chiefs of staff from ECOWAS met in Mali to plan a military operation to remove Gbagbo.[43] But not all African leaders agreed.

Gambia broke ranks recognizing the legality of Gbagbo's election and opposed an ECOWAS military intervention.[44]

The following week, AU chairman Malawian President Bingu wa Mutharika made a consultative visit to Abidjan. After talks with both leaders, Mr. Mutharika promised to present the "proposals" of his "brother and friend" Laurent Gbagbo to the AU summit.[45] Gbagbo called for a vote recount and received some additional support. For instance, Uganda's President Museveni suggested in those days that the UN should not have recognized Ouattara so quickly.[46]

On January 28, 2011, the African Union's Peace and Security Council met in Addis Ababa. It established a panel of five African leaders representing all the regions to make a decision legally binding on all Ivorians.[47]

On February 06, 2011, an AU team arrived at Abidjan to prepare a report on the situation for the five-member heads-of-state panel appointed. On February 20, 2011, the presidents of Chad, Mauritania, South Africa, and Tanzania representing the AU went to Côte d'Ivoire to find a way to resolve the standoff between the country's rival leaders.

The African Union panel's mediation efforts were affected by the heavy fighting in Abidjan's streets, which began when the panel arrived. President Zuma insisted on coming up with an "African solution to an African problem."[48] He called the election results "inconclusive" and suggested a power-sharing agreement followed later by fresh elections.[49]

In those days, the Libya situation was covering the news. Violence on Côte d'Ivoire's streets was combined with a legal discussion: Gbagbo invoked that the country's Constitutional Council, the highest authority on the matter, re-elected him. Ouattara affirmed that he was elected president based on results announced by the Electoral Commission and certified by the United Nations.[50]

By February 25, 2011, the situation escalated into a non-international armed conflict between pro-Gbagbo forces and armed forces loyal to Alassane Ouattara, which allegedly committed war crimes in Douékoué. As fighting spreads through the country, all talk of a power-sharing agreement started to vanish.[51]

AU Panel Recommendations

In March 2011, the situation deteriorated further as forces loyal to Laurent Gbagbo resorted to heavy weapons against protesters. On March 10, the AU panel presented its recommendations. Ouattara attended the meeting held in Ethiopia, but Gbagbo sent two delegates.

The AU panel reaffirmed Ouattara's electoral victory and recommended that Gbagbo step down; called on the Constitutional Council to swear in Ouattara as president; suggested that a national unity government be formed; and called for the establishment of a national peace and reconciliation process based on the Ouagadougou Political Agreement.[52]

The AU Panel did not recommend international justice but rather establishing a "Truth and Reconciliation Commission" and adopting an amnesty law. The amnesty would cover "all acts and offenses committed in relation with the post-electoral crisis" and provide "full immunity for all those who held the office of President of the Republic or that of Prime Minister, as well as senior officers of the Armed Forces and Security Forces."[53]

The AU Panel reserved particular criticism for the Constitutional Council.[54] It also observed that former President Gbagbo had held office for a decade, a period corresponding to the maximum term that he could have served had he been constitutionally elected to two successive terms of five years. Thus, he had enjoyed a lengthy opportunity to promote peace and reconciliation, an outcome that the panel's report stressed had not been achieved.[55]

The Gbagbo camp rejected the panel's recommendations and considered them to violate the Constitutional Council's ruling. Ouattara accepted the need for a cross-party government "in a framework of reconciliation ... because I want peace," but rejected the notion that it would, at its core, be a power-sharing government with Gbagbo or his close allies. He instead emphasized that he would remain firmly in control.[56]

The UN Security Council Was Authorizing "All Necessary Measures"

Anticipate Violence

At the beginning of March 2011, the International Crisis Group foresaw that "The most likely scenario in the coming months is an armed conflict involving massive violence against civilians, Ivorian and foreign alike, that could provoke unilateral military intervention by neighbors, starting with Burkina Faso."[57]

The BBC Africa's correspondent suggested on March 24 that Côte d'Ivoire could be "worse than Rwanda" and considered it unrealistic that a "blitzkrieg" could transform the situation.[58]

On March 25, 2011, the UN Human Rights Council decided to dispatch an independent, international commission of inquiry to "investigate the facts and circumstances . . . following the presidential election of 28 November 2011."

UN Security Council Resolution 1975

On March 24, 2011, Nigeria's Ambassador sent a letter to the UN Security Council recalling the decision adopted by ECOWAS' heads of state on December 24, 2010, to use "legitimate force, to achieve the goals of the Ivorian people."[59] Nigeria requested the UN Security Council to authorize the UNOCI "to use all necessary means to protect life and property." At the same time, the UN Security Council discussed the *measures* to protect Libya's civilians.[60]

By the beginning of March, Gaddafi's forces were marching toward Benghazi.[61]Côte d'Ivoire and Libya crises were demanding UN Security Council decisions at the same time.

On March 30, 2011, the UN Security Council adopted Resolution 1975 (2011) sponsored by Nigeria and France. Acting under Chapter VII, the Council authorized the "UNOCI, while impartially implementing its mandate, to use all necessary means to carry out its mandate to protect civilians under imminent threat of physical violence." And adopted "targeted sanctions against individuals."[62]

The Council stressed "that those responsible for such serious abuses and violations, including by forces under their control, must be held accountable" and noted "that the International Criminal Court may decide on its jurisdiction over the situation in Côte d'Ivoire on the basis of Article 12, paragraph 3 of the Rome Statute.[63]

During the Council's debate, Nigeria[64] and South Africa fully supported the Resolution.[65] Ambassador Bamba representing Côte d'Ivoire expressed his country's satisfaction with the Resolution and requested a referral to the ICC.[66]

The Office of the Prosecutor Preliminary Examination's Progress and the End of the Conflict

Both sides of the conflict took into consideration our preliminary examination.

On March 15, 2011, the Office of the Prosecutor received a memorandum from lawyers representing President Ouattara, which compiled information on crimes committed in the context of post-election violence.

On March 31, 2011, the Prosecution received a series of documents from Laurent Gbagbo's cabinet, including a "Memorandum on alleged crimes against humanity committed in Côte d'Ivoire."[12]

Throughout March 2011, forces supporting Ouattara were gradually seizing control of much of the country and reached Abidjan at the end of the month. Our preliminary examination process concluded that crimes under the court's jurisdiction were committed, and the situation was admissible. We were worried about the impact of the conflict for civilians in Abidjan and the time required to obtain authorization from the pre-trial chamber to open an investigation.

We made a statement on April 5, 2011, mentioning specifically "alleged mass killings in the Western part of the country" that involved pro-Ouattara forces and warned all the parties to the conflict per our impartiality duty.

We reiterated our invitation to state parties to refer the Côte d'Ivoire situation "to expedite the process" to open an investigation.[67] But the concerned states were afraid to be perceived involved in the judicial proceedings and exposing their nationals' lives in Côte d'Ivoire.

On April 11, military operations conducted by forces loyal to President Alassane Ouattara, backed by helicopters led by UNOCI and French Licorne troops, arrested Laurent Gbagbo. They placed him in President Ouattara's custody. Following Mr. Gbagbo's arrest, the fighting continued for a few weeks.

On May 4, 2011, the Constitutional Council proclaimed Mr. Ouattara the president of Côte d'Ivoire and declared valid the decisions he had previously taken in his function as president.

The Battle for the Narrative

The Russian foreign minister, Sergei Lavrov, questioned the legality of the airstrikes, suggesting the UN peacekeepers may have overstepped their neutral mandate. The chairman of the African Union declared that foreign military intervention was unjustified.[68] President Ouattara was announcing investigations and the establishment of a Truth Commission.

BBC International Development Correspondent indicated the need to investigate the crimes to end impunity, rightly highlighting that it could be "intensely political." The criminal proceedings "would involve probing the roles played by some of the armed men who ultimately brought President Ouattara to power."[69] Showing the disconnection between the legal frames, the BBC did not mention the role of the ICC.

On May 4, 2011, we received a further letter from President Ouattara confirming his request that the ICC Office of the Prosecutor conduct independent and impartial investigations. He considered that "the Ivorian judiciary is not at this stage in the best position to address the most serious of the crimes" committed since November 28, 2010. President Ouattara reiterated his commitment to providing full cooperation with the office in the course of these proceedings.

On June 8, 2011, the UN Commission of Inquiry issued its report confirming the commission of crimes against humanity and war crimes in Côte d'Ivoire.[70] It considered that at least 3,000 persons had been killed between November 28, 2010, and May 28, 2010. The UN Commission of Inquiry report and President Ouattara's letter completed the information needed. We decided to start an investigation immediately that could consolidate the end of violence.

The Office of the Prosecutor Request to Open an Investigation

On June 23, 2011, the Office of the Prosecutor requested authorization from the pre-trial chamber to open an investigation.[71]

Temporal jurisdiction: This requisite became the most disputed issue before the Chambers. The Prosecution presented alleged crimes committed since November 28, 2010. They were under jurisdiction *ratione temporis*, since Côte d'Ivoire accepted the Court's jurisdiction from September 19, 2002, and "for an unspecified period of time." The acceptance of jurisdiction was reaffirmed by letter on December 14, 2010.[72]

We also stated that upon reviewing the supporting material, the chamber might broaden the investigations' temporal scope to events that occurred since September 19, 2002.[73]

b) Material jurisdiction: We affirmed that from February 25, 2011, until May 6, 2011, pro-Gbagbo forces and armed forces loyal to Alassane Ouattara allegedly committed war crimes during a non-international armed conflict.

b.1) Crimes against humanity: The Prosecution considered that the attacks on Abidjan's civilian population were not isolated or spontaneous acts of violence. They were committed *under the leadership of former President Gbagbo to launch violent attacks against persons perceived to support the political opponents in order to retain power.*"[74]

The information showed "that the State apparatus, including the security forces, were colluding with the militia groups, most notably Young Patriots and Liberian mercenaries, in order to execute a plan to attack civilians."[75]

The concept was to defend Côte d'Ivoire against "foreigners," a category that included civilians perceived as pro-Ouattara, either because they had a Muslim name, wore Muslim clothes, or were from the North.

b.2) We estimated *that war crimes might have been committed by pro-Gbagbo forces but also "by individuals linked or belonging to pro-Ouattara forces, namely the New Forces (Forces Nouvelles), renamed the Forces Républicaines de Côte d'Ivoire (FRCI)."* However, identifying the persons who bear the greatest responsibility for ordering or facilitating the crimes remained unclear and *"would be one of the objectives of the envisaged investigation."*

c) Complementarity: The Appeals Chamber unanimously ruled in the Katanga case *"Inaction on the part of a State having jurisdiction (that is, the fact that a State is not investigating or prosecuting, or has not done so) renders a case admissible before the Court, subject to article 17 (1) (d) of the Statute."*[76]

Accordingly, the prosecution attached two confidential, ex parte annexes presenting a preliminary list of persons or groups belonging to or associated with the pro-Gbagbo and pro-Ouattara sides that appear to bear the greatest responsibility for the most serious crimes, with an indication of their specific role. The prosecution affirmed that there were no criminal proceedings against them.

We identified a case opened in France under universal jurisdiction but considered that were no investigations pending against them. And President Ouattara's letter confirmed our assessment.

    d) Gravity: The Prosecution evaluated that people in high-ranking political or command positions had a crucial role in the violence and murders, rapes, and enforced disappearances committed on a large scale. Many of these crimes were committed with cruelty and on ethnic, religious, or politically discriminatory grounds. Sexual violence appears to be part of the widespread and systematic attack against the civilian population. Their aggressors often told victims that they were being raped as a punishment for their ethnicity or political affiliations.

    e) Interest of justice: based on the available information, the Prosecution had no reason to believe that the opening of an investigation into the situation would not be in the interests of justice.

The UN Security Council took note of the ICC activities and did not mention any obstacles.[77]

The Judges' Decisions on Jurisdiction

As mentioned in 2003, Goldsmith and Krasner asserted that international judges would not respect legal limits and that, as a consequence: "ICC jurisdiction can only be expected to expand."[78] The actual chambers decisions showed the opposite, displayed an intense legal debate between the different judges and the lack of connections with any political agenda.

Pre-Trial Chamber III
Pre-Trial Chamber III, with a majority integrated by Judge Elizabeth Odio Benito, and Judge Adrian Fulford, authorized an investigation in Côte d'Ivoire for crimes within the court's jurisdiction committed since November 28, 2010.

The investigation was also allowed concerning continuing crimes that may be committed in the future. Finally, the ruling instructed the prosecutor to revert to the chamber within one month with any additional information available to him on potentially relevant crimes committed between 2002 and 2010.[79]

Presiding Judge Silvia Fernandez de Gurmendi disagreed with the ruling's last two aspects in a partially dissenting vote. All Pre-Trial Chamber III's judges agreed that the court has jurisdiction over crimes allegedly committed in Côte d'Ivoire since September 19, 2002.

The chamber's conflicting views were first, whether to authorize an investigation into crimes that may be committed after the filing date (June 23, 2011) and second, whether to approve an investigation into crimes committed before November 28, 2010.[80]

Regarding the first issue, the majority agreed with the temporal limit established by the decision authorizing the investigation into Kenya's situation. In that precedent, Pre-Trial Chamber II decided that it would be erroneous to widen the time limit of the investigation to include events following the date of the prosecutor's request.[81]

However, Judges Odio Benito and Fulford were worried about the possible commission of new crimes. "Bearing in mind the volatile environment in Côte d'Ivoire, the Chamber finds it necessary to ensure that any grant of authorization covers investigations into 'continuing crimes'—those whose commission extends past the date of the application."

Presiding Judge Fernandez de Gurmendi disagreed on that point. In her view, the limitation of jurisdiction to "continuing crimes . . . might leave out of the investigation underlying acts of war crimes and crimes against humanity that could not be considered as 'continuing crimes,' even if they were part of the same attack or same armed conflict."

Presiding Judge Fernandez de Gurmendi suggested following the criterion established by Pre-Trial Chamber I in the "Mbarushimana" case. In that case, Presiding Judge Cuno Tarfusser, Judge Sylvia Steiner, and Judge Sanji Mmasenono Monageng arrived at a different conclusion. They said that a single situation could include crimes committed after the referral, "insofar as they are sufficiently linked to the situation of crisis referred to the Court as ongoing at the time of the referral."[82] "It is only within the boundaries of the situation of crisis for which the jurisdiction of the Court was activated that subsequent prosecutions can be initiated."[83]

Presiding Judge Fernandez de Gurmendi also strongly disagreed with requesting to the prosecutor more information on the crimes committed before November 2010. She considered that the pre-trial chamber could not be transformed into an investigative chamber looking for additional alleged crimes and suspects independently. She reminded that France's proposal at the Preparatory Committee that pre-trial functions be carried out by "Preliminary Investigation Chambers" was not accepted.[84]

Judge Fernandez de Gurmendi affirmed that "the Chamber has no investigative powers and the possibility granted to victims to express their views should not become the vehicle for a fact-finding exercise by the Chamber that has no basis in the ICC legal framework." She also quoted the Appeals Chamber decision "[m]anifestly, authority for the conduct of investigations vests in the Prosecutor."[85]

The Arrest of Laurent Gbagbo

On November 23, 2011, Pre-Trial Chamber III issued an arrest warrant for Laurent Gbagbo, who was transferred to the court on November 30, 2011. On May 29, 2012, Laurent Gbagbo challenged the court's jurisdiction, alleging that the scope of the Declaration of April 18, 2003, was limited to crimes committed in the context of the September 19, 2002, *coup d'état*. Therefore, it did not provide jurisdiction to the period between December 2010 and April 2011.

The defense submitted that the words "faite pour une durée indéterminée" in the Declaration of April 18, 2003, relate solely to the court's ability to exercise its jurisdiction. It alleged the court might exercise its jurisdiction exclusively to the period preceding the declaration. The defense further argued that Mr. Ouattara was neither the de facto or de jure president of Côte d'Ivoire when the letters of 2010 and 2011 were drafted and could not bind the state.

The case was transferred to Pre-Trial Chamber I, integrated by Presiding Judge Silvia Fernandez de Gurmendi, Judge Hans-Peter Kaul, and Judge Christine Van den Wyngaert. They ruled that nothing in the Declaration of April 2003 indicated Côte d'Ivoire's attempt to restrict the temporal jurisdiction.

The chamber considered that the events between September 19, 2002, and November 28, 2010, were part of a single situation, a circumstance accepted by Gbagbo's defense. The words for "une durée indéterminée," when given their ordinary meaning, make it clear that Côte d'Ivoire accepted the jurisdiction of the court over events from September 19, 2002, onward.

"In addition, upon its reception, the Registrar informed Côte d'Ivoire of the consequences that were attached to the Declaration of April 18, 2003, under rule 44 of the Rules." The chamber ruled that "while States may indeed seek to define the scope of its acceptance, such definition cannot establish arbitrary parameters to a given situation."

The judges stated that nothing in the Declaration of April 18, 2003, indicates Côte d'Ivoire's attempt to restrict the temporal jurisdiction. Accordingly, *"the Chamber deems it unnecessary to address the validity of the letters of 14 December 14, 2010, and May 3, 2011, or the question of the capacity of Mr. Ouattara to bind Côte d'Ivoire on those particular dates."*

On December 12, 2012, the appeal chamber made a different interpretation. It was integrated by Presiding Judge Anita Usacka, Judge Sang-Hyun Song, Judge Sanji Mmasenomo Monageng, Judge Akua Kuenyehia, and Judge Erkki Kourula. It found that the acceptance of jurisdiction may also cover crimes committed after the declaration has been lodged.

Notes

1. Prosecutor v. Laurent Koudou Gbagbo, ICC-02/11-01/11 OA2, Judgment on the appeal of Mr. Laurent Koudou Gbagbo against the decision of Pre-Trial Chamber I on jurisdiction and stay of the proceedings, ¶ 50 (Dec. 12, 2012) https://www.icc-cpi.int/CourtRecords/CR2015_05010.PDF.

2. Ellen Otzen, *Can West Africa Resolve Côte d'Ivoire crisis?*, BBC (Jan. 3, 2011, 3:55 PM), https://www.bbc.co.uk/blogs/africahaveyoursay/2011/01/can-west-africa-resolve-ivory.shtml#sa-link_location=story-body&intlink_from_url=https%3A%2F%2Fwww.bbc.com%2Fnews%2Fworld-africa-12110119&intlink_ts=1596298051248-sa.

3. S.C. Res. 1975, U.N. Doc. S/RES/1975 (Mar. 30, 2011).

4. Situation in the Republic of Côte D'Ivoire, ICC-02/11, Request for authorization of an investigation pursuant to Article 15 (June 23, 2011), https://www.icc-cpi.int/CourtRecords/CR2011_07959.PDF.

5. Norimisu Onishi, *Côte d'Ivoire Ruler Declares Himself Winner*, N.Y. TIMES (Oct. 25, 2000), https://www.nytimes.com/2000/10/25/world/ivory-coast-ruler-declares-himself-winner.html.

6. *Id.*

7. *Id.*

8. *Côte d'Ivoire Profile—Timeline*, BBC News (Jan. 15, 2019), https://www.bbc.com/news/world-africa-13287585.

9. The Associated Press, *Renewed Fighting in Côte d'Ivoire Threatens to Halt Peace Talks*, N.Y. Times (Nov. 30, 2002), https://www.nytimes.com/2002/11/30/world/renewed-fighting-in-ivory-coast-threatens-to-halt-peace-talks.html.

10. Situation in the Republic of Côte D'Ivoire, ICC-02/11, Prosecution's provision of further information regarding potentially relevant crimes committed between 2002 and 2010, ¶ 9 (Nov. 3, 2011) https://www.icc-cpi.int/CourtRecords/CR2011_18008.PDF.

11. *Id.*

12. *Id.*

13. Prosecutor v. Laurent Koudou Gbagbo, ICC-02/11-01/11 OA 2, Judgment on the appeal of Mr. Laurent Koudou Gbagbo against the decision of Pre-Trial Chamber I on jurisdiction and stay of the proceedings, ¶ 51 (Dec 12, 2012), https://www.icc-cpi.int/CourtRecords/CR2015_05010.PDF.

14. Situation in the Republic of Côte D'Ivoire, ICC-02/11, Prosecution's provision of further information regarding potentially relevant crimes committed between 2002 and 2010, ¶ 14 (Nov. 3, 2011), https://www.icc-cpi.int/CourtRecords/CR2011_18008.PDF.

15. S.C. Res. 1527, para. 2, U.N. Doc. S./RES/1527 (Feb. 4, 2004).

16. S.C. Res. 1528, U.N. Doc. S/RES/1528 (Feb. 27, 2004).

17. S.C. Res. 1572, para 7, U.N Doc. S/RES/1572 (Nov. 15, 2004).

18. S.C. Res. 1600, U.N. Doc. S/RES/1600 (May 4, 2005).

19. *Côte d'Ivoire Profile—Timeline*, BBC News (Jan. 15, 2019), https://www.bbc.com/news/world-africa-13287585.

20. Being born in the country does not grant a person Ivorian citizenship. The children of foreigner parents remained "foreigners" according to the Côte d'Ivoire laws.

21. S.C. Res. 1880, para. 4, U.N. Doc. S/RES/1880 (July 30, 2009).

22. S.C. Res. 1933, ¶1, U.N. Doc. S/RES/1933 (June 30, 2010).

23. Ariel Zirulnick, *Five Key Reasons Côte d'Ivoire's Election Led to Civil War*, Christian Science Monitor (Apr. 6, 2011), https://www.csmonitor.com/World/Africa/2011/0406/Five-key-reasons-Ivory-Coast-s-election-led-to-civil-war/Disputed-election-results.

24. *Côte d'Ivoire: UN Plans More Peacekeepers*, BBC News (Jan. 5, 2011), https://www.bbc.com/news/world-africa-12123607.

25. H. E. Blaise Compaore, President of the Faso, H.E. Prof. John Evans Atta-Mills, President of the Republic of Ghana, H.E. Ellen Johnson-Sirleaf, President of the Republic of Liberia, H.E. Amadou Toumani Toure, President of the Republic of Mali, H.E. Dr. Goodluck Ebele Jonathan, President of the Federal Republic of Nigeria, H.E. Maître Abdoulaye Wade, President of the Republic of Senegal, H.E. Faure Essozimna Gnassingbe, President of the Togolese Republic and representatives from Cape Verde, Benin, Gambia and Sierra Leone. Economic Community of West African States (Abuja), *Final Communique on the Extraordinary Session of the Authority of Heads of State and Government on Cote d'Ivoire*, All Africa (Dec. 7, 2010), https://allafrica.com/stories/201012080763.html.

26. The heads of state decided in accordance with ECOWAS Protocol on Democracy and UN Security Council resolutions. *Id.*

27. *Id.*

28. Communique, Peace and Security Council, Communique of the 252nd Meeting of the Peace and Security Council, African Union Communique, PSC/PR/COMM.1(CCLII) (Dec. 9, 2010).

29. S.C. Res. 1962, ¶1, U.N. Doc. S/RES/1962 (Dec. 20, 2010).

30. NICOLAS COOK, CONG. RESEARCH SERV. RS21989 CÔTE D'IVOIRE'S POST-ELECTION CRISIS 8 (2011).

31. Luis Moreno Ocampo, Prosecutor of the International Criminal Court, Statement on the Situation in Côte d'Ivoire (Dec. 21, 2010).

32. Ellen Otzen, *Can West Africa Resolve Côte d'Ivoire Crisis?*, BBC (Jan. 3, 2011), https://www.bbc.co.uk/blogs/africahaveyoursay/2011/01/can-west-africa-resolve-ivory.shtml#sa-link_location=story-body&intlink_from_url=https%3A%2F%2Fwww.bbc.com%2Fnews%2Fworld-africa-12110119&intlink_ts=1596298051248-sa

33. NICOLAS COOK, CONG. RESEARCH SERV. RS21989 CÔTE D'IVOIRE'S POST-ELECTION CRISIS 8 (2011).

34. *Côte d'Ivoire: Africa Mediation Fails to End Stalemate*, BBC NEWS (Jan. 4, 2011), https://www.bbc.com/news/world-africa-12110119.

35. *Id.*

36. U.N. Secretary General, Letter dated Jan. 7, 2011 from the Secretary General addressed to the President of the Security Council, U.N. Doc. S/2011/5 (Jan. 10, 2011).

37. S.C. Res. 1967, ¶4, U.N. Doc. S/RES/1967 (Jan. 19, 2011).

38. *Id.*

39. *Côte d'Ivoire: Odinga Makes Fresh AU Mediation Attempt*, BBC NEWS (Jan. 17, 2011), https://www.bbc.com/news/world-africa-12204139.

40. Rukmini Callimachi, *Côte d'Ivoire: Shooting Erupts, Military Chiefs Meet*, BOSTON (Jan. 18, 2011), http://archive.boston.com/news/world/africa/articles/2011/01/18/shootings_in_ivory_coast_au_mediator_stays/.

41. Gbagbo rejects Kenyan PM as mediator in Côte d'Ivoire's political crisis, BBC (Jan. 20, 2011, 10:44 AM), http://www.bbc.co.uk/worldservice/africa/2011/01/110120_ivory_coast.shtml.

42. Rukmini Callimachi, *Côte d'Ivoire: Shooting Erupts, Military Chiefs Meet*, BOSTON (Jan. 18, 2011), http://archive.boston.com/news/world/africa/articles/2011/01/18/shootings_in_ivory_coast_au_mediator_stays/.

43. *Id.*

44. NICOLAS COOK, CONG. RESEARCH SERV. RS21989 CÔTE D'IVOIRE'S POST-ELECTION CRISIS (2011).

45. *Côte d'Ivoire: AU panel of Leaders to Seek Way Forward*, BBC NEWS (Jan. 29, 2011), https://www.bbc.com/news/world-africa-12314022.

46. *Id.*

47. *Id.*

48. Scott Baldauf, *Côte d'Ivoire Violence Escalates as Mediation Efforts Stall*, CHRISTIAN SCIENCE MONITOR (Feb. 28, 2011), https://www.csmonitor.com/World/Africa/2011/0228/Ivory-Coast-violence-escalates-as-mediation-efforts-stall.

49. *Id.*
50. *Ouattara Pessimistic about AU Mediation for Côte d'Ivoire*, VOA NEWS (Feb. 21, 2011, 7:00 PM), https://www.voanews.com/africa/ouattara-pessimistic-about-au-mediat ion-ivory-coast.
51. Scott Baldauf, *Côte d'Ivoire Violence Escalates as Mediation Efforts Stall*, CHRISTIAN SCIENCE MONITOR (Feb. 28, 2011), https://www.csmonitor.com/World/Africa/2011/ 0228/Ivory-Coast-violence-escalates-as-mediation-efforts-stall.
52. NICOLAS COOK, CONG. RESEARCH SERV. RS21989 CÔTE D'IVOIRE'S POST-ELECTION CRISIS (2011).
53. *Id.*
54. *Id.*
55. *Id.*
56. *Id.*
57. CRISIS GROUP, CÔTE D'IVOIRE: IS WAR THE ONLY OPTION? Africa Report No. 171 (2011).
58. Andrew Harding, *Will the World Prevent Côte d'Ivoire War?*, BBC NEWS (Mar. 24, 2011, 3:28 PM), https://www.bbc.co.uk/blogs/thereporters/andrewharding/2011/03/ will_the_world_prevent_ivory_c.html
59. Security Council, Letter dated Mar. 24, 2011 from the Permanent Representative of Nigeria to the U.N. addressed to the President of the Security Council, U.N. Doc. S/ 2011/182 (Mar. 24, 2011).
60. *Id.*
61. SAMANTHA POWER, THE EDUCATION OF AN IDEALIST 295 (Kindle ed. 2019).
62. S.C. Res. 1975, ¶ 12, U.N. Doc. S/Res/1975 (Mar. 30, 2011).
63. S.C. Res. 1975, para. 11 and 13, U.N. Doc. S/Res/1975 (Mar. 30, 2011).
64. U.N. SCOR, 66th Sess., 6508th mtg. at 3, U.N. Doc. S/OV.6508 (Mar. 30, 2011).
65. *Id.*
66. *Id.*
67. Luis Moreno Ocampo, Prosecutor of the International Criminal Court, Statement in relation to Côte d'Ivoire (Apr. 6, 2011).
68. Barbara Plett, *Did UN Forces Take Sides in Côte d'Ivoire*, BBC NEWS (Apr. 7, 2011), https://www.bbc.com/news/world-africa-13004462.
69. Mark Doyle, *The Politics of Human Rights in Côte d'Ivoire*, BBC NEWS (May 24, 2011), https://www.bbc.com/news/world-africa-13528781.
70. Report of the independent, international commission of inquiry on Côte d'Ivoire, Human Rights Council, 17th Sess., U.N. Doc. A/HRC/17/48 (extract) (June 6, 2011).
71. Situation in the Republic of Côte D'Ivoire, ICC-02/11, Request for authorization of an investigation pursuant to Article 15 (June 23, 2011), https://www.icc-cpi.int/Court Records/CR2011_07959.PDF.
72. *Id.*
73. *Id.*
74. *Id.*
75. *Id.*
76. Prosecutor v. Germain Katanga and Mathieu Ngudjolo Chui, ICC-01/04-01/07 OA 8, Judgment on the Appeal of Mr. Germain Katanga against the Oral Decision of Trial

Chamber II of 12 June 2009 on the Admissibility of the Case ¶ 78 (Sept. 25, 2009), https://www.icc-cpi.int/CourtRecords/CR2009_06998.PDF

77. S.C. Res. 2000, para. 6, U.N. Doc. S/RSS/2000 (July 27, 2011).

78. Jack Goldsmith & Stephen D. Krasner, *The Limits of Idealism*, 132 *Daedalus* 47 (2003)

79. Situation in the Republic of Cote D'Ivoire, ICC-02/11, Corrigendum to "Decision Pursuant to Article 15 of the Rome Statute on the Authorisation of an Investigation into the Situation in the Republic of Côte d'Ivoire" ¶ 213 (Nov. 15, 2011), https://www. icc-cpi.int/CourtRecords/CR2011_18794.PDF.

80. *Id.*

81. Article 53(l)(a) of the Statute, by referring to "a crime [which] has been or is being committed," makes clear that the authorization to investigate may only cover those crimes that have occurred up until the time of the filing of the Prosecutor's Request. Situation in the Republic of Kenya, ICC-01/09, Decision Pursuant to Article 15 of the Rome Statute on the Authorization of an Investigation into the Situation in the Republic of Kenya (Mar. 31, 2010).

82. Prosecutor v. Callixte Mbarushimana, ICC-01/04-01/10, Decision on the Prosecutor's Under Seal Application for a Warrant of Arrest Mbarushimana against Callixte ¶ 6 (Sept. 25, 2010), https://www.icc-cpi.int/CourtRecords/CR2010_06674.PDF.

83. *Id.*

84. Situation in the Republic of Cote D'Ivoire, ICC-02/11, Corrigendum to "Judge Fernandez de Gurmendi's separate and partially dissenting opinion to the Decision Pursuant to Article 15 of the Rome Statute on the Authorisation of an Investigation into the Situation in the Republic of Côte d'Ivoire" ¶ 20 (Oct. 5, 2011)https://www.icc-cpi.int/CourtRecords/CR2011_16840.PDF.

85. *Id.*

22

Jus ad Curiam and *Jus ad Bellum* Decisions in Syria

During the last year of my tenure, war crimes and crimes against humanity were committed in Syria, a state non-party. Writing this book, I realized the importance of reviewing the council dynamic that promoted *jus ad Bellum* decisions in Syria and prevented a *jus ad Curiam* resolution referring the situation to the ICC.

In March 2011, the Arab Spring arrived in Syria. Antigovernment protests broke out in a country that the Assad family has governed for over four decades. Security forces used weapons against demonstrators, and an armed conflict started. In August 2011, President Obama called on Syrian President Bashar al Assad to step down.[1]

The P-5 consensus reached in Libya disappeared in a few months. The UN Security Council, the only global institution, was divided and unable to protect the peace. The United States participated in negotiations promoting the opposition and adopted a *jus ad Bellum* decision in Syria supporting proxy forces. Russia supported military activities and political negotiations that held President Assad's power and condemned foreign armies' interventions in a sovereign country to produce a regime change.[2]

For two years, the Syrian government attacked its citizens, killing 100,000 persons. In March and in August 2013, the Syrian government used chemical weapons to kill around 2,000 people. The last incident crossed a "red line" established by President Obama, to protect US personnel and allies like Turkey, Jordan, and Israel.[3] He announced a military intervention, knowing that it was a decision without legal basis.

Amb. Samantha Power explained that a strike was the only option. She considered that referring Syria to the ICC was not relevant to stop President Assad's use of chemical weapons. However, the UK Parliament and the US Congress did not support President Obama's *jus ad Bellum* decision.

President Putin's intervention facilitated an agreement to dismantle Syria's chemical weapons arsenal. For a few months, the council dynamic changed,

War and Justice in the 21st Century. Luis Moreno Ocampo, Oxford University Press. © Oxford University Press 2022.
DOI: 10.1093/oso/9780197628973.003.0023

and it adopted resolutions by consensus on Syria demanding justice and access to humanitarian assistance. But the conflict in Ukraine created a political confrontation between Western countries and Russia affecting the council dynamics.

Meanwhile, the Islamic State was taking control of parts of Syria. The US Congress adopted a *jus ad Bellum* decision to use armed forces against the Islamic State and other terrorist groups in Syria without the Assad government's consent. Syria became a contained global war by proxy.

Each party involved in the Syria conflict, including the United States and Russia, had its own policy, supported different groups, and chose legal arguments, but the outcome was catastrophic. Over 5.6 million people have fled the country, and 6.9 million are internally displaced as of March 2022.[4] Already in 2016, the UN estimated that 400,000 people had died as a result of the conflict.[5]

In 2014, after the Ukraine conflict started, France tabled a referral to the ICC. Previously, the United States opposed referring the Syrian situation to the ICC. This time, it voted in favor forcing Russia and China to use their veto power to stop the initiative. Everyone understood that a criminal investigation had to prosecute Assad and could investigate the US and Russian personnel.

President Obama consolidated a new blueprint: a combination of high-tech attacks and proxy forces in the ground as a new permanent state of war in sovereign nations not at war with the US. Such a policy affects the international law fundamental principle prohibiting aggression against sovereign states and establishing the state monopoly of violence, a national law fundamental principle.

In 2015, after a brutal attack in Paris, the UN Security Council overcame the divisions and by consensus adopted Resolution 2249, authorizing "all necessary means" against the Islamic State in Syria. The War on Terror became a council policy.

The Syrian Conflict

The Parties Involved

Syria's Arab Spring "became a sectarian war, with the majority Sunnis fighting to overthrow a government in which the minority Allawi monopolized power. Other countries became involved. Iran supported the Assad government, its long-term ally and fellow Shia, and dispatched Hezbollah forces from Lebanon to fight on Assad's behalf. Russia, whose alignment with the Syrian regime dated back to the Cold War era, also supported it."[6]

In August 2012, President Obama was asked what would lead him to use direct military force in Syria. He said, "a red line for us is we start seeing a whole bunch of chemical weapons moving around or being utilized."[7]

As the US president, he focused on US national interest. President Obama was not proposing a humanitarian intervention to protect a hundred of thousands of Syrian victims. Instead, he focused on the control of chemical weapons to protect US personnel and its allies.

Switzerland took the lead on international criminal justice and promoted a collective effort to end impunity. On January 14, 2013, it sent a letter to the UN Security Council on behalf of fifty-seven states calling for referring Syria to the ICC.[8] I learned that the United States requested informally to Switzerland to suspend the request.

There were other voices demanding justice. At the beginning of 2013, Navi Pillay, the UN High Commissioner for Human Rights,[9] and Syria's UN International Commission of Inquiry also proposed the ICC referral to the council.[10] Informally, the United States blocked such proposals.

The conflict became a multi-sided war.[11] The United States vetted and assisted Syrian militias confronting the Assad regime. Qatar and Saudi Arabia supporting proxy forces, and the European Union (EU) in May 2013, gave the conditional green light for the transfer of arms to the Syrian Opposition Council.[12]

The CIA covertly armed and trained the loose coalition of so-called moderate rebels in the Free Syrian Army (FSA). The Pentagon set up and began arming an association called the Syrian Democratic Forces, dominated by the Kurdish YPG (*Yekîneyên Parastina Gel or "People's Protection Units"*).[13] In 2013, Congress authorized the provision of non-lethal assistance to elements of the Syrian opposition.[14]

The former Qatar prime minister admitted his country's support to Al-Nusra, a terrorist group created by Al Qaeda.[15] He explained the coordination to support proxy forces between the United States and some Gulf countries. There were *two operation rooms, one in Jordan and one in Turkey.*[16]

In March 2013, different reports suggested a chemical weapons attack, and the Syrian government asked the United Nations to investigate the incident. UN investigators arrived on the ground in Syria in August 2013, and their arrival coincided with the much larger-scale Ghouta chemical attack.[17] Until those days, almost 100,000 people were killed in Syria, but this chemical attack killing around 2,000 persons crossed President Obama's red line and triggered his reaction.

Most of the Obama administration members proposed "a military strike," and only the chief of staff, Denis McDonough, raised questions about the legal basis for it.[18] President Obama understood that "There was no firm international legal basis for bombing Syria—no argument of self-defense, which justified our actions against al-Qaeda; no UN resolution such as we had had in Libya." But he concluded, "still, the military strike was the preferable option."[19]

Already during his Nobel lecture, President Obama retained his national authority to decide on *jus ad Bellum*. Obama explained the US national interest a few days later. The gassing of Syrian children was "a danger to our security. If we fail to act, the Assad regime will see no reason to stop using chemical weapons. As the ban against these weapons erodes, other tyrants will have no reason to think twice about acquiring poison gas and using them."[20]

President Obama identified US troops and allies as the communities to protect, not the Syrian citizens.[21]

Neither Ban Ki-moon, the UN secretary-general, nor Angela Merkel, Germany's leader, supported the strike.[22] UK Prime Minister Cameron was willing to assist a direct military intervention, but the British Parliament rejected the proposal.[23] Reluctantly, President Obama decided to seek congressional authorization for a *jus ad Bellum* decision in Syria.[24] His administration found that the plan had no backing, even from those that previously had advocated a military operation.[25]

On September 3, 2013, Oona Hathaway published an op-ed presenting the legal argument against a *jus ad Bellum* decision. She stated that US intervention without Security Council authorization would "flout the most fundamental international rule of all—the prohibition on the use of military force, for anything but self-defense, in the absence of Security Council approval. This rule maybe even more important to the world's security—and America's—than the ban on the use of chemical weapons."[26]

Her comments contradicted many US thinkers, but she did not mention an international criminal justice option. Instead, she advocated for economic sanctions and US rhetorical power to shame and pressure Russia and China.

On September 6, Ambassador Samantha Power, then the US permanent representative before the UN, answered Oona Hathaway's arguments, presenting the *jus ad Bellum* decision as to the only efficient option. "At this stage, the diplomatic process is stalled because one side has just been gassed on a massive scale, and the other side so far feels it has gotten away with it. What would words—in the form of belated diplomatic condemnation—achieve?"[27]

Ambassador Power went further and dismissed a *jus ad Curiam* decision referring Syria to the ICC: "What could the International Criminal Court really do, even if Russia or China were to allow a referral? Would a drawn-out legal process really affect the immediate calculus of Assad and those who ordered chemical weapons attacks?"[28]

President Obama was between *impotence or war*: "Over the last two years, my administration has tried diplomacy and sanctions, warning and negotiations—but chemical weapons were still used by the Assad regime."[29] But he did not follow the Nuremberg chief prosecutor's advice: "Only sanctions which reach individuals can peacefully and effectively be enforced."

The decision to go to war trumped the decision to use international criminal justice. Still, there was no political support to implement a *jus ad Bellum* decision. A different political option appeared when President Obama met Russian President Vladimir Putin at the G20. Russia shared President Obama's interest to control the use of chemical weapons, and it offered to work together to convince the Syrian government to give its arsenal up.[30]

The United States and Russia agreement would force Syria to sign the Chemical Weapons Convention, subject to the Organization for the Prohibition of Chemical Weapons (OPCW) inspections. President Obama adjusted to the circumstances and adopted a coercive diplomatic strategy. On September 10, 2013, he asked "the leaders of Congress to postpone a vote to authorize the use of force while we pursue this diplomatic path. Meanwhile, I've ordered our military to maintain their current posture to keep the pressure on Assad and to be in a position to respond if diplomacy fails."[31]

On September 12, 2013, Syria notified the UN of its intention to apply the Chemical Weapons Convention.

President Putin Support for International Law

President Putin published an *op-ed* in the *New York Times* following a long Russian tradition supporting international law, a tradition that ended with the Ukrainian intervention. He affirmed that "A new opportunity to avoid military action has emerged in the past few days. The United States, Russia and all members of the international community must take advantage of the Syrian government's willingness to place its chemical arsenal under international control for subsequent destruction."[32] He described the problem, "Syria is not witnessing a battle for democracy. There are few champions of democracy in Syria. But there are more than enough Qaeda fighters and extremists of all stripes battling the government." He also pointed out to the United States' responsibility without mentioning it directly, "This internal conflict" was "fueled by foreign weapons supplied to the opposition."[33]

President Putin explained, "A strike would increase violence and unleash a new wave of terrorists" promoting nuclear proliferation ". . . if you cannot count on international law, you must find other ways to ensure your security. Thus, a growing number of countries seek to acquire weapons of mass destruction. This is logical: if you have the bomb, no one will touch you."[34]

He agreed with the ACLU that President Obama established a "new normal": "It is alarming that military intervention in internal conflicts in foreign countries has become commonplace for the United States."

In a paragraph that Oona Hathaway and Daniel Shapiro could have drafted, he said, "We are not protecting the Syrian government, but international law. We need to use the United Nations Security Council and believe that preserving law and order in today's complex and turbulent world is one of the few ways to keep international relations from sliding into chaos. . . . force is permitted only in self-defense or by the decision of the Security Council. Anything else is . . . an act of aggression."[35]

President Putin evaluated the military intervention in Afghanistan, Libya, and Iraq and concluded: "force has proved ineffective and pointless." He also indicated the unavoidable killing of civilians: *"No matter how targeted the strikes or how sophisticated the weapons, civilian casualties are inevitable, including the elderly and children, whom the strikes are meant to protect."* President Putin insisted, "We must stop using the language of force and return to the path of civilized diplomatic and political settlement."

President Putin was rooted in a long Russia's tradition. Since the nineteenth century, Russia had advocated for the rule of law internationally, without mentioning the Russian implementation of the rule of law domestically.[36] Already Tsar Nicholas II promoted the 1899 Hague Peace Conference. In an introductory document entitled "Rescript of peace," he "steadfastly opposed the use of armed conflicts as an ordinary means of conducting 'international diplomacy.'"[37]

Stalin, for the wrong reasons, was the leading promoter of the Nuremberg trials. Russia signed the Rome Statute and voted in the UN Security Council to favor the Darfur and Libya referrals. In 2010 President Dmitry Medvedev proclaimed, "The result of the war was the vaccination against Nazism that we all received at Nuremberg, and also the establishment of international organizations to guarantee our world's peace and security."[38]

Syria Joined the Organization for the Prohibition of Chemical Weapons (OPCW)

The consensus between the United States and Russia transformed the Syrian situation in a few days. On September 14, 2013, Syria deposited with the UN secretary-general its instrument of accession to the Chemical Weapons Convention. On September 27, 2013, the UN Security Council unanimously adopted Resolution 2118 (2013), endorsing Syria's chemical weapons program's expeditious destruction, with inspections to begin by October 1. In the event of noncompliance, the council announced "Chapter VII" measures.

During the debate, the UN Secretary-General confirmed that "chemical weapons were used in Syria" and demanded that "The perpetrators of that crime must be brought to justice." He considered Resolution 2118 as historical, but he also highlighted:

> We must never forget that the catalogue of horrors in Syria continues with bombs and tanks, grenades and guns. A red light for one form of weapons does not mean a green light for others; This is not a license to kill with conventional weapons. All the violence must stop. All the guns must fall silent.[39]

Secretary-General Ban Ki-Moon was demanding to protect all the Syrian victims. He challenged without mentioning the previous President Obama's explanation of the need to control the chemical weapons to safeguard just US troops and allies.[40]

The experienced Russian minister of foreign affairs, Sergei Lavrov, was the first speaker at the council emphasizing *"that the resolution sets out a framework for a political and diplomatic settlement of the Syrian crisis."* Without naming the United States, he stated, "Particular responsibility lies with those who back and sponsor the opposition."[41]

Secretary of State John Kerry was also present at the council, commended Russia, supported the *jus ad Bellum* initiative but indicated the advantage of the diplomatic solution:

> Our original objective was to degrade and deter Syria's chemical-weapons capability. The option of military force that President Obama has kept on the table could have achieved that, but tonight's resolution, in fact, accomplishes even more. Through peaceful means, it will for the first time seek to eliminate entirely the nation's chemical-weapons capability.[42]

In a carefully crafted line, Secretary Kerry said, "So we are here united tonight in support of our belief that international institutions do matter; that international norms matter." But he limited the legal commitment exclusively to weapons of mass destruction. "We say with one voice that atrocities carried out with the world's most heinous weapons will not be tolerated."[43]

In less than a week, on October 2, 2013, the new consensus allowed the council to adopt a presidential statement describing the death of more than 100,000 people in Syria and urging all parties to facilitate immediate humanitarian assistance.[44] The entire council recognized the crimes committed and condemned "the widespread violations of human rights and international humanitarian law by the Syrian authorities, as well as any such abuses and violations by armed groups."[45] Without distinguishing between national or international, the council included a strong comment on justice: "to end impunity" and demanding that perpetrators "must be brought to justice."[46]

A few months later, such a presidential statement was followed by a unanimous UN Security Council Resolution 2139(2014), adopted on February 22, condemning the Syrian government and armed groups and demanding justice and access to humanitarian assistance.[47]

During the debate, US Ambassador Samantha Power stated, "At long last, the Security Council has spoken clearly and unanimously about the devastating humanitarian catastrophe unfolding in Syria." She emphasized President Assad's responsibility and "terrorist groups like Al-Nusra and the Islamic State in Iraq and the Levant."[48] She did not comment on the previous support provided to Al-Nusra. Amb Power recognized the consensus and requested action.[49]

Russian Ambassador Vitaly Churkin blamed the council's delay for taking action on the US agenda to promote Assad removal.[50] He focused on assisting the Syrians.[51] He insisted on a political solution adopted by the Syrian people. He concluded, "the Security Council should swiftly proceed to discuss a further draft document on countering terrorist activities in Syria."

French Ambassador Gérard Araud stated that France would continue to stand beside the Syrian people. And he alerted, "Criminals should pay for their crimes." Australia, Chile, and Lithuania proposed to refer the situation to the ICC.

The Ukraine Conflict

The same day the resolution on Syria was adopted unanimously, the conflict in Ukraine transformed the interaction between the United States and Russia. On the same February 22, 2014, the Ukrainian Parliament dismissed President Viktor Yanukovych from office. The speaker of the Ukrainian Parliament became interim president. "A day for the history books," tweeted Geoffrey Pyatt, US ambassador to Ukraine.[52]

President Putin had a different point of view. The Ukrainian president's removal triggered a Russian military intervention, a civil war, a conflict with Europe and deeply affected the United States and Russia's ability to act together. Russia perceived the Ukraine Parliament decision as a coup promoted by Western intervention. It denounced the US policy as a superpower's global domination and complained about NATO expansion.[53] Russia remembered well the promises mentioned by Professor Gaddis.

After a referendum, Crimea seceded from Ukraine and asked to join the Russian Federation.

On March 16, 2014, "President Obama emphasized that the Crimean 'referendum,' which violates the Ukrainian constitution and occurred under the duress of Russian military intervention, would not be recognized by the United States and the international community." He also warned, "of additional costs to be imposed on Russia."[54]

On March 18, 2014, President Putin went ahead. He submitted to the Russian Federal Assembly the treaty creating two new entities within the Russian Federation: the Republic of Crimea and the city of Sevastopol. He explained:

a referendum was held in Crimea on March 16 in full compliance with democratic procedures and international norms. More than 82 percent of the electorate took part in the vote. Over 96 percent of them voted in favor of reuniting with Russia.

The referendum was fair and transparent, and the people of Crimea clearly and convincingly expressed their will and stated that they want to be with Russia.

In people's hearts and minds, Crimea has always been an inseparable part of Russia.

The most recent public opinion surveys conducted here in Russia show that 95 percent of people think that Russia should protect the interests of Russians and members of other ethnic groups living in Crimea.[55]

At the time, Russians constituted 60 percent of Crimea's population. And President Putin explained that the intervention aimed to protect Russians living in Crimea: [W]e had to help create conditions so that the residents of Crimea, for the first time in history, were able to peacefully express their free will regarding their own future.[56] Nationalism works in the United States and Russia. After the Crimea intervention, President Putin's popularity in Russia increased from 60 percent to more than 80 percent.[57]

President Putin invoked Kosovo's legal precedents to justify his decisions and criticized Western leaders. *They say we are violating norms of international law. Firstly, it's a good thing that they at least remember that there exists such a thing as international law—better late than never.*

Moreover, he mentioned that the Crimean authorities invoked "the well-known Kosovo precedent." He equated "the unilateral separation of Kosovo from Serbia" with "what Crimea is doing now." He considered that Kosovo separation "was legitimate and did not require any permission from the country's central authorities." President Putin, quoting US submission to the ICJ, stated "Declarations of independence may, and often do, violate domestic legislation. However, this does not make them violations of international law."[58]

President Putin combined his position on international law with the *realist* idea that states have to protect themselves. *Russia has its own national interests that need to be taken into account and respected.* The corollary of the realist model is to escalate before military threats. And that was President Putin's rationale.

Our western partners, led by the United States of America, prefer not to be guided by international law in their practical policies, but by the rule of the gun."[59] They have lied to us many times, made decisions behind our backs, placed us before an accomplished fact. This happened with NATO's expansion to the East, as well as the deployment of military infrastructure at our borders. Let me note too that we have already heard declarations from Kiev about Ukraine soon joining NATO. NATO remains a military alliance, and we are against having a military alliance making itself at home right in our backyard or in our historic territory.[60]

On March 23, 2014, Michael McFaul, US ambassador before Russia, published an op-ed titled "Confronting Putin's Russia" without mentioning the promises identified by Professor Gaddis. He affirmed:

> *The decision by President Vladimir V. Putin to annex Crimea ended the post–Cold War era in Europe. Since the late Gorbachev-Reagan years, the era was defined by zigzags of cooperation and disputes between Russia and the West, but always with an underlying sense that Russia was gradually joining the international order. No more.*[61]

The world was divided and the narrative too: "The Western press portrays Putin as a new Tsar, a Stalin or a populist aggressor. The Russian press provides a mirror image, talking about Western fascist aggression in and outside of Ukraine."[62]

The New *Jus ad Bellum* Decision on Syria

In 2014, the Obama administration requested authority and funding from Congress to provide lethal support to vetted Syrians in "defending the Syrian people from attacks by the Syrian regime."[63]

But the subsequent advance of the Islamic State changed the US direction. Congress authorized a *Department of Defense-led program to combat terrorist groups active in Syria, defend the United States and its partners from Syria-based terrorist threats.* And urged the Executive to *"promot[e] the conditions for a negotiated settlement to end the conflict in Syria."*[64]

In September 2014, the United States began airstrikes in Syria, with the stated goal of preventing the Islamic State from using Syria as a base for its operations in neighboring Iraq. In October 2014, the Defense Department established Combined Joint Task Force-Operation Inherent Resolve (CJTF-OIR) to "formalize ongoing military actions against the rising threat posed by ISIS in Iraq and Syria." Seventy states cooperated with it.[65]

The United States gradually increased the number of US personnel in Syria, reaching roughly 2,000 by late 2017. They supported local militias and succeeded in retaking, by the end of 2017, nearly all of the territory once held by the Islamic State.[66]

By early 2018, the collapse of IS territorial control in most of Syria was matched by the Syrian government's significant military and territorial gains. But the United States continued demanding Assad removal as *a prerequisite for the provision of reconstruction assistance*.

Syria became a limited world war by proxy. Israel has acknowledged conducting over 200 military strikes in Syria, and Turkey maintains military forces in northern Syria against Kurdish fighters.[67] There were also clashes between state forces. For example, Turkey shot down a Russian plane in December 2015,[68] and the United States, United Kingdom, and France struck Syrian facilities in retaliation for an alleged chemical attack in April 2018.[69]

In the meantime, the number of people displaced exceeded twelve million people, similar to removing New York and Berlin's entire population.[70]

The Increasing Use of Proxy Forces

The United States consolidated a new blueprint: a combination of high-tech attacks and proxy forces in the ground as a new permanent state of war in some nations. It is a neocolonial approach to manage international violence.

"More armed groups have emerged in the past six years than in the past six decades." A study conducted by the American Bar Association considered that "Sponsorship of proxy groups has become a feature of nearly every global conflict." The United States is "one of the world's most visible and robust sponsors of proxy groups."[71]

Mark Mazzeti published in the *New York Times* that President Obama resisted for a while the idea to support proxy forces in Syria. He initially rejected a plan presented in 2012 by General Petraeus, then the CIA director, to arm and train small groups of Syrian rebels in Jordan. Secretary of

State Clinton and Defense Secretary Panetta supported Petraeus's idea, but President Obama rejected that plan. He wanted to know more: "Did this ever work?"[72]

He commissioned in 2012 an internal study analyzing CIA experiences supporting proxy forces.[73] According to the New York Times, the study found that the strategy "rarely works" to achieve US goals, and there are no mentions of the impact in the foreign countries.[74] The study's only success story was the support provided to the *mujahedeen* rebels fighting Soviet troops in Afghanistan during the 1980s.

Interestingly, such an operation, perceived as mission accomplished, trained Pakistan intelligence in supporting the Taliban. It also promoted Osama bin Laden's leadership and the creation of Al Qaeda as a collateral result. September 11 and twenty years of wars are the cost of the success. It is shocking—the inability to learn from the past.

President Obama recognized that there was a problem supporting proxy forces. He said in a New Yorker interview: "I actually asked the C.I.A. to an-alyze examples of America financing and supplying arms to an insurgency in a country that actually worked out well. And they couldn't come up with much."[75]

But the Syrian use of chemical weapons changed his mind. "In April 2013, President Obama secretly authorized the C.I.A. to begin a program to arm the rebels at a base in Jordan."[76] In September 2014, President Obama said he would redouble American efforts by having the Pentagon participate in arming and training rebel forces.[77] Although President Obama originally in-tended for the CIA to arm and train the rebels to fight the Syrian regime, as mentioned, Congress changed the target, shifting to training the rebel forces to fight the Islamic State.[78] That change affected all the operations, the Free Syrian Army couldn't fight at the same time the government and the radical opposition, and it collapsed.

In September 2015, General Petraeus came back with the idea of proxy forces and proposed to reach an agreement with some members of Al-Nusra, a terrorist organization created in Syria by Al Qaeda, to fight against ISIS, and the Syrian government.[79]

Ronan Farrow considered that

> Ironically, it was Obama's non-interventionist, "don't do stupid shit" ap-proach to foreign policy that prompted . . . a legacy of low-footprint in-tervention, and, along with drones, alliances with foreign militaries and

militias were at the heart of that legacy. [Farrow further said]: At the center of that vision was proxy war: over and over again, [President Obama] used the word "partner," referring to foreign militaries or militias doing the bidding of the United States. Why send American sons and daughters to do work that Yemenis and Pakistanis could be paid to do for us?[80]

An ABA study considered that national leaders support proxy forces in foreign conflicts for their short-term national political advantages.[81] Stephen Walt explained the political benefits of using drones, an argument that could be extended to the practice of proxy forces. "The desire to keep the costs to the United States low and the willingness to ignore the costs to others makes it easier to keep today's wars going and makes tomorrow's wars more likely."[82]

The ABA study identified a necessary consequence: *"Proxy warfare creates protracted challenges in establishing the rule of law and a state monopoly on violence in post-conflict settings."*[83] The most consistent violence reducer mechanism in the history of humanity is affected, and there is no analysis of the problem.

The Draft Resolution Referring Syria to the ICC

France championed justice for Syria, and on September 10, 2013, a French draft resolution including a referral to the ICC was leaked to the press.[84] Following conversations with the United Kingdom and the United States, the draft resolution was not tabled.

At the end of March 2014, after the Ukraine intervention created a conflict between Russia and Western countries, the United States gave the green light, and France proposed a Security Council resolution that would refer Syria to the International Criminal Court.[85] France knew that "Russia might well veto such a resolution," but "it could still embarrass the Kremlin, the Syrian government's most important foreign supporter, at a time when the Russians already face isolation over the crisis in Ukraine."[86]

France argued that after more than three years of mass atrocities in Syria, the situation should be referred to the ICC. It reached out to the fifty-eight states signatories of Switzerland's letter on January 14, 2013, to co-sponsor the referral. The United States was on-board. Its concerns about protecting Israel were taken into consideration.[87] The French draft proposing an ICC referral was informally discussed on May 14. The draft resolution had the immediate support of the ICC-11 state parties members of the Security Council,[88] the United States, and Rwanda supporting the ICC.

I learned about the attempt and realized that Russia would exercise its veto. It was evident that an ICC investigation should indict President Assad and triggering regime change. I tried to reach out to US and Russian diplomats to propose a draft resolution that both sides could adopt.

I had presented the idea in a post in *Just Security* in September 2013: "the UN Security Council could refer the Syrian situation to the International Criminal Court with—and here's the first novel point—a future jurisdiction that would start in 2014. A delayed ICC jurisdiction would give all relevant parties incentives to stop committing grave crimes."[89]

A delayed start would put Assad and the rebels on notice that they would face international justice and provide them with meaningful incentives to stop the violence and bring their behavior in line with international law. Second, the delayed start would buy some time for a negotiated settlement, which should include domestic justice, but with a clear deadline. Finally, this approach combines diplomacy with action: it first creates a window for a negotiated settlement, and then, if that fails, it provides clear international authorization to take real action.

I recognized Ambassador Power's argument that a judicial decision without enforcement will not stop the carnage, and I proposed to plan how to enforce the eventual arrest warrants.

> If the United States is ready to strike, it should also be ready to work with other countries to plan effective arrest operations and to integrate judicial decisions with political and military power. President Obama can make the threat of prosecution a credible, preventative measure, employing it as a sword of Damocles; and in order to achieve such effect, he must be ready to implement it if necessary.[90]

I still believe that there are new ways to harmonize the different interests. "Sequencing the timing of the referral could be a new way to combine political negotiations, judicial activities, and arrest operations."

My calls were not answered. China and Russia vetoed the resolution tabled by France.[91] The proposal was called a "publicity stunt" by the Russian ambassador to the UN.[92]

During the debate, French Ambassador Araud considered that France's proposal aimed at re-establishing the council's unity around the values shared by its members. He believed that there was no peace process to protect.[93] He quoted the rejection of impunity as the principle agreed in previous Syria Resolutions 2118 (2013) and 2139 (2113), and the text repeatedly agreed in Darfur and Libya. "Acting in unison, the Council would thereby say that in 2014 people could no longer behave as they did in 1942 or 1994; and that it would not allow the state of barbarity to return." Ambassador Araud foresaw well: "Extending equal impunity to all criminals is not a paradox; there is brotherhood in crime. They refuse to negotiate because they want to be victorious and think they can be. They will not negotiate because they think it is a matter of killing or being killed."[94]

He described the situation in 2014: *more than 160,000 deaths, more than 9 million displaced persons and refugees, a country destroyed, hunger, and epidemics.* There were 60,000 more deaths than just six months before.

He quoted the "Cesar" report, produced at Qatar's request by a group of senior international prosecutors.[95] "A veto would cover up all crimes; it would be a veto against justice. It would give new justification to the French proposal to limit the use of the right of the veto in the case of mass atrocities."

Vitaly Churkin, the Russian ambassador, understood "the motives" to support the referral, "it is hard to witness the destruction, loss of life and suffering of the people." "It is more difficult to discern the motives that led France to initiate the draft and put it to a vote, fully aware in advance of the fate it would meet."

He highlighted the importance of unity between the P5, "when that unity is present, we manage to achieve concrete positive results," and mentioned the destruction of the Syrian chemical stockpile. "Why deal such a blow to P5 unity at this stage?"

He accused the United States of a double standard, approving a draft that establishes an exemption for itself and its citizens. Russia challenged the United State and the United Kingdom to refer Iraq to the ICC to show that they "are truly against impunity."

He also denounced the supply of weapons to "good opposition groups only." "Their list of good guys now includes the Al-Nusra Front, which has openly confessed to a series of brutal terrorist attacks, including the recent one in Aleppo that claimed the lives of dozens of civilians."[96]

"Pursuing regime change by force will prolong the crisis." The referral "is an attempt to use ICC . . . for eventual outside military intervention."[97] He ended: "We are convinced that justice in Syria will eventually prevail. Those guilty of perpetrating grave crimes will be punished, but if that is to happen, peace is needed first and foremost."

Ambassador Wang Min explained that China is *firmly opposed to all violations of international humanitarian law or serious violations of human rights committed by all parties to the conflict in Syria*. However, China had some serious reservations about the referral. First, *China always has reservations concerning the referral by the Security Council of particular country situations to the ICC. This is our principled position. Secondly, to forcibly refer the situation in Syria to the ICC is not conducive either to building trust among all parties in Syria or to an early resumption of the negotiations in Geneva. Thirdly, we believe that the Council should continue holding consultations, rather than forcing a vote on the draft resolution, in order to avoid undermining Council unity. Regrettably, China's approach has not been taken on board; China therefore voted against the draft resolution. The United States, the United Kingdom, and other Western countries have made totally unfounded accusations against China. That is irresponsible and hypocritical.*

China *has continued to uphold an objective and impartial position on the question of Syria. China pursues no self-interest on the issue, much less shield any party, faction, or persons in Syria. As a permanent member of the Council and a responsible member of the international community, China has remained committed to seeking a political settlement to the question of Syria.*[98] US Ambassador Samantha Power followed Professor Oona Hathaway's proposal to adopt a "US rhetorical power to shame and pressure Russia." She spared China and stated:

> Today is accountability for Syria, but it is also about accountability for the Security Council . . . [B]ecause of the decision of the Russian Federation to back the Syrian regime no matter what it does, the Syrian people will not see justice today. They will see crime, but not punishment. A judicial process does more than hold perpetrators accountable. It also allows victims to speak. The vetoes today have prevented the victims of atrocities from testifying at The Hague.[99]

Ambassador Power mentioned the ICC's record in states parties situations:

> In the past, when extraordinary crimes have been carried out, the International Criminal Court has been able to act. Why is it that the people of Uganda, Darfur, Libya, the Central African Republic, the Democratic

Republic of the Congo, Côte d'Ivoire, Mali, and Kenya deserve international and impartial justice, but the Syrian people do not?

She exposed the difference between the automatic ICC's treaty jurisdiction and its ad hoc intervention due to a UN Security Council referral. She asked the question:

> Why should the International Criminal Court pursue accountability for the atrocities in Africa but not those in Syria, where the worst horrors of our time are being perpetrated? For those who have asked the Security Council that very reasonable question, today they have their answer—the Russian and Chinese vetoes.

She selected the framework to fulfill her role in representing the United States. She neither mentioned the previous US decision to stop the Switzerland initiative nor her own observation about the ICC intervention's futility. She ended from high grounds.

> While there may be no accountability before the ICC today for the horrific crimes being carried out against the Syrian people, there should be accountability for those members of the Council that have prevented such accountability.[100]

The UN Security Council did not adopt a *jus ad Curiam* decision providing impartial international criminal justice to the victims in Syria.

The UN Security Council Adoption of the War on Terror

The Ukrainian conflict created frictions between the United States/Europe and Russia and triggered the process to force Russia to veto the ICC referral. Still, it was possible to reach a consensus in adopting resolution 2249 (2015) to confront the Islamic State and Al-Nusra.

Since September 2014, France, one of the prominent critics of the US intervention in Iraq, launched "Opération Chammal," an airstrike military campaign in Iraq against the Islamic State.[101] In October 2015, extremist groups attacked Paris, more than 120 people were killed and 600 injured.[102] The Islamic State claimed that the attacks were retaliation for *Opération Chammal*.[103]

Francois Hollande, the socialist French president, assumed the duty of revenge. He denounced the extremist attacks as an "act of war" that must be countered "mercilessly."[104] France expanded its airstrikes to Syria, targeting ISIS's so-called capital in Raqqa, and its interior minister, Bernard Cazeneuve, said the raids were a direct retaliation for the Paris attacks.[105] The European Union, for the first time, activated the mutual solidarity clause.[106]

France opposed US intervention in Iraq in 2003 but a decade later promoted UN Security Council Resolution 2249. The resolution authorized to "take all necessary measures" on the territory under the Islamic State's control in Syria and Iraq to prevent and suppress terrorist groups, designated by the UN Security Council.[107]

Besides all the previous discussions, China and Russia fully supported the decision.

"The Chinese Government firmly opposes all forms of terrorism and firmly combats all violent terrorist crimes that challenge human civilization. We will further strengthen our cooperation with the international community on counter-terrorism in order to safeguard world peace and stability."[108]

The Russian Ambassador said:

The Council has taken a number of important decisions aimed at strengthening the international community's fight against terrorism and adapting it to new threats and the changing tactics of terrorists. Resolution 2199 (2015), on combating the financing of terrorism by cutting off attempts to gain financing through the illegal trade in oil, was adopted in February at Russia's initiative.[109]

Following the Council *jus ad Bellum* decision, the United States, United Kingdom, France, Australia, Denmark, Norway, the Netherlands, and Belgium conducted military operations in Syria against ISIS, invoking Resolution 2249.[110] Such military interventions would be an additional obstacle to allow impartial criminal investigations and prosecutions.

Notes

1. Armed Conflict in Syria: Overview and U.S. Response. Updated July 27, 2020 Congressional ResearchService, https://crsreports.congress.gov/product/pdf/RL/RL33487

2. US experts are not following well the transformation produced by the Rome Statute and the Russia position. For instance, Michael McFaul, a Stanford professor and Obama ambassador in Moscow, analyzed Russia position on Libya without even mentioning the fact thar Russia voted in favor of the Darfur referral. He wrongly considered that in February 2011, Susan Rice secured Russian support for the first resolution on Libya, UNSCR 1970. Mc Faul did not mention that such a resolution included the ICC referral. MICHAEL MCFAUL, FROM COLD WAR TO HOT PEACE: AN AMERICAN AMBASSADOR IN PUTIN'S RUSSIA 222 (Kindle ed. 2018).

3. "Over time, our troops would again face the prospect of chemical warfare on the battlefield. If fighting spills beyond Syria's borders, these weapons could threaten allies like Turkey, Jordan, and Israel. And a failure to stand against the use of chemical weapons would weaken prohibitions against other weapons of mass destruction, and embolden Assad's ally, Iran—which must decide whether to ignore international law by building a nuclear weapon, or to take a more peaceful path." *President Obama Addresses the Nation on Syria*, THE WHITE HOUSE (Sept. 10, 2013), https://obamawhi tehouse.archives.gov/photos-and-video/video/2013/09/10/president-obama-addres ses-nation-syria#transcript.

4. Eleven years on, mounting challenges push many displaced Syrians to the brink, **UNHCR, report**. https://www.unhcr.org/en-us/news/briefing/2022/3/623055174/ eleven-years-mounting-challenges-push-displaced-syrians-brink.html.

5. Independent International Commission of Inquiry on the Syrian Arab Republic, https://www.ohchr.org/EN/HRBodies/HRC/IICISyria/Pages/AboutCoI.aspx.

6. MICHAEL MANDELBAUM, MISSION FAILURE 305–06 (Kindle ed. 2016).

7. BEN RHODES, THE WORLD AS IT IS 224 (Kindle ed. 2018).

8. Letter to the UN Security Council from the Switzerland government states https:// www.newsd.admin.ch/newsd/message/attachments/29293.pdf. *See also* Switzerland asks the UN Security Council to refer the serious crimes committed in Syria to the International Criminal Court. Federal Department of Foreign Affairs, https: https:// www.admin.ch/gov/en/start/documentation/media-releases.msg-id-47431.html

9. Pillay renews call to refer Syria to world criminal court, February 13, 2013, https:// www.ohchr.org/en/newsevents/pages/pillaytosecuritycouncil.aspx

10. On February 5, 2013, the Syria's UN International Commission of Inquiry considered that "the ICC *is the appropriate institution for the fight against impunity.*" https://documents-dds-ny.un.org/doc/UNDOC/GEN/G13/106/27/PDF/G1310 627.pdf?OpenElement. The following report of the UN Commission, in September 2013, considered that "The perpetrators of these violations and crimes, on all sides, act in defiance of international law," the report said. "They do not fear accountability. Referral to justice is imperative." Nick Cumming-Bruce, *U.N. Rights Panel Cites Evidence of War Crimes by Both Sides in Syria.* THE NEW YORK TIMES, Sept. 11, 2013, https://www.nytimes.com/2013/09/12/world/middleeast/united-nations-panel-cites-evidence-of-war-crimes-in-syria.html

11. Tom Ruys, *Of Arms, Funding and "Non-lethal Assistance"—Issues Surrounding Third-State Intervention in the Syrian Civil War*, CHINESE JOURNAL OF INTERNATIONAL LAW March 2014, at 13–53, https://doi.org/10.1093/chinesejil/jmu003.

12. *Id.*
13. Ronan Farrow, War on Peace: The End of Diplomacy and the Decline of American Influence 159 (Kindle ed. 2018).
14. Armed Conflict in Syria: Overview and U.S. Response, February 16, 2018 (RL33487), https://www.everycrsreport.com/files/20180216_RL33487_95c44345c9c939c6abfd5 9a1a4b29e3ceccaa390.html
15. Middle East Eye, October 31, 2017, "When the Syria issue started (. . .) anything that was going, it goes to Turkey, and there was coordination with the US forces. And everything was distributed, and happened through US forces and Turks and us (. . .). Maybe a mistake happened that one faction was supported in a certain period, but it was not ISIS, they exaggerated the subject it was not ISIS. Maybe Al Nusra there was a relation. There could have been a relationship, I do not know about this subject, but I say even if there was a relation, when we were told that Al Nusra is not accepted, the support stopped, and the main focus was the liberation of Syria." Available at [https://www.middleeasteye.net/news/qatar-maybe-supported-al-qaeda-syria-says-former-pm.]
16. *Interview with Sheikh Hamad Bin Jassim Al-Thani,* Charlie Rose Videos, https://charlierose.com/videos/30589 (last visited July 7, 2021).
17. The chemical attack took place on August 21, 2013, with reported estimates of at least 281 to 1,729 fatalities, not less than 51 of whom were rebel fighters. The UN investigation revealed that the chemical agents used in the Khan al-Assal chemical attack "bore the same unique hallmarks" as those used in Al-Ghouta attack and that "the perpetrators likely had access to the chemical weapons stockpile of the Syrian military." Stephanie Nebehay, *Chemical Weapons Used in Syria Appear to Come from Army Stockpile: U.N.,* Reuters (Mar. 5, 2014, 8:07 AM), https://www.reuters.com/article/us-syria-crisis-chemical/chemical-weapons-used-in-syria-appear-to-come-from-army-stockpile-u-n-idUSBR EA240SF20140305.
18. Ben Rhodes, The World as It Is 224 (Kindle ed. 2018).
19. Ibid.
20. *President Obama Addresses the Nation on Syria,* The White House (Sept. 10, 2013), https://obamawhitehouse.archives.gov/photos-and-video/video/2013/09/10/presid ent-obama-addresses-nation-syria#transcript.
21. *Id.*
22. Ben Rhodes, The World as It Is? 224 (Kindle ed., 2018).
23. On August 29, 2013, the British Prime Minister David Cameron lost a vote endorsing military action against Syria by 13 votes. The Parliament voted 285–272 against joining US-led strikes on Syria after debating the path to war. *Id.*
24. On September 10, 2013, President Obama delivered a speech on the situation in Syria providing his reasoning. ". . . a targeted strike can make Assad, or any other dictator, think twice before using chemical weapons. Other questions involve the dangers of retaliation. And our ally, Israel, can defend itself with overwhelming force, as well as the unshakeable support of the United States of America." *President Obama Addresses the Nation on Syria,* The White House (Sept. 10, 2013), https://obamawhitehouse.

archives.gov/photos-and-video/video/2013/09/10/president-obama-addresses-nat ion-syria#transcript.

25. "[M]embers of Congress in both parties—including people who had demanded that we take action in Syria—announced that they would vote against authorizing it." BEN RHODES, THE WORLD AS IT IS 224 (Kindle ed. 2018).

26. Ooṇa A. Hathaway & Scott J. Schapiro, *On Syria, a U.N. Vote Isn't Optional*, N.Y. TIMES (Sept. 3, 2013), http://www.nytimes.com/2013/09/04/opinion/on-syria-a-un-vote-isnt-optional.html?_r=0.

27. *Remarks by Ambassador Samantha Power on Syria at the Center for American Progress*, BELFER CENTER HKS (Sept. 6, 2013), https://www.belfercenter.org/publication/rema rks-ambassador-samantha-power-syria-center-american-progress. *See also* Garance Franke-Ruta, *The Ambassador to the UN's Case Against the UN*, ATLANTIC (Sept .6, 2013), https://www.theatlantic.com/international/archive/2013/09/the-ambassador-to-the-uns-case-against-the-un/279439/.

28. *Remarks by Ambassador Samantha Power on Syria at the Center for American Progress*, BELFER CENTER HKS (Sept. 6, 2013), https://www.belfercenter.org/publication/rema rks-ambassador-samantha-power-syria-center-american-progress.

29. *President Obama Addresses the Nation on Syria*, THE WHITE HOUSE (Sept. 10, 2013), https://obamawhitehouse.archives.gov/photos-and-video/video/2013/09/10/presid ent-obama-addresses-nation-syria#transcript.

30. BEN RHODES, THE WORLD AS IT IS 224 (Kindle ed. 2018).

31. *President Obama Addresses the Nation on Syria*, THE WHITE HOUSE (Sept. 10, 2013), https://obamawhitehouse.archives.gov/photos-and-video/video/2013/09/10/presid ent-obama-addresses-nation-syria#transcript.

32. Vladimir V Putin, *A Plea for Caution From Russia*, N.Y. TIMES (Sept. 11, 2013), https://www.nytimes.com/2013/09/12/opinion/putin-plea-for-caution-from-russia-on-syria.html.

33. *Id.*

34. *Id.*

35. "No one wants the United Nations to suffer the fate of the League of Nations, which collapsed because it lacked real leverage. The potential strike by the United States against Syria, despite strong opposition from many countries and major political and religious leaders, including the pope, will result in more innocent victims and esca-lation, potentially spreading the conflict far beyond Syria's borders. A strike would increase violence and unleash a new wave of terrorism. Millions around the world increasingly see America not as a model of democracy but as relying solely on brute force, cobbling coalitions together under the slogan "you're either with us or against us." "I would rather disagree with a case [President Obama] made on American exceptionalism . . . We are all different, but when we ask for the Lord's blessings, we must not forget that God created us equal." *Id.*

36. PETER HOLQUIST, THE RUSSIAN EMPIRE AS A "CIVILIZED STATE": INTERNATIONAL LAW AS PRINCIPLE AND PRACTICE IN IMPERIAL RUSSIA, 1874–1878 (2006).

37. John Mack, *Nicholas II and the Rescript for Peace of 1898: Apostle of Peace or Shrewd Politician?* 31 RUSSIAN HISTORY 83–103 (2004).

38. Dmitry Medvedev, President of Russia, Address at the ceremonial reception to mark the 65th anniversary of victory in the 1941–1945 Great Patriotic War, (May 9, 2010), transcript available at http://eng.kremlin.ru/news/191.

39. *Secretary General Press Encounter Following the Adoption of Security Council Resolution on Syria*, UN SECRETARY GENERAL (Sept. 27, 2013), https://www.un.org/sg/en/content/sg/press-encounter/2013-09-27/secretary-generals-press-encounter-following-adoption-security.

40. "Over time, our troops would again face the prospect of chemical warfare on the battlefield. If fighting spills beyond Syria's borders, these weapons could threaten allies like Turkey, Jordan, and Israel. And a failure to stand against the use of chemical weapons would weaken prohibitions against other weapons of mass destruction, and embolden Assad's ally, Iran—which must decide whether to ignore international law by building a nuclear weapon, or to take a more peaceful path." *President Obama Addresses the Nation on Syria*, THE WHITE HOUSE (Sept. 10, 2013), https://obamawhitehouse.archives.gov/photos-and-video/video/2013/09/10/president-obama-addresses-nation-syria#transcript.

41. UN SCOR 68th Sess., 7038 mtg., U.N. Doc S/PV.7038 Provisional (Sept. 27, 2013).

42. *Id.*

43. *Id.*

44. Press Release, Security Council, Appalled at Deteriorating Humanitarian Situation in Syria, Urges Eased Access for Relief Workers, Including Across Conflict Lines, UN Press Release SC/11138 (Oct. 2, 2013).

45. *Id.*

46. *Id.*

47. Press Release, Security Council Unanimously Adopts Resolution 2139 (2014) to Ease Aid Delivery to Syrians, Provide Relief from 'Chilling Darkness, U.N. Press Release SC/11292 (Feb. 22, 2014).

48. *Id.*

49. *Id.*

50. "The Security Council decided relatively recently to consider the humanitarian situation in Syria, and only after it became clear that attempts to use the deterioration of the humanitarian situation to effect regime change were unsuccessful." UN SCOR, 69th sess., 7116 mtg., U.N. Doc S/PV.7116 Provisional (Feb. 22, 2014).

51. *The resolution adopted today focuses on the need to provide humanitarian access based on a mutual, unpoliticized and impartial approach and in line with the guiding principles of the United Nations in the area of providing humanitarian assistance.* UN SCOR, 69th sess., 7116 mtg., U.N. Doc S/PV.7116 Provisional (Feb. 22, 2014).

52. William Booth, *Ukraine's Parliament Votes to Oust President; Former Prime Minister Is Freed from Prison*, WASH. POST (Feb. 22, 2014), https://www.washingtonpost.com/world/europe/ukraines-yanukovych-missing-as-protesters-take-control-of-presidential-residence-in-kiev/2014/02/22/802f7c6c-9bd2-11e3-ad71-e03637a299c0_story.html

53. "Assurances that the North Atlantic Alliance would not expand eastward—which had been given to the leadership of the Soviet Union—turned out to be empty words, for

NATO's infrastructure has continuously drawn closer to Russian borders." *Russia's Priorities in Europe and the World*, CENTER FOR INT'L RELATIONS AND SUSTAINABLE DEVELOP'T, https://www.cirsd.org/en/horizons/horizons-winter-2015--issue-no2/russias-priorities-in-europe-and-the-world (last visited July 7, 2021).

54. David M. Herszenhorn, *Crimea Votes to Secede from Ukraine as Russian Troops Keep Watch*, N.Y TIMES (Mar. 16, 2014), https://www.nytimes.com/2014/03/17/world/europe/crimea-ukraine-secession-vote-referendum.html.

55. *Address by President of the Russian Federation*, KREMLIN (Mar. 18, 2014), http://en.kremlin.ru/events/president/news/20603.

56. *Id.*

57. *Do You Approve of the Activities of Vladimir Putin as the President (Prime Minister) of Russia?*, STATISTA, https://www.statista.com/statistics/896181/putin-approval-rating-russia/ (last visited July 7, 2021).

58. *Address by President of the Russian Federation*, KREMLIN (Mar. 18, 2014), http://en.kremlin.ru/events/president/news/20603.

59. *This happened in Yugoslavia; we remember 1999 very well. And then, they hit Afghanistan, Iraq, and frankly violated the UN Security Council resolution on Libya, when instead of imposing the so-called no-fly zone over it they started bombing it too. Id.*

60. *Id.*

61. "Instead of hoping that Putin would eventually come back to his senses and seek again to integrate with the West, I declared that this project was over. In its place, I recommended a strategy of selective containment and selective engagement, an update of the strategy I'd proposed in 2012 of selective engagement and selective disengagement." MICHAEL MCFAUL, FROM COLD WAR TO HOT PEACE: AN AMERICAN AMBASSADOR IN PUTIN'S RUSSIA 407 (Kindle ed. 2018).

62. Jaap de Wilde, *The Ukraine Crisis as Explosive Anachronism*, 39 ATLANTISCH PERSPECTIEF 15, 15 (2015).

63. *Armed Conflict in Syria: Overview and U.S. Response*, EVERY CRS REPORT (Feb. 16, 2018), https://www.everycrsreport.com/files/20180216_RL33487_95c44345c9c939c6abfd59a1a4b29e3ceccaa390.html.

64. *Id.*

65. *CJTF-OIR and coalition forces worked to bolster the efforts of local Syrian forces, including graduates of the Syria train and equip program, against the Islamic State. About CJTF-OIR*, OPERATION INHERENT RESOLVE, https://www.inherentresolve.mil/About-CJTF-OIR/ (last visited July 7, 2021).

66. *Armed Conflict in Syria: Overview and U.S. Response*, EVERY CRS REPORT (Feb. 16, 2018), https://www.everycrsreport.com/files/20180216_RL33487_95c44345c9c939c6abfd59a1a4b29e3ceccaa390.htm.

67. CARLA E. HUMUD & CHRISTOPHER M. BLANCHARD, CONG. RESEARCH SERV. RL33487, ARMED CONFLICT IN SYRIA: OVERVIEW AND U.S. RESPONSE 18 (2020).

68. *Turkey's Downing of Russian Warplane—What We Know*, BBC NEWS (Dec. 1, 2015), https://www.bbc.com/news/world-middle-east-34912581.

69. Helene Cooper, Thomas Gibbons-Neff, & Ben Hubbard, *U.S., Britain and France Strike Syria Over Suspected Chemical Weapons Attack*, N.Y. TIMES (Apr. 13, 2018),

https://www.nytimes.com/2018/04/13/world/middleeast/trump-strikes-syria-att
ack.html.

70. *Independent International Commission of Inquiry on the Syrian Arab Republic*, OHCHR, https://www.ohchr.org/EN/HRBodies/HRC/IICISyria/Pages/AboutCoI. aspx (last visited July 7, 2021).

71. Brittany Benowitz & Tommy Ross, *Time to Get a Handle on America's Conduct of Proxy Warfare*, LAWFARE (Apr. 9, 2020, 11:21 AM) https://www.lawfareblog.com/ time-get-handle-americas-conduct-proxy-warfare.

72. Mark Mazzetti, *C.I.A. Study of Covert Aid Fueled Skepticism about Helping Syrian Rebels*, N.Y. TIMES (Oct. 14, 2014), https://www.nytimes.com/2014/10/15/us/polit ics/cia-study-says-arming-rebels-seldom-works.html.

73. *Id.* See also: Obama-commissioned study reported that the outcome of aiding insurgents is rarely democracy. MICHAEL McFAUL, FROM COLD WAR TO HOT PEACE: AN AMERICAN AMBASSADOR IN PUTIN'S RUSSIA 331–32 (Kindle ed. 2018).

74. Mentioning the same report, Michael McFaul said the Obama-commissioned study reported that the outcome of aiding insurgents is rarely democracy. MICHAEL McFAUL, FROM COLD WAR TO HOT PEACE: AN AMERICAN AMBASSADOR IN PUTIN'S RUSSIA 331–32 (Kindle ed. 2018).

75. Mark Mazzetti, *C.I.A. Study of Covert Aid Fueled Skepticism about Helping Syrian Rebels*, N.Y. TIMES (Oct. 14, 2014), https://www.nytimes.com/2014/10/15/us/politics/ cia-study-says-arming-rebels-seldom-works.html. See also: Obama-commissioned study reported that the outcome of aiding insurgents is rarely democracy. MICHAEL McFAUL, FROM COLD WAR TO HOT PEACE: AN AMERICAN AMBASSADOR IN PUTIN'S RUSSIA 331–32 (Kindle ed. 2018).

76. Ibid.

77. *Id.*

78. *Id.*

79. Mark Pomerieau, *Petraeaus Plan to Defeat ISIS*, ATLANTIC (Sept. 1, 2015), https://www. theatlantic.com/notes/2015/09/petraeuss-plan-to-defeat-isis/403264/. Petraeus clarified, "We should under no circumstances try to use or coopt Nusra, an Al Qaeda affiliate in Syria, as an organization against the Islamic State," the former CIA director told CNN. Petraeus argued, "the question, therefore, is whether it might be possible at some point to peel off so-called 'reconcilables' who would be willing to renounce Nusra and align with the moderate opposition (supported by the US and the coalition) to fight against Nusra, ISIL, and Assad." Jake Tapper, *EXCLUSIVE: Petraeus Explains How Jihadists Could Be Peeled Away to Fight ISIS—and Assad*, CNN POLITICS (Sept. 1, 2015). https://www.cnn. com/2015/09/01/politics/david-petraeus-al-qaeda-isis-nusra/index.html.

80. RONAN FARROW, WAR ON PEACE: THE END OF DIPLOMACY AND THE DECLINE OF AMERICAN INFLUENCE 162–63 (Kindle ed. 2018).

81. "Policymakers appear to favor largely short-term considerations (for example, limiting large-scale commitments of their own troops and maintaining deniability) while neglecting the risks. Research doesn't support this calculation." Brittany Benowitz & Tommy Ross, *Time to Get a Handle on America's Conduct of Proxy Warfare*, LAWFARE (Apr. 9, 2020, 11:21 AM) https://www.lawfareblog.com/time-get-handle-americas-conduct-proxy-warfare.

82. STEPHEN M. WALT, THE HELL OF GOOD INTENTIONS 178 (Kindle ed. 2018).

83. Brittany Benowitz & Tommy Ross, *Time to Get a Handle on America's Conduct of Proxy Warfare*, LAWFARE (Apr. 9, 2020, 11:21 AM), https://www.lawfareblog.com/time-get-handle-americas-conduct-proxy-warfare.

84. Louis Chabonneau, *EXCLUSIVE—French Draft, Disliked by Russia, Would Give Syria Chemical Arms Ultimatum*, REUTERS (Sept. 11, 2013, 12:13 AM), https://www.reuters.com/article/syria-crisis-un-draft-french/exclusive-french-draft-disliked-by-russia-would-give-syria-chemical-arms-ultimatum-idINDEE98A01R20130911. Draft resolution available at https://docs.google.com/file/d/0ByLPNZ-eSjJdX29vd2Y3WlNxQWc/view (last visited July 7, 2021).

85. Somini Sengupta, *French Push U.N. to Seek War Crimes Case in Syria*, N.Y. TIMES (Apr. 4, 2014), https://www.nytimes.com/by/somini-sengupta.

86. *Id.*

87. *Id.*

88. Argentina, Australia, Chad, Chile, France, Jordan, Lithuania, Luxembourg, Nigeria, Republic of Korea, and United Kingdom.

89. *If international jurisdiction were established from the beginning of the conflict and if the suspicion that Assad himself was ordering crimes were confirmed, he would have no interest to comply.* Luis Moreno Ocampo, *The ICC as the Sword of Damocles*, JUST SECURITY (Sept. 23, 2013), https://www.justsecurity.org/914/icc-sword-damocles/.

90. *The threat of an ICC intervention supported by arrest operations would provide serious incentives to stop the brutal attacks, to change behavior without changing regime. And it would do so for all parties involved in the conflict and for all the serious crimes. Id.*

91. UN SCOR 69th Sess., 7180th mtg., U.N. Doc S/PV.7180 Provisional (May 22, 2014).

92. Ian Black, *Russian and China Veto Move to Refer Syria to International Criminal Court*, GUARDIAN (May 22, 2014, 4:07 PM), https://www.theguardian.com/world/2014/may/22/russia-china-veto-un-draft-resolution-refer-syria-international-criminal-court.

93. UN SCOR 69th Sess., 7180th mtg., U.N. Doc S/PV.7180 Provisional (May 22, 2014).

94. *Id.*

95. David Crane and Sir Desmond de Silva, QC, former chief prosecutors of the special court for Sierra Leone, and Sir Geoffrey Nice, QC, former prosecutor of the ICTY.

96. UN SCOR 69th Sess., 7180th mtg., U.N. Doc S/PV.7180 Provisional (May 22, 2014).

97. *Id.*

98. *Id.*

99. *Id.*

100. *The outcome of today's vote, disappointing as it is, will not end our pursuit of justice. There is no limit to our determination to see that the victims of the atrocities in Syria and their loved ones receive answers in accordance with the majesty of law. Id.*

101. *Irak: Premières frappes françaises*, MINISTÈRE DES ARMÉES, https://www.defense.gouv.fr/operations/chammal/actualites/irak-premieres-frappes-francaises (last visited Jan. 7, 2021). On January 13, 2015, a few days after the terrorist attack against the

satiric magazine *Charlie Hebdo*, the French Parliament voted almost unanimously (488 to 1) to continue anti-ISIS airstrikes in Iraq.

102. *France: Extremism and Terrorism*, COUNTER-EXTREMISM PROJECT, https://www.counterextremism.com/countries/france (last visited July 7, 2021).

103. Cara Anna, *ISIS Expresses Fury over French Airstrikes in Syria; France Says They Will Continue*, CTV NEWS (Nov. 14, 1:38 PM), https://www.ctvnews.ca/world/isis-expresses-fury-over-french-airstrikes-in-syria-france-says-they-will-continue-1.2658642.

104. Jon Henley & Angelique Chrisafis, *Paris Terror Attacks: Hollande Says Isis Atrocity Was "Act of War,"* GUARDIAN (Nov. 14, 2015, 3:37 PM), https://www.theguardian.com/world/2015/nov/13/paris-attacks-shootings-explosions-hostages.

105. Ben Doherty et al., *Paris Attacks: French Police Launch Raids as Military Strikes Isis in Syria*, GUARDIAN (Nov. 16, 2015, 8:02 AM), https://www.theguardian.com/world/2015/nov/15/paris-attacks-car-found-with-kalashnikovs-as-gunmans-relatives-questioned.

106. UN SCOR 70th Sess., 7565 mtg., at 2 UN Doc. S/PV.7565 Provisional (Nov. 20, 2015).

107. Press Release, Security Council, Security Council "Unequivocally" Condemns ISIL Terrorist Attacks, Unanimously Adopting Text that Determines Extremist Group Poses "Unprecedented" Threat, UN Pres Release SC/12132 (Nov. 20, 2015).

108. UN SCOR 70th Sess., 7565 mtg., at 3 UN Doc. S/PV.7565 Provisional (Nov. 20, 2015).

109. *Id.* at 5.

110. Dustin A. Lewis, Naz K. Modirzadeh, & Gabriella Blum, *Quantum of Silence: Inaction and Jus ad Bellum* and *Annex: HLS PILAC Catalogue of Communications to the Security Council of Measures Taken by United Nations Member States in Purported Exercise of the Right of Self-Defense: October 24, 1945 Through December 31, 2018*, HARVARD LAW SCHOOL PROGRAM ON INTERNATIONAL LAW AND ARMED CONFLICT (2019), available at: http://blogs.harvard.edu/pilac/files/2019/07/Quantum-of-Silence-2019.pdf.

Epilogue

Describing the Office of the Prosecutor's decisions during the *"jus ad Curiam"* phase, the book glanced at the legal systems managing international violence at the beginning of the twenty-first century and their interaction.

The first part of this conclusion summarizes the Office of the Prosecutor's preliminary examination practice, a procedure established by the Rome Statute to identify situations under the court's jurisdiction. The prosecutor *Proprio Motu* authority linked states parties' institutions and the ICC creating the autonomous criminal justice system referred to by Professor James Crawford, the ILC's leader of the Draft Statute in 1994.

Still, the Rome Statute's consistent application by the ICC did not provide consistent outcomes. As Tolstoy said, "the people who participate in the events," defined the results.

Describing the role of national authorities in DRC, Uganda, CAR, Kenya, Guinea, and Colombia, and the involvement of regional organizations, help us to perceive the functioning of the autonomous criminal justice system established by the Rome Statute.

The second part condenses the *War on Terror*'s policy to kill individuals considered enemy combatants in sovereign countries unwilling or unable to control international terrorism. The War on Terror redefined *jus ad Bellum*, including drone attacks and proxy forces.

It also increased the US opposition to the ICC and created obstacles to adopt *jus ad Curiam* decisions in Iraq or Syria that could promote investigations against US personnel or limit diplomatic negotiations. Paradoxically, the *War on Terror* expanded the support for insurgencies.

The third part describes the UN Security Council's *jus ad Curiam* and *jus ad Bellum* practice. Since 1993, the UN Security Council, the only global political authority, could promote international criminal investigations in any UN member. Still, the permanent five members have the discretion to make different decisions, protecting their own or their allies' interests.

The council promoted only justice in Darfur, both war and justice in Libya, or none of the two in Israel or Korea. The UN Security Council supported the execution of the ICC arrest warrants in DRC, authorized the war on terror against the Islamic State in Syria but not justice.

In 2011 the council reached consensus to adopt a *jus ad Curiam* decision referring Libya to the ICC and in 2015 adopting a *jus ad Bellum* decision to implement the War on Terror in Syria. The council and its members choose the legal system to apply.

1. The Rome Statute in Motion

The *Jus ad Curiam*'s Office of the Prosecutor Decisions

Since June 2003, the Office of the Prosecutor adopted fifteen strategic decisions regarding the preliminary examination process:

(1) To identify the situations under the ICC jurisdiction as the Office of the Prosecutor duty. The ICC prosecutor should examine all the situations in state parties falling in the ICC jurisdiction.

(2) To filter the *jus ad Curiam* decisions adopted by the political actors, even by the UN Security Council in Darfur and Libya.

(3) To maximize the impact of the ICC intervention fostering the policy of positive complementarity, promoting national criminal investigations. In 2013, the Assembly of States Parties embraced the concept.[1] Colombia and Guinea were the best outcomes of such a policy.

(4) To adopt gravity as the criterion to select between situations. Such a policy was particularly relevant to identify the first two investigations and to dismiss two preliminary examinations in 2006 in Venezuela and UK personnel in Iraq.

(5) To distinguish between "situation" and "cases." States and the UN Security Council have the authority to limit the time and space of the situation as they did in Uganda or Darfur, but not to define the cases or the suspects to be investigated.

(6) To refine the admissibility analysis adopting the policy to focus investigations against those most responsible. This criterion provided economic viability to the court, helped national institutions to concentrate their efforts, and provided a clear rationale for the complementarity test. The ICC chambers decided that Kenya's

investigations against lower-level individuals did not affect the admissibility of a case against the leaders involved.

(7) To consider the absence of national proceedings as the first criterion to evaluate the admissibility of a situation. There were no national proceedings in the seven situations opened by the Office of the Prosecutor. The ICC chambers consolidated the jurisprudence on "inactivity" without analyzing "inability" or "unwillingness."

(8) To understand the diversity of the local opinions as part of the meaning of the "interest of the victims." There was particular criticism from the Acholi community and international NGOs and commentators against the ICC intervention in Uganda. The Office of the Prosecutor concluded that respecting the victims' interest implies a duty to be mindful of divergent views without affecting the prosecution's respect for its legal mandate.

(9) To differentiate "the interest of justice" under the ICC Office of the Prosecutor authority from the "interest of peace" under the rule of other actors, including states and the UN Security Council. The office refused to expand its judicial mandate and to participate in the negotiations conducted by political actors. Uganda, Colombia, Kenya, Darfur, Libya, and Côte d'Ivoire are applications of such policy. The Juba talks that ended the LRA activities in Northern Uganda were influenced by and respected the legal framework established by the Rome Statute. During Colombia's preliminary examination, three different administrations and other relevant national actors, including paramilitary and guerrilla leaders, negotiated under the Rome Statute's shadow. Colombia displayed the possibility of signing a peace agreement while doing justice, first with the paramilitaries and then with the FARC. It is a model recognized by the Nobel Committee.

(10) To publicly inform the UN Security Council in advance of the request of arrest warrants, respecting the council's authority on international peace and security to suspend investigations per Article 16. The prosecution applied such a policy consistently in the Darfur and Libya situations.

(11) To use its *proprio motu* authority to invite state referrals before requesting authorization to the pre-trial chamber to open an investigation. The office applied the same policy in DRC, Uganda, and Kenya. DRC and Uganda authorities accepted our invitation

confirming the possibility to adopt *jus ad Curiam* decisions in agreement with states interests and increasing cooperation.

(12) To be predictable and respectful in using the prosecutor's *proprio motu* powers. Dissipating the reservations during the Rome Conference, everyone agreed with the independent ICC intervention in Kenya, including its president and prime Minister, the AU, the EU, and the United States.

(13) To obtain cooperation in all the situations under preliminary examination, including from states' non-parties like the United States and Russia, Libya's transitional government, and even Sudan.

(14) To increase the transparency of the preliminary examinations. The prosecution has made public reports since 2011 and invited submissions in Colombia, Palestine, and Kenya.

(15) To protect the ICC judicial integrity by avoiding the judges' involvement during the *jus ad Curiam* phase. The Office of the Prosecutor met Uganda's President Museveni, DRC's President Kabila, Kenya's President Kibaki, Côte d'Ivoire's President Ouattara, and Palestinian ministers to discuss their referral or acceptance of jurisdiction. The prosecution insisted on its exclusive authority to decide when and where to trigger the ICC intervention. During the CAR and Palestine *jus ad Curiam* phase, the approach was challenged. After the end of my tenure, the appeal chamber confirmed it in the decision about the Mavi Marmara incident and authorized to open the Afghanistan investigation.

The *Jus ad Curiam* as a New and Neglected Field

The ICC prosecutor has the legal mandate to decide where the ICC should intervene, challenging traditional ideas on national sovereignty.

There is no academic field fully covering such unprecedented practice. Commentators judged our intervention without analyzing our legal frame, considering their own paradigms or their preferences.[2]

The Office of the Prosecutor rejected demands to apply standards beyond the statute, including (a) expanding the rules of jurisdiction to accept Palestine's requests; (b) balancing the ethnicity of the defendants to avoid an alleged "African bias"; (c) that local constituencies like the Acholis, have the right to stop the Office of the Prosecutor's interventions; (d) to request UN Security Council referrals; and (d) that negotiations for peace agreements should be prioritized on top of the office duties to investigate and to prosecute.

With a long and unique experience, Juan Mendez explained the importance of judicial actors respecting their mandate, even when contradicting political or activist expectations. As mentioned, he explained: "For justice to have a preventive effect, the most important condition is that justice has to follow its own rules."[3]

The African Bias Campaign

The "African bias" campaign launched by President Al Bashir is one of the best examples of replacing the Rome Statute standards for commentators' criteria.

Bashir pretended that the genocide charges against him were baseless and that the ICC "is a tool to terrorize countries that the West thinks are disobedient."[4] He said, "Any government in the world, when facing an armed rebellion, has a constitutional, legal and moral obligation to resist those militants."[5]

Bashir conceded *that mistakes had been made*, but he pretended that the commanders responsible had been tried and punished. "The US Air Force in Afghanistan mistakenly bombed a wedding and killed 147 civilians. But you cannot say that the US President should be tried for this because he is the Commander in Chief of US forces."[6]

Jean Ping, then AU chairperson of the commission, promoted the African Bias campaign, asking, "Why only Africa? Why is the Rome Statute not applied against Israel, Sri Lanka, and Chechnya?"[7] He did not mention that the ICC has no jurisdiction in those situations.

Bashir and his supporters were able to replace the frame of analysis. A genocide against African victims was neglected: "The court is only one mechanism of neo-colonialist policy used by the West against free and independent countries."[8]

There was no African bias, but the repetition of the narrative created a common perception. Equal geographical or ethnic representation of suspects is not a Rome Statute criterion to select situations and cases, but it became the standard of good faith commentators. Many, including representatives of nation-states, scholars, and civil society, ignoring the rules of jurisdiction and admissibility established by the statute, genuinely believe that ICC's focuses on Africa during its first years was a mistake.[9]

The press has difficulties following years of political developments, and the "African bias" became a recurring narrative that replaced the coverage of the Darfur crimes. After a few years, the international media gradually picked up this framing; even prestigious outlets like the BBC, to keep its impartiality, presented the "African bias" as a reasonable opinion.[10]

It is a paradoxical label because Bashir and his supporters used the colonial and "ethnic" arguments to cover up his own "ethnic" crimes against African victims like Hejewa Adam. Bashir "promoted the idea of a polarization between tribes aligned with him, whom he labeled 'Arabs' and the three ethnic groups . . . who became derogatorily referred to as 'Zurgas' (blacks) or 'Africans.'"[11]

Bashir supporters were invoking the Equal Protection Clause of the US Constitution without quoting it and more importantly, without proving a prosecutor *bias*. Under such a principle, defendants have a right not to be prosecuted based on impermissible criteria such as ethnicity, gender, and race.[12] The Rome Statute legal framework was disregarded. The facts, like the massive crimes committed and the absence of national investigations, were ignored.

Staying true to its legal mandate, the ICC was involved in African situations because massive crimes occurred while national authorities conducted no investigations. The refusal to open investigations in Africa would have been an ICC's *bias*.

Nobel Laureate and South African Bishop Desmond Tutu regretted "that the charges against President Bashir are being used to stir up the sentiment that . . . the International Criminal Court is biased against Africa. Justice is in the interest of victims, and the victims of these crimes are African."[13]

Ralph Gonsalves, the prime minister of Saint Vincent and the Grenadines, a group of islands in the Caribbean Sea, had presented the opposite view to the UN General Assembly's annual high-level debate in 2007: the actions of the UN in recent years "have caused the world to wonder about the relative worth of a Sudanese or Rwandan life, versus an Israeli, Chinese, American or European life." He accused the UN of showing "heartless neglect, in practical terms, of the genocidal campaign being waged in Darfur."[14]

The alleged solution proposed by "African bias" critics was to open investigations in other regions, assuming a legal duty to respect ethnic, geographic, or gender diversity. Such opinions ignored a genocide and supported those African leaders committing crimes against Africans.

Besides, when ICC Prosecutor Fatou Bensouda, following her mandate, opened investigations outside Africa in Afghanistan or Palestine, she received a new type of criticism. She was affecting powerful states.

The Respect for the Office of the Prosecutor's Legal Mandate

All of the ICC Office of the Prosecutor's decisions on jurisdiction strictly followed the Rome Statute. In the specific cases, the chambers confirmed all *jus ad Curiam* decisions taken by the Office of the Prosecutor to trigger the court's jurisdiction.

In a paper written in 2003, Goldsmith and Krasner erroneously anticipated that the court would not respect legal limits and concluded, "ICC jurisdiction can only be expected to expand."[15] In 2014, David Bosco reviewed eleven years of the court's activities. He discovered the opposite outcome: "The Prosecutor and other Court officials have also sought not to expand the Court jurisdiction."[16]

David Scheffer, the head of the US delegation at the Rome Conference that led the opposition to the independent prosecutor authority, recognized that the Office of the Prosecutor "developed protocols . . . far more sophisticated than the totally unregulated political decisions by either a state party or the Security Council."[17] Furthermore, Scheffer acknowledges that following "the Security Council and states parties" referrals, the Office of the Prosecutor applied "legal standards" to review the political decisions.[18]

He considered in 2015 that "[f]ollowing a decade of practice, the concept of the Proprio Motu (independent) prosecutor at the International Criminal Court has achieved normality and acceptability, belying the prognostications preceding the conclusion of the Rome Statute in July 1998."[19]

The Relevance of the Rome Statute in the Prevention of Crimes in the Treaty Jurisdiction

The consistent application of the Rome Statute by the ICC did not provide consistent outcomes.

Other actors' efforts defined cooperation to collect evidence, national proceedings and arrest operations. National and international leaders decisions determined the value of the Rome Statute's contribution to preventing crimes.

It took some years, but the Rome Statute significantly contributed to stopping LRA's crimes in Northern Uganda. Uganda and the DRC were in conflict, but both are state parties and cooperated to face the LRA. Sudan, a state non-party, signed an agreement to execute the arrest warrants, and those decisions combined with the ICC arrest warrants removed the LRA from Northern Uganda. For the first time, concerned states and the UN Security Council discussed implementing the ICC's arrest warrants. During the *Juba talks,* those authorities developed a common approach to respecting justice while conducting peace negotiations. The most important outcome of the peace negotiations was the definite marginalization of the LRA in Uganda. More than one million internally displaced people returned to their homes. There are no more night commuters in Gulu.

Invisible Children promoted awareness about the arrest warrants against Joseph Kony, showing that an NGO led by young activists from San Diego could harmonize global efforts to implement the court's decisions.

Invisible Children initially opposed the ICC intervention in Uganda. Still, later it created a global collective action to control the LRA's crimes integrating young people worldwide, victims in Africa, the ICC, and the United States. It engaged with local communities in the DRC and Uganda, the AU, and the region's governments. It participated in the meetings at our office with civil society groups from all over the world. It lobbied the US Congress to pass the "Lord's Resistance Army Disarmament and Northern Uganda Recovery Act," promoting US military efforts to stop Joseph Kony. It also produced the video "Kony 2012," reaching 120 million viewers in merely six days, more than the court's outreach program could ever achieve.

In January 2013, following the Invisible Children campaign, the US Congress agreed to include the ICC in the "reward for justice program," offering financial incentives for the arrest of Kony. As a result, the LRA was drastically reduced, Dominic Ongwen was arrested and transferred to the ICC, and Joseph Kony was forced to hide in Sudan. Young people from the United States and Uganda were able to harmonize state efforts.

The 2013 and 2017 elections in Kenya were more peaceful than in 2007. The ICC was in the people and political elite's minds, but the ICC's contribution in controlling violence is hard to assess. Additionally, the influence of the US interest in Kenya's role in the war on terror in Somalia promoted support to Kenyan authorities.

CAR and the DRC situations show that national states are still the main actors in managing violence. In both situations, crimes continued to be committed.

The Rome Statute had enormous influence in Colombia and Guinea without the opening of an investigation. The Rome Statute was a critical constraint for different actors in Honduras, Georgia, Nigeria, and Israel.

The preliminary examinations of the Palestinian, Venezuelan, and UK personnel situations were closed during my tenure and reopened by ICC Chief Prosecutor Fatou Bensouda following new events. In particular, more crimes were committed in the Venezuela situation. Honduras and Korea were closed after my departure. Nigeria continued facing crimes under the ICC jurisdiction. And the ICC Chief Prosecutor Bensouda decided to open investigations in Georgia and Afghanistan, challenging Russia and the US interventions in both situations.

2. The War on Terror

President Bush improvised a reaction to 9/11, the most severe attack on US soil since Pearl Harbor. The US justice system already had indicted bin Laden, and Chapter 3 presented the options to arrest him and other Al Qaeda members. Lessons from previous failed US experiences, including Vietnam or the 1980s Soviet invasion of Afghanistan,[20] were ignored. Without a proper analysis, the United States launched the War on Terror.

The US military intervention removed the Taliban government in a few weeks, made no relevant efforts to arrest bin Laden, and, similar to what transpired with the Soviet involvement, promoted the insurgency.

The US Congress did not establish a time limit for the War on Terror. The 2001 authorization was used during the following decades by the Bush, Obama, Trump, and Biden administrations.

The US Congress did not define a specific battlefield. Different administrations invoked the authorization to conduct military operations in Afghanistan, but also to deploy and direct US forces in Syria, Iraq, Yemen, Pakistan, Somalia, Djibouti, the Horn of Africa, to engage terrorist groups "around the world" and "on the high seas."[21]

The War on Terror strategy trumped respect for national sovereignty. The different administrations considered that the United States had the right to conduct lethal operations even in a nation "which is not at war with the

US,"[22] when such a country was "'unwilling and unable' to take 'appropriate action' to address" international terrorism.[23]

The target could be a non-state organization or even an individual. The consistent State Department legal opinion is that the United States "has the authority under international law, and the responsibility to its citizens, to use force, including lethal force, to defend itself, including by targeting persons."[24]

US officers received the authority to decide who should be considered a target based on information supplied by unknown sources. The US courts decided they had no jurisdiction to review the standards to identify someone as an enemy combatant.[25]

In April 2016, the secretary of state's legal adviser considered that *it is not necessary as a matter of international law to reassess whether an armed attack is imminent prior to every subsequent action taken against that group, provided that hostilities have not ended.*[26]

Because the United States is not charging individuals with criminal responsibility, it "is not required to provide targets with legal process before the state may use lethal force."[27] A US federal appeals court ruled that prisoners at Guantánamo Bay are not entitled to due process.[28] Afghans had no legal protection against US operations in Afghanistan; their national courts are considered not to have jurisdiction over US soldiers.

The US Congress adopted a *jus ad Curiam* decision promoting the creation of an international court to prosecute Saddam Hussein in November 1998. Still, four years later, Congress replaced it with a *jus ad Bellum* decision. Congress authorized to "use the Armed Forces" against Iraq, circumventing the UN Security Council's authority. It wrongly assumed that Hussein had a stockpile of chemical weapons and planned to distribute them to terrorist organizations. Again, the US military intervention removed the regime but fueled the insurgency. Former members of Hussein's regime created terrorist organizations, including the Islamic State.

In 2009, President Obama had the opportunity to end the War on Terror. He received no alternative plans[29] but advice to shift the focus to Pakistan and away from Afghanistan. The mission should be targeting Al Qaeda and not the Taliban. No one suggested President Obama create a law enforcement intervention specially designed to face Al Qaeda, a non-government criminal network infiltrated in Pakistan. Chapter 17 presented a possible option to start a conversation.

After seven years of the War on Terror, the only new strategy that President Obama received in 2009 was the military counterinsurgency (COIN) manual developed under General David Petraeus and Marine General James Mattis's leadership and applied in Iraq throughout the "surge."

President Obama renewed the *jus ad Bellum* decision in Afghanistan, for a few years applied COIN, and then replaced it with a simple attrition tactic focused on killing "enemies." President Obama applied the policy of targeted killings even more vigorously than President Bush.[30] The War on Terror strategy to kill enemies became the "new normal."[31]

Marine General James Mattis, appointed by President Trump as secretary of defense in 2017, did not insist on going back to COIN. Instead, he suggested being even more aggressive. In his opinion, the strategy needed "to radically change from a slow war of attrition to one of 'annihilation.'"[32]

The 2001 authorization was limited to *those that planned, authorized, committed or aided the 9/11* terrorist attacks. The Bush and Obama administrations expanded this limitation into *forces associated* with Al Qaeda and the Taliban.

Jack Goldsmith considered that the Obama administration *normalized and legitimated* "all of the tenets of Bush preemption."[33]

On January 3, 2020, the Trump administration raised the enemy combatant standard scope and killed in Baghdad Iranian leader Qassem Soleimani and Iraqi Shiite militia leaders. The US strike was against the sovereign Iraqi government's will.[34]

A combination of high-tech attacks and proxy forces was tested in Libya and consolidated in Syria as the new permanent state of war. "Sponsorship of proxy groups has become a feature of nearly every global conflict."[35]

Using Proxy Forces

President Obama commissioned in 2012 an internal study analyzing CIA experiences supporting proxy forces. The study's only success story was the assistance provided to the *mujahedeen* rebels fighting Soviet troops in Afghanistan during the 1980s.[36]

Interestingly, such an operation, perceived as mission accomplished, endorsed Pakistan supporting the Taliban, promoted Osama bin Laden's leadership, and created Al Qaeda as a collateral result. The inability to learn from the past is shocking.

Ronan Farrow was a young US officer working in Afghanistan after 2009 and wrote about his conversation with the CIA handler who brokered some of the relationships with the mujahedeen and continued defending such an idea years later. "Let's be clear about one thing: moderates never won anything," he told Farrow. "Moderates. Don't. Win. Wars."[37]

Enforcing the law is the power of the moderates. The use of military forces did not provide a victory.

Afghanistan

The 9/11 terrorist attack killed 3,000 people. The reaction multiplied the loss of life fifty times. About 157,000 people have been killed in the Afghanistan war between 2001/2019. More than 43,000 of those killed have been civilians.[38]

The number of Western coalition soldiers killed in Afghanistan between 2001 and 2020 reached 3,594; and 2,450 were US soldiers.[39]

The war has also inflicted invisible wounds. In 2009, the Afghan Ministry of Public Health reported that two-thirds of Afghans suffer from mental health problems.[40]

At the end of his tenure, President Trump realized that the military strategy did not work, engaged in negotiations with Taliban leaders, accepted their conditions, and forced the Afghan government to release 5,000 Taliban soldiers in prison.[41]

On August 31, 2021, the United States concluded its military engagement in Afghanistan and the Taliban returned to power.

Iraq

No one knows with certainty how many people have been killed and wounded in Iraq since the 2003 United States invasion. However, we know that over 182,000 civilians have died from direct war-related violence caused by the US, its allies, the Iraqi military and police, and opposition forces from the time of the invasion through November 2018.[42]

Syria

Syria's population was around 21,500,000 in 2010, and ten years later, the conflict removed more than half of it. As of April 2018, over 5.6 million people have fled the country, and 6.6 million are internally displaced. Already in 2016, the UN estimated that 400,000 people had died as a result of the conflict.[43]

The September 2020 Syria's Commission of Inquiry report documented continuing human rights violations by nearly every fighting force controlling territory across the country. It also highlighted an increase in patterns of targeted abuse, such as assassinations, sexual and gender-based violence, and looting or appropriation of private property.[44]

The War on Terror Negative Deterrent Impact

Even those who considered that the War on Terror is respecting the law should agree that as a policy, it is counterproductive and is also detrimental to civilian protection.[45]

Chapter 18 presents the paradox: the War on Terror has a negative deterrent impact; it fuels "*support for the insurgency.*"[46] General McChrystal labeled as *insurgency math* the transformation of friends and family into terrorists produced by the killing strategy.

The NBER report confirmed "the 'revenge' effect"[47] identified by General McChrystal. A different study confirmed, "when Western forces inflicted harm, their support went down, and that of the Taliban went up."[48] Piazza and Choi compared data from 1970 to 2005 and concluded that states experience more terrorism after being subject to military interventions.[49] John Tirman described the phenomenon: "the US military was battling an insurgency that was to some important degree one of its own making, and the methods of battling it only intensified that very response of resistance."[50] Confirming his opinion, the number of Islamist extremist fighters in 2018 was 270 percent higher than 2001.[51] *In late 2001 Al Qaeda counted only a few hundred mujahidin, and IS did not exist at all.*[52]

Instead of galvanizing an international community around basic legal principles, the war model promoted people resorting to violence to defend their community. A British teacher felt "directly responsible for protecting and avenging my Muslim brothers and sisters"[53] and became a suicide bomber killing himself and six persons in London's tube. He was not alone. *More than 30,000 Muslims and converts to Islam from some 100 countries have gone to Syria and other jihadi theatres of war in recent years to join IS, Jabhat al Nusra and, to a lesser extent, other jihadist groups.*[54]

John Brennan, CIA head during the Obama administration, exposed a return to tribalism. "More people are shifting their allegiances away from the nation-state and toward sub-national groups and identities, leading societies that once embraced a national identity to fracture along ethnic and sectarian lines."[55]

The Conflict between Justice and the War on Terror

President Clinton opposed the adoption of the Rome Statute and ended up signing it on the last possible day, aiming to improve US ability to protect its personnel, not to ratify it.[56] The Congress adopted in August 2002 the American Service Members Protection Act (ASPA) to "ensure that our soldiers and government officials are not exposed to the prospect of politicized prosecutions and investigations."[57] ASPA prohibited US cooperation with the ICC, including funding or sharing classified information. It authorized the president to take any necessary action to rescue US personnel handed over to the ICC.

US Permanent Representative John D. Negroponte stated: "*The American system of justice can be trusted to punish crimes, including war crimes or crimes against humanity, committed by an American—and we pledge to do so.*"[58]

The abuse of prisoners in Abu Ghraib challenged such a commitment. Secretary of Defense Donald Rumsfeld blamed low-ranking officers and announced further inquiries: "Watch how a democracy deals with wrongdoing."[59] But the US fulfilled neither Ambassador Negroponte's promise nor Rumsfeld's forecast.

President Obama's adoption of the *War on Terror* policy and his interest to keep a working relationship with the Republican Party inclined his administration to protect those involved in torture and disappearance. His administration confronted Congress members investigating torture methods, the media request for information, and people committed to doing justice.

President Trump stretched the protection policy showing opposition to any judicial investigation, including the US military justice system. He pardoned two Army Officers charged with war crimes and restored a Navy SEAL officer's rank previously acquitted by a military jury on all but a minor count. At a November 2019 political rally, Trump brought two of them on stage, claiming that he had "stuck up for three great warriors against the deep state."[60]

The ICC investigation in Afghanistan increased the conflict with the United States. The Trump administration revoked the ICC prosecutor visa in April 2019 and after, in September 2020, "designated" the prosecutor "for having directly engaged in an effort to investigate US personnel."

Beyond the different presidents' personalities, there is a constant: US strategy to address international terrorism is in open confrontation with any independent judicial scrutiny, whether national or international. Neither a high-ranking officer nor a member of the US administration was prosecuted for the policy of torture adopted. The involvement of the US troops in Iraq and Syria prevented any possibility to refer those situations to the ICC.

The Interaction between the War on Terror and the ICC in Different Situations

The War on Terror created a permanent interest influencing US decisions worldwide and transforming into enemies those opposing it. The US 2002 National Defense Strategy exposed the International Criminal Court as a fundamental constraint that should be faced.[61] The US National Security Strategy set out by President Obama in 2010 presented self-interest as an explicit policy: "[W]e are supporting the ICC's prosecution of those cases that advance US interests and values."[62]

The LRA was considered a terrorist group, promoting US support to Uganda and the ICC investigation. As mentioned, Congress adopted the "Lord's Resistance Army Disarmament and Northern Uganda Recovery Act of 2009" facilitated by Invisible Children, and the Obama administration made efforts to arrest Joseph Kony.

President Bush himself became the biggest supporter of the arrest warrant against President Bashir. The goal of obtaining Sudan's support in the War on Terror contributed to the absence of efforts to implement the arrest warrant against President Bashir during the Obama administration.

However, Gaddafi's assistance in the War on Terror did not stop the United States from supporting the adoption of *jus ad Curiam* and *jus ad Bellum* decisions at the UN Security Council to face Libya's situation. The United

States supported the ICC investigation in Kenya and, at the same time, the goal of obtaining Kenya's military involvement to control Islamic groups in Somalia promoted support to President Kenyatta.

Chief Prosecutor Fatou Bensouda received a US sanction, applied to drug dealers and terrorists, for investigating the same crimes of torture that President Obama and the US Senate recognized.

In 1945, Justice Jackson alerted about the forever war impact. Two weeks before his appointment to lead efforts at Nuremberg, Justice Jackson spoke at Washington, DC. He highlighted, "It ought to be clear by this time that personal freedom, at least of the kind and degree we have known in this country, is inconsistent with the necessities of total war and incompatible with a state of militarization in readiness for one. Awareness of the effect of war on our fundamental law should bring home to our people the imperative and practical nature of our striving for a rule of law among the nations."[63]

Jackson foresaw the NSA interference with US. citizens' communications, the increased militarization of the domestic police activities, and the attacks against the US constitutional system.

3. UN Security Council

World War II winners led the adoption of the UN Charter, transforming their military and political power into legal authority. The law conferred them a permanent seat at the UN Security Council and veto power. Any council decision must respect the interests of the five permanent members. They are legally authorized to impose their will over the other 188 UN members.

Consequently, the US hostility against ICC eliminated any expectation that the court would ever achieve a constructive relationship with the UN Security Council. Besides, China's policy does not support the intervention of international criminal justice; instead, it promotes stability and respect for sovereignty. Russia, was a Rome Statute supporter until November 2016, when the ICC scrutinized its intervention in Georgia and the Ukrainian conflict. France and the United Kingdom, the only permanent members who are also state parties, protected the Rome Statute project and mobilized the council's non-permanent members to impose their will in referring Darfur and Libya.

On June 30, 2002, while the Bush administration was planning the Iraq intervention, precisely one day before the ICC jurisdiction came into effect, the

United States vetoed a resolution to extend the UN Mission in Bosnia and Herzegovina. The United States was demanding ICC immunity to non-state parties' staff. In agreement with the United Kingdom, the French ambassador suggested Article 16 as a solution to preemptively protect US personnel while respecting the statute's legal architecture.

The council, by consensus, adopted Resolution 1422/2002 under Article 16 of the Rome Statute, suspending ICC investigations against UN Peacekeepers belonging to states non-parties of the Rome Statute. One year later, and four days before my swearing in, it was renewed by Resolution 1497/2003. This time France, Germany, and Syria abstained. The United States expressed its intention to renew such a decision for further twelve-month periods "for as long as might be necessary."[64] After the ICC became operational and the Abu Ghraib scandal, there was no support to reintroduce an Article 16 decision protecting states' non-parties personnel.

The council precedents are influential, but they are not limiting new and different agreements. For instance, after its initial opposition to the Iraq military intervention in 2003, the UN Security Council adjusted to the post-invasion situation, focused on humanitarian assistance, and ended up recognizing the occupation. Each council decision is the consequence of an agreement between its members' interests.

Following a UK initiative, the United States accepted some support for ICC activities in DRC, a country deeply affected by a regional war. In October 2004, the council expanded the MONUC mandate to include support implementing the ICC arrest warrants.[65]

Unexpectedly and against the US and China's wishes, in March 2005, the UN Security Council made a *jus ad Curiam* decision and referred the Darfur situation to the ICC. How did it happen? There was not a single decision maker. *The people who participate in the events* made a difference.

Nine of the UN Security Council's fifteen members were states parties of the Rome Statute committed to doing justice for atrocity crimes. France UN permanent representative at New York, Ambassador Jean-Marc de la Sablière, led the "ICC-9" and imposed the Darfur referral.

The academic debates about UN Security Council's reforms focused on including new permanent members do not include how the Rome Statute adoption changed the council's dynamic.

In April 2006, the council discussed plans to implement the International Criminal Court's arrest warrants against LRA's leaders in DRC and Sudan. The council did not strengthen the military capacity of the UN peacekeeping missions but supported the Juba talks frame, remained involved in the negotiations with the LRA, and supported the ICC intervention.

In December 2006, to respect the council's authority to suspend our investigations, I announced our intentions to request the first arrest warrants during our briefing on Darfur. But the council was not prepared to implement them.

I met with a UN permanent representative of a state party who wanted to discuss how to take advantage of our intervention to solve the Darfur conflict. I suggested putting pressure on the Sudan government to remove and jail Minister Harun, sending a clear message that the Darfur crimes had to stop.

The ambassador said, "It is a great idea, but we don't know how to do something like that. We have two strategies: bombing or nothing. We threaten with the bombing, and as soon they start a negotiation, we do nothing." During the meeting, I was thinking that the ambassador was joking. Later, I learned that he was describing reality. The council considers ICC just as a tool to promote negotiations.

During my briefing in December 2007, I warned the UN Security Council that we would request new arrest warrants. I confirmed my decision in my briefing to the council in June 2008. My announcement triggered a series of political reactions exposing states' reluctance to confront a head of state.

In the following years, I confirmed that the agreement between the UN Security Council members to adopt a *jus ad Curiam* decision did not include support for the subsequent implementation of the *jus in Curiae* decisions, particularly the arrest warrants' enforcement.

In February 2011, following the Darfur precedent's language, the UN Security Council referred the Libya situation to the ICC by consensus. France and the United Kingdom drafted a resolution identical to the Darfur referral. The Obama administration could not oppose the language previously accepted by the Bush administration.

The Arab League supported the referral, and the Libyan representatives requested it. South Africa, representing the AU, endorsed the Libyan ambassador's demands, facilitating India and China's positive vote.

In March 2011, the council authorized the military intervention in Libya. Germany, India, and Brazil, candidates to be permanent members, plus China and Russia abstained. The same month, at the request of ECOWAS' heads of state, the UN Security Council authorized the UN mission "to use all necessary means" to protect civilians in Côte d'Ivoire while noting the ICC intervention.[66] The Council kept mentioning in its resolutions the advances of the ICC intervention in Côte d'Ivoire."

The council refused to discuss Article 16 in CAR and transferred to the Assembly of States Parties a similar Kenya's request. The Bush administration threatened to veto an Article 16 decision in favor of President Bashir. Under Gaddafi's leadership, AU invoked such council's refusal to forbid cooperation with ICC concerning the arrest of a head of state.

In my last briefing to the council, on June 5, 2012, states recognized the ICC's work and openly presented their different approaches to enforce the court decisions in Darfur.

The United States proposed political isolation. It "urged all States to refrain from providing political or financial support to the Sudanese suspects subject to ICC arrest warrants and to bring diplomatic pressure to bear on States that invite or host these individuals."

The US representative concluded, "Continued impunity and a lack of accountability for heinous crimes fuel resentment, reprisals, and conflict in Darfur." The US representative could condemn impunity at the council's room while his country negotiated with the Bashir administration in Khartoum.

Russia considered justice a matter of time. It "supports the work of the ICC in ensuring the irreversibility of sanctions for the most grievous crimes that trouble the whole of the international community."

South Africa supported the court but stated that "the Council should utilize the Court as a tool to promote political dialogue in the search for peace and justice in Darfur."

And China emphasized the priority of political agreements: *"We hope that the efforts of the ICC on the issue of Darfur will facilitate the political settlement of the question of Darfur."*[67]

The debates presented the council's political role and the multiple legal systems working in parallel. The council members could choose the legal system that would apply.

The council did not establish obligations to non-states parties to implement the arrest warrants in Darfur nor Libya and could not adopt a common policy to implement them. The ICC pre-trial chamber did not recognize the council's interest in political negotiations rather than justice. It ruled in the Bashir case:

When the Security Council, acting under Chapter VII of the UN Charter, refers a situation to the Court as constituting a threat to international peace and security, it is expected that the Council would respond by way of taking such measures which are considered appropriate. Otherwise, if there is no follow-up action on the part of the Security Council, any referral by the Council to the ICC under Chapter VII would never achieve its ultimate goal, namely, to put an end to impunity. Accordingly, any such referral would become futile.[68]

I invited Samantha Power, former US permanent representative before the UN, as a guest speaker to my class at Harvard, and she explained the council's dynamic. Each resolution adopted by the council requires enormous efforts to harmonize different interests. A new council resolution providing a mechanism to enforce the arrest warrants in Darfur in 2009 would have required a further negotiation to rearrange the various political interests. It was not possible.

Poker is a suitable metaphor to describe the UN Security Council dynamic. The UN charter and poker rules do not change, but the players receive different cards on each hand, so the outcomes vary. Besides, five players at the council have the authority to cancel the hands when they don't like their cards. Still, the fifteen players continue playing, and they can influence others without showing their cards.

And yet the council has global power on *jus ad Bellum* and *jus ad Curiam*. In each situation, the council's members choose the legal system to apply: the UN Security Council could confer power to states to use force and to international prosecutors and judges to conduct criminal proceedings or none of both options. The council could define the international criminal justice temporal and territorial jurisdiction and who should execute the arrest warrants.

The UN Security Council authorized international criminal justice in Darfur and Libya. Acting under its legal authority, the council refused to send to the ICC's the Iraq, Israel, Syria, and Korea situations. It also authorized the War on Terror against the Islamic State in Syria.

On October 17, 2012, the Council had a meeting on *"Peace and Justice, with a special focus on the role of the International Criminal Court."* The UN press release said that *"[w]hen the floor was opened for discussion, many of the nearly 60 speakers participating in the meeting applauded the achievements of the International Criminal Court and its relationship with the Council."*[69]

Whenever there is a political agreement, the council can now rely on a permanent and independent International Criminal Court.

Notes

1. Review Conference of the Rome Statute, Stocktaking of international criminal justice, Complementarity ¶ 4, RC/11 Annex V (c). ICC-ASP/12/S/012 (Apr. 12, 2013).
2. KATHRYN SIKKINK, EVIDENCE FOR HOPE 17 (Kindle ed. 2017).
3. Juan Mendez, *Justice and Prevention, in* THE INTERNATIONAL CRIMINAL COURT AND COMPLEMENTARITY: FROM THEORY TO PRACTICE 33, 36 (Kindle ed. 2011).
4. **Sam Dealey,** *Omar al-Bashir: Sudan's Wanted Man,* TIME (Aug. **13, 2009),** http://content.time.com/time/world/article/0,8599,1916107,00.html.
5. *Id.*
6. *Id.*
7. David Bosco, *Why Is the International Criminal Court picking only on Africa?,* THE WASHINGTON POST (March 29, 2013), https://www.washingtonpost.com/opinions/why-is-the-international-criminal-court-picking-only-on-africa/2013/03/29/cb9bf5da-96f7-11e2-97cd-3d8c1afe4f0f_story.html
8. *Arrest warrant draws Sudan scorn,* BBC **(March 5, 2009)** http://news.bbc.co.uk/1/hi/world/africa/7924982.stm
9. O. Emmanuel & A. Hope. (2018). *The Contentious Relationship between Africa and the International Criminal Court (ICC),* J. L. & CONFLICT RESOLUTION, 10(3), 19–31.
10. Karen Allen, *Is This the End of the International Criminal Court?,* BBC NEWS (Oct. 24, 2016), http://www.bbc.com/news/world-africa-37750978; and referred the possible ICC "collapse." Milton Nkosi, *What South Africa Leaving the International Criminal Court Would Mean,* BBC NEWS (Oct. 14, 2015), http://www.bbc.co.uk/news/world-africa-34509342.
11. Scott Baldauf, *Sudan 101: Is the Darfur Conflict a Fight between Arabs and Africans?,* THE CHRISTIAN SCIENCE MONITOR (Apr. 26, 2010), https://www.csmonitor.com/World/Africa/2010/0426/Sudan-101-Is-the-Darfur-conflict-a-fight-between-Arabs-and-Africans.
12. MAXIMO LANGER & DAVID ALAN SKLANSKY, PROSECUTORS AND DEMOCRACY: A CROSS-NATIONAL STUDY (ASCL Studies in Comparative Law) (2017).
13. *Desmond Tutu, Will Africa Let Sudan Off the Hook?,* THE NEW YORK TIMES (March 2, 2009), https://www.nytimes.com/2009/03/03/opinion/03tutu.html
14. *UN Actions to End Darfur 'Genocide' Too Little, Too Late – Saint Vincent Leader,* UN NEWS (September 28, 2007), https://news.un.org/en/story/2007/09/233682-un-actions-end-darfur-genocide-too-little-too-late-saint-vincent-leader
15. Jack Goldsmith & Stephen D. Krasner, *The Limits of Idealism,* 132 DAEDALUS 47, 54 (2003).
16. DAVID BOSCO, ROUGH JUSTICE, THE INTERNATIONAL CRIMINAL COURT IN A WORLD OF POWER POLITICS 185 (Kindle ed. 2014).

17. *Id.*

18. *Id.*

19. David Scheffer, *False Alarm about the* Proprio Motu *Prosecutor, in* THE FIRST GLOBAL PROSECUTOR: PROMISE AND CONSTRAINTS (LAW, MEANING AND VIOLENCE) 29, 29 (Martha Minow, C. Core True-Frost et al. eds., Kindle ed. 2015).

20. UNITED STATES ARMY, LESSONS FROM THE WAR IN AFGHANISTAN 2 (Army Department Declassification Release, 1989), *available at* https://nsarchive2.gwu.edu/NSAEBB/NSAEBB57/us11.pdf.

21. THE PRESIDENT OF THE UNITED STATES, REPORT ON THE LEGAL AND POLICY FRAMEWORKS GUIDING THE UNITED STATES' USE OF MILITARY FORCE AND RELATED NATIONAL SECURITY OPERATIONS (2016).

22. JACK GOLDSMITH, POWER AND CONSTRAINT: THE ACCOUNTABLE PRESIDENCY AFTER 9/11 13–15 (Kindle ed. 2012). *See Civilian Casualties & Collateral Damage*, LAWFARE, https://www.lawfareblog.com/civilian-casualties-collateral-damage (last visited Mar. 10, 2020).

23. Benjamin Wittes, *State Department Legal Adviser Brian Egan's Speech at ASIL*, LAWFARE (Apr. 8, 2016, 8:36 AM), https://www.lawfareblog.com/state-department-legal-adviser-brian-egans-speech-asil. *See also* ROSA BROOKS, HOW EVERYTHING BECAME WAR AND THE MILITARY BECAME EVERYTHING: TALES FROM THE PENTAGON 285 (Kindle ed. 2016).

24. Harold Hongju Koh, Legal Adviser at the US Department of State, Speech at the Annual Meeting of the American Society of International Law (Mar. 25, 2010), *available at* https://www.state.gov/documents/organization/179305.pdf

25. OWEN FISS & TREVOR SUTTON, A WAR LIKE NO OTHER: THE CONSTITUTION IN A TIME OF TERROR 264–65 (Kindle ed. 2004).

26. Benjamin Wittes, *State Department Legal Adviser Brian Egan's Speech at ASIL*, LAWFARE (Apr. 8, 2016, 8:36 AM), https://www.lawfareblog.com/state-department-legal-adviser-brian-egans-speech-asil.

27. Harold Hongju Koh, Legal Adviser at the US Department of State, Speech at the Annual Meeting of the American Society of International Law (Mar. 25, 2010), *available at* https://www.state.gov/documents/organization/179305.pdf.

28. Carol Rosenberg, *Court Rules Guantánamo Detainees Are Not Entitled to Due Process*, N.Y. TIMES (Sept. 2, 2020), https://www.nytimes.com/2020/09/02/us/politics/guantanamo-detainees-due-process.html.

29. "The Obama Administration came to power heralding a radical shift of approach by appearing to have promptly abandoned the 'war on terror' epithet. Media reports that the 'war on terror' was dead were, however, themselves short-lived. In his national security remarks on May 21, 2009, President Obama stated: 'Now let me be clear. We are indeed at war with al Qaeda and its affiliates.'" HELEN DUFFY, THE "WAR ON TERROR" AND THE FRAMEWORK OF INTERNATIONAL LAW 389 (Kindle ed. 2015).

30. JACK GOLDSMITH, POWER AND CONSTRAINT: THE ACCOUNTABLE PRESIDENCY AFTER 9/11 13–15 (Kindle ed. 2012). *See Civilian Casualties & Collateral Damage*, LAWFARE, https://www.lawfareblog.com/civilian-casualties-collateral-damage (last visited Mar. 10, 2020).

31. *Establishing a New Normal. National Security, Civil Liberties, and Human Rights under the Obama Administration, An 18-month Review*, AM. CIVIL LIBERTIES UNION (July 2010), *available at* https://www.aclu.org/sites/default/files/field_document/Establ ishingNewNormal.pdf.

32. BOB WOODWARD, RAGE 4 (Kindle ed. 2020).

33. Jack Goldsmith, *Obama's Embrace of Bush's Preemption Doctrine*, LAWFARE (Apr. 6, 2016, 3:30 PM), https://www.lawfareblog.com/obamas-embrace-bushs-preempt ion-doctrine. Daniel Bethlehem, the principal legal adviser of the UK Foreign & Commonwealth Office from May 2006 to May 2011 challenged Goldsmith's analysis. Daniel Bethlehem, *Not by Any Other Name: A Response to Jack Goldsmith on Obama's Imminence*, LAWFARE (Apr. 7, 2016, 1:51 PM), https://www.lawfareblog.com/not-any-other-name-response-jack-goldsmith-obamas-imminence.

34. Ryan Goodman & Steve Vladeck, *Why the 2002 AUMF Does Not Apply to Iran*, JUST SECURITY (Jan. 9, 2020), https://www.justsecurity.org/67993/why-the-2002-aumf-does-not-apply-to-iran/.

35. Brittany Benotwiz & Tommy Ross, *Time to Get a Handle on America's Conduct on Proxy Warfare*, LAWFARE (Apr. 9, 2020, 11:21 AM), https://www.lawfareblog.com/ time-get-handle-americas-conduct-proxy-warfare.

36. Mike Mazzetti, *C.I.A. Study of Covert Aid Fueled Skepticism about Helping Syrian Rebels*, N.Y. TIMES (Oct. 15, 2014), https://www.nytimes.com/2014/10/15/us/politics/ cia-study-says-arming-rebels-seldom-works.html. See also: Obama-commissioned study reported that the outcome of aiding insurgents is rarely democracy. MICHAEL MCFAUL, FROM COLD WAR TO HOT PEACE: AN AMERICAN AMBASSADOR IN PUTIN'S RUSSIA 331–32 (Kindle ed. 2018).

37. RONAN FARROW, WAR ON PEACE: THE END OF DIPLOMACY AND THE DECLINE OF AMERICAN INFLUENCE 171 (Kindle ed. 2018)

38. *Afghan Civilians*, COSTS OF WAR WATSON INST. INT'L & PUB. AFF. BROWN UNIV., https://watson.brown.edu/costsofwar/costs/human/civilians/afghan (last updated Jan. 2020).

39. Statista Research Dep't, *Number of Fatalities among Western Coalition Soldiers Involved in the Execution of Operation Enduring Freedom from 2001 to 2020*, STATISTA (Feb. 2, 2021), https://www.statista.com/statistics/262894/western-coalition-soldi ers-killed-in-afghanistan/.

40. *Afghan Civilians*, COSTS OF WAR WATSON INST. INT'L & PUB. AFF. BROWN UNIV., https://watson.brown.edu/costsofwar/costs/human/civilians/afghan (last updated Jan. 2020).

41. Mujib Mashal & Fatima Faizi, *Afghanistan to Release Last Taliban Prisoners, Removing Final Hurdle to Talks*, N.Y. TIMES (August 9, 2020), https://www.nytimes.com/2020/ 08/09/world/asia/afghanistan-taliban-prisoners-peace-talks.html

42. *Iraqi Civilians*, COSTS OF WAR WATSON INST. INT'L & PUB. AFF. BROWN UNIV., https:// watson.brown.edu/costsofwar/costs/human/civilians/iraqi (last updated Nov. 2018).

43. *Independent International Commission of Inquiry on the Syrian Arab Republic*, UN HUMAN RIGHTS COUNCIL, https://www.ohchr.org/EN/HRBodies/HRC/IICISyria/ Pages/AboutCoI.aspx (last visited Feb. 18, 2021).

44. *Syria: Bombshell Report Reveals "No Clean Hands" as Horrific Rights Violations Continue*, UN NEWS (Sept. 15, 2020), https://news.un.org/en/story/2020/09/1072 402. See the full report: Report of the Ind. Int'l Comm. of Inquiry on the Syrian Arab Republic, Human Rights Council, 45th Sess. Sept. 14—Oct. 2, 2020, U.N. Doc. A/HC/45/31 (Aug. 14, 2020), *available at* https://undocs.org/A/HRC/45/31.

45. See a comprehensive legal analysis of many US policies in HELEN DUFFY, THE "WAR ON TERROR" AND THE FRAMEWORK OF INTERNATIONAL LAW (Kindle ed. 2015).

46. Ganesh Sitarama, *Counterinsurgency, the War on Terror, and the Laws of War*, 95 VA. L. REV. 1745, 1747 (2009).

47. Luke N. Condra et al., *The Effect of Civilian Casualties in Afghanistan and Iraq* (Nat'l Bureau of Econ. Research, Working Paper 16152, 2011).

48. LAWRENCE FREEDMAN, THE FUTURE OF WAR 207 (Kindle ed. 2017) (ebook) (quoting Jason Lyall, Graeme Blair, & Kosuke Imai, *Explaining Support for Combatants during Wartime: A Survey Experiment in Afghanistan*, AMERICAN POLITICAL SCIENCE REVIEW 107(4) (2013)).

49. James Piazza & Seung-Whan Choi, *International Military Interventions and Transnational Terrorist Backlash*, 62 INT'L STUD. Q. 686, 686 (2018).

50. JOHN TIRMAN, THE DEATHS OF OTHERS (Kindle ed. 2011)(ebook).

51. Eirc Rosand & Alistar Millar, *Nearly 20 Years Later: It's Time to Reset Our Approach to Countering Terrorism*, JUST SECURITY (Nov. 14, 2019), https://www.justsecurity.org/67270/nearly-20-years-later-its-time-to-reset-our-approach-to-countering-terrorism/.

52. Alex P. Schmid, *Public Opinion Survey Data to Measure Sympathy and Support for Islamist Terrorism: A Look at Muslim Opinions on Al Qaeda and IS* 6 (Int'l Cent. for Counter-Terrorism, The Hague, ICCT Research paper Feb. 2017), *available at* https://icct.nl/app/uploads/2017/02/ICCT-Schmid-Muslim-Opinion-Polls-Jan2017-1.pdf..

53. *London bomber: Text in Full*, BBC NEWS (Sept. 1, 2005, 10:01 PM), http://news.bbc.co.uk/2/hi/uk/4206800.stm.

54. Alex P. Schmid, *Public Opinion Survey Data to Measure Sympathy and Support for Islamist Terrorism: A Look at Muslim Opinions on Al Qaeda and IS* 6 (Int'l Cent. for Counter-Terrorism, The Hague, ICCT Research paper Feb. 2017), *available at* https://icct.nl/app/uploads/2017/02/ICCT-Schmid-Muslim-Opinion-Polls-Jan2017-1.pdf.

55. John. O. Brennan, *John Brennan on Transnational Threats to Global Security*, COUNCIL ON FOREIGN RELATIONS (June 29, 2016), https://www.cfr.org/event/john-brennan-transnational-threats-global-security.

56. "[W]e are not abandoning our concerns about significant flaws in the treaty. In particular, we are concerned that when the court comes into existence, it will not only exercise authority over personnel of states that have ratified the treaty but also claim jurisdiction over personnel of states that have not. With signature, however, we will be in a position to influence the evolution of the court. Without signature, we will not." William J. Clinton, *Statement on the Rome Treaty on the International Criminal Court*, WHITE HOUSE (Dec. 31, 2000), https://clintonwhitehouse4.archives.gov/library/hot_releases/December_31_2000.html.

57. Marc Grossman, Under Secretary of State for Political Affairs, Address delivered at Center for Strategic and International Studies (May 6, 2002).

58. John. D. Negroponte, US Permanent Representative to the United Nations, Remarks at stakeout following UN Security Council vote on Resolution 1422, including text explanation of vote (July 12, 2002).

59. David Stout, *Rumsfeld Offers Apology for Abuse of Iraqi Prisoners*, N.Y. TIMES (May 7, 2004), https://www.nytimes.com/2004/05/07/politics/rumsfeld-offers-apology-for-abuse-of-iraqi-prisoners.html.

60. Maggie Haberman, *Trump Brings 2 Officers He Cleared of War Crimes Onstage at Fund-Raiser*, N.Y. TIMES (Dec. 8, 2019), https://www.nytimes.com/2019/12/08/us/politics/trump-war-crimes-pardons.html.

61. THE WHITE HOUSE, 2002 NATIONAL SECURITY STRATEGY OF THE UNITED STATES OF AMERICA (Sept. 17, 2002).

62. THE WHITE HOUSE, UNITED STATES NATIONAL SECURITY STRATEGY (May 2010),

63. The Rule of Law Among Nations By Justice Robert H. Jackson, Associate Justice, Supreme Court of the United States, Washington, D.C. April 13, 1945. Article originally appeared at 31 ABAJ 290 (1945) *Versions of this Jackson speech were published in the Proceedings of the ASIL 10-18, in 31 American Bar Association Journal 290-94 (June 1945)*

64. Press Release, Security Council, Security Council Requests One-Year Extension of UN Peacekeeper Immunity from International Criminal Court, U.N. Press Release SC/7789 (June 12, 2003).

65. The UN Security Council adopted Resolution 1565, authorizing MONUC "to ensure that those responsible for serious violations of human rights and international humanitarian law are brought to justice." Press Release, Security Council, Security Council extends Democratic Republic of Congo mission until 31 March 2005, authorizes additional 5,900 troops, police, U.N. Press Release SC/8203 (Oct. 1, 2004).

66. S.C. Res. 1975, U.N. Doc. S/RES/1975 (Mar. 30, 2011).

67. UN SCOR 57th Sess., 6778th mtg., at 19 U.N. Doc. S/PV.6778 (June 5, 2012).

68. Prosecutor v. Omar Hassan Ahmad Al Bashir, IC-02/05-01/09, Decision on the Non-compliance of the Republic of Chad with the Cooperation Requests Issued by the Court Regarding the Arrest and Surrender of Omar Hassan Ahmad Al-Bashir ¶ 22 (Mar. 26, 2013), https://www.icc-cpi.int/CourtRecords/CR2013_02245.PDF.

69. Press Release, Security Council, Secretary-General Hails International Criminal Court as Centerpiece of "New Age of Accountability," Urges Enhanced Cooperation with Security Council, U.N. Press Release SC/10793 (Oct. 17, 2012).

Final Observations

I lived under a dictatorship that abducted and killed thousands of citizens; as the ICC prosecutor, I examined the most serious conflicts of the twenty-first century. I learned that legal designs are a matter of life or death, and such a characterization is not a metaphor.

Presenting my entire ICC experience as a single *case study* helps to perceive the real functioning of a "fragmented" international legal system.[1]

The operational *international legal order* includes multiple subsystems working simultaneously, *conferring power* to various authorities, and prescribing different and sometimes opposite solutions to the same case. As mentioned, quoting French Professor Mireille Delmas-Marty, "*these are indeed legal, and therefore normative, interactions.*"[2] There is no chaos just complexity.

The International Law Commission's report on *Fragmentation* made a legal design analysis and described the evolution "from a world fragmented into sovereign States," integrated under the UN Security Council on international peace and security "to a world fragmented into specialized 'regimes.' "[3]

The Rome Statute and the War on Terror are the twenty-first-century "specialized regimes" to manage international crimes and terrorism. They are two antagonistic legal models *conferring power* to different authorities and influencing states and the UN Security Council decisions.

Sovereign state parties of the Rome Statute created an international criminal justice system conferring power to the ICC prosecutor to trigger investigations in their territory or against their personnel if they failed to act genuinely.

They reduced their sovereignty to "to put an end to impunity for the perpetrators" of "the most serious crimes of concern to the international community as a whole" to "contribute to their prevention."

Instead, the United States claimed the sovereign right to restrict the sovereignty[4] of a nation "not at war with the US."[5] US officers received the authority to decide when a country was " 'unwilling and unable' to take 'appropriate action' to address" international terrorism.[6]

The US president conferred power to the CIA and the armed forces to kill people *abroad* without providing "targets with legal process before the state may use lethal force." The presidents followed the 2001 congressional authorization to use the armed forces "to protect United States citizens at home and abroad." Most of the War on Terror victims *abroad* are not US citizens and are not covered by the US Constitution; they are aliens living in foreign countries, and their suffering is ignored.[7] The War on Terror legal design is a matter of life protection for US citizens and death for aliens living in foreign countries.

The ongoing War on Terror expands the self-defense authorized by the UN Charter, affecting basic national and international principles, like respect for sovereignty, and the state monopoly of violence.

The War on Terror is a critical obstacle for national and international justice.

The Blind Spot

The book depicts an issue in a consequential blind spot: the results of the normative conflicts. The report on Fragmentation concluded: "A key point made in this study is that normative conflict is endemic to international law." Different actors received the authority to support, attack, or control international criminal justice; and, that is my point: they do it following norms.

The crimes examined during my tenure were not the direct consequence of individual cruelty or the lack of respect for the norms. The leaders' commands triggered institutions to act. Perpetrators of massive atrocities followed instructions and rules, and diplomats and intelligence services worked to consecrate their impunity.

Due obedience is not a legal excuse, but Stanley Milgram's experiment showed that the authorities could influence the behavior of the subordinates more effectively than any threat of prosecution.[8]

Different authorities select the norms to apply. Chapter 5 described how *power-conferring* norms grant specific individuals the right *to participate in the events* and decide the solution for a case. The ICC received a justice mandate, but some state authorities ordered to commit or to cover up international crimes

While our duty as prosecutors was to open investigations to punish crimes, public officers were mandated to imprison or torture dissidents, as allegedly happened in a state party like Venezuela (Chapter 12).

Similarly, the Sudanese government instructed the entire state apparatus to commit Darfur's crimes. Security and armed forces followed very well-planned orders and respected chains of command. Ambassadors promoted cover-ups and political negotiations. Intelligence operations distracted the attention and influenced the international media, first denying the genocide, then attributing the attacks to *Janjaweed* militias, and later alleging an ICC's *African bias.*

Obstructing justice would be regarded as a crime at the national level. President Richard Nixon had to resign when charged with obstruction of justice and abuse of power after the Watergate scandal. Still, political leaders have the legal authority to interfere with criminal justice in the international field and to instruct diplomats and intelligence agencies to do it.

The Bush administration opposed the International Criminal Court as a formal policy.[9] President Obama did not try to enforce the arrest warrants against President Bashir instead his administration used them as leverage to negotiate cooperation on the War on Terror and to consolidate the South of Sudan's independence.

In the Syrian conflict, Switzerland, supported by fifty-seven states, promoted a collective effort to end impunity but, first the United States, and after Russia and China opposed to refer the situation to the ICC (see Chapter 22).

The Obama administration also forced the release of a CIA member arrested in Panama at the request of the Italian justice accused of abducting a terrorist suspect in Milan. President Trump *designated* the ICC prosecutor for planning to investigate tortures committed by US personnel in Afghanistan, crimes that Congress recognized. Chapter 18 mentions these and more examples. Presidents Bush, Obama and Trump; and Russian and Chinese leaders acted within their normative frame. In a legal sense, they did not *abuse power.*

One of the biggest twenty-first century's life-or-death problems is not a matter of villains or heroes; rather, it is the consequence of a fragmented and contradictory international legal design.

The Contradictions of a Fragmented Global Legal System

The attack at Kunduz Hospital is an excellent example of the problem I present in these final pages. The United States launched the War on Terror in

Afghanistan in 2001. In 2009 President Obama confirmed the *jus ad Bellum* decision in Afghanistan.

Following such a decision, in October 2015, US personnel fired 211 shells on the Kunduz Hospital operated by *Médecins Sans Frontières* (Doctors Without Borders), killing forty-two persons. The US officers were following instructions, but they could have been involved in the commission of war crimes while doing so.

The United States investigated sixteen US personnel and concluded that some of them "arbitrarily" chose a target, failed to "distinguish between combatants or civilians," and engaged in a "facially disproportionate" attack. Still, the only sanctions were either administrative or disciplinary.[10] *Médecins Sans Frontières* made a fundamental point: "We were not satisfied that an independent, impartial investigation could be carried out by the parties involved."[11] As mentioned in Chapter 18, in 1873, the ICRC cofounder noted that states at war have no interest in punishing crimes committed by their own soldiers.[12]

During his Nobel lecture in 2009, President Obama affirmed the US discretionary authority to adopt *jus ad Bellum* decisions while promising strict respect for *jus in Bello* (see Chapter 17).[13] But Chapter 18 shows the Bush, Obama, and Trump administrations protecting the US personnel involved in crimes in Afghanistan from national and international investigations. Loyalty is the supreme value during a fight.

The blind spot conceals the political leader's decisions. Naz K. Modirzadeh. discussing with Ryan Goodman, made the point, "A debate over the law of armed conflict should not eclipse arguments about the legality of the use of force. Indeed, the most important concern in this domain . . . It's that the US will go to war in more and more places without a sufficient justification."[14]

The authorization to use military force and its consequences should be the central debate on the *War on Terror*. The vast majority of those many hundred thousand killed by different parties in Iraq and Afghanistan were not murdered by US troops, but they are victims of wars triggered by the United States. The discussion on war crimes should not cover the effects of launching the war.[15]

That is the central point of *Humane*, Samuel Moyn's most recent book. "Americans had a torture debate. It diverted them from deliberating on the deeper choice they were making to ignore constraints on starting war in the first place." "We fight war crimes but have forgotten the crime of war."[16]

Hanna Arendt and Franz Kafka, quoted by Michael Reisman, explained the leader's responsibility in launching wars and imprisoning people.

Hanna Arendt presented Nazi atrocities committed by ordinary people following leaders' criminal instructions. During the 1960s, she wrote about the case in Israel against Adolf Eichmann, who had executed Hitler's orders to send millions of Jews to the gas chambers. She spoke about "the banality of evil," pointing out that Eichmann was not a "villain."

On the contrary, Eichmann "had always been a law-abiding citizen." He explained to Israel's judges how meticulously he fulfilled his duties, arguing that "a law was a law, there could be no exceptions," and accusing "those in power" of having abused his "obedience."[17] Even the worst criminals follow norms and recognize authorities.

In *The Trial*, Franz Kafka unveils the impact of *power-conferring* norms. As soon as the subordinates recognize the leader's authority, they follow the commands. The jailer explains to the prisoner that "We are humble subordinates who can scarcely find our way through a legal document and have nothing to do with your case (. . .), but we are quite capable of grasping the fact that the high authorities we serve before they will order an arrest such as this, must be quite well informed about the reasons for the arrest and the person of the prisoner."[18]

Kafka's dialogue could explain the operators' decision to shoot the weapons against the Kunduz Hospital, a target defined by unknown intelligence sources. Kafka also could enlighten the case of Mohamedou Ould Slahi, who spent fifteen years in Guantánamo and other prisons under US authority without charges.[19] "I only have the law," he said.[20] In 2010 a US federal judge ordered his release. Still, the Obama administration relied on the information provided by the confessions obtained under duress during the Bush administration, appealed such a decision, and Mohamedou Ould Slahi remained in Guantánamo for another six years.[21] A film, *The Mauritanian*, exposed his case.

The national and international legal architecture is a matter of life or death because it defines who the rulers are, the scope of their authority, and the legal system to apply. They can launch and expand the War on Terror and demarcate the rules implemented by their subordinates, including shooting at the Kunduz Hospital or keeping Mohamedou Ould Slahi as a prisoner without charges for fifteen years.

What Is the Relationship between Legal Designs and Individual Efforts Presented by This Book?

Jorge Luis Borges wrote a poem called "The Just" describing the importance of individual contributions to achieve global purposes:

> (. . .) *The potter, contemplating color and form.*
> *The typographer who set this page well, though it may not please him (. . .)*
> *She who prefers the others to be right.*
> *These people, without knowing, are saving the world.*

The book mapped many individual contributions to put the Rome Statute in motion, from the Nuremberg trial and the 1998 Rome Conference to the Court's establishment and operations. The list includes political leaders, NGOs, national authorities amending laws, and even constitutions, to ratify the statute.

All those actors also played a crucial role since 2003. The states parties prevented and prosecuted crimes under the Rome Statute. They also financed the ICC activities, cooperated during the investigations, and arrested those sought by the Court upon request. Some of them took initiatives at the UN Security Council to refer Darfur and Libya. Others participated actively in the Assembly of States Parties like Botswana or the Colombian president or the dozens of nations pushing for justice in Syria.

Ambassador Dabashi's request for an ICC referral at the beginning of Libya's rebellion shows the possibilities to produce a radical transformation offered by the adoption of the Rome Statute (see Chapter 19).[22] Chapter 10 describes the crucial role of Goungaye Wanfiyo, a civil society leader that promoted the Central African Republic referral.

Although there is still ample discretion in international affairs, the victims have access to a permanent institution committed to protecting their rights. Hundreds of them agreed to testify and transformed their painful stories into evidence.

The staff members of the ICC's different organs made enormous efforts to fulfill their mandate, providing the registry's services, obtaining cooperation in New York, or interviewing former child soldiers in the DRC bush.

In The Hague, the prosecution, the victims' representatives, the defense lawyers, and the judges making final rulings ensured fair trials.

As in any court, the ICC judges make the final decisions on the defendants' responsibility based on the evidence and the law. But, unlike any other court, the ICC's decisions impact the citizens and the institutions of more than one hundred states parties and beyond. *Jus in Curiae* rulings influenced decisions adopted around the world by different actors.

The Rome Statute articulated activities across time and space, creating a shared goal and forming a global *"shadow"* (see Chapter 9). In 2010, the UN Secretary-General Ban Ki-Moon summarized: *the ICC casts an increasingly long shadow, which those who would commit crimes against humanity have clearly come to fear.*[23]

Still, the court's rulings did not guarantee the Rome Statute's implementation by other actors. National leaders have different *preferences* and provide commands to soldiers or instructions to diplomats and intelligence agencies favorable or conflicting with the Rome Statute.

David Bosco analyzed the first ten years of the ICC activities, recognizing that "powerful states that imagined that they could marginalize or control the Court might themselves adjusting to its activities." But, as mentioned, his findings did not change his "realist" frame: "that international organizations often serve as vehicles for major-power influence."[24]

I partially agree with Bosco. Big powers' *preferences* can take advantage of the Rome Statute, asking the ICC to investigate their enemies' situation, blocking investigations against their friends, or refusing to implement arrest warrants. But the statute and the ICC also provide new possibilities to other preferences.

I participated and witnessed the struggle of national and international actors to impose their legal frameworks, promoting clashes between people fulfilling opposite obligations.[25] As in any network, each node follows its own interests, and such a controversial dynamic affects the results. *The potter, contemplating color and form,* would *not save the world* if others received daily instructions to destroy all the potter's production.

David Kennedy explained how decisions are made in a network without centralized authorities: "The internationalization of politics means the legalization of politics. Every agent of the state, of the city, of the region, acts and interacts on the basis of delegated powers, through the instruments of decision and rule and judgment."[26] The work of the Rome Statute would provide innumerable examples of a "New World order" based on networks presented in 2004 by Anne Marie Slaughter.[27]

Since 2009, the consistent outcome of the contradictory global legal system managing violence is a new record of displaced people worldwide, reaching more than ninety million persons. Until Russia invaded Ukraine, there were almost no classic wars between states in the twenty-first century; victims were escaping from "persecution, conflict, violence, human rights violations and events alarming public order."[28]

Hejewa Adam and Nadia Murad are just two prominent examples. The war in Afghanistan, Iraq, and Syria produced millions of forcibly displaced people and undesired immigration to Europe, transforming national leaders' attitudes. It is a failure by design.

The Technical Discussions and the Contradictory Preferences

I spent a significant part of my time as the ICC prosecutor reviewing the security of witnesses and investigators, overviewing the investigations, and supervising our litigation before the judges.

I was tempted to clarify some of the controversies about the efficiency of the ICC investigations and the quality of our litigation activity. Still, I concluded that it is essential to highlight the entire system created by the statute.

The ILC's report on "Fragmentation" explained that "Normative conflicts do not arise as technical 'mistakes' that could be 'avoided' by a more sophisticated way of legal reasoning." Instead, new legal regimes emerge "as responses to new preferences."[29]

During my tenure, the tensions between contradictory preferences like political interest to provide impunity and justice demands were present when Muammar Gaddafi and Omar Al Bashir mobilized the AU to protect their power.

Burundi and the Philippines' leaders were allegedly involved in the commission of crimes against humanity and decided to withdraw from the Rome Statute. Their resolutions were a matter of *preferences; they* had the legal authority to adopt such decisions and could "not be 'avoided' by a more sophisticated way of legal reasoning."

During the last twenty years, the United States has *preferred* to use armed forces to protect its citizens. Senator Rod Grams stated, "[T]he greatest force for peace on this Earth is not an international court; it is the United States military."[30]

US politicians learned to take advantage of the fears produced by terrorists to maintain or increase their power. Army officers are struggling to find a proper strategy, and scholars are not presenting options. Aliens living in foreign countries are not represented in the US debate.

The US legal system, unable to effectively manage global problems combined with a fragmented international legal model, produced a civilization's regression.

As former CIA head John Brennan alerted, the lack of a collective frame created a return to tribalism.[31] Brennan was referring to the Middle East, but even democratic states are returning to *tribalism*. In September 2001, the authorization to kill enemies was adopted by Congress exclusively "to protect United States citizens," not the rest of humanity.

The War on Terror is a gigantic step back to the Old-World Order developed by Grotius in 1625 (see Chapter 3). President Obama consecrated the War on Terror started by Bush and, in his 2009 Nobel Prize lecture, supported its expansion through humanitarian interventions (Chapter 17).

The War on Terror model promotes violence in other nations, demands impunity, and opposes justice efforts.[32] It also neutralizes the national and international mechanisms to control terrorism financing. Most remarkable, as General McChrystal and different experts' reports show, it will perpetuate terrorism (see Chapter 17).

The War on Terror affects the rule of law in the United States, and it disrupts the sovereignty of Pakistan, Iraq, Syria, and other countries. Intelligence agencies and proxy forces are interacting in foreign countries, profoundly affecting the factor identified as the most consistent violence reducer in the history of humanity: "a state that uses a monopoly of force to protect its citizens from one another."[33]

The end of the Afghanistan occupation is not the end of the conflict between both models. A permanent War on Terror using drones and proxy forces to eliminate enemies in foreign countries continues, and its consequences could be more dangerous than terrorism itself.[34]

I described the problem to my son, and he gave me an excellent metaphor to present the risk.

He introduced me to *Fortnite Battle Royale*, one of the most popular online games with 350 million registered users. It is based on the same premises of the War on Terror: to eliminate all the enemies. There are up to 100 players competing in each game. All of them are enemies, and the winner must kill all the other players. By design, the champion will be left alone.

Harmonizing Contradictory Mandates

"War appears to be as old as mankind, but peace is a modern invention." That is how Michael Howard, a military historian professor at Oxford and Yale, opened his short and fundamental book: *The Invention of Peace.* He alerted, "Peace is not an order natural to mankind: it is artificial, intricate, and highly volatile."[35]

How to create permanent peace in the time of a *forever* War on Terror and a renewed Cold War? No procedure is established, no one is in charge, and no academic discipline covers the entire problem. Hejewa Adam expected a solution from those who went to school, but there is no school to prepare such a solution; it must be invented.

How to improve international terrorism control and increase the Rome Statute's contribution to preventing the most serious crimes? One of the main findings of the ILC's report is that "no homogenous, hierarchical metasystem is realistically available" to solve "the emergence of conflicting rules and overlapping legal regimes."[36] A World Constitution to harmonize all the preferences would not be adopted in the near future.

Harmonizing legal mandates at the international level is the crucial task ahead. Imagine two different traffic lights at a street corner, one green and the other red at the same time. How could we ensure that cars would stop? The solution is not to improve respect for the red light but to harmonize both.

Stanley Milgram's famous experiment shows the impact of divided authority. Sixty-five percent of ordinary citizens were prepared to give severe electrical shocks to other individuals when ordered by a single expert figure. The compliance dropped to 0 percent when two "professors" proscribed opposite commands.[37]

How to coordinate impartial justice and the War on Terror? It would require designing new law enforcement mechanisms to face international terrorism. Criminal investigations could be combined with intelligence and special forces, eliminating the policy to kill people as the primary strategy and reducing the opposition to impartial institutions.[38] Chapter 17 presents a new global mechanism to face international terrorism reducing friction between the different models as an option to discuss.

Technologies for Public Purpose

This book aims to help new generations to develop innovative approaches. A technological revolution, the invention of the printing press in the fifteenth century, slowly created and extended a legal system to establish peace. Artificial intelligence is producing a similar global social and economic transformation in just a few decades. We should be technologically savvy but learn from the past.

Thousands of Holocaust survivors interviewed by the Shoah Foundation agreed that education is crucial to preventing the repetition of such tragedies. During the Nazi regime, two Jewish lawyers educated in Poland, Raphael Lemkin and Hersch Lauterpach, defined two of the four crimes under the Rome Statute: genocide and crimes against humanity.[39]

Education transformed people with difficult experiences into international justice leaders as Sheriff Bassiouni,[40] Ben Ferencz,[41] Navi Pillay,[42] and Judge Sang-Hyun Song.[43]

In the twenty-first century, educational efforts to provide equal rights and protect majorities and minorities should be adjusted. They should cross national and regional borders and include various disciplines, particularly artificial intelligence.

Humanity is technologically connected but still institutionally divided into nonhomogeneous 193 sovereign states. We celebrate technological innovations, including drones and other weapons to kill with precision and dismiss innovations in global institutions.[44] During the first Cold War, powerful states used proxy forces to avoid open wars, and now they can add drones to kill. New technologies are at the service of an old institutional model.

The regional human rights systems and the Rome Statute consolidation in just two decades are significant achievements to protect individuals, but they are not the end of history. Such institutions should trigger other innovations integrating international protection of some rights and an efficient mechanism to control global terrorism.

As Kathryn Sikkink described, activists and NGOs are exposing the crimes and demanding justice. They should add a new method to their toolbox: to identify who the decision makers are and how to influence them. A great example is the Coalition for the International Criminal Court during the Rome Conference, interacting with states representatives who *participated in the events* as Philippe Kirsch, Phani Daskalopoulou-Livada, Rolf Fife, and Silvia Fernandez. It is possible to identify national or international agents making decisions and integrating their *"preferences"* to manage the conflicts.

The question is how to put new technologies at the service of a worldwide public purpose to make legal designs to control violence more effective.

In 1945, Justice Robert Jackson mentioned the difficulties to transform global habits, a comment that is applicable to the current global order. He said that conflicts create opportunities to: *"to reshape some institutions and practices which sheer inertia would otherwise make invulnerable."*[45]

Invisible Children provided the best example of a civil society group integrating states' efforts using "YouTube," a 2005 technology. How to keep innovating?

To avoid the consolidation of tribalism, the twenty-first century is requesting new technologies to improve the international protection of each and all individuals.

For the last two centuries, there have been social demands to protect specific groups like Afro-Americans, Armenians, Jewish, Tutsi, or Darfuris. There is also a global battle to protect women in different circumstances, including sexual harassment in Hollywood and massive rapes in Darfur. Are we demanding protection exclusively for our group in our country? Or for majorities and minorities, Israelis and Palestinians? and everywhere, in Hollywood, Minneapolis, Syria, Venezuela, and Iraq.

Humanity's legal protection is the opposite of cultural appropriation. Foreigners' life should be respected; they could not be collateral damage in a War on Terror. Terrorists should be treated as criminals, not as enemies.[46]

The nineteenth-century campaign to end the slave trade harmonizing diverse constituencies, combining Quakers' principles with economic incentives, and sustained for decades is an example to consider.

The goal is to create new models integrating solutions for different groups' demands, protecting freedom and peace for Hejewa Adam, Nadia Murad, and each person in the world.[47]

Victory is not a world without violence; it is impossible to create a global or domestic community without conflicts. Success is to learn how to use new technologies to establish peaceful models to manage violence, and failure is not to try. The battle for justice is endless, but the war should not be.

Notes

1. IGE F. DEKKER & WOTER G. WERNER, GOVERNANCE AND INTERNATIONAL LEGAL THEORY 23 (Publications of the Institute of Public International Law of the University of Utrecht, 2004).

2. Mireille Delmas-Marty, Ordering Pluralism. A Conceptual Framework for Understanding the Transnational Legal World 14–15 (Naomi Norbergm trans., 2009).

3. "Fragmentation of international law: Difficulties arising from the diversification and expansion of international law." Rept. of the Study Group of the Int'l L. Comm., 58th Sess., 1 May–9 June and 3 July–11 Aug., 2006, U.N. Doc. A/CN.4/L.682 (Apr. 13, 2006) (finalized by Martti Koskenniemi).

4. Hans J. Morgenthau, *The Problem of Sovereignty Reconsidered*, 48 Colum. L. Rev., 341, 344–45 (1948).

5. Jack Goldsmith, Power and Constraint: The Accountable Presidency After 9/11 13–15 (Kindle ed. 2012). *See Civilian Casualties & Collateral Damage*, Lawfare, https://www.lawfareblog.com/civilian-casualties-collateral-damage (last visited Mar. 10, 2020).

6. Benjamin Wittes, *State Department Legal Adviser Brian Egan's Speech at ASIL*, Lawfare (Apr. 8, 2016, 8:36 AM), https://www.lawfareblog.com/state-department-legal-adviser-brian-egans-speech-asil. *See also* Rosa Brooks, How Everything Became War and the Military Became Everything: Tales from the Pentagon 285 (Kindle ed. 2016).

7. "One of the most remarkable aspects of American wars is how little we discuss the victims who are not Americans." John Tirman, The Deaths of Others 3 (Kindle ed. 2013).

8. "Two third of the ordinary people that participated in the Stanley Milgram experiment conducted at Yale University during the 50s tried to inflict very serious electric shocks to other individuals in order to please the authority." W. Michael Reisman, The Quest For World Order and Human Dignity in the Twenty First Century: Constitutive Process And Individual Commitment (2012).

9. In September 2002, President Bush adopted a US National Security Strategy promising effort *to ensure that our efforts to meet our global security commitments . . . are not impaired by the potential for investigations, inquiry, or prosecution by the International Criminal Court*, The White House, 2002 National Security Strategy of the United States of America (Sept. 17, 2002).

10. Brian L. Cox, *Five Years On: Military Accountability and the Attack on the MSF Trauma Center in Kunduz*, Just Security (Oct. 12, 2020), https://www.justsecurity.org/72665/five-years-on-military-accountability-and-the-attack-on-the-msf-trauma-center-in-kunduz/.

11. MSF, On October 3, 2015, US airstrikes destroyed our trauma hospital in Kunduz, Afghanistan, killing 42 people, https://www.msf.org/kunduz-hospital-attack-depth.

12. Christopher Keith Hall, *The First Proposal for a Permanent International Criminal Court*, 38 Int'l Rev. of the Red Cross 57 (1998).

13. Barack Obama, 44th President of the US, A Just and Lasting Peace, Nobel Lecture Oslo (Dec. 10, 2009) (transcript available at https://www.nobelprize.org/prizes/peace/2009/obama/lecture/).

14. Naz Modirzadeh, Reframing the Debate: A Response to Ryan Goodman's Memo to the Human Rights Community, https://www.lawfareblog.com/reframing-debate-response-ryan-goodmans-memo-human-rights-community

15. Ben Ferencz is suggesting that launching a war is a crime against humanity because inevitably, a *jus ad Bellum* decision would produce attacks against the civilian population.

16. SAMUEL MOYN, HUMANE, HOW AMERICA ABANDONED PEACE AND REINVENTED WAR 11–13 (Kindle ed. 2021)

17. "The trouble with Eichmann was precisely that so many were like him, and that the many were neither perverted nor sadistic, that they were and still are, terribly and terrifyingly normal." HANNA ARENDT, EICHMANN IN JERUSALEM 66 (1963).

18. FRANZ KAFKA, THE TRIAL, DEFINITIVE EDITION 10 (W. Muir trans., 1972 (1925)). W. MICHAEL REISMAN, THE QUEST FOR WORLD ORDER AND HUMAN DIGNITY IN THE TWENTY FIRST CENTURY: CONSTITUTIVE PROCESS AND INDIVIDUAL COMMITMENT (2012).

19. He was arrested in Mauritania in November 2001, transferred to a black site in Jordania, interrogated for eight months, then he was transferred to Afghanistan and finally Guantánamo. He was subjected to "enhanced interrogation techniques." https://www.amnesty.org/en/documents/amr51/149/2006/en/

20. "And if the law fails me, I'm done. There is nothing else left for me." https://www.nytimes.com/2021/09/12/us/politics/torture-post-9-11.html

21. Spencer S. Hsu, *U.S. Appeals Court: How Do You Quit al-Qaeda?*, https://www.washingtonpost.com/wpdyn/content/article/2010/09/17/AR2010091706657_pf.html

22. Catharine MacKinnon imports from chaos theory the concept that small actions can have highly complex and significant impacts. She showed how political activists could use the fragmented legal systems to produce radical transformations and promote gender equality. CATHARINE MACKINNON, BUTTERFLY POLITICAL, CHANGING THE WORLD FOR WOMEN (2017)

23. Ban Ki-moon. *We Must Get Justice*, https://www.un.org/africarenewal/web-features/we-must-get-justice

24. DAVID BOSCO, ROUGH JUSTICE, THE INTERNATIONAL CRIMINAL COURT IN A WORLD OF POWER POLITICS 187 (Kindle ed. 2014)

25. Ruti Teitel made a significant effort to integrate different *duty-imposing* norms, the law of war, international human rights, and international criminal law, into a single legal framework: *Humanity's law*. RUTI G. TEITEL, HUMANITY'S LAW (2013). Marti Koskenniemi commented: "Humanity law is attractive precisely because it may be expressed in any number of absolute norms that point in different directions simultaneously." He emphasized the role of the decision makers in implementing such norms: "Language—however absolute—does not cease to defer to process; there is always a further question to be asked: who is it that rules the process?" Martti Koskenniemi, *Humanity's Law by Ruti G. Teitel*, 26 ETHICS & INT'L AFF. 395, 396–397 (2012)(book review).

    Prof Teitel made a realist rebuttal. Her goal was to understand the "ascendancy of humanity-based discourse 'in diplomacy and international institutions,' . . . to identify

the roots of this discourse, to elucidate its specific politics and the agents that prop-
agate it." Ethics & Int'l Aff. 27, no.2 (2013), 233–34.© 2013 Carnegie Council for
Ethics in International Affairs

26. David Kennedy, *The Mystery of Global Governance*, 34 Ohio N.U.L. Rev. 821, 848
(2008).

27. Anne-Marie Slaughter, A New world order, 4 Princeton University Press
(Kindle ed. 2004).

28. Global trends report. https://www.unhcr.org/flagship-reports/globaltrends/

29. Rept. of the Study Group of the Int'l L. Comm., 58th Sess., 1 May–9 June and 3
July–11 Aug., 2006, U.N. Doc. A/CN.4/L.682 (Apr. 13, 2006) (finalized by Martti
Koskenniemi).

30. The International Criminal Court: Protecting American Servicemen and Officials
from the Threat of International Prosecution: Hearing Before the H. Comm. On
Foreign Relations, 106th Cong. (2000).

31. See Epilogue, endnote 61.

32. In 1994 the United Nations Development Programme (UNDP) proposed the concept of human security. It published a report arguing that the concept of security has
"for too long been interpreted narrowly: as security of territory from external aggression, or as protection of national interests in foreign policy or as global security from
a nuclear holocaust. It has been related more to nation states than to people." Later
Mary Kaldor and other experts tried to develop a comprehensive framework. Mary
Kaldor & Shannon Beebe, The Ultimate Weapon Is No Weapon: Human
Security and the New Rules of War and Peace 6. (Kindle ed. 1974)

33. Steven Pinker, The Better Angels of Our Nature: Why Violence Has
Declined 680 (Kindle ed. 2011).

34. *The failures in Iraq and Afghanistan obscure what experts say is the striking success of
a multilateral effort that extends to as many as 85 countries.* Mark Landler, *20 Years
On, the War on Terror Grinds Along, With No End in Sight*, https://www.nytimes.com/
2021/09/10/world/europe/war-on-terror-bush-biden-qaeda.html

35. Michael Howard, The Invention of Peace: Reflection on War and
International Order (New ed. 2001).

36. Rept. of the Study Group of the Int'l L. Comm., 58th Sess., 1 May–9 June and 3
July–11 Aug., 2006, U.N. Doc. A/CN.4/L.682 (Apr. 13, 2006) (finalized by Martti
Koskenniemi).

37. "The subject is confronted with two incompatible prescriptions for action, each
issued by an authoritative figure . . . Of 20 subjects, one broke off before the disagreement and 18 stopped at precisely the point where the disagreement between the
authorities first occurred. Another broke off one step beyond this point. It is clear that
the disagreement between the authorities completely paralyzed action." Milgram
Stanley, Obedience to Authority 107 (Kindle ed. 1974).

38. In 2010, two Harvard professors, Philippe Heymann, a former US deputy attorney
general with extensive experience in criminal justice; and Gabriella Blum, a former
Israel Defense Forces legal advisor and a global expert on international humanitarian
law, made a joint effort to present a new approach to control international terrorism.

They considered that neither the law enforcement model applicable during peace nor the war paradigm could deal with international terrorism. They thought that it would take decades to create a new model. Gabrielle Blum & Philippe Heyman, Laws, Outlaws, and Terrorists: Lessons from the War on Terrorism 140–43 (Kindle ed. 2010).

39. *See* Philippe Sands, East West Street (2017).

40. Bassiouni was born in Egypt, studied there and also in France, Switzerland, and the United States. He fought for his country during the Suez Crisis in 1956, and was wounded and decorated for his courage. He was arrested in Egypt for criticizing Nasser and in France for training Algerian members of the resistance. https://www.theguardian.com/world/2017/oct/22/cherif-bassiouni-obituary

41. Ben Ferencz was born in Transylvania, escaped from persecution in Europe at the beginning of the twentieth century, and obtained a scholarship to Harvard. When he was twenty-eight years old, he became the chief prosecutor of the Einsatzgruppen case at Nuremberg, the biggest murder case in human history. He dedicated his life to educating us on the consequences of the war. He repeated and repeated US President General Dwight Eisenhower's quote, *"the world no longer has a choice between force and law. If civilization is to survive, it must choose the rule of law."* https://benferencz.org/news/letter-from-ben-ferencz-re-obama-farewell-to-military/

42. Navi Pillay's ancestors were Indian forced workers imported to South Africa, and her neighbors financed her legal studies in Durban. As a lawyer, Navi Pillay represented Mandela's comrades in Robben Island, transforming the social perception from enemies to prisoners with rights. For more than two decades, she fought for equality during the *apartheid* regime. Later, she became a judge in South Africa, ICTR's judge and president, ICC's judge and vice president, and the UN High Commissioner for Human Rights.

43. Born in South Korea, Song experienced the Japanese occupation, the Second World War, and the Korean War and witnessed firsthand the atrocities of war. His grandfather was a leading figure in the "independence movement" during the Japanese occupation of Korea and was assassinated because of his political convictions. These harsh experiences drive Song in his dedication to human rights and his ambition to alleviate suffering. https://justiceleaders.org/leaders/sang-hyun-song/

44. Thomas Friedman, a senior journalist from the *New York Times* with enormous experience in international conflicts, wrote *The World Is Flat* describing the changes produced by technology and recognized that al-Qaeda and other terrorist networks could also *collaborate*. However, he is not even mentioning the possibility of creating a global public system to manage violence and other problems. The legal design is almost invisible. Thomas Friedman, The Word Is Flat: A Brief History of the Twenty-First Century (Kindle ed. 2007).

45. The Rule of Law Among Nations By Justice Robert H. Jackson, Associate Justice, Supreme Court of the United States, Washington, D.C., April 13, 1945. Article originally appeared at 31 ABAJ 290 (1945) *Versions of this Jackson* speech were published in the Proceedings of the ASIL 10–18, in 31 American Bar Association Journal 290–94 (June 1945) and in Temple Law Quarterly.

46. Samuel Moyn invites us to acknowledge how recent and contingent international rights are. "True, rights have long existed, but they were from the beginning part of the authority of the state, not invoked to transcend it." SAMUEL MOYN, THE LAST UTOPIA: HUMAN RIGHTS IN HISTORY 82 (Kindle ed. 2010).

47. That is the Rome Statute's goal that I presented at the conclusion of my swearing-in speech in 2003: "We must learn: there is no safe haven for life and freedom if we fail to protect the rights of any person in any country of the world."

Index

For the benefit of digital users, indexed terms that span two pages (e.g., 52–53) may, on occasion, appear on only one of those pages.

Notes are indicated by an italic *n*, following the page number.